CHARACTERS OF BLOOD

Characters of Blood

BLACK HEROISM IN
THE TRANSATLANTIC
IMAGINATION

CELESTE-MARIE BERNIER

UNIVERSITY OF VIRGINIA PRESS

Charlottesville and London

University of Virginia Press

© 2012 by the Rector and Visitors of the University of Virginia

All rights reserved

Printed in the United States of America on acid-free paper

First published 2012

9 8 7 6 5 4 3 2 1

Library of Congress Cataloging-in-Publication Data

Bernier, Celeste-Marie.

  Characters of blood : black heroism in the transatlantic imagination /
Celeste-Marie Bernier.

    p.   cm.

Includes bibliographical references and index.

ISBN 978-0-8139-3324-5 (cloth : acid-free paper) — ISBN 978-0-8139-3325-2 (e-book)

1. Blacks in literature. 2. Blacks in art. 3. Heroes in literature. 4. Heroes in art. 5.
Slavery in literature. 6. Slavery in art. I. Title.

PN56.3.B55B47 2012

809'.8896—dc23

        2012015852

Title spread illustration: John Childs, *Joseph Cinque Addressing His Compatriots on
Board the Spanish Schooner. Amistad,* 1839 (Chicago History Museum)

For

ANDY, TINA, *and* GEORGE GREEN

In loving memory of my mother,

MAUREEN BERNIER,

and my grandmothers,

CECILIA MARY BERNIER *and*

SADIE MCKEEVER

Does the color of my skin impair my honor
and my bravery?
—TOUSSAINT LOUVERTURE

I must go back to the days of my infancy,
and even before I was born.
—NATHANIEL TURNER

Brothers, I am resolved that it is better to die
than be a white man's slave.
—SENGBE PIEH

Now the war begun.
—SOJOURNER TRUTH

I am only the painter.
—FREDERICK DOUGLASS

No one will take me back alive;
I shall fight for my liberty.
—HARRIET TUBMAN

CONTENTS

ILLUSTRATIONS

Across the centuries, acts and arts of black heroism have inspired a provocative, experimental, and self-reflexive intellectual, political, and aesthetic
tradition. At war with monolithic conceptualizations of black diasporic histories, the lives and works of six iconic African, African American, and African Caribbean men and women—Toussaint Louverture, Nathaniel Turner,
Sengbe Pieh, Sojourner Truth, Frederick Douglass, and Harriet Tubman—
have played a key role in the construction and theorizing of an alternative
visual and textual archive. Regardless of their survival as symbolic touchstones, however, scholars have yet to do justice either to their complex bodies of work or to their multifaceted lives. Such failures have not only resulted
in interpretative difficulties regarding the sheer range and extent of their signifying practices but have also made it almost impossible to investigate their
widespread rejection of dominant histories and official records. For Louverture, Turner, Pieh, Truth, Douglass, and Tubman, acts and arts of radical reimagining remained integral to their vociferous challenge to white amnesia
and to the racist distortions enacted by national and transatlantic sites and
sights of memory. Remarkably defying the limitations imposed by their own
fallible mortality, the legacies of these Black men and women constitute a
generating and galvanizing force as they live on in poetry, song, public monuments, murals, portraits, plays, statuary, historical volumes, religious tracts,
slave narratives, novels, and oratory, among many more diverse forms.

A Black artist's challenge to the white-supremacist trade in the taboo life
and exalted death of Nathaniel Turner provides a particularly powerful place
from which to begin this intellectual and cultural history of black heroism.
William H. Johnson painted his controversial work *Nat Turner* in 1945, representing a forceful, if ambivalent, testament to this historical figure's revolutionary idealism. "In all my years of painting," Johnson emphasizes, "I have
had one absorbing and inspired idea, and have worked toward it with an un-
yielding zeal—to give, in simple and stark form—the story of the Negro as
he has existed."[1] Fully aware of the ways in which the "story of the Negro" had
been vilified by white racist sympathizers and proslavery apologists over the
centuries, Johnson refused to reimagine Nathaniel Turner as an inhumane
fiend engaged in barbaric acts of violence. Rather, in Johnson's work Turner
signifies as an apocryphal prophet and freedom fighter and, as such, as a

historical figure mythologized for enacting diverse arts of resistance within a black folkloric and literary tradition. A tour de force, Johnson's painting bears witness to the difficulties arising from the fact that in the twentieth no less than the nineteenth century, there remains no official visual or textual language within which to categorize Turner. Instead, the widespread preference among white historians, politicians, artists, and writers alike has been for relying on demonic descriptions. These have not only dehumanized this historical figure but have guaranteed, rather paradoxically, that his life and death have simultaneously remained both well-worn and underexplored territory.

In striking and very immediate ways, this painting offers a compelling opening to this book. In these pages, I investigate the politicized aesthetics and aestheticized politics at work in textual and visual materials produced by, and purporting to represent, Toussaint Louverture, Nathaniel Turner, Sengbe Pieh, Sojourner Truth, Frederick Douglass, and Harriet Tubman, all formerly enslaved and self-emancipated historical figures who have since operated as heroic icons in a transatlantic milieu. In an eclectic array of works produced over a long time frame and across diverse national boundaries, these six Black historical figures occupy the eye of the storm in debates over African, African Caribbean, and African American memorializations and representations. Lacunae, distortion, and obfuscation have characterized white national official archives to such an extent that Black revolutionaries such as Turner, as well as African American artists and writers including Johnson, have not only chosen but have been forced to engage in acts and arts of reimagining even to begin to dramatize their otherwise elided subjectivities. Sensationalized as an extreme case, Turner's life and death represent an especially compelling point of origin for mapping the obfuscated legacies of Black male and female heroic figures. Because his acts and arts of radical resistance functioned as the catalyst for the majority of his subsequent memorializations, Turner provides a forceful introduction to the equally multifaceted practices and slippery personae of Louverture, Pieh, Truth, Douglass, and Tubman. In self-reflexive ways, they have remained equally committed to playing a key role in the formation—as well as the perpetuation—of a complex continuum of black male and female resistance.

Regardless of the fact that Johnson's painting has suffered from significant critical neglect, his portrait of Turner performs fundamental revisionist work regarding visual narratives of black heroism. Here, he rejected the authority of white mainstream caricatured representations that appeared in the immediate aftermath of Turner's revolution in 1831. While there was and remains a dearth of images purporting to portray this controversial figure in the popular imagination, in the majority of those that did appear, Turner was and remains little more than an underdeveloped, anonymous, and even antiheroic, stock figure. Committed to setting the skewed historical record straight, Johnson created an individualized and idealized portrait of Turner. As a stark contrast to popularly reproduced illustrations dramatizing this historical figure as a disheveled and murderous-looking fugitive from slavery, his Turner is well dressed and wears a green waistcoat and socks, white shirt, blue trousers, black jacket, and cravat. At first glance, this formal clothing resonates with the typically elegant attire of former enslaved men and women turned writers. Across the eighteenth century, frontispieces of individuals such as Olaudah Equiano and Phillis Wheatley engaged in a radical reappropriation of Western fashion styles to ensure their portrayal not only as quintessential embodiments of a black civilized humanity but also as agents of their own destiny, however circumscribed by white editorial conventions. Yet a closer examination of Johnson's painting soon reveals the ways in which his jarring color scheme complicates any such straightforward associations of the black body with elite forms of acculturation. His work daringly emphasizes similarities between Turner's clothing and the exaggerated costumes of blacked-up white minstrel performers that dominated the nineteenth- and even early twentieth-century theatrical stage. By deliberately courting rather than flinching from such problematic comparisons, Johnson destabilized white tendencies toward endorsing one-dimensional dramatizations of Black historical figures. These worked to obscure, if not annihilate entirely, the elided complexities of seemingly unrecognized Black subjectivities. According to his self-reflexive and multilayered aesthetic practices, any such polarizing paradigms resulted in, at best, monolithic archetypes and, at worst, stereotypical reimaginings that colluded in racist strategies of dehumanization.

Representing a radical departure from white official archives, which relied on grotesque detail in their racist portrayals of black physiognomies, Johnson provides only the barest outlines of Turner's facial features. Adopting a seemingly untutored artistic style, he dramatizes pared-down delineations of Turner's eyelashes, eyebrows, and carefully trimmed goatee. Thwarting white racist tendencies toward endorsing gross exaggerations of black masculinity, his minimalist approach lays claim to Turner's enduring symbolism as a mythological touchstone. Clearly, Johnson's determination to minimize Turner's facial features works in two ways. First, this strategy speaks to the absence of any carefully observed authentic portraiture of Turner within the white-dominated records. Second, Johnson's technique guarantees that deliberate and unmistakable physical parallels can be made between Turner's mythical physiognomy and his own. As Kimberly Pinder argues, "Johnson's black Christ makes the conflation of the sympathetic devout and suffering savior even more literal by including a self-portrait."[2] As a signifier of the psychological, political, and aesthetic deaths visited upon the body of Johnson no less than Turner, his decision to keep the eyes of his Black male subject closed explicitly engages with a politics and poetics of seeing and nonseeing regarding black male representation. More tellingly still, Johnson's decision to invite comparisons between the fated nineteenth-century Black freedom fighter and the difficulties faced by twentieth-century Black artists may well be interpreted, with hindsight, as a prophecy of his own horrifying descent into insanity during the final decades of his life.

Pinder's observation regarding Johnson's construction of Turner as a "black Christ" speaks to the powerful way in which this artist reimagines this historical figure in terms of Christological debates. In iconographic ways, Johnson's Turner appears as a sacrificial martyr, as his well-dressed and civilized body hangs from a symbolically cross-shaped tree. And yet, for Johnson, his martyrdom functions not as a passive capitulation to white oppressive forces but as an empowered declaration of black radical activism. Relying on symbolic formal details such as the angular edges of his black bow tie, Johnson legitimizes Turner's spiritual strivings for redemption by replicating the contours of the cross. Equally, his hyper- if not surreal use of color operates in powerful ways, as Turner's green waistcoat and socks replicate the color of one of the tree limbs from which his lifeless body hangs. Such a technique accentuates his body as a site not only of death but of resurrection: the tree is both his final resting place and a symbol of a biblical "tree of life." Painted in 1945 at the height of segregation and at the end of World War II, Johnson's dramatization of Turner's hanging body critiques clear-cut definitions of black male heroism while also exposing the changing contexts of black persecution that came to the fore in the decades following the end of slavery. Johnson's Turner bears witness to the atrocities of slavery to indict the ongoing survival of white racist ideologies. Signifying upon the conventions of lynching photography, he demonstrates that acts and arts of black resistance were repeatedly met with barbarous white vengeance in spectacular twentieth-century ritual killings. Dramatizing not only the horrifying rise of lynchings during the late nineteenth and early twentieth centuries, Johnson also condemned the discrimination experienced by African Americans serving in the military during both world wars. Directly confronting white racism as enacted on an international stage, Johnson may even have created this painting to indict Nazi persecution: the formal properties of the rope from which Turner hangs are suggestive of half of a swastika. Perhaps he foregrounded this symbolic association to encourage cross-racial solidarity and identification among diverse oppressed groups, irrespective of race or nationhood.

Relying on a layered aesthetic vision, Johnson generated further iconographic ambiguities from the ways in which he narratively constructed the graveyard in his work. Turner's body hangs before a segregated burial ground, as rows of white and black crosses divide the picture plane while fiery red and orange streaks of paint smear a burnt sienna sky. These pink, beige, yellow, brown, lilac, and red crosses run the full color spectrum to situate the artist's composite Turner/Johnson figure within an apocryphal landscape. Symbolizing an array of black and white shades of skin coloration, these grave markings establish Johnson's preference for multifarious rather than bifurcated notions of racial difference. Equally, he exposes the realities of racially skewed and horrifying social conditions that guaranteed that black and white bodies remained segregated even in death. Signifying upon the traumas and horrors of World Wars I and II, therefore, Johnson's inclusion of these mass burial sites condemn injustices enacted against black military personnel. Across the centuries, African American soldiers have been perpetually relegated to labor duties and have had to fight for the right to combat status due to white fears regarding the spectacle of armed Black men. More horrifyingly still, they have repeatedly been given the dehumanizing job of "reburying the dead" in the aftermath of bloodied conflicts.[3] Carefully painting anonymous rows of white crosses, Johnson's portrait exposes the racist injustices enacted by national military cemeteries which sought solely to eulogize white sacrifice. In unmistakable ways, his painting explicitly evokes the iconography of Arlington National Cemetery in Washington, DC, a symbol of white national supremacy, to problematize its importance as a site of black memorialization. According to Johnson's bold reenvisioning, the viewer is only able to interpret white sacrifice through the horrific spectacle of a hanging black body. Rejecting existing racially coded parameters of white national heroism, his new and alternative model encompasses diverse rather than mutually exclusive constructions of black and white revolutionary activism.

More revealingly still, Johnson's dramatization of black martyrdom and death comes to grips with the history of segregated burial grounds in the United States. Here, he testifies to the shocking historical practice by which whites repeatedly denied funeral rites to Black women, men, and children, both enslaved and free. Nowhere are these issues more prevalent than in the relatively recent controversies surrounding the discovery in downtown Manhattan during the 1990s of the eighteenth-century "Negroes Burying Ground" or African Burial Ground, from which "more than 400 burials" have been excavated.[4] These groundbreaking discoveries leave critics such as Edward Rothstein at a loss: he asks, "Where are the 'memorials'" that will "provide the ground for a people's memory?"[5] Recently, such concerns have been partly assuaged by the construction of an awe-inspiring marble monument, an edifice emotively accompanied by seven burial mounds. These sacred graves signify not only upon the excavated but also upon the unrecovered bodies of these African women, children, and men. As a work painted decades before, Johnson's portrait establishes how the tragic phenomenon of the "missing memorial" finds particular force in Turner's fate. As a radical break with historical precedent, his painting performs the long-awaited work of commemoration by providing Turner with an aggrandized site of memorialization for the first time.

In the final analysis, any straightforward endorsement of the black male body as a site of Christological persecution and triumphant sacrifice is far from the whole story in this portrait. Ultimately, Johnson's painting signifies as a declaration of radical black resistance. Demonstrating his determination to challenge any straightforward reimaginings of Turner's martyrdom, sheets of blank paper, a rifle, a machete, and a knife appear in the bottom right corner of his canvas. These well-chosen symbolic objects speak to Turner's repeatedly elided creativity, a subject that perhaps would have been lost to history if it had not been for the testimony of the white radical abolitionist Thomas Wentworth Higginson. "He [Turner] had some mechanical ingenuity also; experimentalized very early in making paper, gun-powder, pottery, and in other arts," he claims.[6] Vociferously protesting against white biases within the dominant historical record, Johnson's inclusion of these white sheets suggests a history of black heroism that has either remained unwritten or has been invisibilized. According to his vision, Turner is a tabula rasa or terra incognita not only within white racist archives but also insofar as acts and arts of black radical artistic reimagining are concerned.

As a work of revisionist artistry as well as of radical history, Johnson's painting does justice not only to Turner's prowess in papermaking but also to his expertise in manufacturing gunpowder. Simultaneously celebrating violent and intellectual forms of protest, Johnson juxtaposes weaponry with textual materials to provide a self-portrait capable of dramatizing Higginson's ambiguous references to Turner's accomplishments in undefined "other arts." Self-reflexively experimental, Johnson's own artistic practices bear witness to Turner's coded use of language as well as his innovations in mechanical and artistic forms. Recognizing this historical figure as one we can only imagine but never fully know, he fought to encourage audiences not to shy away from Turner's psychological complexity. For Johnson, Turner's legacies encompass diverse forms of physical, spiritual, historical, intellectual, and aesthetic rebellion, while his performed resistances clearly also shed light on the lives and works of Toussaint Louverture, Sengbe Pieh, Sojourner Truth, Frederick Douglass, and Harriet Tubman examined in this book.

In clear-cut ways, Johnson's portrait of Turner collapses the political and aesthetic boundaries between the struggles for self-representation confronting an enslaved hero and those encountered by a twentieth-century Black artist. Experimenting with conventions of self-portraiture, Johnson the artist inspires imaginative, empathetic engagement from his viewers by assuming the guise of Turner, an elided and distorted historical figure whose multiple identities have continued to proliferate as a combination of myth, memory, and legend within the transatlantic imagination. Mapping aesthetic experimentation onto political modes of resistance, Johnson argues that the Black artist's burden remains no less incendiary, fearful, and radical than the Black revolutionary's vision. Therefore, his painting of Turner can be inserted into a heroic continuum according to which acts of black militancy remain indivisible from arts of black creativity. For Johnson, a visual and symbolic equivalence between the Black freedom fighter and the Black artist offered proof that constructions of black masculinity remained fraught aesthetic and ideological terrain across both the nineteenth and twentieth centuries.

Adopting a self-reflexive approach, Johnson's experimental constructions of Turner as a malleable icon refute white anti- and proslavery tendencies toward creating polarized representations of Black male heroic figures. Refusing to endorse Black men as either demons or deities, he celebrates a psychologically and historically complex middle ground. More especially, his visual memorialization of Turner blurs the boundaries between artificially polarized constructions of passive versus active black heroism. Notably, these models have maintained their grip in the popular white Western imagination over an extended historical period and an expansive geographical context. According to these prescriptive definitions, Black heroic figures have been and continue to be stripped of complexities solely to be memorialized as slain martyrs or bloodstained avengers. Offering a stark contrast, Johnson's portrait engages with Turner's signifying capabilities, not only as a rebel and revolutionary but as an author, agent, activist, and artist. For

Johnson, Turner is "cutting a figure," as theorized by Richard Powell in his recent analysis of the subversive, signifying practices of Black male and female subjects during slavery.[7] Clearly, his theoretical model applies not only to Turner but also to Louverture, Pieh, Truth, Douglass, and Tubman, as they similarly transgressed the boundaries of dominant forms and practices to engage in radical acts and arts of self-representation.

More problematically, while the blank sheets of paper that Johnson prominently includes offer a symbolic indictment of whiteness as the normative standard in the historical archive, they may well also speak to undocumented feats of black female heroism, a major source of intellectual, political, and ideological debate discussed in this book. As an anonymous writer for the *Richmond Whig* proclaimed in the immediate aftermath of Turner's rebellion, "I have in my possession, some papers given up by his [Turner's] wife under the lash—they are filled with hieroglyphical characters, conveying no definite meaning. The characters on the oldest paper, apparently appear to have been traced with blood."[8] As a figure barely documented in any visual or textual archive, Turner's wife's life and, in particular, her body, rival Turner's in similarly functioning as a site of persecution and martyrdom. While problematic gendered paradigms have prevented her from signifying as a Black Christ or messiah, she nonetheless operates as a talisman of suffering, even in the face of her widespread neglect. As activists committed to confronting the erasure of enslaved female bodies throughout U.S. history, Sojourner Truth and Harriet Tubman figure prominently in this book. Examining their vast and yet profoundly underresearched literary and oratorical archives, I come to grips with their distorted and elided signifying practices. As their lives and works demonstrate, black female heroism has been a casualty not only of white dominant archives but also of revisionist attempts to commemorate black male exceptionalism.

As detailed above, the anonymous nineteenth-century reporter's ambiguous references to Turner's coded use of a symbolic language—"characters" that he had "traced with blood"—resonates powerfully with a letter written by an unknown Black man known simply as "Nero." Arriving in Southampton County immediately following Turner's revolutionary activism in late 1831, Nero's letter sought to strike terror into white slaveholders. He proclaimed, "Little do you know how many letters in cypher pass through your post office . . . though you would not be the wiser if you were to see them, for they are past your finding out—till you hear from us in characters of blood."[9] Clearly, Turner's "hieroglyphical characters," which he purportedly "traced in blood," can be usefully understood in the context of Nero's "characters of blood." In this regard, many iconic and unknown Black figures, both enslaved and free, typically experimented with the inextricable relationship between coded systems of signification and overt enactments of violence. As both an incendiary phrase and an apocalyptic statement, "characters of blood" operates not only as a compelling trope but also as a theoretical structuring motif for this book as a whole. While on the one hand, "characters" signals diverse modes of resistance by suggesting a cryptic code via signs, symbols, and textual fragments, on the other, "blood" dramatizes competing forms of heroism by signifying not only upon violence and death but also upon martyrdom, sacrifice, and resistance as enacted through genealogical bloodlines. Decades later, this powerful phrase was to be given new life as Frederick Douglass delivered an incendiary speech, "The Mission of the War," against the epic backdrop of the American Civil War in 1864. In this address, he offered a powerful warning: "But if . . . this potent teacher, whose lessons are written in characters of blood, and thundered to us from a hundred battle-fields shall fail, we shall go down, as we shall deserve to go down, as a warning to all other nations which shall come after us."[10] While there is no evidence to suggest that he had any knowledge of Nero's prior use of this radicalizing trope in the 1830s, for Douglass, agitating not only for black freedom but for black rights in the 1860s, "characters of blood" endured as a powerful touchstone and talisman. Exalting not in a separatist call for black vengeance and retribution as did Nero, however, Douglass's "characters of blood" resonate as "lessons" to be learned. In unequivocal ways, Douglass sought to educate audiences, Black and white, regarding the moral, political, and social transformations that could be realized only by a divinely inspired violence enacted in the service of idealism.

Ultimately, the radical force of Johnson's portrait derives from his provocative engagement with Turner's ambiguous legacies. In compelling ways, therefore, Johnson's work may well be interpreted as sharing affinities with the concerns of the contemporary cultural theorist, writer, and activist Amiri Baraka. Charting the "discovery" of the Black artist Thornton Dial by the white art critic Bill Arnett, Baraka exalts in a black will to agency, remarking, "Dial would not tell him, Arnett, a white man, what the paintings meant."[11] Recognizing the tenacity of widespread racist tendencies toward reductive fixity and distortion regarding black humanity, for Baraka, Dial's strategies of withholding constitute subversive acts and arts of resistance. Contemplating Dial's mixed-media abstract canvases consisting of cacophonous explosions of color, texture, and found materials, he explains, "The dynamic smashing explosions shaped of paint, rug, wood, found objects are telling a mean tale."[12] Reimagining the perspective of Dial himself, he warns, "You don't want to hear this tale, boss. . . . It scare me. Shit, suppose Nat Turner painted?"[13]

Deciding to conjoin a "mean tale" with the speculation "Suppose Nat Turner painted?" Baraka offers a compelling variation upon Johnson's "story of the negro." Far from didactic or straightforwardly representational, Dial's abstract canvases celebrate strategies of concealment to refute any pretensions toward revelation that might lead to easy emotional purging on the part of his audiences as they presume to know, presume to feel, and presume to understand. One of his works, *I Am a Man, I Always Am* (1994), dramatizes black masculinity as a site of ambiguity. Experimenting with both layered abstraction and nonrepresentational play, he defies the ways in which white artists and writers create works grossly reliant upon reductive black caricature.[14] Just as Dial creates difficult, destabilizing paintings that signify as sites of visual as well as political and artistic conflict in a contemporary era, Johnson's much earlier work similarly foregrounds aesthetic process. Working decades apart and across contrasting bodies of work, both artists transgress formal and thematic boundaries to sustain rather than elide the paradoxes of diverse Black male subjectivities.

Baraka's enigmatic question "Suppose Nat Turner painted?" operates in the same way as the ambiguous signifying practices of Johnson's *Nat Turner*. Both Baraka's question and Johnson's portrait cut to the heart of debates discussed in this book regarding the ways in which Turner—as well as Louverture, Pieh, Truth, Douglass, and Tubman—all engaged in self-reflexive acts and arts of self-representation. As I argue, these African, African Caribbean, and African American figures lived and died to become creators or "painters" of their own representations. Constituting yet another art if not act of heroism, and out of both necessity and design, they influenced the parameters of their own reimagining. As artists and activists they experimented with their status as slippery signifiers to establish the parameters for their own malleable symbolism. In this regard, their radical poetics testify to a coming to consciousness of the aesthetic and political necessity of a will to self-expression as a way of challenging and even working to transcend finite distortions and lacunae dominant within white official archives.

Across their lives and works, Louverture, Turner, Pieh, Truth, Douglass, and Tubman endorsed a myriad of strategies designed not only to intervene into but actively to put flesh on the bare bones of a skeletal historical record. Safeguarding their survival, they provide points of departure for reimaginings that have since emerged over an expansive time period and transatlantic milieu. Consequently, I am concerned with mapping two archives in this book: The first consists of material remarkable for the ways in which these originatory figures generated their own processes of textual and visual significations. The second encompasses the body of works generated as a result of the multifarious ways in which nineteenth-, twentieth-, and twenty-first-century writers, artists, and political activists riffed off extant primary archival representations to subvert and challenge lacunae within white mainstream histories.

Refusing to tell either a "mean tale" or a "story of the negro" directly, ellipsis and fragmentation are fundamental to the wide-ranging and groundbreaking representations by and of these formerly enslaved heroic figures. Adopting a wide variety of experimental approaches, these historical figures themselves—but also later writers and artists—have engaged in aesthetic experimentation to refute reductive representations of black male and female heroism within the popular transatlantic imagination. For an array of artists, authors, and activists, self-reflexive aesthetic practices offer powerful ways in which to disrupt white mainstream tendencies toward graphic display as well as to subvert the perpetual trade in black male and female bodies as commodified spectacles for white consumption. As I show in these pages, formerly enslaved heroic black male figures can only be liberated from ongoing forces of marginalization and racist annihilation by evoking a process by which, as bell hooks insists, as scholars and audiences we "must set our imaginations free."[15] Only then will it become possible to begin to do justice to Louverture, Turner, Pieh, Truth, Douglass, and Tubman's various "characters of blood" as we explore the politics and poetics of otherwise excessively sensationalized, grossly oversimplified, and willfully misunderstood acts and arts of black male and female heroism.

ACKNOWLEDGMENTS

This book is written with heartfelt thanks to Judie Newman, whose friendship, kindness, generosity, and inspirational intellectual rigor brought this book to life. I would also like to thank Cathie Brettschneider and Susan Castillo for their wonderful expertise and much-treasured guidance, without which this book would not have been possible. I am enormously grateful to the groundbreaking scholars Marcus Wood, Jeffrey Stewart, Bill Lawson, Alan Rice, and Fionnghuala Sweeney as their wonderful insights have stimulated new approaches and directions in my research. Equally, I owe an enormous debt of gratitude to George Lipsitz and John Stauffer, whose superlative knowledge and creativity have played a key role in the completion of this book. During the writing and researching of this book, Zoe Trodd and her groundbreaking insights have had a real formative influence; many key insights emerged from our conversations and intellectual exchange. This book has benefited enormously from Iyunolou Osagie's and James McGowan's exceptional generosity and brilliant scholarship. I would like to thank Debra Priestly and Lubaina Himid for their enormous kindness in sharing their wonderful and inspirational work with me. I am profoundly grateful to Charlie Haffner and Raymond DeSouza-George for their exceptional generosity in so kindly providing me with their unpublished play scripts. I also wish to thank the Beneicke Rare Book Library, Yale University, for access to Owen Dodson's "Play Script Commissioned by Talladega College Performed There April, 1939, Amistad" (unpublished, second holograph, Owen Dodson Collection, box 1, folder 30) and the Schlesinger Library, Radcliffe Institute, Harvard University, for access to June Jordan's "In the Spirit of Sojourner Truth" (unpublished manuscript, 1978, June Jordan Papers, 1936–2002).

My profound and grateful thanks go to the Leverhulme Trust in the United Kingdom for its wonderful generosity in awarding me a Philip Leverhulme Prize in the History of Art in 2010, which has financed the inclusion of full-color plates in this book. I would also like to thank the W. E. B. Du Bois Institute for African and African American Research at Harvard University for a Sheila Biddle Ford Foundation fellowship, which made the completion of this decade-long project possible. I am profoundly grateful to Henry Louis Gates Jr. for his inspirational scholarship and generosity as well as the outstanding team at the W. E. B. Du Bois Institute: Sheldon Cheek, Karen Dalton, Vera Grant, Delphine Kwankam, Abby Wolf, Tom Woljeko, and Donald Yacovone, among many others. I am deeply indebted to the wonderful friendships I made with all the fellows, but I would especially like to thank Barbara Rodriguez and Deborah Willis, both dear friends and exceptional scholars. I would like to dedicate this book to the memory of Emory Elliott, an outstanding scholar whose exceptional support and generosity made all the difference in the conceptualization of this project.

The outstanding scholarly environment at the University of Nottingham remains a source of ongoing support and inspiration, and I would like to thank John Fagg, Anthony Hutchison, Richard King, Stephanie Lewthwaite, Graham Locke, Ruth Maxey, Sharon Monteith, Sinéad Moynihan, Dave Murray, Judie Newman, Maria Ryan, Bevan Sewell, and Graham Thompson for their expertise and great friendship. I would also like to extend my profound thanks to my graduate students Rebecca Cobby, Hannah Durkin, and Donna-Marie Urbanowicz. At the University of Nottingham library, Alison Stevens's kindness, patience, and resourcefulness have been invaluable in tracking down elusive materials.

On a personal note, I would like to thank my brilliant and inspirational friends: Richard "Big Bro" Anderson; Erica Arthur; Susy Billingham; Ian Brookes; Owen Butler; Jacqui Clay; Marion Connor; Jean Darnbrough; Claire, Ant, Daisy, and Charlotte Freeman; Helen Henry; Travis Jacobs; Stephanie "Ern" Lewthwaite; Becca Lloyd; Maha Marouan; Ruth, Olly, and Rebecca Maxey; Ann and Paul McQueen; Steve Moore; Sinead Moynihan; Cathki "Little C" Nash; Helen "H" Oakley; Champa Patel; Luca Prono; Gillian Roberts; Neil Roberts; Barbara Rodriguez; Lisa Rull; Maria Ryan; Brenda, Axel, and Riley Schaefer; Bevan Sewell; Helen Taylor; Tash and Dillon Tetley; Graham Thompson; Zoe Trodd; Robin Vandome; Tricia Welsh; Alex Kent Williamson; Sara Wood; and Stuart Wright. I would also like to thank Mike Walker and Marion Bussetti for all their wonderful love and kindness. This book was finished at 179 Prospect Street, a stop on the Underground Railroad and a bridge away from Mansfield Street, Stonehouse, and Ballymoney.

This book is written in loving memory of my mother, Maureen Bernier; and my father, Nicholas Louis Bernier; my grandmothers, Sadie McKeever and Cecilia Mary Bernier; my uncle, Lawrence Robert Bernier; and my great uncle, Frank Bussetti. Finally, this book is written for my wonderful husband, Andy Green, as well as my dearly loved and much treasured mother- and father-in-law, Mama Tina and Captain George.

CHARACTERS OF BLOOD

"On a beautiful morning in the month of June, while strolling about Tra-falgar Square, I was attracted to the base of the Nelson column, where a crowd was standing gazing at the bas-relief representations of some of the great naval exploits of the man whose statue stands on the top of the pillar." So writes the nineteenth-century enslaved African American fugitive turned free man, author, orator, and historian William Wells Brown describing a visit to London in the opening to his sketch "Visit of a Fugitive Slave to the Grave of Wilberforce," which appeared in Julia Griffiths's antislavery gift book, *Autographs for Freedom,* published in the United States and Great Britain in 1854. Tellingly, Brown remained unimpressed by portrayals of white Euro-pean manhood until he made a crucial discovery. "Being no admirer of war-like heroes, I was on the point of turning away, when I perceived among the figures (which were as large as life) a full-blooded African," he observed. On one of the bronze panels designed by William Railton and built in 1840–43, he was astonished to see a "full-blooded African with as white a set of teeth as ever I had seen, and all the other peculiarities of feature that distinguish that race of the human family, with musket in hand and a dejected counte-nance, which told that he had been in the heat of the battle, and shared with the other soldiers the pain in the loss of their commander" (see figure 1).[1] As a forceful work of protest, Brown's provocative vignette celebrates Brit-ish inclusivity only to denounce the gross inequalities enacted by official U.S. representations of black and white heroism on iconic sites of public memorialization.

Deeply traumatized by the soul-destroying effects of white American racism, Brown was uplifted by contemplating a European monument that exaggerated racial differences not to dehumanize but to aggrandize black manhood. Although the unknown soldier's physiognomy relies on stereo-typical features that betray the artist's indebtedness to racist caricature, his prominent inclusion in such an iconic site of military prowess signaled, for Brown, some kind of official attempt to recuperate black bodies within a white national imaginary. Much to Brown's surprise, the artist was keen

FIGURE 1. William Railton, Nelson's Column, "ENGLAND EXPECTS EVERY
MAN WILL DO HIS DUTY," 1840–43. (Courtesy of Richard Anderson)

to memorialize black humanity according to white social and political ideologies for purposes of elevation rather than denigration. As he concedes,
the effect was instantaneous: "As soon as I saw my sable brother, I felt more
at home, and remained longer than I had intended. Here was the Negro, as
black a man as was ever imported from the coast of Africa, represented in his
proper place by the side of Lord Nelson, on one of England's proudest monuments."[2] Dissatisfied with the power of the image alone, the artist chose to
accompany this bas-relief of an unknown African soldier standing alongside
his white compatriots with the caption "ENGLAND EXPECTS EVERY MAN
WILL DO HIS DUTY." As a powerful declaration of black national belonging, this textual description succeeds in positioning an otherwise problematic representation of a typically exoticized African masculinity within a
patriotic white British paradigm. As Brown understood it, the spectacle of
African heroism was writ large in a monument otherwise seemingly solely
devoted to eulogizing white male bravery. For Brown, therefore, this bronze

panel was to be celebrated for its candor regarding the powerful yet repeatedly neglected reality that overwhelming numbers of Africans fought in the army and navy during the Napoleonic Wars. Still visible today, this panel bears witness to an empowered black masculinity as the body and face of this unknown, erect, and armed African soldier come to life in stark contrast to the dejected countenances and prostrate bodies of white soldiers.

For Brown, caught up in the idealistic possibilities of transatlantic memorialization, no monument could be further from perpetuating racist constructions of black bodies as objects of trade, spectacles of entertainment, or proofs in moral suasionist discourse. More powerfully still, the official representation of black male heroism provided on this white British site inspired Brown to reflect upon American injustices. "How different, thought I, was the position assigned to the colored man on similar monuments in the United States," he protests.[3] According to Brown, a transatlantic milieu accentuated national inequalities by legitimizing his indictment of the immorality not only of American slavery but of white governmental tendencies toward commemorative rituals of black erasure. "Some years since, while standing under the shade of the monument erected to the memory of the brave Americans who fell at the storming of Fort Griswold, Connecticut," he explains, "I felt a degree of pride as I beheld the names of two Africans who had fallen in the fight, yet I was grieved but not surprised to find their names colonized off, and a line drawn between them and the whites." As Brown saw it, the act of forgetting remained inscribed in the art of remembering within white American memorials, which worked to displace and diminish black male heroism. "This was in keeping with American historical injustice to its colored heroes," he concedes, stating, "The conspicuous place assigned to this representative of an injured race, by the side of one of England's greatest heroes, brought vividly before my eye the wrongs of Africa and the philanthropic man of Great Britain."[4] Balancing one national context against another, Brown condemns American inequalities to expose the different ways in which white official transatlantic sites memorialized black heroism. Trading in illusory constructions of an idealized British humanitarianism, he was able not only to rally international support to the antislavery movement but also to reinforce his attack on white North American racism.

Groton Monument, the U.S. memorial to which Brown refers, was erected in 1830 to commemorate white struggles for emancipation in the bloody battle against British forces at Fort Griswold, Connecticut, in 1781. His evocation of this particular conflict exposes a terrible hypocrisy. Brown was appalled that white Americans had retained a system of slavery—even in the face of having fought and won their own freedom—because they had felt not only colonized but in fact fettered by the constitutional monarchy of England during the colonial era. While the monument survives today, the original "List of men who fell at Fort Griswold, Sept. 6, 1781" that so offended Brown is currently only on view within the stone edifice. Particularly offensive to Brown was the fact that this marble record exalted in feats of white American male martyrdom by providing an alphabetical list of the dead that tellingly excluded the "(Colored Men) Sambo Latham" and "Jordan Freeman," both added as an afterthought.[5] Such a stone inscription is not to be confused with the bronze plaque added to the memorial gate nearly a hundred years later in 1911. Performing the work of revisionist history, this tablet reinserts Jordan and Freedom into a newly unsegregated alphabetical list that includes "JORDAN FREEMAN (NEGRO)" and "LAMBO LATHAM (NEGRO)," significantly no longer identified by the racist designation "Sambo." As Sidney and Emma Nogrady Kaplan report, William Anderson, a "black man" present at the dedication of this monument, was incensed at the white-authored misrepresentations of Black men provided in the original text. "One of these men was the brother of my grandmother, by the name of Lambert, but called Lambo,—since chiselled on the marble monument by the American classic appellation of 'Sambo,'" he explains.[6] Far from the exalted visualization of black manhood provided within a British context in Nelson's Column, as Brown shows, political and social lacunae remained the defining characteristic of white American sites of memory. Here, writ large, was incontrovertible proof that black male heroism remained off limits within a white-dominated national imaginary.

As a forceful declaration of black independence, Brown's politicized juxtaposition of white American amnesia with European official sites of memorialization sheds light on many of the fundamental concerns of this book. In these pages, I examine not only an array of visual and textual materials created by Toussaint Louverture, Nathaniel Turner, Sengbe Pieh, Sojourner Truth, Frederick Douglass, and Harriet Tubman but also the contemporaneous and subsequent nineteenth-, twentieth-, and twenty-first-century archive inspired by and indebted to their lives and works. I come to grips with multifarious textual and visual strategies of black heroic representation that encompass a long time frame and wide-ranging transatlantic milieu. Adopting an interdisciplinary framework, I counter mainstream and marginal tendencies toward fragmentation and obfuscation to explore the diverse ways in which these African, African Caribbean, and African American historical figures were and are reimagined across diverse social and political contexts as well as a gamut of aesthetic forms. One of my aims is to address the ways in which the majority of current scholarship fails to investigate these heroic figures either within a comparative perspective or a transatlantic context or even over an extensive historical period. By engaging with a powerful and multifaceted yet barely excavated archive, I am guided by Marcus Wood's observation that "when it comes to the official memory of slavery the slaves are still iconically imprisoned within the visual rhetoric of disempowerment, stereotypification, and passivity."[7] Vilified and demonized if not discounted altogether, the "liberty or death" freedom fighters Louverture, Turner, Pieh, Truth, Douglass, and Tubman have typically remained beyond the pale of white mainstream discourse and iconography. At the same time, they have generated a wealth of textual and visual representations that constitute a distinct intellectual, political, and aesthetic tradition.

In recent decades, there has been a proliferation of outstanding scholarship devoted to excavating and examining these enslaved heroes and heroines as individualized subjects. Working in an alternative vein to this extant criticism, however, I adopt a comparative framework to situate these historical figures within a multifaceted transatlantic tradition. Clearly, while I have decided to focus this book upon Louverture, Turner, Pieh, Truth, Douglass, and Tubman, strong claims can be made that I could just as easily have investigated representations of Phillis Wheatley, Olaudah Equiano, Harriet Jacobs, Denmark Vesey, Gabriel Prosser, Henry Highland Garnet, "Solitude," Bussa, Nanny of the Maroons, Sam Sharpe, Robert Young, Mary Prince, Robert Wedderburn, and Margaret Garner, among many others. And yet there is a rationale for examining these particular figures. Appearing and reappearing across the centuries, Louverture, Turner, Pieh, Truth, Douglass, and Tubman have played a key role in inaugurating as well as influencing a political, historical, and cultural tradition of black male and female heroism both within and beyond the United States. At the same time, while they are indispensable to a black transatlantic tradition of antislavery activism and literary and visual culture, many other enslaved men and women turned activists and writers—including even such iconic figures as Nanny of the Maroons, "Solitude," Denmark Vesey, Gabriel Prosser, Margaret Garner, and Madison Washington—have not been represented nearly so widely in poetry, novels, drama, sculpture, murals, portrait painting, photography, or historical writings. Repeatedly emerging at fundamental epochs of transatlantic history, Louverture, Turner, Pieh, Truth, Douglass, and Tubman all signify as pioneers of diverse forms of political, physical, aesthetic, moral, cultural, and intellectual resistance. Ultimately, the perpetuation and recirculation

of their lives and works within a U.S. and transatlantic context more generally bears witness to their status as imaginative touchstones within a forceful
continuum of black male and female heroism.

Countering the lack of scholarship devoted to examining eclectic forms of
black heroism within a transatlantic imagination, I identify a wealth of textual and visual materials in this book. These cut across diverse printing technologies and cultures as I analyze historical tracts, daguerreotypes, etchings,
sculpture, fine art portraiture, poetry, novels, plays, essays, tracts, speeches,
murals, graffiti, mixed-media installations, and performance art. As visual
and textual works produced and disseminated across the United States,
Africa, and Europe, this wide-ranging archive not only revisits but resists
lacunae in official records and mainstream sites of memorialization. Working with the aim of beginning to do justice to neglected materials, I investigate imaginative and historical textual and visual works produced by major
African, African American, African Caribbean, European, and European
American authors and artists in relation to those produced by neglected
and critically ignored writers and creators. This approach complicates mainstream accounts of transatlantic black heroism to shed light on the difficulties of understanding major historical icons whom we may think we know
and concerning whom a great deal is written and yet for whom distortion
and myopia have remained the dominant characteristics in the historical archives. Writing an intellectual and cultural history of black heroism, I excavate well-known and little-discussed visual and textual materials in order to
examine acts and arts of "slave agency" and denounce the double standards
by which, as Wood argues, "slave thought and slave cultures are not allowed
a presence, a life."[8]

My purpose in examining historical figures such as Sojourner Truth,
Frederick Douglass, and Harriet Tubman—all of whom were officially sanctioned by white mainstream abolitionists, however much they were persecuted by proslavery racists—alongside the more controversial figures of
Toussaint Louverture, Nathaniel Turner, and Sengbe Pieh, each of whom
were subjected to vilification and demonization on the grounds that their
liberation struggles necessitated acts of violence, is to complicate monolithic and reductive definitions of black heroism. I implode ideologically
inflected boundaries to contest artificially imposed demarcations that categorize Black men and women according to prescriptive heroic, unheroic,
and even antiheroic constructions. The same rules apply for seemingly well-
documented and celebrated Black heroic figures as apply for misrepresented

or underresearched figures. Scholars must read against the grain to counter facile assumptions and trouble seemingly still waters.

Rejecting oversimplified paradigms, a comparative approach makes it possible to examine Truth's experimental identities alongside her overtly politicized maternal constructions, to reinterpret Tubman's coded performances in the context of her physical liberation work on the Underground Railroad, and to reexamine the signifying practices by which Douglass endorsed a philosophy of art for art's sake at the same time that he demanded conversion to the abolitionist cause via incendiary rhetoric. This all-encompassing theoretical framework also makes it possible to reevaluate Louverture's linguistic experimentation—in his use of parables and allegories—as an extension of rather than a departure from his physical militancy. A comparative approach no less allows scholars to understand Turner's widely misinterpreted use of imagery and rhetorical appeal as inextricable from his advocacy of violence. Such a wide-ranging interpretative framework also facilitates attempts to situate Pieh's elided, if not entirely erased, African identity in conjunction with his antislavery persona as a spectacular exhibit. As I argue in this book, bifurcated categorizations of black heroism impose artificial polarizations that fail to take account of the role played by contradiction and paradox as diverse Louvertures, Turners, Piehs, Truths, Douglasses, and Tubmans circulated in an array of literary, historical, and aesthetic forms. As the malleable symbolism dramatized by eclectic representations of black male and female heroism demonstrates, any quest to penetrate beneath obfuscations within the archive to recover an essential or even historically verifiable heroic figure is not only illusory but ultimately doomed to failure.

Symptomatic of the extent to which black heroism has remained unmappable terrain, over the centuries many writers and artists have fought and lost significant battles to convince publishers and readers not only of the political and historical significance but even of the legitimacy of their heroic subjects. Writing to W. E. B. Du Bois, one of his most famous authors, the publisher Ellis P. Oberholtzer was embarrassed to admit that Frederick Douglass was off limits as a biographical subject because Booker T. Washington had decided he would write the official history. In response, Du Bois's alternative proposal was that "the subject for me would be Nat Turner." Oberholtzer was skeptical: "Is there sufficient material for such a purpose, and could he be made to appear as anything more than a deluded prophet who led a little band of men armed with scythes and broad axes?"[9] "In my opinion no single man before 1850 had a greater influence on Southern legislation & feeling than Nat Turner," was Du Bois's unequivocal reply. He insisted, "There is abundant material for his life & times." This declaration failed to convince, however, as Du Bois instead produced a biography of the controversial white freedom fighter and martyr John Brown. A key aim of the present book, therefore, is to explore a wealth of both overexamined and underresearched material in order to investigate the difficulties presented by the fact that while Black historical figures such as Douglass, for example, remain enduringly canonical icons, radical revolutionaries such as Turner exist as their unpalatable shadow, memorialized as barbarous, murderous, and quintessentially "antiheroic."

The white researcher Earl Conrad similarly faced seemingly insurmountable barriers in the 1930s in his search for a publisher for his biography of Harriet Tubman. "Nearly all of the New York City publishers saw and turned down this story," he writes. "'What?' they said, 'a black woman? Why are you writing the story of a black woman? Who can she possibly be? What could she possibly have done?'" Finally, his work was published with a black press because he had "won the respect of the black community."[10] Appearing in very different political contexts, both Du Bois's and Conrad's negative experiences attest to widespread difficulties confronting authors and artists in convincing white publishers, patrons, and audiences that formerly enslaved men and women such as Turner or Tubman were significant for their heroism. Equally, the scantiness of Turner's and Tubman's archives is telling regarding the ways in which they—as well as Pieh, Louverture, and Truth—were repeatedly misunderstood because of lacunae generated by racist assumptions within white mainstream historical records. Surprisingly, the memory of Frederick Douglass, a much more famous and celebrated figure, has similarly suffered from distortions and misrepresentations that have worked to elide his complexities and endorse illusory oversimplifications.

Given the persistence of racist ideologies in both self-conscious and unconscious ways, it is essential that oratorical and textual works by Toussaint Louverture, Nathaniel Turner, Sengbe Pieh, Sojourner Truth, Frederick Douglass, and Harriet Tubman be reexamined in conjunction with the diverse materials produced by subsequent writers and artists. Similarly engaged in imploding dominant modes of thought and representation, they no less transgressed intellectual, historical, and artistic boundaries to dramatize fundamental, if elided and obscured, aspects of black heroism. One purpose of this study is to analyze both earlier and later works in order to identify and examine the formative role these figures played in influencing as well as inaugurating a diverse aesthetic, political, and historical tradition. Restructuring the parameters within which to represent black male and female resistance within a diasporic context, by both necessity and design, these heroic figures engaged with groundbreaking constructions of multiple selves in their writings, oratory, and diverse performances. As a point of origin, they inserted themselves into, at the same time that they redefined, a multifaceted, diasporic tradition of black male and female heroism.

Louverture, Truth, Turner, Pieh, Douglass, and Tubman all engaged in experimental visual, oratorical, and textual practices designed to challenge the tendencies toward reductive fixity that were otherwise inextricable from the nefarious practices of slavery. As an institution and a national ideology, the North American system of chattel slavery provided legal ballast to objectified categorizations of Black women, children, and men as they were repeatedly exploited as objects of sale, entertainment, scientific enquiry, and even anthropological investigation. Therefore, the sheer fact of the lives and works of Louverture, Turner, Pieh, Truth, Douglass, and Tubman has not only worked to sabotage fraudulent theories regarding racist stereotypes but has also countered dominant anti- no less than proslavery discourses that reimagined Black men and women as no more than spectacular commodities or bodies of evidence. Theirs was both a politicized aesthetic and an aestheticized politics, as strategies of disguise, masquerade, and indirection became their modus operandi in the face of dehumanizing social and political contexts. Spanning generations and lifetimes, their acts and arts have resulted in the creation of a revisionist archive that has ensured their survival as seemingly transcendent icons of a living, breathing black female and male humanity, both illusory and mythical but also palpable and historically real. Far from dead, these enslaved heroes and heroines have lived and subsequently continue to relive in the transatlantic imagination by proliferating in multiple incarnations, many of which they themselves galvanized via their own literature, oratory, songs, and visual representations. As I argue, eclectic and experimental reimaginings of enslaved male and female heroism are indebted to the linguistic manipulation and self-expressive forms of Louverture, Turner, Pieh, Truth, Douglass, and Tubman as authors and artists.

Adopting a long time frame, this book traces black heroic legacies across the nineteenth, twentieth, and twenty-first centuries not only to examine works produced by Louverture, Turner, Pieh, Truth, Douglass, and Tubman but also to identify and analyze the diverse texts they directly and indirectly inspired. Their multiple forms of self-representation have influenced writers and artists working not only in the United States but also in the Caribbean, Africa, Canada, and Europe with the result that their visual and textual materials constitute a rich and frequently neglected tradition. Overall, in this study I am centrally concerned with the larger organic processes by which biographical mythologies were and have been reinvented and continuously regenerated across this period. Consequently, this book charts the complex processes of cultural evolution by which originatory works—such as Louverture's and Turner's prison narratives, Truth's and Pieh's oratory, Tubman's ambiguous use of song and Douglass's intellectual, literary, and philosophical forays into narrative production—provided the creative source material for a second archive consisting of later adaptations by numerous writers and artists.

Clearly, the legacies of these formerly enslaved women and men resonate beyond their immediate historical contexts and on into the late nineteenth, twentieth, and twenty-first centuries. Their acts and arts of imagining and reimagining remain intrinsic to this subsequent vast archive in which artists and activists not only seek to inspire empathetic responses from diverse audiences but also rely on strategies of defamiliarization to stimulate dispassionate analysis and inspire a politicized engagement. While this book is far from comprehensive or encyclopedic, my purpose is to introduce readers to neglected writers and artists while at the same time encouraging scholars to engage with more familiar writers and artists in new ways. A comparative perspective not only allows for a reevaluation and recuperation of radical Black heroic figures who have existed seemingly beyond the pale of white representation but also illuminates otherwise elided tensions within more accepted icons. My aim in undertaking research into obscure as well as more renowned writers and artists is to reveal the ways in which the experimental tendencies of lesser-known texts shed fresh light on existing works we think we know well. Thus a reevaluation of existing theoretical models and approaches becomes possible as we begin to interrogate the illusory foundations of frequently polarized and reductive representations.

The rationale for selecting this diverse but limited array of historical, political, and literary texts and artworks has been influenced not only by their thematic content and formal structure but also by the date of publication. As readers will note, each chapter includes at least one work from the following epochs: the height of chattel slavery in nineteenth-century North America; the Depression era in the 1930s and 1940s; the decades commonly identified as the twentieth-century civil rights movement in the 1950s, 1960s, and 1970s; and, finally, the soi-disant "post–civil rights" period of the 1990s–2000s down to the present day. While this study addresses the fact that diverse texts devoted to black heroism proliferated beyond these defining moments, my purpose in selecting these particular epochs is to pinpoint the historical, social, and political uses and reuses of these heroic figures as they were reimagined and remembered to suit differing agendas, audiences, and movements. As this book demonstrates, Louverture, Turner, Pieh, Truth, Douglass, and Tubman all operated not only as talismans of injustice, sacrifice, and suffering but also as signifiers capable of breathing fresh life into radical movements by acting as imaginative symbols for further resistance and reimagining. Yet this is not the whole story. Numerous historical, political, social, and artistic texts were created outside of these specific temporal boundaries. Emerging both before and after as much as within the eye of the storm of these key eras, a rich array of visual and textual materials testifies to the intellectual necessity of working with blurred rather than categorical definitions of the relationships between historical periods. Adopting experimental and eclectic approaches, countless writers and artists have established the evolving roles and changing symbolism of these diverse Black heroic figures. As reimagined to suit shifting contexts, their lives and legacies bear witness not only to a continuum of black male and female resistance but also to a rich and experimental aesthetic tradition.

Challenging national boundaries, I investigate multifaceted representations of diverse forms of black male and female heroism as disseminated within a transatlantic imagination. While four of the six heroic figures discussed in this book (Nathaniel Turner, Sojourner Truth, Frederick Douglass, and Harriet Tubman) are African American, one is African Caribbean (the Haitian revolutionary Toussaint Louverture) and the other African (the Sierra Leonean–born freedom fighter Sengbe Pieh). Thus, while the chapters are structured according to four key historical moments roughly defined as slavery, the Depression, the civil rights movement, and the "post–civil rights" era, each also includes at least one transatlantic text—i.e., a work produced in a non-U.S. context including Africa, France, Great Britain, the Caribbean, and First Nations Canada. At the same time that these heroic figures and texts differ in national origin, textual and visual memorializations of Black heroic figures as produced within a U.S. context form the focus of this study. A major organizing principle emerges, therefore, from the decision to restrict the study to all works published or translated into English. A comparative book examining works representing black heroism in the United States, the Caribbean, Africa, and Europe in their original languages is still to be written. For the benefit of readers, this study includes color as well as black and white reproductions of an array of paintings, drawings, woodcuts, prints, photographs, statuary, and mixed-media installations. As a brief selection of well-known and neglected works produced across a range of genres and over a long time frame, this archive offers a condensed visual introduction to the book's interdisciplinary exploration of acts and arts of representing, memorializing, and reimagining black heroism.

Any scholar engaged in examining elided and distorted representations of black male heroism in a transatlantic imagination necessarily encounters even greater obstacles in mapping a black female heroic tradition. It is no exaggeration to state that distortions, lacunae, and misrepresentations have all but erased any traces of a black female heroic tradition in the white-dominated mainstream. Repeatedly subjugated and displaced, if not entirely annihilated by the masculine biases of European and European American as well as African and African American male writers and artists, acts and arts of black female heroism are frequently both profoundly underresearched and widely misunderstood. Therefore, one of the main aims of this book is not only to illuminate but to contest and reconfigure existing intellectual, political, and aesthetic barriers to representing black female heroism. In this regard, Frances Smith Foster incisively exposes the flawed premises at work within intellectual and political biases that define Black men as the sole bearers of "the heroic spirits once enslaved." "Mention the slave woman," she explains, "and noble images fade." "In the popular imagination, she stands on the auction block, nameless, stripped to the waist," she writes.[11] Few formerly enslaved female authors were more persecuted by this paradox in the nineteenth century than Harriet Jacobs, author of *Incidents in the Life of a Slave Girl*, published in 1861. As a writer forced to engage in literary experimentation, she battled to tell her narrative as "if it was the life of a Heroine with no degradation associated with it," as she fought to endorse her belief in a "liberty or death" ethos.[12]

To begin to address these injustices, black female heroism must, first and foremost, be understood on its own terms rather than in conjunction with a black male continuum of resistance. The only way to ensure full recognition of the strategies by which African American women reconfigured, adapted, and contested the boundaries of black, no less than white, male forms of heroism is to construct an independent theoretical model. Regardless of their widespread fame as historical icons and touchstones for black female liberation, the radicalism of such self-emancipated liberators as Sojourner Truth and Harriet Tubman has been repeatedly obscured or denied. As declarations of independence, their signifying performances remain inextricable from their search for political, social, and artistic freedoms. Their diverse strategies include oratorical performance and linguistic subterfuge as they repeatedly fought for the right to sexual agency and to express ideological resistance to white domestic values. Equally, they manipulated their visual and textual legacies in a battle for ownership over the wealth generated by their laboring bodies in order to protect the sanctity of black familial relationships. Moreover, Tubman and Truth experimented with oratorical performances in their ideological commitment to challenging the political legitimacy of literacy as any verifiable proof of black equal humanity. Their diverse forms of performative storytelling operate in conjunction with self-stylized manipulations of dress and facial expressions to insist upon black female psychological and aesthetic complexities. Above all else, Truth and Tubman warred against the problematic tendency, exhibited by pro- and antislavery sympathizers alike, toward memorializing black female heroism solely according to masculine paradigms. This strategy was frequently understood as the only clear-cut way in which to reclaim these formerly enslaved activists as freedom fighters within a European American heroic paradigm. While Truth was forced to bare not only her breasts but also her muscular arm to conjoin her exceptional strength with her femininity in the minds of her audiences, so too Tubman's life and works encountered the gender biases even of such radical men as John Brown, for whom she was the "most of a man naturally that I ever met with."[13]

As the opening to this introduction demonstrates, William Wells Brown's anger at the ways in which Black men had been "colonized off" succeeds in rejecting white American racism by betraying his masculine biases. Far from atypical, Brown's gendered resistance underscores his similarities with the majority of Black male antislavery activists—including Douglass—whose focus was equally upon the distortions and violations enacted upon black male bodies within white official histories. Thus one defining aim of this book is to interrogate Douglass's exploration of the archetypal figure of the "heroic slave"—an icon he later reconceptualized during the Civil War as the "black hero"—as both a radically revisionist and yet profoundly problematic model. Following from Brown, at the same time that he rejected the legitimacy of white mainstream archives, Douglass reinstituted black male representations as the standard default of African, African Caribbean, and African American heroisms.

The intellectual, political, and aesthetic practices of Sojourner Truth and Harriet Tubman offer powerful and alternative ways in which to confront the distortions embedded within and generated by dominant forms of black male knowledge. Across their lives and works, they challenged the ways in which the concept of the "heroic slave" or "black hero" for Douglass, Brown,

and countless other writers, artists, and activists was problematically configured as male. In these pages, I draw out the key features of a black heroic female tradition, recognizing, as Hazel Carby argues, "In many complex ways
the politics and language of gender over determine the representation of
the black male rebel and produce a politics and aesthetics of the black male
body."[14] As self-reflexive negotiators of the terrain of black female physical
representations and linguistic signifying, Truth's and Tubman's multiple existences rejected not only white male and female strategies of appropriation
and erasure but also black male tendencies toward denying or commodifying
feats of black female heroism. More especially, as freedom fighters working
across stereotypically feminized and masculine domains, Truth and Tubman
worked to reposition the black female figure, not solely as a self-sacrificing
martyr or catalyst to black male heroism, but as a revolutionary and quintessential liberator in her own right.

In a republican nation forged from the shackles of monarchical corrup-
tion, white American models of heroism have long been the subject of political, social, historical, and cultural debate. Roger D. Abrahams, Cora Kaplan,
David Lambert, Robert Penn Warren, Dixon Wecter, and Joseph Campbell
are among a number of scholars who usefully theorize the intersections
between heroism—typically identified as male—and social construction,
mythological symbolism, and legendary reimagining. More particularly, in
the early nineteenth century, the white British writer Thomas Carlyle, a pioneering theorist and philosopher of white European and masculine forms
of heroism, produced seminal works including *On Heroes, Hero-Worship,
and the Heroic in History,* a collection of essays published in 1840. Betraying
his ideological biases, at the start of this work he describes his subject matter as consisting solely of "Great Men, their manner of appearance in our
world's business, how they have shaped themselves in the world's history,
what ideas men formed of them, what work they did;—on Heroes, namely,
and on their reception and performance, what I call Hero-worship and the
Heroic in human affairs." Drawing solely on European classical and modern
male icons such as William Shakespeare, Napoléon Bonaparte, and Oliver
Cromwell, Carlyle positions exceptional forms of white masculinity as not
only representing but actually embodying the forces of history. "Universal
History, the history of what man has accomplished in this world, is at bottom the History of the Great Men who have worked here," he insists. Any
cursory examination quickly reveals that Carlyle's panegyric is defined by
exclusionary practices. His all-white, all-male, and exclusively European pantheon promulgates six heroic types—"Divinity," "Prophet," "Poet," "Priest,"

"Man of Letters," and "King"—to offer "some glimpses into the very marrow of the world's history." In providing the reader with "glimpses" into his perfidious selection criteria, he betrays his racist and ideologically fraught interpretations of a heroism which nefariously masquerades as "universal" and "world" history.[15] For a scholar and historian who was capable of writing the vitriolic and racist polemic "Occasional Discourse on the Nigger Question," published in 1853, the same year in which Douglass's *The Heroic Slave* appeared to both British and North American audiences, black heroism was beyond his comprehension. "I decidedly like poor quashee," he offensively declares.[16]

Rejecting Carlyle's overtly Europeanized framework that perpetuates Old World hierarchies, Ralph Waldo Emerson took this deeply problematic philosophical and intellectual model to task in his essay "Heroism," published a year later. Contesting the model's usefulness in any serious attempt to define heroism, Emerson endorsed categorizations that, in contrast to Carlyle, spoke specifically to an American context. In so doing, he recuperates an idealized vision of heroism, which he understood as inextricable from the redemptive force of violence. "To this military attitude of the soul we give the name of Heroism," he argues. "Its rudest form is the contempt for safety and ease, which makes the attractiveness of war."[17] Simply arguing that heroism "is the extreme of individual nature," he insists, "we must profoundly revere it" as he shores up his convictions regarding the didactic and spiritual function of heroic figures as role models.[18] "Heroism feels and never reasons, and therefore is always right," he explains, thereby vindicating his belief in the historical power of emotional rather than intellectual realities. Refusing to draw solely on classical European models, however, he cites white American sacrifice in the context of slavery as his preferred parable. "It is but the other day that the brave Lovejoy gave his breast to the bullets of a mob, for the rights of free speech and opinion, and died when it was better not to live," he writes.[19]

On the surface, Emerson's decision to celebrate Elijah P. Lovejoy as the quintessential white victim, martyred in the service of black freedom, succeeds in perpetuating Carlyle's biases by similarly eliding historical representations of black heroism. Yet, as is clear from his other essays and speeches on the rights of humanity, Emerson was not averse to extolling black male heroism, if not as the normative standard, then at least as proof of equal humanity. For example, a few years later, in "An Address on the Emancipation of the Negroes in the British West Indies," delivered on August 1, 1844, he took issue with proslavery racist appraisals of black inhumanity. "If the black man is feeble, and not important to the existing race, not on a parity with the best race, the black man must serve, and be exterminated," he initially seems to assert, adding, however, that "if the black man carries in his bosom an indispensable element of a new and coming civilization, for the sake of that element, no wrong, nor strength, nor circumstance, can hurt him: he will survive and play his part."[20]

In clear-cut ways, Emerson exalts in instances of black male heroism to offer tangible proof of his belief in black humanity: "So now, the arrival in the world of such men as Toussaint, and the Haytian heroes, or of the leaders of their race in Barbadoes and Jamaica, outweighs in good omen all the English and American humanity." Therefore, for Emerson, who was problematically preoccupied with seemingly exceptional black icons, Louverture clearly functions as both a man and an "anti-slave" and, as such, an archetypal figure in possession of sufficient political, intellectual, and ideological weight to silence racist detractors such as Carlyle. As shown in his other writings, even Carlyle was fascinated and horrified to admit that "society, it is understood, does not in any age, prevent a man for being what he *can* be. A sooty African *can* become a Toussaint L'Ouverture, a murderous, Three-fingered Jack.'"[21] Offensively denigrating Louverture as a "murderous" and "sooty African," he ultimately rejects any potential associations of black masculinity with heroism. Instead, he foregrounds theatrical adaptations in the legendary persona of enslaved man turned subversive trickster, "Three-fingerer Jack," to exclude Louverture from an exceptional pantheon of "universal" white heroes.

As Cora Kaplan writes, "Philosophers, poets, novelists, political thinkers were busy *theorizing* heroism, arguing about its job description, giving it a special place in the definition of what makes man in the generic, but also in the gendered and the ethnic or racial sense, fully human" throughout this early period.[22] This definitional process has since been further developed by Roger Abrahams in his determination to establish "Some Varieties of Heroes in America." Beginning with the disclaimer "The deeds of heroes are sung throughout the world, but the concept of heroic action is by no means universal," he rejects Carlyle's earlier suppositions. "The actions we consider heroic reflect a view of life which is based upon contested values and a social hierarchy built on the model of a male-centered family," he explains.[23] Reframing the intellectual positions of Carlyle and others, Abrahams's essential revisionist work explores heroism as a relative concept heavily dependent upon social and political biases. As Kaplan writes, "Modern heroism emerges as an effect of the creation of republics and democracies—the more equality, the more heroes. Heroic identifications, together with the inevitable discontents and disappointments, were, we might say, a narrative process of idealization and disenchantment, central to the making of modern subjectivity."[24] Her view that processes of heroic formation remain integral to "modern subjectivity" construction bears witness to the political, historical, moral, and aesthetic importance of comparatively reexamining the otherwise elided tradition of black heroism on offer within works produced by African, African Caribbean, and African American activists and artists.

More recently, Jerry Bryant's research focuses upon the African American literary canon to situate the intersections between masculinity and heroism within a context of victimization and violence. "In the most morally simplified cases, white violence against blacks produces a victim, black violence against whites a hero," he argues, summarizing, "Victims and heroes tend to be constantly shifting and changing shapes." Here, Bryant's sense of "changing shapes" speaks to the multifaceted black heroic continuum examined in this book. According to this approach, boundaries between victims, martyrs, and exceptional icons become blurred and reconfigured in the search for new ways of overturning static and reductive representations of black heroism. Bryant also gets to the heart of a key concern for the heroic figures discussed in this volume by exposing the fact that "for most American whites, to speak of a black 'hero' is a contradiction in terms."[25] Fully aware of the ways in which their public and private identities would be reimagined and reused to suit diverse political agendas, Louverture, Turner, Pieh, Truth, Tubman, and Douglass all engaged with multiple forms of self-representation. Ultimately, they shared a determination to exert control over the interpretative parameters within which to reconstitute black male and female heroism. As I demonstrate in this book, black male and female heroism remains a repeatedly distorted if not entirely elided or taboo subject within the white American national imaginary. If we accept David Lambert's assessment that "the creation of national heroes is part of the ongoing project of what a nation 'means,'" any such cultural, political, and intellectual difficulties speak to the extent to which men and women such as Louverture, Turner, Pieh, Truth, Douglass, and Tubman have been subject to censure for problematizing, if not outright rejecting, dominant and exclusionary constructions of nationhood.[26] Repeatedly engaging in acts and arts of self-representation across their lives and works, they fought against national distortion and amnesia by interrogating the extent to which "heroic reputations are also reproduced through namings of space and the construction of public statuary, and contested through the same symbolic landscape."[27]

In *Heroic Reputations and Exemplary Lives,* Geoffrey Cubitt and Allen Warren similarly debate "the ways in which notions of exemplarity have helped to shape the cultural uses of heroic figures."[28] And yet, for the formerly enslaved men and women discussed in this book, exemplarity is a fraught issue. Living and dying beyond the pale of white official representations, these Black heroic figures have not only had to fight for the right to a recognition of their exceptionalism but also for control over their subsequent "cultural uses" and, more powerfully, misuses. In this respect, Cubitt's understanding that typically heroic figures are "cultural constructions reflecting the values and ideologies of the societies in which they are produced" is only part of the story.[29] For the Black men and women discussed in this book, heroism originates in the act and art of reclaiming their right to dominant "values and ideologies" at the same time that they have continued to fight for autonomy over their "cultural constructions." In this regard, it makes very little sense even to begin to try to differentiate between that which Cubitt defines as the "complex relationships between lives lived, lives imagined and lives textually reproduced."[30] In the context of the racist biases embedded within white national imaginaries, black acts and arts of self-representation exist in slippery relation to dominant modes of representation as formerly enslaved men and women contest the accuracies of any mainstream attempts to extrapolate their "lives" as "lived."

While Bryant and many other scholars—including Albert Murray, Fred O. Weldon, and William L. Van Deburg—focus on African American folk heroism, John W. Roberts's determination to problematize seemingly neutral categorizations of heroism is pivotal to this book. In contrast to Lambert and Cubitt, he directly extrapolates the ways in which heroism remains a relative concept that is simultaneously dependent upon social, political, and aesthetic contexts. "We often use the term 'hero' as if it denoted a universally recognized character type, and the concept of 'heroism' as if it referred to a generally accepted behavioral category," he argues, adding, "In reality, figures (both real and mythic) and actions dubbed heroic in one context or by one group of people may be viewed as ordinary or even criminal in another context or by other groups, or even by the same ones at different times."[31] Roberts's insistence on the role played by social, political, and historical contexts in refocusing the lens through which we reconstruct and reimagine heroism is integral to the theoretical framework of this study. Similarly, although he adopts a very different focus, Van Deburg's conviction that "heroism is constantly evolving," reflects this book's emphasis upon the importance of a plethora of circulating, nonfixed, and fluid identity constructions.[32]

According to this radical conceptualization, representations of Louverture, Turner, Pieh, Truth, Douglass, and Tubman have been and are continually adapted and reconfigured to suit diverse social and political contexts.

Refracted across gender, national, and class boundaries, acts and arts of black male and female heroism problematize seemingly straightforward white mainstream constructions of Black men and women solely as bodies of entertainment, exhibition, and evidence. As demonstrated in the lives and deaths of the historical figures examined in this book, heroism was not a monolithic, fixed, or linear concept. Far from it. The cultivation of multiple political and historical personae by men and women like Turner attests to the extent to which they deliberately failed to fit white abolitionist teleologies of cathartic uplift by refusing to follow any singular journey from slavery to emancipation. At the same time, their ambiguous identities countered proslavery discourses that endorsed reductive caricature and bestialized stereotyping. Any examination of their textual and visual representations produced within a transatlantic imagination reveals that black heroism must be understood as encompassing a continuum of diverse forms of resistance.

Simultaneously engaging in diverse feats of military conflict, physical resistance, performative subterfuge, diplomatic negotiation, spiritual prophecy, and, of course, self-reflexive manipulations of language, the iconic Black men and women examined in this study rejected their "nonbeing" status to exalt instead in a newfound mythic and iconic exceptionalism that defied easy categorization. Thus, while for Toussaint Louverture heroism was based on the interrelationship between war and a fight for national independence, for Turner heroism was bound up in acts of spiritual and physical redemption as he cultivated an apocryphal martyrdom rooted in self-conceptualizations as a Black messiah and redeemer. In contrast, for Pieh it was essential that his linguistic prowess mirror his physical performances as he fought to unshackle himself from antiheroic dismissal via reductive caricature. Instead, he positioned his actions within a "give me liberty or give me death" paradigm as he sought to reconfigure his otherwise othered Africanness and situate his rebellion within a white American national framework.

Truth's heroism as a self-appointed preacher remains inextricable from sexual and domestic politics as she laid claim to her right not only to a maternal role but to the ownership of her body. Truth boldly rejected literacy in favor of oratorical protest in order to testify to her radical awareness regarding the ideological biases embedded within dominant textual discourses. On the surface, nothing could be further from Douglass's strategies, as his heroism not only functioned as a source of self-representation and self-identification but was also integral to his determination to transgress dominant boundaries of literary expression and philosophical inquiry. Probe deeper, however, and it can be argued that across Truth's no less than Douglass's life and works, she similarly interrogated the parameters for black cultural representation by equally experimenting with textual and visual languages to become her own "work of art." Conjoining physical resistance with a coded use of song and oratory, Tubman fought to destabilize prescriptive and seemingly mutually exclusive constructions of black male and female heroism.

Across the centuries, oversimplified and artificially polarized paradigms of black male and female heroism and antiheroism have continued to prevail in the popular white American imagination. Arguably, these problematic tendencies are most powerfully encapsulated in the nineteenth-century white abolitionist author Harriet Beecher Stowe's renowned and yet infamous novels, *Uncle Tom's Cabin* (1852) and *Dred: A Tale of the Great Dismal Swamp* (1856). Existing in seemingly compatible ways with popular racist discourses and iconography, her black male protagonists have functioned as symbolic touchstones for monolithic definitions of a black male heroism as defined by the "passive heroic" paradigm on the one hand and the "active heroic" model on the other. As I show in this book, the multifaceted and eclectic lives and works of Toussaint Louverture, Nathaniel Turner, Sengbe Pieh, Sojourner Truth, Frederick Douglass, and Harriet Tubman offer a powerful counternarrative that not only complicates but rejects such flawed demarcations. Proliferating over the centuries and across a range of genres and national contexts, the textual and visual materials they created and inspired exist in uneasy relation to any such oversimplified dualisms. Instead, their acts and arts of resistance testify to a multifaceted and shifting continuum of black male and female heroism.

Regardless, Stowe's bifurcated representations have continued to dominate the political, cultural, and national landscape. As testament to their endurance, Wilson Moses singles out the "myth of Uncle Tom" as particularly "difficult to untangle" as he traces the extent to which myths of "slave servility" and "slave resistance" have remained inextricable from the "related symbols of Nat Turner and Uncle Tom."[33] For Moses, these competing mythologies constitute two sides of the same coin and thereby provide a powerful way in which to explain the exclusion of black male heroism from white mainstream histories. As saints or sinners, deities or demons, martyrs or murderers, black male heroes in particular have been repeatedly denied their humanity, not only in official archives and dominant sites of memorialization, but also in mass culture. At the same time, these monolithic models of black male heroism that leave no room for psychological complexity or moral fallibility have emerged at the cost of black female heroism. In forceful ways, while debates rage over artificially polarized representations of Uncle Tom and Dred as either incendiary freedom fighters or passive martyrs, the shadow archive of black female heroism is almost entirely eradicated. As the white North American mainstream visual and textual archive reveals, there was and is no intellectual, political, social, cultural, or aesthetic middle ground within which to conceptualize black male and female heroism. Psychologically complex and multifaceted portraits that work to do justice to black individualized subjectivities were off limits. Black men and women have been conceptualized solely as either barbaric fiends in an array of proslavery atrocity literatures or as sacrificial martyrs in didactic, seemingly redemptive antislavery tracts. Furthermore, any brief examination of white historical and cultural developments soon reveals that these essentialized and oppositional models have gained rather than conceded ground in the twentieth and twenty-first centuries—a telling indictment of their ongoing nefarious grip on the popular imagination.

Thus, these paradigms are still basically in situ in the artificially polarized and misplaced constructions of a martyred and saintly Martin Luther King Jr., perceived as a Christological symbol of a conciliatory integrationism, on the one hand, and in problematic reimaginings of a demonized Malcolm X, as the repository of a vengeful black nationalism, on the other. "They are perceived as having stood at opposite extremes on the spectrum of black leadership, representing different organizations and political-religious perspectives," Lewis V. Baldwin writes.[34] And yet white mainstream attempts to represent these iconic figures according to artificial polarizations have encountered powerful resistance in the lives and works of King and Malcolm X. Engaging in self-reflexive practices and multiple acts and arts of resistance, they themselves bore witness to their incisive understanding of the damaging role that these dominant conceptualizations and mythologies of a monolithic black masculinity played in the white national imaginary. Knowingly and deliberately resisting their bifurcated associations with either "dream" or "nightmare," as recently theorized by James H. Cone, the subversive political and linguistic strategies of Martin Luther King and Malcolm X shed light on the no less elided ambiguities and complexities that differentiate the formerly enslaved historical figures discussed in this book.[35] Scholarly recognition of the ways in which Louverture, Pieh, Turner, and even Tubman have been excessively demonized while Truth and Douglass have been redemptively assimilated into the white mainstream provides a useful way in which to implode artificial barriers and endorse a multifaceted continuum of black male and female resistance.

Controversies over the parameters of black male and female heroism maintain their grip across the centuries. Such debates clearly reveal the diverse ways in which processes of hero worship intersect with the persistence—psychologically, politically, historically, ideologically, and culturally—of white supremacist ideals within enduring constructs of American nationalism. Ever the outsider, the outlaw, and the misunderstood other, Black men and women including Louverture, Turner, Pieh, Truth, Douglass, and Tubman remain sites and sights of contestation. Yet, in the face of such annihilating contexts, black acts and arts of heroism constitute a powerful countertradition by speaking to the ways in which black male and female historical figures have fought to destabilize and deconstruct white national paradigms. In this book, therefore, I examine not only the act of black heroism but, perhaps more importantly, the art of black heroism. Thus, while dominant white models sought to effect the cultural, political, social, and historical erasure of Black male and female heroic figures, repeated instances of black agency and artistry have secured their resurrection. Surviving and adapting across differing eras, their malleable personae continue to proliferate across diverse cultural materials in order to galvanize social change.[36]

Over the centuries, Toussaint Louverture, Nathaniel Turner, Sengbe Pieh, Sojourner Truth, Frederick Douglass, and Harriet Tubman signify as political, social, historical, and cultural touchstones within African, African American, Caribbean, European, and European American imaginaries. However slippery and elusive, these heroic figures have been and are reimagined and re-created by both renowned and neglected, Black and white, female and male writers and artists from diverse national backgrounds. As talismans, these figures circulate not only as iconic exemplars but also as representative individuals capable of encompassing the untold histories of anonymous women, children, and men engaged in unmemorialized acts and arts of resistance. However problematically, Louverture, Turner, Pieh, Truth, Douglass, and Tubman reemerge not only as exceptional individuals but as representative surrogates for elided and distorted black male and female histories that have been subjected to violation throughout the centuries and across a transatlantic milieu. As individual heroic enslaved liberators, Louverture, Turner, Pieh, Truth, Douglass, and Tubman operate as representative icons, as their palpable ambiguities and unresolved tensions speak to, if not for, those undocumented and unmemorialized black diasporic lives, which, of necessity, can only be reimagined and re-created from dissatisfying fragments.

Thus the memorialization of Louverture's martyrdom signifies on the untold experiences of numerous Black soldiers who died in his military campaigns. Similarly, Turner's invective against slavery and subsequent execution bears witness to his largely anonymous enslaved supporters who were equally victimized by white vengeance in bloody reprisals. As one of the very few enslaved Africans to return from the Middle Passage, Pieh symbolizes the undocumented lives of the men and women engaged in multifarious acts of resistance aboard the slave ship, still a subject for debate in current scholarship. For Sojourner Truth, it was essential that she embody the suffering of the archetypal mother enslaved in the South, even though she herself had experienced life as an enslaved woman in the North. Across his diverse writings, oratory, and photographic representations, Douglass positioned himself as a witness to his own as well as to unrecognized feats of male and female enslaved heroism as he documented the widespread existence of black radicalism in his works. Such was also the case for Tubman and her undocumented missions to rescue hundreds of enslaved women, men, and children, the majority of whose lives can be commemorated solely through her heroic acts.

In reimagining the multiple legacies of Louverture, Turner, Pieh, Truth, Douglass, and Tubman, the aim of this book is to resist displacing the undocumented lives of those anonymous enslaved heroes whose legacies are lost to history, literature, and the visual arts but whose complex existences remain integral to memorializations of known and unknown acts and arts of enslaved heroism. In this regard, one of the most startling discoveries of African American art history in the twentieth-century speaks to white mainstream neglect of black female quilting traditions in Gee's Bend, Alabama. As the works of such contemporary African American quilters as Arlonzia Pettway, Annie E. Pettway, Mary Lee Bendolph, Annie Mae Young, and Loretta Pettway demonstrate, both their enslaved female forebears and they themselves repeatedly had no choice but to create quilts to ensure black familial survival and counter the annihilating effects of extreme poverty. However constrained by their oppressive circumstances, historic and contemporary black female quilters have continued to piece cloth fragments together to create ambiguous visual archives. As a measure of the phenomenal loss to social as well as art history, the earliest quilts by unmemorialized enslaved women have not survived. And yet the quilts of earlier enslaved women, no less living and dying in a poverty-stricken world in which all materials must be reused and recycled, are far from entirely lost. Similarly suffering from a lack of resources, their descendents have frequently only been able to create their own quilts by salvaging fragments from their earlier, frequently disintegrating artifacts.

One particularly powerful example of African American female quilting traditions can be found in Missouri Pettway's blocks-and-strips workclothes quilt made in 1942. Created from "cotton, corduroy, cotton sacking material," this quilt testifies to untold histories of black male and female heroism. Arlonzia Pettway, Missouri Pettway's daughter and herself a quilt maker, powerfully explains the cross-generational, collaborative art process by which this quilt was made following the death of her father: "Mama say, 'I going to take his work clothes, shape them into a quilt to remember him, and cover up under it for love.' She take his old pants legs and shirttails, take all the clothes he had, just enough to make that quilt, and I helped her tore them up."[37] An epic-sized quilt consisting of large blocks of color, this artifact speaks to a very different site of black male memorialization in comparison with William Wells Brown's witnessing of the African soldier included on Nelson's Column nearly a hundred years previously. The textured fabric of this quilt is a far cry from such one-dimensional, seemingly representational reconstructions of a black male body etched into stone. Rather, and in the artistic hands of Missouri Pettway and her daughter, an unnamed Black man's history comes to life in a wordless, nonrepresentational visual narrative designed not for consumption by unknown audiences but, as Alice Walker powerfully writes in her short story, for "everyday use" within a domestic setting.[38]

Reflecting no pristine, shiny stone surfaces, the rectangular and square strips of blue, white, gray, and red fabric are stained, discolored, and faded. No iconic, idealized or cleaned-up reinterpretation of black lived realities, these markings provide a useful map of black survival in the face of impoverished circumstances. They not only memorialize death but bear witness to lives as lived in frayed and worn seams representative of "all the clothes he had." As a way to "remember him," Pettway's quilt does not represent a rarefied, decorative art object but rather an artifact designed for use in her determination to "cover up under it for love." As a symbol not only of her husband's life and death but also of her own untold personal history, this quilt commemorates both absent and present black male and female bodies. Clearly, Pettway memorializes the loss of her husband's physical existence only to celebrate his spiritual and emotional transcendence as he lives on in black female creativity. In this regard, the act of viewing this quilt as exhibited on museum walls rather than in its original domestic setting decontextualizes this object and runs the risk of violating, if not entirely erasing, the quilter's original vision in much the same way that the grave markers of the stone sculptor and ex-enslaved artist William Edmondson have been removed from his yard and robbed of their origins as a result of their exhibition under glass cases in art galleries.[39]

As a work created out of a desire not to protest but to commemorate, Pettway's quilt bears witness to the hardships of black poverty via the partial fragments of this man's clothing, which were only "just enough to make this quilt." As shown with Pettway's quilt, powerful reimaginings of black male history are made possible only through black female acts of storytelling. Variously pieced together squares of differing sizes and colors function as visual chapters testifying to an "imaginative inner life" regarding black emotional, social, and political realities otherwise elided within white mainstream representations.[40] As this book tracing acts and art of black male and female enslaved heroism across the centuries demonstrates, a far-reaching but neglected tradition exists, consisting of artifacts and artworks that run the full gamut by encompassing not only public statues but also private quilts. Countering ellipses and fragmentation, these diverse works memorialize the symbolic as well as the imaginative legacies of enslaved heroic figures within a transatlantic milieu.

As forces of resistance "hidden in plain view," Toussaint Louverture, Nathaniel Turner, Sengbe Pieh, Sojourner Truth, Frederick Douglass, and Harriet Tubman have all assumed radical, transformative, and transgressive identities across the centuries. Proliferating in multiples guises, their lives and works have gained rather than lost momentum. No mean feat, they have survived regardless of an outpouring of a wealth of skewed narratives generated in order to obscure, if not annihilate, the complexities of Black subjectivities. Constituting a powerful counterarchive, the multitudinous representations of Louverture, Turner, Pieh, Truth, Douglass, and Tubman on offer in historical volumes, political tracts, eclectic literary works, as well as a plethora of art objects testify to the role played by aesthetic experimentation in the recovery not only of erased and misinterpreted histories but also of unimagined lives. Born or sold into slavery, none of these heroes died in slavery. The oratorical, writerly, performative, physical, intellectual, moral, and spiritual modes of resistance in their acts and arts of heroism secured black liberation. Straining beyond the actualities of their bodily existences, they operated as controversial sites of contestation within both proslavery and abolitionist discourses by assuming multiple symbolic, imaginative, and psychological realities via their reincarnation as icons, myths, and talismans. Clearly in no ways averse to, but actively engaged in, an "attempt to play the *hero*," Louverture, Turner, Tubman, Pieh, Truth, and Douglass all fought to overcome taboo issues related to black iconic representation.[41]

Writing in the mid-twentieth century, Langston Hughes recognized the significance of such a multifaceted heritage in his essay "The Need for Heroes." He did not hold back from articulating a sense of outrage at the fact that "Harriet Tubman, Sojourner Truth, Frederick Douglass, Nat Turner were worthy of an odyssey—a great creative series of biographies and novels—but I don't find them on the shelves of our library."[42] However much they are missing from library shelves, numerous Toussaint Louvertures, Nathaniel Turners, Sengbe Piehs, Sojourner Truths, Frederick Douglasses, and Harriet Tubmans have played a key role regarding their reimaginings within a transatlantic imagination. Their kaleidoscopic "odysseys" shed light on the political and aesthetic realities of a multifaceted and yet neglected African, African American, and African Caribbean heroic continuum, the full extent of which is only mappable via multiple intellectual, political, and aesthetic journeys not only of discovery but also of recovery. As I argue in this book, multiple Louvertures, Turners, Piehs, Truths, Douglasses, and Tubmans come to life across a gamut of visual, literary, political, and historical contexts. As touchstones whose symbolism extends beyond their lifetimes, the lives and works of the Black heroes examined in this book have not only inaugurated but have also played a key role vis-à-vis inspirational legacies of black heroism within the transatlantic imagination. In this regard, an unflinching recognition of the importance of white racist omissions, distortions, and lacunae in perpetuating black failures of knowing is a source not of despair but of hope. As I argue in this book, nefarious attempts to effect black dehumanization and annihilation have paradoxically laid the foundations for an alternative political, aesthetic, and intellectual tradition. Refusing to sacrifice either their memory or their legacies, Toussaint Louverture, Nathaniel Turner, Sengbe Pieh, Sojourner Truth, Frederick Douglass, and Harriet Tubman have all performed—at the same time that they have inspired—radical and revisionist acts and arts of heroism within the transatlantic imaginary.

CHAPTER 1 "I SHED MY BLOOD"

TOUSSAINT LOUVERTURE, MYTH,

HISTORY, AND THE TRANSATLANTIC

IMAGINATION

On November 4, 1941, Ralph Ellison published "Mister Toussan" in a radical magazine titled the *New Masses*. As a dramatic engagement with white official history and black oral folk culture, Ellison's short story establishes the fundamental role played by black male heroism in the lives of his impoverished Black child protagonists, Riley and Buster. Re-created as a mythical legend for both boys living in unjust social circumstances, Toussaint Louverture's memory sparks their resistance to white mainstream stereotypes. These work not only to dismiss but to eradicate any epic associations that might potentially equate black manhood to heroism. Buster informs Riley, "All them Africa guys ain't really that lazy," citing as proof "one of the African guys named Toussan what she [his teacher] said whipped Napoleon!" Tellingly, Riley's response is one of incredulity: "Now how come you have to start lying?"[1] Showing "lying" as the only way of telling the truth regarding diverse forms of African Caribbean heroism as enacted in the Americas, Buster and Riley's conversation testifies to Ellison's conviction regarding the intellectual and cultural necessity of textual and oratorical signifying as the only way in which to recuperate and dignify otherwise erased black histories. Adopting a call-and-response narrative structure, Ellison's "Mister Toussan" alternates between hagiographic affirmation and fearful skepticism to dramatize his rejection of official truths as freely endorsed by white-dominant archives. Thus Ellison foregrounds the necessity of acts and arts of reimagining even to begin to re-create Toussaint Louverture as both a symbol and icon.

Rupturing any illusions regarding the potential of white public discourse to provide accurate representations of black history, Ellison's "Mister Toussan" problematizes the boundaries between white mainstream and black marginal sites of knowing. Thus he argues for the intellectual necessity of an imaginative recovery of black historical exemplars in this work. Re-creating Louverture as a malleable touchstone for diverse contexts of subjugation and resistance, Ellison sought to create new narratives of black liberation.

Betraying a determination to position black heroism as a lens through which to indict ongoing political injustices, his narrator eulogizes Louverture's memory in the same breath that he condemns the actions of "Ole Rogan," a racist white neighbor who denies Riley and Buster any share in his abundant supply of cherries simply because they are "little nigguhs."[2] As "Mister Toussan" bears witness, a resurrection of Louverture's memory within African American communities speaks directly to ongoing realities of black social, political, and cultural disfranchisement as maintained within twentieth-century U.S. systems of segregation.

More tellingly still, Ellison's "Mister Toussan" argues for the necessity of a creative engagement with Louverture's mythic legacies as the only way in which to contest dominant stereotypes generated by discriminatory educational systems that collude in racist constructions of a white national memory. Exposing the woeful inaccuracies of Buster's so-called evidence that purports to establish the inferiority of African peoples, Riley seeks solace in oral traditions within his own family: "My old man says that over there they got kings and diamonds and gold and ivory." Functioning as both a transgressive and celebratory counternarrative, Riley's account of his father's mythical engagement with an imagined Africa inculcates race pride by providing a radical alternative to white denials of black diasporic histories. He identifies Louverture as "one of the African guys" to endorse his iconic symbolism as an enslaved African who is not only equal to whites but fully capable of reversing the skewed power dynamics of slavery by demonstrating no fear of "whipping" white European manhood. Ellison ensures that Riley's initial disbelief in the fact of black heroism is replaced with a sense of psychological liberation: Buster's performance holds inspirational sway over him, as he "felt the excitement of a story rise up."[3] Functioning more as an imagined myth than as historical matter, the memory of Louverture plays an integral role in Ellison's call-and-response recovery of black male heroism as a blueprint for social, political, and cultural advancement. As dramatized in "Mister Toussan," black oral histories form the bulwark of Ellison's psychological, political, and aesthetic resistance to the reductive forces of white official records.

Pierre Dominique Toussaint. François Dominique Toussaint. Toussaint Bréda. Toussaint L'Ouverture. Toussaint Louverture. Black Spartacus. General Toussaint. *Fratas baton. Vieux Toussaint.* Black Napoleon. *Le premier des noirs.* Black chief. *"Puissaint Louverture."* A malleable figure within an array of African, Caribbean, and European American visual and textual archives, the memory of Toussaint Louverture encompasses a continuum of black heroic representations. As the subject of countless mythical reimaginings of which Ellison's "Mister Toussan" is only one, diverse memorializations of Louverture both resonate with and depart from the multifaceted representations of Nathaniel Turner, Sengbe Pieh, Sojourner Truth, Frederick Douglass, and Harriet Tubman, which have no less appeared over the centuries. Regardless of the extent to which contradictory portrayals of Louverture differ in terms of political biases, genre, or aesthetic experimentation, his memory has suffered from gross oversimplifications, according to which he has been categorized as either a barbaric demon or as a spiritual redeemer. These reductive polarizations speak to widespread racist attempts to dehumanize Black male and female subjectivities by artificially closing down rather than opening up imaginative possibilities vis-à-vis identity politics.

More particularly, in the wake of breaking news testifying to the bloody realities of Haitian revolutionary violence, Europe was awash with terror at the potent specter of black militancy. Almost instantly, this fear gave way to "anti-black atrocity literatures focused on Haiti," which, as Marcus Wood suggests, "became increasingly popular in the United States."[4] Repeatedly appearing at the center of such demonic accounts was Toussaint Louverture, a highly contested historical figure who, on the surface, seemed to exist beyond the pale of white heroic representation as little more than Carlyle's "sooty African." Yet the brutal political exploitation suffered by Louverture and his memory at the hands of proslavery apologists soon encountered a powerful counternarrative in a celebratory, primarily black-originated North American revisionist archive. Against a backdrop of white generated "anti-black atrocity literatures," abolitionist activists on both sides of the Atlantic galvanized a radical oppositional discourse and iconography as they fought to do justice to Toussaint Louverture's otherwise denigrated personae. According to their recuperative visions, which traded in no less imaginary constructions, an alternative array of self-sacrificing, deified, and superhuman Louvertures bore witness to shifting political contexts of black disenfranchisement and subjugation.

However seemingly relegated to the margins of official sites of European, Caribbean, and American memory, Toussaint Louverture has been immortalized in diverse works of poetry, plays, songs, novels, lithographs, sculptures, paintings, and murals. Louverture's multiple identities as part symbol, part icon, part revolutionary leader, part incendiary militant, and part political philosopher have remained constantly in flux across a gamut of aesthetic forms and national imaginaries. He has remained an enduring touchstone for radical white and black memorializations throughout the centuries and into the contemporary era. For black radical sympathizers and activists alike, his role as catalyst to the founding of the first black republic in the Western Hemisphere offers the ultimate proof regarding the possibilities of an epic black masculinity that operates not only as a profound source of inspiration but also as a defense against charges of black male inferiority. As an embodiment of the spectacle of black male radical militancy in the service of aggrandized military conflict rather than reactionary resistance, Louverture's heroism and mythology have historically and politically symbolized war as fought on ideological and intellectual grounds.

Despite his Haitian origins, Louverture's symbolism and iconicity have been repeatedly reimagined within an African American cultural and intellectual tradition. Yet, according to Susan Belasco, "Scholars have tended to underestimate the importance of the figure of the foreign Toussaint L'Ouverture in the American abolitionist movement, concentrating instead on the role of American slaves who dared to rebel, such as Denmark Vesey and Nat Turner."[5] Such a view clearly speaks to the problems presented by U.S.-centered paradigms of black resistance that collude in exaggerated emphases upon exceptional African American figures at the cost of under-researched and elided African Caribbean male and female icons. These neglected historical figures include not only Louverture but also Bussa, Solitude, "Nanny of the Maroons," and Sam Sharpe, among many more. And yet, palpably enduring as a symbolic founding father of black U.S. histories of radicalism regardless of white racist materials intent on demonizing his life and works, Louverture's memory has consistently overshadowed that of Vesey and Prosser, if not even that of Turner, by functioning as a point of origin for the revisionist reimaginings of black male heroism that have since gained momentum within a national and transatlantic milieu. Perhaps, and in ways not dissimilar to Sengbe Pieh as a Sierra Leonean, Louverture's heroism represents less of a risk to activists, artists, and writers. In comparison with U.S.-born Turner, Tubman, Truth, and Douglass, Louverture and Pieh have existed beyond the pale of a white U.S. national imaginary. Thus, they may well have offered antislavery campaigners a potentially less incendiary way into celebrating an otherwise terrorizing spectacle of formerly enslaved heroism. Regardless of these distinctions, for Louverture—no less than for Pieh, Douglass, Truth, Tubman, and Turner—the fight for agency remains paramount.

Recognizing, as Charles Forsdick argues, that he would be "mythologized, allegorized and instrumentalized in a number of ideological and moral causes," Louverture engaged in acts of self-representation designed to retain control over his legacy both within and beyond his own lifetime.[6] Thus the impetus among historians, writers, and artists to create a Louverture in their own image can only ever remain partial in light of his own signifying practices. However, Louverture's experimental use of a symbolic language in his written and oratorical discourse is still very much the subject of ongoing and emerging research. Therefore, it is imperative that scholars reexamine his radical uses of language within the context of the vast white mainstream textual visual archive, which continues to proliferate an array of contrasting Louvertures. Consisting of diverse portraits and reimaginings, these images complicate any straightforward tendencies either to "fix" or categorically "know" Louverture's physiognomy or physicality. In stark contrast, his own array of diverse materials, including speeches, letters, legal proclamations and documents, as well as a final prison narrative à la Nathaniel Turner, provide a workable body of materials indispensable to extrapolating the otherwise often obscured complexities of this multifaceted historical figure.

Acts and arts of reimagining remain imperative to the recovery of the multiple lives and deaths of Louverture. Equally, they speak to the overall need to develop a critical awareness that will make an in-depth examination of original works by other iconic Black male and female heroic figures including Nathaniel Turner, Sengbe Pieh, Sojourner Truth, Harriet Tubman, and Frederick Douglass possible. Clearly, these are all historical figures we may think we know but for whom it is still necessary to problematize seemingly straightforward representations by revisiting lacunae in the historical records. For example, ambiguities of naming ultimately reveal Louverture's agency in his determination to inhabit multiple personae via various incarnations as an archetypal soldier, revolutionary, laborer, politician, father, and diplomat. "Although most historians refer to him as L'Ouverture, he always . . . signed himself Louverture," Wenda Parkinson explains, adding, "He said to Laveaux once laughingly, 'I thought it was a good name for bravery.'"[7] Clearly, Louverture's reliance on the metaphor "louverture," or "the opening," speaks to the necessity of transitional as well as transformational upheavals vis-à-vis black male and female identity formation across this period. Such an apocryphal use of nomenclature also foregrounds Louverture's endorsement of revolutionary idealism, as he ensured his enduring significance not as a force of ad hoc, bestialized resistance but as an abstract embodiment of ideological principles.

Ultimately, a lack of historical or political certainty regarding Toussaint Louverture's symbolic use of naming testifies to his autonomy. Even in the early period, he inaugurated yet refused to fix the parameters for his own symbolism by adopting a slippery relationship to nomenclature. Moreover, his decision to engage in mythic processes of becoming testify to ambiguities of selfhood that betray his multiple affinities with the other historical figures discussed in this book. For example, naming was not only integral to Sojourner Truth's symbolic transformation from Isabella Baumfree and Frederick Douglass's transition from Frederick Augustus Washington Bailey but equally essential to Sengbe Pieh's liberation from Europeanizing identifications according to which he was known solely as Joseph Cinque. Equally, Harriet Tubman's transformation from hunted criminal to biblical redeemer was partly made possible on the grounds that she had become known within black folkloric reimaginings by the spiritual appellation "Moses." For Frederick Douglass and many other Black radicals, "Nat" Turner was always "Nathaniel" Turner as they fought repeated tendencies within legal discourse not only to abbreviate his first name but also to remove his surname altogether. Clearly, there was a concerted effort among white memorialists to erase the violations enacted upon black bodies by white paternal ancestry by instead favoring an insidious denial of the tangled skeins of black and white genealogies.

Across the centuries and on both sides of the Atlantic, Louverture has proved a controversial talisman for shifting memorializations. As Cora Kaplan argues, the vast array of historical, political, and artistic representations of Toussaint Louverture as produced across varying national frameworks and chronological time periods establish diverse paradoxes regarding black male subjectivity. These works bear witness to the extent to which he embodied "the contested figure of the modern black hero." As she argues, Louverture inaugurated a paradigmatic shift within black heroic identity formation by establishing "a set of possibilities and questions for the future of people of African descent that had not previously existed."[8] Thus the emergence of repeated yet varying memorializations of Louverture by Haitian, African American, and European American authors and artists was designed to counter racist exclusions and lacunae within the official records. This tradition was continued into the twentieth century by many "black intellectuals, poets and artists" who "made Toussaint's career the basis for the rethinking of the meaning of heroism" as they debated "new questions about the heroic, identification and cultural identity."[9]

As research into this extensive yet neglected visual and textual archive reveals, obliterations of Louverture's historical prominence attest to nothing more than nefarious tendencies to whitewash black history. Contradictions, ambiguities, and distortions proliferate across multifaceted works of art, politics, and history as writers and artists reimagine infinitely collaged and mythological Toussaint Louvertures. Refusing to shy away from Louverture as an unknowable, indefinable, and yet groundbreaking figure, a wealth of neglected and well-known visual and textual materials testify to his signifying possibilities, many of which are still unexamined. Even during his own lifetime, Louverture engaged in various practices designed to overturn polarized racist categorizations and defy mainstream caricatures as he refuted the popular trade in black bodies as authentic proofs. As he served simultaneously as a symbol of both iconic and anonymous forms of black male heroism within a diasporic as well as a transatlantic imagination, for the majority of writers and artists lacunae and fragmentation surrounding Toussaint Louverture operate not to dispossess but to empower his diverse representations. As both paradox and possibility, Louverture remains a source of fascination not only for white European and white American but also for African American and African Caribbean radicals, revolutionaries, and artists emerging over the centuries.

DEBATING THE "TRUE LIKENESS" OF TOUSSAINT LOUVERTURE IN NINETEENTH-CENTURY LITHOGRAPHS AND ENGRAVINGS

"The absence of any authentic portrait from the life of Toussaint Louverture is remarkable," Hugh Honour notes.[10] Similarly, Grégory Pierrot states, "There are no known pictorial representations of Toussaint Louverture made prior to 1802 in France, in the United Kingdom or in Santo Domingo."[11] Typically, early lithographs and engravings capitalizing upon distorted physical representations of Louverture shed light on white mainstream tendencies toward trading in exaggerated delineations of his physiognomy and physicality. However, with the exception of Fritz Daguillard's recent excavation of Louverture's visual archive and scholarly explorations by Matthew Clavin and Grégory Pierrot, these lithographs and engravings have suffered from significant critical neglect.

Writing in the mid-nineteenth century as "Ethiop," the Black radical writer and theorist William J. Wilson published an article titled "Picture VII—Toussaint L'ouverture," in which he imagines he is standing before an unidentified portrait of this heroic leader. Subtitled "Afric-American Picture Gallery— Second Paper," this article was published in the *Anglo-African Magazine*. As Ivy G. Wilson has recently written, the persona of "Ethiop" functioned as "the conceit through which Wilson offers his thoughts on art and culture" at the same time that he shored up his conviction that "the progress of the race will be determined by black participation in the arts." "Pictures are teachings by example. From them we often derive our best lessons," observes "Ethiop," laying claim to the didactic value not only of such works but also of Black heroic figures as offering instructional stimulus to social change. "A picture of a great man with whose acts we are familiar, calls up the whole history of his times," he asserts, exalting in the symbolic importance and political value of such iconic portraits. Seeming to gaze upon a visual representation of black rather than white heroism, "Ethiop" is paradoxically reminded not of the inconsistent realities embedded in the Declaration of Independence but of its potential as a reusable blueprint authorizing black visionary idealism. He is inspired to hope for a future era when "its broad and eternal principles, will be fully recognized by, and applied to the entire American people." For Wilson as "Ethiop," Louverture exists not only as an embodiment of the radical force of black Haitian heroism but also as a mythic figure whose legacy provides an apocryphal framework within which to expose white American inequalities. Thus his projection into an idealized future is made possible only through the existence of men such as Louverture who offer proof of black "greatness."[12]

Just as Douglass in his celebration of Louverture before British audiences refused to "extol his merits," so Wilson as "Ethiop" too proclaims, "Far be it from me to venture to a description of . . . the picture of the man," for, as he modestly protests, "I have no pencil and no pen with which I can do it." Even in the act of seemingly viewing a portrait of Louverture, he refuses to shy away from the failures of textual representations, preferring to celebrate Louverture's seemingly unquantifiable magnitude instead. For this writer, Louverture's very existence refutes scientific and political discourses associating black humanity with inferiority and barbarism. Exalting in the power of artistic portraiture, he urges, "The whole history from first to last of this Island and this people is vividly brought before the mind, by merely this likeness of the inimitable Toussaint L'Overture." As he sees it, Louverture's originality lay in the ways in which his memory functioned to aggrandize a form of black male heroism that was not divorced from, but fully encompassed, the "whole history" of Haiti as well as of its "people."[13]

The ambiguities surrounding Wilson's construction of not only an imagined persona but an imaginary portrait of Louverture bear witness to the widespread difficulties that continue to afflict this historical figure's visual archive. Recognizing that a wealth of diverse and often contradictory representations of Louverture were popularly consumed during this early period, here I focus on the following images in particular, all of which are readily available in Fritz Daguillard's invaluable exhibition catalog: *Toussaint Louverture*, a "color engraving" by an artist identified solely as "Jean" and published in Paris in 1802; *Toussaint Louverture*, an undated, anonymous image that represents a clear variation on Nicolas Eustache Maurin's lithograph published in 1838 (see figure 2); and *Reunion of the Louverture Family*, an anonymous lithograph that circulated from 1822 onwards (see figure 3).[14] As an astute critic of these early representations, Daguillard argues, "Portraits of Toussaint Louverture are many and bear little resemblance to one another." As he notes, such a "variety of likenesses" may well have emerged because of the marketability of Louverture's iconic representations given that "attaching his name to a work upgraded its value."[15] Capitalizing on Louverture's exceptionalism, therefore, antislavery artists traded on his signifying possibilities simultaneously as a political icon, heroic exemplar, war hero, and revolutionary liberator. Holding firm at the other end of the spectrum, proslavery apologists endorsed racist representations of Louverture as a barbarous and grotesque African. Such a diverse array of visual representations oscillate between portraits of Louverture as an embodiment of abolitionist prophesy on the one hand and his symbolism as an incarnation of proslavery fear on the other.

According to Daguillard, *Toussaint Louverture, Leader of the Insurgent Blacks of Saint Domingue* was created by an artist named "Jean" and published in Paris in 1802.[16] As one of the few color representations, Jean's is a striking image. Brandishing aloft his sword and seated astride a rearing steed, a heroic Louverture appears in full military regalia as visually dramatized by the opulent textures of his red, white, and blue clothing decorated with gold embroidery. This symbolic use of color operates as an iconographic signifier of Louverture's ambivalent relationship to France during his tumultuous rise and fall as military leader. As Daguillard notes, "Toussaint is often shown on horseback," and yet, while in this work "the horse is brown," frequently the "horse seems to be Bel Argent (Silver Shadow), the famous white steed that Louverture rode."[17] Jean's decision not to reproduce "Bel Argent," a famed folkloric symbol typically associated with Louverture, may have originated in a determination to resist constructing this figure as an exceptional icon so as not to detract from his relationship to black collective activism (i.e., as a way of exalting in his role as a typical rather than iconic "leader of the insurgent blacks"). However, such an overt fictionalizing of the historical record may also have succeeded in compounding Louverture's mythology yet further by displacing pretensions to realism in favor of dramatic and symbolic reimaginings.

While for Daguillard, "It is difficult to discern the facial features" of Louverture in full-body engravings, here we see his detailed rather than caricatured physiognomy.[18] The unknown illustrator takes pains to individualize his identity by dramatizing his prominent brow, expressive eyes, and resolute mouth in order to build upon Louverture's status as a visionary leader rather than as a ferocious type. The blackness of his skin—typically evoked to denote exaggerated demarcations of racial difference—is offset by the apocryphal color of his clothing. Such visual symbolism evokes both the French tricolor and the U.S. flag to suggest that the artist reimagined black militancy as a transnational, but no less patriotic, independence struggle. In this depiction of the leader as a solitary figure, Louverture's brandished sword appears more symbolic than real. Seeming not to have committed violence, he is portrayed as unsullied by war, as his enemies remain abstract because unseen in this print. As Srinivas Aravamudan argues, this portrait "imitates and revises the traditional equestrian statues in Europe."[19] Moreover, as reproduced in a work that recuperates black male heroism within a Europeanized tradition of white military activity, Louverture's sword operates in the same way that visual representations of ownership of the pen signified in the frontispieces of early transatlantic slave narratives written by Black men and women. In compelling ways, they relied on portraits emphasizing their status as authors in order to signal their adherence to the supposed moral values of Western civilization. Both recuperative and revisionist, Jean's work refuses to stray far from "traditional" iconography. Thus the illustrator succeeds in satiating the conciliatory demands of white European and American audiences by effecting a visual cleansing of Louverture's heroism.

Toussaint Louverture, a work for which no date or author is known, is a direct reproduction of the French artist Nicolas Eustache Maurin's lithograph, which appeared a few decades later in 1838 (see figure 2). Acknowledging the popularity of Maurin's image, Daguillard asserts that this representation "will doubtless go down in History, as the true likeness of Toussaint Louverture." However, this work inhabits difficult terrain as one of the few portrayals of Louverture in profile, a problematic arena for black visual representation. Clear-cut difficulties arise from the profiled view's associations with scientific racism via the popular circulation of black physiognomies as anthropological diagrams and criminalized reproductions. Yet Daguillard speculates that Maurin's image may have a basis in historical fact when he notes, "Those who saw Louverture have often commented on his prognathism, which is especially striking in this portrait. He owed his salient lower jaw to the loss of his teeth and of part of the upper maxillary during a skirmish."[20] While Louverture's exaggerated profile risks endorsing caricatured representations of black masculinity in this work, these appropriations are not born out by the delicacy of his facial features. His etched eyebrows, detailed eyes, and minutely reproduced lashes combine with his styled hair, round diminutive nose, and high cheekbones to counter charges of gross caricature. Ornate clothing—including the excessively nuanced leaf embroidery on his jacket and collar, patterning on his buttons, tassels on his epaulettes, and plume on his tricornered hat—contribute to the overall impression that Maurin's Louverture occupies an exalted status. A symbolic use of dress lends yet further ballast to Marcus Rainsford's eyewitness descriptions of Louverture. "His uniform was a kind of blue jacket, with a large red cape falling over the shoulders; red cuffs, with eight rows of lace on the arms, and a pair of gold epaulettes thrown back; scarlet waistcoat and pantaloons, with half boots; round hat, with a red feather, and a national cockade," he purports to have observed from life.[21]

However, as Daguillard explains, reductive readings of this image can coexist with aggrandized interpretations. "Perhaps Maurin, in the same spirit of derision, also caricatured Toussaint by exaggerating the thickness of his lips and the prominence of his jaw," he speculates.[22] By contrast, as Richard Powell argues, "As problematic as Maurin's rendering of Toussaint L'Ouverture is, there is also something visually arresting about it."[23] Rather than the didactic image "Ethiop" applauded, Maurin's lithograph exalts in physiognomic complexities to introduce psychological depth to otherwise problematic surface portrayals of Louverture. Consistent with Louverture's existing iconography, Maurin's Black subject remains first and foremost an epic, visionary leader rather than a war hero. Both his contemplative gaze and disassociation from any historical context via an absence of symbolic properties reinforces his identity as a theorist and strategist rather than as a soldier mired in bloody combat. Equally, the fact that Louverture's handwritten signature overshadows the printed record of his name on this lithograph invites parallels with the frontispieces of slave narratives, which typically combine textual and visual evidence to vindicate black authority. Such associations are revealing regarding the textual and visual slippages created by an array of black signifying practices. Just as enslaved narrators communicated their stories regardless of white attempts to intervene and shape their radical uses of language, so Louverture may have obtained symbolic iconicity in this image regardless of Maurin's problematic assumptions. Perhaps it is in

FIGURE 2. Anon., *Toussaint Louverture*, n.d.
(Prints and Photographs Division, Library of Congress)

recognition of these difficulties and unreconciled tensions that Jacob Lawrence "used Maurin's work as the basis for his portrait of Louverture."[24]

Daguillard's recent research identifies *Reunion of the Louverture Family*, an anonymous lithograph created in 1822, as *Le Gal. Toussaint-L'ouverture, a qui Gal. Leclerc avait envoyé* (see figure 3). "Different episodes of Louverture's life have inspired graphic artists, in particular his reunion with his children upon their return to Haiti with Abbott Coisnon," he observes, acknowledging, however, that "all of these works are pure fantasy." A highly sentimentalized and imaginative re-creation of an archetypal abolitionist tableau, this work deifies the black family as spiritual sanctuary. As an image particularly suited to a radical antislavery political agenda, Louverture appears here as the only erect figure. By comparison, his wife and two children prostrate themselves before him, gripping tightly to his clothing in supplicating gestures as they seek his protection. In depicting a "romantic scene" with no basis in any representation of historical reality, the illustrator may have signified on its enduring importance as a mythical reimagining of the emotional complexities of the black domestic sphere. This work may, therefore, have been created to transgress boundaries of nation and race by encouraging white audiences to imaginative empathetic identification with Louverture's history.[25]

Dramatic juxtapositions communicate Louverture's exceptionalism in this image, as one of his sons kneels before him with clasped hands. Adopting the pose of the supplicant enslaved figure of Josiah Wedgwood's imagining in "Am I Not a Man and a Brother?," the bowed body of Louverture's son suggests that it is his father and not a white paternal authority figure who has the power to effect black redemption. While the partially obscured white tutor, all but lost to the historical record, stands clothed in black and in the shadow to the left of the image, the artist carefully illuminates Louverture's delineated physiognomy. As a Black heroic figure dressed in a white military uniform, he appears in the light of the open doorway to signify his role as an "opening" not only for his own family but also, by a sentimental sleight of hand, for the body politic. Conceding, "It is not known why he chose the name Louverture or L'Ouverture," Wenda Parkinson speculates regarding the origins of his choice of naming that "in Vodun there is a prayer to Legba to 'open the gates.'"[26] Simultaneously fulfilling the roles of paternal leader, deity, abolitionist, and prophet, these excessively sentimentalized reimaginings of Louverture invert racist hierarchies with the result that it is the white man who appears solely as adjunct and guide to the Black man, who instead fulfills the role of quintessential heroic archetype.

FIGURE 3. Anon., *Le Gal. Toussaint-L'ouverture, a qui Gal. Leclerc avait envoyé*, n.d. (Prints and Photographs Division, Library of Congress)

"Portraits of Louverture are as inscrutable as the man himself," Daguillard explains, admitting that, "faced with dozens of portraits, I am unable to tell you which one truly depicts my hero." The sheer fact of such a wide range of lithographs and engravings that emerge in the aftermath of Louverture's death mitigate against polarized bifurcations of this figure within either a European imagination or national consciousness. Offering a blueprint for future commemorations, Louverture appears in a variety of guises, including ex-enslaved freedom fighter, spiritual seer, paternal authority, and Europeanized war hero. As Daguillard suggests, such an array of competing iconographic portrayals not only "revolutionized the depiction of the black man at that time" but also provided "the first manifestation of black power."[27] Clearly, Louverture functions as a symbol of black male empowerment in works that refuse to shy away from black masculinity as a locus of contradiction and paradox.

Thought-provoking ambivalences regarding this iconic figure testify to the extent to which Louverture fascinated audiences, on the one hand as an icon of black masculinity, and on the other as an exemplar visually recodified to fit European and white male American definitions of an exceptional heroism. Therefore, these early lithographs and engravings of Louverture introduce key difficulties in this book. A clear tension exists regarding the extent to which visual and textual archives seemingly engaged in recovering exceptional Black heroic figures had the reverse effect by assimilating black social, political, and historical differences and thereby obscuring a black heroic continuum. Similarly, Louverture's lack of control over his iconography—given that none of these images were commissioned portraits—must not be overlooked. In this regard, Louverture was as vulnerable as Nathaniel Turner or Sengbe Pieh, both of whom were susceptible to reactionary reimaginings of their bodies and face as popularized by a racist public seeking to sensationalize black acts and arts of resistance. These associations of black masculinity with dispossession also shed light on the signifying power and radical politics of Douglass, Truth, and Tubman, as they commissioned photographic portraits to celebrate a multiplicity of individualized black male and female subjectivities. However problematic, Toussaint Louverture's multilayered iconography nonetheless sheds light upon black battles against white strategies of racist stereotyping not only within a transatlantic milieu but also within the context of an increasingly militant antebellum United States.

"This Negro left hardly a line for history to feed upon." So concludes the African American novelist, essayist, and editor Pauline Hopkins as early as 1901, lamenting the absence of works written by Toussaint Louverture.[28] Nearly half a century previously, the white American scholar Charles W. Elliott similarly observed, "What thoughts, what struggles, what hopes had taken shape in the black brain no man knows, for Toussaint was a man of few words, and he left no writings."[29] Yet the barely excavated historical and cultural archive that has since been expertly mined by leading scholars such as C. L. R. James, David Geggus, Charles Forsdick, and Philip Kaisary tells a different story. "The correspondence of Toussaint L'Ouverture is vast, and remains to a great degree unpublished," Nick Nesbitt has observed as recently as 2008.[30] A wealth of both translated and untranslated materials exists, including Louverture's military correspondence, political writings, and historical documentation as well as his prison narrative, *Memoir of Toussaint L'Ouverture,* completed shortly before his death from starvation and maltreatment by Napoléon Bonaparte.[31] As Laurent Dubois argues, an enormous repository of his public and private letters represents an invaluable resource providing access to "his actions and ideals."[32] However, significant problems of language have led to transcription issues. As a result, the majority of scholarship, including my own analysis in this chapter, continues to engage with Louverture's body of materials from at least one remove by reinterpreting his works through the lens of various translators. Such is no less the case regarding Sengbe Pieh, for whom language barriers, poor translations, and almost nonexistent record keeping have made it impossible to recover his scant oral testimony with any accuracy.

"We know that Toussaint could write only phonetic creole," Parkinson observes, noting that "he dictated painstakingly, speaking, then listening carefully as his draft was read back to him, then altering and re-dictating until the end result satisfied his perfectionist mind."[33] Louverture's meticulousness clearly attests to his determination to define the parameters of his own memorializations. He recognized the symbolic potential of language either to reduce or to liberate black self-representations. As more than that of just a self-conscious author, Louverture's prose style betrays a powerful command of narrative form. However inflected by his own political agenda designed to aggrandize Louverture as a paragon of black revolutionary consciousness, C. L. R. James observes he was not only the "born soldier but" also "the born writer," as he "habitually wrote and spoke like a philosopher."[34] Incorporating parable, simile, metaphor, and rhetorical questioning, Louverture's symbolic style inaugurates many of the mythical facets of his biography. Occupying a middle ground between existential reimagining and the seemingly historically real, Louverture envisioned a formative role for his textual archive as a point of origin for the aesthetic and political tropes that were subsequently to characterize his future memorializations.

As a declaration of independence from racist calumny designed to annihilate black selfhood, Louverture's autobiography, *The Memoir of General Toussaint L'Ouverture, Written by Himself,* memorializes the traumas he endured following his imprisonment. Such a preoccupation is made manifest not only through this work's symbolic and mythic properties but also within the context of its discovery. As Deborah Jenson writes, a "handwritten autobiographical fragment [was] found wrapped in his headscarf" upon "his death."[35] An artifact literally unwrapped from his own skin, this work betrays an inextricable relationship between the black male body and text not only in his use of language—according to which he reimagined his body as a site of wounding—but also by the sheer fact that his testimony was concealed within his "headscarf." Clearly, this piece of clothing operates as a symbol both of an ancestral African heritage and an enslaved existence, as I explore in more depth later in this book in relation to Sojourner Truth's artful manipulation of such a garment. Equally, the subtitle, *Written by Himself,* functions not only as an authenticating device but also as a vindication of black autonomy. As a very early foundational text within that which was a transatlantic, but which was to become a North American, slave narrative tradition, his work functions as a manifesto of individual rights, bearing witness to a black equal, if not superior, humanity.

Working within a narrative genre premised on the assumption that Black women, children, and men were on "trial" as they fought for the right to their humanity during slavery, Louverture's *Memoir* oscillates between explication and obfuscation as he testifies to the importance of narrative indirection as political stratagem. Constructing an impassioned self-defense as a critique against white racism, his careful description of an exceptional military prowess can be understood as an implicit refutation of proslavery emphases upon black inferiority. As an "'author' of authentic memoirs," for Daniel Desormeaux, Louverture is "the first of the black memorialists."[36] He played a formative role in nuancing, editing, and reimagining his history for mass public consumption, both across national contexts and beyond temporal frameworks. If Louverture's memoir functions as a slave narrative, however, it can only be identified as such in full recognition of the fact that, like Nathaniel Turner, he was unfree at the time of writing, yet, unlike Turner, he was not even given the hollow ritual of an empty trial. Poignantly realizing the futility of physical redemption during his own lifetime, Louverture shared Nathaniel Turner's and the white revolutionary turned martyr John Brown's determination to produce literary self-expressions that would set the parameters for their own future mythic legacies. For Louverture, his memoir functioned as a dramatic confession that testified to his realization regarding the difficulties of communicating black heroism as he cultivated an exceptional rather than representative heroic status. Far from the anonymous and formerly enslaved Black subject writing himself into being through autobiography, Louverture signifies on his renown to create a public "memoir" that actively reframes existing knowledge regarding his life and works.

Written in France toward the end of his life, Louverture's memoir first appeared in English in the white British abolitionist John R. Beard's translation, *The Life of Toussaint L'Ouverture*, published decades later in Boston (1863). Publishing his translation in the context of the American Civil War, Beard admitted to a revisionist motivation in returning to Louverture's history. "A hope of affording some aid to the sacred cause of freedom, specially as involved in the extinction of slavery, and in the removal of the prejudices on which servitude mainly depends, has induced the author to prepare the present work for the press," he explains. Dismissing in one sweep the existence of a wealth of black literature—not only slave narratives but also speeches, essays, political pamphlets, historiographical works, and journalistic reportage—he was outraged: "The blacks have no authors; their cause, consequently, has not yet been pleaded." Ostensibly recuperating Louverture within a separatist African paradigm, Beard's essentialist rhetoric notes that "he was wholly without white blood." "Small in person, he was of a repulsive aspect, and having a difficult utterance, he spoke with as little elegance as grammar. Yet, his were words of power. . . . A man of few words, and powerful imagination, he sometimes uttered his ideas in parables," he writes. However troubling regarding his overtly racist use of language in an excessive reliance upon that which he demonizes as his "repulsive aspect," Beard's emphasis upon Louverture's "words of power" and "powerful imagination" gesture toward new ways of reexamining this figure's dismissed and distorted oeuvre. Playing an integral role in the formation of the first black republic in the Western Hemisphere, Louverture functioned as an inspirational talisman in the United States, irrespective of the stranglehold of white racist discourses and iconographies surrounding his mythological representations. Working within an abolitionist agenda, therefore, Beard foregrounds Louverture's representative status in order to vindicate black equality. "While, however, the world has seen but one Toussaint L'Ouverture, this history sets forth many black men who were possessed of great faculties, and accomplished great deeds," he observes.[37] Thus Beard experimented with multiple "Louvertures" not only to reinforce his symbolic status but also to reject monolithic constructions of black masculinity. For one Louverture, he implies, the underexplored historical record reveals many others.

"It is my duty to render to the French Government an exact account of my conduct. I shall relate the facts with all the simplicity and frankness of an old soldier, adding to them the reflections that naturally suggest themselves. In short, I shall tell the truth, though it be against myself." So Louverture freely admits at the start of his memoir.[38] Fearlessly, he lays bare his autobiographical persona by bearing witness to a humanized individualism rather than a flawless exceptionalism. Inaugurating alternative paradigms for black male selfhood in this work, he immediately departs from the slave narrative tradition according to which writers were burdened with the responsibility of trading in idealized self-representations. Instead, Louverture accentuates the seeming veracity of his narrative by confessing his intention to testify, even if it be "against myself." He creates a psychologically complex self-portrait in his determination to convince his readership concerning his refusal to flinch from internal contradictions and paradoxical representations. As further evidence of his determination to persuade audiences of his veracity, Louverture replicates generic conventions according to which ex-enslaved writers avowed "simplicity and frankness." Thus a lack of literary embellishment seemingly provides uncut access to an "unvarnished tale" vis-à-vis the testimony of enslaved subjects. Just as Louverture's humble self-effacement as an "old soldier" provides the rhetorical sleight of hand by which he wrong-foots audience expectations regarding his multifaceted identity constructions, so too his claims to a direct literary style are no less performative, as he seemingly satiates yet subverts prescriptive white authenticity demands.

Similarly, Louverture's *Memoir* performatively cultivates a subjugated relationship to the white French body politic. At face value, he seemed determined to provide an "exact account" of his actions as the only way to fulfill his "duty." This was no less the concern of enslaved narrators who enhanced their social critique by revealing excessive faith in, only to expose the failures of, a flawed white American democracy. For Louverture, however, any determination to conciliate white European power was clearly not at the cost of literary stratagem. Exalting in the work of black aggrandizement, he departed from racist mandates that argued that he needed to establish equality solely by vindicating black humanity. Ultimately, he interpreted his revolutionary acts as inaugurating an unprecedented mode of black governance based on egalitarian idealism. "The island had attained a degree of splendor which it had never before seen. And all this—I dare to say it—was my work," he declares.[39]

Throughout his *Memoir*, Louverture relishes in the political uses of juxtaposition to illuminate black honesty and bravery against a backdrop of white cowardice and duplicity. Repeatedly celebrating black superior morality, he exposes the heinous crimes enacted by white men, including the actions of one military general in particular whom he refused to name in order to accentuate his symbolism as a touchstone of white barbarity. "I then demanded a conference with him. But Couppé had not time to execute my orders; they fired upon us at twenty-five steps from the barrier," Louverture narrates. Suffering deprecations from yet another French commander whom he does name as General Rochambeau, Louverture signals the complexity of his subversive practices. Rejecting physical resistance in favor of written protest in this work, he opts for impassioned rhetorical questioning as the only bloodless way of "manifesting my indignation to the general." He asks, "why he had ordered the massacre of those brave soldiers who had only followed the orders given them," speculating, "Was this the recompense that the French Government had promised them?"[40] Insisting on the ideological foundations for war, Louverture exposes white European hypocrisy to eulogize black valor.

A far cry from his opening performance as an "old soldier," Louverture heightens his intellectual and political authority by including his own correspondence as an integral part of his *Memoir*. Selecting excerpts from his own letters, he challenged dominant white publishing frameworks to become his own editor as he fought to legitimize the necessity of his emergence as a freedom fighter. "I concluded by saying to Gen. Rochambeau, that 'I would fight to the last to avenge the death of these brave soldiers, for my own liberty, and to reestablish tranquility and order in the colony,'" he quotes himself as saying. Such polemical rhetoric clearly accounts for Louverture's appeal to Beard and other abolitionists, as he articulated a "liberty or death" ethos that chimed in immediate ways with a white American heroic tradition. Working within the parameters established by numerous formerly enslaved narrators who were new to written forms and who portrayed acts of rebellion as the last recourse in black self-defense against white barbarity,

Louverture condemns General Leclerc's violence as the sole catalyst to his resistance: "If he persisted in his invasion, he would force me to defend myself, although I had but few troops." Signifying on his dual identities as soldier and writer, Louverture insists on his status as both a self-sacrificing martyr and incendiary revolutionary. More particularly, Louverture represents his protest against the inhumane violence of Leclerc as symptomatic of nefarious attempts by whites not only to divide and rule but to deny black heroism by constructing seemingly incontestable parallels between his actions and white slaveholding practices. "Did he not try to instigate the laborers to rise, by persuading them that I treated them like slaves, and that he had come to break their chains?" he rhetorically asks. Defending his work ethic as a bulwark of liberty, Louverture vindicates his position and underscores the radical egalitarianism of his new constitution. "If I did oblige my fellow-countrymen to work, it was to teach them the value of true liberty," he asserts.[41]

Performing as the patriotic citizen of France par excellence, Louverture minimizes black difference by recuperating his representational possibilities according to preestablished Europeanized frameworks of heroism at the same time that he consolidates his status as proof of the possibilities of black civilization. Rather than exalting in an exceptional invincibility, Louverture chooses not to shy away from martyrdom by providing graphic descriptions of his near-death experiences. He indicts the ways in which one of Leclerc's commanders, General Maurepas, "carried his audacity so far as to oppose me when I marched against him to force him to submit to his chief, and to retake the territory and the town which he had invaded! The day that he dared to fire upon me, a ball cut the plume from my hat." Suffering no physical injury, however, Louverture expresses outrage regarding the violations enacted upon his clothing, a symbolic extension of his political persona and a signifier of his iconic exceptionalism. He also admits to anger regarding white French determinations to vilify his actions. "Why was all the evil which had been done and the disorders which had existed imputed to me?" he wonders, unequivocally concluding, "It is not right to attribute to me more wrong than I deserve." Ceasing his performances as a quintessential French patriot, here Louverture assumes the role of black arbiter of justice to expose white barbarity. Eschewing personal grievances, he favors not only safeguarding the nation but protecting vulnerable and powerless masses of enslaved women and men otherwise afflicted by unimaginable atrocities. "Considering all the misfortunes which the colony had already suffered, the dwellings destroyed, assassinations committed, the violence exercised even upon women, I forgot all the wrongs which had been done me, to think only of the happiness of the island and the interest of the Government," Louverture explains.[42] Clearly, his seeming capitulation to the "interest of the Government" operates as a smokescreen to conceal his equivocal language as he describes his efforts to protect his new nation by "any means necessary."

Throughout his *Memoir*, Louverture condemns white racist generals not only for engaging in unnecessary acts of violence that resulted in black acts of physical self-defense but also for their failure to admit to the existence of black heroism. As he writes, "If from the beginning I had been treated as I should have been, not a single shot would have been fired." He communicates his outrage at the depredations to which he bore witness: "I saw that all my houses had been pillaged and even the coffers of my laborers carried off." Louverture's reportage-style description of his arrest castigates white enactments of injustice via a poetics of undertelling. Forcing audiences to reimagine the horrifying realities, he requires them to piece fragments of the narrative together: "An aide-de-camp of Gen. Leclerc entered, accompanied by a large number of soldiers, who surrounded me, seized me, bound me as a criminal, and conducted me on board the frigate Créole."[43] His pared-down narrative dispenses with sentimental rhetoric to encourage audiences to empathetic identification regarding black bodies as sites of violation.

More particularly, Louverture's *Memoir* exposes the barbarity and cowardice of various leaders, including General Brunet. For example, he explains how the general "treated my family with great cruelty" by deploying "a detachment of troops to the house where I had been living with a part of my family, mostly women, children, and laborers" and then "ordered them to set it on fire, compelling the unhappy victims to fly half-naked to the woods."[44] Shifting emphasis from persecutions he himself has endured, he condemns white depredations against Black women, children, and workers more generally, whom he saw as defenseless "unhappy victims" of society. These accounts of en masse suffering provide a displaced portal through which Louverture magnifies his experiences by aggrandizing the terrors endured by his "half-naked" family. He exalts not in an isolated but in a fully encompassing model of black male heroism as inextricable from domestic relations. At the same time that Rainsford interpreted Louverture as "free from the affectation of sentiment," his *Memoir* reveals he was not averse to manipulating emotion in the service of radical protest.[45] Countering the paternalism of objectifying exhibitions that circulated in white mainstream iconography, Louverture alternately adopts strategies of revelation and concealment.

Oscillating between minimalist undertelling and excessive narration, he describes his journey to France on board the *Héros* as unequivocally hellish. "I endured not only great fatigue, but also every species of hardship, while my wife and children received treatment from which their sex and rank should have preserved them," he states.[46] These admissions regarding his own "great fatigue" combine with enigmatic references to "every species of hardship" not only to heighten the horrors of the unspecified "treatment" of his innocent family but to expose white villainy. In self-reflexive ways, he accentuates the political and symbolic importance of black bodies as loci of persecution.

For Louverture, the origin of white acts of violence and violation upon the bodies of Black women, children, and men was clear. "Doubtless, I owe this treatment to my color; but my color,—my color,—has it hindered me from serving my country with zeal and fidelity? Does the color of my skin impair my honor and my bravery?" he questions.[47] Appearing for the first time in a memoir otherwise preoccupied with self-justification, Louverture's impassioned denunciations of racist strategies of appropriation and objectification appear at a critical juncture in the text. Following his seeming capitulation to white authority by which he engages in self-representations constructed according to white Western mores, this critique betrays his radical protest as he sought to inspire outrage by rejecting racist rhetoric. In compelling ways, Louverture's rhetorical questioning and symbolic repetition of the word "color" reject white myopic distortions of black selfhood. In a radical move, he testifies to the horrifying realities of black male suffering by admitting to his powerlessness as a protector of black domesticity, no less a concern of Turner, Truth, Pieh, Douglass, and Tubman as they fought—physically, emotionally, intellectually—for the right to protect their families and communities torn apart by slavery.

Clearly, Louverture was aware of his totemic power for future generations not only in spite of, but also because of, his impending martyrdom. As a powerful preface to Douglass's mid-nineteenth century concept of "living parchments," Louverture's *Memoir* establishes haunting equivalences between body and text. His is an impassioned denunciation of black bodies as sites and sights of violation within a white transatlantic imaginary:

They have taken forcible possession of my papers in order to charge me with crimes which I have never committed; but I have nothing to fear; this correspondence is sufficient to justify me. They have sent me to France destitute of everything; they have seized my property and my papers, and have spread atrocious calumnies concerning me. Is it not like cutting off a man's legs and telling him to walk? Is it not like cutting out a man's tongue and telling him to talk? Is it not burying a man alive?[48]

Louverture's bold and declarative claims expose white "calumnies" by bearing witness to the misuses and abuses of black histories. Recognizing that even his own testimony ran the risk of reappropriation by proponents of slavery, for Louverture white ownership of his "papers" wreaked devastation by perpetuating racist fabrications of his identity. In one heartrending move, he was denied access, not only to his private testimony but, and more importantly, to his public memory.

Throughout the *Memoir*, Louverture's powerful imagery shifts from clear-cut denunciations to an impassioned self-defense as he equates the denial of linguistic expression to physical trauma. Relying on metaphors of amputation as well as symbolic death, he documents the loss not only of his archive but also of its fabricated reincarnations. Clearly, his powerful imagery sought to get to the heart of the psychological and existential annihilations effected by racist mythologies. More particularly, his metaphor of a living death evokes diverse states of enslavement to suggest not only bodily and psychological mutilation but also a state of nonbeing. "I have been a slave; I am willing to own it; but I have never received reproaches from my masters," he asserts.[49] His admission not only revels in his status as a moral paragon superior to whites but also attests to slavery as a source of superheroic empowerment rather than shame regarding black endurance in the face of white-enforced suffering.

Overall, Louverture's *Memoir* legitimizes a graphic account of black male violence by adopting deliberate practices of textual layering. For Louverture, black male heroism was symptomatic of white racist injustices as well as a tradition of black exceptional bravery. "I gained a famous victory over the English in a battle," he reveals, admitting, "This battle was so fierce that the roads were filled with the dead, and rivers of blood were seen on every side. I took all the baggage and ammunition of the enemy, and a large number of prisoners." Clearly, Louverture's denunciation of black "half-naked" bodies ravaged by whites authorizes his graphic narration of retaliatory black violence. He interprets his body, an elusive signifier, as a text upon which a history of resistance and bravery in the service of a newly envisioned patriotism could be written:

I shed my blood for my country; I received a ball in the right hip which remains there still; I received a violent blow on the head from a canon-ball, which knocked out the greater part of my teeth, and loosened the rest. In short, I received upon different occasions seventeen wounds, whose honourable scars still remain.[50]

Overall, Louverture's history of black physical mutilation and scarification signifies upon white abolitionist displays of enslaved victimization but with a crucial difference. His graphic exposé purporting to mathematical accuracy—"seventeen wounds"—attests not to black objectification but to agency. As his writing reveals, he chose to engage in these conflicts not out of necessity for self-preservation but out of free will in support of his revolutionary idealism as expressed in his stark admission, "I shed my blood for my country."

"If I were to record the various services which I have rendered the Government, I should need many volumes, and even then should not finish them," he argues.[51] Thus Louverture's *Memoir* testifies to the failures of the written archive to document the realities of a black male heroism otherwise marginalized or excluded by nefarious racist practices. Moreover, the scraps of shot and wounds that "still remain" dramatize the black male body as a site of survival regardless of victimization. Such compelling imagery also offers irrefutable proof of the enduring symbolism of the persecuted and soon-to-be-martyred black male body as a locus for physical and psychological resistance. Louverture's appeal to Napoléon Bonaparte in his *Memoir* makes for heartrending reading. "First Consul, father of all soldiers, upright judge, defender of innocence, pronounce my destiny," he begs, declaring, "My wounds are deep; apply to them the healing remedy which will prevent them from opening anew; you are the physician; I rely entirely upon your justice and wisdom!"[52] Here, he engages in hagiographic language self-reflexively to appease white French tyranny by eulogizing European military process. By insisting on his status as an "old soldier," Louverture foregrounds his importance as an archetypal warrior, regardless of white rituals of black dehumanization. Engaging in political arts of performed subjugation, he identifies Bonaparte as a paternal authority only in order to encourage empathy across racial boundaries. Seeming to capitulate to Bonaparte's omniscience, Louverture eulogizes his morality in an attempt to inspire the white leader to transcend his immoral failings by recognizing black superiority. Therefore, Louverture's appeal to Bonaparte to heal his "deep wounds" so that they would not "open anew" denies any illusory constructions of clear-cut hierarchies between black and white manhood.

Regarding his *Memoir*, Desormeaux writes that Louverture "seems torn between two models: chivalrous heroism (the model of spectacular action that would speak for itself), and an acute sense of honor (the aristocratic model in which the desire to write his illustrious life and increase his renown has become a spiritual quest)."[53] Deftly manipulating separatist versus conciliatory racial identity politics, Louverture's *Memoir* introduces a multiplicity of heroic paradigms, as he simultaneously remains part chivalrous, part aristocratic, part African, part European, part ex-enslaved icon, and part republican leader. His life and works as a "born writer" reveal his projection of a heroic self engaged in acts and arts of resistance. Adopting a performative mask through which to minimize racial differences and annihilate racist hierarchies, he functioned as the black commander in "whiteface." Ever adept at manipulating language and genre, Louverture's consummate abilities as a writer demonstrate that he himself played a fundamental role as the point of origin for tropes within his own subsequent memorializations.

"Let us go forth to plant the tree of liberty, breaking the chains of those of our brothers still held captive under the shameful yoke of slavery." So Louverture urges in an impassioned "Address to Soldiers for the Universal Destruction of Slavery," delivered on May 18, 1797, in which he denounces slavery by appealing to a black brotherhood of men. In his "Letter to the French Directory," written in November of the same year, he similarly adopts a "liberty or death" ethos. "We have known how to confront danger to obtain our liberty, and we will know how to confront death to preserve it," he declares.[54] An exceptional orator as well as military commander and writer, Louverture rejected racist inequalities by experimenting with complex symbolism. As one reporter notes, "Into a glass vase filled with kernels of black corn he mixed a few white kernels," before which Louverture "said to those around him: 'You are the black kernels, the whites who would reenslave you are the white kernels,'" as he then "shook the vase and, presenting it to their fascinated eyes, exclaimed, as if inspired, 'See the white ones only here and there?'—that is to say, consider the whites in proportion to yourselves."[55] As this story testifies, Louverture's preference was for coded systems of textual and oratorical representation as he fought to secure black self-empowerment and agency. Relying on symbolic vignettes to communicate his own "characters of blood," Louverture recognized that his life and works constituted an iconic blueprint of black male heroism for subsequent authors, artists, and activists.

"Until she spoke the slave ship, followed by hungry sharks, greedy to de-vour the dead and dying slaves flung overboard to feed them, ploughed in peace the South Atlantic painting the sea with the Negro's blood." So reads Frederick Douglass's haunting description of the Haitian Revolution, which he dramatizes as a powerful catalyst to black heroism in a lecture delivered at the World's Columbian Exposition in 1893. "It was she [Haiti] who first awoke the Christian world to a sense of 'the danger of goading too far the energy that slumbers in a black man's arm,'" he observes. As far as the "Chris-tian world" was concerned, "The Negro was in its estimation a sheep like creature, having no rights which white men were bound to respect, a docile animal," Douglass states, adding, "The mission of Haiti was . . . to give to the world a new and true revelation of the black man's character."[56] Speaking in the postbellum era, Douglass here idealizes Louverture as the "true revela-tion" of the heroic possibilities of black masculinity, as he fought not against slavery but against the survival of its nefarious "spirit" in the repeated spec-tacle of lynchings. For Douglass, writing here and elsewhere in his manu-scripts devoted to Toussaint Louverture, this heroic figure gained intensified power by becoming an abstraction, or "an unanswerable argument."[57] For Douglass, a Louverture disassociated from corporeal realities functioned as the quintessential symbol in his fight against the injustices and distortions perpetuated by white textual, legal, linguistic, and political acts of violation.

A pioneering historian and philosopher of a black heroic tradition, Doug-lass was not alone in his desire to memorialize Toussaint Louverture in the nineteenth century. Outpourings of writings and artworks throughout this early period attest to his groundbreaking significance as the inspiration for an overwhelming number of Black and white writers, artists, and historians on both sides of the Atlantic. As Michael Dash observes, "The impulse to celebrate the Haitian struggle for independence as an heroic and exemplary act is evident in the nineteenth century literary imagination."[58] Perhaps, however, it was more specifically the opportunity to deify and aggrandize Louverture that galvanized such representational strategies. In this regard, Douglass's awareness of the corrupting influences of a racist moral atmo-sphere sheds light on the realization of a multitude of writers that predomi-nantly white models of black male heroism were mired in a fraught political, moral, and psychological terrain from which they could only be liberated by creative revisioning.

"Public memory of Louverture influenced the American abolitionist movement throughout the nineteenth century," Matthew Clavin writes.[59] Yet Louverture's memory epitomizes tensions and contradictions within competing methods of antislavery resistance, as he was portrayed in diverse ways and to suit differing agendas, depending upon the national origin and racial identity of the writer or artist. As a powerful figure within the black antislavery arsenal in particular, Louverture was the subject of dramatizations not only by Frederick Douglass but also by William Wells Brown, James McCune Smith, James T. Holly, John Mercer Langston, Prince Saunders, and William G. Allen. Such was no less the case among white philosophers, politicians, and writers as his memory assumed center stage in works by Lydia Maria Child, William Wordsworth, Thomas Wentworth Higginson, Harriet Martineau, John Greenleaf Whittier, and Thomas Branagan, among many others. Narrowing down this wealth of materials, I focus particularly upon *St. Domingo: Its Revolutions and Its Patriots,* a lecture published in 1855 by the ex-enslaved fugitive, historian, and orator William Wells Brown, as well as the famous speech *Toussaint L'Ouverture: The Hero of St. Domingo,* repeatedly delivered by the white antislavery activist and writer Wendell Phillips and printed on the eve of the Civil War in 1861. As seminal works, these addresses extrapolate key facets of Louverture's legacies, particularly as they relate to shifting constellations of black masculinity and revolutionary politics within white and black U.S. antislavery discourses.

Critics remain conflicted regarding representations of Louverture's heroism, an ongoing source of controversy throughout the nineteenth century. "For antebellum free blacks, one might have expected the Haitian Revolution to have furnished a powerful, heroic antislavery image. It did not," Bruce Dain observes.[60] Similarly, George Tyson argues, "American blacks have shown relatively little interest."[61] Yet, according to Mitchell Kachun, a wealth of works appeared in which "L'Ouverture was lionized" because he epitomized "qualities of leadership, independence, and sacrifice."[62] At the same time, Clavin suggests, "Abolitionists tried to soften the rock hard image of this indomitable black warrior."[63] Such contradictory legacies surrounding Louverture are testament not only to the shifting political, social, and historical biases of their originators but also to this iconic figure himself and his adept manipulation of his cultural archive.

Recognizing that the Haitian Revolution functioned in the dominant white transatlantic racist imagination as a source of atrocity literatures purporting to reveal the innate barbarity of Black men and women if "unnaturally" liberated from slavery, a wealth of writers and artists sought to gain sympathy for Louverture as a tragic victim and martyr persecuted by Napoléon Bonaparte's treachery. Various authors—including Brown and Douglass—worked within a black radical tradition as they sought to substitute passive martyrological narratives with reimaginings of Louverture as a transcendent heroic archetype. In equal measure but with different results, black and white reimaginings of Louverture repeatedly refused to endorse polarized constructions of a black exemplary masculinity. Instead, they relied on Louverture's example to engage with the complex parameters of a slippery black heroic continuum. Across their works, they debated whether it was possible to identify a spectrum of mutually inclusive and relative rather than absolute and nonnegotiable categorizations of black heroism. Mapping blurred boundaries between "soft" and "rock hard" constructions, these fluid conceptualizations contributed to multifaceted reimaginings of Louverture as a Black male heroic figure ever adaptable to diverse historical eras and political agendas.

"And the American slaves are only waiting the opportunity of wiping out their wrongs in the blood of their oppressors. No revolution ever turned up greater heroes than that of St. Domingo. But no historian has yet done them justice." So William Wells Brown declares in his lecture *St. Domingo: Its Revolutions and Its Patriots,* delivered to transatlantic audiences in London and Philadelphia during 1854, at the height of black radical abolitionist activism. Brown's Louverture operates as a talisman expressive of the inevitability of African American militancy in the defense of human rights. Interpreting black agency as an antidote to white persecution, Brown opens with one of Frederick Douglass's favorite quotations from Lord Byron's *Childe Harold:* "Hereditary bondsmen. Know ye not / Who would be free, themselves must strike the blow." For Brown, as for Douglass, black moral outrage not only exposed white racist persecution but also justified black militancy. "Right is the most dangerous of weapons,—woe to him who leaves it to his enemies," he counsels.[64] Adopting a familiar trope within antislavery literature, Brown foregrounds Louverture's exceptionalism as a mechanism by which to heighten the spuriousness of black male and female subjugation during slavery.

Just as Olaudah Equiano had been lauded as the "African prince" toward the close of the eighteenth century, Brown reimagines monarchical origins for Louverture by narrating that he was "the grandson of the King of Armadas, one of the most wealthy, powerful, and influential monarchs on the west coast of Africa." No vision could be further from Carlyle's "sooty African." As Brown writes, "Toussaint was a man of prepossessing appearance, of middle stature, and possessed an iron frame. His dignified, calm, and unaffected features, and broad and well-developed forehead, would cause him to be selected in any company of men, as one who was born for a leader."[65] Substituting one racist fiction for another, Brown self-consciously engages with the penchant—exhibited among white European and American elites throughout this period—of situating enslaved Africans within a soi-disant noble tradition. Such a tendency had been popularized centuries before by white British writers, including Aphra Behn in her dramatic work *Oroonoko; or, The Royal Slave,* published as early as 1688. For white transatlantic audiences, only men and women from within a mythic and imagined African aristocracy could be allowed to be revolutionary and heroic, as further revealed by the mythologized "noble chief" Sengbe Pieh's enduring success in the popular imagination. By cultivating such associations, therefore, Brown seemingly aligns himself with this tradition in order to parody its oversimplified assumptions. Adopting an ambiguous poetics, he simultaneously encompasses assimilationist and radically oppositional discourse in this speech.

Deliberately endorsing physical prowess as inextricable from intellectual profundity, Brown's provocative descriptions dramatize Louverture's exceptional body as a site of corporeal no less than psychological and moral superiority. His is no arbitrarily given birthright—as per monarchical assumptions of power—but rather one he earned through his cultivation of self-made attributes. Adopting tropes similar to those dramatically on offer in Douglass's novella, *The Heroic Slave,* Brown's references to Louverture's "iron frame," which he interprets as inextricable from a "prepossessing appearance" and "well-developed forehead," testify to a widespread determination among Black abolitionists to endorse violence as a legitimate protest against intellectual, emotional, and physical injustices. For Brown no less than Douglass, Holly, Allen, Smith, and others, Louverture's military prowess was motivated solely by abstract idealism in the service of moral resistance. "It might be said that an inward and prophetic genius revealed to him the omnipotence of a firm and unwearied adherence to a principle," he suggests.[66] According to Brown, Douglass, and a wealth of other Black politicians, writers, and artists, enslaved men and women were made and not born. Exceptional, heroic archetypes such as Louverture fulfilled their exemplary potential regardless of the subjugating forces of Atlantic slavery.

A problematic dualism clearly emerges in Brown's writing concerning the split between iconic and anonymous feats of black male heroism. In *St. Domingo,* he navigates the divide between exceptional historical figures on the one hand and the anonymous millions of men and women held in captivity on the other. As a result, a dangerous implication emerges by running the risk of suggesting that those who lived and died in slavery were somehow inferior and may even have been complicit in their own oppression. Such a difficulty remains key to ambivalences within Louverture's multiple legacies, as writers and artists preferred to minimize individualized constructions in favor of exalting in his signifying practices as a representative icon or "unanswerable argument." For this reason, even in this early period, Brown knowingly countered isolationist portrayals of Louverture to dramatize "his superior knowledge of the character of his race" instead.[67] However reappropriated and reconfigured, Brown's Louverture is ultimately far from sanitized, as he functioned not only as a spectacular embodiment of white terror but also as a catalyst to black heroism. Refusing to flinch from alienating his white listeners, Brown reexamines Louverture in the context of a dangerous nineteenth-century comparison. "Like Nat Turner, the Spartacus of the Southampton revolt, who fled with his brave band to the Virginia swamps, Toussaint and his generals took to the mountains," he observes. Suggesting even the slightest hint of similarities between Turner's and Louverture's revolutionary stratagems risked vilifying Louverture by association with Turner, demonized as the quintessential signifier of black vengeance within the United States. Damningly, Brown endorses a conterminous rather than a bifurcated understanding of black male exceptionalism by situating Louverture and Turner within a heroic continuum of resistance. He also engages in rhetorical questioning to communicate his vision of inevitable black apocalyptic violence by prophesying, "Who knows but that a Toussaint, a Christophe, a Rigaud, a Clervaux, and a Dessalines may some day appear in the Southern States of this Union?"[68] Testifying to his awareness of Louverture's significance within a pantheon of diasporic heroism, Brown bears witness to Louverture's representative rather than exceptional iconic status.

For Brown as well as other Black writers, archetypal Black revolutionary exemplars in general and, most significantly, Louverture in particular, provided a portal through which the heroism of an unindividualized mass of enslaved manhood could be celebrated:

> The spirit that caused the blacks to take up arms, and to shed their blood
> in the American revolutionary war, is still amongst the slaves of the south,
> and, if we are not mistaken, the day is not far distant when the revolution

of St. Domingo will be reenacted in South Carolina and Louisiana. The Haytian revolution was not unlike that which liberated the slaves of Sparta.[69]

Recontextualizing Louverture according to acts of black male heroism as performed during not only the Haitian Revolution but the "American revolutionary war," Brown reinterprets this African Caribbean heroic figure as a transcendent embodiment of a black U.S. militant "spirit." Equally, Brown adopts Douglass's self-reflexive tactic of persistently returning to ancient Western classical models—including the antiquarian freedom fighter Spartacus—on the grounds that the dominant white male rhetorical traditions within which he operated similarly supported their arguments by such seemingly learned examples. Seeking to legitimize Louverture's status as an exemplary icon, Brown translates his revolutionary ideology into familiar terms for purposes not of assimilation but of radical recognition and subversion.

Deliberately shifting national frameworks in this speech, Brown juxtaposes geographical locales to justify black emancipation as a matter not of principle but of self-preservation as he seemingly courts racist fears regarding the specter of violent black manhood. Realizing the inefficacy of ideological, moral, and political forms of protest in converting white audiences to an awareness of black equality, on the surface Brown capitulates to irrational prejudices in order to secure his greater aim of abolition. Therefore, his classical allusion to Spartacus legitimizes black radicalism on white terms by evoking an ancient European civilization as the social and political standard for diverse forms of African heroism. Yet his use of a comparative heroic framework encompassing diverse forms of European heroism ultimately establishes his authority, no less than Louverture's, as a learned orator and authoritative interpreter of black historical sites of conflict and memorialization.

Returning to Douglass's emphasis upon Haiti as a stage upon which the "black man's character" could be tried and tested, Brown insists on "reviewing the character of Toussaint" on the grounds that "his very name became a tower of strength to his friends and a terror to his foes." As Brown recognized, the most powerful way in which to dramatize black heroism for his white audiences was by assimilating Louverture's memory within a white American context:

> Toussaint's career as a Christian, a statesman, and a general, will lose nothing by a comparison with that of Washington. . . . Toussaint's government

made liberty its watchword incorporated in its constitution, abolished the slave-trade, and made freedom universal amongst the people. Washington's government incorporated slavery and the slave-trade, and enacted laws by which chains were fastened upon the limbs of millions of people.

Brown's abolitionist tactic of comparing competing models of white and black male heroism reversed popular assumptions by denigrating Washington as a white man because he lacked the egalitarian vision of a Black man, Louverture. Paradoxically, however, he applauds the white general's antiheroic actions for creating the inequitable conditions in which black militancy was forced to appear. Brown graphically prophesies the specter of a violent "contest" according to which "the indignation of the slaves of the South would kindle a fire so hot that it would melt their chains, drop by drop until not a single link would remain; and the revolution that was commenced in 1776 would then be finished."[70] Brown's metaphorical correlation of molten shackles with a visionary embodiment of white American idealism worked to galvanize black social protest by fusing physical and ideological realities. Thus he vouchsafed his conviction that the promise of white national political idealism could only ever be realized by black revolutionary militancy.

As a recurring symbol within a nineteenth-century African American literary, political, and artistic imagination, Louverture has remained the subject of profoundly diverse and dramatically inconsistent representations. In particular, the journalist, orator, and shoemaker James T. Holly was mesmerized by "the daring deeds of dreadless heroism performed by a Toussaint" in his speech "The Negro Race, Self-Government, and the Haitian Revolution."[71] Adopting a tactic similar to Brown's, Holly recuperates Louverture according to generic models of white male heroism, describing him as "another Washington," a benevolent force engaged in constructing "a plan that comprehended in its scope the well-being of the masses of humanity." By comparison, the renowned physician, writer, and activist James McCune Smith delivered a lecture in 1841 in which he foregrounded Louverture's philosophical profundity. Smith celebrates Louverture's "lofty intellect," which "always delighted to effect its object rather by the tangled mazes of diplomacy than by the strong arm of physical force." Shying away from graphic comparisons with Turner, Smith's Louverture is far more of a pacifist than Brown's, as he engaged in a "bloodless conquest" in refutation of white racist assumptions regarding the "natural inferiority of the Negro race."[72] According to John Mercer Langston, Louverture's history represented a rallying call both to black militancy and radical solidarity. "Let us, then, disfranchised

Americans, take new courage; for our cause and the cause of the slave shall triumph gloriously," he insists.[73] Simultaneously invoking a Black Washington, a Haitian Turner, and an African Spartacus, this rich tapestry of black memorializations testifies to Louverture's conflicting and ambiguous symbolism as a talisman of military, ideological, and political subversion within an African American imaginary.

Depicting Louverture as a no less aggrandized but varyingly configured emblem of antislavery discourse within white American memorializations, Wendell Phillips immortalizes Louverture in his famed lecture "Toussaint L'Ouverture." Delivered a few years later than Brown's oration, on the eve of the Civil War in 1861, this speech was "among the most popular orations of the time."[74] Seemingly motivated by a determination to provide an unequivocal description of his controversial subject matter, Phillips unveils the life of "one of the most remarkable men of the last generation—the great St. Domingo chief, Toussaint L'Ouverture, an unmixed Negro, with no drop of white blood in his veins." Rather than adopting Brown's technique of eulogizing Louverture's mythologized regal origins, Phillips directs his invective toward white ignorance to insist that, contrary to racist supposition, he possessed "no drop of white blood." "If anything, therefore, that I say of him tonight moves your admiration, remember, the black race claims it all—we have no part nor lot in it," Phillips clarifies.[75] Such an avowal of immutable differences between the races explicitly endorsed essentialized constructions of racial separatism in the service of a radicalized antislavery agenda. Just as Brown equivocates in order to legitimize Louverture's heroism as inspired by patriotic fervor, so Phillips evokes racist theories of black difference to reject nefarious practices of white appropriation. For Phillips, no less than for Douglass, Louverture signifies as a metonymic emblem or "argument" of black equality rather than as a flesh-and-blood individual, as both activists sought to provoke a reformist conscience in their audiences. Clearly, Phillips, Brown, and Douglass—in addition to many others—were determined to transform the scant historical record surrounding Louverture into a creative source of empowerment on the grounds that such lacunae necessitated acts and arts of radical reimagining.

"My sketch is at once a biography and an argument," Philips summarizes, admitting to Louverture's primary rhetorical significance as an intellectual embodiment of abstract antislavery principles. Yet, however groundbreaking, his lecture betrays white racist paternalist biases that risk undermining his vision of utopian egalitarianism. Barely taking breath from exalting in separatist constructions of black male heroism, he endorses white superiority in the very act of critiquing dominant strategies of racist exclusion. "I attempt the Quixotic effort to convince you that the Negro blood, instead of standing at the bottom of the list, is entitled, if judged either by its great men or its masses, either by its courage, its purpose, or its endurance, to take a place as near ours as any other blood known in history," he informs his white audiences.[76] Deciding to insert the telling equivocation of "a place as near ours as any other" Phillips colludes in racist hierarchies that potentially detract from his radical endorsement of the equality of "Negro blood." Such a tactic was no doubt effective, however, in galvanizing and empowering white audiences ready to support the antislavery cause only by liberating a particular vision of a black shackled rather than equal humanity as they fought to protect the status quo. Just as Josiah Wedgwood's "Am I Not a Man and a Brother?" medallion testifies to white spirituality by requiring their acts of emancipation over and above a recognition of the arts of black enslaved experiences, Phillips' vision of black heroism is less a vindication of African Caribbean humanity and more a celebration of white moral supremacy.

Well aware of white racist strategies of black dehumanization, however, Phillips was determined to radicalize his rhetoric yet further by exposing white violent excesses during slavery in order to deflate charges of black bestiality. "I am about to open to you a chapter of bloody history—no doubt of it," he concedes, seemingly admitting to the horrifying realities of black revolutionary activism. "Who set the example?" he asks, to which he provides his own reply: "Our race. And if the black man learned the lesson but too well, it does not lie in our lips to complain." Adapting the biblical conviction that we "reap what we sow," Phillips reconfigures black violence not as a sign of barbaric militancy but as necessary self-defense in the face of white villainy. However, this strategy also risked displacing black agency by suggesting that Louverture's actions were not motivated by a revolutionary consciousness as they instead betrayed his importance as little more than a cultural and political cipher for whites. This view is scarcely fair, however, as Phillips's self-reflexivity betrays his own awareness regarding his limitations. "During this whole struggle, the record is—written, mark you, by the white man—the whole picture from the pencil of the white race," he emphasizes.[77] A powerful admission, Phillips's declaration repeats with variation Douglass's condemnation of "chattel records" no less than Brown's critique of historiographical injustices. Thus Phillips's realization paved the way not only for resistance to white-dominated historical discourses but also for identifying the biases unconsciously embedded within his own account.

A critical sensitivity to Phillips's multilayered protest strategies is essential in coming to grips with his groundbreaking refusal to shy away from white violence. With the exception of Louverture's own historical archive, he was one of the first writers to focus on the horrors of racist reprisals. He argues, for instance, that "for one life the negro took in battle, in hot and bloody fight, the white race took, in the cool malignity of revenge, three to answer for it." Phillips's determination to indict the horrifying practices by which enslaved men, women, and children became Black sacrificial martyrs to white clamorings for revenge invites comparisons to the terrifying aftermath of Turner's rebellion, a similarly horrifying example of racist injustices carried out by vigilante mob law and as enacted in the United States. More tellingly still, Phillips not only exposes inaccuracies within dominant historical archives but also debates white nefarious practices of monumentalism and memorialization:

> Were I here to tell you the story of Washington, I should take it from your hearts—you, who think no marble white enough on which to carve the name of the Father of this country. I am about to tell you the story of a negro who has left hardly one written line. I am to glean it from the reluctant testimony of . . . men who despised him as a negro and a slave.[78]

Phillips's provocative juxtaposition refuses to flinch from critiquing entrenched systems of white heroic adulation by exposing the excessive memorialization of national heroic figures such as Washington. While there was "no marble white enough" for Washington's heroism, Louverture's was the "story of a negro" hidden from history, whose neglect necessitated Phillips's imaginative reconstruction of black heroism from the distorted fragments of a "reluctant testimony."

According to Phillips, white reinterpretations of black historical realities were justified on the grounds that Louverture had "left hardly one written line," helping to perpetuate fallacies regarding his archival lacunae in order to legitimize the proliferation of his own diverse re-creations. However radical and groundbreaking, therefore, Phillips's speech ultimately conceptualizes Louverture according to essentialized paradigms that subjected Africans and African Americans to dehumanizing polarizations as either deities or demons, heroes or villains, saints or sinners, and yet never as multifaceted, psychologically complex social and political equals. "But there never was a race that, weakened and degraded by such chattel slavery, tore off its own fetters forged them into swords, and won its liberty on the battlefield, but one, and that was the black government," Phillips concludes, thereby again exalting in a hagiographic and one-dimensional interpretation of Louverture's iconic exceptionalism.[79]

By comparison, the majority of white nineteenth-century representations of Louverture's heroism speak to yet further political, historical, and ideological conflicts regarding black masculinity. For example, Ralph Waldo Emerson's essay "Character" exalts in black heroic prowess solely by exposing the physical bonds of slavery as meaningless in the face of black bravery. "Is an iron handcuff so immutable a bond?" he asks, arguing, "Suppose a slaver on the coast of Guinea should take on board a gang of negroes, which should contain persons of the stamp of Toussaint L'Ouverture."[80] Decades later, as works by Brown and Phillips prophesied, Louverture's heroism took center stage during the American Civil War in light of his status as an embodiment of black revolutionary violence.[81] As Wood writes, "The myth of Toussaint was of vital importance to English and American abolitionists" in establishing "an uncomplicated way of presenting an idealized pro-black version of the Haitian Revolution with which to counter the pro-slavery atrocity literatures."[82] For example, in *Toussaint L'Ouverture,* published in 1863, James R. Beard asks, *"Are Negroes fit for Officers?"* answering, "We are entering on that debate now. The Life of Toussaint may help to end it."[83] Similarly, the military commander and staunch abolitionist Thomas Wentworth Higginson commended his "color-sergeant," Sergeant Prince Rivers, on the grounds that "he makes Toussaint perfectly intelligible."[84] Sharing Phillips's concerns regarding the problems of the white historical record, Lydia Maria Child was one of the first writers to identify a black historical tradition as a source of political and aesthetic empowerment. "When the Africans have writers of their own, we shall hear their efforts for liberty called by the true title of heroism in a glorious cause," she writes.[85]

Embracing an alternative vision of black heroism, in 1870, the white American artist Anne Whitney created *Toussaint-Louverture,* a marble sculpture whose location is still unknown (see figure 4).[86] All that remains is a photograph of the plaster statue, in which she depicts Toussaint in atypical guise as a half-seated figure, his face and body poised and leaning toward the viewer. In radical opposition to the kneeling black subject of Wedgwood's imagination, however, Whitney's Louverture is no subjugated figure as he is instead shown primed for action and ready to do battle. Furthermore, his overtly Africanized physiognomy and the carefully carved textures of his hair combine with his exemplary and heightened musculature to signal a radical break with existing visual representations. Cultivating an idealized form in this sculpture, she endorses Louverture's heroic and exemplary status according to black rather than white aestheticized standards. Clearly, the body and face of Whitney's Louverture have little in common with eighteenth- or nineteenth-century lithographs and engravings purporting to represent his body and face, or even with contemporary works documenting black exemplary humanity such as the African and Native American sculptor Edmonia Lewis's *Forever Free* (1867). Yet the classical contours of Louverture's physiognomy as sculpted by Whitney can be situated within white standardized conventions regarding an aggrandized exceptionalism as she exalts in his mythic status. The upper half of his body clad in only short trousers, is fully on display to the viewer. However, rather than offering the Black man's body up for white consumption in spectacular display, Lewis presents Louverture as guarding his own physique with a hand placed in front of his body as he adopts a half-concealed posture. However imbued with problematic assumptions, therefore, a rich array of black and white oratory, sculpture, essays, and literary adaptations establishes Toussaint Louverture's enduring significance as a fluctuating and varyingly reimagined symbol during the nineteenth century.

"THE BLACK MAN'S NECESSARY MASKS": JACOB LAWRENCE'S *THE LIFE OF TOUSSAINT L'OUVERTURE* SERIES (1938)

"This story is to help fill a long-continuing void. The Negro youth of the world has been taught that the black race has no great traditions, no characters of world importance, no record of substantial contribution to civilization." So writes the Black dramatist Leslie Pinckney Hill as justification for his play *Toussaint L'Ouverture: A Dramatic Work*, published in 1928. Adapting Louverture's example to suit emerging eras of segregation and lynch law, Hill's work provides an apt bridge between nineteenth- and twentieth-century representations of this heroic figure. More specifically, various continuities arise from his determination to resist racist stereotypes as well as his experimentation with art as a politicized site of black heroic reimagining. "A worthy literature reared upon authentic records of achievement is the present spiritual need of the race," he urges. "For centuries the Negro had to dream and sing and cover his will to be free by mummery, mystery and buffoonery" Hill asserts, adding, "He is still the world's accepted scaramouche. Every guise, attitude, or dialect conveying that character has had ample freedom and hospitality. Not so heroic conduct or creative genius."[87]

FIGURE 4. Anne Whitney, *Toussaint-Louverture,* 1870. (Courtesy of the Wellesley College Archives)

On the surface, according to Hill, African and African American enslaved women and men exist beyond the pale of a "heroic" pantheon. He exalts in the fact that they engaged in survival strategies devised to establish that "this white world" had failed "to penetrate the black man's necessary masks." Celebrating Louverture's memory as a touchstone for black signification, he theorized this historical figure in terms of black rituals of disguise and masking. In forceful ways, he mapped the inextricable relationships among Louverture, performativity, and the body as sites of resistance. A leitmotif for black collective freedoms, Hill's Louverture signifies as a self-sacrificing liberator eloquently articulating his own vision of equality: "It is not, then, to make one race supreme / That we must fight, but to make all men free."

As a work debating the politics and poetics of black heroic representations, Hill's play introduces key features of the renowned artist Jacob Lawrence's *The Life of Toussaint L'Ouverture*, created a decade later in 1938. A forty-one-panel work executed in "tempera on paper," Lawrence's multifaceted series signals a stark departure from conventions proliferating in marginal and mainstream representations of Louverture. His pioneering experimentation with mixed-media textual and visual narratives endorses new approaches to representations of black male heroism.[88] More significantly, Lawrence's *Toussaint L'Ouverture* series inaugurates the visual and textual vocabulary as well as the aesthetic milieu for his later historic works, including *The Life of Frederick Douglass* (1938–39) and *The Life of Harriet Tubman* (1939–40).

While Lawrence's representation of Louverture's history addresses a fundamental epoch in Haitian history, Harlem clearly provides the political and aesthetic backdrop. In an interview, he admits to listening to "street corner orators talking about social issues and things of that kind." "We were in the Depression," Lawrence explains. "We had Negro history clubs in the schools and the libraries. And teachers and various people were speaking of Frederick Douglass, Toussaint L'Ouverture, Harriet Tubman."[89] Recuperating and revising Louverture's heroism, which he recontextualizes alongside the activism of African American heroic figures, Lawrence seeks to use his memory to protest against racist injustices within U.S. political, social, and historical contexts. Far from clear cut, Lawrence's aesthetic vision represents no cathartic trajectory of black uplift. Rather, he complicates Louverture's seeming epic transcendence over his dehumanizing conditions by refusing to shy away from his victimization and martyrdom. As a series designed to provide a displaced forum within which to examine the soul-destroying effects of deprivation and discrimination in the contemporary era, Lawrence categorizes Louverture as an enslaved laborer turned liberator, soldier, statesman, and martyr. Louverture's memory serves an integral function in Lawrence's exploration of the multiple roles and "necessary masks" adopted by Black women and men in their ongoing determination to survive contemporary society. "Out of the community," Lawrence insists regarding his inspiration for the series, "people speaking about these things, about liberation, . . . people like this became the symbol of what people would talk about." For Lawrence, Louverture resonates not only as an iconic signifier of historical resistance but also as a lens through which to debate contemporary injustices. "As a youngster I guess I wanted an identity," he explains, noting that "it made for a very colorful method, working in a series form, telling a story."[90] Such interrelationships between political consciousness and narrative experimentation betray Lawrence's more general endorsement of a politicized aesthetics and an aestheticized politics vis-à-vis representations of black male and female heroism.

Creating an array of narratives within his work on the grounds that it was "the only way I could tell a full story," Lawrence constructs his series from multiple vignettes. His reimagining of black military prowess, political leadership, violent conflict, death, loss, and sacrifice all starkly contrast to white betrayal and cowardice as perpetuated by the dual horrors of slavery and colonization.[91] An eclectic researcher, he was indebted to eighteenth- and nineteenth-century lithographs and drawings as well as historical, literary, and oratorical works for his dramatizations of Louverture. Self-reflexively interweaving text and image, he recycles and revisits dominant iconography in conjunction with literary and historical motifs. Thus he obtains not so much "a full story" as a multifaceted array of layered narratives whose interpretative dynamics can only be identified by direct audience engagement.

A groundbreaking work within not only Lawrence's oeuvre but also European American and African American art history, *The Life of Toussaint L'Ouverture* has received scant critical attention. As one of the few scholars to examine this series, Cora Kaplan incisively argues that Lawrence creates "a cartoon that simultaneously strips the history down to its essential parts and raises it to legend, pictorially representing its emblematic, epic moments."[92] This emphasis on his stark use of minimalism illuminates Lawrence's development of a symbolic language through muted colors, stylized figuration, and dramatic composition. Lawrence relies on these techniques to wage war on the emotional erasures effected by an excessive discourse of sentimentality. He insists that his viewers and readers engage in an imaginative and emotive critique of reductive historical records. "The absence of light and dark modeling relates to Lawrence's aversion to overpersonalizing the features of his heroes in the *Toussaint* series," Patricia Hills observes.[93] A lack of individualized specificity across his panels establishes Lawrence's determination to minimize difference by signifying upon Louverture's history as a foundation for black political resistance in the contemporary era. Perhaps another way of interpreting such anonymity, however, can be identified by situating his angular bodies alongside Leslie Pinckney Hill's theories of black performativity and masking. Adopting a technique of undertelling via stylized, symbolic compositions that withhold detail, Lawrence's aesthetic practices of concealment and revelation proliferate a multiplicity of representations designed to subvert stereotypical forms of didactic exposition regarding Louverture's heroism.

Reimagining a plethora of Louvertures, Lawrence not only revisits lacunae within dominant memory but also signifies on his importance as a defamiliarizing lens through which to expose twentieth-century political struggles against social and historical injustices. As an incendiary protest artist whose anger has often gone unrecognized, Lawrence finds in Louverture a displaced forum within which not only to denounce black sacrifice and martyrdom but also to condemn white perfidy, terror, and immoral barbarity in his own era. For Hills, Lawrence's series exalts in an exceptional individualism, as "the forty-one panels on Toussaint . . . focus single-mindedly on the heroism of Toussaint and his men."[94] Yet in this series Lawrence endorses a continuum of black heroism by encompassing both celebrated and unknown forms of resistance. A challenging, ambiguous, and aesthetically experimental work, Lawrence's series dramatizes Louverture's heroism via juxtapositions not only between text and image but also between image and image in his layered narrative. "Jacob Lawrence did his own research for *The Toussaint L'Ouverture* series and wrote his own captions," but the "exact sources have been forgotten," Grant Spradling explains.[95] The unverifiable and ambiguous origins of Lawrence's literary reinterpretations testify to his belief in the political and moral responsibility of his audiences to engage in imaginative recovery. His use of an abstract-figurative mode works to intensify the dramatic and emotional force at the heart of his symbolic compositions. As David Driskell observes, "It is in this manner of composing and staging art that Lawrence awakens the social consciousness in all of us."[96] Politically engaged and aesthetically avant-garde, Lawrence's *Toussaint L'Ouverture* operates as a visual and textual montage. Signifying upon lacunae within official archives, he urges audiences to an imaginative identification with black male heroism.

"I like narration," Lawrence admits regarding the storytelling impetus undergirding his work.[97] The early panels in *Toussaint L'Ouverture* constitute narratives within narratives, as he provides compelling triptychs heightened by factual and emotive captioning. The captions to panels 5, 6, and 7 read, "Slave trade reaches its height in Haiti, 1730"; "The birth of Toussaint L'Ouverture, May 20, 1743. Both of Toussaint's parents were slaves"; and "As a child, Toussaint heard the twang of the planter's whip and saw the blood stream from the bodies of slaves."[98] As forceful, layered vignettes, these panels provide destabilizing and emotive effects by alternating between panoramic overviews and intimate close-ups. Offering a powerful indictment of white immorality, the first of these works denounces the evils of the slave trade. Here, he contrasts the affluent and well-dressed bodies and individualized physiognomies of white men and women with a prostrate, huddled, and indistinguishable mass of enslaved black figures. While the expressions on the white faces are clearly on view, Lawrence distinguishes his Black subjects only by their enlarged eyes and masklike physiognomies. Concealing his subjects' emotions, Lawrence compels his viewers to experience outrage via symbolic reimagining rather than a process of invasive and objectifying appropriation as he resists the reductive problematics at work in strategies of didactic explication. He also includes a black pieta in the foreground of this image to dramatize the pathos of an unidentified Black woman holding a baby to her body. Thus he amplifies his reinterpretation of Louverture's iconic heroism as emerging within otherwise anonymized histories of suffering.

Dramatizing a visual dialogue between panels, his next painting is characterized by repetition with variation as Louverture's mother cradles the diminutive form of Louverture as a baby. Lawrence's symbolic use of color—the mother and child in both works are similarly wrapped in white and yellow cloth—aggrandizes Louverture's exceptionalism by situating his birth within a wider context exposing the horrifying white trade in black bodies. At the same time, the typicality of the clothing of both Louverture and his mother breaks new ground by situating Black women and children within a tradition of black female, rather than male, resistance. This view can be further substantiated in light of the earlier prominence of these colors in the ceremonial dress of Queen Anacanca, a historical figure whom Lawrence argues led the war against Columbus's colonization mission.[99] Lawrence's ambiguous sixth panel reveals Louverture's poverty-stricken origins as interlocking and askew grid-like patterns on the cabin ceiling and walls symbolize confinement. Painstaking details such as roughly forged nails hammered into the bedpost suggest transition and transformation in order to communicate makeshift and improvised strategies of survival. In this regard, his use of a domestic interior resonates with the imagery of his *Migration of the Negro* series, created scarcely three years later, as he offers further proof of his politicized use of historical injustices to critique contemporary inequalities.[100] As his aesthetic practices reveal, Lawrence rejected didacticism and excessive sentimentality as effective narrative tools. Instead, he relies on a pared-down simplicity onto which audiences were encouraged to project their emotions and arrive at an individualized sense of trauma.

Hills observes that "Lawrence's artistic style seems especially fitting for such a depersonalized epic," explaining, "His expressive cubism, with its flat shapes, controlled outlines, and limited range of color, kept the emotion restrained and the conceptual goals clear, and moved the sequences in measured cadences." Lawrence's angular stylization and minimalist iconography in this series bears witness to his defamiliarizing strategies designed to rupture straightforward interpretations and inspire audience empathetic engagement. As Hills further observes, "The skilled delivery and pace of a folktale find their analogues in Lawrence's pairing and sequencing of his panels."[101] For Lawrence, graphic visualizations of white barbarity combine with those of black subjugation to dominate panel 7 as the final work in this narrative within a narrative. In this image, Lawrence dramatizes prostrate, mangled, and heaped bodies of muscular, half-naked Black men begging for mercy from a villainous white man whose horrifying presence is accentuated by the deathly pallor of his white clothing and the fact that he wields a brown whip. By comparison, enslaved black bodies remain indistinguishable and unindividualized, as his use of white circles to symbolize eyes does little to detract from their faceless anonymity.

The threatening posture of the white male figure dominating this panel clearly arises from his angular stylization. A hunched-over shoulder results in the partial concealment of his eyes as if to further politicize processes of seeing and condemn his loss of humanity as he is shown just before he strikes this array of powerless black bodies. More startlingly still, this scene functions as a rite of passage for a young Louverture as Lawrence graphically dramatizes the horrors implied by his caption, "As a child, Toussaint heard the twang of the planter's whip and saw the blood stream." Overtly engaging with the act and art of bearing witness, Lawrence's decision to replicate the angular stylization of the white man's hunched-over body in the diminutive form of Louverture—here portrayed as a child—confirms Wendell Phillips's nineteenth-century view that black violence emerges solely as a mirror to white barbarity. Surprisingly, Lawrence defines his aesthetic practices as inspired by necessity during this period by insisting he painted "the only way I knew to paint." Such a view is difficult to substantiate, however, in light of Lawrence's highly stylized and symbolic imagery, which betrays his preference for dramatizing both a layered multiplicity of perspectives and an array of narratives.[102]

The caption accompanying panel 10 reads, "The cruelty of the planters toward the slaves drove the slaves to revolt, 1776. Those revolts, which kept cropping up from time to time, finally came to a head in the rebellion" (see plate 1). A compositional tour de force, this work reproduces the violent actions of the slaveholder dramatized in Lawrence's seventh panel with a key variation. In this work, he replaces the broken bodies of enslaved men and women with a single prostrate black figure bound by rope yet still similarly engaged in supplicatory prayer, as he delineates his subject's hands with uncharacteristic detail. Snaking across the ground, the unfurled end of a rope binds the enslaved man's feet to accentuate black powerlessness via a visual call-and-response relationship to the frayed end of the whip. Boldly reversing dominant associations, this symbolic object dramatizes black resistance by evoking formal similarities to the broken shackle hanging in the concluding panel of the whole series. In this final work, Lawrence eulogizes Louverture's "liberal leadership" by problematizing Dessalines's reign, as he appears "beside a broken chain" and unequivocally in the guise of "a dictator."[103]

In panel 10, Lawrence substitutes the diminutive form of Louverture—who had appeared in panel 7 as a witness to black suffering—with a shackled group of barely individualized enslaved men and women to accentuate their collective role as witness to an anonymous man's suffering. He thus highlights the extent to which competing forms of an iconic black male heroism forcefully operate as representative of the mass experiences of enslaved black victims. In contrast to the young Louverture, however, these enslaved women and men confront the viewer with enlarged eyes that resonate with those of the men and women in panel 5 as if in further condemnation of the terror and pathos of slavery. Drawing attention to the representative status of his male and female subjects, Lawrence emphasizes their unindividualized physiognomies in this work. By comparison, his detailed emphasis upon the haunting intricacies of their yellow-colored shackles testifies to a continuum of black resistance. For Lawrence, an iconic and anonymous male and female heroic continuum alternately characterized by subversion and seeming complicity represents a multifaceted fight for survival in the face of subjugation. More particularly, Lawrence's symbolic use of the color yellow draws attention to the cross the white man wears on his chest to secure an ironic indictment of white barbarity in the service of a soi-disant civilizing Christianity.

The drama of this haunting composition arises from Lawrence's macabre use of symmetry. In this work, the contours of the white man's yellow cross mirror the hand-drawn, improvised structure of the crimson red crucifix etched onto the prostrate body of the bound Black man. This metaphorical parallel accentuates the Black man's bloodied scars to suggest his significance as a signifier of black spiritual redemption via physical sacrifice. Adopting a symbolic use of red in this work, Lawrence foregrounds the Black man's bloodred scarification not only by accentuating the red mouths of the enslaved men and women but also by writing his own signature in red. Refusing to flinch from dramatizing black victimization, he thereby situates these bound and shackled bodies within a continuum that encompasses not only physical rebellion in "revolt" but also aesthetic resistance, as the artwork itself represents an act of protest in his decision to sign his name in red. In this multifaceted painting, Lawrence's powerful symmetry relies on angular constructions of white and black male bodies. While the white man's arms bear left, the Black man's turn to the right to suggest that, if joined together, they would form a crucifix. Such a radical envisioning of a biracial body engaged in acts of self-sacrifice communicates Lawrence's integrationist vision of radical resistance.

Appearing in the early part of his *Toussaint L'Ouverture* series, Lawrence's graphic visions testifying to white barbarity offer a powerful prelude to his overtly physical dramatizations of black violence in later works such as panel 12, "Jean Francois, first Black to rebel in Haiti," and panel 19, for which the unequivocal caption partially reads, "The Blacks formed into large bands and slaughtered every Mulatto and White they encountered" (see plate 2).[104] Panel 12 offers a radical reversal of the black-whip-wielding white man in panel 10 by including a Black man with a masklike face holding aloft a white sword. In this figure, distinctive only in his enlarged white eyes and bared teeth, Lawrence upsets power hierarchies by inverting the positions of his black and white bodies in order to expose the arbitrariness of black subjugation in slavery. In this work, it is as if the dead have been brought back to life, as these half-naked Black men betray visual similarities with the bound men and women populating earlier panels but now with a key difference: they carry rifles in their hands and raise their fists as they march in solidarity with a common cause.

As an even more violent spectacle, panel 19 depicts a tortuous dance of the macabre as black and white bodies engage in violent conflict. Offering a powerful reversal of inequalities in this work, Black armed men stand over the mutilated bodies of vulnerable whites shown falling or lying prostrate. In a powerful volte face, white bodies assume the position of typically enslaved black subjects, as they are repeatedly exhibited with their hands outstretched and begging for mercy. While white facial features indicate fear and horror with wide eyes and open mouths in this panel, Lawrence obscures the black physiognomies of his formerly enslaved revolutionaries by revealing only a white slit for an eye, heightening ambiguity in their masklike faces. Replacing the earlier yellow shackles with weaponry as they now wield yellow spears, Lawrence confirms the extent to which black violence originated as self-defense against white barbarity. Compellingly, one of Lawrence's unidentified black male subjects holds the face of a white woman while her hands are outstretched as if begging for mercy. Thus Lawrence offers an unsanitized and uncensored exposure of ongoing racial conflict in his critique of twentieth-century contexts of segregation and lynch law.

"General Toussaint L'Ouverture, Statesman and military genius, esteemed by the Spaniards, feared by the English, dreaded by the French, hated by the planters, and reverenced by the Blacks." So reads the caption accompanying panel 20, a work in which Lawrence exalts in Louverture's shifting subjectivities (see plate 3).[105] As Daguillard, Hills, and Powell observe, this portrait of Louverture in profiled view was directly inspired by Nicolas Eustache Maurin's problematic lithograph created a century before, on which the anonymous image *Toussaint Louverture* was based (see figure 2). As Powell observes, Louverture functions for Lawrence as "a contemporary, Depression-era liberator: a decorated yet faceless dignitary, leading the charge against economic and racial injustice in style."[106] Yet Louverture's decision to reproduce Louverture's clothing in this image may well reveal his determination to accentuate his individualism. While his physiognomy lacks the detailed intricacy of the original etching, Lawrence's silhouetted and overlapping use of brown- and black-layered color re-creates Louverture as an enigmatic and disguised yet emotionally evocative and individualized heroic subject. Lawrence borrows from abstract stylizations characteristic of some forms of African sculpture and popularized by other Black painters including his teacher, Charles Alston. He attributes an elongated neck and chin and extended mouth to Louverture to evoke a mythologized diasporic heritage. Moreover, Lawrence's elongation of Louverture's face aggrandizes his forehead to heighten intellectualism over and above military prowess.

Clearly, Powell's invaluable question "Were Belley, Toussaint, and their modern black brethren in fact 'in disguise?'" highlights Lawrence's subversive strategies by returning to Leslie Pinckney Hill's emphasis upon the "black man's necessary masks," as he insists that "through their sartorial and corporeal expressivity they embodied an aesthetic departure that ruptured the white cultural order."[107] Overall, Lawrence experimented with an aesthetics of rupture in order to heighten his emphasis upon formal and thematic ambiguities within his *Toussaint L'Ouverture* series. For Lawrence, a transgressive and experimental use of form effectively dramatizes Louverture's various performances as an enslaved man turned politician, warrior, laborer, father, writer, and philosopher. Similarly, for the African American writer Arna Bontemps writing in *Drums at Dusk,* a novel published contemporaneously in 1940, Louverture operates as a mythic symbol of survival. Exalting in Louverture's exceptionalism, Bontemps insists, "Toussaint was not to be considered with the ordinary run of black flesh." For Bontemps, no less than for Lawrence and Hill, varying textual and visual constructions of Louverture attest to inextricable relationships between black masculinity, disguise, and theatrical performance. "In that fighting old Toussaint was sure to have a part. A flash of benign confidence gleamed on the coachman's masklike face," so Bontemps's narrator prophesies.[108]

"I SEE THE DEAD": ÉDOUARD GLISSANT'S *MONSIEUR TOUSSAINT* (1961, 1981)

As a catalyst for black pride and a talisman against white injustices, Toussaint Louverture has played a key role in diverse representations that have gained center stage within the English- and French-speaking Caribbean imagination over the centuries. In his seminal twentieth-century work on the Haitian Revolution, *The Black Jacobins,* first published in 1938, the Trinidadian author C. L. R. James vindicates Louverture as a symbol of black male agency and exceptionalism. "I was tired of reading and hearing about Africans being oppressed and persecuted in Africa, in the Middle Passage, in the USA and all over the Caribbean," he writes, admitting, "I made up my mind that I would write a book in which Africans or peoples of African descent . . . would themselves be taking action on a grand scale and shaping other people to their own needs." Situating Louverture within a context of resistance movements at a grassroots level, James contests the parameters of "Great man" history by insisting that "it was the slaves who had made the revolution." And yet he also laid the framework for subsequent aggrandizing mythologies by endorsing Louverture's exceptionalism. "By a phenomenon often observed, the individual leadership responsible for this unique achievement was almost entirely the work of a single man—Toussaint L'Ouverture," he argues.[109]

Critical to James's vision of Louverture as an exceptional icon is his status as "a slave till he was forty-five."[110] However, as David Geggus reveals, this myth has been shattered by recent research that establishes "that Toussaint was no longer a slave at the time of the French Revolution."[111] This discovery complicates tendencies among many Black and white writers to endorse an overly simplified cathartic vision by vouching for a paradigmatic and monolithic transformation of the former enslaved man into an archetypal, static heroic freedom fighter. Yet James himself was determined not to reimagine Louverture in isolation, as he admits that "Toussaint did not make the revolution, it was the revolution that made Toussaint."[112] James refused to sensationalize Louverture, whom he defended as "no phenomenon, no Negro freak"; for James he functioned as a touchstone for black revolutionary ideology and as a representative symbol of black heroism rather than an aberration.[113] Interestingly, this was not the first time James had grappled with Louverture's history, as he had previously written a play—originally titled *Toussaint L'Ouverture* and subsequently changed to *The Black Jacobins* (1938)—in which he unashamedly sought to recuperate Louverture as a "fantastic Negro."[114]

Alternatively, for the Martinican writer, poet, and founder of the Negritude Movement Aimé Césaire, writing decades later during the tumultuous political era of the 1960s, Louverture functions metonymically and as "a historical articulation" because of his prominent location at "the center, undoubtedly, of West Indian history."[115] Writing in *Cahier d'un retour au pays natal,* his groundbreaking poetical work first published in French in 1939 and subsequently translated into English as *Notebook of a Return to the Native Land* by Clayton Eshleman and Annette Smith, Césaire dramatizes Louverture's plight in terms similar to James's, deploring the fate of "a lone man defying the white screams of white death." In powerful and dramatic ways, he transgresses James's seemingly omniscient historical framework by adopting an interiority of perspective in order to reimagine Louverture's elided psychological paradoxes. Césaire's Louverture gives powerful voice to poignant realizations regarding his political, historical, and social legacies. "And I say to myself Bordeaux and Nantes and Liverpool and New York and San Francisco / not an inch of this world devoid of my fingerprint," his Louverture proclaims.[116] Operating as a signifier for his radical belief in negritude, Césaire's Louverture celebrates his status as a militant revolutionary. Refusing to shy away from this African Caribbean hero's battle for a "ferocious freedom," he exalts in the fact that there is "So much blood in my memory!"[117] Ultimately betraying more similarities to than differences from James's historical and dramatic works, however, as Dash argues, Césaire's *Notebook* equally "reduced the impact of the Haitian Revolution to the exiled and isolated figure of Toussaint Louverture."[118] In Césaire's poetical work, however, Louverture is depicted as a troubled talisman for collective suffering. "We the vomit of slave ships / Hail to the three centuries which uphold my civil rights and my minimized blood! / My heroism, what a farce!" Césaire's Louverture laments.[119] These lines testify to Césaire's self-conscious interrogation, and even deconstruction, of the parameters of black male heroism as he actively strained beyond Jamesian hagiography in his literary reimagining of Louverture. According to this version, he not only does not shy away from the dehumanizing realities of mass suffering in a black humanity reduced to "vomit" but also critiques illusory dramatizations of Louverture as an epic, transcendent icon.

For the Haitian poet René Depestre, writing a few decades later, Louverture's memory remains a no less slippery site of transatlantic heroism. In 1967 Depestre published *Un arc-en-ciel pour L'occident Chrétien,* a poetical work subsequently translated into English as *A Rainbow for the Christian West* by John McBride and Paul Vangelisti. Following from Césaire's forceful constructions of Louverture as an ambivalent locus of black male heroism, Depestre shifts geographical locale to situate Louverture within a U.S. national imaginary. As he explains in an interview, "The gods descend to the South of the United States in the blood of the poet there to do vengeance for oppression."[120] Similarly following from James, however, in his "Ode to Toussaint L'Ouverture" included in *A Rainbow for the Christian West,* Depestre debates the iconic hero's relationship to anonymous Black men and women suffering in slavery. He apocryphally writes of Louverture's ascent from among "an enslaved people" as "he happened like a cry piercing a house asleep / as if a blood were dying at the first blisters of a curse."[121] For Depestre no less than Césaire, Louverture operates as black male heroic icon and a psychological and metaphorical site not only of wounding but also of healing, given his capacity to function, as memorialized by James, as an exceptional individual in order to effect self-transformation. Tackling violence more directly, however, Depestre's Louverture mitigates against his "scars" by foregrounding the necessity for "black wrath."[122] As Philip Kaisary argues, Depestre "reverses and manipulates race stereotypes in order to celebrate indigenous and black histories and cultures that have been denigrated by the Christian West's project of colonialism."[123] Clearly, however much they differ, for C. L. R. James, Aimé Césaire, René Depestre, and, as we shall see below, Édouard Glissant, a Martinican author, philosopher, and critic, Louverture's memory and symbolism are not only inextricable from anticolonialist, antislavery and anti-Western worldviews but are also integral to their formulation of a revisionist and constantly evolving black diasporic consciousness.

"Yet the present work is not politically inspired; rather it is linked to what I would call, paradoxically, a *prophetic vision of the past.* For those whose history has been reduced by others to darkness and despair, the recovery of the near or distant past is imperative," writes Édouard Glissant in his preface to the first edition of *Monsieur Toussaint,* published in French in 1961. Translated into English by Juris Silenieks as recently as 1981, his work signifies as a point of both continuity and rupture vis-à-vis works by James, Césaire, and Depestre. For Glissant, reimagining and re-creating Louverture's legacy not only constitutes an act of resistance to black historical erasure, as it did for these writers, but also much more overtly symbolizes an idealized engagement with the transformative and transcendental possibilities of black male heroism. As Forsdick suggests, Glissant's work constitutes a radical break with the tradition established by James, Césaire, and Depestre in that his construction is "far removed from the upright *Négritude* of the romanticized liberator to which James had alluded and which became central to Césaire's reworking of the Toussaint myth."[124] Bereft of hagiographic and epic associations, Glissant's Louverture embodies psychological complexity and ambivalent mythologies.

Resituating Louverture's radical history alongside a pantheon of elided legends such as Mama Dio, a "Voodoo Priestess," and Mackandal, a "maroon, i.e. runaway slave," Glissant writes, "Toussaint's relations with his deceased companions arise from a tradition . . . of casual communication with the dead." Describing Mackandal as "a black maroon of the preceding century, who appears to Toussaint as a sort of primeval conscience," he argues for patterns of influence within a spiritual continuum that have been written out of white official testimonies.[125] According to Glissant, therefore, Louverture was no lone freedom fighter, as his heroism did not originate in a vacuum. Rather, he was inspired by the religious faith, military strategy, and political ideology of earlier Black radicals who had lived and died within a Caribbean context. Appearing not in literary or political isolation, Glissant's theatrical adaptation can be situated within existing black radical Francophone and English Caribbean theatrical traditions. These have long debated Louverture's memory in relation to issues of nationhood, war, heroism, black masculinity, identity, and social reform. As Martin Banham, Errol Hill, and George Woodyard observe, "Few events in modern history have engendered the writing of as many plays as the Haitian war of independence." Despite the fact that "most of these plays originated in Haiti," a transatlantic tradition can be identified on the grounds that "about one-third came from writers in England, France, Germany, Ivory Coast, Martinique, St. Lucia, Sweden and the United States."[126]

According to VèVè A. Clark, "From 1796 thought 1975, a total of sixty-three plays concerned with the Haitian Revolution were either performed or published." Glissant's work can thus be situated within a movement of "political theatre" that sought to "show how decolonization, like the period of original settlement, promoted cultural invisibility and dismemory." As Clark demonstrates, Glissant's play, which interprets Louverture as a metonymic signifier of the Haitian Revolution, continues in the vein of other popular works including Alphonse de Lamartine's *Toussaint Louverture* (1848), Jean Brierre's *Adieu à la Marseillaise* (1934), Eugene O'Neill's *Emperor Jones* (1920), and Aimé Césaire's *La Tragedie du Roi Christophe* (1963). Across their experimental plays, Glissant and other dramatists challenge dominant historiographical modes and political frameworks. They adopt a self-reflexive approach to black heroism in order to take "*representation* or mimesis, *misrepresentation*, and *re-presentation*" as their subject matter.[127] The revisionist and radical works of Glissant and his contemporaries push the boundaries of aesthetic experimentation to interrogate the politics and poetics of black heroic identity construction.

As Silenieks argues, Glissant's drama relies upon literary experimentation "to arrive at a more dynamic aesthetics capable of expressing the Afro-Caribbean realities." For example, Glissant's *Monsieur Toussaint* ruptures temporal frameworks to counter the legitimacy of historical chronologies and generate dramatic tension by exalting in an emotional logic produced by the "simultaneity of the two time frames in which Toussaint lives (that of the insular space and that of the prison)." As Silenieks suggests, Glissant's narrative practice exposes the "structures and the modes of perception of the Afro-Caribbean mind," given that "these devices reflect Time" that "is not perceived as an irreversible and evanescing flow but rather as a cyclic return that assures a permanence partaken by the living and the dead as well as by those not yet born—a feature of many African beliefs."[128] Refusing to shy away from his political, ideological, and spiritual conflicts with dead freedom fighters, Glissant reimagines Louverture as a Caribbean rather than African American or European American heroic figure. Thus Glissant's Louverture not only receives advice from the dead—as in Mama Dio's insistence that he realize the extent of the white prison guard's racism: "To him you're just a beribboned puppet"—but is also reclaimed by Mackandal's chant, "We bear him with us."[129] Glissant's nonlinear perspective memorializes Louverture's relationship to his ancestors within a politicized continuum and national framework. As Madison Smartt Bell argues, Glissant "situates the black general in a newly evolving Caribbean literary tradition."[130]

Glissant's Louverture's candid description of slavery as a state of nonbeing and existential nihilism provides a powerful backdrop to his epic and yet problematic transformation into a heroic exemplar in this play. "I was a good slave. One who knows nothing and learns nothing," he confesses to his wife at the start of this drama. Successfully unshackling himself from self-hatred and survival strategies born of moral expediency, he later not only experiences a self-sacrificing epiphany—he realizes he must fight "for the freedom of all"—but also recognizes the contemporary significance of his ancestors, whom he invites to bear witness as he commands, "Open your eyes to blood, slaughter, madness."[131] Such hard-hitting candor regarding the gritty spectacle of carnage betrays Glissant's determination not to sanitize but to radicalize and spiritualize Louverture's violence within a Caribbean perspective. Thus, Glissant sought to engage his audiences by recuperating Louverture not as a transcendent individual but as a historical figure enmeshed in a network of social and political relations. As Henry Cohen argues, his "theatre is intended to function in the collective life of the people as the dramatized historical recitations of West African *griots* do, as a mechanism to guarantee the ideological and cultural cohesiveness of the community."[132] Foregrounding ellipses and fragmentation in his experimental dramatic style, Glissant encourages solidarity among diverse audiences within the black diaspora.

For Cohen, Glissant's work debates "the problem of heroism."[133] In a candid admission of his own moral weaknesses, Glissant's Louverture informs Mackandal that his graphic and impassioned resolution to enact heroism was born of an involuntary blindness—"For three months I tried not to see the bodies"—to which Mackandal's answer is unequivocal: "Three months are long, for those who die every day." In forceful ways, Glissant's *Monsieur Toussaint* testifies to a multifaceted heroic continuum within which Louverture plays only a part. Such a legacy consists not solely of his morally ambivalent strategies of denial and epiphany regarding violence but also Mackandal's graphic insistence upon a direct engagement with the realities afflicting persecuted Black men and women. Ultimately, therefore, Glissant dramatizes the African Caribbean origins of Louverture's heroism as emerging out of a call-and-response relationship to acts and arts of ancestral resistance. Glissant imbues Louverture, no longer solely a mortal figure, with the mythological consciousness of his forebears, as he gains legendary insight by bearing witness to centuries of suffering and finally admits, "I see the dead."[134] Glissant's decision to situate Louverture's legendary status solely within a Haitian political and aesthetic context represents a stark departure from previous representations. Glissant's Louverture emerges out of the shadow of white racist archival representation in order to vindicate his militancy solely as the result of an "impossible choice" presented by the realities of white barbarity. As a result, Louverture is not only critiqued by but accountable to "the dead," as his ability to see their mutilated histories renders his resistance to white hegemonic power inevitable.

"Don't tell your tale, Toussaint, for the dead will not hear you!" cautions the "voodoo priestess" Mama Dio. On the surface, Glissant's drama exposes the failures either of language or narrative ever to recuperate Louverture's memory. Exalting in the political necessity of a refusal to tell, he instead emphasizes the importance of strategies of withholding for black empowerment. Yet Glissant's Louverture's defiant "I will not omit a single word!" rejects his ancestor's advice. Thus he controversially stakes his claim to independence not only from European slaveholders but also from his Black revolutionary forbears. For Glissant, Louverture's radicalism emerges not from endorsing tropes of masking and disguise but by promulgating strategies of explication as integral to processes of both black vindication and white denunciation. Frustrated by the demands made on him by the dead, Louverture asks one apparition: "Am I to cut out my tongue and pin it on your uniform?"[135] For Glissant, images of self-mutilation are tied to a loss of language as he exposes the disempowering realities of silence and its role in perpetuating black subjugation and even destruction.

Glissant's *Monsieur Toussaint* dramatizes psychological and physical sites of political and racial contestation regarding the "never-ending conflict between the living and the dead." Fighting for independence, Louverture insists, "Now that I've given my life for the living, I must thrust the dead back into death!" The battles of the self-sacrificing martyr Louverture arise from psychological conflicts with his ancestors as he grapples with an elusive and marginalized black heroic legacy. "All the work, the victories and conquests, all to end in the darkness of a prison cell. From here I lead a sad masquerade," Louverture laments near the end of his life as Glissant interrogates interrelated associations of black masculinity, performance, spectacle, and death. "If I write 'Toussaint,' Macaïa leans over and spells out 'traitor.' I write the word 'Republic' and Mackandal thinks it is 'delusion,'" explains Louverture as he is forced to admit, "I do not know how to write."[136] In the context of the fact that the historical Louverture wrote himself into being through memoir and legal documentation, such an admission gets to the heart of debates surrounding absence and presence, revelation and concealment, telling and untelling in order to confront this historical figure's ambivalent position within a black heroic tradition. As compellingly articulated by the African theater director Femi Euba, who embarked on the challenging task of staging Glissant's play at Louisiana State University in 1989–90, "the question raised by Édouard Glissant" remains one of "black leadership."[137]

A radical, avant-garde, and experimental work, Glissant's *Monsieur Toussaint* is one of the first to engage explicitly with self-annihilation, paradox, and contradiction vis-à-vis memorializations of Louverture within an African Caribbean heroic continuum. Simultaneously encompassing diverse forms of moral, political, philosophical, and social resistance, Glissant's work crosses national boundaries in resonating with the African American playwright Lorraine Hansberry's fragment "Toussaint: A Drama: Excerpt from Act I of a Work in Progress," a work first broadcast on national television in 1961 in which she insists, "L'Ouverture was not a God; he was a man."[138] Similarly refusing to shy away from his mortality, Glissant's Louverture is portrayed as meditating on human fallibility when he proclaims, "I am dead."[139] As preoccupied as Glissant with challenging the boundaries between life and death, the African American poet and dramatist Ntozake Shangee's *For Colored Girls Who Have Considered Suicide When the Rainbow Is Enuf,* published in 1977, reframes Louverture's multifaceted legacies to legitimize diverse strategies of black female resistance in a contemporary era. For Shangee, no less than Glissant and Hansberry, Louverture remains a site of both hyperinvisibility and hypervisibility. As "the lady in brown" frankly admits regarding the dangerous politics of perception in this work, "There waznt nobody cd see Toussaint cept me."[140]

"LE PASSAGE POUR HERO": REMEMBERING AND REIMAGINING TOUSSAINT LOUVERTURE IN THE PAINTINGS OF JEAN-MICHEL BASQUIAT AND ÉDOUARD DUVAL-CARRIÉ

In 2001, the African American author Charles S. Johnson published his short story "A Report from St. Domingue," in which he celebrates Toussaint Louverture as "a magnificent figure of manhood."[141] However, such "magnificence" has been interrogated not only by Édouard Glissant but also, and more recently, in works by the contemporary Haitian artist Édouard Duval-Carrié and the New York icon and former street artist turned cause célèbre Jean-Michel Basquiat, an artist of Haitian and Puerto Rican descent. For both artists, Louverture's heroism occupies fraught political, social, historical, and aesthetic terrain. Basquiat's and Duval-Carrié's challenging works expose the political and social lacunae generated by mythological reimaginings of Louverture's heroism in the last few decades. According to their aesthetic and political vision, his symbolic status as an iconic exemplar and representative emblem have obscured and even denied the multifaceted and complex lives of an anonymous mass of enslaved women, men, and children. Dramatizing the atrocities of slavery directly in only a handful of paintings, Basquiat's seven-panel work titled *Toussaint L'Overture vs. Savonarola* provides a forceful meditation upon black male heroism as an absent presence in official histories. Louverture's memory equally occupies the eye of the storm in Duval-Carrié's aestheticized as well as politicized juxtapositions of slavery within a contemporary era of black disfranchisement, as signaled by ongoing economic and social persecutions in present-day Haiti. Starkly contrasting in his approach if not in his thematic conflicts to Basquiat, Duval-Carrié has produced numerous works dramatizing Louverture. These include not only *Mural Toussaint,* painted on a school wall in Florida in 2002, but also a series of paintings such as *La voix des sans voix* (1994), *Le passage pour hero* (2003), *Le General Toussaint enfumé* (2003), and *Toussaint L'Ouverture* (2004), to name but a few. And yet, as in Basquiat's case vis-à-vis his creation of *Slave Auction*—a heavily collaged single work in which anonymous bodies testify to the dehumanizing horrors of the trade—these works exist in problematic relation to Duval-Carrié other installations, such as *Le retable des neufs esclaves* (1989), in which he rejects iconic heroism in favor of dramatizing the horrors of the Middle Passage.

Despite his renown as a painter of elliptical canvases, Basquiat gained prominence and notoriety in the early 1980s as a street artist. He started by etching powerful slogans and striking images onto the exterior walls of buildings across the urban sprawl of New York City. Vociferously protesting the corporate capitalism of a commodified white mainstream art world, he opted for the tag "SAMO"—an abbreviation for "same old shit"—followed by a copyright symbol. Appearing next to the abstract impossibilities of his textual fragments, Basquiat's acronym testifies to his self-conscious association of the artist's role with social and political protest. Tackling the legacies of slavery, labor, oppression, and forces of market capitalism, his spray-painted, cryptic, and stark slogans—"ORIGIN OF COTTON," "Man made," and "SAMO © MICROWAVE & VIDEO X-SISTANCE 'BIG-MAC CERTIFICATE' FOR X-MAS"—constitute a powerful antiauthoritarian archive. These early statements confront the death of the artist—"SAMO © IS DEAD"—not only as an act of existential nihilism but also as an act of aesthetic liberation. Explicitly debating the topic of heroism, he writes, "'GREAT BLACK' MEN. CXXXIV" in enormous black letters on a gray brick wall. As minimalist slogans that refuse to tell, these multilayered statements both shed light upon and complicate the unresolved tensions and semantic riddles of his later paintings. Relying on enmeshed yet split-apart visual and textual fragments across his diverse artistic reimaginings, he grapples with black bodies as loci of amnesia and trauma. Ever occupying the liminal status of the outsider guerilla artist, he self-consciously works beyond the bounds of official representation to reinvent black revolutionary legends as sites of dissidence and resistance. Across both his life and works, therefore, Basquiat's aesthetic inheritance as a New York graffiti artist remains inextricable from his later experimental, self-reflexive practices as a painter.

Basquiat famously defines his subject matter as "royalty, heroism, and the streets" and admits that his art is "about 80% anger." Luca Marenzi catalogs Basquiat's *Toussaint L'Overture vs. Savonarola*, a mixed-media work, as being constructed from "acrylic, oil stick and Xerox collage on canvas."[142] As Richard D. Marshall notes, this painting consists of "seven separate canvases that are hinged together" and result in "no discernible narrative."[143] Yet any clear-cut identification of textual absences risks eliding Basquiat's preferred protest aesthetic as characterized by inversion, implosion, and antilinearity in his dismissal of sanitized teleologies of moral uplift. As his eclectic works reveal, he rejected straightforward structures stereotypically associated with transformational narratives of cathartic moralizing. As nonredemptive reimaginings of black male heroic representation, Basquiat's cacophonous canvases accentuate rather than detract from his interest in thematic discontinuities. Instead, his challenging works consist of layers of paint, collaged fragments, and handwritten textual scraps to bear witness to his determination to animate his abstract and abstract-figurative iconographies. His uneasy aesthetic tensions encourage audiences to engage interactively with his seemingly impenetrable subject matter.

Juxtaposing and interweaving diverse textual panels with works constructed from abstract blocks of color as well as portraits not only of the Haitian revolutionary Toussaint Louverture but also of Girolamo Savonarola, an executed and controversial Italian martyr of the fifteenth century, Basquiat constructs *Toussaint L'Overture vs. Savonarola* from a series of seemingly disparate vignettes in order to bear witness to racist legacies of spiritual persecution and historical erasure. In this regard, while the evocation of Savonarola can never be categorically explained, his association with extreme religious censorship and persecution may indirectly reflect upon Basquiat's protest against the racist structures of amnesia surrounding Louverture. If a torturing, barbaric white persecutor can take center stage in official archives, why is it that a heroic "Great Black Man" is excluded and erased? In an original and bold move, Basquiat's decision to explore Toussaint Louverture's heroism in the context not of black persecution but of a white religious leader martyred by the Catholic authorities is revealing. He obfuscates rather than exalts in iconic, celebratory constructions of black male heroism by associating his black icon with an ambivalent white historical figure.

Basquiat constructs a compelling visual dialogue between the first and second panels in this work. Simultaneously including fragments of text and pseudodiagrammatic line drawings, he engages with black memorialization as a locus of intellectual, political, and aesthetic paradox. Crossed-out and underlined handwritten textual fragments dominate his first two panels as he includes words and phrases such as "FREE," "IRON," "NAPOLEON," "LIBERTY," "MALCOM X," "POWER + MONEY (VALUE)," "ACTUAL SIZ NEGR," "COTTON" and "HISTORY." Insisting upon the imaginative possibilities generated by fractured, seemingly polarized discourses, Basquiat thwarts any clear-cut narratives tending toward reductive interpretations of black spectacular consumption, commodification, or even cultural appropriation in this work. For political and aesthetic purposes, broken textual fragments appear alongside various drawings, such as those of a diminutive creature labeled "BABOON"; a robotic figure titled "DARWIN"; an anonymous head-and-shoulder portrait of a male icon, "AL JOLSON"; as well as the derogatory figure of a faceless Black man toting burdens next to the word "COTTON." Histories of black subjugation as communicated by spectacles of enslaved labor, discourses of scientific racism, and bestialized caricature are displaced and interrogated in Basquiat's oeuvre.

The political implications of Basquiat's highly abstract third and sixth panels are inescapable in this multipanel work. The left-hand third of panel 3 consists of a monolithic block of white color, while the right-hand side is covered in a bloodred swathe of paint out of which an indefinable black abstract shape emerges. With this contrast, Basquiat may well have sought to provide an abstract examination of black and white bodies as sites of racial conflict and violence in this painting. Similarly, panel 6 consists of a black canvas painted white through which black blocks of color appear and may well have been created in order to crystallize debates associating the black body with dissolution, fragmentation, and erasure. Deeply unconvinced by the didactic function of role models, Basquiat's experimental work interrogates the difficulties generated by polarized representations of a seemingly monolithic black male heroism. He supports this view further by reproducing a masklike but unknown portrait in this painting. Thwarting potential revisionist tendencies toward iconic adulation, he portrays an anonymous, nonidealized physiognomy constructed from enlarged eyes, nose, and teeth as well as red hair and green skin. With characteristic ambiguity, the text reads, "OHIO," thereby defying attempts at interpretation or recognition to reinforce his meditation upon the failures of memorialization instead.

This is not the case in Basquiat's final panel, however. His crossed-through but still visible title "L'Overture, T." appears beneath an abstract head-and-shoulder portrait of Louverture. Atypically for Basquiat's work, Louverture's physiognomy betrays some indebtedness to historical precedent. Noticeably, Basquiat provides an individualized and recognizable mouth, eye, nose, and facial hair as he draws one half of his face in delicately etched lines. Yet the other half reverts to a stark stylization by providing only a black, bare outline to contrast with a sepulcher white skin tone. Basquiat's Louverture is both empowered and dispossessed, as he wears a black hat while a disembodied hand suspended beside his torso brandishes a sword. Re-creating Louverture as a Janus-faced and even indecipherable figure in this work, Basquiat provides kaleidoscopic representations of Louverture as a simultaneously European, African, and Caribbean freedom fighter. Complicating his painting yet further, Basquiat includes textual fragments next to Louverture's physiognomy that are almost impossible to decipher in photographic reproduction. The one possible exception is "1ST COAT," which may refer not only to the absence of Louverture's military clothing but also to Basquiat's aesthetic techniques of painterly layering. Unafraid of rupturing any painterly illusions, Basquiat encourages audiences not to immerse themselves in his work but to engage intellectually and critically with his subject matter. He further destabilizes Louverture's iconic status by engaging in subversive word play via a semantic shift of naming. According to Basquiat, Louverture's legendary symbolism emerges not from his status as "l'ouverture," or "the opening," but from his "overt" behavior, as the rest of the word is crossed out to suggest his ongoing preoccupation with Louverture's iconic fame and mythological status.

In comparison with Basquiat's elliptical works, which defy the legitimacy of any artificially imposed parameters within which to dramatize black hero-ism, Duval-Carrié's visual "chronicles" are explicitly characterized by an educational imperative. "Haiti is a country of people who are unfortunately illiterate and the image is essential," he explains.[144] He provides a "problem-fraught presentation of heroes" in order to engage with their mythical signifi-cance as political, social, and historical touchstones of reform. Duval-Carrié created one of his most haunting paintings, *La voix des sans voix*, in 1994 "after the coup d'état that ended the first regime of President Jean-Bertrand Aristide in 1991."[145] Here the prostrate and persecuted body of Aristide lies before his contemporary persecutors and in front of historical portraits of "Mackandal," "Pétion," "Dessalines," and, of course, "Toussaint." Duval-Carrié identifies these historical figures by inserting their names into gilt-edged frames as he celebrates a black heroic continuum by blurring the bound-aries between the contemporary era and a historical past. More particularly, Duval-Carrié's decision to paint the slogan "LA VOIX DES SANS VOIX" in enlarged red and white lettering and between painted representations of his historical heroic figures as well as Aristide's body ruptures temporal frame-works to dramatize the cyclical nature of black struggle.

In stark contrast, Duval-Carrié's provocative canvas *Le passage pour hero,* painted in 2003, underscores his indebtedness to nineteenth-century visual representations by portraying Louverture in the typical equestrian pose. Yet he heightens dramatic tension by including a symbolic twist: the burnished orange-red backdrop is literally disintegrating. Abstract, jagged blocks of black and green color bleed across the canvas to suggest the ongoing anni-hilation and distortion of black historical heroism in a twenty-first century context. Juxtaposing a backdrop of palm trees with an urban skyline, he sig-nifies upon the dehumanizing encroachment of modernity onto historical traditions. As this painting demonstrates, Duval-Carrié's emphasis is upon the ways in which the "myth of the hero, which was lavished on the revo-lutionary generals, has only served to enlarge the role of the Haitian army and its glorious past," regardless of the fact that "the reality . . . is far from glorious."[146] Thus his portrayal of a eulogized Louverture arrayed in glori-ous clothing exists in a call-and-response relationship to the ghostly pallor of Basquiat's antiheroic reinterpretations of this figure. Regardless of their differences, both artists rely on painterly swathes of black color to split their canvases apart as they accentuate distortion and loss. Foregrounding Louverture's distorted physiognomy, Basquiat and Duval-Carrié indict the ongoing forms of degradation generated by slavery and its nefarious contem-porary legacies.

In the contemporary era, Toussaint Louverture's multiple legacies remain a source of inspiration not only for renowned painters such as Jean-Michel Basquiat and Édouard Duval-Carrié but also for anonymous street artists. Working beyond the parameters of the high art world, these artists created countless works in the wake of Jean-Bertrand Aristide's presidential election in 1990. "From one end of Haiti to the other, walls and fences were painted with portraits of Aristide and of Haiti's revolutionary heroes," Karen McCarthy Brown observes.[147] Engaging more overtly with Louverture's legacy than Basquiat ever did in his urban slogans, one such anonymously produced, solitary portrait of Louverture consists only of the barest facial details. This unknown artist relies on minimalist techniques to accentuate Louverture's masklike status and thereby signify upon his malleable symbolism and political ambiguity as a reusable icon.[148] As diverse historical and contemporary representations in oratory, literature, fine art, and documentary film attest, artists and writers have continued to remake multiple Toussaint Louvertures in their own image across the centuries. Interrogating the parameters within which to represent black male heroism, these works testify to his signifying possibilities not only as a force of political, social, and historical change but also as a stimulus to aesthetic experimentation.

In the last few years, Scot French has debated the difficult question of why there is no film dramatizing the life and death of Nathaniel Turner. Steven Spielberg's success in securing funding to direct *Amistad,* a film devoted to Sengbe Pieh, sheds further light on the cultural and historical reality that Turner is a much more problematic historical figure for mainstream Hollywood, a reality quickly explained by the fact that U.S.-born Turner's bloody revolution was enacted close to home and on U.S. soil, while Sierra Leonean leader Pieh's took place at sea. Yet, in comparison with Pieh, Louverture's memory remains as mired in controversy as that of Turner. The African American actor and director Danny Glover recently admitted to facing insurmountable barriers in his unsuccessful attempts to secure financial support for his epic film, *Toussaint,* a project currently locked in production battles. As he explains, "Producers said 'It's a nice project, a great project ... where are the white heroes?'"[149] Regarding the script for the film, in which Don Cheadle has been cast in the starring role and for which the release date has been repeatedly postponed, Philip Kaisary celebrates the fact that it is "one of the more meticulous, historically aware, and aesthetically achieved narratives of the Haitian Revolution."[150] As these ongoing controversies reveal, the topic of black diasporic male heroism remains taboo not only within the mainstream film industry but also within the contemporary era more generally. Audiences are still not ready to see popular representations of Black heroic figures engaged in acts and arts of resistance to white authority.

Difficulties surrounding the controversial Toussaint Louverture's memory introduce the key motifs of lacunae, paradox, fragmentation, distortion, and loss, which no less characterize representations of Nathaniel Turner, a similarly ambivalent figure demonized for his "work of death." As reusable and recyclable historical icons reimagined across the centuries, both Louverture and Turner signify as sites of black male wounding and dispossession as well as of healing and empowerment in their controversial acts of black male militancy. Speaking less than a decade ago, René Depestre wondered, "On this 7 April 2003, what can Toussaint Louverture do for an unprecedented renewal of the solidarity between France and Haiti? What can his lofty ideals of justice and rights still do to help the Haitian people rise as never before towards democracy?" Admitting to experiencing "a *Louverturian sensibility*," Depestre bears witness to this iconic figure's enduring mythical, historical, and political legacies.[151] Taking his view even further as we shift heroic contexts, is it not equally possible to map a "Turnerian sensibility"?

CHAPTER 2 "N.T. 11 11 31" NATHANIEL TURNER,

SYMBOLISM, MEMORIALIZATION, AND AN

EXPERIMENTAL POETICS

"THE KNIGHTLIEST OF THE KNIGHTLY RACE / WHO SINCE THE DAYS OF OLD / HAVE KEPT THE LAMP OF CHIVALRY / ALIGHT IN HEARTS OF GOLD." So reads the inscription carved onto the base of a Confederate memorial close to the capitol in Montgomery, Alabama, in the American South. This edifice starkly memorializes a horrifying history of racial terrorism in defense of white masculinity by exalting in the "knightliest of the knightly race" as custodians of the "lamp of chivalry." As recently as November 14, 2007, "N.T. 11 11 31" was found spray-painted onto the monument.[1] The incendiary overtones of this unequivocal message written by an unknown hand demand recognition. Spectral black text authoritatively obliterates the pale grayness of official lettering in a bold statement of radicalism. A haunting display of impassioned denunciation, these cryptic numbers and letters reject mythical symbolism associating whiteness with honor and "chivalry." A powerful irony is communicated in the fact that "the knightly race" is the only text not partially covered by black spray paint, while the mixture of numbers and letters renders the message meaningless to those with no prior knowledge regarding this historical event.

Clearly, "N.T." is Nathaniel Turner, the leader of the Southampton revolution that was enacted by enslaved men during August 1831 and led to the deaths of fifty-five whites and countless numbers of enslaved women and men in brutal reprisals. As an unauthorized statement spray-painted onto official white stone, "N.T. 11 11 31" documents Turner's presence through absence by telling yet refusing to tell. Transgressing the authority of a public space sacred to white memory and regardless of the fact that we do not know his or her gender or racial identity, the artist suggests that Turner's heroism can be more forcefully recovered within an unofficial black folkloric imagination. As Henry Tragle insists, "Nat Turner did exist as a folk-hero to several generations of black men and women."[2] While easily dismissible among whites as the unintelligible graffiti of disaffected youth, this enigmatic message symbolizes resistance for audiences within African American communities. According to this graffiti artist's definition of history, this monument memorializing a white supremacist's vision of the "knightly race" operates as a battleground for the struggle over memory. More damningly still, Desiree Hunter's article "Alabama Capitol's Confederate Monument Vandalized," published in the *Decatur Daily News* includes a photograph confirming that more than graffiti was discovered on the monument. As she writes, an unknown individual climbed over the fence not only to spray coded markings onto the stone base but also to paint the grayed stone face and hands of one of the Confederate soldiers black. As an indication of the seriousness with which they confronted this act, the Alabama Division of the Sons of Confederate Veterans immediately advertised "a $1,000 reward for the arrest and conviction of those responsible," claiming that these actions represented a "hate crime."[3] Just as a reward notice was posted for Nathaniel Turner's body in the nineteenth century, so too a price has been placed upon the quest for his memory in the twenty-first century. Further speculations by whites in the article even go so far as to suggest that the defilement of their monument was likely to have taken place on November 11 rather than November 14, a date that remains significant not only as "Veterans Day" but also as the day upon which Turner was executed to satiate a white public clamoring for his death.

As these recent events reveal, Turner's power resides not so much in the realities of a life lived but in his mythical symbolism, as fallacies regarding his biography continue to proliferate in the national imagination and popular memory. His ambivalent history operates not only as the record of a repeatedly misunderstood heroic legacy but also as an evocative catalyst to an untold tradition of black resistance. As a slippery site of violation and violence, his body and memory constitute an alternative slave narrative. As the antithesis of white gradualist abolitionism, Turner's multiple legacies were forged in polemical controversy and proslavery vilification. White-generated oral histories, reward notices, newspaper narratives, engravings, and literary adaptations all emerged in the wake of his rebellion, attesting to his widespread distortion and mystification. Unique for its enigmatic wordlessness, this bold artist's graffiti statement celebrates the impossibility of reconstructing Turner with any historical accuracy. Who he was, how he lived, and what he believed, let alone what he looked like, are sites of virulent contestation. In powerful ways, Turner remains as much a fugitive to history as the countless anonymous enslaved men, women, and children who similarly fought for their freedom but whose defiant feats of feigned pregnancy, sexual resistance, work stoppage, poison, arson, physical combat, and flight will never be fully known because so many left no firsthand testimony behind.

Six thousand slave narratives testify to the haunting losses of four million enslaved women, men, and children and the emotional, political, and social realities of slavery. Across the centuries, the battles over Turner's memory prove beyond any doubt that the life and works of the militant black heroic revolutionary remain unpalatable to white American audiences.

Like Louverture's, Turner's heroism can only begin to come alive and make sense if scholars engage imaginatively rather than factually with his legacy. For shackled men and women like Louverture and Turner no less than Sengbe Pieh, Sojourner Truth, Frederick Douglass, and Harriet Tubman, acts and arts of enslaved heroism remain incomprehensible so long as audiences and scholars continue to search for an iconic history categorized by verifiable data and authentic truths. A sparse statement, "N.T. 11 11 31" offers a cryptic code that can only be broken by the reader's imagination, which, as the formerly enslaved poet Phillis Wheatley argued centuries earlier in her poem "On Imagination," remains an enigmatic power. "Who can sing thy force?" she wondered, admitting, "There in one view we grasp the mighty whole / Or with new worlds amaze th'unbounded soul."[4] For Wheatley and numerous other Black authors writing in an era of chattel slavery, the imagination represented a portal to a liberated vision of the world by offering a way of accessing the domain of the "unbounded soul." Defiant, and unknown because unknowable, for centuries the "mighty whole" of Nathaniel Turner's legacy has been reinvented within a transatlantic as well as a national imagination.

As a recurrent figure in historical and contemporary African American culture, Turner's life haunts rather than inhabits sites of official public memory. As Kirk Savage argues, "Public monuments were meant to yield resolution and consensus, not to prolong conflict." "History was supposed to be a chronicle of heroic accomplishments, not a series of messy disputes with unresolved outcomes," he emphasizes.[5] Far from providing any moral, intellectual, or aesthetic closure, the historical memory of Turner remains as unresolved as representations of the elusive figure himself. Thus the work of this graffiti artist represents just one of the first unorthodox attempts at commemorating Black male heroic icons whose lives and works exist beyond the pale of white official memorialization. Such an act of defacing—for which read, editorializing—white mainstream monuments reverses their mythological symbolism to ensure that they become the text upon which hidden histories of black rebellion can be written. In contrast to Louverture, Truth, Pieh, Tubman, and Douglass—all of whom have monuments erected in their honor variously in the United States, Africa, and the Caribbean—Nathaniel Turner's heroism is still subject to historical, political, and cultural censure.

Ideological yet warring, Turner's radicalism remains the heroism that cannot speak its name. Repeatedly subjected to grotesque oversimplifications, white audiences have been intent upon perpetuating sensationalized representations of this historical figure. Representing no teleology of black moral uplift, Turner's revolutionary violence endorses proslavery fears regarding the specter of an unfettered black masculinity. Moreover, his memory denies white abolitionists catharsis by refusing their adherents any moral purging in spiritual redemption. Black engineered and black imagined, the Southampton revolt is the unspeakable antithesis of the white British potter Josiah Wedgwood's "Am I Not a Man and a Brother?" antislavery medallion, which traded in the spectacle of kneeling shackled black masculinity begging for white alms. As Marcus Wood writes regarding the nefarious effects of this piece of antislavery propaganda, "The Abolition seal is a semiotic nexus, a net for containing the black male and female."[6] Turner's rebellion shook the foundations not only of antislavery but also of proslavery ideology to the very core by not asking but declaring, "I am a man, your brother," a radical slogan first used by the white British abolitionist Elizabeth Heyrick as she demolished the passive basis of Wedgwood's aphorism in her pamphlet *Immediate, Not Gradual Abolition,* published in London as early as 1825.[7] In telling ways, the difficulties embedded in memorializations of Turner can unlock other oversimplifications in current scholarship by revealing the all too straightforward representations of Louverture, Pieh, Truth, Douglass, and Tubman. Their histories may be more remembered and knowable, but ambiguities and distortions remain that confirm that their lives and works are as unfathomable as those of Turner. Similarly demanding an imaginative engagement with the limitations of white mainstream knowledge, they no less require scholars to engage in a revisionist politics and poetics of unknowing in order to celebrate multifarious rather than monolithic representations of black heroism.

Surviving as a controversial figure within the popular American and European imagination over the last one hundred and eighty years, Turner remains the repeated subject of newspaper accounts, historical volumes, lithographs, drawings and paintings, sensational and instructional literature, poetry, drama, and, most recently, a documentary and a multivolume graphic novel. A useful place from which to begin to excavate representations of Turner the historical figure in conjunction with Turner the symbol can be found by exploring various dramatizations in the popular press along-side contemporaneous drawings and paintings created to fire primarily white audiences' imaginations. Notably, the multifaceted iconography and textual inventions of early representations betray ambivalences within multi-faceted constructions of Turner's heroism as portrayed in written and visual archives. More myth than matter, the imaginative landscape of Nathaniel Turner's legacy is a swirling quicksand of half-told, half-revealed vignettes in which he has typically assumed a pseudohistorical existence that defies fixity or categorization. This is not cause for despair but for hope, however, as writ-ers and artists attempt to create a Nathaniel Turner in their own image to no avail. The multifarious legacies of Turner remain as resistant to objectifica-tion and stasis in the twentieth and twenty-first centuries as they did in the nineteenth. A patchwork scholarship of juxtaposed literary, historical, and cultural parts—fully cognizant of the limitations within dominant intellec-tual frameworks—alone has the potential to recuperate a usable if enigmatic Turner. To ask the real Nathaniel Turner to please stand up is to deny, obfus-cate, and annihilate the intellectual, aesthetic, and political circulation of his multiple personae across multiple forms and diverse contexts.

"A GENUINE SON OF AFRICA": MAPPING NATHANIEL TURNER'S LEGACIES ACROSS RACIAL BOUNDARIES

Nat. "Ol' Prophet Nat." "General Nat." The "Great Bandit." These are just a few of the names used to identify Turner within white mainstream racist and popular historical and political archives. I adhere to "Nathaniel Turner" on the grounds that Frederick Douglass, Henry Highland Garnet, and many other Black radicals recuperated his full name in a political condemnation of racist naming practices. While his name may remain hotly debated, Gov-ernor John Floyd's "Proclamation" issued in the immediate aftermath of Turner's revolution with the offer of a "reward of five hundred dollars" for his apprehension ostensibly offers a verifiable physical description of this his-torical figure:

Nat is between 30 & 35 years old, 5 feet 6 or 8 inches high, weighs between 150 and 160 lbs, rather bright complexion, but not a mulatto—broad shouldered—large flat nose—large eyes—broad flat feet—rather knock-kneed—walks brisk and active—hair on the top of the head very thin—no beard except on the upper lip, and the tip of the chin—a scar on one of his temples—also one on the back of his neck—a large knob on one of the bones of his right arm near the wrist produced by a blow.[8]

However steeped in racist biases, this proclamation is likely to bear some resemblance to a factual representation of Turner simply because it was published with the desperate hope of satiating white vengeance by apprehending this freedom fighter. Critics have commented upon two key aspects of this notice: Turner's "bright complexion," carefully described as "not" that of "a mulatto," and the itemization of his injuries, which white abolitionists such as Thomas Wentworth Higginson believed "look suspicious." "It must therefore remain an open question, whether the scars and the knot were produced by black hands or by white," he concludes.[9] Any evidence indicative of instances of black male victimization clearly remained precious currency in the abolitionist era. The majority of white campaigners were determined to effect emancipation by converting white audiences to slavery's atrocities solely by presenting a sanctified panorama of noble, flawless Black victims worthy of white pity. Turner exists as the archetypal, shackled enslaved Black man in this notice and, as such, as an emblem of paternalist sympathy rather than an apocryphal figure of vengeance. Yet this penchant among sympathetic whites for reimagining Turner as a victim was almost instantly replaced with visions of Turner as the epitome of a superheroic invincibility within the black popular imagination.

Across the centuries, Turner's memory has been transformed to suit differing political agendas. These range from his demonic appearances in proslavery atrocity literatures to his circulation as a divine symbol in hagiographic texts written to inculcate race pride and endorse black fights for civil rights. Complicating matters further, and in addition to the denial of his experiences of physical violation, Turner's possibly mixed-race ancestry represents a highly contentious yet little-discussed issue that has been repeatedly excised from both black and white memorializations but for very different reasons. On the one hand, white nineteenth- and twentieth-century depictions of Turner reveled in his blackness. A contemporary and anonymous, presumably white writer, given his or her overreliance on stereotyping, agreed with this reward notice only to suggest that "he is of darker hue, and his eyes, though large, are not prominent—they are very long, deeply seated in his head and have rather a sinister expression."[10] For Black writers, however, this "darker hue" was a source not of despair but of hope in symbolizing an endorsement of black pride in a reimagined African legacy. Equally, for William Wells Brown writing in the 1860s during an era desperate for Black heroes, Turner's "unmixed African descent" functioned as a touchstone for black empowerment. "In stature, he was under the middle size, long-armed, round-shouldered, and strongly marked with the African features," he writes.[11] This was equally the case for white radicals such as Higginson, for whom Turner was "a short, stout, powerfully built person, of dark mulatto complexion and strongly marked African features."[12] Similarly, during 1883 amid the volatile years of Reconstruction, which saw the meteoric rise of lynching as a white terrorist means to police black "freedoms," the Black historian George Washington Williams describes Turner as "quite low in stature, dark," a man who "had the genuine African features. His eyes were small but sharp, and gleamed like fire when he was talking about his 'mission.'"[13] Cumulatively, such malleable descriptions testify to Black writers' collective attempts to recuperate Turner's blackness as an unequivocal signifier of black heroism. For Williams and others, it was essential that Turner's physicality be reconfigured according to a perceived Africanness so as to celebrate his psychological complexity and physical militancy within a black diasporic heroic tradition.

Turner's advocates have especially confronted the racist, polarizing rhetoric of proslavery apologists. For white writers such as Stephen Beauregard Weeks, Turner's allegedly "genuine African features" were accentuated to condemn this historical figure as "small and somewhat feeble in body."[14] In the face of his widespread white vilification, however, Turner had a defender in an unlikely source. The early white scholar of the rebellion William Drewry took time out from lamenting the suffering of Turner's "victims" to describe this historical figure not solely in typically essentialist terms as "a stout, black negro of the pure African type" but also as a man who possessed "considerable mental ability and wide information."[15] Disappointingly, however, Drewry's focus upon Turner's intellect proves the exception rather than the rule, as attraction and repulsion remain the defining features characterizing white attempts to rationalize representations of Turner. Fighting to situate his memory within the context of scientific discourses of black inferiority, the vast majority of white-authored representations deflect attention away from any potentially clear-cut heroic associations.

For the vast majority of Black activists, Turner's physical stature was of little interest, as they sought to do justice to his historical and mythical legacies. Recognizing the political implications of his shifting symbolism, as early as 1843 in his "Address to the Slaves," the former enslaved man and freedom fighter Henry Highland Garnet describes Turner as motivated by idealism. "He was goaded to desperation by wrong and injustice," he states.[16] Scarcely over a decade after Turner's rebellion, Garnet's speech attests to his sensitivity regarding the role played by racial biases as well as nefarious dominant social, political, and aesthetic contexts in the shaping of Turner's memory. Speaking on the eve of the American Civil War in 1861, Frederick Douglass gave an equally impassioned speech titled "A Black Hero," to which Turner's memory was no less integral. "Love of liberty," Douglass informs audiences, "inspired Denmark Vesey, Nathaniel Turner, Madison Washington, Toussaint L'Ouverture, Shields Green, Copeland, and other Negro heroes."[17] Signifying beyond Turner's status as an exceptional icon, Douglass was keen to situate his memory within a pantheon of unrecorded black heroism in order to inspire enslaved and free men to acts of martial heroism during the Civil War.

A source of ongoing controversy, Turner's memory sparked heated debates in the post-emancipation era when an anonymous Black writer in the *New York Age* opposed Frederick Douglass Jr.'s recommendation that there be a monument in honor of John Brown on the grounds that his "memory stands no immediate prospect of vanishing into oblivion." For this diehard radical, "Nat Turner was a black hero." He writes, "He preferred death to slavery. He ought to have a monument. White men care nothing for his memory." "It is quite remarkable," the writer persists, "that whenever colored men move that somebody's memory be perpetuated, that somebody's memory is always a white man's."[18] A centuries-old phenomenon, battles over commemorating Turner's memory follow racial fault lines by illuminating tensions not only of discrimination but also of internalized racism as Black and white memorialists paradoxically oscillate between conciliatory and radical politics. For the white scholar Herbert Aptheker, Turner's legacy remains clear: "Nat Turner sought the liberation of the negro people."[19] Similarly, the Black critic and activist Vincent Harding describes Turner as a "sign in himself" on the grounds that his signifying abilities defy psychological, moral, historical, or political confinement.[20] In stark contrast, Lerone Bennett Jr. not only situates Turner within a black heroic male tradition but also argues for a direct correlation between the art of protest and the act of physical resistance: "Nat Turner was David Walker's word made flesh." According to Bennett, Turner stripped away white illusions of black passivity and emasculation. As Bennett observes, "After Nat's insurrection, it was no longer possible for men to pretend. There were men in the slave quarters. One could not always depend on their masks."[21] Bennett's evocation of the mask, a forceful trope no less associated with Louverture, Pieh, Truth, Douglass, and Tubman, provides an apt symbol with which to explore the multi-edged ambiguities of Turner's self-representations and multifaceted legacies. By emphasizing black agency via disguise and masking, Bennett sheds light on the necessity of theorizing the difficult yet inextricable relationships among the body, language, spectacle, and performance. In no uncertain terms, Turner's history and memory occupy the eye of the storm regarding the facts and fictions of black heroic identity constructions.

NAMELESS, BODILESS, FACELESS: EARLY VISUAL MEMORIALIZATIONS OF NATHANIEL TURNER

Any scrutiny of nineteenth-century visual representations of Nathaniel Turner immediately reveals that they are as riven with conflict as written accounts of his life. As Kenneth Greenberg argues, the fact that he is a "difficult figure for historians to reconstruct" testifies to distortions within both visual and written interpretations of Turner.[22] A case in point is the anonymously produced, controversial woodcut titled *Horrid Massacre in Virginia*, a work designed not only to commemorate the rebellion but also to confirm white audience fears regarding the terrifying spectacle of black on white violence (see figure 5). Appearing in the immediate aftermath of Nathaniel Turner's revolution, this image was circulated as an illustration in Samuel Warner's account, *An Authentic and Impartial Narrative of the Tragical Scene which was Witnessed in Southampton County,* published a month before Gray's *Confessions of Nat Turner* in 1831.[23] Self-explanatory captions indicative of white trials and tribulations summarize this work's four-part structure. Hypersensationalized and explicitly sentimentalized, these depictions were designed to send shivers down the spine of white audiences: "Fig. 1, a Mother intreating for the lives of her children.—2. Mr Travis, cruelly murdered by his own Slaves.—3. Mr Barrow, who bravely defended himself until his wife escaped.—4. A comp. of mounted Dragoons in pursuit of the Blacks."

A deeply flawed work, *Horrid Massacre in Virginia* infamously provides a demonic depiction of barbarous, indistinguishable enslaved Black men engaged in full-scale revolt rather than revolutionary heroism. Wielding swords and axes, these armed Black men represent the antithesis to the deified, prostrate bodies of well-dressed whites shown begging for mercy. This image is striking for Turner's absence, as ambiguous visual clues make it difficult to identify which figure was intended as his portrait. Such an attempt to minimize and even eradicate Turner's presence by rendering his physiognomy and figure indistinguishable from the mass of enslaved men is indicative of

FIGURE 5. Samuel Warner, *Horrid Massacre in Virginia,* woodcut illustration in *Authentic and Impartial Narrative of the Tragical Scene which was Witnessed in Southampton County,* 1831. (Rare Book and Special Collections Division, Library of Congress)

white racist strategies of historical distortion. This tactical removal confirms the racist biases at work within white mainstream records, which made the memorialization of black heroism almost impossible. Despite his status as a white antislavery radical, Thomas Wentworth Higginson conceded, "The biographies of slaves can hardly be individualized, they belong to the class," unwittingly testifying to the failures, even of sympathetic whites, to recognize the sublime possibilities presented by romanticized reimaginings of black male heroism.[24] Any attempt to engage seriously with Turner's religious beliefs and political ideology, or even his psychological coming to consciousness of the ideological injustices of slavery, is therefore far more typical of the African American than the European American archive. Yet in the face of white determination not only to dilute but to deny his radicalism, both Turner's actions and his subsequent testimony guarantee his emergence as an "individualized" figure no less than as a symbol for the "biographies of slaves" otherwise fettered by dehumanizing "chattel records."[25]

As the opening textual descriptions accompanying *Horrid Massacre* dramatize, the anonymous artist of this work—most likely white, given the appearance of this image within a white-authored tract as well as its clear indebtedness to stereotyped representations of Black subjects—exalts in white heroism in the face of indiscriminate acts of a seemingly generic black barbarity. In this woodcut, individualized white men and women appear as paragons of self-sacrifice in contrast to a murderous mass of caricatured Black men. Moreover, a uniform blackness reinforces the Black men's grossly exaggerated facial features to prevent the viewer from distinguishing one from the other. By comparison, the white women, men, and children all possess clearly differentiated physiognomies and idiosyncratic clothing. Yet any detailed study of Warner's tract itself reveals that he ascribed far greater agency to Turner than does this accompanying illustration. In stark contrast, Warner provides polemical yet far from generic descriptions of an "artful black" who fraternized with "Plantation Negroes" in order "to persuade and to prepare them in the most sly and artful manner to become the instruments of their slaughter!"[26] No such view of Turner, "artful" or otherwise, appears within this woodcut. Instead, a mass of faceless enslaved Black men are portrayed according to racist conventions that deny their masculinity. Instead, the artist endorses prejudicial and deeply flawed depictions of a homogenous blackness.

Nonetheless, this scene may be far more radical than the artist intended. Wittingly or not, this unknown illustrator reverses the racial dynamics of the "Am I Not a Man and a Brother?" tableau of the Wedgwood medallion by substituting the body of the enslaved victim with that of the white man, now on his knees begging for mercy. In contrast to the original image, in which black humanity operates as a symbol of white spiritual redemption via moral uplift, a double vision of black rebellion is presented here: on the one hand, one of militancy, as an enslaved man, most likely Turner, wields two swords above the head of his white owner, Travis, in a gesture of apocryphal vengeance and, on the other, one of clemency, as another Black man clasps a white man's hand in a gesture of brotherhood, as if in radical fulfillment of this racially inverted "Am I Not a Man and a Brother?" tableau. The idea that Turner may be represented in either or both men extrapolates ambivalences integral to Gray's *Confessions of Nat Turner,* a work in which he remains both a military commander committed to the atrocities of war but also a peaceable visionary working for revolutionary change and for whom violence was a necessary but short-lived means to reform.

While accurate likenesses of Frederick Douglass, Harriet Tubman, Sengbe Pieh, and Sojourner Truth exist as drawings, etchings, portraits, and

daguerreotypes, Nathaniel Turner's and Toussaint Louverture's physiognomies and corporealities remain a representational battlefield. Henry Tragle's
volume reproduces the majority of the portraits of Turner: an "unknown" and
undated drawing illustrating the press coverage at the time; a likeness from
William Sidney Drewry's oral history–inspired account, *The Southampton
Insurrection,* published in 1900 (see figure 6); and an undated portrait "most
likely after a rendering by" William Ernest Braxton, an African American artist who came to prominence during the Harlem Renaissance.[27] The first image, a drawing reproduced in the newspaper accounts at the time, portrays a
typically unindividualized Turner wearing a round-brimmed hat and working clothes as if to deflate any epic associations. Yet the illustrator counters
charges of racist genericism by distinctively etching his features: the specificities of a strong jaw line, large inquisitive eyes, and angular cheekbones all have
the potential to foreground Turner's internal fight for agency. Thus a defiant
enigmaticism characterizes Turner's physiognomy in this work, as the artist
succeeds, however problematically, in gesturing toward his ambiguous subjectivity. The cross-hatched lines and bold contours complicate Turner's facial expression to create an image that is far more unequivocal in its self-possession
and authority than Drewry's later portrait, which depicts a pensive Turner as
he contemplates the reader from beneath a similarly round-brimmed hat.

Taking a very different approach, Drewry's often-reproduced image portrays Turner's facial features in order to suggest benignity in large eyes, soft
cheeks, and an expressionless or possibly even "masked" mouth (figure 6).
Detracting attention away from Turner's physiognomy, however, his portrayal emphasizes the roughness of his working clothes as if to diminish his
militancy by suggesting his similarities to an antiheroic laborer of nonthreat-
ening aspect. More damningly still, Drewry adheres to mainstream stereotyped conventions regarding visual representations of black masculinity, as
Turner's exaggerated facial features resonate with the black minstrel figure of
white plantation mythology. Regardless of these potentially problematic associations, however, both Drewry's illustration and the previously discussed,
anonymously produced image succeed in documenting Turner's confrontational gaze by relying on a minimalist use of detail as they successfully dramatize his identity as an "artful," masked radical.

Ultimately a far more empowered image, the drawing purportedly created
by the underresearched Black landscape and portrait painter William Ernest
Braxton offers a symbolic and revisionist merger of these earlier drawings.
Both the broad-brimmed hat and working man's clothes are again portrayed
in this work, but here they seem to be included to counter associations of

FIGURE 6. William Drewry, *Nat Turner*, 1900, from *The Southampton Insurrection* (Washington, DC: O'Neal, 1900).

Turner with the military regalia of Toussaint Louverture, the European aristocratic clothing of Frederick Douglass, or even the classical dress of Sengbe Pieh. Rather, this work invites explicit parallels between Turner's functional clothing and the understated laboring attire of Sojourner Truth and Harriet Tubman, both of whom operated as grassroots campaigners immersed within, rather than detached from, the everyday lives of black communities. Speaking "as" rather than "for," theirs, no less than Turner's, was a heroism born of a clear identification with the plight of unknown Black women and men.

Cultivating further ambiguities vis-à-vis Turner's physiognomy, Braxton follows from these earlier adaptations by relying on a masked facial structure, as soft and jagged facial features contribute to his enigmatic gaze. Ultimately, his work bears witness to Turner's individualism by rejecting the stereotyped lips and eyes of Drewry's work as well as the angular simplification of the anonymous illustration. Braxton favored a detailed portrait of unmitigated intensity; both pensive and contemplative, Turner impassively confronts the viewer in his reimagining. In this work, the absence either of caricature or iconic oversimplification regarding Turner's physiognomy successfully removes obstacles that might prevent the reader from engaging directly with his humanity and individualism. Despite their differences, all three drawings rely on shading and crisscrossed lines at the edges of Turner's face in order to darken his otherwise light skin tones. Albeit in different ways, these artists signify upon Turner's possible racial ambiguity in order to expose ambivalences within white historical records. Regardless of their problematic aspects, these early images represent Turner as a far more multifaceted heroic figure than either J. D. Torrey's undated and popularly reproduced full-color work *Nat Turner Talking with His Confederates* or the anonymous drawing *Discovery of Nat Turner*, which appeared in 1881.[28] Ultimately, while we can verify very little regarding Turner's biographical history, these cultural materials expose the tensions at work within the diverse representations of Turner provided by white historical archives. Any polarized attempts to recover Turner within the written archive as either an enslaved murderer or a biblical prophet clearly perpetuate rather than eradicate ongoing difficulties. Equally, the emerging visual iconography reflects a wider problem identified by Greenberg, who observes, "Even in our fantasies, we have been unable to restore the name, face, and body of a man who lost them all so many years ago."[29] In an era of racist fixity, acts and arts of reimagining are therefore essential to attempts not only to extrapolate but to reconstruct multiple Nathaniel Turners otherwise caught within distorting bodies of evidence.

"I HAVE NOTHING MORE TO SAY": NATHANIEL
TURNER'S TEXTUAL EXPERIMENTS IN THOMAS R.
GRAY'S *CONFESSIONS OF NAT TURNER* (1831)

The racially problematic nineteenth-century visual and literary representations of Nathaniel Turner that took center stage in the aftermath of his war on slavery encountered an immediate challenge from an unlikely witness. The white lawyer Thomas R. Gray's *The Confessions of Nat Turner*, published in 1831 in the wake of Turner's execution, is controversial not only as a work that demonizes and yet deifies Turner's memory but also, and above all else, as a text that represents the conflicting lives and deaths of this heroic figure. An instantaneous publishing sensation, this work proved wildly popular, as technological advancements resulted in an overwhelming print run of "fifty thousand copies."[30] Such success quickly established Gray's commercial eye for "capitalizing on public curiosity."[31] Securing a powerful legacy, the multilayered and contradictory portrait of Turner that emerges from this work remains a force with which to be reckoned by influencing subsequent adaptations. As a multivoiced text, this work provides groundbreaking representations of Turner's multiple personae as a freedom fighter, preacher, philosopher, martyr, messiah, and architect of his own symbolism. The fact that Gray's racist vision of Turner has remained far less offensive or problematic for many Black activists writing in the 1960s and beyond than the twentieth-century literary adaptation by the white southerner William Styron alone merits a critical reappraisal of this complex work. And its very endurance may well be explained on the grounds that Turner himself played a key role not only as a protagonist but as a coauthor of this collaborative work. As Mary Kemp Davis notes, "Gray's text is generally accepted as the Ur-text of the revolt, even though its authenticity has been repeatedly challenged."[32] Such an argument counters the assessment of Bryan Rommel-Ruiz, who writes, "While they [readers] can get a glimpse of Turner's perspective, in the end it is Gray's authorship that frames their understanding of Turner and the rebellion."[33] In the face of such pessimism, clear-cut evidence of Turner's signifying practices confirms that he possessed the ultimate authority in this text. He engaged in knowing performances by inhabiting diverse radical personae as he fought to expose the limitations of Gray's knowledge. As Walter C. Rucker argues, "Slave rebel Nat Turner fits very close this description of the typical slave conjurer."[34]

Before examining the complex facets of the Turner/Gray text, it is essential to recognize, as Marcus Wood emphasizes, that the "*Confessions* is, in formal terms, a straightforward contribution to the gallows confession pamphlet literatures." A hybrid work, this text effectively works "to combine slave narrative, liberation theology, and the popular confessional form of the criminal's 'last dying testament.'" Notable for its eclecticism, this body of evidence testifies to Turner's articulation of multiple identities, as he succeeded in communicating his ambiguous personae irrespective of dominant white tendencies toward black erasure. Wresting editorial control from Gray at key moments, Turner secured his authoritative status regardless of this work's similarities to the dominant conventions of European "gallows confessions" literature, an infamous genre that popularly relied on sensationalism and flawed moralizing in order to eradicate the psychological complexities of its soi-disant deviant subjects. As Wood observes, "Popular forms of publishing relating to criminality could be used to drown out or erase slave insurrection as an expression of slave liberation." Relishing both in black sensationalism and white voyeuristic experiences of terror, such literature sought in Turner's case to deflect attention away from black spiritual justifications for resistance. According to this dominant schema, the emphasis was very much upon physical militancy as a way of delegitimizing enslaved testimony in order to consign black heroism to historical oblivion.

Yet, regardless of these nefarious attempts to distort his testimony, Turner's apocryphal status as a formerly enslaved revolutionary emerges almost entirely unscathed in this work. Working against these difficulties, he recast himself not only as a martyred victim but also as a self-conscious freedom fighter, ideologically and spiritually at war with slavery. Thus Turner's triumph speaks to Wood's suggestion that "gallows confessions were a form capable of empowering and indeed biographically establishing the previously disempowered."[35] As black masculinity was not only likely to be physically killed off but also had the potential to be spiritually and politically reborn in this controversial and paradoxical literary genre, Turner rejected oppressive forces designed to eradicate black testimony in *The Confessions*. In a bid to retain his autonomy, therefore, he foregrounded lacunae and omission, thus refusing to conform to white expectations that demanded that he provide a full "confession."

The radical and groundbreaking elements of the Turner/Gray *Confessions,* a work frequently interpreted as an aberrant text in the history of the slave narrative, can be further contextualized by comparison with a widely neglected antecedent whose full title reads, *The Dying Confession of Pomp, A Negro Man, Who Was Executed at Ipswich, on the 6th August 1795, for Murdering Capt. Charles Furbush, of Andover, Taken from the Mouth of the Prisoner, and Penned by Jonathan Plummer.* In contrast to Turner and Gray's ambiguous narration, which repeatedly vouches for the black male protagonist's reticence with regard to taking a white man's life, Pomp's testimony includes a seemingly no-holds-barred admission of guilt. Graphically narrating his retributive act of violence against his white master, he purportedly declares, "I raised the ax before he awaked and at two blows, I so effectually did the job for him, that he never after even stretched himself."[36] Far from acting upon the guidance of divine intervention à la Turner, Pomp is portrayed as a powerless individual whose unstable mentality offers the sole explanation for his actions. "I was frequently troubled with convulsion fits and sometimes crazy in such a degree," he allegedly admits. Read in this context, Gray's determination to interpret Turner as just such a black "fanatic" falls down in light of the space given to his philosophical, intellectual, and moral meditations in this much more radical and dialogic "confessions." Such was not the fate of Pomp, a figure whose complexities were all but annihilated by Jonathan Plummer, his white amanuensis. While Plummer had seeming free rein to editorialize black humanity, for Gray it was impossible to conclude that his Black subject's "mental improvements were extremely small" because he was confronted with the forceful reality of Turner's authorial presence in this text.[37] Wood's suggestion that "Pomp consequently emerges as a shadow consciousness" can be adapted to the Turner/Gray Confessions to argue that Gray functions as the white "shadow" to Turner's black "consciousness" in this groundbreaking and far more challenging work.[38]

Neither The Dying Confession of Pomp nor the Turner/Gray Confessions appeared in isolation. Far from aberrant texts, they can be situated within a tradition of "dying confessions" delivered by incarcerated Black men similarly facing execution. These include The Life and Dying Speech of Arthur, a Negro Man; Who Was Executed at Worcester (1768); Sketches of the Life of Joseph Mountain, a Negro, Who Was Executed at New-Haven (1790); and The Address of Abraham Johnstone, a Black Man, Who Was Hanged at Woodbury (1797). Yet in comparison to the testimonies of men such as Joseph Mountain and a man known solely as Arthur, Turner's "confessions" are startlingly different not only because they do not condemn a Black man for rape or sexual assault but also because he is the only protagonist who succeeds in portraying his actions as those of a martyr. Betraying no such complexity, Mountain confides, "I die a death justly merited by my crimes," while Arthur interprets the fact that he has been "sentenced to be hanged" as "but too just a Reward for many notorious Crimes."[39] Nothing could be further from Turner, who faces death by demanding, "Was not Christ crucified."

Overall, the Turner/Gray collaboration remains controversial because of the lack of consensus regarding the white interviewer's ambivalent representations of his Black protagonist. For many, these tensions reveal his unwillingness or, more likely, inability to capture Turner's multifaceted personae. Yet, as we have briefly seen, Gray's complex narrative strategy in privileging ambiguity operates in stark contrast to other black "gallows literature." For example, Plummer's presumption of an all-knowing relationship with Pomp was far more typical and speaks directly to a white gradualist nineteenth-century abolitionist era in which the trade in verifiable truths and objectified black bodies was at a premium. Nothing could be further from Turner and Gray's far more collaborative and dialogic work. Defying white editorial control, Turner was no textually submissive Pomp or voiceless Joseph or Arthur. Instead, he relied on multifaceted techniques to shore up his status as a revolutionary and psychologically complex protagonist. Rather than a monolithic, savage archetype, the "Nat Turner" of this prison narrative encompasses multiple incarnations as an African griot, enslaved orator, folklorist, preacher, and militant. In forceful ways, these varied personae testify to Turner's determination to reject his status as an emblem of shackled black masculinity. Rather, he favored accessing a model of black humanity that was yet to be conceived, let alone endorsed within white mainstream editorial, no less than legal, jurisdiction.

Startlingly, for a work intent on establishing its veracity, no frontispiece accompanies this publication. "A copy of the likeness by John Crawley of Norfolk, supposedly published with Gray's *Confessions,* has yet to be found," Tragle concedes.[40] Paradoxically, even the fact that various scholars remain at a loss regarding whether this "likeness" exists ultimately represents a form of freedom regarding attempts to memorialize Turner. Turner's very absence points to a key departure from dominant abolitionist conventions, according to which slave narratives were required to include frontispieces so as to satiate white audiences demanding the exhibition of Black subjects as bodies of evidence. Thus the very corporeality of Turner's body no less than the mythology of his legacy gained authority by remaining at large: unknown, indefinable, and constantly malleable in popular memory.

On the surface, as narrated in this work, Turner's response to the judge— "I have nothing more to say"—no less than his apparent readiness to speak to Gray, seems to capitulate to white hegemonic dominance. However, a closer examination of his experimental modes of literary and oratorical address, as well as his manipulation of diverse audiences, both imagined and real, reveals his multilayered engagement with linguistic strategies of ellipsis and masking in this text. Both techniques speak to his complex politics of reform. Refusing to explain his actions, Turner's was no "confession" but instead a blueprint for revolutionary black male heroism. Critics make too little of the fact that Turner himself was the first audience for his "confessions." As the court records note, "Col. Trezvant . . . narrated Nat's Confession to him, as follows *(his Confession as given to Mr. Gray)*."[41] Only after he had heard this text did he declare, "I have nothing more to say"; thus he had the power to endorse the authenticity of *The Confessions* by attesting to the legitimacy or lack thereof of his own version of events. Clearly, Turner recognized the fallacy of a white racist judicial system for which his trial was, at worst, a vigilante crucifixion and, at best, a theatrical performance. Instead, he preferred to vocalize his history in a literary sphere in which he may well have believed there was some possibility of being heard, unfettered, across the centuries.

In striking ways, Turner's seemingly unequivocal declaration, "I have nothing more to say," exists in powerful relation to the generic conventions of white martyrological narratives. Clearly, a dominant tradition of white self-sacrifice was established as early as the sixteenth century by the English writer John Foxe in his magnum opus, the *Book of Martyrs*. Appearing in multiple editions over the centuries, this didactic yet entertaining tract became a popular staple of a European immigrant's moral education in the Puritan colonies of the New World. Readers of this work were promised access to "the lives of 'true' Christian believers who were condemned to death because of their religious convictions."[42] For men and women eager to be both terrified and shocked at the same time that they were emotionally and spiritually purged by visceral tales of persecution and torture, these white martyrological narratives functioned as catalysts for individual redemption but were also sought out, more ignobly, for their entertainment value. This work held great national sway by endorsing a dominant heroic paradigm according to which suffering, passivity, and martyrdom offered the only route to heroic exceptionalism. As Hazel Catherine Wolf argues, this powerful tradition was to ensure that "by the third decade of the nineteenth century the martyr concept was a revered American tradition."[43] Perhaps cognizant of the belief that martyrdom was for whites only, Turner concomitantly engaged in physical militancy and linguistic withholding to insert himself radically into the accepted pantheon of an otherwise all-white heroic imaginary. Thus he fought to join Elijah P. Lovejoy, William Lloyd Garrison, and Prudence Crandall as a Black martyr no less celebrated for laying his body on the line in the pursuit of antislavery reform. Yet, although he sought to ensure his legendary status as a revolutionary freedom fighter dying for the cause, he complicated models straightforwardly associating black heroism with passive martyrdom. Far from advocating militant action as the sole catalyst to self-sacrifice, Turner engaged in textual resistances. Deliberately crafting his testimony to assume editorial control of Gray's *Confessions,* he relied on signifying practices that worked to defy white racist attempts to commodify or appropriate black masculinity.

The critic John King's emphasis upon "the martyrologist's active role in the framing of narrative" in his discussion of the composition of Foxe's *Book of Martyrs* is useful in attempting to come to grips with the complexities of the Turner/Gray text. Their subjects betraying no fear in dying, as King observes, these vignettes were "renowned for recording last words" as "martyrs behaved in accordance with the *ars moriendi* ('art of dying'), which presumed that a 'good death' functioned as a testimonial to dying in a state of grace." "In attempting to silence martyrs, bailiffs acknowledged the power of final words," he writes.[44] No attempt to silence Turner was necessary, however. Readily stating, "I have nothing more to say," he deliberately courted a narrative poetics of withholding. I would argue that in so doing Turner singlehandedly ensured that his historical record would be characterized by lacunae that were far more liberating than the explicatory confines of abolitionist slave narratives or proslavery propaganda, both of which operated via evidential proofs in a desire to know and thereby fix black identities.

Any recognition of Turner's self-appointed role as a military leader and divine seer is inextricable from his experimental poetics, as these work to radicalize otherwise seemingly capitulatory moments in this text. Examples include his pains to eulogize his white owner, Joseph Travis, who "was to me a kind master, and placed the greatest confidence in me." As read within the context of Turner's determination to foreground ambiguities rather than certainties, this statement functions less as a celebration of white philanthropy than as an endorsement of black heroic liberation enacted on ideological rather than ad hoc grounds. According to textual representations of Turner's interrogation of the enslaved man Will, his emphasis was less upon resisting slavery and more upon the fight for emancipation. As he admits, "I . . . asked Will how came he there, he answered, his life was worth no more than others, and his liberty as dear to him. I asked him if he thought to obtain it? He said he would, or loose [*sic*] his life."[45] Insisting upon the relationship between "thought" and the effort to "obtain" "liberty," Turner via Gray fought to offer up his own powerful self-portrait as an enlightened leader in the war on slavery. Adopting a literary poetics of artful juxtaposition in his oratory, Turner expounds upon his ideological, moral, psychological, spiritual, and physical war for black "liberty." The fact that he had "no cause to complain" of his master's "treatment" suggests a possible motive for his willingness to talk to Gray. As an accomplished preacher and orator spreading the "word" among enslaved audiences before his martyrdom, Turner may have hoped this text would reach Black audiences and encourage them to revolt on the grounds not of personal grievance but of ideological principle.

"No firm truth can be established from such an incoherent text, or from the silhouette of the man," writes William Styron.[46] Yet the seeming lack of a white critical consensus regarding Turner establishes the necessity for black imaginative re-creation in order to put flesh onto the bones of his fragmented and marginalized representations. In this multivocal text that continues to provoke controversial debate, Turner resisted white vilification by outlining his own "silhouette" in the gaps created by Gray's ignorance. Working with an experimental literary poetics, he endorsed ambivalent constructions of a multifaceted selfhood as he fought to reformulate the parameters of an apocryphal black male heroism. Walking a linguistic tightrope, he manipulated a plethora of selves to open up rather than close off meaning. In persuasive ways, his poetics undermine Greenberg's determination to celebrate Gray's text as the "triumph of a single name: Nat Turner."[47] Rather, as Davis argues, "The text contains not just *two* but *many* Nat Turners."[48]

In contrast to Gray—a misguided, biased, and insensitive reader of Turner's personae—it is essential that we engage imaginatively with Turner's intellectual clues to read against the grain of these enigmatic "confessions." Albert Stone captures this work's ambiguities by describing it as simultaneously "a firsthand account, a polemical argument, and a mythic portrait."[49] Part political tract, part slave narrative, part religious treatise, part military memoir, and part instructional manual for prospective Black revolutionaries, the Turner/Gray *Confessions* provides white and Black audiences with the spectacle of black physical prowess as inextricably conjoined to a series of linguistic performances. As Eric Sundquist warns, "Too concentrated a focus on the repressive mechanisms of Gray's text . . . can blind us to the unique revelatory powers of Nat's own story."[50] Turner's historical memory is both present and absent within this dominant site of textual representation, as both he and Gray engaged in acts and arts of concealment and revelation.

Writing in the *Richmond Enquirer* on November 25, 1831, an anonymous reviewer triumphantly identifies a fundamental "defect" in the "style" of Gray's *Confessions,* insisting that "the language is far superior to what Nat Turner could have employed."[51] This criticism draws attention to Gray's radical decision not to follow preestablished white conventions, according to which black dialect was consistently portrayed according to the degrading markers of blackface minstrelsy. In a historically unprecedented move, Gray instead relied upon poetic and literary language to dramatize Turner's voice. He thus effectively re-created the controversial figure of Turner as an individualized, if problematic, rather than straightforwardly stereotypical historic figure. By not only running the risk of but actually positively encouraging "doubt" regarding the "authenticity" of his text, Gray paradoxically affirmed Turner's veracity. No less seemingly aberrant than his violent actions, Turner's eloquence constitutes an act of incendiary protest and bolsters Gray's claim that "his own account of the conspiracy is submitted to the public, without comment."[52] Perhaps Turner had "nothing more to say" because Gray took his job seriously, regardless of white criticism and his own prejudices. Incarcerated, shackled, and biding his time before his execution, Turner worked collaboratively with Gray within the framework of an "as told to" slave narrative to provide a powerful, if mediated, display of black authorial agency. The literary dynamics of *The Confessions* testify to a complex interplay between black and white voices and thus underscore Turner's signifying oratorical practices. As a Black subject working within the confines of a white publishing agenda, Turner's linguistic strategies offer a rich example of African American tendencies toward masked discourses, a self-reflexive strategy that Phillis Wheatley identified over fifty years before in observing that "Ethiopians Speak / Sometimes by simile."[53]

Regardless of his exertion of multiple freedoms, Nathaniel Turner remains an absent presence throughout Gray's *Confessions* as he negotiates the difficult terrain of black psychological invisibility as typically compounded by corporeal hyper visibility. The literary poetics of withholding that characterize his negotiation of Gray's authorial practice provide a useful interpretative framework for readers of early works of African American literature more generally. As Sundquist notes, "Turner was far more than Gray's *equal,* as a man and certainly also as an 'author.'" As he emphasizes, the "constantly effaced historical figure of 'Nat Turner'" operates as "a clear signification of neither Turner's nor Gray's intentions alone but instead a joint semiotic construction."[54] While I would agree that Gray's *Confessions* can be analyzed as a collaborative text indicative of a self-reflexive linguistic tapestry, I would contest the claim that Turner was "effaced" in this work. Rather, he plays a leading rather than dual role in shaping its "semiotic construction."

Gray's recourse to theatrical language following his "cross examination" of Turner—"He is a complete fanatic, or plays his part most admirably"— addresses this heroic liberator's capacity for disguise and obfuscation, as he granted his interviewer no concessions vis-à-vis his multifarious performances of multiple identities.[55] Such a view casts doubt upon Jean Fagan Yellin's claim that "just as the insurrectionist's name belonged to his master . . . so the *Confessions* are the work of . . . Thomas Gray, not of the rebel Nat."[56] Liberating fictions of black heroic representations belong as much to Turner as to Gray, as this enslaved man created his own mythologies of selfhood. On first glance, Gray's preface "To the Public" suggests that it was in fact his rather than Turner's authenticity that was in doubt as he fought to establish his authority as the enslaved African American's transcriber.

Simultaneously insisting upon "little or no variation," he downplayed even as he foregrounded his editorial influence over his text.[57] His disclaimer may well have operated in the same way as those that typically opened slave narratives and in which authors proclaimed to give an "unvarnished" tale. Just as they artfully succumbed to complex narrative techniques in a self-conscious "varnishing" of their narrative, Gray's literary ventriloquism is shown as necessitating aesthetic experimentation. Yet as close textual analysis seems to suggest, the embellishment of this narrative was effected not by Gray but by Turner himself as the ultimate author and protagonist.

A powerful disjuncture exists between Gray's description of Turner's actions and Turner's reported first-person narration in this text. Gray describes Turner as a "gloomy fanatic" who "was revolving in the recesses of his own dark, bewildered, and overwrought mind, schemes of indiscriminate massacre to the whites." In stark contrast, however, Turner's rational coherence and far from "bewildered" perspective almost immediately reframe Gray's injunction that he intended only to discuss his "motives." Instead, Turner testifies to his long memory by exploring the tessellated relationships between black ancestry and biography in this work. "You have asked me to give a history of the motives which induced me to undertake the late insurrection, as you call it," Turner summarizes, clarifying, "To do so I must go back to the days of my infancy, and even before I was born."[58] Turner's determination to establish his own origins by adopting, yet adapting, conventions from the seemingly panoramic beginnings of a slave narrative compounds his critique of white authenticity. He defies Gray's preference for defining his revolution as an insurrection by challenging his terminology as he insists, "as you call it." Thus, his interventions establish his and Gray's engagement in a dynamic "semiotic construction" by emphasizing the Black man's right to editorialize the white man's language.

Admitting to his participation in folkloric belief systems, Turner provides a heroic framing for his actions throughout *The Confessions* to accentuate his exceptional role within the black community. "Being at play with other children," he explains, "I was telling them something, which my mother overhearing, said it had happened before I was born—I stuck to my story, however, and related something which went, in her opinion, to confirm it."[59] As shown here, Turner's decision to evoke oral histories within the black community attests to his self-reflexivity regarding storytelling conventions. As refracted through Gray, Turner's statements constitute a series of choreographed performances. Clearly, his insistence that "I stuck to my story" operates as a declaration of independence by vouching for his right to aesthetic experimentation. Straying beyond his own national origins, Turner draws on a mythic diasporic heritage to evoke a temporal no place in which slavery has only an imaginary existence. In this regard, he establishes his creative autonomy via cross-generational memory not only to overshadow Gray's textual insertions but also to consolidate his own authority.

However mediated by Gray's editorial presence, Turner's testimony dramatizes a black familial legacy unshackled by slavery:

> My father and mother strengthened me in this my first impression, saying in my presence, I was intended for some great purpose, which they had always thought from certain marks on my head and breast—[a parcel of excrescences which I believe are not at all uncommon, particularly among negroes, as I have seen several with the same. In this case he has either cut them off or they have nearly disappeared].[60]

Turner's forceful admission regarding familial networks overshadows Gray's skepticism. Thus the white man's attempts to discredit the Black heroic figure fail in light of his celebration of a black ancestral prophesy. An inconclusive physical examination ensures that Turner retained authority regarding his "great purpose" by requiring audiences to have faith in unverifiable, but no less powerful, black traditions and belief systems.

As both author and activist, Turner cultivates an iconic exceptionalism by celebrating a seemingly innate rather than learned knowledge throughout this text. Rejecting any pretensions to the ethos of a Benjamin Franklinian self-made man as cultivated in such diverse ways by Sojourner Truth and Frederick Douglass, Turner instead lauds automatic knowledge within black enslaved communities. In contrast to the majority of Black self-emancipated male and female narrators who painstakingly describe their acquisition of literacy to ensure that the white reader is left in no doubt regarding their intellectual credentials, the self-confessed features of Turner's narration are amnesia and mysticism. "I had no recollection whatever of learning the alphabet," he writes, explaining, "I began spelling the names of different objects—this was a source of wonder to all in the neighborhood, particularly the blacks." Repeatedly rejecting white authenticity dictates, Turner withholds verifiable details in favor of endorsing enigmatic generalizations. Thus he consolidates his symbolic status within the black community in order to reaffirm his hidden agenda of reaching enslaved audiences. While Gray may have written for white readers in his desire to demystify a "sad affair . . . wrapt in mystery," Turner spoke to Black audiences to ensure his mythology would live on by encouraging diverse acts of resistance.[61]

Cultivating mythic, legendary, and superheroic capabilities, Turner celebrates his ability not solely to act but to theorize in this hybrid work. "I was reflecting on many things that would present themselves to my imagination," he explains, "and whenever an opportunity occurred of looking at a book . . . I would find many things that the fertility of my own imagination had depicted to me before."[62] According to his testimony, therefore, Turner's emphasis was not upon white injustices but upon pride in a black heritage as he fought for the survival of oral traditions in a foregrounding of folkloric memory. According to Turner's conception, the aim for this work, neither an abolitionist text nor a didactic work of protest, was that it should function as a philosophical manifesto of black liberation by securing his proliferation of multiple, seemingly contradictory identities. A celebration of black ancestry combines with intellectual and spiritual prowess to reinforce his belief in the fact that the "fertility of my own imagination" gave life to "many things," none of which he documents. Clearly, his interest was in Black rather than white audiences, for whom such explanations represented a waste of words. As Turner was all too aware, the fight for the right to a psychological inner life was tantamount to emotional and intellectual emancipation. Ultimately, his identities remained unmappable terrain for white audiences, to whom black male humanity was not only unconstitutional but unimaginable, even for white abolitionists struggling to recognize black equality.

Turner and Gray's eclectic *Confessions* soon shifts from providing an account of Turner's imaginative faculties to describing his practical skills. As a result, this work represents not only a philosophical treatise on the rights of the Black man but also an instructional manual for future Black revolutionaries. Turner is shown describing his interest "in making experiments in casting different things in moulds made of earth, in attempting to make paper, gunpowder, and many other experiments, that although I could not perfect, yet convinced me of its practicability if I had the means." As a vindication of agency, "never surrender" is Turner's subtext to his Black audience—keep on making "experiments" even if you have not the "means," as one day these will be available. Such opaque references to these "many other experiments" operate by obfuscation in the face of seeming explication to insist upon Turner's textual authority. He consolidates the claim made by Gray's footnote, "When questioned as to the manner of manufacturing those different articles, he was found well informed on the subject." Such formal attempts to verify Turner's claims appear lackluster besides his own ostensible description of his experimental practices. Just as David Walker intended his *Appeal to the Coloured Citizens of the World* to be read aloud to Black audiences, it is no stretch to argue that, as an accomplished preacher, Turner had a similar aim in mind for his own work. Thus Turner's "confessions" foreground the political necessity of his performances. "Having soon discovered to be great, I must appear so, and therefore studiously avoided mixing in society, and wrapped myself in mystery," he emphasizes.[63] Signaling his awareness of the political and social mileage to be found in deliberate obfuscations or "mysteries," he adopts a narrative strategy characterized by a refusal to tell according to any preestablished white conventions.

A defining feature of the Turner/Gray *Confessions* emerges from Turner's insistence upon the ideological basis for his systematic and revolutionary war against slavery. "Now finding I had arrived to man's estate, and was a slave, and these revelations being made known to me," he confesses, "I began to direct my attention to this great object, to fulfill the purpose for which, by this time, I felt assured I was intended." Here, Turner's sense of a noble purpose or a "great object" combines with his belief in predestination not only to communicate his sense of the inevitability of war but also to diminish his personal responsibility by suggesting he acted as an instrument of divine will, yet another reiteration of his Christlike affinities. As preparation for his "great object," therefore, Turner contextualizes his later "insurrection" by describing earlier heroic feats. "I was placed under an overseer from whom I ranaway [*sic*]—and after remaining in the woods thirty days, I returned, to the astonishment of the negroes on the plantation, who thought I had made my escape to some other part of the country, as my father had done before," he explains.[64] The question here is not why did he return but why did he leave? Again, Turner reveals very little to readers forced to imagine his rationale regarding a black revolutionary activism born of free will rather than oppressive coercion.

Turner articulates his flight and return solely by summarizing the responses from members of the black community. "And the negroes found fault," he concedes, "and murmured against me, saying that if they had any sense they would not serve any master in the world." Their responses not only testify to a widespread discontentment with slavery, and thereby aggrandize Turner's militancy by shattering myths regarding slavery as a benevolent institution, but they also explain his return. Committed to a "great object," he escaped not for personal reasons of injustice but on ideological grounds. As a founding father of black radicalism within the United States, his heroism emerges not within a vacuum but according to a tradition of anonymous feats of black resistance. For Turner, his voluntary return to slavery inaugurates his work as a freedom fighter: "And about this time I had a vision—and I saw white spirits and black spirits engaged in battle, . . . and I heard a voice saying, 'Such is your luck, such you are called to see.'" He thus justifies heroic resistance as a necessity given his powerlessness in the face of a divine prophecy inexorably leading him to war. He describes how "while laboring in the field, I discovered drops of blood on the corn as though it were dew from heaven—and I communicated it to many, both white and black . . . —and I then found on the leaves in the woods hieroglyphic characters, and numbers."[65]

Turner's discussion of coded communications via a symbolic language that he alone was able to interpret accentuates his role as a soothsayer graphically prophesying the bloodshed of war. A question-and-answer exchange between Gray, who asks, "Do you not find yourself mistaken now?" and Turner, who replies, "Was not Christ crucified," further vindicates this enslaved hero's spiritual as well as physical militancy.[66] Tellingly written as a statement, Turner's decision to answer Gray's question with a declaration masquerading as a rhetorical question remains symptomatic of his staged responses to white editorial control. Throughout this work, Turner repeatedly reminds readers of his ideological principles in order to render his critique of American national politics irrefutable.

In forceful ways, John King's assessment that in much earlier works such as the *Book of Martyrs* "the reader encounters repeated examples of the most pervasive typological application, imitation of Christ" can be usefully applied to the Turner/Gray work.[67] Similarly in this text, Turner cultivates his martyred status as a vengeful yet apocryphal divine force not only to galvanize moral opposition to the barbaric horrors of slavery but also to legitimize black revolutionary activism by situating his actions within a religious framework. Turner's narrative betrays the extent to which he borrowed from the language of popular prophecy to endorse his own status as a black revolutionary. As Wilson Moses argues, Turner's memory is best understood according to "the Afro-American messianic myth," which "thrived because its rhetoric is familiar to the people of the United States, who envision themselves as a 'redeemer people.'" By recuperating himself as both a retributive messiah and a martyr suffering from white spiritual persecution, Turner fought to deify his memory in order to counter proslavery dehumanizations. As Moses argues, "While Turner was superficially reminiscent of the wrathful, retributive messiah, he had actually merged this identity with that of the sacrificial, long-suffering Jesus."[68] Simultaneously inhabiting multiple guises as a "political revolutionary, a religious martyr, and even as a Christological substitute," Turner resisted any forms of moral, social, political, or spiritual crucifixion as he fought to ensure that his body and memory retained their importance as shifting sites of social critique, political transformation, and moral redemption.[69]

One of the most surprising "confessions" in Turner's text emerges from his free admission ascribing his seeming military shortcomings to a reluctance to kill. At the beginning of the revolution, Turner admits, "I entered my master's chamber, it being dark, I could not give a death blow." Succeeding only once by effecting the death of "Miss Margaret," he explains how, "after repeated blows with a sword, I killed her by a blow on the head, with a fence rail." While Turner's minimalist factual narration may lack gory detail, he nonetheless refuses to shy away from the moral relativism of war. Thus he celebrates his role as a military commander by admitting, "We remained some time at the barn, where we paraded," and claims, "I formed them in a line as soldiers, and after carrying them through all the manoeuvres I was master of, marched them off." Working within the tradition of Toussaint Louverture's stratagem rather than Denmark Vesey's and Gabrielle Prosser's ad hoc insurgency, Turner displays his knowledge regarding military formations. "I took my station in the rear, and as it 'twas my object to carry terror and devastation wherever we went, I placed fifteen or twenty of the best armed and most to be relied on, in front," he declares. Both these and later statements lay claim to Turner's recognition of this text's legacy as a military memoir and as an instructional manual for future Black revolutionaries rather than as a religious tract or as a cautionary tale of black violence.[70] For Alexis Joyner, H. Khalif Khalifah, and James Magee, "It is quite possible 'the work of death' description was by Nat Turner," as he "came to the conclusion that killing slave owners was the only way to free Black captives."[71] By describing death as "work," Turner divests his acts of violence of their gothic associations. Rather, he relies on a dispassionate use of language actively to reclaim his actions within the context of rational performances, which he defines as a dutiful necessity undertaken solely in the service of survival.

Awaiting execution, Turner was uninterested in exonerating his behavior to appease whites. Instead, he recognized that his legacy would lie in his capacity to create his own mythology as an inspiration for future Black radical activists. Thus he narrates his capture via ellipsis rather than explication not only to resist the entertainment value of his "confessions" but also to demonstrate that his interest was in commemorating black warfare rather than personal sacrifice. "I had many hair breadth escapes, which your time will not permit you to relate. I am here loaded with chains, and willing to suffer the fate that awaits me," he informs Gray. Unable to prevent his circulation as a spectacle of shackled black humanity exposed for eager consumption by whites, Turner was aware of his legendary status among Black audiences. Clearly, the Turner/Gray *Confessions* provides a space within which Turner regains his freedom by pioneering a textual politics and poetics according to which he imaginatively re-created himself as both an author and activist: he became his own "painter," as argued in the preface to this book. Regardless of Gray's attempt to undertake a thorough "cross examination" of the Black man's testimony, therefore, this "heroic slave" defied his white interlocutor's political agenda. More particularly, Turner exposed the limitations of Gray's philosophical understanding as he was forced to a candid admission regarding his failures at comprehension, leading Gray to declare, "I shall not attempt to describe the effect of his narrative."[72] Decades later, Osborne Perry Anderson, one of the few Black freedom fighters who survived John Brown's Harper's Ferry raid, testifies to the symbolic importance of Turner's diverse strategies of performative subterfuge, which remained key to black survival. "Vague hints, careful blinds, are Nat Turner's entire make-up to save detection," he states.[73]

Admitting that Turner was capable of "daring to raise his manacled hands to heaven, with a spirit soaring above the attributes of man," Gray was an unlikely source for celebrating black moral superiority.[74] While Mary Kemp Davis is right to applaud the Turner/Gray work for its generic hybridity as "a complex document with affinities to the slave narrative, the spiritual autobiography as conversion narrative, and the criminal confession," there are also deliberate similarities with the military memoir in the tradition of earlier works such as Toussaint Louverture's prison document. Similarly, Davis's argument that Gray "unwittingly created all kinds of texts within his text" can be more appropriately applied to Turner's authorial strategies of experimentation with an array of literary conventions and seemingly disguised patterns of oral testimony.[75] While William Andrews makes a crucial intervention by stating that the "meaning of Nat Turner is perpetually postponed and relative," in light of his existence as a "product of the dynamics of the text itself," clearly his self-reflexive practices signify beyond his passive status as "product" to betray his active role as a producer.[76]

On the eve of the Civil War and nearly thirty years following its initial publication, in 1859 the Turner/Gray *Confessions* was reprinted in the *Anglo-African Magazine* and accompanied by an anonymous article, most likely written, as Zoe Trodd and John Stauffer note, by the editor James McCune Smith.[77] Titled "Brown & Nat Turner: An Editor's Comparison," the article urges recognition of the historical origins of black revolutionary activism by predicting, "There can be no long delay in the choice of methods. If John Brown's be not soon adopted by the free North, then Nat Turner's will be by the enslaved South."[78] Working to conflate Brown's and Turner's revolutionary dissidence, the author aggrandizes Turner as archetypal liberator. He inverts typical descriptions of Turner as a "black John Brown" to reinterpret John Brown as a white hero in blackface, apocryphal only as a sacrificial and warring white Nathaniel Turner.

Appearing only a few years later in 1867, William Wells Brown's historical volume, *The Negro in the American Rebellion,* exalts in Turner's symbolic status as a folkloric touchstone for anonymous feats of black heroism. Condemning white immorality, he applauds black self-sacrifice in the imagined life of an unknown enslaved man, "Jim," who saves his white master from Turner's rebellion and yet fails to repress his newfound sense of a right to liberty. As Brown reimagines, "He handed his pistol to his master, and said, 'I cannot help you hunt down these men: they, like myself, want to be free. Sir, I am tired of the life of a slave: please give me my freedom, or shoot me on the spot.'" A horrifyingly predictable outcome ensues: "Capt. Harris took the weapon, and pointed it at the slave. Jim, putting his right hand upon his heart, said, 'This is the spot; aim here.' The captain fired, then the slave fell dead at his feet."[79] By recording the life and death of "Jim," an imaginary historical figure, Brown dramatizes undocumented and even invented feats of anonymous black male heroism within the context of Turner's iconic status as a legendary figure. Thus he reinterprets black resistance as a continuum encompassing diverse forms of sacrificial martyrdom and revolutionary activism. As yet another revision of the Wedgwood tableau, the enslaved Black man lying prostrate at the white man's feet does not register hope in the prospect of white philanthropy but despair in white villainy, as the black body becomes a talisman of white moral condemnation. Writing in the post–Civil War era, Brown recognized that dead Black men were morally more useful than living Black men in light of ongoing white racist predilections for Black sacrificial martyrs as the rightful and legitimate heirs of emancipation.

Decades later, the twentieth-century Black reporter George Coleman Moore was less interested in black martyrdom as he instead celebrates Turner as a symbol of violence. Reimagining that Turner did not come quietly when facing capture by Benjamin Phipps, he writes, "His first impulse was to slash him with the blade, but he thought better of it when he saw the revolver in Phipps' hand. Nat was commanded to surrender but refused." Writing against a backdrop of an early twentieth-century context of Ku Klux Klan revivals and disillusionment following World War I, the rise of lynchings, and the consolidation of segregation laws, Moore evokes Turner's memory in the context of black male resistance to exalt in survival rather than sacrifice. "Exhausted and weary, outnumbered and discouraged, abused by whites and abandoned by his own people, Nat Turner permitted himself to be captured," he concludes.[80] For Moore and other Black reporters writing in this much later period, the focus was not upon gauging white sympathies but on galvanizing black grassroots activism, arguably no less a preoccupation of Turner as he sought to inspire future acts of liberation. Writing in the *Chicago Defender* in this period, Joseph C. Coles breaks further ground by introducing new stories to Turner's mythic arsenal, which operate along similar lines. "Because he dared to agitate among the slaves his master turned him over to a slave-breaker to be beaten into submission," he writes, "but instead of the slave-breaker breaking Nat Turner, Prophet Nat, as he was called, broke him."[81] Celebrating black wish fulfillment against a historical backdrop of powerlessness, Coles relishes in the ultimate triumph of Nathaniel Turner's legacies. Break or be broken—black masculinity in the nineteenth no less than the twentieth century had no choice but to engage in military, moral, ideological, and aesthetic resistance in the pursuit of racial equality.

"PHONY LEGENDS": STERLING BROWN'S POETICIZED MEMORIAL OF NATHANIEL TURNER

"Forgetting has been a way, but that's changing," Sterling Brown argues. "That's another good thing about the Black Movement; the heroes are coming back into their own," he declares.[82] As Brown notes, key contemporary activists within the twentieth century sought to revise and reinvent new mythologies for Black heroes, such as Nathaniel Turner, not only to counter political and cultural misinterpretations but also to inculcate black pride by insisting on their didactic importance as role models. The imaginative reincarnations of historical figures such as Turner no less than Louverture, Douglass, Truth, Tubman, and Pieh signal a sea change in black cultural history. As a political and historical subject, in the twentieth century slavery became reconfigured not as a history of white shame and moral culpability but as a source of black radicalism. Celebrated for aesthetic, political, and historical strategies of resistance, exceptional individuals were recuperated as symbols for black activism in order to inspire black political and cultural liberation in the present and future eras. Thus Turner's memory continued to resonate within urban and rural black communities in early twentieth-century poetical works such as Sterling Brown's "Remembering Nat Turner" and Melvin Tolson's "Dark Sympathy" as well as paintings by Johnny Otis, Malvin Gray Johnson, and William H. Johnson, among others. Regardless of their formal and stylistic differences, powerful consistencies emerge across these diverse representations, particularly as they relate to debates regarding memorialization and folkloric history as well as battles over visual and textual language and the formal parameters of black heroic representation. Across the early decades of the twentieth century, Black and white writers and artists re-create a usable plethora of imagined Nathaniel Turners to resist the injustices of a segregated "Jim Crow" post–World War I Depression era.

Appearing more than a century after Turner's rebellion and execution, Sterling Brown's "Remembering Nat Turner" confronts the ongoing difficulties besetting any attempts to memorialize such an elided and taboo black historical figure. More particularly, his paradoxes of poetic personae address cross-racial tensions as well as the distortions perpetuated by both Black and white communities' fights for ownership of Turner's history. For Brown, these remain as fraught in the post-emancipation era as they were during slavery, as his poem begins: "we followed the trail that old Nat took / . . . / In his angry stab for freedom." Relying on the collective pronoun "we," Brown reflects upon the black community's will to remember, as he collapses temporal boundaries in order to reclaim Turner's "angry stab for freedom" as if it were their own. His exposure of the cultural and historical violations enacted upon black history by a racially circumscribed forgetting speaks to Brown's radical indictment of similar holes within the black folkloric imagination. As his poetic persona observes, "The Negroes had only the faintest recollections." A montage of anonymous voices attest to lacunae within black knowledge as one protagonist speculates, "I heard something, sometime; I doan jis remember what."[83] On the surface, Brown's poetic message appears to indict the loss of black oral traditions, exposing a new generation's irresponsibility regarding the memory of slavery as they had rejected, to their cost, the significance of these legacies for future activism.

However, does the reading change if we interpret Brown's unnamed narrators as white? In this context, perhaps the Black community members' refusal to speak, "I doan jis remember," communicates a poetics of withholding designed to protect Turner's memory. Such an interpretation has the potential to heighten awareness regarding black authorial acts of willful masking and theatricality as expressed not only in literary texts but also in fragments of oratorical conjecture. In this reading Brown's experimental poetics reinforce ambiguities of narrative voice to sustain the idea that Turner's memory remained so incendiary that his legacy is a story for black ears only, thereby emphasizing yet greater parallels between suffering during segregation and slavery's persecutions. The cultural work of putting flesh onto the bones of Turner's skeletal history provides the galvanizing force that undergirds Brown's poem. Scripting interpretative ambiguity into the structure of his poem, Brown encourages readers and viewers to engage imaginatively with Turner's multiple legacies.

Brown's use of poetic juxtaposition functions not only to challenge white official pretensions to historical accuracy but also to engage directly with the vagaries proliferating within a black community imagination. Reversing the power dynamics of Gray's text, he editorializes white factual claims and thus exposes the inaccuracies of the story of an aged white female witness who delights in describing Turner as a murderous vigilante prowling with "axe in hand." In stark contrast, Brown's unequivocal poetic aside dismisses her testimony by stating that, according to her view, this event took place "in a house built long after Nat was dead."[84] Exposing the racialized parameters at work in dominant sites of historical memory, Brown explores the differences between African American witnesses who frankly admitted their ignorance and white overinflated pretensions to knowledge. Thus Brown condemns the nefarious influences of imagined fictions that continue to masquerade as factual truths within white communities. Rather, he endorses literary subterfuge as a means to justify disguise as a political necessity among black communities, as individuals necessarily adopted a complex poetics of telling and untelling to ensure their cultural preservation. Above all else, Brown indicts racist ignorance by condemning the testimony of an anonymous white woman who had "given a lot of phony legends about Nat Turner" as he admits to a determination "to set in contrast what she would say and what the actual facts were."[85]

Brown's narrative poetics of juxtaposition or "contrast" expose the fallacies and distortions perpetuated by white racist myths that were complicit in refuting memorializations of "Remembering Nat Turner." According to this schema, white acts of misremembering represent a worse crime than black amnesia, as one is born of a desire to distort in the service of "phony legends," while the other is symptomatic of a widespread white annihilation of black culture. As Brown informs an interviewer, "I showed that she [the white woman] had misinformation, and my folks had no information." Ultimately, therefore, Brown's ballad dramatizes the ways in which African

Americans have remained unwitting perpetrators of the erasures of their own histories in light of obfuscations within the dominant records. "That's survival and just the bare necessities of life which made it so that they'd forget it," Brown explains. "In it I was very disheartened by the loss of his memory," he concedes, thereby defending his recourse to a structuring principle of absence and erasure across his oeuvre.[86] And yet, as "Remembering Nat Turner" demonstrates, loss can be countered by a poetic engagement with imaginative acts of memorialization. Remarkable for its lyrical beauty and intellectual complexity, Brown's poem belies Albert Stone's critique of it as possessing "little emotional or ideological bite." His view that this text "skirts the dangerous realities" does little justice to Brown's forceful exploration of the mechanisms by which Black historical figures have been erased within white mainstream memorializations.[87] As Brown philosophizes, any alleged historical "realities" surrounding Turner remain illusory in light of the power of racist mythologies to effect historical distortion.

Brown's aesthetic strategies boldly displace Turner as a heroic presence not only to indict white mainstream lacunae regarding black history but also to expose rituals of forgetting perpetuated within black culture. His works make it possible to understand why even such a celebrated Black writer as Langston Hughes omitted Turner from his pioneering volume *American Negro Heroes,* while Golden Legacy comic books founded during the Black Power era erased him entirely from their pantheon of archetypal Black leaders. Suspended on a knife edge, Nathaniel Turner's biography reflects political and moral tensions for Black no less than white artists and writers. Rejecting such conflicting legacies, Brown challenged the historical legitimacy of "phony legends" by providing imaginative reconstructions of multiple Nathaniel Turners, all of whom signified as reusable antidotes to victimized spectacles of black masculinity.

Such was equally the case for African American painters such as William Johnson, whose portrait *Nat Turner* I discuss in the preface to this book. While on the surface Johnson's painting appears to conciliate a white-supremacist vision of black passivity and death, a brief consideration of this portrait in the context of works by other twentieth-century Black artists reveals that his portrait is in fact far more incendiary. One such work is Malvin Gray Johnson's portrait *Nat Turner,* a similarly neglected painting created more than a decade before Johnson's in 1934 (see plate 4). Rather than providing covert references to Turner's various artistic abilities, Malvin Johnson's Turner appears as an almost entirely faceless figure, surrounded solely by symbols of black enslavement. Framed with reproductions of chains, a slave cabin, a whip, a white stone edifice, and a white fence, Gray Johnson's work testifies to black powerlessness and white cruelty. Refusing to sanitize black suffering, Johnson's portrait offers a visual denunciation of the unspeakable realities that not only afflicted black masculinity in the white slaveholding South but also survived, undiminished, in the white-supremacist, segregated South of the interwar years.

Thus Gray Johnson's work may well provide a more unequivocal celebration of black violence than first appears. Far from the solitary hanging body of William Johnson's work, his Turner stands between two other enslaved heroic figures, armed with a torch and rifle, as he himself holds what appears to be a sword that has been broken in battle. Perhaps, then, Gray Johnson's Turner runs less risk of being dismissed as a touchstone for black martyrdom, as he is instead portrayed as a military leader mired in the heat of conflict. Yet however much they may differ regarding their endorsement of diverse forms of black male resistance, the physiognomies of both Gray Johnson's and William Johnson's Turner remain similarly ambiguous and unreadable. Across an array of literary and visuals works, early twentieth-century Black artists and writers such as Brown, William Johnson, and Malvin Gray Johnson exalt in Turner's memory as a mythic touchstone regarding the physical indeterminacy of black heroism. In the particular case of Turner, they foreground psychological ambiguity so as to refute white mainstream tendencies toward commodifying the complex yet misinterpreted subjectivities of this slippery icon.

"A GOTHIC FIGURE": NATHANIEL TURNER IN
THE BLACK AND WHITE IMAGINATIONS OF
ROBERT HAYDEN AND WILLIAM STYRON

Groundbreakingly adopting a first-person perspective, Robert Hayden's poem "The Ballad of Nat Turner" displaces the primacy of historical accounts to construct an alternative, imagined persona for this enslaved man turned legend. His mythic landscape compellingly reimagines Turner as walking "where Ibo warriors / hung shadowless." Directly contextualizing Turner's heroism in relation to "Ibo warriors," Hayden transgresses national boundaries to insert the historical figure's militancy in a continuum of black diasporic suffering. Signifying upon multiple meanings, he not only appeals to imagined African origins in references to black "warriors" that "hung shadowless" but also critiques lynching as a spectacle within the United

States. For Hayden, dying black bodies operate as ambiguous repositories of memory. His narrator bears witness to their suffering by asking, "Is this the sign . . . forepromised me?"[88] Far from being a "sign in himself" as Harding notes, Hayden's Turner embodies ambivalent paradoxes, as he remains paralyzed by fear and desperate for an external "sign" that would emotionally and intellectually empower his actions. However mythically reimagined, Hayden admits to his reliance upon historical research for his creation of Turner. "I very often study old prints, illustrations in books, old posters, photographs," he notes, adding that this "research helps me to visualize my characters and their setting." Yet according to Hayden's vision, material details remain secondary to metaphysical questions. "It's not the facts per se that make the poem" but rather "what the imagination does with the facts," he emphasizes.[89]

Hayden's experimental use of language relies on the power of reimagining to reject tendencies toward oversimplifying Turner's spirituality and heroic leadership. Instead, he gives poignant utterance to Turner's self-doubt in a persecuting sense of nihilistic abandonment. Frail, mortal, and vulnerable, Hayden's Turner is a tragic hero of epic and mythic proportions whose humanity paradoxically testifies to his iconic exceptionalism. In "The Ballad of Nat Turner" and other poetical works, Hayden's shocking art of rupture condemns untold histories of black suffering. "As I studied accounts of the rebellion," Hayden explains, "what interested me was not the bloodshed but Nat Turner himself, his characteristics, his personality." Sublime, transcendent, and quintessentially Romantic, Hayden's Turner may well have been inspired by official historical records but signifies beyond them. Reimagining Turner as confessing that the "conqueror faces . . . were like mine," Hayden endorses a language of racial transcendence by adopting a rhetoric of sameness rather than difference regarding universalities of human conflict, war, and resurfacing trauma. Bearing witness to his sense of Turner's apocryphal presence, which he admits "greatly stimulated my imagination," Hayden describes him as "a gothic figure, as a rather frightening kind of vengeful mystic."[90] In this regard, Hayden's work fought to capture the complex performative poetics of Turner's multiple selves.

Yet just as Brown relies on amnesia, Hayden embraces failure by admitting, "I don't know that I really got 'inside' Nat Turner," despite the fact that he "read a great deal about him."[91] In this regard, Hayden's recognition of the failures of historical documentation in countering incontrovertible proofs regarding Turner's moral and psychological complexities are useful for approaching controversies surrounding the white southern writer William

Styron's novel *Confessions of Nat Turner,* published in 1967. Seemingly un-aware of the challenges he faced in unlocking the "inside" of such an unfath-omable historical figure as Turner, Styron argues he was inspired to write this novel to correct widespread neglect within official histories. Thus he seemingly shares Sterling Brown's determination to challenge the sparsity of Turner's memorialization, as his history was denied any formal monument other than a "historical highway marker."[92] For Styron, such a seeming lack of historical information legitimizes his literary creativity. "I had to create him out of whole cloth because there is no sense of his personality in either the 'Confessions' or the trial records. So he is a product of my imagination," he insists.[93]

Subsequent and ongoing controversies establish that Styron underesti-mated the prior multifaceted existences of Nathaniel Turner within black historical and folkloric memory. As Styron's novel shows, he ultimately ar-gued for the existence of verifiable truths regarding Turner. Depicted as "a person of conspicuous ghastliness" plagued by psychosis rather than spiri-tual prophecies regarding the promise of black redemption, Styron's Turner masquerades as a historical icon by performing as a gothic other. Fully encapsulating white normative standards of black antiheroism, he is char-acterized by hyperbestialized sexuality, irrational primitivism, and avowed insanity. In light of Styron's excessive reliance upon hyperbolic language and sensationalized representations relishing in taboo, his conviction that he awarded Turner "dimensions of humanity that were almost totally absent in the documentary evidence" is impossible to sustain.[94] Clearly, Turner's hu-manity was far less on trial for the nineteenth-century southerner Gray, for whom he possessed a "spirit soaring above the attributes of man," than it was for the twentieth-century southerner Styron, whose Turner philosophizes that "in order to buy some advantage from a white man it is better . . . to si-lently wrap oneself up in one's niggerness."[95]

Writing during the height of the twentieth-century civil rights era, Sty-ron returned audiences to a period of slavery by admitting that his major source was the Turner/Gray *Confessions,* which he believed was "genuine." "I was generally disposed to use it as a guideline, a *loose* guideline, for my own narrative," he claims.[96] However, Styron's four-hundred-page novel strays far from Gray's twenty-page text to create a substantially different work that has since elicited polarized responses, prompting both excessive adulation and excessive condemnation. Black activists, philosophers, and writers were so angered that they published a lengthy intellectual tract titled *Ten Black Writ-ers Respond,* in which they demanded that Styron engage with their moral and political outrage. As Barbara Foley suggests, Styron's determination to have it both ways left him wide open to censure on the grounds that "the ambiguous generic premise of *Confessions of Nat Turner* reflects the author's desire to enjoy simultaneously the benefits of legendary reshaping and those of documentary veracity."[97] Styron's claiming both imaginative free rein and historical legitimacy powerfully reflects upon the eras of slavery and civil rights as sites of the struggle over memory in white American national discourse more generally. As Joyner, Khalifah, and Magee write, "Styron's book is a vain attempt to blur, ignore or misrepresent Black People in the history books."[98] Undoubtedly, the most outrageous and reprehensible aspect of Styron's treatment lies in the way in which he systematically layers unpleasantly calculated and systematically racist sexual stereotypes onto Turner. As far as extant evidence is concerned, one of the most striking aspects of Turner's aborted revolution lay in the noted historical reality that none of the white victims were sexually abused in any way. Yet Styron thoroughly abuses this archival fact to create a fantastical spectacle of Turner as a quintessential embodiment of black barbarous masculinity.

"One of the most striking aspects of the institution" of slavery, Styron believes, "is the fact that in the 250 years of its existence in America, it was singularly free of organized uprisings, plots, and rebellions."[99] Clearly, Styron's misunderstanding regarding black histories of resistance results in cataclysmic distortions, as he imagines Turner as an aberrant rather than representative historic figure. Guilty of reprehensible ignorance regarding diverse forms of black radicalism, Styron myopically defines black rebellion solely according to the terms of full-scale male-led resistance movements, with the result that he whitewashes black history. Tellingly, as Greenberg argues, the "controversy of the 1960s offers us a view of the real Nat Turner as a man with a 'blank' face rather than as one with a 'black' or 'bright' face."[100] For Greenberg's construction of "blank," it is also possible to substitute "unreadable" as a means of beginning to unpack ambiguities concerning Turner's history, which remain, at worst, unrecognized by white writers such as Styron and, at best, unresolved in the bid for racial and national ownership of his memory in twentieth- and twenty-first-century controversies.

Styron's novel has the potential to wreak disproportionate damage in light of a notable dearth of attempts by Black writers to reimagine Turner's legacy in prose. As Davis writes, "There are no novels written by African Americans that portray Gray's Nat Turner."[101] Yet for the majority of Black critics, Styron's book does little to fill this hole. As Sterling Brown asserts, "He goes back to the stereotypes."[102] More particularly, Ralph Ellison condemns

Styron's failings as symptomatic of the problems facing white writers' attempts to memorialize black history more generally. "He has to sell *me*, convince me, that despite the racial divisions and antagonisms in the U.S., his received version of history is not drastically opposed to mine," Ellison insists. "Because I am conditioned to assume that his idea of the heroic individual is apt to violate my sense of heroism."[103] Clearly, the inability of a white writer to represent black heroism with any degree of sensitivity or empathy lies at the crux of these difficulties. As Albert Murray argues, Styron's construction of Turner was symptomatic of widespread failings within the white male literary imagination. "The slightest notion of a black compatriot as a storybook hero compels him to equate the strongest Negroes with the most helpless," he suggests.[104] For Vincent Harding it is "the killing without conviction which marks Styron's black-white man indelibly as a twentieth-century anti-hero."[105] Advocating an entirely different position, James Baldwin is more forgiving. "I hope it starts a tremendous fight, so that people will learn what they really think about each other," he concedes.[106]

Yet few bridges have been crossed in the "tremendous fight" that the book has generated, particularly given its complicity in securing seemingly fixed and immutable constructions of black heroic identity formation. As Julius Lester suggests, the book promises little hope, given that "Styron's novel is no different from the many editorials by white writers and politicians telling blacks that violence is wrong."[107] Refusing to engage with these debates, Styron indulges in flawed perceptions of the reasons for black criticisms regarding his strategies of heroic construction vis-à-vis Turner. That his Turner "did not correspond, on the crudest level, to a kind of stereotypical cardboard black hero," Styron writes, "is what disturbed the black critics of the book more than anything else."[108] Clearly, Styron misreads the antagonism toward his representations of Turner not as being based on his one-dimensional racist portrayals but as being rooted in an illusory desire among Black audiences for an idealized archetype: such was not the case. Styron is equally far from immune to castigation by white critics, as Herbert Aptheker forcefully declares, "Styron has stolen the real Nat Turner."[109] Yet, regardless of the forcefulness of Aptheker's claims, if debates regarding battles over the ownership of Turner across the centuries prove anything, it is that no "real" heroic figure exists that can be accessed either through historical representation, folkloric memory, or imaginative re-creation.

At the outset, Styron's "Author's Note" urges historical veracity by claiming, "I have rarely departed from the *known* facts about Nat Turner," yet he insists on the right to artistic license, by admitting "I have allowed myself the utmost freedom of imagination."[110] Bolstering a pseudofictional emphasis upon authenticity, he includes excerpts from Gray's narrative. Co-opting white abolitionist truth-telling traditions of the nineteenth century, he thereby seeks to legitimize his imaginative re-creation. As Charles Joyner argues, however, the novel "takes the form of a pastiche of the slave narrative genre."[111] Clearly, Styron's relationship to the slave narrative genre is troubled and ill-conceived. In explicit ways, he relies on stereotypes to denigrate blackness and establish his "possessive investment in whiteness." As George Lipsitz expertly contends, "The artificial construction of whiteness almost always come to possess white people themselves unless they develop antiracist identities."[112] A lack of self-reflexivity regarding some of the more troubling aspects of his text therefore prevents Styron's rejection of "antiracist identities." Instead, his exploration of Turner's torturing self-hatred functions as nothing less than a racist endorsement of a white-imagined model of black masculinity.

Despite its limitations, Styron's novel does, however, begin to illuminate some omissions and obfuscations within literary constructions of Turner. In his novel he demonstrates a keen if flawed insight into Turner's performances of a stereotyped blackness, a later fascination for the Black graphic novelist Kyle Baker. Such insight is shown when the fictive Turner justifies begging for food from a white prison guard by saying, "Big talk will fetch you nothing but nigger talk might work." Revealing Turner to be an artful manipulator of language, Styron tackles important concepts related to black subterfuge via an imagined interrogation of Turner's relationship with Gray. As his Turner explains, "I managed if not completely to stifle my dislike, then to mask it," thereby celebrating black subversive arts of disguise. Yet Styron fails to resist reverting to portraying a problematically corporeal rather than spiritual Turner, a man he re-creates as ultimately motivated by physical want rather than by ideological principle. "If I was to be hung come what may, what purpose could be served by withholding a 'confession,' especially when it might augment in some small way my final physical relief?" his Turner asks. Similarly, Styron's excessive reliance upon racist imagery ascribes a radical self-hatred to Turner when he states that "my black shit-eating people were surely like flies."[113]

Yet, supporting the view that Styron struggled to construct psychologically complex protagonists, black or white, his dramatization of Gray is also heavily caricatured. As a white southern racist buffoon, Styron's Gray is physically repelling, with "discolored blotches on his flushed face," while his language is generic, "the quintessence of white folks' talk." By comparison, however troubled, his portrayal of Turner is much more multifaceted and characterized by staged ambiguities that render his strategies of black representation contradictory, conflictual, and not easily read. Working beyond its limitations, Styron's *Confessions* does therefore display some sensitivity to a necessity for ellipsis in his narrative. He reimagines an illuminating cross-racial exchange between Turner and Gray in the heroic figure's response to his white interviewer's question regarding why he killed his benevolent owner, Joseph Travis. Turner comments, "That I can't give no reply to, Mr Gray," adding in an aside to the reader, "And I couldn't—not because there was no reply to the question, but because there were matters which had to be withheld even from a confession." Such unexpected nuances make it disappointing to interpret at face value Styron's facile and clear-cut racist representations of Turner's realization regarding his renown as a "comic nigger minister of the gospel." However, such reductive comments ultimately testify to Styron's own problematic confession that "I fell under the spell of négritude, fascinated by black people and their folkways, their labor and religion and especially their music." Clearly, his attraction to and repulsion from Turner as a heroic Black icon undermines any radical possibilities by colluding in his own "anxiety about my secret passion for blackness."[114]

Overall, Styron confronts historical controversies as a platform upon which to interrogate racial tensions dominant within contemporary society. "I'm sure that my early fascination with Nat Turner came from pondering the parallels between his time and my own society," he admits, suggesting that contemporary conditions "were not really so different from the days of slavery."[115] "I want the book to exist on its own terms as an American tragedy," Styron asserts, explaining, "You can see Nat Turner as an archetypal American tragic hero, but this doesn't make Rap Brown an archetypal American hero. . . . I think violence on a purely psychic level can be cathartic in the best sense of the word—it can satisfy the Negro's longing to assert his identity. But I don't think that's enough in 1967."[116] And yet, writing against a backdrop of the fight for civil rights, assassinations, racist persecutions, and urban rioting in the 1960s, Styron reimagines the complexities of Turner's motivations—sexual, moral, physical, intellectual, and spiritual—only to testify to his failures of knowing, as he endorses one-dimensional and racist constructions of black male activism as existing beyond the pale of white official heroism. Such a focus on the seemingly irrational foundations of black violence does little either to unpack widespread legacies of white racist injustice or to begin to map the full spectrum of black civil rights and Black Power activism.

Even more riskily, Styron undermines the reader's potential for moral outrage against slavery by including problematic events, most notably his narration of Turner's mother's rape. As Styron's Turner admits, "I do not know whether the sound I hear now is the merest whisper of a giggle ('Uh-huh, aw-*right*,' she seems to murmur)." While such a scene foregrounds subversive black female performances in the face of white male annihilation, Styron's prose runs the horrifying risk of replicating racist ideologies surrounding black femininity and myths of hypersexuality. According to his literary vision, enslaved Black women were willful participants in enforced acts of their own violation. More generally, one of the most difficult aspects regarding Styron's memorialization of Turner concerns his emphasis upon black internalizations of whiteness. "So near to the white people, I absorb their language daily," his Turner admits. In this context, Turner's racist denigration of enslaved cabin life exposes class differences in order to consolidate myths of black inferiority. His Turner is appalled by "the odor—the stink of sweat and grease and piss and nigger offal," as he admits that "despite myself, the blood shame, the disgrace I felt at being a nigger also, was as sharp as a sword through my guts."[117] According to Styron's text, therefore, these forms of internalized racism gave birth to a bitter self-hatred that not only opposes any potential heroic constructions of Turner as a self-appointed redeemer of black suffering but also risks belittling the undocumented lives of anonymous Black men, women, and children living and dying in slavery. As recent archaeological excavations leading to the discovery of possessions distinctive for their political, spiritual, and aesthetic significance demonstrate, the histories and belief systems of otherwise anonymous enslaved men and women are far more rich and diverse than Styron's narrow racist judgments would have us believe.

More damningly still, Styron's novel repeatedly foregrounds Turner's desires for whiteness in projected fantasies of racial role reversals, a classic example of which occurs at the moment in which he waits for his master in a plantation temporarily bereft of white ownership. Enjoying a brief respite from slavery, Styron's Turner relishes in the fact that "for a fleeting moment instead I owned all, and so exercised the privilege of ownership by unlacing my fly and pissing loudly on the same worn stone where dainty tiptoeing feet had gained the veranda steps." This act of public defilement that sees Turner urinating on white architectural splendor explicitly endorses racist stereotyping. For Styron, Turner is a man confined by a base physicality rather than a military leader possessing ideological control over his own body, let alone his men. As he fails to assert his own worth in preferred fantasies of whiteness—"How white I was!"—it is hard to believe in Styron's Turner's spiritual and philosophical convictions regarding the need for a race war to end slavery. Moreover, Styron's color symbolism betrays his endorsement of white exceptionalism, as black heroism repeatedly pales in the face of white martyrdom. For instance, he dramatizes his celebratory portrayal of masters such as Travis fighting for their freedom in the following language: "His gaunt work-worn face was the hue of his white night-shirt—but at last how brave he was!"[118] While the Turner/Gray *Confessions* had documented the white man's admiration for the Black man in spite of his racist beliefs over a century before—Gray admitted to Turner's "uncommon share of intelligence"—Styron's *Confessions* places undue emphasis upon the Black man's involuntary respect for, and inferiority to, the white man.[119]

Against this backdrop, Styron's subsequent emphasis upon Turner's new-found heroic identity as he galvanizes resistance among enslaved men lacks conviction. Resisting white bestial rhetoric in one speech, Styron's Turner claims, "You is *men*, brothers, *men* not beasts of the field! . . . Where oh where, my brothers, is yo' pride?" Yet readers remain uncertain regarding the extent of Turner's "pride," given Styron's focus upon his indulgences in an imagined whiteness, moments that are repeatedly followed by deflation: "my blackness immediately returned, the fantasy, dissolved." Clearly, his ability to sway black audiences—"My language was theirs, I spoke it as if it were a second tongue"—sits uneasily with his aping of white social mores.[120]

Despite the overwhelming praise awarded to Styron for this Pulitzer prize–winning novel, Black scholars and activists have amassed voluminous protests, some of which were published in 1968 in the essay collection *William Styron's Nat Turner: Ten Black Writers Respond*, reissued more recently as *The Second Crucifixion of Nat Turner* in 1997.[121] "I realized that *Nat Turner* was not, in this case, an aesthetic object but a political whipping boy," Styron conceded in response to these works.[122] However, his defensive view fails to engage with the genuine problems and widespread distortions of black history perpetuated not only by himself but by other white mainstream writers and artists. While Ernest Kaiser argues that "Styron cannot see Turner as the hero he was," for Alvin F. Poussaint, Styron's cultivation of a "white-worship language" meant that "Nat Turner didn't come out as some heroic character that you wanted to emulate."[123] As Lerone Bennett Jr. observes, "Styron has, in fact, replaced Thomas Gray, the author of the first *Confessions*, as Nat Turner's Last White Man."[124] Tellingly, Turner suffers from far more problematic distortion and silencing in Styron's work than he does as the Black heroic subject of his own and Gray's literary imagination. As Harding argues, "The man reported by Gray far overshadows the character created by Styron."[125] The most likely explanation for this inversion of power hierarchies arises from the fact that Turner played a key role in the earlier work. Ultimately, white-authored texts such as Styron's cause John Oliver Killens to despair, "Perhaps it is impossible for white Americans . . . to grant to the black man epic and heroic proportions."[126] "Nat Turner is a hero awaiting an interpreter equal to his heroic place in history," John Henrik Clarke similarly declares.[127]

A source of hope in the face of despair regarding white literary efforts, Daniel Panger's novel *Ol' Prophet Nat* was published contemporaneously with Styron's in 1967 and offers new possibilities regarding white memorializations of black heroism. Rejecting any pretensions toward panoramic comprehension, Panger's imagined first-person re-creation of Turner's voice directly exposes the difficulties facing any white writer determined to grapple with the complexities of his legendary status. Rather than an authoritative owner of black history, Panger's unnamed narrator is respectful and deferential, as revealed in his reaction to the anonymous Black taxi driver who first mentions Turner's name to him: *"I wanted to ask who Nat Turner was, but the way the man had said the name made me feel that my not knowing was a sign of ignorance."* In an explicit meditation upon the failures of white knowing, Panger's narrator engages in an imaginative process of historical recovery as illustrated by his discovery of Turner's Bible in a secondhand bookstore. "The ample margins of the page were choked with crabbed handwriting, half-faded, crowded, tiny, almost unreadable," he describes.[128] In forceful ways, therefore, Panger's dramatic emphasis upon the recovery of a fictional historical artifact engages thoughtfully with Turner's absent presences. Just as the unknown contemporary graffiti artist fought to editorialize white mainstream memorials, Panger reimagines Turner's words within the marginalia of a Bible in order to critique the racially circumscribed parameters of white Western Christianity. Destabilizing the authorizing power of a white narrative framework more generally, Panger experiments with a black text written in the margins of a historical artifact to generate "an ironic tension between the two portraits."[129] Thus, while Stone critiques Panger for representing Turner solely via "a portrait drawn in stark outline," his skeletal technique in fact has the potential to liberate alternative forms of black heroic reimagining.[130] Placing the onus upon the reader to read against the grain, Panger dramatizes Turner's legacy as possessing an alternative life away from the distorting records on offer in white racist archives.

Working within the tradition of a shackled Turner striving for a voice

PLATE 1. Jacob Lawrence, panel 10, "The cruelty of the planters toward the slaves drove the slaves to revolt," *Toussaint L'Ouverture* series, 1938. (Courtesy of the Amistad Research Center; © ARS, NY and DACS, London 2011)

PLATE 2. Jacob Lawrence, panel 19, "The Blacks formed into large bands and slaughtered every Mulatto and White they encountered," *Toussaint L'Ouverture* series, 1938. (Courtesy of the Amistad Research Center; © ARS, NY and DACS, London 2011)

PLATE 3. Jacob Lawrence, panel 20, "General Toussaint L'Ouverture, Statesman and military genius, esteemed by the Spaniards, feared by the English, dreaded by the French, hated by the planters, and reverenced by the Blacks," *Toussaint L'Ouverture* series, 1938. (Courtesy of the Amistad Research Center; © ARS, NY and DACS, London 2011)

PLATE 4. Malvin Gray Johnson, *Nat Turner*, 1934. (Art and Artifacts Division, Schomburg Center for Research in Black Culture, The New York Public Library, Astor, Lenox and Tilden Foundations)

PLATE 5. Anon., *Joseph Cinquez, Leader of the Gang of Negroes Who Killed Captain Ramon Ferrers and the Cook on Board the Spanish Schooner Amistad,* 1839. (Stanley-Whitman House, Farmington, Conn.)

PLATE 6. Nathaniel Jocelyn, *Joseph Cinque*, 1840.
(The New Haven Museum and Historical Society)

PLATE 7. Romare Bearden, *Prince Cinque,* 1971. (Prints and Photographs Division, Library of Congress, © Romare Bearden Foundation/ DACS, London/ VAGA, New York 2011)

PLATE 8. Charles White, *Five Great American Negroes*, 1939–40.
(© 1939–40 The Charles White Archives, Collection of Howard University Gallery of Art)

(*opposite*)

PLATE 9. Jacob Lawrence, panel 10, *Frederick Douglass* series, 1938–39.
(Courtesy of Hampton University Museum, Hampton, Va.; © ARS, NY and DACS, London 2011)

PLATE 10. Leroy Foster, *The Life and Times of Frederick Douglass*, 1973. (Detroit Public Library)

PLATE 11. Mike Alewitz, *Move or Die,* 1999. (Courtesy of Mike Alewitz)

PLATE 12. Jacob Lawrence, *Forward*, 1967.
(Courtesy of North Carolina Museum of Art; © ARS, NY and DACS, London 2011)

(*opposite*)
PLATE 13. Jacob Lawrence, panel 2, *Harriet Tubman* series (1939–40).
(Courtesy of Hampton University Museum, Hampton, Va.; © ARS, NY and
DACS, London 2011)

PLATE 14. Jacob Lawrence, panel 7, *Harriet Tubman* series (1939–40).
(Courtesy of Hampton University Museum, Hampton, Va.; © ARS, NY and DACS,
London 20011)

PLATE 15. William H. Johnson, *Harriet Tubman*, 1945.
(Smithsonian American Art Museum, Gift of the Harmon Foundation)

PLATE 16. Debra Priestly, *Strange Fruit 2*, 2001.
(Courtesy of Debra Priestly; photo by Becket Logan)

within Gray's no less than Styron's text, Panger explicitly denounces white failures of omniscience. *"Several of the words were smeared, and try as I might I could not decipher them,"* his narrator concedes. In contrast to Styron's Turner, therefore, a historical figure who remains imprisoned in a cage of whiteness born of his own construction, the heroic possibilities of Panger's Turner are positioned within a clear-cut tradition of diverse forms of black resistance. For Panger, exceptional feats of black male heroism are indivisible from anonymous acts of enslaved resistance. "I looked at the faces of the men and women and of the several boys who had fought as bravely as any man," his Turner explains.[131] For these reasons, Panger's construction of Turner represents a more fitting tribute to an ongoing black struggle for civil rights. He documents Turner as a Black heroic role model in intellectual and moral dialogue with his community rather than as a bathetic stereotype persecuted by white racist delusions and imaginary demons. The fact that Panger's is the forgotten novel and not Styron's, however, ultimately attests to Turner's historical and cultural legacies as more likely to capture a white mainstream imagination when characterized by a racist vilification of black masculinity.

However fraught with shifting complexities, Turner's memory remained powerful currency at the height of mid-twentieth century civil rights and Black Power movements. In "Dig on This," an anonymous article published in the *Black Panther* newspaper in 1967, the writer proclaims, "NAT TURNER . . . MARCUS GARVEY . . . DU BOIS . . . PAUL ROBESON . . . ROBERT WILLIAMS . . . MALCOLM. NO MORE! NO MORE!"[132] As a historical figure recuperated and reimagined as the founding father of black cultural, intellectual, and philosophical resistance, Turner has repeatedly signified as a point of origin for radical protest movements. As Larry Neal writes, "There is a tension throughout our communities. The ghosts of that tension are Nat Turner, Martin Delaney, Booker T. Washington, Frederick Douglass . . . and a whole panoply of mythical heroes."[133] Speaking in a New York radio address in 1969, at the height of black struggles for social rights, Kathleen Cleaver relies on Turner's legacies to condemn internalized racist structures. "We know that Nat Turner was not betrayed by crackers. He was betrayed by bootlicking, uncle tomming niggers. They must be dealt with in a revolutionary manner," she avows.[134] In this regard, Neal's sense of the "tension" within black communities can be usefully understood in the context of Cleaver's conviction as she radically came to grips with Turner's memory as a site of black ambivalence rather than unity. For Eldridge Cleaver, however, Turner operates less as a reflection of psychological fissures within Black communities than as an apocalyptic indictment of white injustices. "From the long heart-breaking days of slavery and the heroic uprising led by Nat Turner, down to the cold blooded murder of brother Fred Hampton in his sleep, our people's flesh and blood has been shed in an endless stream in a hopeless effort by our oppressor to drown our search for freedom and liberation," he insists.[135]

"Beginning a New Series: Search for a Black Past," Roger Butterfield's article published in *Life* magazine during the tumultuous year of 1968, adopts a very different approach to Turner's memorialization. While Butterfield's article includes painted and photographic reproductions of Douglass, Tubman, Pieh, and Truth, stark and uninhabited landscape photographs are all that testify to Turner's heroism. Captioned "Nathaniel Francis' house (right) where Nat's men killed five whites" and "The rebels brought a broadax to their clandestine meeting place," these photographs portray an arcadian idyll—cloudless blue skies, sandy yellow earth, and rich green vegetation. As works in which there is no sign of black humanity, these images reduce the mythic potency and political power of Turner's legacies to an impenetrable abstraction.[136] Existing beyond the pale of straightforward memorializations and in the face of painstaking representations of Louverture, Douglass, Tubman, Truth, and Pieh, Turner signifies as both myth and symbol, all the more haunting because of his scarcely tangible existences that reinforce the failure of white attempts at black heroic memorialization.

"L'ANGE NOIR": CATHERINE HERMARY-VIEILLE'S
NAT TURNER'S TRAGIC SEARCH FOR FREEDOM:
FROM DEPRIVATION TO VENGEANCE (2002)

"In memory of the more than one million African, men, women, and children, who, over the span of two centuries in the course of their journey from Africa to America, a journey that came to be known as the Middle Passage, died while enduring conditions so horrific as to be unimaginable." So reads Catherine Hermary-Vieille's dedication, in which she provides a powerful summary of the inhumanities of the transatlantic trade at the start of her novel *Nat Turner's Tragic Search for Freedom: From Deprivation to Vengeance.* Throughout this work, she emphasizes the failures of white official sites and sights of imagining by reinforcing the dramatic necessity of a politics and poetics of unknowing vis-à-vis black representation. First published as *L'ange Noir* (The black angel) in France in 1998, this novel was translated into

English by Robin Orr Bodkin and published with a new title by Trafford, a Canadian press, in 2002. Hermary-Vieille's preface invokes not only white American brutality but also European acts of atrocity by interpreting slavery as a global phenomenon. "The French, English, Dutch, and Portuguese perpetrated this crime against humanity to the benefit and gain of all the Americas," she states.[137] Hers is not an American South in isolation, therefore, as she reconfigures Turner's heroism as inextricable from a diasporic struggle for human rights.

"Whereas Styron's novel puts into play an idiosyncratic view of Nat Turner—a '"madman,'" Bodkin argues in his translator's note, "Hermary-Vieille's crisp French narrative ends up conveying an epic struggle that far exceeds the mere individuals or institutions of which it is comprised." Portraying Turner as a heroic figure working to overthrow transatlantic histories of white barbarity, Hermary-Vieille shares Kyle Baker's later preference for what Bodkin describes as "beginning at the beginning." As Bodkin writes, Hermary-Vieille's literary emphasis is upon a poetics of transatlantic identification. Bodkin observes that in Hermary-Vieille's novel, "the reader follows a painful journey that leads from deprivation to vengeance." In her precise narrative style, her "crystalline prose paints a vivid portrait" that "requires a keen eye on the part of the translator."[138] As a novel that has obtained such accolades as the *Prix Littéraire du Quartier Latin* just as "France commemorated its 150th anniversary of the end to slavery," this work memorializes Turner's heroism within a transatlantic framework explicitly to condemn white European inhumanity no less than white American barbarity. Yet any works testifying to a history of abolitionism rather than slavery raise the problematic specter of a desire, if not to clean up, then to simplify historical complexities by trading in linear narratives of white progress and black redemption. Considered in this light, Hermary-Vieille's recovery of Turner's heroism runs the risk of distorting, merely by simplifying, the untold atrocities of slavery.

In a stark departure from the key tropes proliferating across Nathaniel Turner's cultural legacies in the United States, Hermary-Vieille preempts Baker's later focus upon the enslaved hero's mother. She reimagines Turner's mother, Yodith, an entirely fictional character absent from historical accounts, as an exceptional fighter: "Everyone knew that no ferocious beast would ever get the best of Yodith without a fight to the death." Significantly, this militant rigor speaks to her determination to fight a white male slave trader as he forces her to board a slave ship in Africa. As she is bolstered by the "anger that was keeping her alive," his mother's experiences of physical violation inspire the narrator to applaud her militancy through rhetorical questioning: "What else did she have to fear?" For Hermary-Vieille, Yodith's subversive, multilayered acts encompass not only physical militancy but also cultural resistance as demonstrated via clothing, song, storytelling, spiritual prophecy, and rituals of food preparation. In contrast to Styron's, therefore, Hermary-Vieille's Turner does not emerge in a "near-vacuum" but with a pre-existing heritage and ancestry fully intact, as his mother provides a template for black heroism in her refusal to be complicit with her own violation.[139]

Just as Panger situates Turner's heroism within the context of a multifaceted tradition of African American resistance, Hermary-Vieille forges even stronger bonds by alluding indirectly to Toussaint Louverture's heroism. As one of the few writers to document the subversive networks of oral communication that existed among enslaved men and women, she is careful to dramatize the impression of an enslaved man, Noah, that "it was going to be up to black people to look after themselves just as they had done down in Santo Domingo." Shortly following this prophesy, Turner is born and his ancestral and pan-African context emphasized: "She [Yodith] would give birth at long last to the little man that her grandfather had always hoped for." More particularly, Hermary-Vieille traces the effect of Gabriel Prosser's thwarted rebellion upon Yodith shortly before Turner's birth, as "its failure really bothered her." Dramatizing an unequivocal militancy born of a pride in her African heritage, Yodith lays the foundations for Turner's heroism on the grounds that "no one would ever convince her that a black person's desire to be free was wrong or unlawful." At the same time, Hermary-Vieille exposes the limitations of black female resistance: "She could never break those bonds by herself, but Nat, her son who bore God's markings, would find a way to do it."[140] While offering a very daring revisionist narrative of this revolution by introducing black female radicalism to accounts of Turner's heroism, Hermary-Vieille nonetheless risks downplaying the protests of enslaved women in favor of feats of exceptional resistance as performed by enslaved men. While official statistics suggest that the majority of runaways were men, voluminous scholarship reveals that women played a fundamental role in protesting slavery not only by physical acts of rebellion but also by manipulating sexual politics, feigning pregnancy, poisoning food, committing arson, gaining literacy, and delivering speeches while escaping and assisting others to escape, as well as raising families within networks of social dissidence.

Bearing witness to a long legacy of suffering within the black community, Hermary-Vieille's novel reimagines Turner's father's punishment following his escape attempt as a key factor in Turner's own subsequent heroic self-construction. "As his [Turner's] eyes clung to his father's silhouette, his only other perception was the whistling sound of the whip cutting through the heavy air," she writes. Such a spectacle of black male victimization legitimates Turner's subsequent acts of violence by showing the extent to which it was learned by white example. Working to interrogate stereotyped notions of racial difference, hers is an archetypal, heroic construction of black activism, given that "Nat was pretty adamant when it came to the idea of leadership. The individual destined to guide his people would have to be pure of heart and deed." More particularly, Hermary-Vieille's decision to exalt in Turner's failure to "strike on the Fourth of July" crosses transatlantic borders to draw upon an explicitly black revolutionary heritage within the Caribbean. After Turner fails to stage the revolt to coincide with white American Independence, she dramatizes Turner's new date, "August twenty-second," as selected on the grounds that it was "when their Haitian brothers had revolted."[141] Thus she prefers not to focus upon Louverture's iconic heroism, aggrandizing instead the otherwise anonymous feats of transatlantic black resistance enacted by his "Haitian brothers."

Overall, Hermary-Vieille's reconstruction of Turner as an exceptional Black heroic figure results in a far less ambivalent text than Styron's novel. In compelling ways, she relies on aesthetic experimentation to interrogate both the politics and poetics of black representation and memorialization. Reimagining Turner as motivated by a desire to intervene in official distortions within the historical record, she emphasizes how "he just could not let white people continue to ignore or misrepresent his mission." Refusing to flinch from difficult questions, Hermary-Vieille dramatizes the complexities of black heroism through the individual perceptions of a Black shoemaker. He debates his guilt at the fact that he had not joined Turner's revolution by despairing, "What was the meaning of Nat's sacrifice?" "Would the poor man be remembered as nothing more than the incarnation of evil itself?" he speculates in an attempt to come to grips with Turner's ambivalent legacies.[142] In self-reflexive ways, Hermary-Vieille's novel offers a meditation upon the processes of black memorialization. And yet she provides self-reflexive dramatizations of Turner's multifaceted heroism to examine his mythological resonance across international contexts. If this novel warrants any criticism, however, it would be that Hermary-Vieille's construction of Turner shies away from some of the conflicts regarding black male heroism that lie at the heart of other more radical works, such as Baker's unequivocal graphic novel. In contrast to Styron, Hermary-Vieille endorses a white abolitionist paradigm by adhering to a teleology of black uplift via allusions to a diasporic heroic continuum whose origins lie not only in Africa but also in the Caribbean.

Significantly, Hermary-Vieille's novel was not the first attempt by a non-American-born author to reimagine Turner's rebellion. In 1978, Alfred Celestine was one of the first to do so in over a century, since the British novelist C. P. R. James memorialized Turner's heroism in his epic novel, *The Old Dominion; or, The Southampton Massacre*, published as early as 1856, excluding of course Harriet Beecher Stowe's *Dred: A Tale of the Great Dismal Swamp*, a work indebted to historical representations of Turner in its dramatizations of the enslaved visionary Dred. Published only a few decades ago, Celestine's poetry collection *The Confessions of Nat Turner* engages with the burden of commemoration by celebrating a multiplicity of perspectives. Repeated phrases such as "an unbearable memory" and a "slaughtered history" testify to the fact that both memory and history operate as sites of black violation in his work. Portraying Turner as a representative of elided histories, Celestine endorses an alternative politics and poetics of representation regarding black heroism. As his narrator proclaims, "The dead plunge their voices like needles / In my veins and speak through my blood." Such graphic imagery maps the corporeal onto the spiritual to reinforce the enduring significance of the bleeding and prostrate black body as both irrefutable proof and moral spectacle. Across his collection, his atemporal narratives elucidate Turner's collective symbolism, as his memory signifies beyond national, racial, and historical boundaries to speak to diasporic struggles. By reframing black violence as a site of haunting, Celestine urges his readers to engage in emotional, psychological, and historical acts of exorcism as the only way in which to secure the imaginative recovery of a black male heroism that cannot speak its name.[143]

VIOLENCE, HEROISM, AND AN EXPERIMENTAL VISUAL POETICS IN KYLE BAKER'S *NAT TURNER* (2008)

"Who was the man who was important enough to be mentioned in *all* the history books, yet is never spoken about at length?" asks Kyle Baker in the preface to his graphic novel *Nat Turner*, a work "dedicated to free people everywhere" and published in 2008. Signposting his dissatisfaction with the dominant political and cultural archive, he was outraged to discover a dearth of materials commemorating Turner's heroism. "I can go to a bookstore and find dozens of books about Harriet Tubman, Abraham Lincoln, or George

Washington Carver," he admits only to discover, "I may find one about Nat Turner."[144] Baker's recognition of the ways in which Turner has been both vilified and erased in favor of seemingly more mainstream and acceptable Black icons critiques the artificial polarizations of seemingly heroic versus antiheroic constructions of black historical identities. Overall, his text rejects racist paradigms according to which Turner's acts have been excessively demonized at the same time that even more mainstream figures such as Tubman have had their incendiary radicalism downplayed. Countering such omissions and distortions, Baker's experimental juxtapositions of text and image re-create and reimagine Turner as a symbol of cross-generational change for Black audiences. "He's one of my heroes, and he is a hero to all Black people," Baker insists, arguing, "When I was a kid, we didn't have any Black comic book heroes that were created by Black people for Black people."[145]

An avant-garde work, Baker's *Nat Turner* sets out to rectify these omissions by providing an in-depth dramatization of this historical figure's struggle for freedom. Furthermore, he explicitly draws parallels between black male heroism and the search for agency by Black artists. "In the tradition of my hero Nat Turner, I went out and found books about being a publisher," he writes.[146] "My books are published exactly as I've written and drawn them," Baker emphasizes. As a powerful declaration of independence, Baker's insistence upon the parallels between historic acts of heroism and the search for authorial control illuminates the ongoing insidious effects of white publishing constraints as they persist into the twenty-first century.[147] For Baker, Turner's heroism operates as a platform upon which he advocates black artistic autonomy via the right to ownership over his textual production. Thus his narrative strategy has much in common with William H. Johnson's determination to rely on self-portraiture in his constructions of Turner. Over seventy years previously, Johnson clearly set a precedent for the ways in which both the artist and the formerly enslaved rebel's personae would become politically and aesthetically merged. Baker's four-part structure, consisting of "Home," "Education," "Freedom," and "Triumph," testifies to his hybrid use of genre in this work. He signifies upon the ways in which many early Black writers had to engage with white mainstream conventions of the slave narrative in order to enter the marketplace and secure the moral conversion of their white audiences. Thus the skeletal outline of Baker's *Nat Turner* maps the trajectory of the classic slave narrative by dramatizing the importance of autobiographical origins; the acquisition of literacy; the liberation struggle; family dynamics; and, finally, an epiphanic coming to consciousness of the necessity of self-emancipation. In his opening image Baker portrays a pair of eyes suspended on an all-black background. Black hands clasp a white book, which emits glimmerings of light to symbolize the interpretative dynamics at work in the acts and arts of reading. By contrasting a white book with black hands, Baker's stark use of color symbolism critiques the ideological supremacy of whiteness and the racialized biases within official records. At the same time, his visual technique debates tensions between black visibility and hyperinvisibility as he dramatizes a black body suspended in nothingness. Thus he maps an educational and political imperative onto his experimental aesthetics in this work. Moreover, the black text of Baker's frontispiece lays a bold claim to authorship by typographically and pictorially juxtaposing "KYLE BAKER" with "NAT TURNER." Thus he insists upon providing a visual reenactment of his formal revision of white systems of knowledge throughout this work.

The ideological, philosophical, social, and historical forces at work in black male subjugation lie at the heart of Baker's subject matter. As he argues, "In my research I learned that this is accomplished by destroying the slave's mind." For Baker, Turner's militancy lies not in his acts of violence but in his intellectual resistance. "Nat Turner broke the law, learned to read and write, and the rest is history," he argues. Such a focus upon cultural resistance explains Baker's decision to preface his work with a visual depiction of a pair of disembodied eyes and hands as they pour over a white book while they are suspended in a black void. Deciding to fuse social responsibilities with moral instruction and aesthetic experimentation, Baker appeals directly to a young Black audience. "If a man in Nat Turner's circumstances was able to change history, imagine what you can do with the freedom you have today," he speculates.[148] Baker's *Nat Turner* investigates the extent to which Turner's memory remains taboo within official scholarship and popular representations. "I wanted to know how a person nobody wanted to talk about could be arguably one of the most important men in American history," he explains.[149] In his haunting and groundbreaking graphic novel, Baker combines historical testimony with aesthetic experimentation to create an imaginative retelling. His graphic novel brings this chapter full circle by overtly returning readers to the Turner/Gray *Confessions*. Other than brief excerpts from the *Memoir of Captain Theodore Canot: Twenty Years of an African Slaver,* the Turner/Gray work is the only other historical publication cited in this text. Just as Turner knowingly contested the white racist parameters of Gray's narrative frame, Baker's poetics riff not only off mainstream literary representations but also existing iconography as he adopts an experimental practice of visual quoting to powerful effect. As Leroy Douresseaux comments, "What makes

Nat Turner stand out as an exceptional work is the efficient and powerful use of visual language."[150] Consequently, Baker's aesthetic practice is characterized by messy and blurred surfaces as he provides an unsanitized vision of Turner's rebellion. Refusing to shy away from black acts of violence, he dramatizes black heroism as a necessity in light of widespread acts of white male barbarity. As Scott Cederlund notes, "Most of this book was created with ink and charcoal, giving a textured and physical presence to the book."[151]

Baker's aesthetic technique is compelling, fast-paced, and dramatic in this tour de force. Contrasting horizontal and vertical, full-, half- , and quarter-page images as well as etched-in foregrounds balanced against muted backgrounds, he juxtaposes internal and external realities to create dramatic tension and fracture narrative resolution. As difficult images that defy interpretation, his panels encourage emotive responses in their hard-hitting, unrelenting content. Adopting the same literary practice as Hermary-Vieille, Baker's first part, "Home," begins in a mythic Africa. Thus he locates Turner's origins in the heroism of his mother, who resists slavery by both violent self-defense and a suicide attempt.[152] One of the most forceful images in part 1 can therefore be found in Turner's mother's arrival on the west coast of Africa. Superimposing graphically drawn figures onto historical iconography, Baker's aesthetic technique is reminiscent of Carrie Mae Weems's experimentation with nineteenth-century daguerreotypes of Black men and women in her print series *From Here I Saw What Happened and I Cried* (1995–96).[153] In a stark full-page image, the naked body of Turner's mother appears in haunting silhouette as Baker powerfully accentuates her exaggerated facial profile and contorted limbs (see figure 7). She struggles against her chains while white hands are shown disappearing after having obviously just removed her scraps of gray clothing. Her body folds in upon itself, with knees bent together, legs outstretched, and breasts displayed in profile. Running no interpretative risks here, Baker quickly rejects any potentially victimized visions of Turner's mother, as the image that follows shows her engaged in violent self-defense, punching a white man with her foot. Fearlessly, she confronts the barrel of a gun, which is no less directed toward the reader as Baker insists on the necessity for audience empathetic identification.[154] Turner's mother is no "giggling" figure complicit in her own violation as portrayed by Styron. Instead, she bears witness to a black female incendiary activism that acts as a legitimate point of origin for Turner's protest. In this context, Baker's imaginative re-creation testifies to acts and arts of black female resistance that result not solely from necessity but also from deliberate design.

FIGURE 7. Kyle Baker, *Nat Turner,* 2008, p. 33. (*Nat Turner* © 2008, Kyle Baker; published by Harry N. Abrams, Inc., New York; all rights reserved)

According to Baker's imagining, only the slightest chink of white appears next to this black female's genitalia to accentuate overlapping concerns with the image in the background. Tellingly, the background of this drawing contributes to illusions of authenticity by providing a faithful re-creation of an early historical illustration showing the horrors of enslaved men and women paraded in coffles on their journey through the African interior. Baker adapts this image to suit his graphic novel by superimposing the silhouetted figure of Turner's mother onto this earlier work. Thus he collapses the horrors of the physical journey in the interior with those of the Middle Passage by including a historical illustration of a slave ship in the far distance. Just as the anonymous graffiti artist chose to deface the official Confederate memorial by etching "N.T. 11 11 31" onto its gray stone, Baker literally graffities over historical documents to counter their status as standard representational fare. In a daring move, he reinserts the realities of suffering black bodies into slavery's frequently cleaned-up images in order to create revisionist visual narratives, which he positions in fraught relation with dominant memorializations. Close-ups of body parts—fists, legs, faces—combine with enigmatic silhouettes and historical iconography to create a complex visual archive inspired by a determination to foreground black agency.

Baker encourages further recognition of the representative significance of Turner's mother's reimagined story by providing a series of visual quotations from yet other historical paintings. Variously depicting a slave ship hold, a slave revolt, and a group of enslaved men and women seated on board deck, these nineteenth-century historical images contribute to Baker's discordant tapestries, which blur the boundaries between iconic and anonymous enslaved histories. Across this work, he exposes a major flaw in the slave narrative genre, according to which a single author was burdened with the task of providing panoramic insights into seemingly representative experiences during slavery. The first part of Baker's *Nat Turner* reveals his mother bearing witness to the suffering of anonymous multitudes on slave ships via whippings, mutilation, infanticide, and scenes of dead black bodies eaten by vermin. She represents the point of origin for Turner's mythic memories as had even been conceded in the Turner/Gray text. In this regard, Baker introduces excerpts from the Turner/Gray *Confessions* to substantiate Turner's narration of events experienced before his birth.

Across his work, Baker eulogizes the transformative possibilities of black acts of storytelling once unloosened from their white narrative moorings. In this work, he provides a visual depiction of Turner talking to enslaved children while the wordless imagery of a speech balloon does not flinch from showing a black baby being fed to sharks at the same time that Turner's shocked mother bears witness to his narration (see figure 8). Baker represents Turner as a storyteller via a visual image rather than textual language as he illustrates his excerpts from the Turner/Gray *Confessions* by dramatizing a black silhouetted baby falling into the jaws of a white shark. In this way, he suggests that he is offering just one possible and imagined view of Turner's nineteenth-century insistence that the "Lord had shewn me things that had happened before my birth."[155] As Baker demonstrates, neither white historical documentation nor black folkloric memory can provide us with any idea as to what it was that Turner was "shewn." By juxtaposing text and image, Baker provides a montage of visual and literary quoting, not only to fracture any pretensions toward factuality, but also to endorse the mythical significance of Turner's own self-re-creations.

Baker's second part, "Education," explicitly situates Turner's fight for literacy within the context of black community resistance. In a shocking image, he portrays the horrific fate of an elderly enslaved man who is shown strung up and whipped as his hands are severed from his body as punishment for his incendiary drumming (see figure 9). Condemning white barbarity, he contrasts the "BOOM B-B-BOOM" of this enslaved man's drums with the "CLANG CLANG" of the white master class as they summon Black men and women to enslaved labor. Here, Baker celebrates diverse forms of black cultural resistance, as many opposed their suffering not only by playing the drums but also by engaging in song and the acquisition of literacy. Adhering to a haunting art of juxtaposition, Baker includes contrasting panels, one depicting a white child holding a black doll and surrounded by all the luxuries of wealth and another reimagining a young Turner contemplating childish drawings within an empty slave cabin.[156] Rejecting the sanitized histories of slavery as provided by official records and white popular reimaginings, Baker justifies Turner's revolution as emerging from a burning sense of injustice against atrocity.

As a testament to Baker's determination not to flinch from carnage, black and white violence takes dramatic center stage in part 3. An array of bleeding and mutilated body parts are brought to life by cacophonies of shading and angular lines, which enhance the realism of his subjects' musculature. Horrifyingly contorted and dying white bodies are shown with severed limbs and mangled clothing as they are strewn across domestic scenes of blood-smeared doors, broken paintings, turned-over furniture and rumpled beds. His starkly etched lines and powerful shading dramatize black militancy via bloodstained footprints as he provides a gothic reimagining of Douglass's

FROM THE CONFESSIONS OF NAT TURNER

"It is here necessary to relate this circumstance—trifling as it may seem, it was the commencement of that belief which has grown with time, and even now, sir, in this dungeon, helpless and forsaken as I am, I cannot divest myself of it. Being at play with other children, when three or four years old, I was telling them something which my mother, overhearing, said it had happened before I was born— I stuck to my story, however, and related some things which went, in her opinion, to confirm it—others being called on were greatly astonished, knowing that these things had happened, and caused them to say in my hearing, I surely would be a prophet, as the Lord had shown me things that had happened before my birth."

FIGURE 8. Kyle Baker, *Nat Turner,* 2008, p. 57. (*Nat Turner* © 2008, Kyle Baker; published by Harry N. Abrams, Inc., New York; all rights reserved)

FIGURE 9. Kyle Baker, *Nat Turner*, 2008, p. 65. (*Nat Turner* © 2008, Kyle Baker; published by Harry N. Abrams, Inc., New York; all rights reserved)

apocryphal words regarding slavery's bloody trail.[157] In a graphic departure from the majority of memorializations, however, Baker does not shy away from the horror of Turner's "confessions" as narrated to Gray. He illustrates the scene in which Gray's Turner explains, "There was a little infant sleeping in a cradle, that was forgotten, until we had left the house and gone some distance, when Henry and Will returned and killed it."[158] Here, Baker juxtaposes scant, controversial text with a haunting image providing a close-up of Turner's contemplative face. More powerfully still, Baker reinserts a missing context for this narration by providing a graphic image in which Turner remembers his futile fight to save his own children from the auction block, an incident that is nowhere to be found in the white historical records (see figure 10). Across this experimental work, Baker performs essential revisionist work. He reimagines the historical and social contexts of Turner's rebellion otherwise elided by racist omissions not only within the Turner/Gray text but also within official trial records and reward notices.

A later image depicting armed enslaved men marching through the undergrowth visually recalls Baker's earlier representations of a coffle in which enslaved men and women were shackled together. Thus he relies on repetition with variation vis-à-vis visual quoting in order to provide a powerful endorsement and justification for the spectacle of black violent resistance. No longer held captive, Black men walk in a military parade with uplifted firearms while white families lie broken and powerless. As a testament to ambiguities of historical representation and conflicts within memorialization, a heavier reliance on text with diminished snapshot illustrations characterizes this section of Baker's graphic novel.[159] These textual and visual sequences bear witness to an art of juxtaposed fragments that operate as touchstones for the whole. In various small images, he repeats parts of objects including a black fist holding an ax, blood spatterings, a sword, a severed white hand (a powerful visual contrast with the earlier severed black hands of the African drummer), a firing gun, prostrate white bodies, and reproductions of historical photographs showing the white households reprinted in Drewry's history. As Bill Sherman notes, Baker "effectively alternates large panels with tinier images to evoke the piecemeal violence of this disorderly rebellion."[160] This visual practice signifies upon the fragmented and distorted representations of black heroism within white mainstream histories. Baker thereby places the onus upon the reader to reject problematic sites of memorialization by engaging in acts of reimagining.

Startlingly, the image on the page facing the opening of part 4, "Triumph," revisits the iconography not of slavery but of twentieth-century lynching

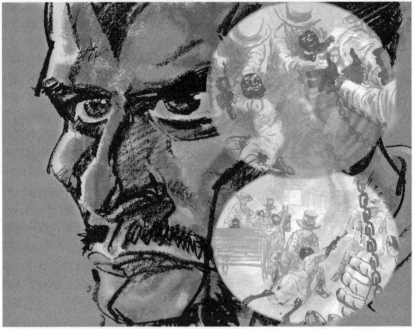

FIGURE 10. Kyle Baker, *Nat Turner,* 2008, p. 120. (*Nat Turner* © 2008, Kyle Baker; published by Harry N. Abrams, Inc., New York; all rights reserved)

photography by showing Turner's mutilated and faceless body hanging from a tree. However, Baker blurs temporal boundaries via the nineteenth-century clothing of the all-white spectators. As an apocryphal image, this work compounds the view that, for many, Turner's greatest significance lay in death rather than in life. However, Baker undermines any initial vicious glee as portrayed in the graphically contorted faces of his white witnesses by introducing existential uncertainty. Behind Turner's body, the clouds break into a sea of whiteness, while a bird flies into the air as if to suggest spiritual transcendence.[161] As Sherman notes, this "10-page wordless sequence depicting Turner's hanging . . . is a graphic tour-de-force."[162] But preferring not to end the book there, Baker ultimately juxtaposes Turner's resistance through death with the subversive act of an enslaved female who is shown as having stolen a copy of the Turner/Gray *Confessions*. As she disappears to read this work in the dark, Baker recalls his opening image, similarly showing disembodied eyes and hands as an anonymous individual reads a book in blackness. For Baker, even racist texts such as Gray's remain integral to the perpetuation of Turner's legendary mythology. A "cross-section of a slave ship, circa 1700s" appears as the final image of Baker's novel and offers a stark departure from his typically iconic representations of Turner's heroism. Baker's inclusion of this image visually reproducing the slave ship *Brookes* functions as metonymic shorthand for the Middle Passage and as a reminder not of exceptional but of anonymous heroism.[163]

Clearly, George Washington Williams's claim that "to every dealer in flesh and blood the 'Nat. Turner insurrection' was a stroke of poetic justice" provides an apt summary for Baker's dramatization of the multiple lives of this heroic leader.[164] Here, Baker relies on experimental techniques not only to situate Turner's memorializations beyond official white archives but also to engage with folkloric legacies proliferating within black oral culture. As one anonymous and undated song warned not long after the rebellion, Turner's was a superhuman power:

> You mought be rich as cream
> And drive your coach and four-horse team,
> But you can't keep de world from moverin' round
> Nor keep Nat Turner from gainin' ground.[165]

"No stone marks the resting-place of this martyr to freedom," George Washington Williams writes, observing that Turner's is a more visceral legacy: "The image of Nat. Turner is carved on the fleshy tablets of four million hearts."[166] Operating in powerful contrast to widespread memorializations of the heroic histories of Toussaint Louverture, Sengbe Pieh, Frederick Douglass, Harriet Tubman, and Sojourner Truth, Nathaniel Turner's legacy remains a far greater site of paradox and distortion. Repeatedly excised from official histories, his heroism has been commemorated in a diverse array of fictional adaptations and literary retellings as well as in black folkloric memories. As F. Roy Johnson argues, "Every aspect of 'Old Nat's War' or 'Nat's Fray,' as it usually was called was fought and re-fought, especially for the benefit of the young people and before almost every hearth-place." Such ongoing complexities of memorialization signify upon Turner's unfinished legacies and living histories. "The mark of the imaginative story teller," Johnson insists, "was left on most of the tales, and several devices to sharpen appeal—pathos, horror and novelty included—were utilized."[167] As Johnson explains, the role of the "imaginative storyteller" provides an indispensable way in which to debate the necessity for a creative engagement among scholars, no less than members of the community, even to begin to capture the emotional and symbolic intricacies of Turner's historical paradoxes.

For Malcolm X, emerging prominently in the mid-twentieth century, Turner's legacy proved an inspirational catalyst. During his period of imprisonment, Malcolm X experienced an epiphany as he discovered reading—"I had never been so truly free in my life"—only to experience disappointment in a haunting realization that "when white men had written history books, the black man simply had been left out." In the face of widespread black victimization, however, he found hope in Turner's warfare by celebrating the fact that "Nat Turner wasn't going around preaching pie-in-the-sky and 'nonviolent' freedom for the black man."[168] Perhaps more surprisingly, Turner's memory equally endures as a source of empowerment within a twentieth-century black female literary tradition. Writing in her first autobiography, *I Know Why the Caged Bird Sings,* Maya Angelou invokes Turner's resistance as a bulwark against white male attempts to violate black history. In describing her high school graduation, she indicts white speakers for their denial of black humanity in oratorical performances calculated to reduce the identities of their academic audiences to "maids and farmers, handymen and washerwomen." As she observes, "Then I wished that Gabriel Prosser and

Nat Turner had killed all whitefolks in their beds."[169] Tellingly, Angelou's apocalyptic vision of the ideological necessity of a race war rejects centuries of black annihilation by recuperating Turner as a quintessential freedom fighter.

A desire to come closer to Turner by following in his footsteps has a no less palpable resonance with twenty-first-century members of the Black Liberation Army. As recently as January 2009, on the night of President Barack Obama's inauguration, they reenacted Turner's journey. They also continue to organize "Nat Turner Trail Tours," which they describe as "a regular tour by the Authors to the 'battle sites' during the revolt by Nat Turner and the Black Liberation Army of 1831." More particularly, Alexis Joyner, H. Khalif Khalifah, and James Magee express the hope that "perhaps we'll be able to obtain something to pass on that may serve to motivate the Black youth of today to commit themselves to a life of struggle to free Black people as did Nat Turner."[170] For Lerone Bennett Jr. and other Black radicals, Nathaniel Turner's body and memory remain a site of reusable heroism. Across the centuries, Turner has become renowned as the "prototype of twentieth century revolutionaries," as his legacies continue to be mapped onto the struggles for black rights in the contemporary era. And yet widespread resentment endures, as Turner remains a "black slave who has not yet received his due in history" and "the gaping wound he opened still runs."[171] Such an emphasis upon the necessity of imaginative re-creation gets to the heart of the matter regarding ongoing mythologies and lacunae in memorializations of Nathaniel Turner. Henry Louis Gates Jr.'s speculation that "there is no Nat Turner back there whole to be retrieved" and "you would have to go and create Nat Turner" remains integral to the imaginative recovery not only of Nathaniel Turner but also of Toussaint Louverture, Sojourner Truth, Harriet Tubman, and above all, the Sierra Leonean–born leader of the *Amistad* rebellion, Sengbe Pieh.[172]

CHAPTER 3 "NO RIGHT TO BE A HERO"

SENGBE PIEH, RESISTANCE, REPRESENTATION,

AND THE POLITICS OF SEEING

"To commemorate the heroism of the Amistad Africans and those who shared in their quest for freedom, [in] 1989 [the] Amistad Committee commissioned this sculpture by Ed Hamilton and dedicated it on September 26 1992." So reads the stone lettering incised on the granite base of the African American artist Ed Hamilton's bronze monument commemorating the heroism of Sengbe Pieh and the *Amistad* Africans (figure 11). The memorial stands in New Haven, Connecticut, the city in which these enslaved individuals were put on trial for "mutiny and murder." Adopting a tripartite structure, as Hamilton explains, "The memorial deals with the three phases of the Amistad Incident. The first side depicts Sengbe Pieh in Africa before he and the other Africans were kidnapped. The backside is a scene of the courtroom trial. The third side is Cinque ready to board the ship, *The Gentleman,* back to his homeland."[1] In the same way that the contemporary replica of the *Amistad* currently traveling around the globe has been designed as a "floating history museum," Hamilton's memorial similarly possesses an educational imperative. Dedicated to raising his viewers' awareness not only regarding the realities of black resistance but also of the atrocities of slavery, his forceful work dramatizes black male heroism as inextricable from the horrors of the Middle Passage. Thus he relies on the symbolic inclusion of "the prow of a ship" as the structuring backdrop to his three vignettes.[2]

More powerfully still, he refuses to shy away from the ways in which even radical memorials fall far short in their attempts to capture the dramatizations enacted by the transatlantic slave trade. Repeatedly, Hamilton juxtaposes iconic with unknown forms of heroism in order to foreground the difficulties of black memorialization. Across his panels, the diminutive yet anonymous bodies of enslaved Africans haunt the background of his large-scale representations of Sengbe Pieh's exceptionalism. Barely individualized, these Black men and women appear as part of the backdrop to insist upon Pieh's collective responsibility as well as his symbolic and cultural resonance within a diasporic imaginary. Their presence speaks to the overwhelming absence of the *Amistad* Africans, not only within the images produced in the

FIGURE 11. Ed Hamilton, *Amistad Memorial*, 1992. (Courtesy of Helen Bralesford)

immediate aftermath of the event, but also in the subsequent visual archive. Rendering his protest yet more visceral, Hamilton also includes a very different fourth panel, which he inserts on the top of this monument as a compelling tour de force. Here, he makes his protest against any pretensions toward exalting in an exceptional black heroic paradigm even more clear by undertaking an act of "guerilla memorialization," as recently theorized by Alan Rice.[3]

"The top of the Memorial is a result of the emotional level of my personal experiences researching for information about slave trading," Hamilton explains. "It depicts the body parts of Africans who were thrown or jumped overboard from slave ships."[4] "Could this be our brother, Foone, who drowned in the Farmington Canal? Or, you could say that this figure, awash in the vastness of an ocean, represents the souls of the many Africans who did not finish *their* journey of the Middle Passage," he speculates. As an emotionally charged vignette that relies heavily upon abstraction to signify upon the failures of seeing, Hamilton's fourth panel vouches for the unimaginable horror of the slave trade. As depicted here, the anonymity of mass suffering far outweighs any redemptive possibilities on offer within seemingly uplifting reimaginings of black iconic heroism. Dense textures of engulfing waves combine with stray limbs to communicate the torture and pain of black bodies torn apart by the Middle Passage. More particularly, the bony fingers of a floating severed hand repeat with variation Hamilton's construction of Pieh's own hand on the panels beneath, as if to challenge the redemptive catharsis suggested by reductive representations of his heroism. Yet the fact that this section is solely on view for those standing above the memorial is revealing. "From the second floor of City Hall, you look down and contemplate this final view of the Memorial," Hamilton emphasizes. Visible only to those occupying an official authoritative space in city hall, Hamilton's final panel condemns and critiques the emotional possibilities of institutionalized sites of memory. The fact that this is a history that remains invisible to viewers on the ground ensures that it is ultimately only the epic vision of Pieh as an aggrandized and heroic ex-enslaved man that dominates the public face of this memorial. And therein lies the crux of the problem regarding historic and contemporary memorializations of the *Amistad* rebellion: however demonized and vilified, Sengbe Pieh remains the sole catalyst to commemoration.

Scarcely less than a decade following Nathaniel Turner's legendary challenge to white power in the American South, the Sierra Leonean–born leader of the *Amistad* slave ship rebellion of 1839, Sengbe Pieh became a no less shifting yet scarcely tangible figure within African, African American, and European American memory. As Frederick Dalzell writes, "Cinque was more than flesh and blood," signifying instead as an ambiguous "icon, a figure embodying powerful, sometimes contradictory symbols and meanings."[5] As Hamilton cautions, however much he shook the foundations of transatlantic slavery to their very core, Pieh's heroism must nonetheless be remembered against a powerful backdrop of the lost legacies of the "sixty million and more" enslaved women, men, and children who lived and died during the Middle Passage.[6] One in a million, he rewrote history by reentering the "Door of No Return." Disembarking in chains from the European slaver *Amistad* onto the shores of the United States, Pieh returned to Africa a free man following his dramatic execution of a successful slave ship rebellion. After zigzagging up the eastern coastline of the United States in thwarted attempts to redirect the ship back home following their subjugation of the white crew, this African leader and his followers were incarcerated by white authorities at New Haven, Connecticut. As legal battles raged over the following two years, Sengbe Pieh became a cause célèbre for the *Amistad* Africans' heroism. In contrast to Ed Hamilton's determination to use the *Amistad* to memorialize the untold histories of enslaved men, women, and children forcibly enslaved during the Middle Passage, for the majority of writers and artists Pieh's example remains the dominant, iconic touchstone for black heroism.

Vastly different from the problematic representations not only of Nathaniel Turner but also of Toussaint Louverture, Harriet Tubman, Frederick Douglass, and Sojourner Truth that circulated within dominant white discourse and iconography in the United States, Sengbe Pieh's memory exists in an alternative ideological space to traditions of African American or African Caribbean heroisms. As recuperated and reimagined according to a clearly delineated, if repeatedly misunderstood and mythologized Africanity, Pieh offered compelling new possibilities for nineteenth-century radical U.S. antislavery sympathizers. For the majority of the white abolitionists who exalted in Pieh's political possibilities, the fact that he spoke an unknown language and was of an entirely different national origin was a distinct advantage. Refusing to shy away from but accentuating his status as an exaggerated spectacle of racial otherness, they were seemingly free to reconstruct his identity as unproblematically heroic. Thus, in contrast to Louverture, who was denigrated in atrocity literatures, Pieh was unknown terrain, both a tabula rasa and terra incognita of black exceptionalism and activism. Similarly, as a seemingly pure African who was not of mixed-race descent—a problem confronting Douglass and arguably even Turner, as he was repeatedly described as being of "bright" complexion in the official historical record—Pieh's status as a freedom fighter existed in an alternative ideological framework to ex-enslaved African Americans engaged in militant resistance on U.S. soil. In this regard, the privileging of a fixed, othered, and excessively sensationalized Africanity for Sengbe Pieh functions in the white North American imaginary as a displaced forum within which to denounce the injustices of the white trade in black bodies and to begin to countenance the ideological realities of black violence. Such a possible freedom of representation was ultimately off limits to Louverture, as Haiti was much closer to home. In the decades following the Haitian revolution, white planter refugees poured into the American South and caused a furor by telling sensational tales in which Louverture figured as an embodiment of a hyperblack masculine barbarity.

Both Iyunolu Osagie and Marcus Rediker address key issues regarding competing constructions of Pieh's Africanity in their pioneering scholarship in this vastly neglected area.[7] Clearly, black male revolutionary heroism as enacted by a Sierra Leonean who led a successful slave ship rebellion after which he returned to Africa was very different from black male revolutionary heroism as endorsed by African American men or women who had been or were enslaved fugitives destined never to settle away from the American mainland. In contrast to Harriet Tubman and Frederick Douglass, for whom reward notices were posted in order to secure their recapture, and Sojourner Truth, whose former master sought her out following her escape, Pieh's regained freedom did not represent a loss of American property. As we see with kaleidoscopic representations of Douglass, Truth, and Tubman, the position of the African American former enslaved man or woman repeatedly necessitated an agonized and ambiguous reconstruction of multifarious and often conflicting identities when it came to definitions of black heroism. Thus it is no exaggeration to state that acts and arts of African American male and female heroism are clearly made unstable by the very existence of Pieh and even of Louverture. The very fact of Pieh's Africanity—however mythologically constructed—worked in ways similar to Louverture's African Caribbean origins paradoxically to accentuate national and racial differences and ensure that both icons were conceptualized and reimagined not only within but beyond the boundaries of a white American revolutionary idealism. Consistently othered and clearly never able to become an American, in contrast to Tubman, Truth, Turner, and Douglass, Pieh posed even less danger than Louverture either to the racist hierarchies of white American society or to dominant national ideologies.

Across the centuries, multifaceted representations of Sengbe Pieh have appeared in newspaper accounts and across various works including wax models, panoramas, public lectures, diagrams, poetry, painting, sculpture, monuments, quilts, dramas, novels, film, murals, theatrical reenactments, and street art. These works attest to Pieh's cultural significance and the necessity of engaging in imaginative reconstruction in order to recover any more than the bare bones of his heroism. In the same way that Nathaniel Turner's face and body remain sites of virulent contestation, debates continue to rage concerning not only Sengbe Pieh's African identity but also his use of language and his physicality. Even his name has become a transatlantic battleground in the light of African, Spanish, and Anglican influences. In the contemporary era, many scholars and artists have finally settled upon the Sierra Leonean name Sengbe Pieh in recognition of his Mende origins. In just the same way that memorializations of Turner may elide at the same time that they operate as a substitute for the anonymous heroism of his fellow enslaved liberators granted no record in official archives, Pieh's iconic status runs the risk of displacing the hidden histories of his fellow freedom fighters equally engaged in incendiary activism. As with Turner, strategies of black commemoration frequently inscribe the art of forgetting within the act of remembering. Such historical oversights remain symptomatic of a general tendency to misinterpret, if not outright reject, black incendiary activism.

"Although the Amistad case is well documented and was widely known in the nineteenth century," Osagie writes, "it has until recently been largely ignored."[8] Controversies are therefore ongoing regarding representations of Sengbe Pieh not only in paintings and drawings by white artists such as Nathaniel Jocelyn and John Barber but also in anonymously produced illustrations, scientific diagrams, and newspaper reportage as disseminated to eager audiences throughout the period. Such an outpouring of contradictory images underscores Dalzell's conviction that "we have little to work with to reconstruct his biography."[9] In this regard, it is necessary to account for my decision to focus upon nineteenth-century illustrations and newspaper coverage in this book rather than the literary adaptations partly inspired by this revolt, such as Herman Melville's extensively examined Benito Cereno, published in 1855. I work with the view that the visual materials and reportage purporting to historical accuracy and characterized by fragmented disjuncture, rather than fictional restructuring, have the potential to illuminate the politics and poetics of black representation in specific ways. While Black heroic figures such as Artufal, who paces the deck in performative chains in Melville's novella, are undoubtedly inspired by Sengbe Pieh, these and other literary representations are so mediated as to have become symbolically distinct from original investigations alleging to be based on eyewitness testimony. Self-reflexive commentary regarding the difficulties of remembering and recovering black male heroism is far more an overt feature of reports published in the wake of this slave ship mutiny than it is of explicitly imaginary narratives. Overall, while I am indebted to Osagie's determination to examine the "Amistad story as an interdisciplinary text," it is useful to narrow her interpretative frame to analyze Sengbe Pieh himself as an "interdisciplinary text."[10] Signifying across literary, filmic, visual, and historical representations, as Richard Powell writes, Pieh "seems to have almost immediately entered American folklore." For Howard Jones, Pieh has "become a black folk hero," while James Oliver and Lois Horton similarly argue that Sengbe Pieh functions as a "symbol of black manhood."[11] Across the centuries, his Sierra Leonean ancestry clearly functions in problematic ways as a metonymic shorthand for the continent as a whole. Simultaneously, Pieh signifies as part symbol, part folkloric figure, part icon, and even part historical embodiment of multiple constructions of a mythic and reimagined Africa.

"THE HERO OF THIS BLOODY TRAGEDY": SENGBE PIEH AND SYMBOLIC REIMAGINING IN FINE ART PORTRAITURE AND SCIENTIFIC ILLUSTRATION

"Ultimately, the battle for the Amistad prisoners' freedom was bound up with the image projected of them," Robin Kelley argues. As he explains, the role of Black and white abolitionists was to challenge those who "had difficulty seeing black people as anything else but Coons, Sambos, and savages unfit for liberty."[12] As the plethora of mass-market and high-art texts and artifacts memorializing the *Amistad* demonstrates, Black and white artists and writers transgress the boundaries of aesthetic experimentation to create symbolic reimaginings rather than stereotypical representations of Sengbe Pieh. The various works produced within an antislavery context include an array of critically neglected newspaper illustrations, a phrenological diagram, a series of woodcuts by the white campaigner John W. Barber to accompany his tract *History of the Amistad Captives,* and, broadening into high-art portraiture, the white artist Nathaniel Jocelyn's famous painting *Joseph Cinque.* As Powell observes, these works "fueled an already-established market for abolitionist imagery."[13] Preferring to memorialize epic and heroic rather than bathetic and antiheroic representations of Sengbe Pieh, these artists and writers countered racist depictions proliferating in proslavery reports, cartoons, and tracts. The very existence of these multifaceted portraits complicates Jones's view that Pieh was solely interpreted as "a romanticized figure."[14]

Joseph Cinquez, Leader of the gang of Negroes who killed Captain Ramon Ferrers and the Cook on board the Spanish Schooner Amistad, an anonymous drawing, appeared in 1839 and is prominent among these early illustrations (plate 5). On first glance, Pieh appears as a solitary, seemingly "romanti-cized" figure standing on the deck of the *Amistad*. Fully clothed in white trousers and a red shirt, Pieh initially functions as a representative icon of an exceptional black masculinity according to standardized models of white civilization. The unknown artist plays with notions of black male physical objectification and eroticized difference to accentuate his essentialized oth-erness, visualizing an idealized representation of Pieh problematically to detach his portrayal from bathetic associations with a seemingly indistin-guishable "gang of Negroes." And yet, in forceful ways, the artist also trans-gresses ideologically fraught boundaries between savagery and civilization in order to interrogate stereotyped representations of black physicality. The detailed depiction of Pieh's physiognomy, as he stands fully erect rather than on his knees begging for mercy or engaged in mutinous conduct, highlights his delicate eyes, nose, mouth, and strong chin to draw attention to his con-templative gaze. The illustrator thereby radically contrasts Pieh's detailed physiognomy with the barely distinguishable contours of his hands as if to celebrate black intellectualism over and above physical prowess. At the same time, however, still starker contradictions emerge from the inclusion of sym-bolic details. Pieh's right hand rests on a machete that itself stands on a piece of wood, possibly included to symbolize the auction block. Boldly signify-ing black violence and resistance, this artist references an auction block on a slave ship to condemn the U.S. internal trade no less than the international traffic in enslaved peoples. The image relies on exhaustive details regarding the ship's rigging metonymically to reference the transatlantic trade and the en-masse deportation of black bodies during the Middle Passage.

"JOSEPH CINQUEZ, the brave Congolese chief, who prefers death to Slav-ery, and who now lies in Jail in Irons at New Haven Conn. awaiting his trial for daring for freedom." So reads the caption accompanying James Sheffield's lithograph that circulated immediately after the rebellion in 1839 (figure 12). Adopting an overtly antislavery perspective, he eulogizes black difference to celebrate the *Amistad* rebellion as an African liberation struggle. According to Elizabeth Alexander, Sheffield "drew illustrations of Cinque to accompany news articles, reportedly while the African was chained on deck."[15] Yet no chains appear in this image. Instead, Sheffield foregrounds ambiguities of black heroic representation by portraying only Pieh's head and upper body. His clothing consists of a smudged white garment, the tonal variations of which reinforce the pale shading of his otherwise dark-skinned face and neck. Sheffield's decision to include only Pieh's face and upper body further intensifies his portrait by focusing the viewer's attention upon his detailed physiognomy. Pieh's emotionally charged facial expression confronts the viewer as if to insist on white moral conversion to antislavery activism. A reporter writing at the time described it as a "most accurate likeness."[16] Not flinching from psychological ambiguity, Sheffield's image ultimately exalts in individualized constructions of a psychologically complex black subjectivity.

More tellingly still, this illustration bears witness to Sheffield's dissatisfaction with the power of visual iconography in isolation. It can be situated within the tradition of slave narrative frontispieces, as it accompanies a purported reproduction of Sengbe Pieh's "Speech to His Comrade Slaves after Murdering the Captain & C. and Getting Possession of the Vessel and Cargo." As Maggie Sale argues, the difficulties of translation between Mende and English make it unlikely that this speech has any basis in fact. Regardless of its inaccuracies, perhaps the aim of this textual excerpt was solely to minimize difference by "Americanizing" Pieh's "Africanized" feats of resistance. According to Sheffield's caption, Pieh delivered the following speech to his fellow enslaved Africans:

> Brothers, we have done that which we purposed, our hands are now clean for we have Striven to regain the precious heritage we received from our fathers. We have only to persevere. Where the Sun rises there is our home, our brothers, our fathers. Do not seek to defeat my orders, if so I shall sacrifice any one who would endanger the rest.[17]

Celebrating overt references to his African heritage, family relationships, and the grisly necessities of war, Pieh's purported speech cultivates explicit parallels between black heroism and the rhetoric undergirding idealized reimaginings of a white American national pursuit of equal rights.

The rallying cry of the white founding father Patrick Henry, "Give me liberty or give me death," reverberates across Pieh's speech as if to contextualize his revolutionary fervor and desire for a new society according to egalitarian principles. In this regard, Pieh's determination, "Brothers, I am resolved that it is better to die than be a white man's slave," resonates with the typical use made by African American abolitionists of a white heroic paradigm. Moreover, this speech can be easily situated within an African American heroic tradition in light of the ways in which Pieh's determination not to flinch from the necessity of black sacrifice as conjoined to militancy resonates with the philosophy of Black U.S.-born radicals such as Harriet Tubman. During her liberation raids from the South, she repeatedly urged enslaved men and women to "Go on or die." Equally, Pieh's protection of a "precious heritage" harks back to Nathaniel Turner's sense of the necessity of an apocalyptic

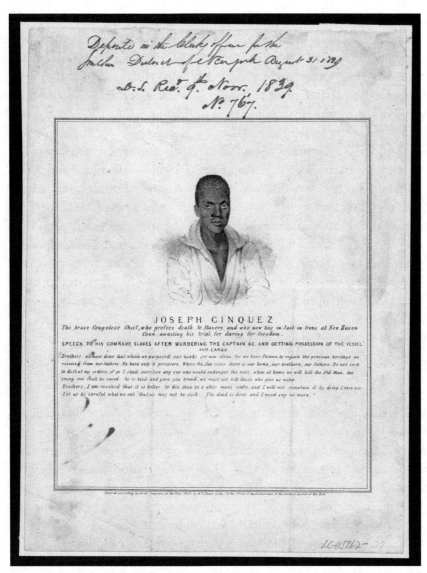

FIGURE 12. James Sheffield, *Joseph Cinquez, the Brave Congolese Chief, Who Prefers Death to Slavery,* 1839. (Prints and Photographs Division, Library of Congress)

cleansing emerging from his understanding of the importance of black ancestral legacies.

John Childs's starkly contrasting lithograph *Joseph Cinque Addressing His Compatriots on Board the Spanish Schooner, Amistad, 26 Aug 1839* was also printed in 1839 (see figure 13). As one of the few images to dramatize Sengbe Pieh alongside the other enslaved *Amistad* Africans, the immediate context of the mutiny is unmistakable in this work. Childs not only depicts the slave ship itself but also dramatizes Pieh as surrounded by enslaved women, men, and children in various attitudes of rapt attention. In contrast to the patterned and improvised clothing of the surviving enslaved men and women, however, Pieh's white attire underscores his exceptionalism. Adopting the guise of the storyteller or preacher in Childs's work, he cultivates the role of a visionary by refusing to maintain eye contact with his Black audience. Instead, Child accentuates not only his griot but also his spiritual, seer-like status by portraying Pieh as gesturing upward with his right hand and downward with his left, providing a symbolic reenactment of the cross. Rather than including a machete to symbolize black agency, here Childs's detailed representation of Pieh's hands aggrandizes linguistic and oratorical prowess over and above feats of physical resistance. On the surface, Childs replicates white abolitionist tendencies toward editorializing black testimony as in the slave narrative genre. He problematically legitimizes his dominant narrative of black heroism by including white sailors and officials as witnesses among Pieh's audience. Yet Childs' aesthetic ultimately complicates such straightforward readings. Relying on formal juxtaposition, he includes mirrored forms of white and black masculinity to provide a radical endorsement of equality. Thus Pieh's erect figure can be understood as reflecting an almost identical pose to that of an unknown white official standing beside him and attired in military clothing. Acting as an interpretative guide for the audience in this work, the white official looks on in admiration and works to establish Pieh's superiority by suggesting that his oratorical prowess was successful in securing at least this white man's moral conversion. Equally, while the facial features of the other enslaved figures either verge on caricature or are scarcely discernible, Pieh's physiognomy is clearly defined, as Childs works against white tendencies toward black dehumanization.

Scarcely a year later, John Warner Barber published *A History of the Amistad Captives,* a pamphlet intended as a dramatic vindication of black male heroism. Yet the comparative lack of any individualized depictions of black bodies in the militant drawing of the frontispiece—*Death of Capt. Ferrer, the Captain of the Amistad*—recalls Warner's *Horrid Massacre in Virginia* by dramatizing anonymous enslaved Africans engaged in violent resistance. However, an African standing in the background who bears witness to the revolt while wearing a toga-style white cloth is easy to miss. Opening up an interpretative space between the viewer and the spectacle of black male violence, he possesses an elevated status over the mass of homogenously portrayed Africans. His individualized physiognomy reinforces his iconic status

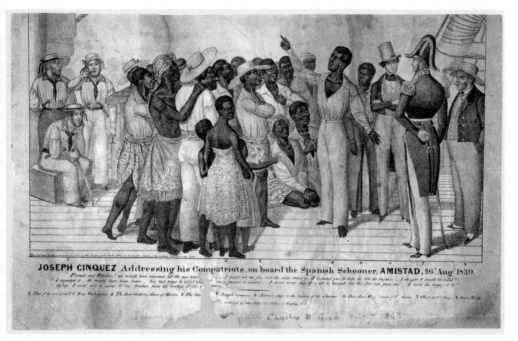

FIGURE 13. John Childs, *Joseph Cinque Addressing His Compatriots on Board the Spanish Schooner, Amistad*, 1839. (Chicago History Museum)

to suggest his resemblance to the mythologized Sengbe Pieh as re-created within a U.S. abolitionist imagination and as symbolically divorced from reductive emphases upon physical militancy. Clearly, Barber's preference was not for a vengeful Pieh but for Pieh as a martyred heroic leader.

Supporting this view, Barber includes an illustration in which he portrays a group of enslaved men crammed into a slave ship (see figure 14). The caption reads, "The above engraving shows the position as described by Cingue and his companions, in which they were confined on board the slaver, during their passage from Africa."[18] Powerfully titled *3 Feet 3 In. High,* Barber's carefully delineated rows of shackled feet accentuate the anonymity communicated by his decision to exhibit the enslaved men's faces only in profile. In this way, he captures the dehumanizing violations enacted upon black bodies and described by the ex–slave trader John Newton as a process by which they were packed "like books upon a shelf."[19] Excluding any individualized human subjects purporting to represent Sengbe Pieh—perhaps with the exception of the figure on the far right, whose eyes, nose, and mouth are depicted in more detail—Barber testifies to the anonymity of mass suffering to expose the atrocities of the Middle Passage. As these various nineteenth-century images show, Barber, Childs, and many other writers and artists were caught in a double bind. Faced with the difficulties of reconstructing iconic versus anonymous forms of black heroism, they oscillated between endorsing and challenging the extent to which Pieh functioned as a symbol for elided enslaved histories.

Complicating any tendencies toward providing a solitary dramatization of Pieh, Barber's individualized series of silhouetted portraits purport to represent the *Amistad* Africans. Tellingly, however, this sequence begins with a profiled view of Pieh to which Barber appends the following brief biography (figure 15):

> (1.) SING-GUE [Cin-gue] (generally spelt *Cinquez*), was born in Ma-ni, in Dzho-poa, *i.e.* in *the open land,* in the Men-di country. The distance from Mani to Lomboko, he says, is ten suns, or days. His mother is dead, and he lived with his father. He has a wife and three children, one son and two daughters. His son's name is *Ge-waw,* (God.). His king, Ka-lum-bo, lived at Kaw-men-di, a large town in the Mendi country. He is a planter of rice, and never owned or sold slaves. He was seized by four men, when traveling in the road, and his right hand tied to his neck.[20]

A lack of imaginative detail combines with exaggerated pretensions to scientific accuracy to suggest parallels between this spartan work and diagrammatic representations ostensibly providing an authentic reproduction of Pieh's physiognomy. Barber's detailed portrayal of black facial features is likely to have originated in some form of factual accuracy. As he explains, they were "taken by a pentagraph from the wax figures now exhibiting through the country," which he and various others in the press at the time describe as providing "striking and accurate likenesses of the Africans."[21] Yet Barber's profiled view of Sengbe Pieh ultimately exhibits tendencies toward caricature in its lack of detail, which contrasts with the anatomically in-depth representations of Pieh's physiognomy provided by other illustrators. Probe deeper, however, and the textured detail of his hair and ambiguity of his solemn expression, as communicated by his meticulously delineated eyes and closed mouth, begin to suggest psychological and moral complexities.

Clearly, Barber's Sengbe Pieh is an understated representation in comparison with the next image, "No. 2," titled "GI-LA-BA-RU, [Gra-beau] *have mercy on me,*" a work in which his emphasis upon this enslaved man's moustache and goatee risks exoticizing black difference and thereby minimizing psychological depth.[22] Furthermore, the pseudoscientific approach to defining Pieh's name masquerades as dictionary terminology as if to reflect upon

FIGURE 14. John Barber, *3 Feet 3 In. High,* from *A History of the Amistad Captives* (New Haven, CT: E. L. and J. W. Barber, 1840). (Documenting the American South, University of North Carolina, Chapel Hill)

white enlightenment attempts to quantify and define black male heroism according to an illusory search for linguistic and physical fixity. Such a sparse biography signifies as a miniaturized slave narrative by stimulating the emotional projection of his audiences via cathartic reimaginings designed to defy lacunae within the historical record. While Sidney Kaplan commends Barber's work for the "full treatment given to the characters and histories of the mutineers as unique human beings and Africans," these visual illustrations succeed because they are anything but "full."[23] Clearly, Barber's silhouetted forms encourage imaginative engagement by foregrounding absence rather than presence as he provides seemingly verifiable yet curiously insubstantial representations of black masculinity.

More particularly, similarities can be traced between Barber's profiled view of Pieh and the line drawing created by the white scientist L. N. Fowler to accompany his article "Phrenological Developments of Joseph Cinquez, Alias Giingqua," published in the *American Phrenological Journal and Miscellany* in the same year. As Fowler told eager white audiences, he visited Pieh in his cell and "took in plaster of Paris an exact likeness of his head, which is now deposited in my cabinet, and may be examined by any person."[24] As an authenticating device, he invites readers to "examine" Sengbe Pieh's head in order to encourage audience interaction, as viewers are urged to collude in a spectacular consumption of the Black man's face and body as specimen. Thus, his soi-disant analytical approach highlights the political role played by performative rituals of white witnessing, as black bodies were made available as evidence within abolitionist discourse and iconography during this

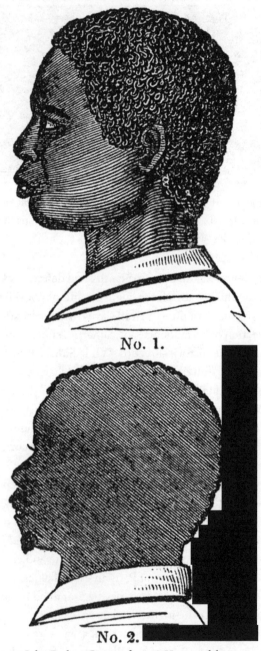

No. 1.

No. 2.

FIGURE 15. John Barber, *Cin-gue,* from *A History of the Amistad Captives* (New Haven, CT: E. L. and J. W. Barber, 1840). (Documenting the American South, University of North Carolina, Chapel Hill)

period. Dissatisfied with textual explanations alone, Fowler illustrates his article with a drawing representing a "cut, taken from this cast." However problematic, this image offering only a bare outline of Pieh's head goes some way in countering hyperphysical or overly sexualized representations of this historical figure as popularized in the white mainstream imagination.[25] Such a fate no less afflicted Nathaniel Turner, as one racist writer avowed that, following his execution, his "head was placed in the hands of science, and the writer has often seen its strangely shaped skull."[26]

Constituting a radical tour de force in Pieh's visual archive, the nineteenth-century white abolitionist artist Nathaniel Jocelyn's painting *Joseph Cinque* appeared in the same year as Fowler's phrenological diagram (plate 6). Recognizing that this work has become the "most important antislavery portrait of a black person from the period," Powell notices how "the portrait—with its dark figure and lighter background—reverses the tonal dynamic of portraits in which Caucasian figures dominant [sic] a darker visual landscape."[27] As the ur-image for all subsequent visual adaptations, Jocelyn's painting represents the visual equivalent to Turner's representation in the Turner/Gray prison narrative. The Black businessman, abolitionist, and Underground Railroad coordinator Robert Purvis commissioned Jocelyn to paint this work in order to document "the Hero of the Amistad." "I had it painted almost fifty years ago, by Nathaniel Jocelyn, then a well-known artist, whom I sent to New Haven to obtain sittings from Sinque," Powell told an interviewer for the *Philadelphia Inquirer* in 1889.[28] Perhaps for the first time in the history of the Black hero in the United States, a Black patron dictated the terms for painting an enslaved heroic figure to a white painter. Ultimately, Purvis's philanthropic act was located in a desire to eulogize black exceptionalism, as he admitted he was motivated by "my admiration for this man Sinque's courage."[29] The anonymous reporter's decision to subtitle his article "One of Robert Purvis's Relics" attests to the painting's spiritual significance as an object for veneration and as a work that traces a black heroic legacy beyond the boundaries of the United States and across a diasporic imaginary.

Situating Sengbe Pieh within an archetypal and imaginary African landscape, Jocelyn's painting sets a precedent for subsequent reimaginings of this heroic figure by African, African American, and European American artists. Rolling mountains and luscious vegetation trade on primitivist myths to dramatize black heroic origins as emerging within a seemingly natural, innocent, atemporal, and pre-European arcadia. As Alexander suggests, "The painting of a proud young African posed against an idyllic native background seems far removed from America's national slavery controversy." Visual and stylistic details suggest that Jocelyn most likely created this work to enhance associations of Pieh with the "noble savage" archetype. For white American audiences, the work may well have resonated with seventeenth-century portraits of Native Americans produced for propaganda purposes by European settlers. Yet Jocelyn's symbolic dramatization of a burnished pink- and gray-hued sky prophesies tumultuous weather, forcefully challenging overly idealized interpretations of this painting as providing only metaphorical representations of an otherwise absent "slavery controversy." Thus Alexander's claim that a graphic visualization of the mutiny would have instead "focused attention on the abolitionists' cause" is debatable. Jocelyn dismissed associating Pieh with visceral proofs on the grounds that they would have played into widespread caricatures of black vengeance.[30]

Simultaneously drawing on African and European influences, Joceyln's Pieh appears in a white toga evocative of "ancient and tribal dress" which works to establish a "classical" framework within which to aggrandize black heroism in this portrait.[31] A far cry from the enslaved black male of the American South shown popularly dancing on the minstrel stage, eating melons on the plantation in popular cartoons, crying on the abolitionist lecture circuit, or wielding weaponry in acts of black ferocity, Jocelyn's Sengbe Pieh is extraordinary not only for his aestheticized and heroic musculature but also for his stillness. Painterly textures lend a sculptured quality to the bronze surfaces of his skin to vouchsafe the painter's determination to create a heroic figure capable of inspiring sublime awe in audiences as a work of art. Such was no less the preoccupation of Frederick Douglass as he sought not only to circumvent but to reject black objectification within political discourse. More statuesque than flesh and blood, Jocelyn's Sengbe Pieh is no object of sale, entertainment, or villainous fear. Instead, he functions as a mythic archetype reimagined to transcend the frailties of the body in the external realm via an embodiment of spiritual and internal ambiguities. Meticulous details such as the play of light and dark accentuate Pieh's physical strength by allowing the viewer to trace not only the bones and veins underneath the surface of his torso but also the lines on his forehead as the artist insists on his intellectual capabilities.

Powell perceptively identifies a "high degree of sensuousness" in Jocelyn's work.[32] Undoubtedly, this artist provides the viewer with a highly aestheticized black body to heighten mythic constructions of Pieh's exemplary masculinity and reinforce his idealized status as a "work of art." Furthermore, his enigmatic facial expression operates in stark contrast to Wedgwood's medallion and the popularly reproduced daguerreotype of the slave Gordon (see figure 19), both of which traded in generic black bodies for white consumption. By comparison, Pieh's personal history remains untold in this image, as Jocelyn not only minimizes African cultural specificities but also omits physical details of the *Amistad* rebellion. "He eliminated elements from Cinque's culture that were termed barbaric by western mores and thereby inappropriate for a hero," Alexander argues, noting, "Not visible are the incised tattoos known to have been on Cinque's body."[33] Equally, Pieh's regal bearing accentuates the absence of shackles or ritual scarification to oppose pro- and even antislavery spectacles of the barbarous, tribal other and of the bleeding, violated enslaved man. Exalting in a myth of black origins, this painting refuses to depict the enslaved rebel leader Joseph Cinque as memorialized within contemporary U.S. reportage. Instead, Jocelyn immortalizes Pieh as a royal dignitary within a European "Oroonoko" tradition. According to this mythic schema, he reimagines Pieh as a historical figure within an imagined ancestral setting and prior to his encounter with the dehumanizing persecutions inflicted by Europeans. The mottled blue and pink sky not only symbolizes political upheaval by prophesying a storm but also compounds the ambiguity of Pieh's expression to endorse his psychological complexity. However, Jocelyn's painting of black innocence in Africa rather than black experience in the United States equally does not flinch from exoticizing black difference to indict white national paradoxes.

"Do you know that that painting was the cause of freeing several hundred slaves and settling forever the rights of freedom to slaves who sought refuge on British soil?" Purvis asked an interviewer in 1889. By far the greatest legacy of this painting resides in the claims he made toward the end of his life that this work played an integral role in the unfolding legacies of black male resistance during slavery. Purvis exalted in the notion, yet to be proved or disproved, that this work inspired Madison Washington's heroism on board the *Creole* slave ship rebellion only two years later in November 1841. If Washington was inspired by the painting, it was not by the spectacle of black violence but by Pieh himself as a visual embodiment of black pride that he was inspired. Purvis showed the painting to Washington, a fugitive passing through Purvis's house (a station on the Underground Railroad), as an educational tool illustrating feats of black heroism. "I showed Washington this painting and he asked me who it represented," he explains. "I told him the story of Sinque, and he became intensely interested. He drank in every word and greatly admired the hero's courage and intelligence."[34] In contrast to the Black soldiers encouraged to fight in the American Civil War following their exposure to the lacerations on Gordon's back, therefore, Washington was inspired to acts of heroism by the representation of black masculinity not only as artistic spectacle but as unfettered by American slavery and in a mythic communion with an African heritage. Tellingly, Washington did not witness the mutiny in this painting but instead had to reimagine it from this portrait. Such a story supports Frederick Douglass's recognition of the importance of visual iconography, no less than literary language, in effecting political change by aestheticizing as well as politicizing representations of black masculinity.

The fascinating legacy of this painting does not end there, as Purvis faced further controversies when he submitted this work to the Academy of the Fine Arts in Philadelphia. "A bitter fight followed between the managers and seceders, which finally resulted in victory for the latter," he concedes. What was the root of their opposition to the work? According to Purvis, "Their principle objection to the painting was that its subject was a hero, and they considered that a black man had no right to be a hero."[35] For a contemporary reporter writing in the *Colored American* regarding the subsequent circulation of Jocelyn's painting as a popular and inexpensively reproduced mezzotint engraving copied from the original by the white artist John Sartain, "Robert Purvis has done himself great honor, in causing to have so correct a likeness taken of him on steel, to be handed down to posterity."[36] As the various political, aesthetic, and ideological tensions proliferating across all visual representations of Sengbe Pieh attest, the "black man's right to be a hero" remains a site of virulent contestation. Excluded from the Philadelphia Museum of the Fine Arts, Sartain's mezzotint engravings of Jocelyn's original painting had pride of place in the homes of countless radical Black abolitionists, including, perhaps more famously, a private residence in Cedar Hill, Anacostia, Washington, DC—home of Frederick Douglass.

A "DUMPISH LOOKING NEGRO" VERSUS A "LION-LIKE CHARACTER": BLACK AND WHITE MEMORIALIZATIONS OF SENGBE PIEH IN HISTORICAL REPORTAGE

While Sengbe Pieh's musculature and physiognomy present far less difficulty regarding strategies of memorialization than those of Nathaniel Turner, translation issues and linguistic differences similar to those besetting Toussaint Louverture's legacy have established seemingly insurmountable barriers regarding any firsthand recovery of Pieh's testimony. With only one or two letters written in English by Sengbe Pieh available in the historical archive, Black and white writers alike have been forced to engage in imaginative reconstructions of his use of language, however much they have laid claim to their accuracy. Unsurprisingly, newspaper interpretations of Pieh's oratorical voice differ according to pro- or antislavery sympathies as well as racial and regional divides. As Sale argues, "Initial reports most startlingly reveal the bedrock assumptions of those who represented them."[37] Such a view further supports the claims made here that imaginary narratives of black heroism typically reveal far more regarding their shifting contexts of publication and biases of authorship than they do concerning the historical figures themselves. One useful way of engaging with such a diverse array of opinions is to compare and contrast accounts published within white-run newspapers—such as the *New York Journal of Commerce* and the *New York Morning Herald*—with reports that appeared in the *Colored American,* a pioneering black publication intent upon problematizing otherwise polarized representations of Sengbe Pieh.[38]

As proof of their abolitionist leanings, Pieh's heroism remained a key attraction for writers in the *New York Journal of Commerce* in the immediate aftermath of the rebellion. Barely weeks after his capture, an article described "Cinques" in epic terms as "the master spirit and hero of this bloody tragedy." While exalting in his exemplary musculature and equality with whites—"He is said to be a match for any two men on board the schooner"—the anonymous writer concedes, "He is a negro who would command in New Orleans, under the hammer, at least $1500." The northern antislavery writer's decision to interpret black worth according to a monetary value system established by the proslavery South risked colluding in racist systems of black objectification and appropriation. Moreover, this description is accompanied by qualifying observations regarding Pieh's capacity for vicious violence as exemplified by the fact that "the backs of several poor negroes are scored with the scars of blows inflicted by his lash to keep them in subjection."[39] Such an admission is revealing regarding the contradictions embedded even in antislavery constructions of Pieh's exceptional status. In repeated instances, he is castigated as a barbarous villain who wielded the "lash" as indiscriminately as any white slaveholder.

In stark contrast, the *New York Morning Herald* betrays its proslavery biases by evoking the spectacle of Sengbe Pieh to effect moral suasion in reverse. Clearly, the *Herald* sought to transform antislavery beliefs into proslavery vindication. "A look at the *hero* and his *compatriots* had wrought an instantaneous change in his sentiments," one reporter writes regarding his own reactions, which he records in the third-person, noting, "Instead of a

chivalrous leader with the dignified and graceful bearing of Othello, impart-
ing energy and confidence to his intelligent and devoted followers, he saw
a sullen, dumpish looking negro." Just the previous day, the same newspaper had published a description of Sengbe Pieh as a "blubber-lipped, sullen
looking negro, not half as intelligent or striking in appearance as every third
black you meet on the docks of New York."[40] One writer became so infuri-
ated that he laid down the gauntlet: "Let the reader conceive to himself a
sturdy, sullen, desperate, oily-looking negro, with all the most repulsive features of the Mingolian race, and then make a hero of him if he can."[41] As these
statements demonstrate, the majority of early proslavery reporters display a
fascination with not only the act but with the art of black representation as
they engaged in the unmaking rather than the making of black heroism.

Lending their support to charges of black physical inferiority, racist authors undermined Sengbe Pieh's significance by relying on problematic
reimaginings of his use of language, as they exhibited no qualms in interpreting fabricated fictional translations as authentic bodies of evidence. As one
writer reports, Pieh's speech consisted of "Thuigua bootah, moo, tuab, jum
yah gobblety," a statement that he had no qualms in translating as "Cinguez
knows the white man to be a fool."[42] In satirizing black language as gibber-
ish, this reporter anticipates the difficulties facing Sojourner Truth. A few
decades later, she was to become increasingly wearied by perpetual representations of her language as "Tickety-ump-ump-nicky-nacky" and repeatedly
denounced white vitriolic determinations to deny black female oratorical
prowess. Yet with regard to Pieh's memory, many antislavery supporters
soon redeployed the tools of the proslavery arsenal by transforming seeming
weaknesses regarding linguistic obfuscation into political strengths. As one
writer translated Pieh for his readers: "He says, 'if you were in my country
and could not talk with any body, you would want to learn our language; I
want to learn yours.'"[43] Such a rhetorical technique turns the tables on racist strategies of exoticizing black difference to exalt in African sameness and
shift national frameworks—"if you were in my country"—thereby to wrong-
foot any pretensions to white U.S. supremacy in the fight for racial equality.

Unsurprisingly, Sengbe Pieh's sophisticated manipulation of language
and action in his performative oratory remained a favored subject among his
radical antislavery supporters. Perhaps the most famous example emerges
from his dynamic courtroom narration of the Middle Passage. According
to various reports, he relied on physical gestures to dramatize his otherwise
minimalist description of the horrific treatment he and the other *Amistad*
Africans endured. When Pieh describes how the slave buyer "Pepe" "came

and felt of them," an anonymous reporter explains in an aside: "Jingua here described how Pepe felt of the Africans to ascertain if they are healthy and sound." Similarly, just as Pieh reports, "They were chained coming from Africa to Havana, hands and feet," the reporter notes, "Jingua here described the manner in which they were packed on board the slaver."[44] A self-reflexive manipulator of both performative and oratorical modes, Sengbe Pieh relied on signifying performances to overcome the limitations of language, evoking his own body as incontrovertible proof of an otherwise bare-bones narration of the Middle Passage. As he realized, the atrocities of his and the *Amistad* Africans' suffering would remain incomprehensible to audiences if he failed to provide a physical reenactment to supplement his oratorical reimaginings.

During this period, the *Charleston Courier* reported two speeches that it alleged Sengbe Pieh had given to the enslaved Africans aboard the *Amistad* shortly after capture. "Although other accounts confirmed that Cinque made two speeches," Sale argues, "the printed text of the speeches is deeply suspect."[45] Regardless of the very real issues presented by debates over historical veracity, however, these speeches are revealing concerning the seeming Americanizing processes at work within contemporary black heroic memorializations. According to an unknown translator, Pieh's first speech reads as follows:

> Friends and Brothers—We would have returned but the sun was against us. I would not see you serve the white man, so I induced you to help me kill the Captain. I thought I should be killed—I expected it. It would have been better. You had better be killed than live many moons in misery. I shall be hanged, I think, every day. But this does not pain me. I could die happy, if by dying I could save so many of my brothers from the bondage of the white man.[46]

Such a forceful reimagining of his military leadership establishes Pieh as preoccupied with a sense of social responsibility, as he insists that he resisted white oppression solely to benefit the black community on board the ship. According to this transcript, his epic language foregrounds self-sacrifice in a "liberty or death" ethos, as he advocates spiritual martyrdom over and above the realities of black enslavement. As confirmation that his transcriber sought proof of black agency rather than annihilation, s/he focuses upon Pieh's statement that this horror "does not pain me" to exalt not in black vulnerability but invincibility.

Yet another fragment of Sengbe Pieh's oratory subverts white male authority by exalting in an ambiguous if archetypally heroic identity:

My brothers I am once more among you, having deceived the enemy of our race by saying I had doubloons. I came to tell you that you have only one chance for death, and I will help you, make the people here kill you. It is better for you to do this, and then you will not only avert bondage yourselves, but prevent the entailment of unnumbered wrongs on your children. Come—come with me then—.[47]

Pieh is here shown condemning white depravity and endorsing his own superior morality. He exalts in a determination to convince the enslaved *Amistad* Africans that the act of forcing whites to commit murder represents the only moral choice in order to save future generations. For Pieh, the grisly spectacle of slavery in the American South represents a reality far worse than death. As Sale argues, these speeches "further the characterization of Cinque as a masculine, noble savage,"[48] perhaps suggesting that his oratorical performances replicate the representational strategies at work in his visual archive. As if fully aware of the isolationist difficulties presented by black male exceptionalism, both speeches portray Pieh as a representative heroic leader determined to legitimize his actions solely within the context of black communal resistance.

Taking a very different approach, the white radical abolitionist Lydia Maria Child also documents Pieh's oratorical powers in her writings. Describing a speech he gave on the abolitionist lecture circuit that she witnessed firsthand, she writes, "His style of eloquence was perfectly electrifying. He moved rapidly about the pulpit, his eye flashed, his tones were vehement, his motions graceful, and his gestures, though taught by nature, were in the highest style of dramatic art. He seemed to hold the hearts of his companions chained to the magic of his voice."[49] Unperturbed by her inability to comprehend Pieh's language as he spoke in his "native tongue," she exalts in his "eloquence." According to Child, Pieh succeeded in emotionally and spiritually shackling his audiences by holding them enraptured and in sublime awe of the "dramatic art" of his oratory that worked not in isolation from, but in close relation to, the empowered spectacle of his body.

In stark contrast to white mainstream memorializations, Black writers publishing articles in the black newspaper press frequently legitimized Sengbe Pieh's heroism with direct comparisons to white exemplary figures. For example, one reporter communicated Pieh's "lion-like character" by suggesting, "His eye is deep, heavy—the cloudy iris extending up behind the brow almost inexpressive, and yet as if volcanoes of action might be asleep behind it. It looks like the black sea or the ocean in a calm—an unenlightened eye, as Webster's would have looked, had he been bred in the desert, among the lions, as Cinguea was."[50] The association of Pieh's "lion-like character" with the white American statesman and orator Daniel Webster not only transgresses racial demarcations but constructs a model of black manhood diametrically opposed to the "dumpish-looking negro" popularized in white-authored accounts. The use of natural imagery not only attests to the significance of environmental factors in affecting human conditioning but also aggrandizes romanticized mythical notions of African difference. As another Black reporter argues, "The spirit that prompted Patrick Henry to exclaim on a memorable occasion, 'Give me liberty, or give me death,' that same spirit fired the bosom and nerved the arm of the daring yet generous African. Joseph Cinquez is more than a hero."[51] The idea that, for Black audiences, Sengbe Pieh represents "more than a hero" ultimately lays claim to his mythic and symbolic status within a revisionist, black-authored intellectual and cultural tradition.

Black writers were suspicious regarding the ways in which white mainstream strategies of memorialization commodified and appropriated black male heroism. Writing of the white-authored play *The Black Schooner; or, The Pirate Slavery Amistad,* published in the same year as the rebellion but now lost to the textual record, Judie Newman writes, "It does not seem to have evoked much sympathy for the slaves; the playbill emphasizes the 'terrible doom' which was very nearly suffered by Inez, the Captain's daughter, at the hands of Cinques, the chief mutineer."[52] Clearly, these racist reimaginings of Sengbe Pieh and the *Amistad* Africans created a sensation not by dramatizing black heroism but by salaciously dramatizing white female victims as exposed to an imaginary black sexual threat. Such was no less the case in a contemporary white newspaper illustration titled *The Captured Africans of the Amistad,* which relishes in an apocalyptic vision of miscegenation by providing a racist caricature of Sengbe Pieh: here, he is shown engaging in a passionate and taboo embrace with a seemingly genteel white woman.

All such profoundly racist, skewed, and problematic adaptations of black heroism took the white national imagination by storm. One reporter went so far as to castigate the proliferation of mass-media representations of Sengbe Pieh by commenting, "Our shameless people have made merchandise of the likeness of Cingues."[53] For this writer and many others, Pieh remained a sacred symbol whose authority could be violated not only by racist abuse but also by overuse as a marketable commodity. Yet Pieh ultimately retained agency through his "unknowable aspects," which guaranteed his survival as a mythical and revered legendary figure. Working to counter dominant vilifying constructions, the celebratory efforts of Black newspaper reporters and writers were committed to creating a new literary tradition in which Pieh was unequivocally represented as embodying a call to arms. For example, for James Monroe Whitfield writing in the poem "To Cinque," published in 1853, Pieh was an inspirational touchstone as a "truly noble chief, / Who scorned to live a cowering slave."[54]

PERFORMANCE AND "RE-MEMORY" IN HALE WOODRUFF'S AND OWEN DODSON'S "HEROIC SAGAS"

"The Amistad revolt was revisited in 1939 not only as a commemorative symbol of black achievement, but also as a 're-memory' of history," Iyunolu Folayan Osagie observes. As she notes, Owen Dodson's play Amistad "was to premiere at Talladega College in Alabama, April 1939" as "part of a larger centennial celebration during which . . . the famous Amistad murals by Hale Aspacio Woodruff were unveiled."[55] "While at Yale, Owen Dodson was commissioned by Talladega College in Alabama . . . to write a play for its Founders' Day Centennial Celebration and the dedication of a new library" on the subject of the Amistad revolt, Bernard L. Peterson Jr. explains.[56] Formal differences notwithstanding, both Woodruff's mural series and Dodson's dramatic adaptation remain inextricably linked by their spectacular and theatrical reimagining of black male heroism. Painted and performed primarily for Black audiences within a black educational context, Dodson's and Woodruff's works broke new ground in the history of African American memorializations of the Amistad. More particularly, their reimaginings of enslaved heroism spoke directly to 1930s struggles regarding poverty and racism. Dodson's play reflected "the historical challenges of the Great Depression years in the struggles of Africans on board La Amistad."[57] At the same time, W. E. B. Du Bois argues that Woodruff's Amistad mural series was rooted in a heroic history of black enslaved resistance in order to indict segregation. "Woodruff of Atlanta dropped his wet brushes, packed the rainbow in his knapsack and rode post-haste and Jim Crow into Alabama," he relates, adding, "There he dreamed upon the walls of Savery Library, the thing of color and beauty . . . to keep the memory of Cinque of the Friendship (La Amistad) and of the day when he and his men, with their staunch white friends, struck a blow for the freedom of mankind."[58] In contrast to Dodson's play dramatizing interracial conflict alongside unity, Woodruff's idealized mural offers a vision of cross-racial collaboration. Creating their works to meet the needs of black social and political life in the early twentieth century, both artist and playwright fought to "keep the memory" of black history alive by generating role models as touchstones for black inspiration in the ongoing fight for civil rights.

The search for a literary and visual language in which to represent multifaceted constructions of a heroic black masculinity undergirds Woodruff's and Dodson's experimental poetics. "It is difficult enough to create everyday, flesh-and-blood characters in our dramas," Dodson admits, "but," he asks, "how do we recreate those who moved among us with heroic force and nobility, remembered so vividly by family, friends, great artists . . . all who sustained their lives because there was a man among them who cared? "[59] Dodson's question acknowledges not only the significance of oral traditions in the struggle for black memorializations but also the relationship between black history and the fight for psychological, physical, and cultural survival in a contemporary era, an issue no less confronting Hale Woodruff. "The mural was painted in honor of the slaves and their mutiny and their final freedom," Woodruff explains.[60] Yet far more than to "honor" slavery, he created this work to counter charges of willful forgetting that plagued older generations within the black community. "Many of the youngsters today, young painters and sculptors, seem to believe that we old timers didn't concern ourselves with the Negro problem," Woodruff observes, admitting, "This to me was a great Negro problem. Because these Africans comported themselves magnificently, you know, and finally won their freedom."[61] As Edmund Barry Gaither writes, Woodruff and Dodson were, quite simply, committed to portraying "heroic sagas from black history."[62]

As Romare Bearden and Harry Henderson note, "In 1966 Woodruff showed slides of his *Amistad* murals in Sierra Leone to descendants of the mutineers who made African and American history," with the direct result that "this experience sharpened his awareness of the cultural diversity of African peoples, evoking a wish for their unity."[63] In the 1960s, Woodruff adapted his 1930s exploration of Sengbe Pieh's and the *Amistad* Africans' heroism not only to speak to a transatlantic context but also to assert black pride in a radicalized civil rights era. Crystallizing the mythic importance of collaborative "rememories," he sought to identify symbolic patterns of ancestry to unite Black peoples within the African Diaspora. Across their works, Woodruff's and Dodson's experimental aesthetic practices heightened the possibilities of identification among their Black audiences by reimagining Sengbe Pieh and the *Amistad* Africans as psychologically complex individuals. By dramatizing a historical event that occurred beyond national boundaries, they protested against U.S. segregation and racial terrorism within a transatlantic framework. Hale Woodruff's three-part mural series *The Mutiny aboard the Amistad, The Amistad Slaves on Trial at New Haven, Connecticut,* and *The Return to Africa, 1842* presents multifaceted transatlantic narratives eulogizing black male heroism.[64] As Gaither notes, Woodruff's mythic and symbolic depictions of Africans both at war and at liberty were deeply inspired by historical research, as he "found a rich body of study materials, including paintings and prints made at the time."[65] Dissatisfied with the power of the visual mode alone, Woodruff accompanied his epic murals with poetic stanzas derived from Dodson's lyrical text in order to juxtapose historically inspired visual narratives with dramatic textual reimaginings. These works betray an important relationship to his Black audiences, as "the viewer is positioned as an observer with a window onto the scene."[66]

Woodruff's cultivation of an "observer" role for his Black viewers undergirds his experimentation with abstract-figurative techniques in these works. Creating moral, psychological, and historical detachment from his viewers, he sought to ensure their dispassionate engagement, not only with a reusable past, but with a reusable memory. Across these panels, he dramatizes feats of African resistance as grounds for future activism for African Americans within the United States. For James Porter, these murals not only attest to Woodruff's exceptional technique in "a fine sense of design" but also reveal his preoccupation with a "retrospective imagination," which he saw as "as indispensable to the great mural artist as to the historian."[67] Woodruff's archival research combines with his imaginative prowess to create epic reconstructions of a mythic, as well as a seemingly "real," historical moment of black heroism.

The first mural in the series, Woodruff's *Mutiny aboard the Amistad,* celebrates black male agency by providing a tumultuous close up of the revolt, as symbolically characterized by stark juxtapositions in this chaotic full-color panel. Offering one of the few visual dramatizations of black male violence as spectacle, Woodruff revises Barber's earlier woodcut *Death of Captain Ferrer* to create anatomically individualized and physically differentiated African bodies in this work. Colliding body parts combine to provide a spectacle of exemplary black manhood, as black and brown torsos, arms, legs, fists, and physiognomies contrast with the pinkish white coloration of a demonized white crew: we see only their raised hands and contorted faces begging for mercy. Blackness and whiteness operate as both myth and matter in this first mural. White clothing wrapped around the Africans' waists contrasts with not only the European's white shirts but also the steel gleam of the ex-enslaved men's machetes to focus viewers' attention upon Woodruff's representation of these individualized black bodies.

A self-consciously choreographed work, Woodruff's mural depicts simultaneous and seemingly intertwined feats of black male heroism. He provides four main pairings of Black and white men to reverse assumptions regarding black passivity, which otherwise dominated white abolitionist iconography: in this work, Black men raise machetes over prostrate white men to secure their physical subjugation. Far from the stillness of Jocelyn's portrait, Woodruff's mural offers fast-paced drama via stark, visual juxtapositions of black and white bodies as he provides abstract reimaginings of violence. As Gaither writes, "subplots are clearly evident" in Woodruff's *Amistad* murals. In this regard, he experimented with the narrative series format to include multiple vignettes in which he simultaneously documents black bravery and white cowardice.[68] A key theme in Woodruff's first mural concerns black witnessing, as he includes an enslaved audience in the background of this work. Such a technique references his Black viewers to reinforce parallels between antislavery resistance and ongoing freedom struggles in the contemporary era. At the same time, Woodruff refutes generic spectacles of black ferocity in this multipanel work by relying on historical sources to individualize his Black freedom fighters. Dramatic tensions emerge, therefore, from his juxtaposition of the Africans' distinctive facial features with the partially revealed, barely profiled physiognomies of a mass of indistinguishable whites.

Sengbe Pieh takes center stage in Woodruff's first panel, as a prominent Black freedom fighter—presumably Pieh—is shown successfully overpowering a white man whom he clutches by the throat as he wields a machete over his body. Testifying to white murder and not black death, this work dramatizes black heroism rather than white martyrdom. Recognizing the need for black community activism to defeat segregation and disfranchisement in the contemporary era, Woodruff represents Pieh's heroism in unity with the armed militancy of other enslaved men. As Gaither writes, "Cinque, the leader of the revolt and therefore its central figure, shares the spotlight with his lieutenants."[69] Woodruff's dynamic experimentation with a rich use of color in *Mutiny aboard the Amistad* generates visual drama to elicit emotional responses from his audiences. Creating powerful contrasts between his horrific subject matter and a highly aestheticized and symbolic use of blacks, browns, whites, pinks, reds, and blues, he evokes death, violence, and loss. Such a technique resonates throughout African American art history, as numerous other twentieth-century artists have created similarly powerful effects by foregrounding a disjuncture between highly aestheticized forms and shocking subject matter. Woodruff excludes visceral matter in favor of stylized and abstracted representations of human forms, thus displacing horrific realities in favor of an epic symbolism. According to Lizzetta LeFalle-Collins and Shirfa M. Goldman, "*The Mutiny Aboard the Amistad, 1839,* uses directional lines as a compositional device to suggest conflict and struggle."[70] Such a view vouchsafes close relationships between aesthetic experimentation and political radicalism in Woodruff's work, particularly in light of the fact that he relied on "space shortage" to heighten physical tensions of cross-racial violence.[71]

Dissatisfied with the signifying possibilities of the visual mode in isolation, Woodruff accompanies his murals with direct quotations from Dodson's prose. The poetic caption to his first panel testifies to black collective agency in the fight for emancipation: "The Schooner will be ours / Ours to steer back, by the sun, to our shore / To freedom."[72] Dodson's lyrical text provides a powerful accompaniment to the spectacle of collaborative black heroism as dramatized in Woodruff's mural. Yet the context of this speech within Dodson's manuscript testifies to the playwright's preferred focus upon an exceptional, iconic heroism. In the original context, these words formed part of a longer oration in which Dodson's Sengbe Pieh asserts his authority by reassuring fearful black voices as they collectively lament, "We will die."[73] Woodruff, on the other hand, addresses contemporary issues across his mural series by explicitly linking the fight for physical emancipation with an awareness of ancestral origins and a commitment to national belonging. Thus he selects another poetic caption from Dodson's play, which foretells communal victory: "Our hands free. / Our legs walking with a big stride / And our faces upward to our Mountains."[74] In one of the first visual representations of Sengbe Pieh created by an African American artist for African and African American audiences, Woodruff's celebration of an African rather than an American homeland for Sengbe Pieh exalts in his reimagined African heritage as a source of pride.

Self-reflexively engaged in complicating his representations of black exemplary heroism in this work, Woodruff includes a powerful countervignette in *Mutiny aboard the Amistad.* He adopts a technique, barely noticeable on first glance, of symmetrical mirroring in the bottom right-hand corner of this work. Thus he juxtaposes the prostrate body of a white man—with hands outstretched as if to defend himself against the African wielding a machete above him—with the lifeless body of an enslaved Black man whose flattened torso, limp-lying arm, and expressionless face all testify to black sacrifice in death. Here, Woodruff provides layered histories of slavery to bear witness to a continuum of black male heroism that consists not only of violent overthrow but also of sacrificial martyrdom. In this work, Woodruff dramatizes the realities of African American suffering in a historical era to come to grips with the horrifying conditions afflicting black humanity in a contemporary context of racist persecution. Refuting oversimplified visions of racial conflict, his vision of black resistance endorses a heroic continuum that runs the gamut from self-sacrifice to warfare. In this regard, his inclusion of a dead black body may have been a legitimizing technique designed to render black-on-white violence palatable for white audiences otherwise incapable of sympathizing with acts of seemingly unprovoked black barbarity, the epitome of which was still Nathaniel Turner's seemingly unimaginable rebellion.

The second panel, *The Amistad Slaves on Trial,* provides a center-stage reimagining of the erect figure of Sengbe Pieh. Fascinatingly, his detailed physiognomy exists in a call-and-response relationship to Woodruff's representations of black manhood as visualized in the first mural. However, his facial features as depicted in this work may well suggest that Pieh is not in fact the central black male shown standing over the prostrate white man in the first mural. Instead, in light of their physical similarities, Woodruff may have intended to represent Pieh in the freedom fighter who appears to the left of the main figure. By comparison, this figure is shown engaged in hand-to-hand combat with a white man as they stand facing each other in a mirrored pose suggestive of equality. According to this alternative visual reimagining of Pieh, he holds up a machete and clutches the white man's wrist to prevent him from using his rifle. At the same time, another enslaved man brandishes an identical weapon to suggest that collaborative forms of black male heroism were as great a necessity in the Jim Crow era as they were during slavery. Ultimately, such a call-and-response relationship between panels not only ruptures any pretensions toward straightforward uplift narratives but also problematizes representations of black male heroism. Ultimately, Woodruff's layered vignettes cast doubt upon his own assertion that "in the Talladega murals I was able to employ a linear style."[75]

In contrast to Woodruff's historically inspired physiognomies and aggrandized representations of Black and white individuals in the trial scene, Woodruff's choice of Dodson's poetic text as caption to this scene exposes a great irony: "Men standing up for justice and truth / Men standing up with fire in their voices / For the honor of America and democracy."[76] Satirizing white American national values, Dodson's and Woodruff's visual and textual works indict white endorsements of moral relativism through flawed definitions of "justice and truth" that do little to exalt American "honor." Moreover, Woodruff's powerful use of color—as revealed by the blue walls and yellow floor of the trial scene—variously recall the colors of the sea and deck of the slave ship of the first mural to reinforce thematic parallels across these panels. Symbolically juxtaposing the social laws of the land with the natural environment of the sea, Woodruff aggrandizes black resistance by arguing for a discourse of human rights unfettered by artificially constructed societal boundaries. Woodruff's second panel visualizes W. E. B. Du Bois's convictions regarding the "color line" as the "problem" of the twentieth century by dramatizing predominantly Black and white groups as seated in opposition to each other in the courtroom. In a powerful departure, he revises typical nineteenth-century representations of Sengbe Pieh as clothed in a toga, barefoot, and half-naked. Instead, he wears European clothing to dramatize his assimilation into western values. Nonetheless, the individualized clothing and physiognomies of the enslaved men on trial are characterized by idiosyncratic details to subvert otherwise generalized records complicit in racial stereotyping. Lined foreheads, closed mouths, and expressive eyes all contrast with the blank passivity of white faces to suggest black psychological complexity and agency. More powerfully still, black faces leaning toward one another teach an invaluable moral lesson by establishing the persistence of community links and social interaction despite white attempts to divide and defeat black resistance movements.

Woodruff's final panel, *The Return to Africa,* repeats with variation the symbolic composition of the first mural. Black and white bodies are no longer locked in battle, however, but in cooperation with one another according to his vision of an integrated utopia. Juxtaposed with his inclusion of a white philanthropist, possibly Lewis Tappan, Woodruff's Sengbe Pieh gestures toward the ship in which they were destined to return free. At the same time he carries paper, indicative of educational prowess, and a staff, suggestive of his political authority. As Woodruff's mural attests, black struggles for independence are far from over. In the same way that Jocelyn's Sengbe Pieh looks into the distance against an apocryphal sky in his canvas painted one hundred years before, so too does Woodruff's Pieh as he prophesies future conflict in twentieth-century African struggles against European colonization. Such a view is no less supported by the subjugated body of a bent-over Black man carrying books and looking toward Pieh. He offers confirmation of Woodruff's realization regarding the ongoing nefarious influences not only of a western education but also of spiritual colonization and its problematic legacies for African peoples. "This time black freedom moves in her sides / And the fighters for this freedom have sent the race / To teach the heathens in the hunter's land."[77] Thus Woodruff again relies on excerpts from Dodson's play for his accompanying caption as he celebrates a reversal of white power hierarchies. And yet, Dodson's narrator in the play ultimately qualifies any endorsement of "black freedom" by suggesting that "nothing has healed these days, / The scars are in the spirit / Not the bone."[78] Across both their works, Dodson and Woodruff refuse to idealize African male heroism in order to shore up their critique of white abolitionist tendencies toward monolithic archetypes as well as of oversimplified mainstream stereotypical perceptions of Africa in their own era. Both writer and painter prophesy diasporic acts of rebellion—"The fire is lit / The smoke is rising . . . rising"—not only to celebrate twentieth-century African freedom struggles against colonial authority but also to gesture toward ongoing issues in contemporary international as well as national politics.[79]

"The *Amistad* murals present Woodruff as a gifted visual storyteller capable of assimilating a huge amount of data and reworking it into a coherent statement," Gaither argues.[80] Yet Woodruff's symbolic color scheme and claustrophobic compositions document thematic and political tensions to resist any clear-cut "coherence." Instead, he relies on strategies of aesthetic experimentation imaginatively to recover otherwise elided tensions and distortions. However, the appearance of Woodruff's mural on the walls of Talladega College "underscores the vital role played in American art by historically black institutions."[81] Woodruff's mural series provides panoramic representations of black male resistance to inculcate pride via the cultivation of role models as he seeks to appeal to a mythic sense of origins otherwise obliterated by the Middle Passage. These works transgress aesthetic boundaries to reflect his belief in "a certain amount of 'artistic distance,'" on the grounds that "to get at a thing, you've got to get away from it, and then come to it in your own terms."[82] For Woodruff no less than Dodson, the realities of twentieth-century injustices not only made any straightforward eulogies of black resistance during slavery impossible but also challenged any sanitized beliefs in the finality of struggle. For artists and activists working in an increasingly militant civil rights era a few decades later, Hale Woodruff's and Owen Dodson's haunting dramatizations shed light on the difficulties of memorializing reusable Black heroic icons within contemporary black liberation movements.

HEROISM, ANTIHEROISM, AND EXPERIMENTAL REPRESENTATIONS OF SENGBE PIEH IN WORKS BY ROBERT HAYDEN AND ROMARE BEARDEN

Experimental aesthetic techniques combine with groundbreaking subject matter to collapse any artificial boundaries between Sengbe Pieh's heroism and antiheroism in Robert Hayden's thought-provoking poem "Middle Passage." Hayden extensively revised this series of poetical vignettes, originally written in 1945, for republication in *A Ballad of Remembrance,* published in 1962 to suit an increasingly militant civil rights era. Throughout this poem, he explores Sengbe Pieh as a mythic talisman of the anonymous heroism of those suffering the "voyage through death" of the Middle Passage.[83] For Hayden, Pieh operates as a symbol or "deathless primaveral image" of centuries-old fights for emancipation as well as of the lost histories of black suffering during the enforced deportation of Africans during the Middle Passage or Black Holocaust.[84] According to Hayden's aesthetic, acts and arts of black male heroism remain indivisible from both myth and matter. Relying on formal innovations, he inspires audience engagement by contesting lacunae within white official records. According to Hayden, Pieh's memory possesses symbolic significance as a "life that transfigures many lives."[85] Pieh's representative status as an embodiment of multiple and elided black histories lies at the heart of his poem, which revels in communal rather than solitary heroism. As Fred Fetrow argues, Hayden's "'anti-epic' approach ennobles Cinquez, an 'anti-hero' who represents his race, and is thus used by Hayden to celebrate the real subject of his poem—the heroic struggle for freedom by the black victims of 'Middle Passage.'"[86] As Hayden explains, the "Middle Passage" provided him with the opportunity not only to examine "themes from Negro history and folklore" but also "to reaffirm the Negro struggle as part of the long human struggle toward freedom."[87] Defiant regarding the ability of a symmetrical and measured poetic framework ever to do justice to his radical subject matter, he engages in formal innovation to arrive at "something really my own, something patterned, wild, and free."[88] Originality in aesthetic experimentation combines with innovation in historical representation to structure Hayden's reimagining of the "Negro struggle" in this work.

Hayden's reimagining of Pieh and the *Amistad* Africans counters mainstream white amnesia by celebrating an unequivocal belief in black protest. While the "past is for most Americans, unfortunately, rather meaningless," Hayden explains, "some of us are aware of it as a long, tortuous, and often bloody process of becoming, of psychic evolution—a process continuing today." Such a realization of the past as both "process" and "evolution" underscores Hayden's belief in the imaginative power of formal ambiguity over and above the reductive limitations of thematic closure. He admits, "I revise endlessly." Not only is this lack of resolution integral to Hayden's aesthetic and political determination to map formal ambiguity onto thematic issues, but it also plays a vital role in his theory of protest. Compulsively editing his poetry in recognition of the failures of conventional forms ever fully to represent black heroism, he displays a commitment to a philosophy of art for art's sake in order to challenge fixed systems of representation. He explains, "I wanted to approach those things as an artist and not as a propagandist," recognizing, "Art is not escape, but a way of finding order in chaos, a way of confronting life." Hayden foregrounds the role played by aesthetic experimentation not only as a process but as a language through which he is able to "find order" and "confront life" as he reconfigures, no less than reimagines, otherwise elided realities. Furthermore, across his works, Hayden cultivates "aesthetic and psychic distance" by "speaking through a mask, a persona" in order to encourage a dispassionate and intellectual engagement in his readers.[89]

Adopting a politics and poetics of ellipsis, Hayden's "Middle Passage" exposes absences within the white official historical records in order to dramatize the integral role played by the imagination in memorializing black heroism. The first parts of the poem provide a panoramic, if fragmented, view of the Middle Passage not only to indict white slaveholding brutality but also to condemn the ways in which African royalty colluded with Europeans to ensure the perpetuation of transatlantic slavery. In contrast, the final section specifically dramatizes the *Amistad* and Sengbe Pieh as he begins with a powerful opening that includes the apocryphal phrase "shuttles in the rocking loom of history, / the dark ships move." Much has been made by critics of Hayden's image of history as a weaving loom, as he appropriated the symbolic power of an experimental tapestry of diasporic testimonies. His comparison between slave ships and "shuttles" is no less significant if we consider that shuttles in operation are imperceptible to the human eye. Hayden's trope unveils his aesthetic mechanics as requiring creative reimagining—via the reader's active engagement—in order to prevent the nihilistic dissolution of his subject matter into nothingness. In this work, Hayden equally relies on repetition with variation to document a "Voyage through death, / voyage whose chartings are unlove."[90] Hayden's idea of "unlove" operates in conjunction with "death" to open up an alternative space within which to reconceptualize complicated emotional responses to the difficult histories of slavery. Just as Hayden's rocking loom weaves multiple threads to dispense with polarized representations of white versus black histories, so the idea of "unlove" opens up an alternative moral continuum according to which positive and negative values lose their potency. In the same way that Jocelyn's painting of Sengbe Pieh foregrounds visual untelling to provide complex representations of an exceptional heroic individualism, Hayden self-consciously cultivates ambiguities of literary language. He highlights lacunae in the historical record to dramatize a mythic re-creation of black manhood as ideally suited to the civil rights era.

In a revealing departure from many earlier representations of the *Amistad* mutiny, Hayden's "Middle Passage" betrays its similarities to Ed Hamilton's monument with which I opened this chapter by detracting attention away from Pieh's heroism to confront the anonymity of black trauma as experienced during the transatlantic trade. Breaking yet more new ground, Hayden's "Middle Passage" narrates black male heroism from the perspective of a white crew member appalled that white men were defeated by "murderous Africans" as he singles Pieh out as a "surly brute" who played a key role in inspiring the "ghastly work."[91] An experimental poetics of symbolic reimagining characterizes twentieth-century works such as Hayden's "Middle Passage." As Vera M. Kutzinski argues, "The historical (and poetic) truth that emerges from these shifting surfaces is the *limbo* of Hayden's ever-transfiguring poetic imagination."[92] Such an emphasis upon the "limbo" of Hayden's "imagination" provides an apt trope for understanding his poetic representation of Sengbe Pieh. A provocative historical figure to Hayden, Pieh operates as a mythic repository and site for reconfiguring heroic and antiheroic histories as repeatedly unrecorded in the "voyage through death." As Hayden's "Middle Passage" testifies, it is important not to read "deathless" as "immortal," as Hayden's Sengbe Pieh represents a finite embodiment of black heroic individualism, ever in dialogue with and inextricable from an untold mass of enslaved suffering.

Created only a few years later in 1971, Romare Bearden's screen print titled *Prince Cinque* (see plate 7) signifies on many of these poetic revisions to Pieh's visual archive. A full-color work constructed from collaged fragments and torn papers and employing a symbolic use of composition and color, Bearden's image documents black heroism through Pieh's detailed physiognomy in which he accentuates his furrowed brow and contemplative gaze. Yet his immediate shift in perspective provides panoramic representations of diminutive black and brown figures engaged in rebellion. Thus he shares Hamilton's and Hayden's determination to destabilize the boundaries between iconic and anonymous feats of heroism. And yet, on the surface, Bearden's representation of black mutiny straightforwardly recalls the anonymous woodcut *Horrid Massacre in Virginia* (figure 5). A similarly indiscriminate mass of black and brown men wield machetes and knives, while a dying white man possesses the only individualized facial features in contrast to a mass of generic, silhouetted black physiognomies. As a visual fulfillment of Turner's prophecy of "black and white spirits engaged in battle," the white man's upraised arm gesturing surrender is visually complemented by raised black arms burdened by weaponry.

The Black men engaged in revolt in Bearden's print are highly stylized, as he relies upon abstract figurative forms to provide an angular depiction of their bodies. Favoring a stripped-down, iconic physicality, he individualizes some faces, while he leaves others almost entirely obscured. Ultimately overshadowing his miniaturized figures with a mythically enlarged representation of Sengbe Pieh, he exalts in an iconic black heroic presence otherwise missing not only from woodcuts such as *Horrid Massacre* but also from Hayden's "Middle Passage," in which black exceptionalism remains a subject of debate. Moreover, Bearden's decision to juxtapose "Prince Cinque's" detailed physiognomy with a grayed outline of Africa heightens Pieh's exceptionalism by mapping the black male body within a diasporic context. A setting bloodred sun exists in a visual call-and-response relationship to the graphic red markings incised on the mutilated white body martyred in this work. Refusing to flinch from horrific realities, Bearden accentuates his juxtaposed representations of black and white sacrifice against a crimson sea. Moreover, the setting sun partially reflected on Pieh's forehead celebrates Africa as a mythic locus of memory and cultural pride as well as a catalyst to diasporic heroism.

Startlingly, a strip of blue divides Pieh's otherwise detailed and realistic physiognomy to recall not only the blue outline he provides of the northernmost part of the African continent but also the backdrop that offsets the freedom fighters' radical resistance. Such a symbolic use of color is suggestive not only of death—as the sea evokes the Middle Passage—but also of emotional and creative liberation in the blues as an aesthetic tradition. Bearden also suggests black spiritual emancipation by including a black cross to the far right of the print. He thus critiques white fallacies of Christianity in order to memorialize the lives of the unknown dead. The destabilizing blue line that splits Pieh's face in half foregrounds ambiguity as integral to representations of black heroism and suggests that he wears a mask. The brown and black composition of Pieh's skin visually complements the skin tones of the rebelling black and brown figures to suggest reciprocity in communal solidarity. And yet, as if to prophesy acts of racist supremacy, jagged and triangular white shapes haunt the edges of this piece to evoke hate groups such as the Ku Klux Klan, as further signified by the inclusion of a black cross as an emblem of black sacrifice.

In multifaceted ways, Bearden complicates his celebration of Pieh's exceptional royal status in *Prince Cinque* in order to relate his heroism directly to community activism. Thus he situates both this exemplary figure and the *Amistad* rebellion within the context of the civil rights struggles of the 1970s. In forceful ways, Bearden's work dramatizes his increasing dissatisfaction with passive resistance by eulogizing the rise of Black Power as he refuses to shy away from the violent spectacle of black rebellion. His symbolic color scheme of blacks, whites, grays, browns, blues, and reds in *Prince Cinque* evokes multifaceted racial and national lineages as he urges the ongoing necessity of African resistance in transatlantic and diasporic contexts. Reimagining Pieh's heroism, Bearden may well have opted for this aggrandized subject matter to counter misunderstandings regarding his work within diasporic Black communities. "To many of my own people, I learn, my work was very disgusting and morbid," he concedes, admitting he faced criticism for visualizing "a type of Negro that they were trying to get away from."[93] His fraught juxtapositions and symbolic use of color in a fragmented picture plane exalt in a new heroic "type" constructed solely for black emulation. Bearden's experimental visual poetics operate via fragmentation and ellipsis to provide only partial representations of Pieh's heroic feats. Thus he places the onus upon the viewer to reimagine and re-create from the dislocated yet harmonious parts.

A well-researched work, Bearden's *Prince Cinque* is a visual quotation of historical texts including John W. Barber's representation of the mutiny in *A History of the Amistad Captives* (1840)—particularly in the group depiction of the Africans—and Nathaniel Jocelyn's portrait *Joseph Cinque* (1841), as shown in his indebtedness to his interpretation of Pieh's detailed physiognomy. Such clear-cut aesthetic influences demonstrate Bearden's preference for signifying upon, at the same time that he interrogates, the limitations of seemingly authenticated white-generated historical works. As he suggests, "The power of the artistic imagination and vision is such that we can accept as credible a new symbolic sense of reality, for very often the world of the artist is more real, more compelling than the world it supposedly represents."[94] For Bearden and many other artists and writers, the transformative power of the imagination provides not only a gateway to a heightened and "symbolic sense of reality" but also a way into the hidden histories of Sengbe Pieh no less than Toussaint Louverture, Nathaniel Turner, Sojourner Truth, Frederick Douglass, and Harriet Tubman. For African American writers and activists such as Hayden and Bearden, Pieh's heroism operates both as a symbol of mythic possibility and as a talisman against racist persecutions in the twentieth century. As Maya Angelou poignantly writes, "The story of Cinque and his heroism brought light into a time of great darkness: my childhood. When mobs of angry whites took a black man and lynched him in my small Arkansas town."[95] However ambivalent and historically ambiguous, Sengbe Pieh signified in the mid-twentieth-century African American imagination as an alternative to white polarized representations of black masculinity.

"YOU SEE NOTHING SON": ANCESTRY, ORAL HISTORIES, AND DIASPORIC LOSS IN CHARLIE HAFFNER'S *AMISTAD KATA KATA* (1988) AND RAYMOND DESOUZA-GEORGE'S *BROKEN HANDCUFF (GIVE ME FREE)* (1994)

"Sengbe Pieh was a Mende farmer whose extraordinary courage in resisting slavery earned him a lasting place in the histories of Sierra Leone and the United States." So reads the opening to "Sengbe Pieh," a brief biographical sketch subtitled "Hero of the Amistad Revolt" and included in the revised edition of *Sierra Leonean Heroes*, published in 1988. Notably, the page facing these brief descriptions of Pieh's actions as a freedom fighter provides a black-and-white reproduction of Jocelyn's painting, newly retitled *Sengbe Pieh*. No artist's name is given, thereby offering further confirmation that this portrait was reused and recycled to fit a variety of social and political contexts. As President Major-General Dr. J. S. Momoh writes in his introduction to the volume, "This edition should therefore go a long way towards building up greater awareness of the rich diversity of our culture, increasing our respect for our greater leaders, and fostering national unity." For African political leaders, writers, and artists alike, Pieh operates as a symbol for lost ancestral genealogies within Sierra Leonean history. As the unnamed writer of his biographical sketch insists, "Sengbe Pieh deserves to be recognized as one of the most famous and influential Sierra Leoneans who ever lived."[96] A number of contemporary Sierra Leonean writers have created theatrical dramatizations of Pieh's heroism, including Charlie Haffner and Raymond DeSouza-George in their respective works, *Amistad Kata Kata* (1988) and

Broken Handcuff (Give Me Free) (1994). These dramatic adaptations foreground the importance of communal memory to endorse malleable constructions of a black male heroism as reimagined to function as a corrective to the myopia of racist historical archives.

Against a backdrop of historical misunderstanding regarding the *Amistad* revolt, Osagie writes that "commemorative processes now in place have ignited the nation's imagination."[97] Thus Haffner's and DeSouza-George's performative adaptations represent just two among many of the new cultural materials devoted to Pieh's heroism that have appeared in Sierra Leone. These materials include not only textual works but also "wall paintings, cement sculptures, public monuments, and road-side decorations in the shape of military weapons painted in army camouflage." Tellingly, a reproduction of Pieh as portrayed by Jocelyn appeared on the "500 leone note," representing the "first time that Sierra Leone has issued currency notes with portraits of historical figures."[98] Numerous street artists have also relied heavily on the white American Jocelyn's portrayal of black heroism in the person of Sengbe Pieh as the basis for their works. For example, the Sierra Leonean painter Alusine Bangura adapts Jocelyn's portrait in a mural in which he individualizes Pieh's facial features in symbolic ways. Refusing to flinch from black heroism as a site of conflict, he foregrounds unreconciled complexities of black selfhood through paradoxes of naming by titling his work *Sengbe Pieh or Joseph Cinque*. Thus he employs a twentieth-century variation upon a centuries-old practice that began in works such as Olaudah Equiano's slave narrative, *The Interesting Narrative of the Life of Olaudah Equiano, or Gustavus Vassa, the African,* first published in 1789. As Bangura's title demonstrates, he was no less devoted to Africanized versus Europeanized ambiguities of identity as encapsulated by a split use of naming.[99] Equally, Amadu Tarawalie's mural *Sengbe Pieh and ECOMOG* takes Jocelyn's painting as his inspiration in an effort to document Pieh's often elided militancy. He not only foregrounds weaponry by including a spear but also reproduces flags from different African countries in an homage to black diasporic power.[100] Such various global patterns of exchange signify on Pieh's memory and support William McFeely's view that "African American history is no longer simply American; it is transatlantic."[101] If, as Robert Purvis believed, Nathaniel Jocelyn's painting of Sengbe Pieh inspired Madison Washington's acts of resistance in the Caribbean, Pieh's transatlantic influences have no less endured in the twentieth and twenty-first centuries, as he has "emerged as an unofficial symbol of the revolution" in Sierra Leone.[102]

As director of the Freetong Players, which Joseph Opala describes as "the foremost theatre group in the country," Charlie Haffner was fascinated by Sengbe Pieh and the *Amistad* revolt.[103] As one of his teachers, Opala bears witness to Haffner's early radicalism by explaining,

> When I appealed to my students to devote their artistic talents to creating symbols of national pride based on Sierra Leone's history and culture, Charlie scoffed; "I'm going to use music and drama to expose the APC for what it's doing to my country," he said. If you're that confrontational, I said, you'll just go to jail. "So what," he answered. "Do you think I'm afraid of that?"

Recognizing Haffner's militancy, Opala channeled the burgeoning playwright's radicalism by urging him to engage in an imaginative recovery of black historic exemplars. "I saw a light go on in Charlie Haffner's eyes during those lectures on the Amistad Revolt," he explains. "One day he stopped me and said, with quiet conviction, that he had seen the point."[104] A direct result of this intellectual epiphany, Haffner's play *Amistad Kata Kata* offers an imaginary substitute for armed physical resistance by relying on aesthetic experimentation to secure historical commemoration.

Written during a period of revolutionary upheaval in Sierra Leone, Haffner's drama speaks to his immediate context. Creating this work to raise awareness of the history of black heroism among Black audiences, he writes to inculcate ancestral pride in the face of communal erasure. As Osagie explains, Haffner's play "helped to awaken the cultural and political consciousness of the Sierra Leonean people during the military coup of 1992."[105] Subtitled *A Play Celebrating Sengbe Pieh the "Hero of the Amistad Revolt,"* Haffner's *Amistad Kata Kata* opens with stage directions that establish his intellectual and thematic focus. As he writes, a "student of history is conducting research on historical figures of the past." As both an ancestral figure and griot for African history, "Grama" educates this "Student," an unnamed representative of an ignorant generation, by stating that "our people have a tradition, which is based on belief that a person survives after death." Exasperated by the fallacies of a written legacy, she exalts in African oral traditions to insist, "You see nothing son. You bookmen and leaders fail to see that it is our ancestors that offer us guidance and counseling throughout our never-ending stream of life."[106]

Grama's insistence upon a direct correlation between a written heritage and the failures of seeing betrays Haffner's emphasis upon the difficulties of a textual or visual language ever to recover more than partial or distorted representations of black male heroism. As Osagie explains, Haffner's drama comes to grips with "the tendency to elevate the written word to the place of *fact* and the oral to the place of *fiction*" within African culture. "This form of hierarchizing," he adds, "comes with the power and privilege of Western education."[107] According to Haffner, such westernized systems of knowledge contribute to a political, historical, and aesthetic blindness within African cultures. As Grama insists, "It is a great tragedy that he [Pieh] is not remembered at all by his own people."[108] Clearly, Haffner's experimental drama is as much concerned with the processes of memorialization as it is with reconfiguring the boundaries of black male heroism.

Haffner's play signifies upon the problems within the official historical archives by examining the different ways in which memory is preserved. In forceful ways, the Student's preoccupation with a search for facts—"Sengbe Pieh, lived between 1813 and 1839. Wait . . . give me one minute . . . Grama . . . please"—critiques memorializations that fail to engage in imaginative reconstructions of black history. Haffner's elliptical framework does not shy away from lacunae and fragmentation, as Grama makes no response to the Student's insistent bid for confirmation; his plea "Grama . . . Grama" meets with silence. It is as if Haffner is suggesting that Grama is a reluctant listener to written and seemingly official histories, which do little justice to feats of black male heroism as re-created in oral histories. Convincingly, the student's reliance on written information—"I read that SENGBE PIEH is well known in many parts of the United States of America . . . eh . . . as well as 'JOSEPH CINQUE'"—is undermined by Grama's derision: "What *(laughs again, coughs)* YOZFI KINZI? *(Laughter still).*"[109] Haffner's phonetic spelling of Sengbe Pieh's Europeanized name as reinvented by Grama signifies not only upon national ambiguities but also on competing memorial practices. According to Haffner's conceptualization, western systems of knowledge privilege scientific discourse, while African traditions exalt in mythic and symbolic legacies as characterized by a poetic reimagining.

At a key moment, Haffner's *Amistad Kata Kata* foregrounds ceremonial ritual to restore black pride. The majority of the dramatic action takes place "AT THE SHRINE" at which the "chief priest" evokes the sacred dead to save contemporary society from its "plight." In this scene, one worshipper, Gbote, makes the following plea: "Pardon Sengbe, pardon your children," as the sins of the father are remapped to expose the sins of the children. Here, Haffner provides audiences with a way of reliving Sengbe Pieh's history, as his "ghost" ruptures linear teleologies by narrating the story of his captivity and revolt via flashback. At the same time, Haffner uses a militant tableaux to exalt in feats of black heroism. His stage directions read, "In a flash back suddenly Sengbe Pieh is ambushed by a group of strong men carrying ropes, sticks. There is a struggle and Sengbe is eventually overpowered." As dramatized here, Pieh's resistance reinforces both his heroic exceptionalism and his mythic significance as the conduit for elided histories. According to Haffner's vision, he represents the untold narratives of the enslaved *Amistad* Africans such as Gilabaro, Kimbo, Fuleh, and Kali. Throughout the play, Haffner foregrounds acts of reimagining as integral to recovering Sengbe Pieh's status as an exemplary historical figure. As Pieh tells the enslaved Africans on board the *Amistad*—repeatedly described solely as "others"— "I am ready, whether you join me or not, I am ready to fight the white men single-handedly... *(Again mixed responses)*." In noting their "mixed responses" to Pieh's call to heroism, Haffner directly confronts political and cultural tensions among the enslaved Africans. As they gain greater conviction and rally around the cause, however, these little-known figures ultimately offer a source of strength for individual heroic icons such as Sengbe Pieh. As he acknowledges, "Your renewed spirit has suddenly intensified my courage and willpower to fight the white man to the last tooth." According to Haffner, Pieh's emphasis upon the necessity of a return to Africa is far greater in this play than in most other memorializations. "You see, we are only just beginning our struggle to regain our freedom. This ship is not Africa, and until we get home, we are not free," he emphasizes.[110] Haffner repeatedly refuses to recuperate Sengbe Pieh's heroism within an American national framework. Instead, he situates his memory within the trials and tribulations of a mythically subjugated and imaginary Africa.

By comparison, as Osagie writes, Raymond DeSouza-George's *The Broken Handcuff (Give Me Free)*, subtitled *Presenting the Spirit of Sengbe Pieh, a Neglected Sierra Leonean Hero* and written less than a decade later, "explores the broader historical and social implications of cultural memory."[111] Across this stark and unequivocal work, DeSouza-George relies on traumatic symbolism. As his stage directions suggest, "A giant handcuff stands against the back wall," while the "stage is littered with dry leaves and other symbols of slavery." Echoing Haffner's approach, DeSouza-George's iconic image transgresses temporal frameworks to juxtapose the unresolved moral, historical, psychological, and political legacies of slavery with the ongoing difficulties confronting a contemporary era. Condemning black apathy, he insists on the need for black solidarity in the fight for civil rights. As one character laments, "Nobody wants to do anything if somebody else can do it." In a daring move, DeSouza-George breaks with existing memorializations to critique African complicity in the slave trade:

THIRD NATIVE: For God's sake *dakpe* don't do it—No, *dakpe* don't give me away.

SECOND NATIVE: Give you away? Free? No, we are going to sell you.[112]

Beginning his play by denouncing the plight of unnamed "brothers" bought and sold within an African context, DeSouza-George juxtaposes iconic with unknown forms of heroism not to foreground cultural pride but to offer a political indictment of black, no less than white, complicity with slavery.

"We fought for freedom, then used the freedom to sully our brothers, our fathers, our mothers, our wives, sons and daughters. . . . We killed ourselves in those sales and are still killing our heroes with dishonour," explains Lavalie, one of DeSouza-George's Black heroic leaders. Throughout the play, DeSouza-George makes a direct connection between historical amnesia and cultural and national annihilation. He provides a frank discussion of the realities of black victimization in order to dramatize the deaths rather than lives of Black heroic figures. As Lavalie insists, enslaved African heroes suffer from "the reality of a living death through the ignominy of feeling and sometimes even accepting that they were less than human in the eyes of their fellow men." Concluding with a candid admission, "Is it any different among us today?" he renders parallels between black suffering in slavery and a contemporary racist era more concrete. More powerfully still, he indicts any seeming acquiescence to animalizing rhetoric, which leads not only to black dehumanization but also deheroization. "We gullibly embrace all those things, which are constantly telling us we are a people without roots, without heroes, without pride?" Lavalie asks as he condemns the nefarious effects of black internalizations of white values. For DeSouza-George, the only source of hope is educational enlightenment and its capacity to stimulate social and political change. As Lavalie concludes, "Even history is willing to, and can teach, when a people learn to listen and act," to which the "People" respond in unison, "If you will die, die fighting to be free."[113]

In provocative ways, DeSouza-George's *Broken Handcuff* situates Sengbe Pieh's heroism within the context of an array of Black male legendary figures not only to dramatize a militant tradition but also to provide a searing critique of white missionary zeal as enacted upon a mythologized African continent. A founding father of African heroism, Bai Bureh, critiques the white "Governor Clarkson" by stating, "You pretended to be philanthropic, but your people have drastically changed the tone of your feelings for my people." In this context, the ghost of Sengbe Pieh appears explicitly to denounce the nefarious impact of white western colonialism upon black societies.

As DeSouza-George's Pieh argues, the white official Clarkson "made sure that he left our brothers holding the mirror so that we could continue looking at his reflection." Yet he does not shy away from ascribing blame to enslaved Africans by indicting contemporary forgetting. "Our people on the other side . . . don't know us, and we are blood brothers, same flesh and bone," he laments.[114] DeSouza-George gets to the heart of difficulties regarding black memorializations by providing daring, imaginative retellings throughout *The Broken Handcuff*, which risk replicating traumas by reducing soi-disant epic figures to bathetic insignificance. As Sengbe Pieh explains, "To tell you and show you all the details of how I was sold, how my countrymen were sold into slavery, will be like going through the experience all over again." For this reason, he asks his audience to re-create this traumatic history for themselves: "Just imagine the worst situation you think a man can be subjected to in terms of losing his freedom," he insists. Betraying an ambivalent perspective on violence in this work, DeSouza-George relies on indirection to narrate Sengbe Pieh's mutiny in a stage direction: "Sounds of anguish, choking and terror fill the air as they dance out the attack. Lighting could go with strobe effect to accentuate the pace and horror. A few deaths."[115] Documenting the failures of visual or textual languages to provide multifaceted representations of black violence, he debates Pieh's slippery significance within national memory in order to highlight his integral yet marginalized role within Sierra Leonean history. "Captured 1839. Returned 1842. (To audience). Returned to what?" Lavalie concludes, finding hope in the fact that "he remains a link between two great continents."[116] Signifying as a "link" rather than as a forgotten figure existing solely in a state of political and historical "limbo," Sengbe Pieh is reimagined in Haffner's and DeSouza-George's theatrical adaptations as both a national symbol and a transatlantic icon. According to their visions, Pieh's epic history signifies as a rallying cry designed to galvanize African pride in the ongoing fight for civil rights. Both playwrights betray a political, social, and aesthetic determination to resist the ongoing realities of racist persecution in the twentieth and twenty-first centuries.

THE "UNSPEAKABLE": HYPER-(IN)VISIBILITY VERSUS SPECTACULAR EXHIBITION IN STEVEN SPIELBERG'S *AMISTAD*

"Blood, we need much more blood!" Steven Spielberg exclaimed during his filming of the slave ship rebellion dramatized at the start of his movie

Amistad.[117] In this mainstream cinematic work, he was intent not only upon providing graphic realism but also upon securing heightened visual drama. As producer and major advisor on this film, Deborah Allen was inspired to participate in this production to counter the widespread historical neglect of the *Amistad* in contemporary U.S. memory. "How was it possible that I had never heard of this epic moment in history?" she wonders. Allen sought to create a didactic film that would "inspire others—especially young people—to explore and debate the truths of the past."[118] Despite this ambitious goal, however, the movie has been subject to widespread vilification and critique. As Patrick Rael asks, "Why did we have to get *this* film? Why not Nat Turner's revolt?"[119] Ostensibly engaged in acts and arts of telling or untelling, Spielberg's *Amistad* epitomizes the failures of popular memorializations of black male heroism as reimagined according to a white American national paradigm.

For Robert Forbes, the film's iconography presents insurmountable difficulties by relying on a "powerful aesthetic of racial essentialism which seemed, like the pictorial language and cartoonish rendering of historical actors and events, deliberately to hearken back to the style of the early decades of the century."[120] Similarly, for Jesse Lemisch *Amistad* "is a present-minded Nineties screed for white paternalism and cartoonified black instinctualism and for the archaic notion of history made by great men, particularly great white men."[121] For these critics, Spielberg does not destroy to create but creates to destroy, as they condemn his perceived complicity in "Reinforcing the absence of black agency" through "the film's focus on Cinque as individual hero."[122] This film clearly testifies to the failures of popular attempts to reimagine Pieh's heroism according to white abolitionist normative standards. The determination of Spielberg and his crew to draw on teleologies of uplift seemingly to secure black redemption runs serious risks by replicating white mainstream tendencies toward black historical objectification and annihilation.

Spielberg's stylized and graphic representation of Sengbe Pieh's role in the mutiny aboard the *Amistad* lies at the heart of controversies in the critical reception of the film. Stripped down and shot in starkly contrasting blacks, browns, whites, and reds simultaneously to signify violence and racial difference, the opening scene provides the viewer with close-ups of Pieh's body parts. The discordant cinematography reveals a Black man's eyes, lips, teeth, and fingers—all later revealed to be those of Sengbe Pieh—as he works to liberate himself from his shackles with a nail found in the ship's deck, while sweat drips down his face. In a gritty image, his bloodied fingers desperately work the nail free, while a dramatic chiaroscuro operates to conceal and reveal his exemplary physicality. Here, Spielberg insists upon Pieh's interpretative ambiguity at the same time that he exalts in his exceptional physicality. Very rapidly in this opening scene, an upward camera angle reveals Pieh's entire face for the first time as he gazes in fearful contemplation at the liberated nail—a metonymic signifier of his freedom—while the viewer is given full access to his naked yet idealized torso. Audiences gain access to Sengbe Pieh's face, visually framed through his fetters, only by peering up through his shackles. Contrary to the claims of his critics, Spielberg may well have sought to invert racist power hierarchies by placing his audiences in a subjugated position deliberately to recall the subordinated posture typically associated with Wedgwood's kneeling enslaved male icon.

Regardless, Spielberg's overt stylization of Pieh as the spectral embodiment of a violent black masculinity grotesquely replicates minstrelsy theatrics in this scene. His close-ups of rolling eyes and exaggerated physical gestures testifying to a pseudoanimalistic posturing clearly have their origins in racist iconographies. Perhaps, however, Spielberg relies on an excessive use of the grotesque in order to challenge his white mainstream audiences' racism. While he may well deliberately play into fearful spectacles of black ferocity, at the same time, his highly aestheticized representation of Pieh's exemplary musculature recalls Nathaniel Jocelyn's portrait, and his camera shot showing Sengbe Pieh in command of the ship counters minstrelsy-inflected caricatures of black masculinity. In this shot, the director accentuates a statuesque stillness in the bronze contours of Pieh's skin, while his stylized posture testifies to his legendary, iconographic symbolism. Yet Spielberg's cinematographer, Janusz Kaminski, argues that "there's definitely not a romanticism" in the film because "there's no clichéd beauty in the photography."[123] Such a claim fails to convince, however, in light of the fact that the film endorses stylized representations of Pieh's classically beautiful physicality. Such a strategy clearly perpetuates constructions of this heroic enslaved figure as a "noble savage," just as Joceyln's portrait painted over one hundred fifty years before may also have conflated and exaggerated racial differences by recalling the earlier proliferation of an array of problematic and stereotypical portraits of Native Americans as popularly painted by white American artists.

Despite these problematic representations, the film's creators clearly worked hard not to portray Sengbe Pieh as the "individualistic hero figure." Revealingly, in one of the most powerful moments during the rebellion, Pieh is shown plunging a sword into a white man's chest. As a sign of his superlative strength, his weapon penetrates beneath the deck while the camera pans below to scenes of the slave ship hold, in which shackled Africans hold up their chains in distress. The heated criticism regarding Spielberg's representation, or lack thereof, of a black heroic individualism should therefore not detract from his hauntingly successful representation of the Middle Passage, as visually narrated not only in the Africans' plight depicted here but also in Sengbe Pieh's courtroom flashback. As Kaminski explains, he inserted "more contrast into the film by enhancing the shadow area and making the highlights more 'glowy,'" a photographic process that "desaturates color" as a means to heighten historicity via a minimalist, understated visual narrative.[124] These self-reflexive aesthetic techniques work most forcefully in Spielberg's representation of the Middle Passage. The lack of any "clichéd beauty" heightens the emotional power of these scenes, while desaturated tonal variations bear witness to white moral depravity. The decision to have Sengbe Pieh narrate the traumas of the masses of unknown enslaved women, children, and men during the Middle Passage returns us to Hamilton's memorial by testifying to Spielberg's interpretation of this singular heroic icon as inextricable from the histories of black communal suffering. In this impressively well-researched and powerfully acted film, anonymous and naked enslaved Africans suffer ritual humiliation in the "tight-packing" aboard slave ships. Rapes, suicides, and whippings are dramatized without either overt sentimentality or excessive dramatization. Moreover, the fact that Sengbe Pieh is whipped and forcibly held back by a white crew as enslaved women and men are drowned en masse does not exalt in his exceptional heroism at the cost of anonymous black suffering but instead accentuates the suffering resulting from his failures.

Such a reading may even begin to challenge Paul Gilroy's view that in this film, "the Middle Passage has been deliberately and provocatively recovered, but it is rendered in an impossible and deeply contentious manner that offers only the consolation of tears in place of more challenging and imaginative connections."[125] While Gilroy powerfully emphasizes the film's problematic use of visual hyperbole to generate an emotional effect upon its viewers, his sense that this is a substitute for "imaginative connections" is perhaps debatable. As Kaminski suggests, Spielberg worked with "an extremely limited use of complicated camera moves" because he "wanted the composition to resemble a still-life tableau." "We're observing the movie rather than following the action," he argues.[126] Such a dispassionate approach is evident in the film's cinematography, which provides panoramic juxtapositions of rape, suicide, starvation, infanticide, death, and whippings. Arguably, these horrific events take place in quick succession not to encourage but to prevent catharsis via a lack of narrative closure, as an array of colliding, fragmented vignettes dramatize a multiplicity of seemingly unimaginable experiences paradoxically to inspire imaginative engagement. Tellingly, scenes from the Middle Passage signify as haunting sites of commemoration in a film otherwise preoccupied with an oversimplified, paternalistic, and racist aggrandizement of white benevolence via an inflated and highly skewed, mythical celebration of the American judicial system. As such, these diverse memorializations of Sengbe Pieh—undoubtedly as obfuscated, annihilated, and frequently destroyed a historical figure as Sojourner Truth—speak to the fragmented and elided histories of millions of enslaved Africans. Directly appealing to his viewers, Ed Hamilton states, "I will let you, as viewer, debate the meaning of this journey." In powerful ways, Hamilton's decision to invite his audiences to embark on their own psychological and imaginary rites of passage resonates with the demands made of her listeners and viewers centuries before by the performer, activist, and intellectual Sojourner Truth.[127]

CHAPTER 4 "TICKETY-UMP-UMP-NICKY NACKY" RE-CREATING, REKNOWING, AND REFIGURING SOJOURNER TRUTH

As recently as April 2009, the Black female sculptor Artis Lane's bronze bust of Sojourner Truth made history as the first work representing an African American woman to be unveiled before audiences at the Capitol Visitor Center in Washington, DC. Worlds away from the centuries-old circulation of the body and face of the half-naked Black female enslaved woman shackled, on her knees, and begging, "Am I not a woman and a Sister?" this sculpture is startling for its aggrandized scale and forceful physiognomy. No bespectacled Truth benignly seated with her knitting—as was typical of her many photographic performances—Lane's Truth is iconic, uncompromising, and challenging. Speaking at this event, First Lady Michelle Obama, herself a groundbreaking Black female icon, celebrates Truth's powerful legacies as inseparable from her own. "I hope that Sojourner Truth would be proud to see me, a descendent of slaves, serving as the First Lady of the United States of America," she proclaims.[1] Intent not only upon securing this historical figure's approval but upon bearing witness to genealogies of black female resistance, Obama vouchsafes Truth's status as a reusable symbol and touchstone for black female spiritual, political, social, and cultural emancipation. Signifying as a point of origin for the overthrow of nefarious paradigms of gender no less than race subjugation, for Obama, Lane, and many others, Truth functions as an archetypal embodiment of the ongoing fight for black female equality. Similarly, she operates as an emblem of the political necessity for an idealized belief in the inevitability of American progress more generally. In forceful ways, Lane's twenty-first-century memorialization of Truth remains inspired by and indebted to the life and works of this historical figure. Perpetually at war against static, one-dimensional and mythologized representations of black womanhood unless they originated in her own speeches and narratives, Sojourner Truth's life and works testify to her fight to elude fixity and defy definition as she engaged in diverse signifying practices.

African. Legend. Prophet. Orator. Fugitive. Feminist. Performer. Trickster. Mother. Wife. Symbol. Daughter. Heroine. This chapter examines the diverse cultural and historical imagining of Isabella Van Wagenen, or Isabella Baumfree, iconically reborn as Sojourner Truth in a symbolic act of self-naming following her escape from slavery. Even in the early nineteenth century, attempts by white abolitionists such as Gilbert Vale to dismiss Truth as "a poor, coloured, unlettered woman" failed in light of her self-conscious performances. "From our listening to this coloured female, . . . we have discovered that she . . . is not exactly what she seems," he was forced to concede. In telling ways, her deliberate obfuscations of language secured his frustration: "She is not communicative, and if circumstances did not prompt her to tell all she knows, it would be difficult to get at it."[2] An unreadable and contrary figure who was "not exactly what she seems," Truth perpetually defied mainstream understanding of her life and works as she manipulated not only her "as told to" testimony but also her visual and performative representations. Hers was a body, identity, and experience that not only refused to tell but engaged in multiple imaginary narratives of being and becoming. In this regard, she has more in common with Harriet Tubman and Frederick Douglass than with Toussaint Louverture, Sengbe Pieh, or Nathaniel Turner in light not only of their shared signifying performances on the abolitionist stage but also their experimentation with oral testimony and the textual poetics of written biographies.

Sojourner Truth was a philosopher and intellectual who fought against slavery, as did Frederick Douglass, on moral, aesthetical, and ideological grounds. "To the woman who became Sojourner Truth, knowing and being known were always of both material and epistemological significance," writes Nell Irvin Painter, one of her major biographers.[3] Truth's interrogative examination of the processes of "knowing and being known" resonates powerfully with the importance Douglass himself attached to existential and philosophical enquiry, the right to which both of these freedom fighters interpreted as the bedrock of an individual's political freedom. Clearly, Truth's experimentation with the signifying possibilities of multiple mythical identities remains as much a defining feature of her malleable symbolism. As Karen Sánchez-Eppler observes, "The legendary Truth is a figure that the historical Truth herself did much, quite self-consciously, to construct and exploit."[4] Writing much more recently, Xiomara Santamarina defines tendencies either to demonize or heroicize Truth as "a critical dynamic that continually recasts her popularity and agency in polarizing terms: either the illiterate Truth was irredeemably susceptible to her interlocutors' agendas, or she was all-powerful."[5] A self-reflexive performer and orator, Sojourner Truth repeatedly resisted white abolitionist tendencies toward privileging authenticity dictates in a reductive search for verifiable proofs regarding black experiences during slavery. Instead, she excelled as an adept manipulator not only of indirection and signifying but also of humor and irony. For Donna Haraway, Truth was a "trickster figure, a shape changer, who might trouble our notions—all of them: classical, biblical, scientific, modernist, postmodernist, and feminist—of 'the human.'"[6] As Gloria Joseph argues, Truth's "uncanny wit" sheds light on the fact that she "remains one of the Black women whose histories have not adequately been treated." Scholars, Joseph suggests, have tended to oversimplify Truth on the grounds that "rarely is there any mention of the philosophical constructs and revolutionary concepts underlying her words and deeds."[7]

The exceptional physicality and self-reflexive signifying practices of Sojourner Truth and Harriet Tubman, the only two female freedom fighters examined in this book, have been excessively marginalized in comparison with the overwhelming emphasis upon Black male heroic figures by white male and female, no less than Black male, writers and artists, all producing works dramatizing black male heroism across a vast time frame and a transatlantic milieu. As their subversive practices reveal, Tubman and Truth fought against normative masculine biases to exalt in their own newfound status as autonomous freedom fighters. Clearly, Truth's and Tubman's multifaceted and subversive heroic legacies exist in complex relation to African, African Caribbean, and African American male traditions of resistance. In striking ways, their lives and works resisted and reconfigured Douglass's default construction of an exceptional and iconic "heroic slave" or "black hero" as explicable solely according to an overtly masculinist paradigm. Their self-stylizations as tricksters in possession of superheroic bodies could not be further from Douglass's conception of the suffering black female body as a passive catalyst to black male heroism. Reimagining the archetypal freedom fighter Madison Washington's iconic bravery in his novella *The Heroic Slave* for example, Douglass's narration of the death of Madison's wife, Susan Washington, betrays his clear-cut gender biases. His protagonist eulogizes black male heroism as a necessary antidote to black female martyrdom. As Douglass's Madison explains, white slave owners "fired, and my poor wife fell by my side dead, while I received but a slight flesh wound," leaving him with no option but a fight for "liberty or death," as he relates, "I now became desperate, and stood my ground, and awaited their attack over her dead body."[8]

Considered against a backdrop of black female appropriation and marginalization, Truth's philosophical and intellectual resistance functioned in conjunction with and not apart from her exhibition of a mythically exalted physicality to establish a very different model for "the heroic slave" or "Black hero." Recognizing not only white but also black tendencies to objectify and sensationalize black female bodies, Truth conjoined oratorical prowess with physical spectacle in her signifying performances. Equally, Tubman's no less exceptional physicality—manifested in her unprecedented leadership in multiple liberation raids—remained inextricable from her coded performances, as she shared Truth's determination to establish an alternative paradigm for black female heroism. As Lerone Bennett Jr. writes, Sojourner Truth "stands with Harriet Tubman as the archetypal image of a long line of fabulously heroic women."[9] Truth, Tubman, and many other formerly enslaved Black women whose names are both known and unknown to folkloric memory and official histories transgressed aesthetic and political boundaries to transform themselves from "passive victims" into "heroic actors."[10] Engaging in oratorical performances, textual signifying, and grassroots activism, they fought not only for political reform but also for the rights of black womanhood. The tangled skein of their shifting political and historical identities can therefore be understood in the context of a fluid and malleable female heroic continuum that encompasses the elided lives of Harriet Jacobs, Margaret Garner, Nanny of the Maroons, and Solitude, among many others living and dying in the Black diaspora. An attempt to map their difficult legacies has implications not only for reformulating prescriptive categorizations of black femininity but also for contesting unimaginative definitions of black male heroism.

In contrast to critical interpretations of Nathaniel Turner, whom Vincent Harding describes as a "sign in himself," Donna Haraway asks, "What kind of sign is Sojourner Truth?"[11] Refusing to shy away from black female heroism as a site of ambiguity, this question usefully encourages critics to recognize the ways in which a circulating plethora of multiple personae are as much excised from the historical and cultural record for Sojourner Truth as they are for Nathaniel Turner. The extent to which Truth, whose legacies were reinvented across diverse artistic and political reimaginings, functions as a "sign" remains a question scholars are still unable to answer. As her extensive archive reveals, any subsequent aestheticized and politicized representations of Sojourner Truth originated within this freedom fighter's own textual and oratorical performances, as was similarly the case for Toussaint Louverture, Nathaniel Turner, Harriet Tubman, Frederick Douglass, and Sengbe Pieh. Especially her experimentation with the representational possibilities of her body and language reveals that she engaged simultaneously in processes of telling and untelling, being and nonbeing, hearing and nonhearing in order to transgress the boundaries of racist discourse by rejecting white paternal-ism, censorship, and taboo. Writing at the turn of the twentieth century, Pauline E. Hopkins candidly admits her despair at ever being able to do jus-tice to such an enigmatic figure. As she observes, "We cannot hope to give more than a skeleton sketch of the life and good works of Sojourner Truth," and yet she argues, "Through all the scenes of an eventful life one traces the workings of a great mind."[12] Such a rare sensitivity to Truth's "great mind" offers a powerful corrective to a great number of inaccuracies within current scholarship by advocating a far more theorized assessment of her oeuvre. Privileging the internal dynamics of Truth's intellectual life over and above her corporeal realities, Hopkins provides a useful way in which to reconsider theoretical approaches to the overly physically determined and imagined fic-tions of singular rather than multiple Sojourner Truths.

"AN *ORIGINAL*?": SOJOURNER TRUTH IN EARLY ILLUSTRATIONS AND PHOTOGRAPHY

A powerful example of Sojourner Truth's determination to adopt an array of signifying practices to defy both media constraints and the limitations of her social and historical contexts can be found in the politicized circulation of her physiognomy and body in illustrations and photographs circulating both during and after her lifetime. "Come and hear an *original*." So quotes Frances W. Titus as an example of the various newspaper articles that en-couraged readers to witness this "interesting and decidedly original charac-ter," at the same time that they were urged, "Don't forget to purchase her photograph."[13] Against the backdrop of the Civil War, numerous known and unidentified artists reproduced portraits of Sojourner Truth as woodcuts, drawings, photographs, cabinet cards, cartes de visite, and even postcards. As Marcus Wood argues, the proliferation of this diverse imagery was testament to her importance as "another example of an ex-slave campaigner controlling the new technology and the new market in order to make a serious political statement."[14] More particularly, and in light of Truth's self-conscious experi-mentation with ambiguous representations of self via oratory and song, in addition of course to her "as told to" narratives, it is no surprise that she de-liberately complicated the relationship between authenticity and artifice in her photographs. Circulating both as a physical presence on the abolitionist circuit and as a mechanically reproduced copy, she problematized conceptu-alizations of black female selfhood simultaneously as an "original" and as an imitation. While John Stauffer suggests that "Sojourner Truth was possibly more famous for her *cartes de visite* than for her actual presence in abolition meetings," her photographic representations undoubtedly perpetuated her cultivation of multiple identities via familiarity among her purchasers with her physical performances as orator, singer, and activist.[15] In powerful ways, Truth's determination to create a visual archive signaled her preoccupation with establishing ownership over dominant iconographic codes of black female memorialization.

As did numerous ex-enslaved men and women—including Douglass and Tubman, who also chose to be photographed during this period—Truth artfully engaged with the politics and poetics of self-representation. Creating and editing her own visual narratives, she inhabited multiple personae beyond her symbolic identities as an archetypal enslaved figure and as an abolitionist emblem. As Painter argues, evidence of her experimental practices reveal that "Truth's images may appear to be unmediated, the essence of her real self, but in fact they were carefully arranged."[16] As a mutually inclusive visual and textual archive, Truth's plethora of photographs, speeches, songs, and narratives all attest to her resistance to "essences" of any kind, be they biologically fixed definitions of motherhood, scientific labels of racial difference, political identifications as activist outsider, or even historical representations as an enslaved fugitive. As Kathy Glass observes, "she created photographs that could be read as texts" as she traded upon her own absent presences in order to exult "in a constant process of making and unmaking meaning."[17] Such a process of becoming and unbecoming reflects Truth's engagement with the black female body's hypervisibility and invisibility in white mainstream culture. Ultimately, Truth navigated the differences between her "shadow" and her "substance" to counter the widespread commodification of black female bodies simultaneously portrayed as sexualized objects, maternal icons, enslaved laborers, and abolitionist lecturers. An existential sojourner in the pursuit of social, political, and philosophical truths, she shared Edgar Allan Poe's and Oliver Wendell Holmes's fascination with photographic technology not as a way of delineating the realities of a physical self but as a means of liberating the "latent soul."[18]

A useful way to begin analyzing Truth's visual archive is by examining an anonymously produced woodcut included as the frontispiece to Olive Gilbert's first edition of *Narrative of Sojourner Truth, A Northern Slave* (see figure 16). Kathleen Collins speculates that this image may have been "based on a daguerreotype portrait." That is unlikely, however, given that, as Collins herself explains, "there is no record" that Truth had "met a photographer before about 1863."[19] As the earliest known portrait, this woodcut offers an intimate close-up of Truth's head and shoulders clothed in a plain white head scarf and black dress. In Augusta Rohrbach's view, Truth's "head wrap" reflects a dual symbolism, representing not only "her connection to slavery" but also "her African past."[20] According to Helen Griebel, the "head wrap" functioned more particularly as a signifier of African cultural retentions in the face of white attempts to subjugate black ancestral legacies. As Griebel writes, this piece of clothing "may be traced back to West Africa both in its style and in the underlying African world view that encodes that style."[21] Wearing a head wrap that affirmed both black female agency and subjugation, Truth fore-grounded her cultural and political performances as the loyal, devoted, and domesticated enslaved woman in this image as precisely that: a performance. As Richard Powell observes, the "head-wrap" operated as a "floating signifier for black history and feminine pride" by which Truth established her prefer-ence for "floating" rather than fixed identities.[22]

Simply titled *Sojourner Truth,* this woodcut refutes any pretensions to-ward black female objectification in pro- or even antislavery iconography. Relying on a thematic use of naming, this work testifies to her symbolic re-birth into freedom in a coming to consciousness of not just one but mul-tiple newfound identities. In contrast to later full-length photographs, there is no exhibition here of her hand, which was injured during slavery, nor is she depicted within an opulent domestic milieu. On the surface, therefore, this minimalist woodcut exalts solely in Truth's identity as a female laborer. Such a view is compounded by Titus's decision to reproduce this frontis-piece in the second half of *Narrative of Sojourner Truth, A Bondswoman of Olden Time,* to which she added the revealing caption "A Picture taken in the days of her Physical Strength."[23] Yet such is not the whole story. Any in-depth examination of this woodcut quickly establishes its significance in offering an intimate portrait of Truth's physiognomy in order to detract attention away from reductive accounts of her "Physical Strength." No eulogy to her exemplary physique, this illustration features crosshatched lines that meticu-lously delineate her prominent forehead, eyes, nose, and mouth to dramatize her contemplative expression, which resisted white mainstream tendencies toward excessive caricature. The simplicity of the vertically etched lines of her clothing complement the delicate lines on her face both to individualize her portrait and cultivate illusions of authenticity by suggesting that this was a seemingly unmediated visual representation of Truth. These individualiz-ing details work in conjunction with the inclusion of Truth's name as cap-tion to problematize Hertha Pauli's insistence that this "portrait might have

FIGURE 16. Anon., frontispiece, *Narrative of Sojourner Truth, A Northern Slave* (Boston: J. P. Yerrington and Sons, 1850). (Documenting the American South, University of North Carolina, Chapel Hill)

been drawn without seeing her, it was so much the popular image of a Negro house slave or servant."[24]

According to this image, Truth is no archetypal enslaved Black woman but instead a famous icon, as her expressive eyes directly confront the viewer. At the same time, the inclusion of her name—"Sojourner Truth"—gestures toward the necessity for performance and disguise in multiple, staged identities. Clearly, this work reveals Truth exalting in her status as a lone individual who had not only just emerged from slavery but who remained unfettered by the trappings of white bourgeois conventionalism. The absence of any signs of domesticity reinforces the starkness of the image, not only to illuminate Truth's cultivation of an iconic exceptionalism, but also to shed light on her signifying poetics in the narrative itself. According to written accounts of her language, Truth preferred a frequently antisentimental, pared-down use of language in order to counter tendencies among white abolitionists to take ownership over her experiences by remaking her testimony in their own image.

The frontispiece to Truth's first narrative resonates powerfully with an untitled portrait that appeared over a decade later in 1867 during her residence at the Northampton Association utopian settlement. This drawing was produced by one of her contemporaries, the white artist Charles C. Burleigh Jr., an ardent advocate not only of abolitionism but also of women's rights (see figure 17).[25] In this seemingly straightforward celebration of Truth's laboring persona, soft-pencil shading replaces the hard, etched lines of the earlier woodcut. Depicting the formerly enslaved woman bent over a washtub and working at a washboard, Burleigh's Truth is surrounded by pots, pans, and begrimed sheets, all operating as a metonymic shorthand for black female labor. In contrast to the earlier woodcut, her elongated frame is clothed in a plain but elegant dress to reveal the exemplary musculature of her forearms. Here, Truth's face is shown only in profile, as if to suggest an inextricable relationship between the black female body and labor. Yet, as in the earlier image, Burleigh draws attention to her contemplative expression in his radical decision to individualize her facial features. Far from depicting a gross caricature of black female physical strength, Burleigh provides a sensitive portrait of Truth as a dignified, well-dressed Black female subject. Furthermore, his focus upon Truth's ambiguous physiognomy betrays the importance of her intellectual inner life, through which she transcended the limitations of her physical status. Nonetheless, and however unwittingly, this image ultimately underscores class differences by presenting Truth as defined by the tools of her labor rather than by the accoutrements of domestic elitism. Significantly, Burleigh's Truth appears as if she could be in the service of the Truth depicted in later photographs of the 1860s and 1870s as they all portray a genteel woman seated before a hearth and in an ornate domestic interior. In contrast to images representing Truth solely as a domesticated woman engaged in genteel pursuits, Burleigh's drawing nonetheless resonates with the earlier frontispiece to document her mutually inclusive incarnations as a heroic exemplar, maternal icon, domestic laborer, and ex-enslaved woman.

FIGURE 17. Charles Burleigh, untitled portrait of Sojourner Truth, 1867. (Historic Northampton, Northampton, Massachusetts)

An anonymously produced carte de visite, *I Sell the Shadow to Support the Substance* inaugurates an alternative tradition of visualizing another persona for Truth (see figure 18). In contrast to earlier drawings and woodcuts, which provide intimate portraits of Truth engaged in physical labor or wearing plain clothing and scarcely removed from slavery, this photograph dramatizes a full-length, well-dressed Truth gazing into the distance rather than directly at the viewer. The stark lighting illuminates the delicate lines on her forehead to suggest her battle-weary status, while her spectacles provide little barrier to her sorrowful expression. As they illuminate her photographic representations, Truth's eyes tell the stories that her decision to remain illiterate prevented her from writing down firsthand. Truth's clothing is far more ornate in this photograph, as she wears not only the customary white head wrap and shawl but also a striped bodice, patterned sleeves, and a dark full skirt. Standing erect, she appears against a plain backdrop not only to heighten ambiguities regarding domestic values but also to underscore her assumption of a symbolic name, "Sojourner Truth," as if to provide further testament to her ongoing search for a moral and political, rather than a physical, home. Not merely a name she assumed for the protection of her formerly enslaved identity, "Sojourner Truth" operated as a performative mask through which she resisted and politicized white female standards of spirituality, domesticity, and morality. In this image, Truth's pose recalls other key photographs in which she similarly rests her right arm on her cane and makes no attempt to hide her hand injury. At the same time, she dispensed with domestic artifacts as usable properties customarily integral to photographic representations of formerly enslaved female subjects in order to vindicate an empowered vision of black womanhood. Instead, she appears carrying a checked and flower-patterned fabric bag on her left arm. Captioning this image with her by now famously repeated refrain, "I sell the shadow to support the substance," she sought to distinguish between Truth the live original and Truth the reproduced copy.

As Collins argues, Sojourner Truth's caption, "I sell the shadow to support the substance," became "her motto as her reputation grew."[26] Painter emphasizes that it was "as much a part of the rhetoric of the image as the portrait itself."[27] An anonymous reporter quoted Sojourner Truth as claiming:

Speaking of shadows, I wish the *World* to know that when I go among fashionable people in the Church of the Puritans, I do not carry "rations" in my bag; I keep my shadow there. I have good friends enough to give me clothes and rations. I stand on principle, always in one place, so everybody

I SELL THE SHADOW TO SUPPORT THE SUBSTANCE.

SOJOURNER TRUTH.

FIGURE 18. Anon., *I Sell the Shadow to Support the Substance*, Sojourner Truth, three-quarter-length portrait, photographic print on carte de visite mount, 1864. (Prints and Photographs Division, Library of Congress)

knows where to find Sojourner, and I don't want my shadow even to be dogging about here and there and everywhere, so I keep it in this bag.[28]

Favoring her mythic "shadow" over the need for practical "rations," Truth exalted in her importance as a didactic guide to white audiences. More particularly, she distinguished between her physical and intellectual wants by separating her spiritual and metaphysical complexities from her corporeal realities. Ultimately, she concealed her "shadow" to free her "substance" as she fought to ensure that her mechanical representation would not dominate her physical and intellectual performances.

For Nicholas Mirzoeff, "Truth's use of photography shows that another 'shadow archive' was possible."[29] Such a description of Truth's manipulation of a "shadow archive" effectively communicates her preference for creating narratives that signified in complex relation to dominant representational practices. "Her maxim suggests that she wanted to extend the 'aura' of the daguerreotype onto other forms of photography in order to preserve the connection between image and reality, shadow and substance, without distortion," Stauffer argues.[30] Clearly, Truth herself did not see any transparent relationship between her "substance" and "shadow," as she recognized the absence of an "aura" in her multiple photographed reproductions. Describing her "shadow" as "dogging about here and there," she called into question abolitionist proliferations of multiple representations or "shadow archives" of black identities. "In her speeches and conversations," Collins writes, "she made it clear that 'substance' meant not only her bodily requirements, but also the words she used and the ideas she promoted."[31] As her visual archive reveals, Truth complicated seemingly polarized representations between her "shadow" and "substance" to expose the complex relationships between the corporeal and the spiritual, the material and the immaterial, and the authentic and the artificial or fake. Such a reading directly engages with Rohrbach's view that "we might understand 'shadow' to mean 'race:'" "shadow" for Truth seemed to suggest metaphorical rather than physical representations of selfhood as exhibited across diverse media.[32] As her photographic archive reveals, Truth was fascinated by the act and art of representation, as she sought to secure individual agency for Black female subjects more generally by countering their objectifying exhibition in anti- no less than proslavery materials.

Appearing in the same year and on the cusp of the unimaginable atrocities that were to define the Civil War era, the white feminist and radical activist Susan B. Anthony offers further evidence of the importance of Truth's photographic archive as she took to the abolitionist stage in a dramatic fight against a battle-weary audience. Prophesying a postslavery future, she believed that black rights had not yet been won and that the "eyes and the ears of the whole public are now open." "It should be the earnest work of every lover of freedom to give those eyes the right thing to see and those ears the right thing to hear," she insists.[33] Yet just what constituted the "right thing" to "see" and "hear" regarding antislavery materials remained ideologically charged, given the overwhelming predominance of a white philanthropic lens as the default filter. As the fight to end slavery became increasingly militant, Anthony emphasized the power of visual iconography, which she interpreted as working in conjunction with written testimonies to provide emotive portrayals of black suffering as catalysts for white moral reform. As her fellow white abolitionist Angelina Grimké had argued decades earlier, prints and photographs were "powerful appeals" that worked to "expose slavery." "Until the pictures of the slave's sufferings were drawn and held up to public gaze," she observes, "no Northerner had any idea of the cruelty of the system."[34]

Believing "More knowledge is needed," Anthony expresses her frustration with the woeful limitations of white antislavery oratory by taking drastic action to convert her audiences.[35] Clearly, for Anthony, the "right thing" to which her viewers should bear witness was not a series of general pictures but a pair of images providing close-ups of specific individuals: a daguerreotype of an enslaved man from Louisiana named Gordon—which formed the basis for the drawing *Gordon under Medical Inspection* published in *Harper's Weekly* (see figure 19)—and a photograph of Truth as a formerly enslaved northern woman turned orator, performer, and activist (see figure 20).[36] As one reporter notes:

> Miss Anthony held up two photographs to the view of the audience. One represented 'Sojourner Truth,' the heroine of one of Mrs. H. B. Stowe's tales, and the other the bare back of a Louisiana slave. Many of the audience were affected to tears. 'Sojourner Truth' had lost three fingers of one hand, and the Louisiana slave's back bore scars of whipping. She asked every one to suppose that woman was her mother, and that man her father. In that case would they think the time past for discussion and petition? The resolutions were at once unanimously passed.[37]

Anthony's decision to pair a formerly enslaved southern man, Gordon, who had become a soldier during the Civil War, with a northern fugitive enslaved woman, Truth, whose antislavery activism was rooted in self-reflexivity and an experimental folkloric identity, sought to effect white moral conversion by relying on symbolic reimaginings of black male and female histories.

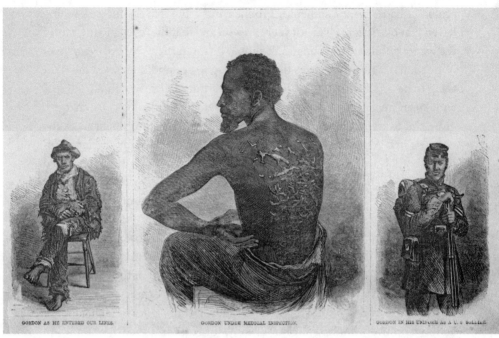

GORDON AS HE ENTERED OUR LINES.   GORDON UNDER MEDICAL INSPECTION.   GORDON IN HIS UNIFORM AS A U. S SOLDIER.

FIGURE 19. Anon., *Gordon as He Entered Our Lines, Gordon under Medical Inspection,* and *Gordon in His Uniform as a U.S. Soldier,* 1863. (Prints and Photographs Division, Library of Congress)

Anthony's determination to urge white audiences to "suppose" that this unrelated Black woman and man were their mother and father sheds light on white abolitionist tendencies toward constructing usable public histories by willfully distorting private and often unknowable black testimonies. Such biases toward maximizing the political possibilities of spectacles of black suffering risked exhibiting black bodies solely as bodies of evidence and, therefore, as significant only as catalysts to white spiritual redemption. Anthony sought to avoid these pitfalls by taking the view that it was not enough that she display these photographs as proofs in a court of law. Instead, she believed it was essential that she imaginatively retell their stories to satiate the demands of her female audience: those capable of being "affected to tears" by understanding black suffering only according to the invented familial mores of a genteel white domesticity. However problematic, the idea that two formerly enslaved Black individuals could act as parents for a white elite ultimately had the potential radically to reverse the codes of slavery as a paternal institution.

According to Painter, the photograph of Sojourner Truth that Anthony decided to exhibit to her audience was an image taken by "Randall of Detroit"

FIGURE 20. Randall, *Sojourner Truth*, 1864. (Courtesy of Burton Historical
Collection, Detroit Public Library)

(figure 20).[38] Stripped of the paraphernalia signifying on a normative bourgeois domesticity that customarily adorned photographs of Truth, Randall's stark portrait portrays her standing, leaning on a cane, and resting on a stone pillar as she appears against a spartan white background. Depending upon whether Anthony relied on Randall's cropped carte de visite or the cabinet card reprinted with Truth's famous caption, "I sell the shadow to support the substance," Anthony's audience may or may not have seen the decorative detail at the base of the stone pillar or the painted backdrop situating this self-emancipated woman in a natural landscape consisting of cliffs, rocks, and sea.[39] Such an idyllic background resonates with Nathaniel Jocelyn's romanticized dramatization of Sengbe Pieh in his decades-earlier portrait *Joseph Cinque* to suggest mythic cultivations of a no less exceptional, heroic identity for Truth: she was a "heroine" for Randall as well as for Anthony.

The overall absence of symbolic properties in this photograph draws attention to Truth's contrasting clothing, a stark white shawl on a plain black dress, as well as her suffering but surviving physicality—graying hair, partially hidden thin hands, lined forehead, thoughtful eyes, and closed mouth—to provide the viewer with seemingly unmediated access to her enigmatic facial expression. The photographer's use of lighting captures the delicate lines on Truth's furrowed brow to accentuate her psychological ambiguity. As this image reveals, Truth's manipulation of her physiognomy creates an array of unreadable expressions, all notable for rivaling Frederick Douglass's experimental practices at work within his daguerreotyped representations. As Mirzoeff notes, "In these carefully posed images, Truth sought to counter the ambivalence of earlier abolitionist photography with a series of well-chosen signs."[40] In this earlier period, these "signs" did not consist of domestic properties as external markers of an equal humanity. Instead, she relied on an ambiguous facial expression alone to operate as a "sign" of black female subjectivity. Anthony equally did not shy away from ambiguities within Truth's iconic mythology, as she chose Randall's minimalist photograph to encourage viewers not only to "discuss" and "petition" but also to reimagine. Yet, as an endorsement of black female emotional complexity, this image reveals that Truth manipulated her physiognomy and bodily posture to resist white abolitionist tendencies, however well-intentioned, toward itemizing black suffering.

This was a luxury unavailable to the comparatively anonymous Gordon, a former enslaved man turned fugitive who was repeatedly represented in the same sensationalizing pose. At first glance, however, Truth purports to provide a similarly uncensored access to black scarification as audiences bear witness to her physical injury. Thus, according to Erlene Stetson and Linda

David, "Like the scarred back, Truth's three lost fingers are a horrific sign of the slave master's brutality."[41] And yet, closer inspection soon betrays Truth's determination to ensure that they remained half-concealed, as she vouch-safed her preference for omitting rather than exhibiting spectacular displays of black female victimization in her visual narratives. In contrast to the *Harper's Weekly* drawing of Gordon, which relies on an artist's cross-hatched rendering of black physicality, the original photograph and subsequent carte de visite copied and circulated by Mathew Brady's studio, and most likely used by Anthony, provided a much more graphic representation of black physical suffering. As Wood writes, this work is "one of the most shocking photographs of an abused slave body ever made."[42] Stark lighting techniques offer a detailed display of the raised welts on Gordon's naked back to foreground the realities of black suffering at the same time that he also appears before a nonspecific white background devoid of properties.

In comparison to Truth's erect posture and fully clothed figure, Gordon sits on a wooden chair with his face half in shadow, while the tactility of the intricate surfaces on his exposed back invite the viewers' touch. His bare furniture contrasts with Truth's classical stone pillar and romanticized landscape to suggest an impoverished and potentially antiheroic domestic environment rather than a romanticized natural world. This symbolic use of properties and backdrops reverses gendered definitions regarding black male heroism as popularized by iconographic woodcuts during the period. According to these generic templates, seemingly archetypal representations of a passive, seated enslaved woman were circulated in stark contrast to visions of black male agency as shown in repeated representations of an enslaved man striding forward regardless of the burdens on his back.[43] For the engravers at *Harper's Weekly*, the image of Gordon's victimization clearly posed a problem. Rather than including this work in isolation, they opted instead to reinsert it as the centerpiece in a compelling triptych of woodcuts captioned "Gordon as He Entered Our Lines," "Gordon under Medical Inspection," and "Gordon in His Uniform as a U.S. Soldier." This "before and after" paradigm succeeds in providing a miniaturized slave narrative by seemingly straightforwardly visualizing the Black man's journey from slavery to freedom.

For Anthony, photographs of Truth's and Gordon's bodies signified as iconic representations of black male and female suffering in order to secure antislavery resolutions where rational arguments had failed. Damningly, the specificities of Truth's and Gordon's biographies remained irrelevant for Anthony, as they instead assumed an iconic status in the service of an antislavery agenda. In clear-cut ways, the exhibition of these photographs operated in the same way as the eighteenth- and nineteenth-century trans-atlantic display of the paraphernalia of torture by white activists, which were initially included as "iron arguments" against slavery.[44] Similarly operating as visual substitutes for the bodies of enslaved women and men, these photographic representations of Gordon and Truth functioned as emblems of archetypal black subjectivities over and above their symbolism as talismans of resistance. Perhaps unsurprisingly, in light of her feminist credentials, Anthony's powerful photographic pairing did attempt to reverse traditional assumptions solely associating black masculinity with heroism. According to Anthony's schema, Truth signified as the archetypal "heroine" or symbol of black resistance, while black male victimization—as represented by Gordon—generated empathy solely as a body of evidence.

In remarkable ways, Truth's plethora of imagined identities proliferate across her photographs as well as in the popular imagination. As Stetson and David note regarding the description of Anthony's speech, one reporter places "'Sojourner Truth' in quotation marks as if this were no real person but another iconic phenomenon" in recognition of her widespread fame.[45] Perhaps it is possible to grant Truth more agency in these and other works than is suggested even by Painter's observation that "as the principal symbol of strength and blackness in the iconography of women's culture, Truth has been bought and sold for more than a century."[46] While this is undoubtedly the case for a number of her representations, photographs such as Randall's establish that Sojourner Truth's relationship to her abolitionist commodity status was far from passive. As these various images indicate, she was engaged in manipulating diverse media to display her own authority. For example, her famed insistence upon "I sell the shadow to support the substance" as epigraph to Randall's photograph reveals not only that she, if anyone, was buying and selling her identity but also that her competing mythologies of selfhood—her "shadow"—were always secondary to a clear-cut sense of her corporeality, her "substance." "By insisting on her control over the financial process," as Mirzoeff writes, "Truth further asserted a freedom to dispose of her own image."[47] Similarly, a too-quick dismissal of Anthony's political and aesthetic objectives in exhibiting Truth and Gordon to her audience risks oversimplifying black ex-enslaved and white abolitionist relationships. However problematic, and as compellingly argued by John Stauffer in *The Black Hearts of Men: Radical Abolitionists and the Transformation of Race,* cross-racial alliances frequently had the potential to transgress the alignments of commodification and appropriation perpetuated by a white abolitionist political and emotional penchant for inspiring sympathy exclusively by trading in spectacular black bodies.

Appearing in the same year, an anonymously produced carte de visite provides yet another variation upon Sojourner Truth's visual iconography as established by Randall and others (see figure 21). In stark contrast to intimate portraits of the black female figure as laborer or as a prophetic traveler in the "truth" carrying her "shadows" bag, Truth sits upright. She takes her place next to a table decorated with a delicately patterned cloth on which appear a vase of flowers and a book, most likely the Bible, as she holds some knitting in her hands. This work provides audiences with the first glimpse of her preference for the bourgeois markers of domesticity that were to characterize many of her later images. As an extensive archive, these works typically showcase the lavish artifacts of an opulent photographer's studio, including ornate chairs, decorative clothing, detailed curtains, excessive mantelpieces, and intricate carpets. Writing of another very similar image in which she adopts an almost identical pose, Wood observes that "given what Sojourner Truth actually did, and what she was really like" images steeped in trappings of bourgeois domesticity "must also surely have an ironic element."[48] "Posing as one of 'them,'" Rohrbach argues, "she uses these objects to trade on the gender norms of nineteenth-century domesticity and establishes an alliance with the white, evangelical, middle-class readers who were her targeted customers."[49] Yet even these seemingly innocuous objects operate as more than talismans of sameness, as Truth politicized ongoing injustices through an accentuation of difference. As revealed in this untitled image dated c. 1860s and held in the Detroit Public Library, Truth's prominent display of a photograph on her lap operates as a self-reflexive evocation of family portraiture by which she testifies not only to missing archives but also to the survival of black genealogies in the face of white strategies of erasure.

Undoubtedly, the simplicity of the domestic properties included in this untitled photograph dated to c. 1860s lack the ornamentation typical of the majority of the later images in her visual archive. A spartan work, this photograph reflects upon Truth's "self-made" identity not only to critique white trappings of respectability but also to eulogize an unquantifiable spiritual richness of soul, which she visualized as far superior to any practical richness in material wealth. Far more than a concession to her white female viewers, this portrait represents a declaration of black female independence. Bearing witness to her emancipation from slavery, she was seemingly able to knit, read, and sit at her own domestic table.

Overall, Truth's use of symbolic properties in this image resonates with other nineteenth-century photographs of formerly enslaved women, including a rare photograph of the quilter Harriet Powers. Clearly, new insights

I Sell the Shadow to Support the Substance.

SOJOURNER TRUTH.

FIGURE 21. Anon., *I Sell the Shadow to Support the Substance,* Sojourner Truth seated at table with knitting and book, three-quarter-length portrait, photographic print on carte de visite mount, ca. 1864. (Prints and Photographs Division, Library of Congress)

emerge regarding Truth's photographic archive if it is read in the context of the underresearched tradition of nineteenth-century black female portraiture. As Kyra Hicks argues in her biography, Powers's carte de visite was taken a few decades later in 1896 or 1897. Significantly, Powers does not hold knitting or a walking cane à la Truth. Rather, a dark scrap of fabric is illuminated against the white backdrop of her abstractly decorated apron.[50] Signifying her artistry via her prowess as a quilter, this symbolic detail reveals that for Powers, just as for Truth, symbolic objects were used to celebrate black female creativity as the subject matter of the photograph. Truth's appearance with a photograph rather than a scrap of cloth as in Powers's image suggests that such mechanical forms of representation in and of themselves constituted an important part of her experimental aesthetic practices. For Truth as well as Powers, seemingly disempowering symbols were reclaimed and repositioned for performative and imaginative purposes. More particularly, situating a Black woman not as an enslaved laborer or servant but as enjoying leisure pursuits within her own domestic sphere, this image has its descendents in twentieth-century paintings by Black artists such as *Mending Socks* by Archibald J. Motley Jr.[51]

Signifying on the act and art of photography, Truth's visual performances refute the flattening possibilities suggested by her mechanical circulation as a technologized icon. "Truth preferred more imaginative representations of herself in speeches, commissioned portraits, and in people's profiles about her," Powell writes.[52] Any acknowledgement of Truth's self-reflexivity provides a rich framework within which to come to grips with the complexities of her experimental practices. Consistently, she pushed the boundaries of visual and oratorical languages to destabilize boundaries and inspire audience engagement. A visual vignette documenting a groundbreaking slice of emancipated black life, as Carla Peterson argues, the "photograph thus came to function for Truth as a form of autobiography, of recorded testimony, of a signature both singular and reproducible, through which she once again hoped in some measure to enter the culture of writing."[53] Peterson is clearly right to identify the textual politics of Truth's iconography, yet her impetus was in fact toward illegibility, as she invited viewers to "read" her images but at the same time emphasized their failures by making it difficult for them to do so. Incorporating a wide array of tropes and motifs, Truth's enigmatic expressions, unreadable physical poses, and symbolic artifacts challenged and ultimately rejected superficial reimaginings of black female experiences as repeatedly manufactured within a white mainstream imagination.

"SOUL AND BODY": LANGUAGE, PERFORMANCE, AND SOJOURNER TRUTH'S ORATORY

For the majority of scholars, Sojourner Truth's illiteracy represents a lost opportunity. As Margaret Washington mourns, if she had "been able to write, Sojourner could have told her story more fully."[54] Carlton Mabee even speculates that she may have "had a learning disability of some kind."[55] Both of these views risk undermining Truth's studied disregard of written testimony in favor of oratory and song. For political and ideological reasons, nontextual media appealed to Truth in offering less mediated forms within which to re-create her personae and articulate her antislavery politics. As Rohrbach argues, "One might say she out-Douglassed Douglass. By remaining illiterate while also being a published 'author,' she retained all the markers of a slave while also claiming her freedom from it."[56] Thus, "She published *as a speaker*, and emphasized the spoken word over the written, what we call today in the language of deconstruction: presence over absence."[57] As a result, Truth's oratory and songs work in conjunction with her photographs to provide an artful tapestry of her self-representations. A knowable and unknowable Truth engaged in both fixity and illusion via mythical reconstructions of self emerges from these materials. In search of multiple "truths," her metaphor of travel or "sojourning" attests to her emphasis upon the limitations of experience as well as upon competing and unresolved forms of representation as dramatized across her oeuvre. Any analysis of written reports of Truth's speeches helps us to identify her radical poetics. She experimented with language to signify upon her "shadow" at the same time that she dramatized her "substance" or body. As she insisted in 1867 in the wake of the Civil War, "I have plead with all the force I had that the day might come that the colored people might own their soul and body."[58]

A desire to stake her moral, aesthetic, and political authority over the "soul and body" of ex-enslaved men and women lies at the heart of Truth's transgressive linguistic representations. As Karlyn Kohrs Campbell argues, she "relied on biblical authority, personal experience, vivid metaphors, and the power of herself as enactment" in her speeches.[59] Yet Truth's oratory has faced substantial critical neglect and, as Drema Lipsomb suggests, "No research has focused on her oratory as deliberative rhetoric."[60] Scholars researching Truth's oratory face almost insurmountable barriers. They confront diverse written representations of her "inimitable voice," as she was ceaselessly subjected to arbitrary revision by an array of white reporters.[61] "The varied ways that her language has been rendered suggest the enormous influence of her transcribers in shaping the texts we have today," Jean Fagan Yellin writes.[62] For Christina Accomando, "A complete picture of Sojourner Truth is impossible, especially given the compromised textual record of her words."[63] The negative connotations of "compromised" risk detracting attention away from problems generated not from transcription errors but from Truth's own artful obfuscations, which intentionally made any "complete picture" impossible.

The multifaceted texts of Truth's speeches reveal that she problematized interpretative possibilities by engaging in ambiguous oratorical performances. Ever intent upon experimenting with linguistic modes, she manipulated Dutch, African, British, and American South accents to effect moral suasion upon her audiences. Speculation that "her accent combined her Dutch background, the language of the unlettered of the day, and possibly some southern black dialect" represents only one possibility regarding the tonal timbre of her voice.[64] As Campbell argues, her northern origins offer "little reason to believe that she spoke in substandard southern dialect."[65] Such controversies betray the similar difficulties confronting scholars attempting to recover the oratorical power of Toussaint Louverture, Sengbe Pieh, or even Nathaniel Turner with any accuracy. Controversially, however, any such misunderstandings served Truth's political agenda. "Rather than correct inaccurate representations of her accent," Rohrbach explains, "Truth promoted and preserved the association with Southern plantation slavery, as it was in her best interest marketwise."[66] In this regard, Suzanne Fitch and Roseann Mandziuk set themselves an impossible task in their collection of her speeches and songs by claiming, "Our intention is to accurately portray Truth by separating out the fact from the myth, and by providing a full examination of her speaking throughout her life."[67]

No clear separation between "fact" and "myth" is possible for such an orator as Truth, as she perpetually experimented with language to refract multiple identities. Neither is any "full examination" possible on the grounds that her language was deliberately obfuscated by white reporters in ways that were not dissimilar to Thomas Gray's thwarted attempt at securing an interpretative framing of Nathaniel Turner's voice. Yet both Turner and Truth found ways to undermine the damaging effects of a white racist filter by liberating themselves from attempts to codify or confine their signifying possibilities. As Yellin argues, Truth's "speeches—however mutilated in transcription . . . bring us as close as we can come to the words of African-American women held in slavery."[68] An especially powerful way in which to come to grips with Truth's multifaceted oratorical legacy is by analyzing differing versions of her iconic "Ar'n't I a Woman?" speech delivered in 1853. Similarly, lesser-known lectures given in 1867 at the First Annual Meeting of the American Equal Rights Association and a few years later on the "Anniversary of Negro Freedom" in 1871 expose the politics and poetics embedded in her experimental engagement with antislavery discourse.

In a notable reversal of earlier white paternalist biases, Frances Titus radicalized Olive Gilbert's first edition of Truth's life, which had ended on the Black woman's forgiveness of the sins of the white master by including a second part titled "Book of Life." Consisting of articles and essays, the materials in this eclectic "book" explicitly engage with diverse strategies of black female memorialization. One of Truth's earliest and most famous speeches, delivered on May 28, 1851, at the Women's Rights Convention and prominently included in this collection, was recorded by the white feminist Frances Dana Gage. Gage's renowned yet controversial reporting of this speech documents Truth's seeming determination to foreground her "substance" over and above her "shadow" by describing how "the leaders of the movement trembled on seeing a tall, gaunt black woman . . . walk with the air of a queen up the aisle." Immediately, the white author destabilizes her potentially degrading juxtaposition by contrasting regal imagery with homespun poverty in order to dramatize black womanhood as a site of difference. As Gage writes, "Old Sojourner, quiet and reticent as the 'Libyan Statue,' sat crouched against the wall."[69] According to her vision, Truth functioned as the contemplative African other, the "Libyan Sibyl" of Harriet Beecher Stowe's and William Wetmore Story's imagining. Yet as a mythical prophetess ever adept at defying white female and male categorizations to effect her own liberation, Truth effected her own transformation from enslaved chattel to self-made performer by defying such annihilating rhetoric. "Slowly from her seat in the corner rose Sojourner Truth, who, till now, had scarcely lifted her head. 'Don't let her speak!' gasped half a dozen. . . . She moved slowly and solemnly to the front, laid her old bonnet at her feet, and turned her great, speaking eyes to me," Gage concedes.[70] Unshackled not only from iconic representations of the seemingly passive enslaved woman—the "Am I Not a Woman and a Sister?" victim—but also from white racist mythic constructions as the "Libyan Sibyl," Truth reverses these problematic representations to effect her own rebirth as a radical feminist orator.

Subordinating her physical presence to her intellectual abilities, Truth communicates profound psychological complexities via her "speaking eyes." Thus she encourages reinterpretations of her physiognomy as an abolitionist text rather than as an objectified proof. As an extension of Douglass's belief that the backs of enslaved men and women functioned as "living parch-ments," Truth ensured that her physiognomy became the "parchment" upon which she recorded not only her victimization but also her militancy. According to Gage, Truth's dramatic rhetoric heightened her logical power by testifying to her refusal to shy away from conflict:

> Well, chilern, whar dar is so much racket dar must be something out o' kilter. I tink dat 'twixt de niggers of de Souf and de women at de Norf all a talkin' 'bout rights, de white men will be in a fix pretty soon. . . . Nobody eber help me into carriage, or ober mud puddles, or gives me any best place [and raising herself to her full height and her voice to a pitch like rolling thunder, she asked], and ar'n't I a woman? Look at me! Look at my arm! [And she bared her right arm to the shoulder, showing her tre-mendous muscular power.] I have plowed, and planted, and gathered into barns, and no man could head me—and ar'n't I a woman? I could work as much and eat as much as a man (when I could get it), and bear de lash as well—and ar'n't I a woman? I have borne thirteen chilern and seen 'em mos' all sold off into slavery, and when I cried out with a mother's grief, none but Jesus heard—and ar'n't I a woman?[71]

Here, Truth galvanizes oratorical power from her ability to juxtapose her physical body with her linguistic presence as she refutes her enslaved status as a commodified object. Such was no less the case for Sengbe Pieh, who similarly relied on performative reenactments to punctuate his spoken tes-timony. Addressing her audience as "chilern," she continues in the vein of Susan B. Anthony by inverting power hierarchies and encouraging white women to see her in a parental role and as their moral and ancestral guide.

As a key speech within her oeuvre, this work communicates Truth's pref-erence for an oratorical poetics of disjuncture as she exposes "something out o' kilter." Relying on rhetorical questioning ("Ar'n't I a woman?"), Truth directly confronts white female racist discourses according to which black femininity functioned as a topic for debate rather than as an automatic right. Moreover, commanding her audiences to "look at me! Look at my arm!" Truth deflated white tendencies toward voyeurism by herself granting au-diences permission to view her body. She overshadows Gage's seemingly factual interjections exalting in Truth's heroic strength by trading in an ob-jectifying rhetoric. At the same time, Truth's celebration of a superhuman ability to "work" and "bear de lash" challenges the racially inflected values of the white "cult of true womanhood," which celebrated black female piety, duty, and passivity.[72] Rejecting white female moral paradigms, Truth sought to consolidate black female difference by engaging in self-conscious performances of an exceptional rather than an aberrant otherness.

In no way symbolizing a violated icon of black female helplessness, Truth's self-reflexive performances foreground intellectualism. "'Den dey talks 'bout dis ting in de head—what dis dey call it?' 'Intellect,' whispered some one near. 'Dat's it honey. What's dat got to do with women's rights or niggers' rights? If my cup won't hold but a pint and yourn holds a quart, wouldn't ye be mean not to let me have my little half-measure full?'" she demands.[73] Truth's artificial display of a consciously crafted, unassuming ignorance inspires a call-and-response relationship with her white audience. Thus she generates empathy by illuminating her intellectualism and radicalism over and above the finite exactitude of her body. Playing the role of the begging supplicant or kneeling enslaved woman in her plea "wouldn't ye be mean," she effects her audience's moral conversion by critiquing their illusory belief in essentialized, racialized hierarchies of "intellect" as off limits to Black female subjects. Painter's suggestion that "the words that Gage quotes Truth speaking are commanding, and they emanate from a superhuman body" attests to Truth's trade on physical fixity only to secure her right to philosophical questioning. Refusing to shy away from linguistic indeterminacy, she complicates her relationship to prescriptive authenticity conventions.[74] A humanist to the very core, Truth rejects artificial hierarchies that endorse intellectual qualifications as a prerequisite to equal rights.

Controversies continue to rage regarding Gage's representation of this speech, not only in light of her candid admission that the depths of Truth's logic eluded her ("I cannot follow her through it all," she confesses), but also because a reporter for the *Anti-Slavery Bugle* recorded Truth's language very differently.[75] Similarly claiming, "It is impossible to transfer it to paper, or convey any adequate idea of the effect it produced upon the audience," this reporter transcribes Truth's voice as follows:

> May I say a few words? . . . I want to say a few words about this matter. I am a woman's rights. I have as much muscle as any man, and can do as much work as any man. I have plowed and reaped and husked and chopped and mowed, and can any man do more than that? I have heard much about the sexes being equal; I can carry as much as any man, and can eat as much too, if I can get it. I am as strong as any man that is now. . . . The poor men seem to be all in confusion, and don't know what to do. Why children, if you have woman's rights give it to her and you will feel better. You will have your own rights, and they wont be so much trouble. I cant read, but I can hear.[76]

As documented here, Truth's transgressive idea that she in fact became "a woman's rights" provides an authoritative declaration of the black female body as the default for a universalizing rhetoric of womanhood. Resisting white mainstream marginalizations and exoticizations, according to this report, Truth rendered the black female experience as the normative standard in vindication of her vociferous critique of white feminist discourses.

Substituting her plea "Ar'n't I a woman?" with the challenge "Can any man do more than that?" this reporter lays bare Truth's insistence upon gender equality to shore up her own exceptional prowess. Equally, by suggesting to her male listeners that if they give women their rights, their own "wont be so much trouble," she supports her arguments that the burden of oppression falls equally on the oppressor as on the oppressed. "I cant read but I can hear," Truth states, thereby exposing her illiteracy not only to foreground her belief in oral culture but also to insist on the need to interrogate the legitimacy of written evidence as authoritative testimony. Such issues related to literary versus oral culture haunted Truth throughout her lifetime. As one reporter noted in a record of a speech given to an American Woman Suffrage Association meeting in 1870, Truth insisted that she "wanted to be reported in a grammatical and smooth way, 'not as if I was saying tickety-ump-ump-nicky-nacky.'"[77] Truth's categorical condemnation of the written record reveals her awareness of the ways in which her language became corrupted within the white mainstream press as writers—Gage prominent among them—sought to satisfy stereotypical agendas for black female representation. Determined to resist such appropriations, Truth went so far as to rely upon children to assist her in evaluating her appearance in print. "I want to see whether these young sprigs of the press do me justice," she explains. "You know, children, I don't read such small stuff as letters, I read men and nations."[78] On the one hand, Truth belittled literacy as a second-rate, diminutive form of knowledge—"small stuff"—but, on the other hand, she recognized the limitations facing her political, moral, and historical legacies in light of the stranglehold over her own self-making that was presented by a distorted printed record over which she had little or no control. In addition to financial pressures, such an awareness may in part explain Truth's decision to agree to various versions of her "as told to" narrative, as she recognized the fundamental role she would be able to play in shaping her written legacies.

The twentieth-century civil rights activist Angela Davis, notes that Truth's "Ar'n't I a Woman?" speech "remains one of the most frequently quoted slogans of the nineteenth-century women's movement." As Davis argues, "Truth tore down the claims that female weakness was incompatible with suffrage—and she did this with irrefutable logic."[79] Veering away from this speech as a quintessential civil rights declaration, however, Donna Haraway focuses instead upon Truth's self-conscious ambiguities of representation. "The change in the shape of the words makes us rethink her story, the grammar of her body and life," she writes.[80] Any such issues related to "rethinking" representations of Truth's "body and life" remain integral to extrapolating her multiple personae. As her complex oeuvre demonstrates, Truth foregrounded intellect and reason over and above physicality to rouse white audiences to a realization regarding the plight of black womanhood and the failures of white sentimental discourse. In a powerful appeal designed to expose white fallacies of justice not only to her white editor, Olive Gilbert, but to her white audience, she repeatedly asked readers not to feel but to "think." "Just think of us! *so* eager for our pleasures, and just foolish enough to keep feeding and feeding ourselves with the idea that we should get what had been thus fairly promised," she explains, adopting a collective voice to exclaim, "And when we think it is almost in our hands, find ourselves flatly denied! Just think! how *could* we bear it?"[81] Ever an adept manipulator of emotional responses, Truth intellectually engaged with her audiences to raise awareness of her signifying performances, lending ballast to Gilbert Vale's view that she was "not exactly what she seems."

"I come from another field—the country of the slave," Truth admits in a lecture delivered over a decade later in New York on May 9, 1867. Describing the world of the enslaved as both a "field" and a "country," Truth not only defamiliarized black history for her white listeners but also cultivated symbolic and mythic national differences. Responding ambivalently to the "loud cheers" of her audience, Truth confessed to an indifference and a seeming lack of authority over their emotions: "I don't know how you will feel when I get through."[82] Truth's trade on the limitations of intellectual knowledge places the onus on her listeners to take moral responsibility for what they were about to hear. According to Alison Piepmeier, Truth was an exemplary orator engaged in a "strategic use of available discourses" designed to secure her status as "a heroic figure."[83] Going a step further, Denise Riley argues, "It's my hope to persuade readers that a new Sojourner Truth might well—except for the catastrophic loss of grace in the wording—issue another plea: 'Ain't I a fluctuating identity?'"[84] However, Deborah McDowell opposes such a view, arguing that "the identity of black feminist criticism, has so far been anything but fluctuating. It has been solidly fixed to a reference schemata and a racial stigmata in a history we've read before."[85]

One way to begin to resolve these tensions is to interpret Truth as both a "substance" and a "shadow." Simultaneously both fixed and fluid, she signified upon her corporeal and immaterial identities to suit differing abolitionist agendas. As a performer, singer, orator, laborer, activist, preacher, and mother, Truth resisted any finalities of interpretation. Her artful proliferation of a multiple array of Truths across her narratives, speeches, and photographs attests less to racist tendencies toward reductive fixity and more to her reluctance to be confined to any one medium. Instead, she encouraged her audiences to reinterpret and reimagine her history and politics from an array of textual and visual fragments. While Fitch and Mandziuk suggest that "the realm of speech became her tool of force," Truth did not shy away from documenting its weaknesses.[86] As a reporter in the *Liberator* noted in 1854, "Sojourner Truth then took the platform, and said she agreed with the last speaker, that the evils of slavery could not be spoken; they could only be *felt*."[87] Despite her ambivalences toward sentimentality as a mode of abolitionist conversion, she was no less skeptical of oratorical performance or the power of rational arguments to end slavery. Undoubtedly, Truth's experimental use of language signified upon the symbolic importance of her body as a spiritual, physical, and psychological site and sight of memorialization. More powerfully still, this belief lay at the heart of "She Pleadeth for Her People," a song she recorded in 1879: "While she bears upon her body / The scars of many a gash, / She pleadeth for her people / That groan beneath the lash."[88]

THE "REAL AFRICAN TYPE": HARRIET BEECHER STOWE, WILLIAM WETMORE STORY, AND MYTHOLOGIZING MULTIPLE SOJOURNER TRUTHS

"Sojourner Truth, The Libyan Sibyl," an essay by the renowned white author Harriet Beecher Stowe, represents a watershed in mythological re-creations of this black female historical figure within a white American imagination. Originally appearing in the *Atlantic Monthly* in 1863 and popularly reprinted ever since, this work was republished in Titus's later edition of Truth's narrative as if to suggest, if not Truth's approval, then her tacit acceptance of Stowe's mythological constructions of her identity. Tellingly, Stowe's essay adopts stylized and theatrical language to dramatize the apocryphal meeting between the ex-enslaved black female activist and the white abolitionist author:

She was evidently a full-blooded African, and though now aged and worn with many hardships, still gave the impression of a physical development which in early youth must have been as fine a specimen of the torrid zone as Cumberworth's celebrated statuette of the Negro Woman at the Fountain. . . . When I recall the events of her life, as she narrated them to me, I imagine her as a living, breathing impersonation of that work of art.[89]

Oblivious to the ways in which she perpetuated mythic inaccuracies regarding her black female protagonist, Stowe not only colludes in dehumanized and exoticized stereotypes of Truth but also wrongly identifies her as African born. Yet, her spiritual objectification notwithstanding, Stowe's aestheticization of Truth as a "breathing impersonation" of a "work of art" inaugurates unprecedented signifying possibilities of which she was most likely unaware but which would have been clear-cut to Truth as a self-reflexive orator and performer.

Although she trades in scientific racism by describing Truth as a "fine specimen," Stowe nevertheless endorses her aesthetic possibilities and signifying practices by associating her with a "work of art." In a rare moment of insight, therefore, Stowe identifies the relationship between Truth's artistic experimentation—via her oratorical and physical performances—and the heroic status she achieved through her aggrandized exceptionalism. While Painter is right to suggest that "Stowe presented a tableau in which she and her family appeared as people of culture who appreciated Sojourner Truth as a primitive *object d'art* and source of entertainment," Stowe's exaltation of Truth as an art object speaks to new and sublime ways by which Black female subjects were able to resist prescriptive white constructions of black womanhood.[90] Thus Stowe's focus upon Truth as a "work of art" unwittingly invites scholars to render parallels between Truth and Douglass far more tangible, particularly given the latter's similar commitment to art as politics. As activists and performers, both Douglass and Truth engaged in a deliberate cultivation of their status as "works of art" as they fought to transcend the confining limits of their repeated exhibition as objectified proofs.

Yet there are serious problems here. While Jean Fagan Yellin forcefully argues that Stowe failed to "present this black rescuer as heroic," perhaps her observation that Stowe's "'Libyan Sibyl' is not an enchained queen, but a mutilate" is more open to question.[91] However, there is little evidence to substantiate the view that Stowe's Truth is a "mutilate." In particular ways, Truth's signifying practices challenge Stowe's attempt to reduce the Black woman solely to a body of evidence or a quintessential "iron argument."[92]

Ceasing to function as entertainment, Truth became her own "work of art" as she circulated as a storyteller and creator of her own visual performances and, in so doing, signified both despite and beyond Stowe's appropriating strategies. During her lifetime, Truth perpetuated her own mythology, the full implications of which remained off limits to Stowe, whose perspective was narrowed by her racist reimagings. Attempting to idealize rather than "mutilate" Truth, Stowe unwittingly inverted the hierarchal relationship between the kneeling enslaved female archetype of abolitionist tableau—"Am I Not a Woman and a Sister?"—and the imagined white sympathizer, in this case herself as paternalistic, philanthropic white woman author. Significantly, she situated herself beneath Truth, whom she reimagined as on a pedestal and within the inflated rhetoric of a universalized, if racially inflected, language of art.

The most enduring legacy of Stowe's ambivalent reimagining of Truth in "The Libyan Sibyl" emerges from her role in inspiring the white American artist William Wetmore Story's marble sculpture *The Libyan Sybil,* a post–Civil War work that appeared in 1868 and was exhibited to great acclaim at the World's Fair in London (see figure 22). Erroneously believing Truth had "passed away from among us as a wave of the sea" while she was still very much alive, Stowe concludes that although her "substance" had left, her "shadow" remains as "her memory still lives in one of the loftiest and most original works of modern art, the Libyan Sibyl, by Mr. Story." As Stowe explains, "When visiting Rome, I related Sojourner's history to Mr. Story" just as "his mind begun to turn to Egypt in search of a type of art which should represent a larger and more vigorous development of nature than the cold elegance of Greek lines."[93] Dissatisfied with the "cold elegance" of art produced within a European Western framework, Story was determined to discover an Egyptian art form characterized by an epic magnitude (for which read "heroic") and a "more vigorous development of nature" (for which read "sensuous, impassioned, irrational and multidimensional").

Borrowing from a deeply problematic and essentialized use of language, Stowe emphasizes, "The history of Sojourner Truth worked in his [Story's] mind and led him into the deeper recesses of the African nature—those unexplored depths of being and feeling, mighty and dark as the gigantic depths of tropical forests, mysterious as the hidden rivers and mines of that burning continent whose life history is yet to be."[94] Deliberately associating Truth with metaphors of the unknown in geographical, emotional, and artistic explorations of natural wildernesses of the land and soul, Stowe here betrays her indebtedness to the language of the white colonizer. She

FIGURE 22. William Wetmore Story, *The Libyan Sibyl*, 1868. (Smithsonian American Art Museum, Bequest of Henry Cabot Lodge through John Ellerton Lodge, 1925.6.3)

interprets Truth's body not only as a mythical embodiment of an unmappable, mythologized African continent but also as a site of prophecy in a "life history" that was "yet to be." Carla Peterson critiques such "metaphoric and symbolic representations of Truth" for "the degree to which they privilege geography—first the geography of continent, then that of the body—over history, ultimately tending towards a dehistoricization of Truth herself."[95]

Yet, while "dehistoricization" carries clear problematic associations, Truth herself cultivated an illusory timelessness in her oratorical performances. Thus she contributed to her own transcendent mythology by accentuating her rootless, abstract "sojourning" toward "truth." Ultimately, Stowe's mistake in proclaiming Truth dead while she was still alive testifies not only to racist myopia but also to Truth's own success in creating a mythological symbolism that transcended the corporeal limitations of her bodily existence.

William Wetmore Story openly acknowledges the abolitionist origins of *The Libyan Sibyl* by describing this work as his "anti-slavery sermon in stone."[96] As he explains:

> I have taken the pure Coptic head and figure, the great massive sphinx-face, full-lipped, long-eyed, low-browed and lowering, and the largely-developed limbs of the African. . . . It is a very massive figure, big-shouldered, large-bosomed, with nothing of the Venus in it, but, as far as I could make it, luxuriant and heroic. She is looking out of her black eyes into futurity and sees the terrible fate of her race. This is the theme of the figure— Slavery on the horizon, and I made her head as melancholy and severe as possible, not at all shirking the real African type . . . —Libyan African, of course, not Congo.[97]

Story's marble sculpture exists in fascinating relation to Edmonia Lewis's works *Forever Free* and *Cleopatra,* both completed during the same period.[98] In very different ways, both Story and Lewis signified upon white Western-ized facial features in their revisualizations of black female bodies at the same time that they traded in exaggerated representations of an imagined Afri-can symbolism. As the pioneering African American art historian Freeman Henry Morris Murray notes, audiences would most likely have found Story's sculpture "less 'African' than Story's description would lead them to expect," as "the popular American conception of the African is the type exemplified by the more outlandish of the captives brought here from the Congo and Niger regions."[99] As an epic work eulogizing an unfettered black female hu-manity, Story's sculpture relies on classical forms to magnify whiteness and communicate an idealized use of symmetry in mythical facial features that bear very little relation to Truth's physiognomy, regardless of his insistence that he "was not at all shirking the real African type." Opting instead to em-body her spiritual capabilities so that her "black eyes" could perceive "the terrible fate of her race," Story may well have been inspired by Truth's own photographic representations. Similarly, he reveled in a psychological em-phasis upon her propensities for intellectual thought.

In this sculpture, Story's substitution of Truth's frail frame—as shown in photographic representations and described by Stowe as a "tall, spare form"—with a "very massive figure, big-shouldered, large-bosomed" establishes his preference for sculpting Truth's "substance" into marble as a substitute for her "shadow" and in recognition of her multiple identities.[100] Challenging the fixity of factual "essences," he attests to the kaleidoscopic shifts at work in her preferred photographic representations and oratorical performances. Thus, while Collins writes that Story's Truth was imaginary, in that he "had never met Sojourner," it is likely that he had seen photographs, which may well have worked on his imagination in conjunction with Stowe's textual narratives.[101] Ultimately, Kirk Savage's view that Story decided "not to portray Truth herself but to create an appropriately distanced piece of ideal sculpture—an ancient and enigmatic *Libyan Sibyl*" may well be inaccurate, given Story's decision to sculpt Truth's identity not only from her "substance" but also from her "shadow archive."[102] Just as Douglass's wrath was repeatedly provoked by his dismissal as a "fine young negro" in the popular press, Truth no less rejected widespread descriptions of her physique as "the real African type." As a form of protest, she created her own countermythology consisting of multiple, shifting, and ambiguous imaginary identities, and it may well be this plethora of self-constructions that Story sought to carve in stone.

Ultimately, Story's greatest difficulty in creating *The Libyan Sibyl* arose from his determination to create a "luxuriant" and "heroic" female figure with "nothing of the Venus in it" and, therefore, as detached as possible from the white American sculptor Hiram Powers's *Greek Slave* (1844), a classical, if controversial, idealization of a vulnerable, shackled white female body popularly circulated in abolitionist contexts as a concession to white moral dictates. Rather than arguing against slavery by using an unmarked, idealized white Westernized female body, Story relishes in Truth's mythic, problematically constructed African otherness to provide competing representations of black female antislavery resistance. Depicting a prophetess rather than a victim, Story's *Libyan Sibyl* is divested of the "cold elegance" of Greek art. At the same time, however, his use of a spartan surface problematically evokes an idealized whiteness rather than a realistic and suffering blackness. For Savage, noting that, "the aesthetic dimension of racial theory cannot be overemphasized," classical sculpture was an antithetical medium within which to represent black heroism. "Sculpture in the classical tradition," he writes, "left no room for an "African American body . . . indelibly scarred" by slavery.[103]

In the same way that she refused to be "dogged" by her "shadow," Truth ultimately rejected white attempts to fix her iconography within the boundaries of a depoliticized symbolism. As one reporter observes, "'She would never listen to Mrs. Stowe's 'Libyan Sibyl.' 'Oh!' she would say, 'I don't want to hear about that old symbol; read me something that is going on *now*, something about this great war.'"[104] Thus Truth rejected white ahistorical and abstract attempts to interpret her identity solely as a "Libyan Sybil." Dismissing this designation out of hand as an "old symbol" unsuited to and unusable in an epic historical moment, Truth rejected fixed interpretations that traded in monolithic Black female identities. While she was more than happy to rely on that "old symbol" as a way of generating sympathy for the plight of enslaved Black women among her white audiences, for herself and her cause Sojourner Truth remained devoted to the militant drama of "this great war."

"LIVING SYMBOLS OF INSPIRATION": JOHN BIGGERS'S CONTRIBUTION OF THE NEGRO WOMAN TO AMERICAN LIFE AND EDUCATION (1952)

"Because of her special role in Negro life, the Negro Woman is the outstanding victim of the socially handicapped Negro group." So writes the twentieth-century African American artist John T. Biggers. Painting his full-color mural *Contribution of the Negro Woman to American Life and Education* onto an interior wall of the Blue Triangle Branch of the Young Women's Christian Association in Houston, Texas, in 1952, he was determined to counter representations of African American women as "outstanding victims." As a companion work, Biggers's unpublished dissertation for a doctorate in education, "The Negro Woman in American Life and Education: A Mural Presentation," written in 1954, represents an invaluable resource for examining the aesthetic and political features of this mural. As he explains, his "choice of a subject matter for a mural grew naturally out of a folk need."[105] Yet during his construction of this work, he encountered virulent opposition from Black female community members who ordered him to "get down from the wall and stop the flagrant disrespect immediately." In the face of such impassioned protest, progress on the mural ceased "until the Y.W.C.A. officials convinced the group that the depiction of black women had value."[106] So while the director, Lilian Jackson, believed that "the mural should portray women of all races," Biggers argued that African American womanhood should be his sole subject matter so that the "occupants of the building could identify themselves with their own background and cultural heritage."[107]

As his response to this furor demonstrates, Biggers created this mural not only to encourage race pride but also to secure black empathetic identification with the elided aspects of African American cultural and political history. More especially, Biggers's dramatization of black female heroism directly confronted the difficult fact that some African Americans, as he argued, remained "ashamed of their own background."[108] Such a reformist ethos and instructional imperative has led Alvia Wardlaw Short to conclude that the mural "constitutes a major contribution to the definition of mural as educational aesthetic."[109] "In a mural expression, actual historical events must by necessity be restricted to the few outstanding examples," Biggers argued, as "those achievements have become symbols for the Negro masses." Thus, in this work, he promulgates a black heroic female paradigm consisting of Harriet Tubman as well as Sojourner Truth, whom he especially singled out as an "outstanding Negro woman and ex-slave who joined the anti-slavery movement." He admired the fact that "this woman journeyed across the land on foot speaking to huge audiences on the evils of slavery, and on the benefit to be derived from woman suffrage."[110]

As exceptional heroic exemplars, Tubman and Truth take center stage in this mural. On the left-hand side of this work, a tall, thin Truth clothed in white stands on a rail track before a captivated Black audience of ex-enslaved men, women, and children. On the right-hand side, the aggrandized figure of Tubman is burdened by makeshift weaponry as she leads a group of men and women into freedom. As Short argues, "Although physically Sojourner Truth has not the bulk of Harriet Tubman, her presence is no less compelling to those listening to her powerful words."[111] Clearly, oratory was no less Biggers's subject in this twentieth-century mural than it was for Truth in the nineteenth century. According to this epic work, Truth's elongated yet frail form gesticulates before an impoverished Black audience as Biggers bears witness to her status as both an archetypal feminist icon and a radical Black abolitionist. "Despite oppression, Harriet Tubman and Sojourner Truth tore open the barriers of restriction," he observes, arguing that "they remain living symbols of inspiration and achievement."[112] Reconfiguring the lives of Truth and Tubman as "living symbols," Biggers insists on their mythical and political relevance to contemporary black freedom struggles.

A determination to document the past in the present lies at the heart of Biggers's ideological and aesthetic agenda. The memory of both Truth and Tubman provides a platform upon which he protests against the horrors of slavery by exposing the fact that black "cultural roots were amputated." Describing his inspiration as "conversations, original songs, and correspondence of Sojourner Truth and Harriet Tubman," Biggers adopts a tripartite structure to dramatize the African American woman's "political history, her social status, and her educational achievements."[113] Thus Biggers's mural was not only inspired by his scholarly work on epic figures such as Truth and Tubman but also by his witnessing of anonymous feats of black female heroism in his own life. Among these experiences was the bravery of his mother, who "saw beauty in practically everything."[114] For Biggers, historical research combines with personal biography to generate emotional and political force. Intent upon dramatizing a continuum of iconic and anonymous forms of female heroism, Biggers dramatizes the "stories told and retold by his grandmother, who was born a slave, concerning the hardships of slavery."[115] For Biggers, Truth operates as a visual lynchpin in this mural via her dialogic relationship to the black community. "The Freedmen, sharecroppers, workmen, and children were included around the teacher, Sojourner Truth," he writes.[116] In this regard, *Contribution of the Negro Woman* represents a declaration of independence for black womanhood by depicting Truth preaching to newly freed men and women while Tubman is shown leading enslaved individuals to liberty. Contrasting methods of black female resistance are juxtaposed in this work, as Truth holds a white scroll in her aged, thin hand, while Tubman brandishes a rifle. Biggers deliberately reinforces these stark comparisons by positioning Truth next to a large but leafless tree—a symbol he describes elsewhere in biblical terms as the "Tree of Life"—while Tubman appears solely as a lone freedom fighter bearing arms. More tellingly still, the earlier sketches of Biggers's mural reveal that the scroll Truth carries attests not only to feminist activism but also to black equality, as it appears to be a "Pet——on," for which read "Petition," for "Land" and "EQUAL RIGHTS F—— WOMEN."[117]

In this work, Biggers juxtaposes black female physical militancy, via Tubman, with educational consciousness-raising, via Truth. These diverse resistance strategies are illustrated not only in their competing physical forms—Truth's body and face are reminiscent of her photographs, while Tubman's sculpted features and larger-than-life physique depart from known depictions—but also by Biggers's stark use of composition in depicting the contrasting male and female figures seated at the feet of both Truth and Tubman. While the Black mother seated at Truth's feet and reading the "Poems and Life of Phyllis Wheatley" to her child is fully clothed, a racially ambiguous and naked woman lies prostrate before Tubman, a hole in her body abstractly suggesting a missing baby. As shown here, Biggers's didactic use of African American educational texts such as Wheatley's poetry collection works to complicate his seemingly straightforward representations of black maternal sacrifice versus redemption. For Biggers, therefore, black female heroism encompasses not only martyrdom and death but also cultural feats of writerly resistance. Representative of the heroic bifurcation in Biggers's representation of iconic leaders, Tubman is associated with unending struggle in ongoing strategies of physical protest. By comparison, Truth symbolizes the transformative power of emotional engagement via her experimentation with oratorical discourse as a means to psychological enlightenment. In this regard, Biggers's decision not to include a portrait of Wheatley, whom he describes as "a lustrous symbol of enlightenment and cultural achievement," is telling. He no doubt favored Truth and Tubman for their illiteracy, which made it possible for him to dramatize the role played by oral culture in cross-generational survival, particularly as he reflected upon his own familial folkloric traditions. "Traits or behavior patterns of patience, endurance, and struggle, handed down through generations of slaves," Biggers admits, "were a part of my fireside education."[118]

Preaching while standing on a train track with a church behind her, Truth's arm gestures toward Tubman's triumph over slavery in her unparalleled black liberation raids. Taken together, theirs is a heroic continuum, as Tubman's activism combines with Truth's oratorical power to confirm their historical and political significance. Across their lifetimes and works, both of these Black female icons engaged in storytelling and oratorical performances. Thus they signified upon their symbolic legacies as ambiguous sites of black female memorialization. Tellingly, Truth's audience consists not only of diverse generations of formerly enslaved African Americans but also of a solitary portrait of an individualized woman whose face is turned to the viewer while she works on a multicolored, patterned quilt. The color symbolism of her blue clothing resonates not only with symbols of labor—as further revealed in a Black man's blue dungarees—but also with emblems of hope in an azure sky, which offsets the confining uniformity of the shotgun houses as they disappear into the distance. More particularly, the yellows, blues, whites, and browns of the working woman's quilt resonate with Biggers's overall color scheme not only to suggest she is sewing memories of slavery but also to draw the viewer's attention to the importance of art as political process. Such a thought-provoking vignette communicates Biggers's self-awareness regarding the mural's function as an artwork in which he demands imaginative engagement from his audiences, a key concern no less confronting Truth during her lifetime.

Biggers's Truth is a fearless transitional figure in this mural as she stands in the middle of an empty train track. He mythically conjoins her memory to John Henry, a folkloric legend perpetually reemerging across the centuries as an exceptional icon of black masculinity. However, Biggers's mural generates further dramatic tension via the colliding bodies of Black women and men as they labor, preach, read, and fight. A compositional tour de force, his work resonates with the first panel of Woodruff's *Amistad* mural series. Biggers similarly accentuates the complexities of human drama through graphic use of "opposing movement, thrust and counterthrust, repetitive rhythms, and ideas of conflict and adjustment."[119] Across his epic mural, therefore, Biggers juxtaposes Truth's transformative use of oratory with militant representations of Tubman to debate the revolutionary potential of diverse forms of cultural and political resistance. Contrasting instances of black victimization with strategies of black self-help, Biggers outlines a heroic continuum that encompasses not only Tubman's physical and radical resistance but also Truth's moral and educational feats of heroism, as they similarly undertook multiple journeys from slavery to freedom. Divided by scrolls, tree limbs, body parts, rifles, tools, and train tracks, this mural's composition challenges any idealistic projections of a linear movement from enslavement to emancipation. Across this work, Biggers troubles archetypal trajectories of black progress by withholding any straightforward endorsements of cathartic teleologies of uplift.

As Biggers's aesthetic and political commitment to a celebration of black female heroism reveals, *Contribution of the Negro Woman* was created as a political, historical, aesthetic, and ideological response to the major twentieth-century African American artist Charles White's earlier mural *Contribution of the Negro to Democracy in America,* created in 1943.[120] Painted on an interior wall at the historically black institute of higher education Hampton University, White's mural eulogizes black male rather than black female heroism. In stark contrast to Biggers's work, White celebrates a heroic masculine continuum as an epic-sized Frederick Douglass embraces a pantheon of Black male heroes including Nathaniel Turner, Crispus Attucks, Denmark Vesey, George Washington Carver, and Booker T. Washington. Yet while Harriet Tubman is entirely missing from this work, Sojourner Truth is prominently included, as she is shown reaching out to touch the hand of a ragged enslaved man. According to White's vision, therefore, she offers new life to black shackled masculinity via a politicized, gendered, and racialized but no less spiritual revisioning of Michelangelo's centuries-earlier vision of God giving life to Adam on the ceiling of the Sistine Chapel in Rome. As inserted into White's work here, Truth figures first and foremost as a transatlantic symbol of redemption and a catalyst for black male physicality. Nonetheless, standing between two icons of black male history, Frederick Douglass and Booker T. Washington, she seems little more than a visual footnote.

Taking issue with this problematic framework, Biggers's revisionist work insists on the primary significance of Truth as the archetypal "negro woman." As his radical mural dramatizes, he applauds the fact that "in the face of insurmountable barriers, her tears, her smiles, and her dreams stimulate a new awakening, a new adjustment, a new horizon." Clearly, John Biggers's *Contribution of the Negro Woman* reimagines Sojourner Truth and Harriet Tubman not only as founding mothers of the contemporary black freedom struggle but also as definers and inaugurators of its "new horizon."[121] More tellingly, he was not the only artist to revise White's vision of Truth. In a powerful charcoal and ink print created decades after his epic mural in 1965 and titled *General Moses (Harriet Tubman),* White himself did haunting justice to a radical and empowered vision of black female militancy. Relying on forceful lines and a symbolic composition, in this pioneering drawing White carried further Biggers's commitment to reimagining Harriet Tubman as a militant force leading the way in the fight for black rights.[122]

"TURN THE FACE OF HISTORY TO YOUR FACE": JUNE JORDAN'S "IN THE SPIRIT OF SOJOURNER TRUTH" (1978)

"blackgirl/slavegirl."[123] "In the Spirit of Sojourner Truth," a collaborative work cocreated by African American poet June Jordan, songwriter Bernice Reagon, and dramatist Ntozake Shangee appeared in 1978. An eclectic, inventive, and discordant work consisting of an array of authorial voices arranged by June Jordan, this theatrical piece dramatizes Sojourner Truth as a malleable icon reinvented for political and moral reuse. More specifically, this dramatic collaboration emerged out of a determination to reject the claims of Michele Wallace's book *Black Macho and the Myth of the Superwoman,* published in 1979. Shocked at Wallace's disparaging comments, Jordan decried this work on the grounds that she denigrated Harriet Tubman and Sojourner Truth as women "whom no man in his right mind would want except, perhaps, patient old Uncle Tom."[124] She was also motivated to create this work following her attendance at a radical meeting of Black female students at which she discovered that their knowledge of black female heroism could be reduced to two names: Sojourner Truth and Harriet Tubman. "I interrupted to observe that now we had *two* names for 482 years of our

Afro-American history," she noted, frustrated at the students' initial struggle to provide any names at all.[125] Transgressing formal boundaries, "In the Spirit of Sojourner Truth" betrays Jordan's conviction that "this invisibility and this silence of the real and various peoples of our country is a political situation of language that every one of us must move against, because our lives depend on it."[126] Jordan, Reagon, and Shangee's experimental text celebrates Truth's multiple personae. Against a backdrop of iconic black male and female hero-ism both historical and contemporary, collaged textual fragments combine to create a challenging work designed to place the onus upon audiences to reimagine both the anonymous and iconic feats characterizing Truth's resis-tance. Shangee, Jordan, and Reagon's determination to document the "spirit" of Sojourner Truth betrays their fascination not only with mythically mapping her heroism onto the legacies of famous civil rights activists but also with the anonymous fights for everyday survival by unsung heroines living and dying during slavery. Their dramatic meditation draws on a long time frame to docu-ment the struggles of the contemporary "blackgirl" within the historical context of the almost insurmountable difficulties afflicting the "slavegirl."

Jordan, Shangee, and Reagon's "In the Spirit of Sojourner Truth" experi-ments with language to transgress the reductive fixity of stereotyped rep-resentations of Black female identities. They exalt in black female battles against psychological, physical, moral, and cultural oppression. By begin-ning this work with Reagon's published song "Had, Took, Misled," written in 1969, these writers situate their dramatic exploration of black female hero-ism within a haunting representation of struggle. "Don't you know, we been had, / Don't you know we been took, / Don't you know we been mislead," writes Reagon in a series of rhetorical questions designed to function as painful rhetorical statements. Yet Jordan's decision to follow this bleak vision of black female powerlessness with an unpublished fragment drawing on her own maternal ancestry confirms her belief in the continuity of survival. Urg-ing her mother to "help me / turn the face of history / *to your face*," she offers a direct appeal to ancestral authority.[127] In this work, Jordan documents the enduring legacy of *"luv"* by generating a plethora of black female identities— "nanny," "granny," "woman"—not only to resist dehumanizing stereotyp-ing but also to endorse a collective sisterhood. Thus she provides a literary equivalent to the Black artist Elizabeth Catlett's *The Negro Woman* (1946–47), a narrative series in which she aggrandizes the lives and deaths of Black women. In this print series, which Catlett retitled *The Black Woman Speaks* following the heightened radicalism of the 1960s, the artist no less eulogizes Truth's heroism in order to situate her oratorical power within the context of a voiceless pantheon of Black female laborers and activists.[128] Similarly, Jordan's plea in this work that her mother "turn the face of history / *to your face*" lays bare her determination to wrest ideological and aesthetic control of black female histories from imprisoning sites of white official discourse.

"Sojourner Truth," the self-explanatory title of Jordan's final poem, written in 1979, renders explicit her imaginative and metaphorical evocations of this historical figure as documented throughout this work. A symbolic as well as political "Sojourner Truth" is clearly the driving force undergirding her inclusion of an array of poetic fragments. She investigates the imaginative and political possibilities of orality and storytelling not only to dramatize but to liberate female histories of suffering. For Jordan, multiple Sojourner Truths intersect to provide competing examinations of violence, stereotyping, protest, and resistance. The handwritten maxim "TURN THE FACE OF HISTORY TO YOUR FACE," repeated from the passage quoted above, powerfully concludes her typescript. In clear-cut ways, Jordan forcefully documents Truth's ambiguities to problematize the difficult relationships between official and unofficial strategies of memorialization. Inspired by diverse protest agendas during the long civil rights era, Jordan's final poem, "Sojourner Truth," explicitly engages with Truth's political activism to celebrate her belief in civil disobedience: "The trolley cars was rollin and the passengers all white / when Sojourner just decided it was time to take a seat." Such a declaration bolsters Jordan, Reagon, and Shangee's earlier representations of black female heroism by trading on Truth's iconic status and capacity for martyrdom: "Sojourner yelled, 'It's me!' / And put her body on the track." Relying on evocative imagery and a rhyming use of repetition, Jordan dramatizes Truth's status as a role model for past and future generations, as evoked by the memorable refrain "Sojourner had to be just crazy / tellin all that kinda truth." Jordan interrogates the boundaries between sanity and insanity in this poem to provide radical reimaginings of an iconic black female heroism. Defying straightforward memorializations, Jordan experiments with a vernacular idiom in phrases such as "talkin bad instead sad" to introduce "flaws" into Truth's otherwise respectable characterization. She presents an anarchic, indefinable folkloric identity for the frequently sanitized historical figure. If Nathaniel Turner remains a "bad man" figure, then Truth is no less a "bad woman" engaged in fearless acts and arts of resistance in support of ongoing black freedom struggles. In this experimental work, Truth's indomitable spirit enables Jordan to map post-Reconstruction hardships onto the aftermath of the struggle for civil rights. As she writes: "she said *I'll ride* / she said *I'll talk*."[129] Jordan's insistence on Truth's determination to access black equal rights celebrates her dual commitment to linguistic and physical resistance, as had been documented much earlier by a nineteenth-century reporter who observed, "She believed in being doers of the word, not hearers only."[130]

Jordan's "Sojourner Truth" resonates in specific ways with another poetical work she includes in this theatrical montage, a work titled "1977: Poem for Mrs. Fannie Lou Hamer." Symptomatic of her determination not to deny parallels between formerly enslaved freedom fighters and contemporary activists, she contends that "whitemen don' / never see Black anybodies without / some violent itch start up." For Jordan, Hamer remains as undaunted by the brutality of a white man's "violent itch" as Truth, whose body suffered multiple vicious beatings during her enslavement. Jordan's direct poetic address dramatizes Hamer's dauntless bravery as whites "beat / you blue beyond the feeling" and yet "failed to stop you." Jordan's experimental use of language, as in her insistence that Hamer was beaten "beyond the feeling," invites parallels with Truth's insistence upon the evocative power of the impossibility of feeling. Jordan's celebration of Hamer's heroism in going to the Laundromat, "that took courage / just to sit there," reinforces domesticity as a site of militant resistance, as varyingly shown by Truth during her own lifetime in her complex relationship to sentimental iconography and its efficacy or inefficacy in establishing black female equality. In this context, Jordan's decision to follow this work with "Ah, Momma," a letter in which she mourns the loss of black female creative possibilities by lamenting to her mother, "you had wanted to be an artist," exposes the traumas effected by black female sacrifice as she demands that her Black female audiences imaginatively fill in the gaps in the service of their own survival.[131]

A transgressive and disjointed work, "In the Spirit of Sojourner Truth" establishes the ongoing need for a collective will to resistance as the only way in which to overpower the struggles afflicting the "blackgirl" in a contemporary era. In this regard, Jordan's Truth operates as a dehistoricized figure laden with archetypal significance. Preferring a pared-down, discordant style Jordan comes to grips with Truth's psychological complexities through a mythopoetic autobiographical search for diverse forms of resistance. As a militant recycling of Truth's legacies, Jordan's avant-garde work can be compared to Robert Hayden's poem "Stars," published in 1975. Similarly exposing the horrors of Truth's domestic life, he establishes her importance as a founding mother of black radicalism. According to Hayden's poetic reimagining, Truth's physical resistance must be powerfully reexamined within the context of her exemplary capacity for philosophical thought. For Hayden, dramatizing the infinite constellations of her intellectualism and signifying practices, Sojourner Truth was an iconic prophet whose "mind," as recognized by Hopkins decades before, was a "star."[132]

"YOU BECOME THE TRICKSTER": LEE MARACLE'S "SOJOURNER'S TRUTH" (1990)

"Each story will require the engaged imagination of the reader," reads the Canadian First Nations writer Lee Maracle's preface to her collection *Sojourner's Truth, and Other Stories*, published in 1990, titled, "You Become the Trickster."[133] The penultimate story in the collection, "Sojourner's Truth," signifies upon relative and fragmented "truths" to reinterpret Native female powerlessness and the fight for agency within symbolic evocations of a mythical, marginalized, and nonwhite heroism. Maracle's experimental poetics transgress the boundaries of language and narrative form to critique racist discourses and expose social inequalities. Dramatizing First Nations and African American female bodies as loci of resistance and reimagining no less than of violence and violation, she engages with issues related to memorialization, historical representation, and empathetic identification. As Maracle explains, "I tried very hard to integrate two mediums: oratory and European story, our sense of metaphor, our use of it, with traditional European metaphor and story form." Her eclectic use of form juxtaposing First Nations and European narrative methods may well have been inspired by Sojourner Truth's own cultivation of generic hybridity as she sought to push the boundaries of formal and linguistic barriers. One way in which to interpret Truth's use of language in her own works is in terms of a recycling aesthetic consisting of collaged and imagined fragments and inspired by African and African American as well as European and European American culture. This complex aesthetic technique foregrounds obfuscation and thus has resonances with First Nations storytelling practices. "When our orators get up to tell a story, there is no explanation," Maracle writes. Admitting to the thematic function of ellipses and fragmentation, Maracle speaks to the extent to which narrative strategies of undertelling within First Nations performances have much in common with Truth's historical and symbolic incarnations as an oratorical trickster. As their works show, Maracle no less than Truth cultivated ambiguity to encourage audiences to interpret across the fragments: "As listener/reader, you become the trickster," she writes.[134]

Maracle adopts a transgressive relationship to form in this short story by inhabiting the first-person perspective of an unnamed dead man. More generally, she indicts the failures of empathy generated by a moral blindness and a lack of self-reflexivity regarding the "truths" of individual selfhood. More sinning than sinned against, the narrator's death forces him to face his mistakes as he confesses that the "lickings I laid on Emma and the kids file through my mind."[135] The orderly connotations of "file" open up a horrific disjuncture by evoking parallels between the spectacle of the slave coffle and contemporary cases of domestic violence as here denounced in the narrator's actions against his own family. Blurring the boundaries between death and life in this text, Maracle contests artificial separations between corporeal and spiritual existences. As Renate Eigenbrod insists, "Links between the dead and the living are a recurring theme in Native literature."[136] In his admission that *the living body of me scarred and twisted the very soul of Emma,"* the narrator's distinction between body and soul signifies upon Truth's earlier negotiation of "shadow" and "substance" to transgress physical boundaries and redefine material realities.[137] For Emma no less than for Truth, a denial of the soul imprisons the body via unwitting collusions in self-erasure and annihilation. The source of horror in this short story arises not from violence but from the unnamed narrator's realization of his own "mind-bending brutality" as he confronts the fact that psychological trauma wreaks irreversible devastation. Maracle's narrator is denied any catharsis, however, as he remains locked in a battle with problematic definitions of selfhood that he encounters in a painful confrontation with memories of the past. Encouraging audiences similarly to "become a trickster" in the search for truths no less enigmatic than "sojourner's truth," Maracle's short story charts the psychological conflicts generated by imaginary and unresolved emotional terrain. While Eigenbrod argues that this text "makes it clear that this truth is a trajectory," Maracle's emphasis upon "rememory" via cyclical patterns of history complicates such oversimplified tendencies toward linear progression or clear-cut emotional purging.[138]

Ultimately, Maracle's short story interrogates the political injustices and racist ideologies inextricable from both white national mythologies and colonialist discourses. Offering an exposé of white histories of black violation, her narrator critiques members of the British House of Lords who argue, "Apartheid is not a question for us to address," by responding, *"I'll bet not. After all, you're the white guys."* Thus, Maracle's decision not to define her narrator's relationship to such unidentified *"white guys"* celebrates racial ambiguity to shore up her critique of racist investments in mythic constructions of a monolithic nonwhite other. Stripping away the narrator's pretensions toward moral superiority, she provides a no-holds-barred confrontation with his "uncomfortable truths" in this work. "I would laugh," he admits, "but the truth stops me and there in the kitchen of my own neighbourhood is Mike, being disgusted by the uppity Blacks 'who had a lotta nerve shooting us,' and the body of me is agreeing." Such a specific emphasis upon the narrator's body's capitulation to racist paradigms offers both despair and hope by divorcing the corporeal from the spiritual in order to advocate the philosophical necessity of an existential search for truth. As the reimagined figure of Jesus explains to the narrator, the *"butchery"* will only end "when the body of people stop hiding from the truth of the spirit."[139] The narrator's response that such a view "seems too simple" testifies to his flawed determination to foreground finite corporeality at the cost of any epiphany regarding the power of his infinite soul. As Eigenbrod suggests, Maracle's story operates by "constructing and then deconstructing racial identifications, and in the end leaving his racial identity indeterminate."[140] Such indeterminacy is thematically, politically, and aesthetically integral to Maracle's short story, as she resists the reductive fixity of stereotyping in order to defy the moral blindness of widespread racist legislation no less than caricature.

A mythopoetic meditation upon black female resistance, Maracle's short story does not flinch from visceral horror, as the narrator redeems Emma's act of violence against her abusive second husband by encouraging empathetic identification. Commenting that she commits murder in order to safeguard the survival of both her body and soul, the narrator admits, "I hear the resounding 'no' from every cell of her flesh." As a fantasy of wish fulfillment, therefore, Emma's violent resistance not only avenges her subjugation but also purges generalized visions of female victimization.

In the final short story in this collection, "World War I," Maracle further aggrandizes Emma's heroism by mapping her private act of defiance onto public histories of national injustices. Defying a realist framework in this story, Maracle resurrects the Scottsboro boys—African American men convicted for a rape they did not commit in the twentieth century—as they join the male narrator at Emma's trial for murder. Breaking temporal boundaries, Maracle establishes a continuum of black male and female sacrifice performed on the altar of white freedoms. She relies on these historical figures from African American history as a platform upon which to communicate the hidden records of black female rebellion. As the reimagined figure of Jesus tells the narrator, their militancy has diasporic reach, as "they have participated in every glorious riot, in every movement of Black resistance from Birmingham in 1948 to Soweto."[141] Thus Maracle's cultivation of parallels between black female fights for survival within the domestic sphere and the nefarious persecution of black masculinity on the international stage issues a call for collective black resistance throughout the diaspora. Working within a tradition of ideological warfare established by militant heroes such as Nathaniel Turner, Maracle's heroine resorts to violence solely because it provides the only means by which she can secure her own redemption.

Overall, Maracle's "Sojourner's Truth" explores an inextricable relationship between "ex-master" and "ex-slave," not only to document the nefarious legacies of the postslavery era but also to challenge artificial political and social boundaries between slave and master, Black and white, and female and male. In this short story, Emma's and Truth's identities merge as the historically resurrected Truth admits, "I was delivered from slavery at fifty-six years ol' and so was she."[142] Thus, Maracle's reimagining of Sojourner Truth via the persecuted and vengeful body of her victimized and racially indeterminate protagonist testifies to the necessity of a continuum of female resistance to counter male oppression. More particularly, she evokes Truth's fraught memory to expose slavery and its legacies as an ongoing locus of physical and psychological trauma. In "Sojourner's Truth," therefore, Maracle places great emphasis upon oratory and song by dramatizing a Truth who insists upon the survival of the black female body via linguistic experimentation and creative expression. *"Who are you?"* the question posed by an unknown voice, legitimizes Truth's affirmation as ventriloquized through Emma that "I'm Sojourner Truth," as Maracle celebrates the inextricable blurring of First Nations and African American identities through both victimization and resistance in this work.[143] Truth's sufferings during slavery legitimize Emma's nonrepentance for her murderous actions as, far from aberrant incidents, they emerge within a long memory of black female victimization. As Eigenbrod argues regarding Maracle's title for "Sojourner's Truth," "The slight modification of the name in the title, the addition of a possessive case, illustrates a slippage reflective of the complexity of the narration."[144] Yet Maracle's emphasis upon Emma's perception of the "light" and "truth" refutes the finalities of narrative ending to effect the ultimate liberation of her "soul" as unfettered by bodily confinement. As she writes, "The truth of this sojourner / has been seen at last."[145] An experimental work, Maracle's "Sojourner's Truth" provides a far more triumphant reinterpretation of the former enslaved woman's legacies than "Sojourner Truth Sings to the Woman Spirit" (1994), a poem written by Kainoa Koeninger in which her recreated persona laments that there are sufferings and injustices that "won't heal."[146]

The ambiguities and ambivalences that constitute Sojourner Truth's literary, political, historical, and visual archive speak to the widespread difficulties inextricable from attempts to memorialize this complex and elided figure. As Painter argues, "She remains more sign than lived existence."[147] Such may similarly be said of an array of artists, writers, and activists working in both the historical and contemporary eras, as they have reused and reimagined but have been unable fully to adapt Truth's multiple personae to fit diverse agendas. More tellingly, in the early period and during her own lifetime, Truth not only remained an enigma within antislavery discourse but also was interpreted as a political and ideological liability by white proslavery apologists.

Rather more shockingly, Truth's activism and radicalism have been disparaged, if not entirely discredited, by some of her most famous African American contemporaries, including, perhaps most famously, Frederick Douglass. For Douglass, Truth was an unreadable, unfathomable, and contrary "sign" but in ways very different from Turner, whom he unequivocally idealized. Revealingly, upon his first meeting with Truth, Douglass did not hesitate to describe her not only as "a strange compound of wit and wisdom, of wild enthusiasm and flint-like common sense" but as "a genuine specimen of the uncultured negro" on the grounds that "she cared very little for elegance of speech or refinement of manners."[148] Readily capitulating to stereotypes, Douglass's problematic language in denouncing Truth as his social and political inferior exposes his own insecurities. His dismissal of her as "strange," "wild," and only able to express "ideas in the oddest forms" represents no small revenge for his resentment that she had not only rejected his determination to act as a "person of culture and refinement" but had also actively sabotaged one of his oratorical performances. This renowned incident took place on the occasion of Douglass's speech advocating greater militancy in the fight to end slavery, at which Truth is variously reported as having asked, "Frederick, is God dead?" or "Frederick, is God gone?"[149] Thus, Douglass's reliance on a discourse of scientific racism to dismiss Truth as a "genuine specimen" and "strange compound" betrays his own need to interpret her failure to participate within existing racist, social structures as precisely that: as evidence of failure rather than as resulting from a principled rejection of white Western ideology.

As an individual ideologically committed to exhibiting rather than eliminating slavery's legacies upon her public personae, Truth rejected the determination on the part of Douglass and others to unfetter themselves from their enslaved personae only by creating artificial demarcations of self-hood that risked perpetuating rather than denying repressed traumas. Class as well as race issues come to the fore here, as Truth's oratorical, nonliterary, and unquantifiable identities expose many of Douglass's internal contradictions, which he actively sought to conceal. By performing as an illiterate naïf, Truth protected herself against the psychological split that increasingly began to haunt Douglass as his formerly enslaved self refused to be sublimated by his newfound and, in many ways, performatively created identity as a free man. As Douglass's anger toward Truth, which he chose to disguise as amused contempt, reveals, he was never at peace with his decision to cultivate his own exceptionalism and minimize difference solely by exhibiting "elegance" and "refinement." Truth's noncompliant, uninhibited, and unrestrained personality that refused to pass within white elite social circles not only directly challenged Douglass's performances as a learned male intellectual but also exposed that which he had lost and compromised in this process. Moreover, the forcefulness of this personal attack reveals more concerning Douglass's own intellectual and psychological contradictions than it does about any ambivalences within Truth herself. Douglass's resistance strategies were very much at odds with Truth's cultivation of an anarchic, discordant, and antiauthoritarian identity. "When a black man's language is quoted," Douglass notes elsewhere, "in order to belittle and degrade him, his ideas are often put in the most grotesque and unreadable English, while the utterances of Negro scholars and authors are ignored. To-day, Sojourner Truth is more readily quoted than Alexander Crummell or Dr. James Mc-Cune Smith."[150] There can be little doubt that Truth's illiteracy, irrationality, and unconventional use of language, which reflected her rejection of, rather than capitulation to, white social mores, was not only repellent but anathema to Douglass.

And yet their diverse works and performances reveal that Truth and Douglass were far from poles apart. Clearly, their self-reflexive signifying practices and manipulations of multiple personae attest to their shared participation within a continuum of black activism and resistance. At the same time that Douglass believed in the "self-made man," Truth avowed, "I am a self-made woman."[151] So while Douglass critiqued her "common sense," "honesty," "industriousness," and "usefulness," these were all values that he repeatedly endorsed as integral to his own newfound pride in black independence and equality. Similarly, as a consummate performer himself, Douglass repeatedly employed oratorical strategies of indirection and irony in his no less complex and frequently satirical use of language and manipulation of a trickster-like status.

Memorializations of both Douglass and Truth, who were equally unwilling to be confined solely to the role of former enslaved laborer, fugitive orator, suffering victim, or even iconic heroic archetype, occupy a continuum. Across their lives and works, they resisted and reconfigured the existing paradigms within which to represent black masculine and feminine identities. Truth, like Douglass, sought to effect the moral and political reform of white abolitionist no less than proslavery ideologies, as she shared his rejection of seemingly immutable and biologically fixed constructions of racial differences. As opposed to and troubled by Frederick Douglass's views on violence, religion, and education in the post–Civil War era as she was, Sojourner Truth's question to the white abolitionist Amy Post in 1866 ultimately betrays her endorsement of Douglass's oratorical prowess and political activism: "'Where's Frederick,' she asked, wondering why 'his voice is not heard in this trying hour.'"[152] More tellingly still, such indebtedness was by no means one way. A few years later in 1870, Douglass himself admitted to audiences in "I Speak To You as an American Citizen," a little-discussed address delivered in Washington, "You know all that I have said, and more than all I have said; but as Sojourner Truth once said, I want you to see that I know it too."[153] Thus while Truth bore witness to the power of Douglass's "voice," Douglass no less testified to Truth's multifaceted signifying poetics in a rare moment of candor and in a bold volte face from his earlier debasements of her intellectual prowess. Directly engaging with her radical displays of knowledge, therefore, Douglass groundbreakingly positioned his self-reflexive performances as not only indebted to but as existing upon a continuum with Truth's own.

In dramatic ways, Truth's politically staged refractions of self resonate powerfully with Douglass's theoretical and aesthetically experimental meditations upon the acts and arts of black radicalism, as both activists signified simultaneously as radical intellectuals and oratorical performers. As her white amanuensis Frances Titus revealed, "A friend not long ago offered to write her life. She told him she was 'not ready to be writ up yet, for she had lots to accomplish first.'"[154] Perpetually determined not to be "writ up," Sojourner Truth's array of multiple and shifting personae attests to a formerly enslaved Black woman's right to intellectual, moral, and philosophical complexities, a right that remains off limits in Douglass's conceptualization of the archetypal "heroic slave."

FREDERICK DOUGLASS'S "LIVING PARCHMENTS"

AND "CHATTEL RECORDS"

Five Great American Negroes, a work painted by the Black artist Charles White between 1939 and 1940, is one of his most famous history murals (see plate 8). White was inspired to create this large-scale, aggrandized spectacle of black cultural and political resistance by a newspaper survey in which Black readers selected Sojourner Truth, Booker T. Washington, Marian Anderson, George Washington Carver, and Frederick Douglass as their representative heroic icons. In contrast to White's mural *Contribution of the Negro to Democracy in America,* painted a few years later in 1943, in which Douglass appears as the founding father of black civil rights activism, *Five Great American Negroes* dramatizes Douglass as the lynchpin in a haunting triptych. Variously depicting diverse ages and incarnations of black heroism, White's array of exceptional icons maps different social and historical epochs in order to trace a nineteenth-century fight against slavery onto twentieth-century struggles for black freedoms. While Booker T. Washington occupies the center of the mural as he stands behind a podium and delivers a speech for the benefit of a Black audience pictured beneath, Douglass appears at his side in the guise of an older statesman.

Refusing to capitulate to dominant representations that favored elder statesman Douglass over and above Douglass the youthful firebrand, White rejects any seemingly conciliatory impetus. He depicts Douglass physically supporting the bent-over body of a young enslaved man who is graphically shown in shackles. Mindful of the ways in which the horrors and injustices of slavery lived on in the early twentieth-century segregationist era, White's symbolism does not flinch from the gritty legacies surrounding black persecution and torture. Rather than standing on an antislavery or even a pro–civil rights podium à la Washington, Douglass and his enslaved alter ego appear to be standing on an auction block. More forcefully still, White relies on apocalyptic color symbolism in his repeated use of brown to accentuate the parallels between the textured surfaces of the enslaved man's skin and the trunk of the tree next to which all three male figures stand. Explicitly signifying upon the visual language of lynching photography, White artfully concretizes the comparisons between slavery and segregation in order to protest against black bodies as sacrificial symbols of racist persecution. His powerful vision of Douglass as literally burdened by a half-naked enslaved man bears visceral witness to this historical figure's often elided paradoxes and ambiguities of selfhood. As part fugitive, part writer, part orator, part activist, and part politician, Douglass experimented with a wealth of identities in his philosophical no less than political fight to secure multiple freedoms.

Any investigation into Douglass's life and works immediately reveals that his psychological contradictions—as captured by twentieth-century artists such as White—have their origin in his own self-reflexive engagement in acts and art of thinking, writing, speaking, and performing. Rejecting iconic fixity or reductive categorization of his own textual and visual representations, Douglass perpetually interrogated boundaries of self-formation to endorse alternative strategies of image making. He engaged in multiple signifying and performative practices artfully designed to secure his own political and aesthetic liberation. Yet as Douglass's twentieth- and twenty-first-century visual and textual legacies demonstrate, for those taking inspiration from his leadership it was imperative that he become not so much a "malleable icon" like Harriet Tubman but in fact a rather more fixed point of origin and compass point for a wide spectrum of protest movements: à la White's visualization, he is repeatedly memorialized as a representative exemplar literally bearing the burdens of slavery's traumas. Frederick Douglass was neither a "fine young negro" nor a kneeling enslaved icon, neither a public orator nor a literary author, neither a politician nor an intellectual, neither a philosopher nor an artist, and neither a heroic nor an iconic representative man. His experimental literary and intellectual practices negotiated all of these categories to create a world of contestation and slippage and become his own "work of art."[1] In stark contrast to Toussaint Louverture, Nathaniel Turner, Sengbe Pieh, Sojourner Truth, Madison Washington, and Harriet Tubman, Douglass was no founder of a black republic; leader of a slave revolution by land or sea; grassroots liberator of enslaved women, children, and men; or even a preacher or spiritual guide. Yet he remains a renowned icon and pioneering symbol of black male resistance across the centuries for his groundbreaking literary works, experimental oratory, self-reflexive photographic performances, and radical advocacy of a militant activism.

"The grand narrative of Douglass' life—an American success story whose hero is the epitome of the American self-made man—reveals enormous inspirational and symbolic power," Waldo E. Martin Jr. writes.[2] Nonetheless, any overly straightforward endorsements of "grand narratives" of Douglass's memory run the risk of endorsing a monolithic and exclusionary model of black male heroism that does little justice to Douglass's contradictions and complexities. On the surface, his visual and textual archive sheds light on his determination to engage in personal reflections of an ennobled selfhood. Yet, ever self-reflexive in his role as quintessential Black heroic figure, as his experimental poetics reveal, he actively transgressed the boundaries of self-representation to signal his awareness of his own identity as a site of paradox and conflict. In this regard, Wilson Jeremiah Moses's view that Douglass's seemingly "unassailable position" renders it essential "for us to ask what we really mean when we speak of an African American hero" speaks to the need to break down typically hagiographic constructions of Douglass's multifaceted personae.[3] Such critiques by Moses and other scholars provide a useful starting point from which to interrogate the problematic parameters for black male heroism as wittingly and unwittingly set up by Douglass himself in the circulation of his public self as an iconic example par excellence.

Directly confronting the difficulties of memorialization and representation within African American history, politics, and culture, Douglass experimented with language, narrative form, and public oratory across his life and works. On the one hand, he subverted typical associations of black bodies with martyrdom in abolitionist rhetoric; on the other, he fought against black objectification as commodified spectacle in white proslavery discourses. Thus Douglass's self-reflexivity provides an alternative position from which to examine Martin's identification of dominant trends within his memorializations. "Popular images of the heroic Douglass, like those of most complex historical heroes, tend to emphasize a simplistic greatness. Typically, there is little, if any, room within these images for contradiction or inconsistency," Martin suggests.[4] Yet Douglass's experimentation with literary and photographic languages vouchsafes his determination to court "contradiction" and "inconsistency" as he resisted white mainstream tendencies toward straightforward exhibitions of black bodies as proofs. As Zoe Trodd observes, a great deal of work needs to be done, as "scholars have only touched on the memory and influence of Douglass."[5] The origins of Douglass's complexities can clearly be traced not only to his multidimensional works but also to his overt theorizing and imaginative and philosophical engagement with experimental approaches to acts and arts of black self-representation. Douglass's autobiographical personae remain inextricable from his engagement with aesthetic and philosophical constructions of a multifaceted black male heroism. "He made his living by cultivating the myth of Frederick Douglass," Moses argues.[6] As Douglass's determination to eulogize a plethora of Black heroic figures—including himself—throughout his lifetime attests, his processes of self-mythologization were not only wide ranging and experimental but also heavily bound up with his meditation upon the political and aesthetic function of representative Black icons otherwise excluded from history. Relying on his own narrative and visual reimaginings as the lens through which to transgress the boundaries for black representation, he fought to access a largely undocumented history of heroism that had typically existed only in folkloric discourse and certainly beyond the pale of a white mainstream imagination.

A compulsive revisionist, Douglass retold, revisualized, and restaged multiple narrative vignettes of selfhood, which he interpolated with iconic feats of black male heroism. For Douglass, imaginative retelling in visual, literary, and oratorical re-creation and reinvention constituted the most radical act of resistance, precisely because of the impossibility, in his view, of reducing the imagination to the bare bones of scientific inquiry or rational investigation. As Robert S. Levine emphasizes, "Perhaps the most heroic aspect of Douglass's efforts to write himself into being as a heroic black leader is his faith in writing itself."[7] Yet Douglass's experimental practices consistently extended beyond the writerly sphere in his experimentation with both the oratorical and photographic modes. Douglass's circulation of his photographic image operated in self-conscious and aesthetically experimental conjunction with his written and oratorical personae to critique white tendencies to lock representations of enslaved men and women within surface paradigms of objectification. Clearly, his intellectual forms of resistance provide new ways of approaching photographs ostensibly of black victimization—such as Gordon's—to appreciate his and many others' frequently elided strategies of "cutting a figure," as recently theorized by Richard Powell, as they established black agency in the face of annihilating subjugation.[8]

Moses's thoughtful questions—"What does it mean to be a hero? What does it mean to have the shaggy-headed leonine portrait of Frederick Douglass staring down at us from the bulletin boards of schoolrooms across America during Black History Month?"—are not new. Such questions regarding definitions of black heroism were ones Douglass himself repeatedly asked, not only of himself, but also of his imaginative reconstructions of Toussaint Louverture, Nathaniel Turner, and Madison Washington, among others, as he sought to reimagine an otherwise elided black iconic heritage. The difficulties and tensions embedded within white abolitionist tendencies to rally audiences to the cause of black suffering by producing images and texts that frequently foregrounded politicized display only to effect psychological erasure were not lost upon Douglass as an ex-enslaved African American turned activist, orator, author, statesman, and philosopher. "Perhaps one reason for our continuing fascination with Douglass is the amorphous quality of his symbolism," Moses argues in an astute recognition of Douglass's ambiguities, which artfully resisted prescriptive tendencies toward reductive fixity.[9] Henry Louis Gates Jr. no less perceptively argues, "Frederick Douglass does not yet exist as a three-dimensional person but as an open-ended system of rhetorical figures and tropes."[10] "Open-endedness" in both theory and practice and as a stimulus to symbolic representation remained Douglass's modus operandi throughout his career, as he complemented acts of protest with arts of reimagining. An experimenter with the possibilities of language, performance, and the fine arts, Douglass devoted a lifetime to ending slavery by reconceptualizing the thematic and formal boundaries within which to represent black selfhood. Nonetheless, unresolved issues related to Douglass's "amorphous symbolism" and simultaneous exploration of "figure and tropes" have ultimately made it difficult for his biographers even to begin to come to grips with his competing construction of diverse black masculinities.

Across his daguerreotypes, photographs, autobiographies, oratory, essays, and single experimental work of historical fiction, Douglass experimented with strategies of political, social, and aesthetic resistance. Popularizing a little-known yet enduring black heroic tradition in these works, he provided himself with new opportunities to problematize and reimagine alternative conceptualizations of black enslaved identities. An exploration of iconic black male heroic figures who had either been distorted or dismissed in the white imagination acted as an aggrandizing backdrop to his own struggles for self-representation across a range of literary, oratorical, and photographic works. In powerful ways, his and their stories became simultaneous emblems and even surrogates for the hidden histories of those anonymous enslaved women, children, and men living and dying in plantation slavery. Douglass's decision to dramatize an array of heroic personae—many of whom he directly associated with his own life—ultimately reflected his understanding of the inextricable ways in which the tensions of an enslaved past could and did exist within a freed present. Just as Barack Obama admitted at the end of the twentieth century that he "had been forced to look inside myself and had found only a great emptiness there," Douglass strained after "glimpses" and "traces" in reconstructions of his own biography and in his reimagining of the lives and deaths of Black heroic men and women, at best lauded or at worst demonized beyond all recognition in official records.[11]

Repeatedly fighting to resist authority not only during his life as an enslaved man but also in his new life as a free man, Douglass repeatedly refracted his imaginative dramatizations of Black heroic icons through an autobiographical lens. He established his shift from a desire solely for physical freedom to the pursuit of simultaneous moral, psychological, intellectual, and social forms of liberation. He was keen to legitimize his self-made exceptionalism within the context of a famed yet poetically and politically displaced black male heroic tradition. Clearly, Douglass's decision to experiment with form and language to dramatize the otherwise hidden histories of Black male iconic figures testifies to his awareness regarding the difficulties he faced concerning his own self-representations. For Douglass, imaginative narratives of black heroism—as repeatedly written out of historical discourse—shared intellectual and imaginative parallels with his determination to liberate the confining parameters within which his own life and work were memorialized.

In his fictionalization of the life of the *Creole* slave ship revolutionary and liberator Madison Washington the historical subject for his only work of fiction, *The Heroic Slave,* published in 1853, his demands of his white audiences were clear cut:

> Let those account for it who can, but there stands the fact, that a man who loved liberty as well as did Patrick Henry,—who deserved it as much as Thomas Jefferson,—and who fought for it with a valor as high, an arm as strong, and against odds as great, as he who led all the armies of the American colonies through the great war for freedom and independence, lives now only in the chattel records of his native State.[12]

Douglass's concept not only of the "heroic slave" but also of "chattel records" is integral to his theoretical understanding of diverse acts and arts of enslaved heroism. Establishing a groundbreaking framework, he challenged the racist paradigms of historical discourse and white mainstream memorializations according to which Black male subjects were distorted and maligned, if not annihilated altogether. Signifying upon absence and ambiguity, Douglass exalted in the role of the recently freed Black writer to create new narratives. Reimagining and re-creating heroic lives otherwise subsumed into "chattel records," he interrogated the boundaries of language to emancipate his own processes of heroic construction from reductive pressures toward fixity. And yet, as his problematic relationship with Sojourner Truth in particular reveals, Douglass's construction of black heroism repeatedly endorsed a problematic and exceptional masculinity as the normative default. During his lifetime, his repeated return to neglected or distorted feats of black male heroism provided the displaced forum within which he vicariously reimagined his own multifaceted oratorical and literary personae. This preference for narrating his own life through the public histories of heroic male icons bore witness to his own psychological ambiguities. Reflective of his iconic status, one of Douglass's key paradoxes concerned his determination to define his own exceptionalism as existing beyond and in contrast to the experiences of the majority of enslaved men and women. In this way, he not only set himself apart from but revealed his commitment to speaking as if he inhabited the individual subjectivities of untold millions shackled in slavery.

Self-consciously interrogating the boundaries between physical and psychological resistance, Douglass was careful to establish in his second narrative, *My Bondage and My Freedom,* that "the overseer had written his character on the living parchment of most of their backs, and left them callous; my back . . . was yet tender."[13] Yet, writing toward the end of his life, he told a different story: "I was called upon to expose even my stripes, and with many misgivings obeyed the summons."[14] As paradoxes across his life and works demonstrate, for Douglass it was imperative that the enslaved body be metaphorically dramatized through literary imagery as a "living parchment" rather than offered up solely as an exhibited body of evidence. His powerful tropes and linguistic sleights of hand not only communicated the realities of traumas enacted upon the enslaved body but also protected black humanity by replacing the finite fixity of physical suffering with the infinite possibilities of textual symbolism. His metaphor of a "living parchment" was inextricable from his belief in "chattel records" as he engaged in a simultaneous experimentation with the intellectual, moral, political, and aesthetic possibilities of black representation. Throughout his lifetime, Douglass increasingly engaged in acts of textual and oratorical reimagining to protest against the objectifying exclusion of black male heroism from official histories. As a result, his radical aesthetic practices freely and involuntarily endorsed fragmentation and ellipsis as the only way in which to signify upon the nefarious effects of white prescriptive definitions of authenticity vis-à-vis black identity construction. Thus the onus is upon critics to recontextualize Douglass's repeated return to the public histories of heroic icons by gaining a heightened awareness of his own ambivalences regarding various processes of self-mythologization.

Any discussion of Douglass's forays into black history would be incomplete without examining his experimentation with visual and textual imagery as a way of shedding light on the importance he attached to the frequently unfathomable but vital relationship between aesthetics and political reform. Such a preoccupation sets him apart from the majority of Black writers, activists, and philosophers engaged in producing works of African American history during this period but perhaps less self-reflexively engaged in the philosophical and aesthetic aspects of this process. As Douglass argued in a speech examining the importance of photography, "The world has no sight more pleasant and hopeful, either for the child, or for the race, than one of these little ones in rapt contemplation of a pure work of art."[15] Both his speeches and writings reveal that art operated similarly for "the child" as for "the race" by inspiring sublime awe and a transcendence of seemingly fixed limitations—political, historical, social—via the all-consuming power of the imagination. Douglass's preoccupation with the transformative powers of a "pure work of art" is revealing concerning his mythic engagement with transitional as well as transformational processes of self-making. He sought to complicate white abolitionists' endorsements of seemingly straightforward, linear trajectories from slavery to emancipation, or from "chattelhood" to "manhood."

Working according to the conviction that the process of appreciating a "work of art" "is one of self-revelation, a comparison of the pure forms of beauty and excellence without, with those which are within," Douglass argued not only for a direct correlation between internal and external realities but also for the power of aesthetic and psychological truths to effect change over socially determinist situations.[16] In palpable ways his sense of freedom emerged not solely from a transgressive exploration of taboo subject matter—a panorama of bleeding, dying, and suffering bodies representative of a symbolic as well as literal "blood-stained gate"—but, and as importantly, from the right to artistic experimentation and to the performance of art for art's sake.[17] Ultimately, Douglass's aesthetic practices were guided by a determination to resist tendencies to inscribe men and women into historical records as "fixed facts." In these and other works, he fought against the deadening forces of iconic monumentalism, static memorialization, and racist commodification, all of which colluded in surface interpretations of men and women as repeatedly confined within reductive photographic images and problematic textual discourse. Maurice S. Lee's view that "Douglass even models for those who read him a kind of interdisciplinary approach" may be adapted beyond Douglass's own experimental practices to the subsequent visual and textual adaptations produced by writers and artists in the twentieth and twenty-first centuries.[18] Multiple Frederick Douglasses come to life not only in his oratory, photography, and diverse writings but also in his enduring legacies. Subsequent writers and artists have remained as determined as Douglass in their fight to re-create this historical figure as a multifaceted and ambiguous heroic icon in their no less self-reflexive "works of art." Writing during the political turmoil of 1968, Julius Lester provides an apt summary of the aesthetic strategies by which Douglass sought to unfetter himself from white mainstream expectations. "He was supposed to be the exhibit, the real thing, and to confine himself to being a 'nigger just escaped from slavery,'" Lester writes, concluding, "Get your tickets! Get your tickets! Real live nigger runaway! Step this way!"[19] Neither the "exhibit" nor the "real thing," Douglass repeatedly signified upon his status as a "work of art" to examine the problematic relationships between "chattel records" and "living parchments" as he sought to endorse malleable constructions of a representative black masculinity.

"THE MAN MAY BE CONSIDERED A FIXED FACT": RADICAL POLITICS, SELF-REFLEXIVE POETICS, AND VISUAL REPRESENTATIONS OF FREDERICK DOUGLASS

"Ambrotypes, Photographs and Electrotypes, good and bad, now adorn or disfigure all our dwellings," observes Douglass in "Pictures and Progress," a speech he delivered in Boston in 1861. "Men of all conditions may see themselves as others see them," he argues. However, at the same time that Douglass celebrated the egalitarian and democratizing possibilities of early photography, he admits that

> pictures are decid[ed]ly conservative. It would be difficult to determine as between a man[']s picture and a man[']s religious creed which of the twain is most conservative in its influence upon him. The one is the measure of the outer man and the other of the in[ner] and both are positive law—on the points to which they apply. Once fairly in the book and the man may be considered a fixed fact, public property.[20]

Douglass's sensitivity to the ways in which "conservative" photographs trade in "fixed facts" in an attempt to record the "inner" via the "outer" man testifies to his determination to signify imaginatively upon the boundaries of form within his own portraits. As his images reveal, Douglass played with ambiguities of tonal variation in contrasts of light and dark as well as a stark, minimalist use of composition. Thus he relied on his own physicality to re-create the black male body as an enigmatic, almost disembodied persona rather than as a scientific specimen. A far cry from the frontispieces that accompanied various editions of his narrative as well as popular media representations, photographs that Douglass himself commissioned resisted his status as "public property." Rather, in these works he cultivated a greater affinity with artistic portraiture over and above the fallacies of representations purporting to scientific exactitude.

In light of Douglass's well-documented dislike of the hand-drawn illustrations accompanying his slave narrative frontispieces as well as an early painted portrait, it is no surprise that he was keen to capitalize on the political and aesthetic possibilities of photography. For Douglass, this new technology seemed to provide the answer to racist caricatures of black physiognomies. Immediately following the inception of the daguerreotyping process, he was keen to capitalize on photography's political and aesthetic possibilities. By the mid-nineteenth century, as Allan Sekula argues, "Photographic portraiture began to perform a role no painted portrait could have performed in the same thorough and rigorous fashion."[21] And it was precisely this thoroughness that attracted Douglass to the medium; it gave whites less scope with which to distort black bodies than was popularly available not only in mainstream portraiture but also in grotesque illustrations and generic runaway slave woodcuts. More particularly, Douglass was excited by the possibility that, as Susan Sontag observes, "Photography, though not an art form in itself, has the peculiar capacity to turn all its subjects into works of art."[22] As he was equally attracted to both the intellectual and the aesthetic properties of the form, Douglass's fascination can also be seen to preempt Roland Barthes's suggestion that "photography is subversive not when it frightens . . . but when it is *pensive*."[23] Across his daguerreotyped portraits, Douglass exalted in photography as a platform upon which a recognition of Black men and women as thinking subjects became possible. For Douglass, the key point was that it was only with the invention of photography that a counterarchive consisting of accurate representations of black humanity became possible. Such technological developments offered the only way out of his powerful realization that "I have never seen a single picture in an American work, designed to give an idea of the mental endowments of the Negro, which did any thing like justice to the subject; nay, that was not infamously distorted."[24]

Alan Trachtenberg's examination of the daguerreotype as "an image [that] lay on the brilliant mirror-like silver surface of a copper plate resting in a small case," which guaranteed "an intimate experience of exact representation" is revealing. As a one-off, nonreproducible object, the daguerreotype "possessed the aura of a unique thing."[25] In many respects, the daguerreotype represented a bridge between public portraits and portrait miniatures, given that, as Robin Frank suggests, "easel portraits present a public self meant to face outward" while "portrait miniatures reveal a private self meant to face inward."[26] As an art form capable of producing unique objects that signified across both public and private realms, the daguerreotype was particularly suited to Douglass's pioneering experimentation with archetypal and iconic self-representations. As Marcus Wood emphasizes, "The multi-valent body of portraiture which evolved around him . . . constitutes something of a master-class in how an African American could control, popularise and manipulate his or her image."[27] Taken together, both Douglass's visual archive and his theoretical examination of photography establish his experimentation with daguerreotyped portraiture, not only to reject white mainstream tendencies toward racist stereotyping but also to counter strategies of appropriation in the visual as well as the political arena.

Just as Sojourner Truth played the game by performing as an icon of black female domesticity to turn the tables on white female overadherence to the slogan "Am I not a woman and a sister?" Douglass pushed the representational boundaries for black masculinity to liberate himself and others from the potentially emasculating appeal "Am I not a man and a brother?" Henry Louis Gates's view that "Douglass was demonstrably concerned with the representation in written language of his public self" can be applied to his experimentation with diverse visual languages. Gates's sense that Douglass "was Representative Man because he was Rhetorical Man, black master of the verbal arts" can be extended to expose his fascination with the transformative possibilities of the visual arts.[28] In stark contrast to photographs of Sojourner Truth and Harriet Tubman, very few of Douglass's stripped-down daguerreotypes, ambrotypes, or photographs include material objects (for an exception see figure 25). For fear of detracting attention away from his monumental and statuesque physical form, the outward expression of his inner complexity and, above all else, his exceptional selfhood were repeatedly the focus of Douglass's radical new gallery of heroic self-portraits.

As *Picturing Frederick Douglass,* the forthcoming book and collaborative project I am working on with Henry Louis Gates Jr., Bill E. Lawson, Sally Pierce, John Stauffer, and Zoe Trodd establishes, Douglass was one of if not the most daguerreotyped and photographed American man, black or white, of the nineteenth century and one of the most important writers to theorize on photography as an art form.[29] While Douglass's visual archive is vast, a brief exploration of a select few of his photographic images as produced

at very different periods during his lifetime is useful here: the white daguerreotypist Samuel J. Miller's *Frederick Douglass* (ca. 1847–52, figure 23);
an untitled and undated image by an unknown photographer held in the
Moorland-Spingarn Research Center; the African American photographer
James P. Ball's *Portrait of Frederick Douglass* (1867, figure 24); and *Frederick
Douglass, Full Length, Seated beside Grandson,* by an unknown photographer
(n.d., figure 25).[30] In many ways atypical of Douglass's visual archive, these
photographs include either a controversial provenance, a rare delineation of
Douglass in profile, or an unusual return to family portraiture in order to
attest, as powerfully as his written texts, not to one but to multiple Frederick Douglasses. "In his early career at least, the textual Douglass often seems
very much at odds with his performative counterpart," Fionnghuala Sweeney
tellingly observes.[31] As he deliberately cultivated inconsistencies and incon-
gruities across not only his "visual persona" but also his "written self," Douglass's photographic theory establishes his determination to retain authority
by rendering his "private self" inviolate because unknowable. Adopting an
aesthetics of disjuncture, Douglass did not shy away from the elliptical incom-
pleteness of photographs, as "he sought to fashion himself as an art object, or
performer."[32] In this way, Douglass's experimental engagement with photography led not only to a visual persona but to visual personae. Creating multiplici-
ties of visual and written selves, he resisted reductive pageantry or spectacular
exhibition in favor of circulating as an unreadable, ambiguous "work of art."

Very little is known regarding the provenance and genealogy of Miller's
daguerreotype (figure 23), a work bought by the Art Institute of Chicago in
the 1990s for a record-breaking sum. As Colin Westerbeck notes, "Unlike
Frederick Douglass himself, the Art Institute's daguerreotype of him is undocumented." Yet the survival of the "daguerreotype's case," which "bears
the name of its maker and the city where he was in business," ensures that
"we have more information about this daguerreotype than about most others of Douglass." Among the most significant features of the recovery of this
image, however, is the daguerreotype with which it was found. "The shoebox
from which the Art Institute's daguerreotype was recovered was a veritable
time capsule of the Abolitionist movement," Westerbeck explains, noting
that "the box also contained a daguerreotype of John Brown."[33] Surprisingly,
Westerbeck makes no mention of the fact that this iconic image of John
Brown was created by one of the few renowned African American daguerre-
otypists, Augustus Washington. Douglass's confrontational engagement
with the viewer in Miller's daguerreotype mirrors Brown's powerful gaze
in Washington's image, as if to suggest a cross-racial history of antislavery

resistance. No less intent upon dramatizing his white subject's exceptional heroism, Washington's representation of Brown focuses upon his upraised palm as a visual signifier of white male sacrifice. If considered in this aesthetic context, in Miller's daguerreotype Douglass was equally engaged in visual practices designed to signify black male suffering, sacrifice, and even potential martyrdom.

A complete volte face from early frontispieces no less than mainstream media representations typically consisting of historical illustration, sheet music reproductions, and paintings, the Frederick Douglass of Miller's daguerreotype is the Frederick Douglass not of his first but of his second autobiography, if of any literary work at all. Photographic subject and artist work together to provide a close up of Douglass's exceptional physiognomy as he confronts the viewer directly with a persecuted yet forceful and empowered, if ultimately masked gaze. In the same way that *My Bondage and My Freedom* is a groundbreaking work critiquing the seeming bare bones of his first autobiography, in which his artfulness had to be communicated indirectly, Douglass's visual persona is infinitely more guarded, ambiguous, and predicated upon a poetics of untelling rather than illustrative exhibition. For Douglass, this image confirms that the photograph no less than the picture represented a tool of aesthetic revision as well as of social and political change. "The picture and the ballad are alike, if not equally social forces—the one reaching and swaying the heart by the eye, and the other by the ear," he insists.[34] Douglass mounted his war on the "heart by the eye" by converting audiences to the injustices of slavery via exemplary feats of self-portraiture. In comparison to painted representations of Douglass including a portrait previously attributed to a white artist, Elisha Hammond, and dated as early as about 1844, hard edges and angular lines structure his face in Miller's daguerreotype to visualize his physiognomy as characterized by symmetry and balance rather than stereotypical contortion or exaggeration. As Westerbeck confirms, Miller's daguerreotype of Douglass, "with its clarity, its precision, and its shirt that buttons right over left (i.e., backward), is unquestionably an original."[35] The Frederick Douglass of Miller's portrayal, an exceptionally defined daguerreotype, is neither partially in shadow nor only half drawn: seemingly inimitable, he possesses the aura of an original rather than a replica. To paraphrase Truth, we can see how he somehow encapsulates both "substance" and "shadow" to get at his corporeal viscerality in conjunction with his spiritual transcendence.

Douglass authorized no shying away from external evidence regarding his hardships in this daguerreotype. A cross-shaped scar appears in infinitesimal

FIGURE 23. Samuel J. Miller, *Frederick Douglass*, 1847–52, cased hall-plate daguerreotype, 14 × 10.6 cm (5½ × 4⅛ in.). (The Art Institute of Chicago, Major Acquisitions Centennial Endowment, 1996.433)

detail to accentuate rather than detract from the profundity of his prominent forehead while clear lines on his physiognomy suggest endurance. At the same time, streaks of white in his otherwise black hair testify to an identity formed in the crucible of slavery. The signifying possibilities of Miller's daguerreotype signal its distance from other early photographic portraits, including an unattributed work created as early as 1845 that depicts a

Douglass with haunted eyes and a far less hardened facial expression.[36] Here he appears in ethereal shadow as if to symbolize his fugitive status through a fugitive representation in this daguerreotype. By comparison, Douglass's posture and physiognomy in Miller's photograph can be understood as a visual embodiment of his conviction concerning the interrelationships between masculinity, idealism, and aesthetics.

Created at the height of Douglass's fame, Miller's image signifies upon his iconic status. In contrast, earlier daguerreotypes betray his barely formed sense of self to record an identity in the process of creation. "Our military heroes look better even in pictures, after winning an important battle, than after losing one," Douglass argues. "The pictures do not change, but we look at them through the favorable or unfavorable prevailing public opinion."[37] Thus Douglass became increasingly aware of the circulation of his images within white mainstream media as he recognized the role played by "public opinion" as the filter for interpretation. In 1845, an unknown Douglass carved himself out of anonymity; by 1855, however, a celebrity Douglass was seeking to encourage ambiguity by cultivating a proliferation of Douglasses. Such an overt engagement with the shifting vagaries of public perception sheds light on his determination to present himself allegorically, mythically, and historically as a grizzled, prematurely aged and yet physically empowered freedom fighter laying down his life on the altar of freedom in this work. Furthermore, those deep lines above his eyebrows, on either side of his nose, and beneath his eyes attest to his "manly beauty," thereby celebrating his status as a "work of art." Here, Douglass is keen to emphasize that his is a beauty not only derived from but made possible solely by suffering.

Overall, Douglass's was a performance not of the minstrel type in this daguerreotype but instead of the artist whose masklike stillness inhabits a multiplicity of guises in order to counter derogatory mainstream representations. This is no generic or unknown Douglass, as, in contrast to frontispieces to his narrative, this daguerreotype speaks for itself by including no reproduction of his name: as a much less mediated image in and of itself, this work represents Douglass's unfettered visual signature. Similarly, the ornate detail of Douglass's flowered waistcoat contrasts with the austerity of his black overcoat and white shirt to heighten the emotional register of his physiognomy, which encompasses a gamut of expressions including sorrow, anger, persecution, loss, and intellectual profundity. In contrast to the frontispieces to Douglass's autobiographies, which directly confront the viewer, Miller's image portrays Douglass according to the traditional gaze of heroic portraiture, in which the subject typically engages in visionary contemplation. And yet, if it is possible to see a direct correlation between Douglass's movement from a bare-bones to a fleshed-out, experimental use of textual language between his two autobiographies, it is no less the case that his visual representations articulate a similar shift. Directing his gaze beyond his audience, Douglass could as easily have been contemplating the past as the future. Thus the anguished yet steely determination of his eyes may record the horrors of his enslaved past rather than his prophetic vision. "The process by which man is able to invert his own subjective consciousness, into the objective form, considered in all its range, is in truth the highest attribute of man[']s nature," Douglass explains.[38] Achieving precisely this semblance of "objective form," Douglass dramatizes his "subjective consciousness" by rendering his internal experiences externally palpable via an intellectual engagement with the picture-making process.

Douglass's daguerreotyped, print, and photographic reproductions frequently evoke stereotypical iconography only to reject its nefarious aspects in favor of illuminating black psychological complexities. One such knowing representation is a diminutive, quarter-plate daguerreotype created by an unknown artist and held in the Moorland-Spingarn Research Center at Howard University. This rare image in his visual archive explicitly indicts racist caricatures of blackness by portraying Douglass's exceptional facial features in profile. In contrast to a wealth of problematic images that accentuate black criminality and bestiality, here Douglass exalts in his own exceptionalism. He is well dressed, and an artful use of lighting emphasizes the symmetrical uniformity and aestheticized proportions of his facial features. In contrast to racist burlesques of blackness, the detailed measurements of Douglass's face are revealed by a vertical line that runs from his strong jaw, chin, mouth, and straight nose to his forehead. In this image, he provides a visual rejection of the racism of scientific diagrams that traded in exhibitions of black inferiority. Denying the viewer access to his physical expression, Douglass recovers the profiled view as the legitimate domain of African American portraiture. While the cross-shaped scar on his forehead remains hidden in this work, a new scar is visible in a long gouged line clearly visible beneath his cheek. Such haunting evidence of physical mutilation ultimately attests to Douglass's battle against slavery, while his unflinching gaze and firmly set mouth subvert tendencies toward objectification by testifying to an inner resolution. Here, Douglass was determined to communicate psychological truths via an interiority of perspective: the "inner" via the "outer" man.

James P. Ball's undated photograph *Portrait of Frederick Douglass* (figure 24) signals the shift from early memorializations of a young, heroic Douglass in various processes of becoming to representations of a fixed elder statesman as typical of later portrayals. Ball's close-up of Douglass's head and shoulders accentuates the grayness of his hair, while his enigmatic expression suggests slippery psychological states of being as he gazes off into the distance. Again, the distinct reproduction of the cross on his forehead works in combination with the deep lines on his face, the texture of his hair, and even the translucent light in his eyes to convey both his corporeal physicality and his spiritual intensity: Ball's Douglass is battle worn, but the photograph does not shy away from the physical effects of suffering and struggle. Painter's view that "Ball's Douglass looks like a nineteenth-century politician in a suit coat, ready for engagement" is scarcely born out by the fragility of the nonfixity of the image.[39]

In this work, Ball illuminates painful uncertainties through his use of lighting in order to accentuate Douglass's lined brow and seemingly translucent eyes. In this regard, Douglass's erect posture and strong gaze contrast with the frailties on the surface of his skin to reflect tensions within his later self-representations, which were less concerned with the processes and more with the emotional and physical aftermath of struggles over identity formation. Psychological ambiguities in his facial expression foreground inner turmoil to underscore his contemplation not only of a future yet to arrive but of a past yet to resolved. An erect and contemplative figure, Douglass appears self-possessed and empowered yet vulnerable and weary. In clear-cut ways, this image lays bare his physical weaknesses to accentuate his spiritual strength in order to provide a self-conscious representation of Douglass as a heroic individual surviving against the odds. Perhaps for the first time, Douglass could not only afford to reveal his vulnerability to a black daguerreotypist and to Black audiences more generally but was also determined to do so in order to dramatize the uncertainty regarding the unwritten future for African Americans. An ever-thinning "living parchment," Douglass's skin appears luminous under Ball's stark use of lighting and tonal variation as if to reassure the viewer regarding his iconic subject's seemingly ageless, firmly set mouth and resolute jaw. The absence of any background detail reinforces Douglass's aggrandized sense of his own status as an enduring symbol of the struggle for black emancipation.

A much later photograph, *Frederick Douglass, Full Length, Seated beside Grandson* provides a rare dramatization of Douglass not as a solitary freedom fighter but as accompanied by his grandson Joseph, a young man who epitomizes a future generation of Black leaders (figure 25). This photograph is one of at least two images taken with Joseph; the other, also an anonymous and undated image, is titled *Frederick Douglass, Full Length, Seated*

FIGURE 24. James P. Ball, *Portrait of Frederick Douglass*, 1867. (Courtesy of Getty Images and Cincinnati Museum Center)

FIGURE 25. Anon., *Frederick Douglass, Full Length, Seated beside Grandson,* n.d. (Prints and Photographs Division, Library of Congress)

beside Grandson, Who Is Playing the Violin. In this work, the photographer's symbolic use of composition provides another rare view of Douglass. Showing Douglass listening to his grandson playing the violin, this photograph establishes the importance of cross-generational exchange to endorse black progress and racial uplift. This image is thus the photographic equivalent of the African American artist Henry Ossawa Tanner's painting *The Banjo*

Lesson (1893), in which a grandfather and grandson similarly share a creative heritage through music.[40] Perhaps Douglass's grandson operates as a spiritual emblem not only for his grandfather's former life but also for his experimentation with an array of artful personae.

Tellingly, Joseph stands to his right in this photograph as he adopts a dignified pose, while Douglass himself remains seated in an ornate armchair. In a turn from earlier portrayals of Douglass before a bare background, the inclusion in this photograph of a few symbolic studio properties, such as a seat decorated with carved lions' heads, represents a new departure in his visual archive. These well-chosen artifacts celebrate Douglass's former leonine mythology and mythic strength in the face of an increasing physical vulnerability. In contrast to Joseph's soft facial features, Douglass's lined physiognomy emphasizes not only a generational shift but also the ongoing role played by historic freedom fighters in inspiring newly established and freed African American communities in the postslavery era. Douglass's white hair contrasts with his grandson's black hair to provide a candid reflection upon his resolution and resistance in this photograph. Douglass is seen here sitting rather than standing, as was typical of his earlier images, not with fists clenched but hands relaxed. He holds what appears to be a newspaper, signaling his ongoing activism as well as his own sense of his enduring significance as a pioneering black editor. The print on the newspaper is as difficult to read as Douglass's facial expression, however, not only suggesting the ambiguity of the future but also insisting that it is still in Douglass's hands.

While the lines on Douglass's face and the cross-shaped scar are visible in this photograph, his square jaw is now hidden by a beard that detracts viewers away from his vulnerability. Instead, he celebrates his resounding mythology as a survivor in the crucible of the antislavery struggle. In stark contrast to Douglass, Joseph stands fully erect, his half-smiling expression contrasting with Douglass's signature ambiguity. Compared to the other studio photograph in which Douglass listens to his grandson play the violin, in this image there is little interaction between the two subjects. Instead, they directly confront the viewer in order to celebrate the importance not only of genealogical bloodlines but of self-reliance and individualism. Whereas the grandson's eyes and unlined face suggest optimism, Douglass's raised eyebrows and ambivalent expression communicate the struggles of the past as etched onto his skin. Thus we see that toward the end of his life, Douglass was careful to craft his heroic self-image as not only inextricable from the living legacies of his antislavery history but as also indebted to his formative experience as an enslaved human being.

Any brief examination of Douglass's visual archive attests to his conviction that "I am only the painter to give form and expression to facts and appeal to the mental experience of all for the fidelity of my pictures." Freely describing himself as a "painter," Douglass explicitly admits to the importance of aesthetic processes in his artfully constructed literary and visual archive. His insistence on the "fidelity of my pictures" lays claim to an authenticity that emerges out of a psychological rather than a physical realism. Just as Amiri Baraka asked if Nathaniel Turner could "paint," as discussed in the preface to this book, Douglass insisted upon his authority as an artist and upon art itself as an act of political resistance. Writing of the importance of pictures that depict "a single living human soul, standing here among us, one of ourselves, occupying the narrow margin of life, and looking away with wondering eyes, with prophetic vision, striving to see the outlines of the vast and silent continents of Eternity," he could have been describing his own photographic images. Described thus, Douglass's self-portraits worked against his status as a mortal, fallible individual to gesture toward his mythical, legendary status as an immortal, divine emblem. "Consciously or unconsciously, we are all man worshippers," he avows.[41] Over the decades, photography became Douglass's favored modus operandi, as his multifaceted and experimental self-portraits testify not only to an iconic black male heroism but also to the enduring symbolism of the black body as a "work of art."

"NO IMAGINED HERO": SELF-REFLEXIVITY AND AESTHETIC EXPERIMENTATION IN FREDERICK DOUGLASS'S *THE HEROIC SLAVE* (1853)

"From that hour, your face seemed to be daguerreotyped on my memory."[42] So Listwell, the allegorically named white abolitionist, explains to Madison Washington, the protagonist of Frederick Douglass's sole work of fiction, *The Heroic Slave*, published in both the United Kingdom and the United States in 1853. An elusive figure allegedly sought to no avail by the white revolutionary John Brown for his raid on Harper's Ferry, Washington was the successful leader of the *Creole* slave ship rebellion of November 7, 1841, which led to the liberation of 134 enslaved men and women off the coast of Nassau, New Providence, in the Bahamas.[43] Notably, Washington has no single chapter devoted to his heroism in this book. The reason for this omission is easily explained. As was the case for Gabriel Prosser, Denmark Vesey, David Walker, and countless other relatively unknown Black historic figures, there are few literary and visual representations of Washington. The important exceptions include the short stories, historical works, and theatrical dramatizations by William Wells Brown, Lydia Maria Child, Pauline E. Hopkins, and Theodore Ward.[44] More tellingly still, and particularly in the context of Listwell's insistence that Washington was "daguerreotyped" in his "memory," there are no engravings, photographs, or portraits purporting to provide an authentic likeness of Washington; neither are there any of Nanny of the Maroons, Denmark Vesey, Gabriel Prosser, or David Walker, while those of Louverture and Turner remain sites of virulent contestation.

A brief exploration of Douglass's literary reimagining of Washington may seem like an irrelevant departure from direct considerations of Douglass's performances. However, Douglass's descriptions of exceptional feats of black male heroism, including those enacted by Washington, illuminate the aesthetic and political dimensions at work within his self-representations. For example, the very absence of any frontispiece accompanying *The Heroic Slave* offered Douglass a golden opportunity by legitimizing his experimental poetics. He was left with no option but to use his imagination to reinterpret his protagonist for otherwise ignorant audiences. This photographic omission renders Listwell's choice of words in describing Washington as "daguerreotyped" on his "memory" even more curious. For audiences and readers in the 1850s, it was Douglass's rather than Washington's physiognomy that was popularly available in daguerreotypes. Such realities concerning Douglass's prominence versus Washington's obscurity render yet more palpable his use of this "heroic slave" as a metaphorical substitute for his own self-portraiture. Unseen and therefore unknown in comparison with Douglass, Washington's physical ambiguities rendered him an ideal conduit for Douglass's displaced projection of a heroic vision of an ennobled selfhood. In this work, he realized that audiences possessing no physical image of Washington would necessarily turn to visual representations of Douglass himself as the only way to reimagine this relatively unknown leader's heroism. As was the case regarding portrayals of Nathaniel Turner and Toussaint Louverture in Douglass's speeches, an absence of visual memorializations of Washington provided Douglass with plenty of scope to encourage audiences to associate this heroic figure more immediately with Douglass himself via rhetorical and literary sleights of hand.

"Daguerreotyping a character was a common trope in abolitionist narration," John Stauffer notes, observing that "a daguerreotype was thought to penetrate the perceiver's soul as well as his mind."[45] Yet the processes of visual appropriation on offer in Douglass's *The Heroic Slave* reverse the seeming power hierarchies regarding the footsore Black man desperately in need of the white man's benevolence. Able to "penetrate the perceiver's soul," Washington, no less than Douglass, gains the ultimate authority in this text by inserting himself into the soul of his viewer via metaphorical evocations of the daguerreotyping process. According to this process, Washington, like Douglass, holds white men such as Listwell in thrall to black masculinity as theatrical embodiment and transcendental spectacle. As Stauffer emphasizes, "Listwell, as someone who has the capacity to 'listen well,' is Douglass' vision of an ideal white man."[46] At the same time, Listwell may well function merely as a backdrop to Douglass's construction of the "ideal black man" via his projected vision of his own iconic exceptionalism. In this regard, the story related by Robert Purvis that, as an enslaved fugitive visiting his household, Washington had seen Nathaniel Jocelyn's portrait of Sengbe Pieh and was inspired to emulate his example supports this interpretation. While no images exist of Washington himself, paintings of men such as Sengbe Pieh—and by extension, as Douglass saw it, of Douglass himself—worked not only to inspire but to give new life to a tradition of black liberation by providing a symbolic stimulus to acts and arts of resistance. As curators at Douglass's final home, Cedar Hill, in the historic Anacostia neighborhood of Washington, DC, have shown, he himself owned a copy of John Sartain's engraving of Jocelyn's portrait and displayed it in his study during his lifetime. Thus Douglass's decision to memorialize Madison Washington, a Black historical figure for whom scant literary dramatizations and no visual representations exist, was clearly far from accidental. Such a narrative strategy betrayed his determination to magnify feats of otherwise nameless and anonymous black male heroism through his own exceptional personae.

Increasingly frustrated with the psychological, intellectual, moral, and physical limitations placed upon him by white American abolitionists, Douglass turned for fictional inspiration not to a retelling of his own life story, as was expected of him, but to the life of Washington. A relatively little-known Black hero, Washington was a figure onto whom Douglass was able to project varying types of a mythological and ambiguous autobiographical selfhood. Douglass not only signified upon acts and arts of daguerreotyping in *The Heroic Slave* but also experimented with the novella form—in addition to theatricalized set pieces—in order to create a series of dramatic monologues. More particularly, he foregrounded generic hybridity to transgress accepted boundaries of anti- and proslavery discourse and visual dramatization. Straining beyond the conventions of the slave narrative genre, he experimented with literary motifs to open up the aesthetic, intellectual, and protest possibilities of black heroic representation in his work. According to this view, neither Douglass nor Washington were "fixed facts," as their identities circulated in alternately interlocking and divergent incarnations. Writing in the preface to her German translation of *My Bondage and My Freedom*, retitled *Sclaverei und Freiheit* and published in 1860, the white German activist, journalist, and writer Ottilie Assing explains, "Instead of an imagined hero, it is the author himself who is at the center of this narrative."[47] Clearly, Washington operated as a no less "imagined hero" for Douglass. Factual absences in Washington's biography provided the stimulus to his development as a mythological figure capable of inspiring sublime awe in ways that invited parallels with Douglass's own self-conscious experimentation with a multifaceted selfhood. In stark contrast to his autobiographical works, Douglass adopted an explicitly experimental literary strategy in *The Heroic Slave*. Seemingly, he retreated from his own exceptionalism only to aggrandize his representative status yet further by a recourse to tropes of a displaced and re-created black male heroism.

Scholarly claims that only begin to suggest parallels between Douglass and Washington can be more forcefully articulated in light of the inextricable political and aesthetic relationships embedded within his oeuvre. John Stauffer's assertion that "Washington suggests something of Douglass' conception of himself" lends ballast to Robert Stepto's insightful view that "Douglass might very possibly have been attracted to Washington's story because it in some measure revises his *own* story."[48] Clearly, Washington became the rhetorical and imaginary platform upon which Douglass argued the case for his own heroism in philosophical and aesthetic no less than political and historical terms. McFeely's conviction that "'The Heroic Slave' was its author's fantasy of his own heroism" can thus be argued on less fantastical and more historically verifiable grounds.[49] Signifying upon his exemplary stature as an orator and enslaved fugitive turned activist, performer, and politician, Douglass invited audiences to replace visions of himself as a "fine young negro"—reminiscent of the parades of "typical negroes" provided in the white mainstream press—with those of a "heroic slave."[50] While William Andrews is right to argue that "Douglass did his part to keep the memory of Madison Washington alive," this tactic reflects equally upon Douglass's self-conscious determination to keep alive the memory not only of Washington but of Douglass himself.[51] Working to memorialize his own legacy within Washington's, Douglass was keen to develop the political and mythological ramifications of his representational status yet further. Signifying upon his and Washington's heroism, he spoke to the barely pieced-together and largely lost histories of those anonymous millions still suffering in slavery and for whom iconic feats of resistance were impossible because of the horrifying realities of their circumstances. As Douglass well knew, for those living and dying in captivity in the U.S. South, Black folkloric figures such as himself, Louverture, Tubman, Truth, Turner, and Pieh served as mythological touchstones integral to cultural survival in creative reimagining.

Ultimately, Douglass was attracted to Washington not only as a projection of his own displaced heroism but also because his historical realities were hidden and characterized by lacunae, a danger that he believed would equally afflict his own subsequent memorializations. Engaging in both celebration ("The state of Virginia is famous in American annals for the multitudinous array of her statesmen and heroes") and critique ("By some strange neglect, *one* of the truest, manliest, and bravest of her children . . . holds now no higher place in the records of that grand old Commonwealth than is held by a horse or an ox"), he exposed the racist paradoxes inextricable from dominant eulogies to whiteness. Tellingly, while he lists Thomas Jefferson and Patrick Henry by name, he evokes George Washington only obliquely, describing Madison Washington more particularly as one who battled for liberty "with a valor as high, an arm as strong, and against odds as great as he who lead all the armies of the American colonies."[52] In this fictionalized work, Douglass highlights racist injustices by leaving George Washington unnamed on the grounds that such an already immortalized white male hero needed no direct evocation, while Black icons such as Madison Washington had to be repeatedly dramatized in light of mainstream tendencies toward racist obfuscation. Indicting white failures to memorialize an enslaved Black Washington, he necessarily evokes the widespread primacy of a free white Washington to attest not only to the skewed biases of the historical record but also to the dehumanizing rhetoric surrounding black male heroism.

Adopting an overtly critical position, Douglass threw down the gauntlet to his white audiences by describing Washington as a heroic figure who "lives now only in the chattel records of his native state." The oxymoronic nature of "living" within "chattel records," surely a historical living death, bears witness to forces of black marginalization, alienation, and cultural erasure as white attempts at "fixity" stultified, if not entirely annihilated, black narratives of progress. "Glimpses of this great character are all that can now be presented," Douglass protests, conceding, "Like the gray peak of a menacing rock on a perilous coast, he is seen by the quivering flash of angry lightning, and he again disappears covered with mystery."[53] In the same way that an absence of daguerreotyped representations empowered Douglass by endorsing the necessity of creatively reimagining Washington, Douglass's dramatization of Washington as a natural phenomenon lays bare his status as a romanticized hero capable of inspiring sublime awe.

Bill Lawson astutely identifies Douglass's use of an iconic exceptionalism in his characterization of Washington. "Here we have Douglass drawing on the Romantic themes of individualism, power, and heroism," he writes.[54] Realizing that he was able only to give "partial satisfaction," Douglass therefore gave free rein both to himself and to his audiences to reimagine and, in so doing, created a malleable model of black masculinity that was resistant to reductive representations. Thus various lacunae regarding Washington's history not only empowered but authorized Douglass's experimental practices throughout *The Heroic Slave*. "Speaking of marks, traces, possibles, and probabilities, we come before our readers," he admits.[55] Seemingly forced to represent an "imagined" rather than an actual "hero" rooted in any kind of historical veracity, Douglass disingenuously argued that he experimented with literary complexity only out of necessity. Writing *The Heroic Slave* at a crucial juncture in his career in 1853, he experimented with the form of the novella for other reasons. He sought not only to dramatize an ambiguous heroic figure but to effect his deliberate transition from the pared-down style of his 1845 *Narrative of the Life of Frederick Douglass, an American Slave* to the elaborate prose of his 1855 *My Bondage and My Freedom*. Such a declaration of agency and artistry made possible his recovery of not one but multiple Frederick Douglasses no less than an array of Madison Washingtons. As a philosophical meditation upon the empowering necessity of imaginative play vis-à-vis representations of black masculinity, Douglass's *The Heroic Slave* resists problematic tendencies toward the exhibition, display, and spectacular consumption of black bodies by white audiences.

Nowhere is this more palpable than in the invented relationship Douglass establishes between Washington and Listwell. A pseudo–William Lloyd Garrison figure ironically so named to leave his inadequacies in plain sight, for Douglass he represented the failures of abolitionist sympathy. He deplored the fact that many antislavery advocates betrayed tendencies toward objectification in an often accidental yet more frequently self-conscious othering of black humanity. Subverting abolitionist dictates that demanded an authentication of black experiences through visual proofs, Douglass was careful to narrate Listwell's conversion to abolitionism as effected by the power of Washington's voice rather than the spectacle of his body. For Douglass, it was imperative that the aural acted not only in conjunction with but also as a stimulus to the visual, as Listwell "caught the sound of a human voice" with the result that, "following the direction of the sound, he descried, among the tall pines, the man whose voice had arrested his attention."[56]

In inescapable ways, Douglass underscores parallels between himself and Washington in this work by introducing white listeners to a form of impassioned antislavery oratory not dissimilar to his own. "But what is freedom to me, or I to it?" his Washington despairs in terms very similar to Douglass's own monologues. He continues, "I am a *slave*,—born a slave, an abject slave,—even before I made part of this breathing world, and scourge was platted for my back; the fetters were forged for my limbs. How mean a thing am I." Douglass encouraged audiences to make comparisons between himself and Washington explicit by attributing his own use of rhetorical questioning and emotive proselytizing to this "heroic slave." Tellingly, Washington operates as a symbol through which Douglass not only refracts his own exceptionalism but also meditates upon the definitions and parameters of heroism itself. By giving sound precedence over sight in this scene, Douglass resists the primacy of the visual spectacle of slavery, complete with all its stereotypical associations regarding black masculinity. Instead, he endorses black male agency by demanding that white audiences engage intellectually, politically, morally, and philosophically with a gamut of black subjectivities. According to Douglass's logic in *The Heroic Slave,* Washington's body was only revealed to Listwell once he had recognized his expert command of language. Thus he "caught, from his hiding place a full view of the unsuspecting speaker" only after he had heard his powerful eloquence.[57]

Vis-à-vis Douglass's characterization of Washington, he endorsed a visual poetics of abstraction rather than physical embodiment across his multiple textual and visual performances. Thus he lauds Washington, celebrated as a heroic vision of black masculinity himself, for his prowess in transcending material confinement via psychological emancipation:

> Madison was of manly form. Tall, symmetrical, round, and strong. In his movements he seemed to combine with the strength of the lion, a lion's elasticity. His torn sleeves disclosed arms like polished iron. His face was "black, but comely." His eye, lit with emotion, kept guard under a brow as dark and as glossy as the raven's wing. His whole appearance betokened Herculean strength, yet there was nothing savage or forbidding in his aspect.... His voice, that unfailing index of the soul, though full and melodious, had that in which it could terrify as well as charm.[58]

Such a hagiographic summary of Washington's exemplary physicality could as easily have functioned as a description of Douglass himself. By insisting on Washington's "manly form," Douglass not only vouches for his similarly exceptional masculinity but also for his competing status as a subject of fine-art portraiture. He accentuates his highly aestheticized features to dramatize statuesque, rather than "fixed," possibilities of black iconic representation. The act and art of "disclosure" in Washington's arms "like polished iron" accentuate the black body's fine-art status to dramatize the ways in which Douglass and Washington both inspired sublime awe and transcendence to effect the moral conversion of their audiences. Moreover, Douglass's leonine attributes, which he here ascribes to Washington, illustrate their shared exceptionalism and malleability. By placing emphasis upon Washington's "eye, lit with emotion," he renders the internal external via the transformative power of the gaze. Douglass's lack of any physical specificity regarding Washington's body testifies to just how difficult he would have been to imagine if audiences had not possessed visual representations of Douglass either in photographic reproductions or literary representations. Curiously abstract phrases—"manly form," "eye lit with emotion," and "Herculean strength"—work to ensure that Washington remains both physically intangible and only symbolically palpable as he, no less than Douglass himself, epitomized mythological abstractions rather than historical truths.

Douglass's *The Heroic Slave* foregrounds a disjuncture between physical appearance and psychological reality to open up possibilities between "outer" representations of "inner" realities. "We have struck for our freedom, and if a true man's heart be in you, you will honor us for the deed. We have done that which you applaud your fathers for doing, and if we were murderers, *so were they*," Washington exclaims to white crew members on board the *Creole*. "The fellow loomed up before me," the white sailor Grant insists, admitting, "I forgot his blackness in the dignity of his manner, and the eloquence of his speech. It seemed as if the souls of both the great dead (whose names he bore) had entered him."[59] Douglass's experimentation with visual staging in this work reverses the subjugated spectacle of Black men on their knees. According to his memorialization, the white man looks upward and in so doing unwittingly references the daguerreotyping processes as described by Stauffer, according to which white men's "souls" are held at the mercy of Black subjects. Thus Douglass condemns white racist failures of perception regarding black physicality and the capacity for revolutionary violence.

Douglass's decision to focus upon a white man's perception of the "eloquence" of Washington's "speech" and the "dignity of his manner" during the rebellion ultimately signifies upon his "heroic slave's" earlier admission regarding the ritual humiliation and exhibition of his body as a spectacle of black torture for white consumption. "I was taken to the house,—chained to a ring-bolt,—my wounds dressed, " Washington narrates. "All the slaves for miles around, were brought to see me. Many slave-holders came with their slaves, using me as proof of the completeness of their power, therefore, and of the impossibility of slaves getting away." In stark contrast to Washington's physical powerlessness as a "proof" of white power in this passage, in the moment of the rebellion Douglass does not indulge in a graphic display of black on white violence, despite the fact that he has before displayed no hesitation in narrating white on black violence when Washington reports his own extraordinary suffering: "I received sixty lashes on my naked back." In stark contrast, Douglass narrates an epic moment of black revolutionary activity solely through black and white dialogic exchange.[60] His decision to dramatize the mutiny only in the margins of his text may well reflect his determination to award heightened symbolic, mythological, and national significance to acts of black physical rebellion by communicating them only through indirection and ellipsis. Douglass's focus upon lacunae or mere "glimpses" of black violence—in contrast to his laying bare white violence for all to see—encouraged audiences to reimagine black heroism. Promulgating a poetics of elliptical fragmentation, therefore, Douglass's aesthetic strategy mythologized his historical subjects to ensure that they signified solely as disembodied spectacles of black male heroism and, as such, were in no way reducible to material realities.

Douglass pushed the boundaries of aesthetic experimentation to celebrate radical models of black male heroism in *The Heroic Slave*. Believing that inspirational narratives of exemplary individualism worked to educate and inspire, he sought to refute mainstream stereotypes regarding black masculinity. Across his life and works, he repeatedly imaginatively displaced his own untold but self-evident heroism onto not only Madison Washington but other major historical exemplars including Toussaint Louverture and Nathaniel Turner. Much later in his career, for example, Douglass became fascinated with Louverture as an "argument" against slavery in his unpublished manuscripts.[61] No less an abstraction than Washington, Louverture signified less as a physical freedom fighter than as an intellectual, historical, and social symbol of black male heroism for Douglass. A range of Douglass's speeches testify to his enduring evocation of a black heroic tradition as reimagined to suit different contexts. For example, in August 1861 he delivered "A Black Hero," in which he eulogized William Tillman's heroism during the Civil War. "Love of liberty alone inspired him and supported him, as it had inspired Denmark Vesey, Nathaniel Turner, Madison Washington, Toussaint

L'Ouverture, Shields Green, Copeland, and other Negro heroes before him," Douglass states.[62] More particularly, on the cusp of the Civil War, he rallied Black troops by exalting in African American military prowess in a speech titled "Fighting Rebels with Only One Hand," in which he celebrates the fact that "noble Shields Green, Nathaniel Turner and Denmark Vesey stand ready to peril every thing at the command of the Government."[63] For Douglass, a representative array of Black heroic male icons functioned as key symbols through which he not only debated issues related to memorialization, nationalism, and civil rights but also addressed controversies surrounding his own self-representations.

The nefarious effects of slavery's racist legacies caused radical revolutionaries such as Malcolm X to reject Douglass's status as a reusable heroic figure in the mid-twentieth century. "Douglass was great," Malcolm X concedes, admitting, however, "I would rather have been taught about Toussaint L'Ouverture. We need to be taught about people who fought, who bled for freedom and made others bleed."[64] Yet as Douglass's earlier turn to Washington's history in *The Heroic Slave* demonstrates, he was as aware as Malcolm X of the limiting dimensions of his own life history in the struggle to end slavery. Refusing to foreground feats of flesh-and-blood exceptionalism in his novella, he instead relied upon a multilayered symbolism to provide a philosophical exploration of the parameters of black male heroism. As part novella, part slave narrative, part autobiography, and part historical tract, *The Heroic Slave* testifies to Douglass's search for a new language and genre within which to dramatize competing constructions of black male heroism. The onus, therefore, is upon us as critics to give greater prominence to *The Heroic Slave*, still a relatively little-discussed work in Douglass's oeuvre. A multifaceted theoretical approach may make it possible to engage simultaneously with the signifying practices of his oratory, writings, and visual archive. Thus it may become possible to engage more fully with his negotiation of black iconicity, as well as the problems of memorializing elided historical figures otherwise subsumed in "chattel records." Regardless, a search for unconfining parameters within which to represent black masculinity clearly undergirded Douglass's emphasis upon existential critique in his philosophical exploration of the nature and type of black masculinity. More tellingly still, nonreductive, disembodied, and abstract representations remain equally inextricable from Douglass's cultivation of part autobiographical, part historical, and part mythological personae.

Among the many tributes to Douglass following his death, as early as 1897 the white American writer Theodore Tilton published a series of sonnets in

Paris. Apart from Douglass himself, he was one of the first memorialists to situate Douglass within a black heroic pantheon. Celebrating the fact that in death Douglass had joined "hero and martyr, Toussaint L'Ouverture," Tilton urges, "He loved a hero." Refusing to shy away from the difficulties presented by his exemplary status, however, in the sonnets Tilton highlights ongoing debates between corporeal absence and spiritual presence by making a heartfelt plea for a statue of Douglass to be forged from the smashed fetters of enslaved women, children, and men. Tilton's imagery follows from Douglass's own textual and visual strategies by fusing corporeal and mythic realities. "Let us," he implores, "mould him a statue of enduring brass / Out of the broken chains of slaves set free!"[65]

"I WANTED TO WRITE ABOUT A BLACK HERO": JACOB LAWRENCE'S AND WILLIAM BRANCH'S SYMBOLIC REIMAGININGS

"The inspiration to paint the Frederick Douglass, Harriet Tubman and John Brown series was motivated by historical events as told to us by the adults of our community," Jacob Lawrence admits.[66] "To us, the men and women of these stories were strong, daring and heroic," he explains, "and therefore we could and did relate to these heroes by means of poetry, song and paint."[67] The inspiration for Lawrence's numerous narrative series, appearing to critical acclaim in the 1930s and 1940s, including his Life of Frederick Douglass series, a work of thirty-two panels painted in 1938–39, arose from his exposure to these legends via oral histories and folkloric testimony. "I grew up during the Depression when older people talked on street corners—we called them soap box speakers, and they would talk about black heroes and heroines," he explains.[68] While I provide an in-depth examination of Lawrence's Life of Frederick Douglass series in a forthcoming article, a brief examination of one of this work's iconic images, panel 10, is illuminating in shedding light on twentieth-century memorializations of Douglass's heroism (see plate 9). This influential painting dramatizes one of the most celebrated moments in Douglass's life history: his repeatedly restaged and reimagined battle with the white "slave-breaker" Edward Covey. A key set piece in Douglass's own narratives and oratorical performances, this epic moment celebrating the rights of black manhood appears in Lawrence's groundbreaking series as an overtly masculinized reimagining of his earlier portrayal of black female heroism. Lawrence's portrayal of Douglass, a visual re-creation of his earlier representation of the enslaved woman Millie's brave resistance to a "flogging" in the third panel of this same series, bears the heroic caption "A second attempt by Covey to flog Douglass was unsuccessful. This was one of the most important incidents in the life of Frederick Douglass: he was never attacked again by Covey. His philosophy: a slave easily flogged is flogged oftener; a slave who resists flogging is flogged less."[69]

In this dramatic image, Lawrence pays homage to Douglass's advocacy of self-defense by celebrating the evocative power of white and black male conflict as heroic spectacle. Refusing to shy away from graphic realities, Lawrence portrays a half-naked Douglass, which, Rebecca Cobby asserts, represents a bold decision that may well have worked to "expose Douglass as uncivilized and animalistic."[70] Yet Lawrence's decision to contrast his graphic exhibition of the black male body with the white man's concealed physicality ultimately works to the latter's disadvantage. Clearly, in contrast to Douglass's heightened physicality as carefully delineated here, Covey's yellow-and-red-checked shirt strips him of any epic righteousness. Instead, the gaudy coloring suggests a comical twist by evoking the excessive designs of theatrical costumes. According to Lawrence's schema, therefore, white masculinity is performative and artificial, while black masculinity is seemingly romanticized and "natural," particularly in light of the visual call-and-response relationship he establishes between the brown hues of Douglass's skin and the similarly brown-colored wooden walls, floor, and tree limbs visible beyond the barn's walls.

Reinforcing his stark composition, Lawrence's symbolic properties accentuate his thematic preoccupation with Douglass's iconic exceptionalism. The piled wood, ax, and hanging horseshoes attest to the dehumanizing realities of black male labor. As Cobby observes, "The unworn horse bridle and shoes on the wall symbolize his resistance to being broken in and affirms the notion that through his act of violence he is a man of agency."[71] Clearly, however, it may also be possible to argue that Lawrence's symbolic positioning of the bridle—as it hangs from a nail on the left-hand side of the painting—is designed to instill haunting associations among his viewers with a noose as a symbol of lynch law and death. Thus, Lawrence did not shy away from complicating any pretensions toward closure or finality in this image on the grounds that, as for many of his contemporaries, the fight to preserve and protect black male bodies otherwise subject to torture and mutilation at the hands of white supremacists was far from over in his own era. As this series demonstrates, it was no less the case for Lawrence than it was for Douglass that black heroic role models signified as symbols for inspiration as well as catalysts for social change. "If these people, who were so much worse off than the people today, could conquer their slavery," Lawrence argues, "we certainly can do the same thing."[72] "Today we can't go about it in the same way," he realizes, arguing, "Any leadership would have to be the type of Frederick Douglass." "How will it come about?" he asks rhetorically. "I don't know. I'm not a politician. I'm an artist, just trying to do my part to bring this thing about."[73] Lawrence's *Life of Frederick Douglass* series was clearly inspired by the same motivation that had guided Douglass himself a century earlier. Both nineteenth-century activist and twentieth-century artist betray a shared determination to use art to memorialize Black heroic figures and inspire social, political, and historical reform.

"I wanted to write about a Black hero. I felt the strong need for black people —and white people as well—to know the wealth of great and positive images in our heritage, images which somehow rarely showed up in works by white writers."[74] So William Branch explains regarding his decision to create a theatrical adaptation of Douglass's life titled *In Splendid Error* and published in 1955. As dramatized for Black audiences, *In Splendid Error* was in the vanguard of Douglass's resurgence during the heightened period of radical civil rights activism in the 1960s and 1970s. According to Melvin G. Williams, Branch's play had a renaissance in the 1970s, as it was "being read—better yet, studied—by men and women on many campuses as a literary milestone along the road to black awareness." And yet, he asks, "Why should a play with a historical character (it was copyrighted under the title *Frederick Douglass*) be offered to a 1954 audience rather than one with a contemporary hero?" Answering his own question, he concedes the need for indirect strategies of resistance, given that "too direct an emphasis on the more explosive social issues of 1954 . . . would have been harder to take."[75] Overall, Branch's theatrical adaptation repeats with variation Douglass's own tried and tested technique of dramatizing historical figures as a displaced lens through which to galvanize radical protest within his own era. As Branch argues, "In Douglass' dilemma I saw uncanny parallels between the pre–Civil War racial-political struggles of the 1850s and the post–World War II racial political climate of the 1950s."[76] These "uncanny parallels" undergird the political uses to which Branch puts Douglass's dramatic tensions in his work. He debates the positive and negative implications of violent versus nonviolent protest by comparing Douglass's life and works to those of the white freedom fighter John Brown. The dramatic force of Branch's theatrical adaptation clearly emerges not from extremist demarcations but from a blurred middle ground, particularly with regard to the efficacy or inefficacy of armed militancy, an increasingly important subject in 1950s America. These contradictions and ambiguities embedded in Branch's multifaceted explorations of black and white male heroism ensure that his reimagined Douglass speaks to the necessity of physical and psychological resistance as the only way in which to complete the unfinished work of a twentieth century still failing to represent a "cradle of democracy."

Written at the height of segregation and on the cusp of an increasingly radical and mass-organized civil rights era, Branch's dramatization of Douglass's conflicted heroism does not flinch from examining this historical figure's political, historical, and moral ambiguities. According to Branch, Douglass's regret regarding John Brown's advocacy of violence highlights his own seemingly tragic flaws, which lie at the heart of ideological tensions within this play. "There are times when the soul's need to unite with men in splendid error tangles agonizingly with cold wisdom and judgment," his Douglass admits, recognizing that "in splendid error he [Brown] had startled the sleeping conscience of the nation and struck a blow for freedom that proves stronger every hour."[77] In contrast to early memorialists seeking to fix representations of Douglass following his death, William Branch's Douglass remains a source of inspiration for the contemporary fight for civil rights not as a one-dimensional icon but as a flawed individual whose acts of heroism encompassed an individual battle against psychological and moral turmoil. As the outpouring of textual and visual works during this period reveals, Douglass's memory was adapted and recycled in order to galvanized diverse modes of resistance across differing political contexts.

"HE DIED IN 1895. / HE IS NOT DEAD": REIMAGINING FREDERICK DOUGLASS IN THE CIVIL RIGHTS ERA

An overwhelming resurgence of multimedia representations of Frederick Douglass in murals, speeches, novels, theatrical adaptations, poetry, paintings, and graphic novels by civil rights and Black Power activists, artists, and writers proliferated in the 1950s, 1960s, and 1970s. Such wide-ranging works signal a dramatic response to his widespread marginalization and distortion in official sites of political and historical memory. As Julius Lester notes, "There is hardly any discussion of Douglass' vast role in the abolitionist movement."[78] Rallying new types of radicalism in 1967, Black Power activists Stokely Carmichael and Charles V. Hamilton turned to Douglass. Insisting that "we have no intention of engaging in the rather meaningless language so common to discussions of race in America," they argued for "a more meaningful language, that of Frederick Douglass, a black American who understood the nature of protest in this society."[79] Carmichael and Hamilton laid claim to Douglass's significance as an intellectual, moral, and political pillar on which to inscribe contemporary forms of black male radicalism. Their reuse of Douglass's memory counters Martin's view that "with this often antiintegrationist, anti-American, and anti-white shift in the movement, Douglass' stock as a heroic symbol declined among certain blacks."[80]

While he may have appeared an incongruous figure in popular resurrections of his memory, Douglass's ambivalences powerfully establish the importance of his reusable symbolism for a range of black protesters seeking to overturn racist injustices. "It has been exceedingly difficult, if not impossible, to exploit him as an unambiguous heroic symbol for their various causes," Martin writes.[81] Yet Douglass's ambiguities prove essential to his applicability and adaptability across a spectrum of diverse forms created by multiple activists and writers. "Frederick Douglass said that no people deserved their rights if they weren't willing to agitate for them," James Forman argues, adding, "We got to make people see that they can fight for their rights." Reimagining Douglass as a reusable icon for black "agitation," Forman was not alone in recognizing his enduring legacy as a talisman for diverse strategies of protest into which he and other activists could breathe fresh life. "We got to take the forms of the man and put our own substance into them and create new forms of our own," he urges. By insisting on the power of language as the cornerstone of radical protest, Forman ruptures temporal frameworks to establish a call-and-response relationship across a heroic continuum. "We got to get the word out. Write our own history. . . . We build on Frederick Douglass and Du Bois; let the young build on us," he argues.[82]

Scarcely less than a decade following the publication of Branch's play, Robert Hayden's sonnet "Frederick Douglass" appears as a symbolic and metaphorical catalyst to his collection *A Ballad of Remembrance,* published in 1962. Differing from the majority of poets celebrating Douglass's exceptional legacy, Hayden extends Branch's dramatization of this historical figure's memory as a site of psychological conflict. Tellingly, Hayden's work begins not by eulogizing Douglass but with a declarative prophecy. "When it is finally ours, this freedom, this liberty, this beautiful / and terrible thing," he writes, only then, he explains, will Douglass be remembered. Relying on a dramatic use of caesura as well as symbolic listing, Hayden encompasses Douglass's various mythic personae—as a fugitive, as a man, as a "Negro," and even as a "Douglass," an archetype of himself—in order to dramatize his singular and multiple identities.[83] His sense of Douglass as "visioning a world" accentuates his prophetic status to reinforce his fight for unrealized utopian ideals. Otherwise remaining atemporal, mythical, and abstract, according to Hayden, Douglass can only be memorialized on the arrival of liberty as a "beautiful / and terrible thing," a source of sublime and transformative power.

Hayden's poetical work refuses to flinch from associating Douglass with physical defeat and psychological struggle. His spectacle of Douglass as a "beaten" victim tells a different story than Douglass's own self-conceptualization as the archetypal defier of white masculinity. Clearly Hayden's Douglass is no heroic freedom fighter but, as Branch also dramatizes, a fallible victim transformed into a philosophical visionary. In a powerful conclusion, Hayden's final lines clarify that Douglass will be remembered "with the lives grown out of his life" rather than with "wreaths of bronze alone."[84] Seemingly rejecting Tilton's turn-of-the-century prophecy that Douglass's "statue of enduring brass" would be forged from the fetters of ex-enslaved women and men, Hayden testifies to the failures of such monuments. Equally, he does not flinch from a nihilistic denunciation of his own form of remembrance by explicitly exposing the inefficacies of poetry and myth no less than "wreaths of bronze" ever to do justice to Douglass's memory. As Hayden emphasizes, access to Douglass's poetical and legendary legacies only becomes possible by freeing "the lives grown out of his life." He interprets Douglass's memory as irrelevant and unusable as long as his representations remain confined within official records or textual adaptation rather than folkloric imagining. Similarly, Langston Hughes's poem "Frederick Douglass: 1817–1895," published in 1966, shares Hayden's conviction regarding the mythological significance of Douglass's legacies as he lays claim to his immortality: "He died in 1895. / He is not dead."[85]

Against a horrifying backdrop of assassinations, murder, and rioting, on November 22, 1968, *Life* magazine published a special issue titled "The Search for a Black Past: Beginning a New Series on Negro History" (see figure 26). Published in the same year as the assassination of Martin Luther King Jr. and on the five-year anniversary of the murder of John F. Kennedy, the somber black cover of this issue assumes the guise of a grave marker. Distinctive for including an enlarged reproduction of a gilt-framed daguerreotype of a young Frederick Douglass, the cover testifies to a Douglass both dead and "not dead." Currently held in the Metropolitan Museum of Art, this early photograph was created by an unknown artist in about 1855, the same year in which *My Bondage and My Freedom* appeared as Douglass's declaration of intellectual and aesthetic as well as political and social independence. A firebrand radical still only in his thirties in this daguerreotype, Douglass's ambiguous yet forceful expression challenges viewers by leaving them in no doubt regarding the suffering to which he bore witness during slavery. Reprinting this image in such an apocryphal twentieth-century context, the editors of *Life* magazine resurrected a mythological Douglass not only to speak to contemporary atrocities—including bombings, unlawful killings, incidents of mob violence and police brutality—but also to remind readers of their point of origin in the eradicated histories of slavery. Douglass's unflinching, conflict-ridden eyes and furrowed brow testify to slavery's elided narratives of sacrifice and resistance. Across his photographic archive, Douglass's haunting facial expression speaks to his significance as a representative of the elided lives of enslaved women, men, and children. Thus he relies on self-portraiture to visualize the ways in which his known and their unknown lives would remain as unfathomable to privileged, myopic whites in the twentieth and twenty-first centuries as they had done in his own context. As Julius Lester argues, his self-reflexive practices guarantee that he communicated his radical resistance in masked ways. "Douglass was not advocating any form of Black Power or telling white folks to go to hell, but he might as well have," Lester explains.[86]

"ABOLITIONIST FREDERICK DOUGLASS" reads the white lettering beneath the reproduction of the daguerreotype on *Life's* front cover. The typeface resonates with the date, "NOVEMBER 22 1968," and the italicized title, *"The Search for a BLACK PAST,"* to establish Douglass as the mythological lynchpin uniting an enslaved past with a seemingly "freed" present. The daguerreotype hangs against a stark black backdrop to ensure that the viewers encounter no obstacle in their exposure to Douglass's powerful gaze. For white editors at *Life* magazine, Douglass not only symbolized but metaphorically embodied a "black past" and its ongoing existence within a black present. Yet for a white middle America unprepared for such a symbol of black radicalism, he was not the representative ex-enslaved man but rather the archetypal "abolitionist," as he was endorsed not within a tradition of black resistance but within the context of a white-originated abolitionism. Clearly, the emphasis upon "search" betrays more than it seems by speaking to Douglass's own lifelong struggle to portray himself as a subject rather than as an object and, therefore, as an individual encompassing multiple self-transformations. The verisimilitude of the gilt-edged frame of this daguerreotype attests not only to its—and by extension, Douglass's—status as a treasured object or "work of art" but also to white determinations to "fix"

FIGURE 26. Frederick Douglass, cover of *Life* magazine, 22 November 1968. (Courtesy of Getty Images and *Life* magazine)

his identity and representations according to particular political agendas. Monochrome tonal variations symbolically reproduce the haunting realities of racial struggle in order to communicate the processes by which horrific legacies of black violation can become revisualized as talismans of resistance. The bloodred background of the title of the magazine resonates with the black, white, and brown coloring of the mass-reproduced daguerreotype to suggest that the lines between life and death were held in perilous balance by the violence of both contemporary and historical eras.

Across the twentieth and twenty-first centuries, images of Douglass proliferated in the black and white press typically to perpetuate polarized memorializations of the historical figure as either a nonconformist revolutionary or as a conciliatory elder statesman. Yet in one particularly forceful work, the African American painter Charles Alston broke with convention by dramatizing a psychologically complex and dramatically ambiguous close-up of Douglass's physiognomy. Appearing as an elder statesmen in his haunting cover of the *Crisis* in February 1969, Alston's Douglass is far from an equivocal figure.[87] Rather, his expressionist aesthetic relies on textured brushstrokes and compelling tonal variations to breathe fresh life into Douglass as an archetypal freedom fighter and mythic touchstone for black liberation. Clearly, for Alston and many other artists and writers, polarized conceptualizations of Douglass failed to do justice not only to his moral, psychological, political, and aesthetic complexities but also to the fact that, as Lester notes, "Douglass refused to be confined to the role they had assigned him."[88]

As another Black artist motivated by a determination to reclaim Douglass's radicalism without denying his emotional and psychological complexities, Leroy Foster painted his experimental mural *Life and Times of Frederick Douglass* in 1973 (see plate 10). According to Michael Harris, this mural portrays "the heroic muscular form of an angry young Douglass breaking the shackles of slavery."[89] Yet in very tangible ways, Foster's dynamic and layered work no less dramatizes the ambiguities surrounding Douglass's multiple personae. While a superheroic reproduction of Douglass's half-naked form iconographically occupies the foreground of this work, Foster rejects chronological coherence in favor of including multiple portraits that testify to an array of Douglasses. Tellingly, Foster's repeated and multifaceted delineations of Douglass's impassioned physiognomies betray his commitment to historical veracity. Refusing to shy away from his indebtedness to Douglass's early daguerreotyped portraits, he provides intricate and individualized visualizations of his subject's frowning brow, confrontational gaze, scarred forehead, and resolute mouth.

Ultimately unable to resist providing a hagiographic dramatization of Douglass's exceptional physique, Foster's epic-sized, pseudo-superhuman portrayal of Douglass dominates this mural to inspire audiences to a sense of awe regarding his aggrandized musculature. This central Douglass overshadows all others, as he is shown as having broken apart his shackles by an exceptional mythical force: smashed fetters hang from his wrists while his

enlarged clenched fist dominates the overall composition. Adopting a layered signifying practice, however, Foster generates additional visual drama
in his mural by blurring the boundaries between Douglass's various incarnations as a radical freedom fighter and as a visionary prophet. Regardless of
the prominence he gives to his epic-sized Douglass, Foster includes an array
of Douglasses that complicate his otherwise excessively iconic and mythologized reimagining of the historical figure. Deliberately engaging with the
paradoxes generated by Douglass's exceptionalism, he juxtaposes diminutive figures in attitudes of distress with brutal and vicious visualizations of
bloodhounds to bear witness to the undocumented horrors of anonymous
lives lived in slavery. As Foster's interrelated vignettes reveal, he reimagined
and re-created the multiple lives and deaths of Douglass not only as a way of
embodying "black history," as Waldo Martin has suggested, but also of signifying the "multifaceted reality of the black liberation struggle."[90] Hauntingly
celebrating the "life and times" not only of Douglass but of unknown Black
women, children, and men, Leroy Foster's mural parades the various ages
of Frederick Douglass in order to interrogate his staying power as both an
exceptional icon and archetypal liberator.

"A MINSTREL *NEVER* SHOWS WHAT'S IN HIS TRICKS BOX!": EXHIBITION, SPECTACLE, AND PERFORMANCE IN DONAL O'KELLY'S *THE CAMBRIA* (2005)

"Inspired by two Irishmen to escape from slavery Frederick Douglass
came to Ireland during the famine. Henceforth he championed the abolition
of slavery, women's rights and Irish freedom." So reads the text of the Frederick Douglass mural recently painted by the white Irish artist Danny Devenny on the "Solidarity Wall," Falls Road, in Belfast, Northern Ireland. This
work transgresses national boundaries by including an enlarged close-up of
Douglass as an elder statesman, rendered yet more dramatic by a powerful
backdrop of bloodred bricks. At the same time, thorny spikes of barbed wire
signify not only the unspeakable horrors of North American slavery but also
the much more recent violent conflict between Protestants and Catholics in
twentieth-century Northern Ireland. Located on a wall designed to represent unity and "solidarity" for a divided city, this public memorial testifies to
Douglass's enduring mythological and political significance as a symbol of
reformist ideals and collective activism in Irish national history. Bill Rolston
notes that "the portrayal of this black activist" was not "unique" in Belfast,

given that in "republican areas, there have been murals depicting Nelson Mandela, Martin Luther King, and Malcolm X."[91] For Devenny and many other muralists who brought this historical figure back to life, it was necessary to reconceptualize and resituate Douglass's legacies within a long tradition of twentieth-century South African and African American civil rights activism.

Adapting Douglass's antislavery protest strategies to fit within a Republican national paradigm, Devenny's work bears witness to his significance as a source of inspiration for diasporic freedom struggles, which continue to exist beyond the fight for civil rights within black and white America. Opting for a provocative juxtaposition of text and image, Devenny quotes Douglass to indict the terrifying paradoxes of Ireland's difficult history. "Perhaps no class has carried prejudice against color to a point more dangerous than have the Irish and yet no people have been more relentlessly oppressed on account of race and religion," the quotation reads. Douglass's frank observation of the inextricable relationship between an enlightened egalitarianism on the one hand and a self-centered bigotry on the other radically offers a displaced historical lens through which to extrapolate Ireland's contemporary paradoxes vis-à-vis human rights discourse. As further proof of this mural's significance as a statement of transatlantic exchange, Devenny painted a companion work on an exterior wall in New Bedford, Massachusetts, in which he also eulogized Douglass's heroism. This highly contrasting mural reproduces Foster's preference for adopting a layered composition, as Devenny similarly creates multiple vignettes dramatizing Douglass's diverse lives. As fraught sites of memorialization, Devenny's murals do not shy away from difficulties of race, class, and national boundaries. Instead, he comes to grips with the lacunae generated by artificially constructed demarcations between victim and victimizer and oppressed and oppressor.

A meditation on the difficulties confronting a nation beset by a history of both liberating and discriminatory practices clearly resonates with the contemporary Irish dramatist and performer Donal O'Kelly's play The Cambria. Subtitled Frederick Douglass' Voyage to Ireland 1845, this work was written in 2005 and has since been performed to transatlantic audiences in Ireland, Great Britain, and the United States. O'Kelly's stage directions indicate that the play "starts in present-day Ireland" to "springboard into the story of Frederick Douglass' voyage to Ireland aboard the Cambria in 1845," a journey that led to his becoming a famed political figure in transatlantic memory.[92] As Sweeney argues, these "transnational encounters were key to Douglass' project of American self-fashioning" because they demonstrated his

determination to eulogize the political practices of one nation only to castigate the injustices of another.[93] Throughout his play, O'Kelly addresses tensions related to race, nationhood, class, and identity—all of which plagued
Douglass during his lifetime—as he reconstructs his heroism within the
context of twenty-first-century conflicts. As a half-memorialized yet half-
forgotten figure, Douglass is both present and absent within a twenty-first-
century Irish national imagination. Thus he operates as a useful icon through
which O'Kelly is able to eulogize histories of redemption in the past in order
to expose the injustices of narratives of enslavement in the present. As Sinéad
Moynihan emphasizes, O'Kelly is a "devotee of a 'theatre of conscience'
philosophy," as Douglass's centuries-old experiences of suffering and racism
provide a platform upon which the playwright is able to condemn existing
inequalities. "Frederick Douglass has become an important figure in cultural
negotiations of race and immigration in contemporary Ireland," she writes.[94]
Similarly, Sweeney astutely observes that O'Kelly's play is "located on the
interface between American slavery, Atlantic culture and the ethical implications of the Irish postcolonial condition." She emphasizes the ways in which
the "play situates Douglass' voyage in the context of contemporary debates
not around multiculturalism, but political asylum and citizenship."[95] Thus
Sweeney introduces Douglass's enduring importance to an Irish national
imagination. He remains an iconic signifier of a disappearing yet powerful
protest tradition, which is resurrected by O'Kelly to address unresolved contemporary inequalities.

With its first scene set in a modern-day airport, the play immediately
establishes the contemporary relevance of O'Kelly's historical framework.
As a history teacher and soi-disant guardian of national memory, Collette
laments the inhumane deportation of her Nigerian student, patriotically
named Patrick, by Irish authorities. As part of O'Kelly's wider meditation
on the role played by community "solidarity" in transgressing class and racial
boundaries, Collette shares her sorrow not with officials but with a laboring man named Vincent, a painter and decorator. In this scene, a distraught
Collette remembers how she implored Patrick to "'think of where you come
from, generations of Irish flung around the globe . . .' But—no use. The plane
was gone to Lagos. Nigeria."[96] In the face of racist bigotry and contemporary
nefarious national practices of political exclusion in Ireland, O'Kelly's play
testifies to the failure of any attempts to draw parallels between the arrival
of recent immigrants from diverse countries and centuries of Irish patterns
of migration. According to this work, ancestry and tradition are rendered
meaningless in the context of racist and prescriptive definitions of genealogy

and race. O'Kelly's Colette directly challenges the parameters of Irish identity formation by describing Patrick's performances of "Robert Emmet's Speech From The Dock." "When Ireland takes her place, among the nations of the earth, then and only then, let my epitaph be writ-*ten!*" she recites.[97] This graphic account of Patrick's reappropriation of Irish nationalist rhetoric clearly speaks to Douglass's preferred modus operandi during his own lifetime. Repeatedly, he juxtaposed unjust nationalist practices by playing one country off against another in order to indict exclusionary practices. O'Kelly challenges the exceptional legacy of a pantheon of white Irish heroes via a satiric use of naming, not only as revealed in Patrick's symbolic appellation but also Colette's sense of irony that she teaches "in O'Connell's Schools." Such a reference to the nineteenth-century radical icon Daniel O'Connell is telling, given that he was a leading figure in Irish struggles for liberation. He plays a significant role later in the play, as Douglass himself is repeatedly described as the "black O'Connell," thereby establishing the political necessity of resurrecting exceptional leaders as instigators of future activism.

Admitting to the inefficacies of her attempts to prevent Patrick's deportation, Collette is comforted by Douglass's oratory: "power concedes nothing without demand."[98] In recent years, this apocryphal phrase has been repeated on both sides of the Atlantic, most powerfully perhaps by Barack Obama during his 2008 presidential election campaign.[99] At the same time that Colette encourages Patrick to repeat the language of the nineteenth-century Irish freedom fighter Robert Emmet, her decision to expose national injustices by quoting an African American man far less renowned in Irish memory is telling. O'Kelly forcefully evokes Douglass's memory to defamiliarize audience expectations and encourage new transnational perspectives on citizenship and asylum debates within Ireland. Seemingly less incendiary because of his historical distance from difficult contemporary issues, such complex memorializations of Douglass radically allow for candid explorations of unresolved inequalities. "Who's Frederick Douglass?" Vincent asks Colette, exposing O'Kelly's engagement with the imaginative and political possibilities presented by Douglass's relative obscurity in contemporary Ireland. Tellingly, Colette replies both with factual clarification—"Frederick Douglass came to Ireland. On a ship . . . Called the Cambria"—and speculation regarding what would happen "if Frederick Douglass . . . came to Ireland NOW."[100]

An early scene in the play compellingly addresses Douglass's centuries-earlier debate regarding the "dangerous" effects of Irish "prejudice against color," as explicitly quoted on Devenny's mural on the Solidarity Wall.

Matilda, a white child, asks Douglass, "Do you sing and dance?" and insists, "You're a minstrel, aren't you?"[101] As Moynihan observes, "O'Kelly engages the often troubling racial politics of minstrelsy" in this work.[102] O'Kelly's Matilda adheres to an immutable notion of racial difference by categorically stating that "slaves are different. My daddy says they don't feel things as much as we do." Communicating Douglass's response via stage directions, "SILENCE FROM FREDERICK," O'Kelly foregrounds the failures of language, a failure that Douglass repeatedly recognized during his own lifetime. Thus he is forced to rely on aesthetic experimentation to resist dominant forms of representation and carve out a space within which to represent Black women and men as dignified subjects rather than as disempowered objects. Resisting the widespread itemization, exhibition, and commodification of Black men, women, and children in pro- and antislavery discourse, Douglass, like O'Kelly, frequently foregrounded the creative possibilities of lacunae as generated by white official failures of memorialization. He understood these failures as a source not of disempowerment but of radical self-realization. Regardless of their differences, according to Douglass and O'Kelly, ambiguities of representation open up possibilities by encouraging audiences to engage with black heroism and individualism in imaginative rather than reductive ways.

A fundamental source of dramatic tension in O'Kelly's *The Cambria* thus emerges from the semiotic slippage between linguistic discourse and artifactual proofs. Failing to realize that Douglass's "box" contains the implements of torture that he exhibits during his antislavery lectures, Matilda gleefully asserts, "I know all about your box of tricks," and begs, "Let me see inside!" O'Kelly's determination to associate black minstrel performances with the exhibition of the visual proofs of the trade as used by abolitionists condemns white racist practices by which Black women, men, and children were bought and sold on the antislavery podium no less than on the theatrical stage and the auction block. Thus he presents these shocking objects of torture within the context of a dramatic spectacle to confront the diverse role these problematic bodies of evidence played in securing white moral conversion. "This is an iron collar which was taken from the neck of a young woman who had escaped from Mobile," O'Kelly's Douglass tells adult audiences on board the *Cambria*. "These are the fetters used in chaining the feet of two slaves together," he declares, heightening the horror by stating, "I was present when they were sawn off the ankles of both screaming men." Clearly, for O'Kelly no less than for Douglass, anxieties regarding the relationship between white material proofs and black dehumanization remain paramount. Repeatedly disassociated from their original context and moral framework, these terrifying objects functioned as slippery signifiers that succeeded in stimulating a horror of the trade but at an unforgivable cost. Thus these seemingly unspeakable "bodies" of evidence ran the risk not only of objectifying but of outright eradicating black suffering by reducing the psychological ambiguities and complexities of male and female experiences solely to physical proofs. More troublingly still, these objects ran the risk of becoming playthings or toys and, as such, a "box of tricks" that succeeded in entertaining white audiences and thereby failed either to educate or galvanize protest, as black bodies were reduced solely to shocking, grotesque spectacle. Douglass's insistence that "a minstrel NEVER shows what's in his tricks box!" confirms O'Kelly's condemnation of blackface minstrelsy by directly equating the properties of its performance with the proofs of the slave trade.[103] Preferring to dramatize Douglass's alternating strategies of concealment and revelation instead, O'Kelly portrays his historical protagonist as both a malleable icon and a consummate performer. In O'Kelly's celebration of his oratorical and textual prowess, Douglass defies slavery's objectifying grip by engaging in experimental practices. Refusing either to show or tell, his signifying strategies forced audiences to admit to lacunae and absence as they were instead encouraged to reimagine black lives as lived during slavery solely from partial fragments and discordant testimonies.

O'Kelly's *The Cambria* dramatizes the need in his contemporary era for not only black but also cross-racial and diasporic solidarity in ways that gesture beyond even Douglass's own reform efforts. In light of the fact that, for O'Kelly, Douglass operates as a transatlantic icon, it is no surprise, that the latter acts as the guiding authority in the final moment of this play. O'Kelly returns audiences to the present-day airport to conclude with Vincent's quoting Douglass, "Power concedes nothing without demand; it never did; and it never will," and Colette's radical redefinition of Douglass the formerly enslaved hero as "Frederick Douglass, one-time asylum-seeker and refugee."[104] As Sweeney argues, "The emphasis is on identity as fluid" in this play.[105] Thus, O'Kelly's Douglass rejects artificial divisions by observing, "I feel at home among the mish-mash of nationalities."[106] Waging war on immutable and fixed identity constructions, Donal O'Kelly's *The Cambria* works to break down prescriptive demarcations as he, like Douglass, refutes the illusory trade in essentialized polarizations of racial and national differences.

Within the last few years, Frederick Douglass has appeared in an array of textual and visual forms, including the Nigerian writer Chimamanda Ngozi Adichie's novel *Half of a Yellow Sun*, published in 2006. A powerful work dramatizing Nigerian life during the civil wars of the twentieth century, it examines the rites of passage of a young boy, Ugwu. In the novel, he makes a life-changing discovery. Following the boy's fearful conscription into the military, Adichie's narrator writes, "He found the book *Narrative of the Life of Frederick Douglass, An American Slave: Written by Himself* slipped into a tight corner beneath the blackboard. On the front page, PROPERTY OF GOVERNMENT COLLEGE was printed in dark blue." Placing it in a different national milieu and temporal framework than its original nineteenth-century U.S. context, Adichie initially positions Douglass's narrative as a tool in the service of the dominant social order. Yet, however rubber-stamped by government authority, Douglass's multiple-edged uses of language succeed in galvanizing grassroots social protest by communicating both gritty realities and antiheroic truths regarding oppressive cycles of captivity. A key passage Ugwu memorizes graphically explains, "*The slaves became as fearful of the tar as of the lash. They find less difficulty from the want of beds, than from the want of time to sleep.*"[107] For Adichie, Douglass's memory reinforces parallels between twentieth-century African civil wars and nineteenth-century histories of U.S. slavery. This comparative perspective works not only to destabilize national boundaries but also to expose continuities of conflict in repeated cycles of oppression perpetuated throughout the diaspora.

The majority of twentieth- and twenty-first-century visual and textual reimaginings of Douglass remain indebted to his own strategies of self-representation. More particularly, they betray a similar determination to resist generic caricature in a reductive stereotyping of his memory. Opting for a different medium from Adichie, in 2000 Vik Muniz created *Frederick Douglass*, a work included in his *Pictures of Ink* series.[108] A "cibachrome print," this image technologically revisits a daguerreotype depicting a middle-aged Frederick Douglass. However, his printing technique contests authenticity claims by foregrounding obfuscation and mediation at the cost of explication. Signifying on the fact that Douglass's image has been endlessly circulated in a diverse array of images, this metaimage is shown in a process of disintegration not only to fragment Douglass's physiognomy but also to heighten audience awareness regarding the artificially constructed origins even of seemingly factual images. Layered gray and black dots of differing sizes appear on a white background in Muniz's work to convey a horrifying sense of black political and social invisibility and erasure as he visualizes the literal corrosion and dissolution of Douglass's skin. For Muniz, a positive becomes a negative, as he relies on a cadaverous pallor to signify upon Douglass's memory as a talisman of suffering and loss. Following from David Hammons's body prints series circulated in the 1970s, Muniz reduces Douglass's image to the skeletal minimalism of an X-ray. Refusing to shy away from metaphors of disintegration and dissolution in the contemporary era, his is a terrifying vision of black male heroism dissolving into nothingness.

As a well-known yet often distorted historical figure, Frederick Douglass remains a site of paradox and uncertainty in contemporary criticism. "Perhaps a great scholar can restore to the life of Douglass its decidedly human face," Henry Louis Gates Jr. perceptively speculates. Appealing to a new "generation of scholars," he asks that they "eschew earlier needs to forge a distinctly Afro-American mythology, complete with our own mythic figures."[109] Clearly, Gates's recognition of the need to commemorate Douglass's "decidedly human face" illuminates the lacunae generated by this historical figure's own philosophical and intellectual commitment to memorializing and defining a mythical pantheon of "heroic slaves" that would speak not only to an elided black heroic tradition but also to his own exceptionalism. As a self-reflexive "living parchment," Douglass was in search of anything but a "human face" in his own self-representations. During his own lifetime, Douglass sought not only to celebrate a legendary tradition of black male exemplars in order to counter racist charges of inferiority but also to offer a displaced forum within which to immortalize his own repeatedly neglected iconography. Across his life, writings, and oratorical performances, Douglass rejected the validity of white "chattel records" by cultivating his own mythic symbolism in a quest to become a transcendent, sublime "work of art."

However much he was engaged in revising and reimagining his own competing mythologies, for Douglass there was no more impressive, if unsung, hero than the enslaved woman turned liberator Harriet Tubman. Breaking with his own conventions, he freely admitted to black female heroic exceptionalism in a testimonial he wrote for *Scenes in the Life of Harriet Tubman,* an "as told to autobiography" written by Sarah Bradford and published in 1869. "You ask for what you do not need when you call upon me for a word of commendation," Douglass informs Tubman, adding, "I need such words from you far more than you can need them from me, especially where your superior labors and devotion to the cause of the lately enslaved of our land are known as I know them." While his testimony—which dispensed with Bradford's narrative authority to address Tubman directly—betrays ongoing inequalities in that his own black male voice is problematically evoked to authenticate feats of black female heroism, he was well aware that Tubman's exceptionalism presented a challenge to his own sense of superiority. "Most that I have done and suffered in the service of our cause has been in public, and I have received much encouragement at every step of the way," he confesses, noting, "You on the other hand have labored in a private way."[110] Blurring the boundaries between male and female, public and private, and heroic and antiheroic identities, Douglass's celebratory constructions of Harriet Tubman eulogize black female heroism as a locus not only of black redemption but also of an iconic exceptionalism that far exceeded his own. As the vastness and variety of his visual and textual archive attests, Douglass engaged in experimental practices throughout his lifetime in a fight not only to vindicate his right to artistry and authorship but also to defy the particular ways in which his body and soul had been bought and sold in very real ways by the white slave owner Hugh Auld as early as 1846. The quest to annihilate Auld's infamous deed of manumission, a document that granted Douglass's legal freedom while inscribing his enslaved origins, undergirded Douglass's life's work as he defied his presence within the "Chattel Records of Baltimore County." For Frederick Douglass, it was the Black man's right to abstract thought, intellectualism, and a belief in art for art's sake that secured the most powerful rejection of his own "chattel record" and effected his transformation of a living death into a deathless life.

"Harriet Tubman: Armed and Dangerous." "Revolution Is a Woman's Work." "Harriet Tubman: Woman Warrior." "The Heroic Struggle of 'General' Tubman." "Tubman Mural with Musket Is Rejected." So read the titles of just a few of the newspaper articles that appeared in 2000 regarding the controversies over the white artist Mike Alewitz's *Move or Die*, a large-scale mural dramatizing the ex-enslaved woman and freedom fighter Harriet Tubman as an armed revolutionary (see plate 11). Alewitz imagined this work, designed in 1999 for an exterior wall of the Associated Black Charities organization in Baltimore, as part of a mural cycle entitled "The Dreams of Harriet Tubman."[1] To this day, virulent criticism has ensured that Alewitz's controversial *Move or Die* exists only as a twenty-by-six-foot banner rather than as a finished mural in situ. Dramatic, stark, and iconic, Alewitz's sketch approximates a finished mural, however, in his powerful depiction of a militant Tubman. In this work, he not only suggests her warrior status—as she wields a rifle in one hand—but also confirms her significance as a spiritual leader, as she carries a lantern in the other. Yet as the reporter Jamie Stiehm explains, this work was "unanimously rejected," not only because the "musket in the mural design stirred an outcry about historical truth vs. contemporary reality," but also because it "condones gun violence."[2]

As Alewitz emphasizes, his decision not to disarm this heroic freedom fighter, despite protests that he should, was born of a determination not to "make Harriet Tubman a meaningless icon."[3] Claiming that Tubman and nineteenth-century abolitionists remained "an inspiration for those who struggle for social justice today," he urges her contemporary relevance.[4] "Then, as now, Harriet was feared not because she carried a gun," Alewitz insists, "but because she organized a mass, militant and uncompromising struggle for social justice."[5] According to Alewitz, the rifle operates as a talisman of black female heroism. For Associated Black Charities director Donna Jones Stanley, however, it was an insult to a community still struggling with slavery's dehumanizing legacies. While she applauds Alewitz's mural because it "started the community discussing slavery, race and history," she alleges that his depiction of Tubman is inauthentic. "It is not historically correct," she observes. "She carried a pistol, not a rifle. It's his vision, but it's our wall."⁶ Although written historical records testify to Alewitz's inaccuracies, visual artifacts from the period substantiate his vision. His iconography has historical origins in an undated nineteenth-century woodcut created by J. C. Darby and similarly showing Tubman with a large rifle (see figure 27). Clearly, folkloric legends of a gun-toting Tubman have retained political currency despite their mythic unrealities. A key issue regarding the problematic reception of this public work emerges from the stranglehold of racist double standards within the national public imagination. As Sara Rimensnyder observes, "Public parks across America are littered with larger-than-life statues of war heroes, most of them carrying guns."⁷ As an exposé of ongoing tendencies toward racist stereotyping and white moral myopia regarding black female heroism, this mural depicting a militant Black heroine inspires controversies that have in no way been an issue for memorials of white public heroes similarly bearing arms. Such difficulties are symptomatic of widespread issues regarding the right to aesthetic experimentation, political representation, and radical reimagining in black memorialization.

A militant freedom fighter and folkloric legend, Harriet Tubman's shifting and fluctuating personae resist categorization. Known variously as Araminta Ross, Harriet Tubman, General Tubman, "Ole Chariot," "Moses," and "Aunt Harriet," her multiple identities illuminate her creative complicity in arts of performative reenactment and acts of naming and testify to her honored place within black folkloric history and memory. Across the centuries, she remains a site of competing mythologies within Caribbean, African, African American, European, and European American imaginations. No less than Toussaint Louverture, Nathaniel Turner, Sengbe Pieh, Sojourner Truth, and Frederick Douglass, Harriet Tubman signifies as a reusable icon for multiple audiences, authors, and artists. For many writers and activists, her biography continues to function as a mythic embodiment of seemingly universal and timeless values of justice, spirituality, and resistance to oppression. Yet, like Louverture, Turner, Pieh, Truth, and Douglass, Tubman herself signaled her authoritative control over the parameters of her diverse representations and heroic legacies. As early as the 1860s, she justifies her heroism on the grounds that "I can't die but once."⁸ While Tubman did in fact die only once, she has since lived hundreds of times over via multiple reimaginings in song, oratory, novels, poetry, plays, and fine art. Such a plethora of multifaceted works vouchsafes her mythic and political centrality to debates regarding black female heroism as remembered and reinvented for twentieth- and twenty-first-century audiences.

As one of her main biographers, Kate Clifford Larson, argues, diverse reconstructions of Tubman testify to "a mythological image of a woman about whose actual life we know little."[9] Such a view is supported by Tubman's niece, Alice H. Brickler, who informed Earl Conrad in a letter dated July 19, 1939, that "many of Aunt Harriet [sic] interesting stories were never written down but were told."[10] Equally, no date, title, or page is given for a report in the *Liberator*, in which the writer concedes the power of Tubman's oratorical performances, admitting that "mere words could do no justice to the speaker."[11] A defier of conventional white attempts to represent black enslaved female suffering, Tubman repeatedly defended her authority, not only as an emancipator of enslaved men and women, but also as a self-conscious interpreter of African American history. As Milton Sernett observes, she, more than many others, was aware of "the malleability of the Tubman myth."[12] Tubman's symbolic ambiguities as a historical figure vouchsafe her engagement in neglected acts and arts of self-reflexive representation that make it possible to extrapolate yet further from David Blight's view that "Tubman had long been a malleable icon of America's antislavery past."[13] While this is no doubt the case, she clearly also engaged imaginatively in recreating her own symbolism, not only to challenge monolithic memorializations of an "antislavery past" but also to denounce a proslavery present. Yet obfuscations proliferate because, illiterate throughout her lifetime, Tubman, like Truth, suffered from the tyranny of the white written record.

Regarding Tubman's shifting identities, a key debate concerns Sernett's preoccupation with the tensions between "the historical Tubman and the symbolic or iconic Tubman—as well as the interplay between myth and history in the crucible of memory." The dearth of verifiable material regarding Tubman's history arises from racist mythologies and political distortions as perpetuated by lacunae within the dominant archive. "There are no Tubman papers as such, no anthologies of collected writings, few documents to query, interpret, and quarrel about," he writes.[14] Several modern biographies of Tubman have been published by scholars seemingly less afflicted by the challenge of sourcing material that confronted Earl Conrad as one of the first researchers determined to memorialize Tubman's legacy. Yet the mere handful of biographies on one of the most significant Black freedom fighters of the nineteenth century represents a staggering hole in African American history. These difficulties speak to Larson's conviction that there remain "limited potential identities available to black women as historical actors."[15]

In the same way that Sojourner Truth rejected polarized representations according to which she was either a poor enslaved woman or a mythologized "Libyan Sybil," Harriet Tubman faced ongoing difficulties in her fight for self-realization as an authoritative agent working for social change. Hers was a lifetime of wresting her heroic personae from audiences intent upon white paternalist constructions of a suffering black female humanity. As Sernett observes, the revisionist determination among artists and authors, Black and white, to re-create Tubman from a scarcity of evidence reveals the "power of myth and of the socio-psychological need to create a black heroine in an American culture saturated with white male historical icons."[16]

Revisionist work is essential in order to engage with Tubman's no less than Truth's determination to become an autonomous agent within untold genealogies of black resistance. As Joanne Braxton argues, these often-elided Black female figures "established a 'wild zone,' or space of difference, from which to wage rebellion against an intemperate, sexist, and slaveholding society."[17] As the scant records suggest, Tubman dug deep to draw on her skills not only as a heroic liberator leading enslaved peoples out of bondage but also as a great orator and performer waging war on the confining parameters within which Black female identities were represented and remembered. For Lerone Bennett, writing in a twentieth-century civil rights context, Harriet Tubman remained a particularly mercurial icon, as she was "born a rebel."[18] As Larson writes, "Tubman's remarkable life, more powerful and extraordinary in its reality, is the stuff of legend and, ultimately, of a true American hero."[19] For Black male and female heroic figures, myths and legends became the only realities as the fight for interpretative control over their imaginative legacies became integral to an array of diverse memorializations and representations.

"IN HARRIET'S LANGUAGE?": HISTORICAL APPROPRIATION, LITERARY VENTRILOQUISM, AND SPECTACULAR COMMODIFICATION IN SARAH BRADFORD'S *SCENES* (1869)

"'No,' said Harriet, 'I hain't got no heart to go and see the sufferings of my people played on de stage. I've heard 'Uncle Tom's Cabin' read, and I tell you Mrs. Stowe's pen hasn't begun to paint what slavery is as I have seen it at the far South. I've seen de *real ting,* and I don't want to see it on no stage or in no teater.'"[20] So Harriet Tubman is reported to observe in *Scenes in the Life of Harriet Tubman,* published in 1869 and the first of the white author

Sarah Bradford's three narratives written to memorialize Tubman as an icon of black female heroism. Laying vehement claim to her authority in declarations such as "I tell you" and "I've seen," here Tubman insists on the right not only to narrate but also to visualize slavery's atrocities for her white audiences. Because she had "seen de *real ting*," she rejects the "stage" or teater" as a legitimate place for exhibiting black suffering. Admitting, "I hain't got no heart," Tubman reverses abolitionist mores to challenge the permissible boundaries of sentimental discourse as a legitimate source of cross-racial identification. Moreover, her astute use of metaphor—"played on de stage" and "hasen't begun to paint"—betrays her use of performative imagery and artistic tropes. Across her life and works, she sought to dramatize the shifting complexities of black experiences and personae that otherwise repeatedly remained off limits to both white authors and audiences. Denouncing the inefficacies of white female literary adaptations, Tubman exalted in her own significance not only as the ultimate authority but also as the only trustworthy "painter" equipped to narrate and visualize slavery's horrors. The idea that she had "seen de *real ting*" offered incontrovertible proof that, however seemingly rooted in historical evidence, any other representation was nothing more than a pale imitation—only ever the "shadow" to Tubman's "substance," to borrow from Sojourner Truth's rhetoric.

As Jean Humez notes, Bradford "omitted" this "revealing anecdote" in her second biography.[21] Far too incendiary, Tubman's critique of white philanthropic representations of slavery risked alienating rather than inspiring white audiences by insisting that their imaginations could never come close to slavery's realities. Regarding Tubman's rejection of the authority of theatrical adaptations of Stowe's novel, it is useful to compare the ways in which this incident was recorded in Bradford's text with later evidence provided by the white philanthropist Samuel Hopkins Adams. Remembering that Tubman was eventually taken to see *Uncle Tom's Cabin* despite her protests, Adams reported that she "was critical of Eliza's escape across the ice, declaring the affair ill-managed and intimating that she could have handled it better. 'Bloodhoun's!' she said disdainfully, eyeing the two disconsolate mastiffs who appeared in the role. 'I nevah made no min' of bloodhoun's.'"[22] Thus if we examine Tubman's rejection of *Uncle Tom's Cabin* as reported in Bradford's text in isolation, it is possible only to argue that she was intent upon exposing white failures to do justice to the atrocities of slavery. However, if we compare this textual record with other fragments of her oral ephemera, it becomes possible to gain additional insight into Tubman's realization regarding her own exceptional heroism over and above her critique of white philanthropy. According to Tubman's testimony as recorded by Adams, she clearly possessed an awareness of the ways in which her own iconic performances far exceeded the heightened drama of any white-authored sentimental novel, however sensationalized or heavily fictionalized for white entertainment.

Clearly, the political, social, and aesthetic tensions generated by the difficult relationship between Bradford as writer and Tubman as illiterate subject no less plagued Sengbe Pieh, Nathaniel Turner, and Sojourner Truth, as they similarly had no choice but to rely on white translations of their testimonies. Only in her second biography, *Harriet Tubman: The Moses of Her People,* did Bradford admit to a new sense of urgency regarding attempts to capture the narrative "in Harriet's language."[23] As discussions revealing Tubman's fight for the right to represent her own experiences reveals, the issue of whose "language" is dramatized in these texts remains fraught terrain. In this regard, it is both illuminating and necessary to reexamine Bradford's first biography, *Scenes,* in conjunction with fragments of Tubman's oral discourse. I support Humez's insistence that researchers examine the "embedded mini-narratives I call her 'core stories,' in which she not only plays a role as a character but also controls the narrative point of view."[24] Therefore, I interweave Bradford's text with excerpts from Humez's invaluable collection of Tubman's oral testimony in an attempt to hear "Harriet's language." In this way, we may begin to come to grips with James McGowan's powerful question "How much of Harriet Tubman's life story has she [Bradford] deprived us?"[25]

Tubman's declaration of moral, political, and artistic authority throughout Bradford's *Scenes* repeatedly counters white editorial attempts to mediate black female testimony. In stark contrast to Sojourner Truth's illuminating, if problematic, relationship with the white abolitionist Olive Gilbert, Bradford's editorializing hand was far less emotionally sensitive. Instead, she exhibited problematic tendencies that resulted in confining, if not denying outright, the exceptionalism of Tubman's heroism. Yet, just as Truth's personae emerges triumphant from the gilded shackles of white paternalist biases, Tubman's artful interventions no less liberate an array of black female representational possibilities. Throughout this work, the reader bears witness to an illiterate protagonist who relies on oratorical conventions in order to narrate revealing vignettes from her personal history as she stakes her claim to authority over the *"real ting."* In this regard, Samuel Hopkins's admission in his introduction to *Scenes* that "the narrative was prepared on the eve of the author's departure for Europe," remains a source of optimism.[26] The fact that Bradford seemingly did not have the time—or much more crucially, the interest—to editorialize Tubman's voice is a key factor in the preference among many scholars for focusing upon this work, rather than her much more heavily mediated second and third biographies. As Sernett suggests, "It is not far-fetched to think of Bradford as the collector or compiler and Moses as the editor of *Scenes*."[27] Perhaps the same could be said, not only of Thomas Gray's textual relationship to Nathaniel Turner, but also of Turner's relationship to Gray. Undoubtedly, Turner shared Tubman's determination to engage in signifying strategies designed to secure self-representation even within the margins of racist ideologies.

The need for critical sensitivity to Tubman's practices of oratorical and literary signifying is compounded by the fact that a consensus existed among her contemporaries regarding her superlative prowess as both performer and orator. Writing as early as 1859, the white abolitionist Thomas Wentworth Higginson explains, "Her tales of adventure are beyond anything in fiction and her ingenuity and generalship are extraordinary." Unable to resist capitulating to stereotypes, however, he admits, "She is jet black and cannot read or write, only talk, besides acting."[28] For Higginson, even in the face of his own racist biases, intellectual acumen and military prowess operate in conjunction with Tubman's performative skills to secure proof of her exceptional individualism. Similarly, the white sympathizer Ednah Cheney freely exalts in Tubman's status as an artist and author, observing, "She has great dramatic power; the scene rises before you as she saw it, and her voice and language change with her different actors."[29] As a political and theatrical performer ever adept at re-creating her experiences so others could see as "she saw it," Tubman sought to inspire imaginative re-creations of historical incidents. Writing in 1905, the white interviewer Emma Telford similarly documents her exceptional storytelling abilities: "As a raconteur, Harriet herself has few equals."[30] A consummate performer, Tubman was no unsophisticated naïf. As her life stories reveal, she self-consciously manipulated audience sympathies to transgress rhetorical and physical boundaries and secure a cultural and political space within which to reenact exemplary feats of black female heroism.

Split critical responses regarding Bradford's first biography underscore its problematic ambiguities. Conrad's insistence that Bradford "did an authentic work, even if it was all too brief" has met with little support.[31] Yet Humez remains convinced that "Tubman's mediated life story contains, I believe, an essential spiritual transformation 'plot' that illuminates the inner sources of her activist life."[32] Such interpretive difficulties necessitate a reexamination of Bradford's text in order to "deconstruct the heroic and heavily mediated tale that Bradford wove about her subject."[33] An artful trickster, Tubman adapted the exemplary skills of performance, disguise, and masking—skills she had perfected in her work as a heroic liberator leading numerous groups of enslaved women, men, and children out of the American South—to suit her experimental uses and reuses of language and oratorical testimony in the postslavery era. At the outset, Tubman's self-reflexive storytelling practices forcefully overturn Bradford's racist presumptions regarding her anticipation of "those who will sneer" at "this *quixotic attempt* to make a heroine of a black woman, and a slave" in this work. Seemingly unable to trust her Black female protagonist because of her own racist presumptions, Bradford betrays her adherence to prescriptive slave narrative conventions, even in the post-emancipation era. "Much has been left out which would have been highly interesting, because of the impossibility of substantiating by the testimony of others the truth of Harriet's statements," she clarifies.[34] Such damning lacunae testifying to white racist myopia illustrate the intellectual and moral importance of adopting a comparative approach to Tubman's multifaceted archive in order to read against the grain of Bradford's bare-bones representations of Tubman's oral testimony. "Through attending to the stories she chose to tell . . . and the way she told them," Humez argues, "readers can create for themselves the closest possible approximation of her own storytelling voice." As she insists, "Tubman shaped the public story of her heroism for an American audience that was polarized by racial politics."[35] According to this view, Bradford's "quixotic attempt" to re-create Tubman's heroism is ultimately most revealing regarding the problematic tensions at work in a white woman's determination to script black female testimony.

Such was no less the case, but for different reasons, for Sojourner Truth, who confronted almost insurmountable difficulties regarding the editorial control exerted upon her autobiography by her first white amanuensis, Olive Gilbert. Writing in her *Narrative of Sojourner Truth,* published in 1850, Gilbert has no qualms in interrupting her narration of Truth's personal experiences to refer obliquely to "a long series of trials in the life of our heroine, which we must pass over in silence; some from motives of delicacy, and others, because the relation of them might inflict undeserved pain on some now living, whom Isabel remembers only with esteem and love." For these reasons, Gilbert emphasizes, "the reader will not be surprised if our narrative appears somewhat tame at this point, and may rest assured that it is not for want of facts, as the most thrilling incidents of this portion of her life are from various motives suppressed."[36] In stark contrast, therefore, to Bradford, who willfully omitted "highly interesting" material regarding Tubman's life solely on the grounds that she could not "substantiate" her story "by the testimony of others," Gilbert censors Truth's story seemingly only to appease the "delicacy" of whites. More tellingly still, her decision to refer in vague terms to a "long series of trials" and to "the most thrilling incidents" works to sensationalize Truth's narrative, thereby reducing the acts of violence and violation visited upon the body and mind of her black female protagonist to little more than a spectacle for white titillation and entertainment.

Bradford's decision to begin *Scenes* by representing Tubman's body simultaneously as an empowered and yet violated spectacle risks reinforcing polarized binaries, which Tubman's, no less than Truth's, experimental language and multiple personae sought to eradicate. Seeming to exalt in Tubman's exceptional strength, Bradford plays into white racist stereotypes of the mythical, hyperphysical enslaved Black woman. As she writes, "Her naturally remarkable power of muscle was so developed that her feats of strength often called forth the wonder of strong laboring men."[37] Across her oral testimony, Tubman herself similarly exalted in the fact that she was physically able to restrain a man so that the surgeons could "saw his laig off," and could herself carry heavy burdens: "I could tote a flour bar'l on one shouldah."[38] As her testimony reveals, Tubman substitutes Bradford's emphasis upon the "wonder" of other men with the power of her own storytelling practices by relying on language to communicate her excessive strength. Seeking to concretize the typically symbolic language used by white writers as both matter and myth, Tubman rendered the psychological and intellectual complexities of black female subjectivity more tangible as she vouchsafed her determination to dramatize slavery as "the real thing."

An anecdote collected by Bradford as late as 1901 revels in Tubman's ability to transform a weakness—the brain injury with which she lived for most of her life—into a strength. "I jes' lay down like a lamb fo' de slaughter," Tubman explains, "an' he [the surgeon] sawed open my skull, an' raised I up, an' now it feels more comfortable. . . . It hurt, ob cose; but I got up."[39] In this story, Tubman foregrounds her exceptional bravery by communicating her determination to engage in a seemingly sacrificial martyrdom only to secure her own survival. At the same time, however, Bradford undermines any potentially radical portrayal of Tubman's "remarkable power of muscle" in *Scenes* by stating, "Thus was she preparing for the life and hardship and endurance which lay before her, for the deeds of daring she was to do, and of which her ignorant and darkened mind at that time never dreamed."[40] Such racist memorializations of Tubman's "darkened mind" confirm that she had to negotiate the same fate as Sojourner Truth. In similar ways, she encountered the failures of a white female editor ever to envisage feats of black female strength as related to, and not distinct from, her intellectual acumen. Clearly, one powerful way in which Tubman in imitation of Truth liberated herself from such racist confines was by experimenting with the signifying possibilities of her oral testimony.

Bradford's primary concern in *Scenes* was to legitimize Tubman's claims to white reader sympathies by portraying her as a specimen of violated black femininity. According to Bradford's written account, Tubman was repeatedly exposed to white tyranny, including the barbaric actions of her white mistress, "Miss Susan," for whom she acted as nurse to her child. "If her weary head dropped, and her hand ceased to rock the cradle, the child would cry out, and then down would come the whip upon the neck and face of the poor weary creature," Bradford emphasizes, voyeuristically adding, "The scars are still plainly visible where the whip cut into the flesh."[41] For Bradford, Tubman's broken skin operated as a "living parchment," legitimizing her right to white female sympathy and redemption. Accordingly, any such clear-cut evidence of suffering operates as a textual sign of scarification to signify the black female body as a site of purity, innocence, and martyrdom and, therefore, deserving of white sympathy as a black paragon of virtue. As Bradford argues, Tubman's "plainly visible" wounds became the text upon which white audiences could project empowered fantasies of philanthropic uplift. According to her vision, and in a complete volte face, theirs was a heroic role as they were given the responsibility of raising up the kneeling enslaved woman in their response to her plea "Am I not a woman and a sister?"

Alternative readings become possible, however, if we consider Bradford's written accounts in relation to fragments of Tubman's oral testimony. Tubman's interviews illuminate her experimental multiple personae, which ran the gamut from idealized victim to freedom fighter. For example, Tubman's interview with Cheney usefully contests Bradford's construction of Tubman as a passive martyr. As Cheney writes, "Araminta found that this [a whipping] was usually a morning exercise; so she prepared for it by putting on all the thick clothes she could procure to protect her skin. She made sufficient outcry, however, to convince her mistress that her blows had full effect."[42] No longer the "poor weary creature" of Bradford's imagining, Tubman portrays herself in her oral archives as a survivor ever adept at manipulating multiple identities via performances of suffering. She exploited the power of language to protect her body from rituals of black female sacrifice by creating a "sufficient outcry." Such a verbal outburst signifies as nothing less than a piece of theater designed to satiate white female desires for enacting vengeance upon black female bodies. For Tubman as well as Truth, the domestic domain became a psychological and physical battleground in which "survival of the fittest" and "by any means necessary" was the rule. As Truth similarly remembers following her sale on the auction block at the age of the nine, "Now the war begun."[43]

As these fragments of oral evidence attest, the epic militancy by which Tubman effected the en-masse liberation of enslaved women, children, and men—the total number of which still remains contested, as too much significance is attached to the futile search for verifiable statistics—had its origins in her subversive performances. As Helen Woodruff Tatlock recalls, "When she was sent to the bedrooms to make up the beds, she would beat up the feather beds, make believe she was working hard, and when she had blown them up she would throw herself in the middle of them."[44] As anecdotes testifying to an anarchic and antiauthoritarian Tubman, these vignettes can be usefully considered in conjunction with Bradford's narrative to expose the white female editor's inability to engage with her Black female protagonist's seemingly antiheroic survival techniques. They reveal Tubman's love of "make believe," which eradicated the power of visible markers of suffering etched onto her skin, as she favored asserting agency in the face of annihilation. Her various oral fragments explain what Bradford left unexplained regarding Tubman's multiple identities, which refused to fit reductive white paradigms. In comparison to Tatlock's account, Bradford's is far more minimalist in omitting such rich details testifying to Tubman's agency. In stark contrast, Bradford simply states, "'Miss Susan' got tired of Harriet, as Harriet was determined she should do, and so abandoned her intention of buying her, and sent her back to her master."[45] Bradford's failure to document the multiplicity of Tubman's survival techniques may have resulted from her fear of alienating a white readership. According to Bradford, her seemingly genteel white female audience would most likely only have been enraged at slavery's horrors as illustrated through the passive exhibition of victimized black female bodies as innocent spectacles.

Bradford's determination to dramatize Tubman's body as a site of black female violation lies at the heart of ongoing controversies in *Scenes:*

> She was next hired out to the man who inflicted upon her the life-long injury from which she is suffering now, by breaking her skull with a weight from the scales. . . . Disabled and sick, her flesh all wasted away, she was

returned to her *owner*. He tried to sell her, but no one would buy her. "Dey said dey wouldn't give a sixpence for me," she said.[46]

Bradford's narration of this defining moment in Tubman's history, which results in her lifelong brain injury, initially works to foreground black female vulnerability. More particularly, her emotive use of phrasing in "disabled," "sick," and "wasted away" not only strips Tubman of psychological complexity but also reduces her body to little more than a skeletal frame. At the same time, however, and most likely unwittingly, Bradford did succeed in aggrandizing Tubman's capacity for heroism. Thus, she celebrates her exceptionalism in going on to lead escaped enslaved men, women, and children to freedom undeterred by her "somnolency."

Even as reported in Bradford's account, it is telling that, in the face of such traumatic experiences, Tubman herself chose not to focus upon her suffering. Taking a different approach, she critiqued her "worth" by satirizing the monetary evaluation of enslaved men, women, and children in order to indict the inhumanity of chattel slavery. Tubman's seemingly straightforward narration, "Dey said dey wouldn't give a sixpence for me," effectively displaces white sentimental dramatizations of black female suffering. Instead, Tubman focuses upon her laboring value within white systems of economic exchange in order to expose the inherent evils of a white trade in which black bodies were sold as commodities. In a bold move, Tubman deliberately admits to black female worthlessness within the economic structure of slavery as an institution only to heighten her value in an emancipated context. Clearly, she understood that by engaging in performances of vulnerability, she would not only signify upon her lack of monetary value but would also endorse her physical freedom, as "no one would buy her." As Tubman well knew, without a prospective purchaser, the patriarchal institution became null and void. In an oratorical sleight of hand, she positions the enslaved body outside the system of financial exchange in order to render the condition of slave ownership hypothetical and irrelevant.

In a telling omission, Bradford's narrative leaves readers in the dark as to why Tubman's "owner" strikes her. The white writer and activist Frank Sanborn redresses this oversight in a letter reprinted in this same biography by giving another explanation for Tubman's disability:

> When the slave was found, the overseer swore he would be whipped, and called on Harriet, among others, to help tie him. She refused, and as the man ran away, she placed herself in the door to stop pursuit. The overseer

caught up a two-pound weight from the counter and threw it at the fugitive, but it fell short and struck Harriet a stunning blow on the head.[47]

According to Sanborn's overtly mythologized heroic schema, Tubman's lifelong injury became a talisman or calling card for her "liberty or death" ethos. His is a highly romanticized Tubman reimagined to rupture stereotypical representations promulgated by Bradford of an enslaved woman engaged in self-sacrificing behavior solely for her own bodily survival. According to Sanborn, Tubman became a larger-than-life superheroic figure instinctively risking her life to save an anonymous male victim of slavery. Her exceptional status as a Black female liberator reversed Frederick Douglass's "heroic slave" paradigm, according to which victimized black female bodies were positioned solely as catalysts to acts of black male heroism. Demonstrating her verbal noncompliance with physical opposition, according to Sanborn, Tubman occupied the liminal space between a white master and a Black enslaved man in order to assume the enslaved man's burden by laying her life on the line to save him. Sanborn's use of this incident aggrandizes Tubman's resistance by dramatizing her feats of heroic self-sacrifice as playing a key role not only in her own survival but also in the redemption of members of the black community. Tellingly, Bradford's second biography, *Moses*, includes a letter written by the white freedom fighter John Brown in which he exalts in Tubman's heroic iconicity, observing, "There is abundant material here and of the right quality."[48] Waging an ongoing war throughout this era and beyond, Truth, Tubman, and many other exceptional figures encountered almost insurmountable odds in their fight to open up a space within which to memorialize black female heroism on its own terms.

Writing in 1905, Emma Telford provides another version of the story of Tubman's brain injury. In a compelling variation, Telford's Tubman describes "the overseer" as "raising up his arm to throw an iron weight at one of the slaves and that was the last I knew." "They carried me to the house all bleeding and fainting," she relates. Tellingly, Tubman explains, "I had no bed, no place to lie down on at all.... I went to work again and there I worked with the blood and sweat rolling down my face till I couldn't see."[49] As a graphic dramatization of the black female body as a site of mutilation and violation, this excerpt downplays feats of archetypal black female heroism. According to this vision, Tubman was simply in the wrong place at the wrong time, engaging in feats of resistance by accident rather than heroic design. Yet, in her interview with Telford, Tubman reveals an early childhood memory otherwise omitted by Bradford. "I used to sleep on the floor in front of the fireplace and there I'd lie and cry and cry," she candidly concedes, explaining, "I used to think all the time. [']If I could only get home and get in my mother's bed!['] And the funny part of that was, she never had a bed in her life. Nothing but a board box nailed up against the wall and straw laid on it."[50] Clearly, this vignette documents a repeated feature of Tubman's archive concerning the failures of the domestic realm to offer any sanctuary for black womanhood. In the context of Tatlock's commentary, Tubman's bald statement unsentimentally vocalizes the horrors of black familial bonds willfully torn apart by white racists during slavery. As this testimony reveals, Tubman was taunted by the futile hope that the comforts of white domesticity could ever be anything more than an illusion for black families. Substituting the horrific realties of a "board box" with the fictional ideal of a "mother's bed," Telford's Tubman impresses the horrifying reality upon her audiences that a comfort that was presumed as a given for whites remained a fantasy for enslaved African Americans.

Telford's representation of Tubman's repeated suffering at the hands of whites accords with the testimony provided by one of her descendants, Harkness Bowery. As he informs Conrad in the 1930s, Tubman "showed me a knot in her side by being struck by one cruel man with a rope with a knot in one end." However, he soon counters any potential association of Tubman with disempowerment by testifying to her acts of resistance as she remained fearlessly undaunted by such brutality. "She was working about the house and for some trivial offense the woman attempted to whip her, to which she would not submit," he claims. Thus he celebrates Tubman's everyday determination to reject white attempts to effect black subjugation. As E. U. A. Brooks records, "On one occasion her master punished her for breach of one of his rules and she in turn bit his knee. From that time forward, he did not punish her again declaring that she had too much temper."[51] Across her lifetime, Tubman's repeated acts of physical resistance provide a dramatic embodiment of Douglass's conviction that "he is whipped oftenest, who is whipped easiest," as, to a greater extent even than Douglass, she was unafraid to repay violence with violence in conjunction with psychological strategem in order to secure black survival.[52]

As Samuel Hopkins Adams emphasizes, again in contrast to Douglass's reticence, during her lifetime Tubman revealed her scars on request to white audiences eager for a glimpse of suffering black womanhood: "She would draw down her dress and exhibit the cruel weals on neck and shoulders." Yet Tubman's responses to questions such as "Didn't it hurt awfully?" exalt in black female militancy rather than passivity: "'Dey nevah make Harriet hollah. I go back dere attawahd.' The gleam in her button-bright eyes indicated a successful raid," Adams notes.[53] In this exchange, rather than making a "sufficient outcry" for self-protection, Tubman associates a withholding of language—"Dey nevah make Harriet hollah"—with exemplary feats of heroism as she underscores her subsequent success as a liberator of enslaved women, children, and men. For Tubman, both silence and language act as springboards to political action in a complex poetics of withholding and exhibition. Tubman consistently betrays her distrust for white abolitionist paradigms that held that moral suasion was effected not only by seemingly explicatory autobiographical testimonies but also by the physical exhibition of black bodies as proofs.

Whereas written accounts suggest that Sojourner Truth experienced a moment of reconciliation with a repentant white master, Bradford's Tubman rejects any such cathartic resolution:

> I prayed all night long for master . . . an' all the time he was bringing people to look at me, an' trying to sell me. . . . Den I changed my prayer. . . . 'Oh Lord, if you ant nebber gwine to change dat man's heart, kill him, Lord, an' take him out ob de way.
>
> Nex' ting I heard old master was dead, an' he died jus' as he libed. Oh, then, it 'peared like I'd give all de world full ob gold, if I had it, to bring dat poor soul back. But I couldn't pray for him no longer.[54]

At first glance, Bradford's text illuminates Tubman's seeming adherence to the role of the stereotypically loyal, self-sacrificing enslaved woman praying for the sins not only of an evil white master who was all the time "trying to sell me" but also for her own moral weaknesses. However, Tubman's excessive dramatization of black female piety ultimately provides her with the means to condemn white male barbarity.

Signifying on her existence solely as an object for white consumption on the grounds that her master "was bringing people to look at me," Tubman's rhetoric artfully shifts from the spiritual supplication characteristic of white abolitionist mores intent solely upon saving black victims to an authoritative demand for divine vengeance as she rejects barbarous attempts to sell her and her family south. To this end, she poignantly describes the realities of the "chain gang" as well as the cotton and rice fields in the context of a horrifying sense of black communal loss: "Dey said I was gwine, an' my brudders, an' sisters." Thus she insists on a direct correlation among plantation slavery, physical suffering, and black genealogical annihilation. In this regard, Tubman's sense of guilt that her prayer results in her white master's death rings hollow in the face of her condemnatory statement that "he died jus' as he libed." As Tubman's rhetoric reveals, black female identities were in flux and on multiple journeys toward moral improvement, while white masculinity remained both ethically and spiritually fixed in reductive paradigms. Her plea that "I'd give all de world full ob gold" to "bring dat poor soul back," contests the efficacy of monetary systems of exchange ever to value or redeem humanity: "poor" signifies ambiguously here to suggest white inferiority rather than pathos by confirming a poverty of the soul. Tubman's explicit condemnation of white inferior immorality offers clear-cut evidence of her radical politics. As Cheney reports in her interview, "When invited into family prayers, she preferred to stay on the landing, and pray for herself; 'and I prayed to God,' she says, 'to make me strong and able to fight, and that's what I've always prayed for ever since.'"[55] Cheney's narration of Tubman's resolution to "stay on the landing" resonates with her earlier determination to stand between the enslaved Black man and the white master. As an ex-enslaved freedom fighter, Tubman exalts in liminal "no places" over and above overtly domesticated or racially circumscribed spaces as she fought to liberate otherwise fixed constructions of black female heroism.

With uncharacteristic frankness, Bradford's *Scenes* tackles a common concern that appears throughout Tubman's oral testimony regarding the political uses of linguistic and performative strategies in the service of survival. As Bradford writes, following her return to the U.S. South, Tubman relayed messages to other enslaved women and men via "communications," which "were generally made by singing," and to which "the uninitiated knew not the hidden meaning." Forced to rely on this system during her own escape attempt regardless of the risk, Tubman here explains, "Whether the Doctor thought her 'imperent' or not, she must sing him farewell." According to Bradford's transcription, Tubman's use of the word "imperent" betrays her rejection of racially inscribed social mores. Instead, she relies on masking as a survival technique via a signifying use of language. Ultimately, *Scenes* gives full reign to Tubman's playfulness in her determination to outwit white slave catchers. Bradford includes moments during which Tubman and other fugitive men and women watched as whites futilely erected runaway slave advertisements. "And den how we laughed," Tubman delights. "*We* was de fools, and *dey* was de wise men; but we wasn't fools enough to go down de high road in broad daylight."[56] Adopting a satirical tone, Bradford's Tubman relishes in the freedoms secured by black male and female subversive practices. Performing as intellectual inferiors, they expose white stupidity by reveling in white slave owners' failures ever to understand black signifying practices.

Taken together, Bradford's *Scenes* and Tubman's many oral statements testify to her reliance on biblical song to communicate coded messages of resistance:

> De first time I go by singing dis hymn, dey don't come out to me ... till I listen if de coast is clar; den when I go back and sing it again, dey come out. But if I sing:
>> Moses go down in Egypt,
>>> Till old Pharo' let me go ...
> Den dey don't come out, for dere's danger in de way.[57]

Thus Tubman's survival strategies demonstrate not only her political use of biblical allegory for subversive purposes but also her repeated engagement with black folkloric symbolism. Signifying on the ritualistic importance of song and improvisation, Tubman cultivates call-and-response relationships between herself and members of an enslaved black community in order to effect their psychological and physical liberation from slavery.

Across her life and works, Tubman celebrates the survival of a multifaceted black culture regardless of white attempts at erasure. A fearless manipulator of black as well as white audiences, Tubman experimented with multiple personae in her simultaneous incarnations as an illiterate enslaved woman, a biblical leader, a political activist, and a theatrical performer as she fought to secure her antislavery agenda. As Cheney writes, "She has needed disguise so often, that she seems to have command over her face, and can banish all expression from her features, and look so stupid that nobody would suspect her of knowing enough to be dangerous."[58] Incendiary yet conciliatory, militant yet passive, Tubman played various identities off against one another in order to defy white reductive attempts to endorse monolithic constructions of a seemingly static black female heroism. For Harriet Tubman, coded messages extended beyond song and oral discourse to include her subversive reliance upon written evidence. In one instance, although unable to write herself, she orchestrated the delivery of a letter from herself to an enslaved man named Jacob, which was purported to be from his son, William Henry Jackson. In this epistle, she relies on an allegorical use of biblical imagery to communicate her determination to rescue her own family. In the guise of Jacob's son, she insists, "Read my letter to the old folks, and give my love to them, and tell my brothers to be always *watching unto prayer,* and when the *good old ship of Zion comes along, to be ready to step aboard.*"[59] In a rare moment of insight, Bradford describes how "white genius having exhausted itself, black genius was called in," as "Jacob saw at once what it meant, but tossed it down, saying, 'Dat letter can't be meant for me, no how. I can't make head nor tail of it.'"[60]

Transgressing gender divides, Tubman adopts the persona of an enslaved Black man both to encourage solidarity within the black community and to effect the liberation of her family. Defying her illiteracy, these actions betray her manipulation of the written form as she subverted official systems of knowledge in order to challenge white authoritative power. Yet this was not the first time she manipulated literacy as a form of political subterfuge. As Tatlock writes, "At another time when she heard men talking about her, she pretended to read a book which she carried. One man remarked, 'This can't be the woman. The one we want can't read or write.' Harriet devoutly hoped this book was right side up."[61] Seemingly endorsing racist stereotypes, this episode fleshes out Bradford's otherwise minstrelsy-inflected trade in a spectacular blackness by testifying to Tubman's repeated performative use of literacy as a way of turning popular mythologies regarding black ignorance to her advantage. Furthermore, as narrated in her final biography, Tubman seems to share Truth's suspicion regarding textual discourse, as she remained similarly conflicted regarding the power of written testimony alone. With a characteristic sense of superiority, Bradford writes, "She seems to have an idea that by laying her hand" on the individual acting as her scribe, "her feelings may be transmitted to the one to whom she is writing."[62] Ultimately, therefore, Tubman relied on her own body as a bulwark against the slipperiness of literary knowledge as she fought to ensure that her amanuenses—including Bradford—should operate as the conduit rather than the interpreter of "her feelings."

Reflecting upon her role as a political theorist as much as an antislavery activist, Tubman's multiple guises as a freedom fighter were inspired by white American Revolutionary ideals, as she not only endorsed but adapted a cult of heroic white masculinity to suit a black female revolutionary ethos. According to Bradford, Tubman admits, "I started with this idea in my head, 'Dere's *two* things I've got a *right* to, and dese are, Death or Liberty—one or tother I mean to have. No one will take me back alive; I shall fight for my liberty, and when de time has come for me to go, de Lord will let dem kill me." Reflecting the same revolutionary creed as Harriet Jacobs, David Walker, Henry Highland Garnet, and Frederick Douglass among many others, Harriet Tubman's exceptional heroism in repeatedly leading enslaved women, children, and men out of slavery can be situated within black radical abolitionist paradigms that endorsed armed self-defense in the pursuit of equal rights. In a bold volte face, Bradford's *Scenes* provides one of the most apocalyptic stories regarding black female heroism:

Sometimes members of her party would become exhausted, foot-sore, and bleeding, and declare they could not go on . . . then there was no remedy but force; the revolver carried by this bold and daring pioneer would be pointed at their heads. 'Dead niggers tell no tales,' said Harriet; 'Go on or die'; and so she compelled them to drag their weary limbs on their northward journey.[63]

In compelling ways, Bradford's religious rhetoric shores up similarities between enslaved flight and a pilgrimage or exodus not only to enhance Tubman's status as a spiritual leader but also to legitimize her use of violence. As recorded here, Tubman's statement "Dead niggers tell no tales" lies at the heart of the ambivalences proliferating within white reimaginings of black heroism. No Sojourner Truth questioning Frederick Douglass's belief in violence by asking, Frederick, *is God dead?*" Harriet Tubman represents a radical, ostensibly more militant and new form of black female heroism, as she follows in Nathaniel Turner's wake by endorsing the necessity of violence to secure black survival.[64]

As popular memory surrounding her acts of liberation attests, Tubman did not shy away from the necessity of violence in the service of self-preservation. As Cheney relates, "If any man gave out, he must be shot. 'Would you really do that?' she was asked. 'Yes,' she replied, 'if he was weak enough to give out, he'd be weak enough to betray us all, and all who had helped us; and do you think I'd let so many die just for one coward man?'" Refusing to sacrifice the many for the one, Tubman was at war not only with the white patriarchal institution but also with gender hierarchies, as she positioned herself—as a female freedom fighter—as the quintessential embodiment of black heroism over and above one "coward man." Arguing her point further, she confided her response to one man's attempted defection as further evidence of this principle in action. "I told the boys to get their guns ready, and shoot him," she explains, confident that "they'd have done it in a minute; but when he heard that, he jumped right up and went on as well as anybody."[65] By unequivocally legitimizing her use of violence, Tubman contributed to her own mythology as a heroic commander in possession of sufficient military authority to organize her troops, execute dissenters, and maintain martial discipline. Rather than having to "point" the revolver at "their heads" herself, as is often narrated or visualized in popular representations, including Lawrence's twentieth-century painting, *Forward* (see plate 12), Tubman seemingly adopted Turner's policy of delegating such acts to others. Thus she offers yet further proof concerning not only their shared military rationale but also their commitment to a black-led and grassroots-based revolutionary and ideological war on slavery. While any comparison between Tubman's and Turner's martial leadership exists beyond the pale for her white editor and audiences, such was not the case for her formerly enslaved and newly emancipated Black audiences living in the postbellum era.

As Larson argues, Bradford's *Scenes* had a debatable influence over memorializations of Tubman, given its "limited publication run of twelve hundred copies," which "did not provide a wide enough circulation to keep Tubman's life story in current memory."[66] In comparison, the competing facts and fictions regarding Tubman's history were made more widely available in her later "as told to" narratives and, more important, in her own abolitionist performances and oral interviews. For Tubman, interviews provided a powerful way both to dramatize graphic realities and to indict the perils of black ignorance during slavery. As Tubman confides to the white interviewer Benjamin Drew in a post-emancipation context, "I grew up like a neglected weed,—ignorant of liberty, having no experience of it."[67] Condemning white slave owners' disregard for black life, she exposes the unnaturalness of slavery as a soi-disant "civilized" institution. Moreover, her later macabre vision of a human harvest of death and vengeance lauds black sacrifice, as she interprets the atrocities of the Civil War in terms similar to Nathaniel Turner's spiritual defense of violence: "and then we heard the rain falling, and that was the drops of blood falling; and then we came to get in the crops, it was dead men that we reaped."[68] Stripped of the sentimentality of much of Bradford's reported testimony, Tubman's stark and nonvernacular use of language challenges racist mythologies regarding oversimplified black female identity constructions.

"From the log cabins of the South have come forth some of our most heroic women, whose words, acts and deeds are a stimulus to us at this hour." So proclaimed Rosetta Douglass-Sprague, Frederick Douglass's daughter, at the National Association of Colored Women's convention toward the end of the nineteenth century. As the author of one of the very few biographies of her mother, Anna Murray Douglass, whose heroism has remained very much in the shadow of her iconic husband, Douglass-Sprague is exultant: "We are pleased to note in the personality of such women as Phillis Wheatley, Margaret Garner, Sojourner Truth and our venerable friend, Harriet Tubman, sterling qualities of head, heart and hand, that hold no insignificant place in the annals of heroic womanhood." Situating Harriet Tubman alongside Sojourner Truth and other Black female writers and activists, Douglass-Sprague insists on Tubman's collective symbolism. As immortalized by

Higginson as the "greatest heroine of the age, " and by Charlotte Forten as "the heroic woman" in her own lifetime, Harriet Tubman's memory remains an enduring source of inspiration in the twentieth and twenty-first centuries. Soon after her death on the cusp of World War I, Booker T. Washington turned to Harriet Tubman as a talisman for future acts of black male as well as black female heroism when he exhorted his Black audiences, "You will be measured by the great life of Harriet Tubman and by her great life all the country is watching you."[69]

HARRIET TUBMAN'S "LIKENESSES" IN
EARLY ILLUSTRATIONS AND PHOTOGRAPHS

"One of her means of security was to carry with her the daguerreotypes of her friends, and show them to each new person," Frank Sanborn remembered, noting, "If they recognized the likeness, then it was all right."[70] This political use of photographic proofs bears witness to Tubman's radical reversal of white abolitionist paradigms according to which black bodies were displayed as evidence for white consumption. Thus Tubman saw a direct relationship between her role as interpreter and arbiter of white identities and black female survival. As enigmatic as she appeared in her oral testimonies and mediated narratives, Tubman's visual archive reveals that she remained equally ambiguous in her experimental "likenesses." Moreover, nineteenth-century woodcuts and photographs represent Harriet Tubman in her interrelated guises as heroic liberator, militant freedom fighter, and founding mother of black female resistance. The following images in particular provide a useful starting point from which to begin examining Tubman's multiple personae: J. C. Darby's military woodcut, which first appeared in Bradford's *Scenes* in 1869 (figure 27); *Harriet Tubman, Full Length Portrait*, H. B. Lindsley's photograph taken sometime between 1860 and 1875 (figure 28); and *Harriet Tubman with Family and Friends, Standing by the Side of Her Barn in Auburn*, created in 1887 by an unknown photographer (figure 29).[71]

"The spirited wood-cut likeness of Harriet, in her costume as scout, was furnished by the kindness of Mr. J. C. Darby, of this city," Samuel Hopkins Adams writes in his introduction to Bradford's *Scenes*.[72] Humez argues that this "image may have been based on an actual photograph taken during the Civil War,"[73] even though no such artifact survives. As one of the most iconic and widely reproduced representations of Tubman in the twentieth century, this woodcut by a little-known illustrator has inspired countless works by

Black and white artists. More powerfully still, as Adams remembers, Tubman herself was "inordinately proud of that woodcut," as "reference to it never failed to loosen her tongue."[74] The fact that this image not only remained a favorite of Tubman's but was also a stimulus to her storytelling performances heightens its social, political, and aesthetic significance. This "spirited woodcut" represents a stark departure from nineteenth-century representations in its endorsement of an explicitly militant black female heroism. Tubman may well have been the first former Black enslaved women to be depicted armed, as her fists clench a long rifle that runs nearly the full length of her body. Appearing as an iconic embodiment of black female militancy, Tubman offers a stark contrast to portraits of Phillis Wheatley, Harriet Jacobs, and even Sojourner Truth, who were all typically portrayed in genteel domestic interiors. More particularly, Tubman's erect figure and militant stance signals her powerful rejection of the association of Black female subjects with passivity. Thus she took to task an array of generically produced woodcuts that typically showed seated and vulnerable enslaved female runaways. In this work, Darby relies on a symbolic use of composition to ensure that the stripes of her dress mirror the slightly tilted vertical position of her weapon. Here, the artist suggests a mutually reciprocal relationship between the black female body and an industrial object typically associated with hypermasculinized forms of violence.

In contrast to Truth, who carried her "shadows" or daguerreotyped self-portraits in her bag, we can speculate that Tubman's satchel, as shown in this woodcut, contained practical supplies or even ammunition manufactured for use in combat. Moreover, Tubman's enigmatic facial expression conveys both her autonomy and psychological depth: à la Douglass and Truth, hers is a physiognomy that refuses to tell. The delicate lines etched onto her face exist in complex visual dialogue with the markings on her hands to communicate the realities of black female labor. This view accords with Humez's assessment that she is "looking directly and unsmilingly out at the viewer—an image that would convey to later generations both African American militant resistance to racial oppression and African American female dignity, strength, and empowerment."[75] While I would agree that this work does indeed provide a visual manifesto of black female heroism, I would also suggest that Tubman secures such empowerment by cultivating a poetics of indirection and undertelling. While it is unclear whether this woodcut was drawn from life or a daguerreotype that has been lost, her enigmatic physiognomy clearly resisted white attempts either to know, quantify, or consume black femininity.

HARRIET TUBMAN.

FIGURE 27. J. C. Darby, frontispiece to Sarah H. Bradford, *Scenes in the Life of Harriet Tubman* (Auburn, NY: W. J. Moses, 1869). (Documenting the American South, University of North Carolina, Chapel Hill)

As the backdrop to this image documents, not for Tubman were the domestic properties of a photographer's studio, the pen and paper of a Phillis Wheatley portrait, or the genteel domesticity of a matriarchal Sojourner Truth performatively seated with her knitting. Instead, Darby creates this drawing at the height of military conflict to locate Tubman's significance within the blood and fire of a Civil War South. Relying on a delicate use of crosshatching, Darby delineates uniform rows of tents against a blank horizon to dramatize the makeshift urgency of war as accentuated by a bare, natural landscape. The entire absence of any signs of human life, black or white, exalts in Tubman's archetypal significance as an iconic liberator while resonating with more popular representations of the army commander Toussaint Louverture, as typically portrayed in the field of battle decades before. As Adams observes, "The woodcut frontispiece of Aunt Sarah's *Scenes in the Life of Harriet Tubman* displays its subject in her scout uniform, 'all fine-an-fitten.'"[76] Betraying his indebtedness to stereotypical markers of black female physicality, however, he describes how "a voluminous bandanna swathes her kinky hair." Nonetheless, close investigation reveals that a rich array of multidirectional patterning characterizes Tubman's clothing in this work, as Darby portrays Tubman wearing a checked head scarf and a striped dress while he relies on a gray-black use of shading to color her three-quarter length coat. Such idiosyncratic detail of Tubman's attire confirms not only her heroic individualism but also her self-identification as a nonexceptional laborer working in the field of slavery. Such asymmetry may also recall African American quilting traditions by which enslaved individuals experimented with break-patterning as a way of protecting the self against malignant spirits. If accurate, these associations potentially encourage further recognition of Tubman's artistry, particularly given her own singular prowess as a quilter. As Cheney notes regarding Tubman's activities during her rescue missions, "By day they lay in the woods; then she pulled out her patchwork, and sewed together little bits, perhaps not more than an inch square, which were afterwards made into comforters for the fugitives in Canada."[77]

Ultimately, Darby's woodcut endorses a vision of Tubman as an exceptional Black female heroic icon by reveling in her significance as a visual embodiment of black community activism. Thus if it did indeed exist, the daguerreotype of this image may also have circulated as a carte de visite to inspire black militancy during the Civil War. Regardless, this image operates ambiguously in its known life as a frontispiece to an "as told to" post–Civil War slave narrative. In contrast to the half-drawn figures of Frederick Douglass or William Wells Brown circulating in the frontispieces of their narratives, Tubman's face and body are fully etched, down to the last detail of her patterned clothing, while her facial expression is carefully delineated. As Darby's woodcut reveals, in both her oratorical and visual performances Tubman signifies upon a post-emancipation context by offering proof that she had effected her own transformation from slavery to freedom. Clearly, a potentially incongruous slippage can be found regarding Darby's radical representation of Tubman in the guise of a soldier and Bradford's textual difficulties regarding the "quixotic attempt" to define black female heroism. Unbesmirched and seemingly unharmed, Darby's Harriet Tubman is unequivocally heroic, as she is shown as having either emerged from the war unscathed or, as is more likely, on her way to combat. Yet Tubman's battles were not to be confined to the military field, as tensions within Bradford's text testify to the necessity of the Black female freedom fighter's ongoing ideological war against social, political, and historical injustices in a post-emancipation context.

"Nurse, spy and scout." So reads the handwritten caption scrawled at the bottom of a photograph created by the little-known photographer H. B. Lindsley and identified in the Library of Congress archives as *Harriet Tubman, Full Length Portrait*, a work dated between 1860 and 1875 (see figure 28). Similarly providing the viewer with a full-length portrait, this image depicts Tubman dressed far more conventionally than in Darby's woodcut. Divested of her military regalia, she stands wearing a single-colored and unpatterned dress decorated solely by an elaborate white necktie. Gone is the head wrap cherished by Truth and understood by many critics as a marker of African difference. Ostensibly, this photographic representation recuperates Tubman's authority according to white Western domestic conventions. The shiny buttons of her dress resonate tellingly with the symbolic properties on view in the studio—the tassels on the chair, the ornate tablecloth and patterned carpet—to render her participation within a white-originated "cult of true womanhood" unmistakable. As a potentially far less radical photograph than Darby's image, therefore, Lindsley's work signifies much more clearly upon the conventions at work within black female portraiture adhered to by Wheatley, Jacobs, and Truth, all of whom were typically surrounded by the paraphernalia of domesticity in their visual representations. Revealingly, Tubman's solitary property in Darby's earlier work—the rifle—is replaced by the power of the written word, as an unopened book rests on the table next to her in this photograph. Here Tubman appears not only as an aging matriarch—as dramatized by her graying hair—but as an unequivocal revolutionary, as hinted at by the masked ambiguities of her facial expression.

Tellingly, given the way the image is lit, the viewer has little access to the frailties of Tubman's face. Instead, both photographer and subject celebrate her intellectual acumen by emphasizing her prominent forehead. Impassive and refusing to tell, Tubman's unreadable physiognomy maintains similarities between this photograph and Darby's woodcut. Thus she foregrounds her self-reflexive strategies of masking and disguise to critique white unknowing vis-à-vis black female identity construction. Regardless of the confining domestic symbolism presented in this studio portrait—which seems a far cry from the battlefields of the U.S. South—Lindsley's is a Tubman about to break free. Significantly, her coat and hat stand on the chair beside her, while her boots are just on view under her dress, suggesting her preparedness for battle by recalling the same exhibition of her feet in Darby's woodcut.

Ultimately, Lindsley's photograph gives prominence to black female militant activism over and above educational resistance, as the closed book is relegated to the background. Instead, the viewer's attention is drawn to a hat and coat, which wait on a chair on which Tubman refuses to sit. In stark contrast to Truth's injured hands, which she repeatedly partially hid, Tubman's hands are prominently displayed. No longer clutching a rifle, here they support her body as if in testament to her exemplary physicality. This photograph reveals an additional block of fabric near the hem of Tubman's dress. At the same time that this patchwork suggests that her dress may have been mended as a result of her ongoing struggles against poverty, it may also testify to her resilience by suggesting that it was torn during one of her many epic struggles for freedom. Clearly, Tubman's life as a freedom fighter bears witness to difficulties regarding the efficacy of traditional female fashions. In a revealing letter, she vouchsafed her preference for radical feminist clothing over traditional attire. "I want, among the rest, a *bloomer* dress, made of some coarse, strong material, to wear on *expeditions*," she insists.[78] However much they differ, it is clear that both Darby's woodcut and Lindsley's photograph exalt in a heroic, iconic, and exceptional Tubman. Both of these works' visions of black femininity challenge racist tendencies to equate black womanhood with objectifying stereotypes otherwise inextricable from plantation slavery.

Both Darby's and Lindsley's artistic and photographic likenesses of a solitary Tubman contrast starkly with her rare appearance in an anonymously produced group photograph variously titled *Harriet Tubman with Family and Friends, Standing by the Side of Her Barn in Auburn* and *Harriet Tubman Standing with a Group of Slaves Whose Escape She Assisted* and taken about 1887 (see figure 29). One of eight Black male and female, adult and child subjects, she stands not in the center but to the far left as if to offer confirmation

FIGURE 28. H. B. Lindsley, *Harriet Tubman, Full Length Portrait*, ca. 1860–75. (Prints and Photographs Division, Library of Congress)

that this is one of her self-deprecating rather than self-aggrandizing performances. Hers is a vision of collective and untold, rather than exceptional and immortalized, heroism as she stands with the youthful members of the group (Gertie Davis, Lee Cheney, Walter Green and Dora Stewart), while the adult men and woman—her husband, Nelson Davis; "Pop" Alexander; and "Blind" Aunty (Sarah) Parker—all remain seated. Clearly, this photograph foregrounds the frailty of an earlier generation only to aggrandize Tubman's mythical exceptionalism by celebrating her enduring legacies. Here, the photographer portrays Tubman as identifying herself with the resilience and health of youth as she stands next to her adopted daughter, Gertie Davis. Taller than Tubman, Davis wears a square-patterned dress with a black buttoned blouse, her hands hidden from view as they are held behind her back. Moreover, her slightly tilted head suggests she is looking downward, contemplating the viewer from a position of authority. Similarly empowered, a young boy, Walter Green, stands on the far side of the image with his arms on his hips in a gesture of self-affirmation. His gray suit communicates his remoteness from domestic and physical labor to suggest his determination to secure social advancement. Green's ambiguous facial expression forcefully affirms black agency by thwarting any pretensions to a pseudophilanthropic and objectifying gaze on the part of white audiences.

Constituting a complex family tableau, these various assertive poses contrast with the diminutive size of the half-hidden figure of Tubman's great—grandniece, Lee Cheney, whose wide eyes and half-open mouth suggest vulnerability. Standing in the center of this photograph, she symbolizes both the past and the future in her seeming frailty and youth. By comparison, Tubman's great-niece, Dora Stewart, stands to the far right of the photograph wearing a white dress and black hat. Visually separated from the other members of the group, in some reproductions she is cut from the photograph entirely, while in others her thoughtful expression is obscured; in either case, her blurred physiognomy exists in powerful relation to the sharp focus of the other family members. With her hands to her side, her worn boots and contemplative, if enigmatic, features contrast with the pristine freshness of her white dress to suggest elided histories of black female struggle. An array of ambivalent representations of black masculinity dominate this photograph in the likenesses of Harriet Tubman's second husband, Nelson Davis, and "Pop" Alexander. Tellingly, Davis's facial features are difficult to read, while the contortions of his furrowed brow, closed mouth, and tensed eyes register a barely suppressed anger. Seated rather than standing, he holds a pipe in his mouth, his hands clasped slightly together, perhaps in a gesture of prayer. A

FIGURE 29. Anon., *Harriet Tubman with Family and Friends, Standing by the Side of Her Barn in Auburn*, 1887. (Photographs and Prints Division, Schomburg Center for Research in Black Culture, The New York Public Library, Astor, Lenox and Tilden Foundations)

large stick is pressed up against his chest; its function is unclear, as it may represent a walking cane, a laboring tool, or even a weapon of self-defense in light of the post-emancipation context of heightened racism. His worn working man's hat, striped shirt, dark trousers, and scuffed boots all poignantly bear witness to a life of grinding poverty and hardship. In this photograph, Davis's unflinching, impassive gaze speaks to internal contradictions, while the fact that he is seemingly both praying and not praying suggests disillusionment in a will to but, ultimately, a lack of faith. In stark contrast, "Pop" Alexander's pose mirrors Davis's to suggest both similarities and differences between the two men. Sitting with one hand resting on his knee, he holds a fan rather than a stick, symbolizing a less militant version of masculinity. In contrast to Davis's working-man's clothes, "Pop" seems better dressed, wearing a white shirt, dark waistcoat, tie, and trousers. His open hands and seemingly more straightforward and half-smiling expression endorse a less radical vision of black masculinity.

As a varying representation of black femininity in this photograph, "Blind" Aunty (Sarah) Parker is dressed entirely in white as she sits hunched over her walking stick in a posture suggestive of physical vulnerability. She does not look at the viewer but instead at her hands, as if to suggest that she has become disconnected from her physical surroundings. The whiteness of her apron symbolizes arduous domestic labor, while the threads visible in her worn black skirt suggest heartbreaking poverty. Parker's hunched-over frame combines with her all-white clothing and walking stick to narrate untold histories of black female struggle. While this is a group photograph, no figure touches another, as their different poses suggest competing responses of pride, anger, denial, resignation and frustration. These men, women, and children all remained confined by their own survival strategies in their fight to transcend the deprivation of their surroundings. Clearly, while set in a post-emancipation era, the complexities of this image attest to the fact that, as Marcus Wood argues, "the familial photographic archive is, in the context of slavery, an agonizing and agonistic space to negotiate."[79]

In this group photograph Tubman is depicted not only in reciprocal relation to these women, children, and men but also on her own terms. Standing as a solitary figure, she adopts a pose typical of her individual photographic representations. Yet, rather than directly confronting the viewer or gazing heroically into the distance, in this image her shoulders are hunched over and her head bowed as if to communicate her masked contemplation of her audience from a seemingly subjugated position. Such an anachronistic portrayal of Tubman as the stereotypically victimized enslaved woman can be best understood in conjunction with her empty bowl. Here she engages in a pragmatic performance designed to secure white charity by accentuating black female physical vulnerability. Contrasting with other heroic portraits of this individualist freedom fighter, in this photograph she self-consciously seems to minimize her strength to gain audience sympathy for the plight of her newly freed black family. Such a reading is born out by other instances in which Tubman was not afraid to perform as the vulnerable enslaved woman begging for white alms to secure the survival of others. As her earlier testimony reveals, Tubman staged sit-ins to secure funds to support her liberation raids to the South. According to Bradford, she avowed, "I'm gwine to Mr.——'s office, an' I ain't gwine to lebe there, an' I ain't gwine to eat or drink till I get enough money to take me down after the old people."[80]

In terms of gender dynamics, while Nelson Davis, Tubman's husband, occupies the foreground of this photograph, she herself stands in the background as if to suggest her voluntary adoption of a subservient role. Yet Tubman's subjugation is only relative when considered in conjunction with her expert use of disguise for survival. Gone are the lavish ruffles around her neck as shown in Lindsley's photograph, as she instead favors a polka-dot necktie, which accentuates only the bare outline of her dark clothing. At the same time, the backdrop plays a fundamental role in Tubman's visual narrative. Nothing could be further from the previous aggrandizing Civil War backgrounds or the opulence of the photographer's studio. Instead, in this image she stands on a dirt floor surrounded by bits of junk in front of what appears to be a cabin wall on which hangs a broken chair. Clearly, these disused domestic artifacts heighten the black family's plight and need for financial succor. At the same time, the complicated array of bodily postures and facial expressions that differentiate these Black men, women, and children as they stand in a row heightens the artificiality of their poses and, by extension, the constructed nature of their histories. Across the decades, this photograph can be situated within the much later, heavily didactic, and frequently objectifying but nonetheless reformist photography of the twentieth-century Farm Security Administration produced during the Depression. Starkly contrasting to Darby's and Lindsley's visions of a solitary Tubman, this photograph attests to Tubman's belief in the inextricable relationship between black female iconic heroism and everyday survival. Constituting a powerful corrective to the obfuscation of black familial histories, this image exists in radical relation to the extant U.S. archive of white "family group portraits," which only "occasionally include black subjects" who appeared solely "as marginal elements in predominantly white family groups."[81]

Following her death in 1913, twentieth-century public attempts to memorialize Harriet Tubman have continued to fall far short of her multifaceted realities. For the pioneering Black art historian Freeman Henry Morris Murray, the bronze memorial unveiled in June 1914 was a crushing disappointment. "It is difficult to view the facial features of this heroine as depicted on this tablet without wincing at what must be called—putting it very mildly—the bald literalness of the portrayal," he explains. He was horrified at the disjuncture cultivated in this memorial between Tubman's "life-history," which he describes as "a romance and a hero tale combined," and the debilitating vision of her physical form as etched in bronze. For Murray, the sculptor had failed by representing "her features as shriveled, mis-shapen and pitifully distorted."[82] Yet such references to her "mis-shapen" distortions may in fact attest to the success of her performances. As her oratorical, visual, and textual archive reveals, Harriet Tubman self-reflexively engaged in acts and arts of political, social, and historical resistance as she fought to secure her legendary symbolism as a "malleable icon."[83]

"THE NEGRO WOMAN WAS NEVER INCLUDED IN AMERICAN HISTORY": JACOB LAWRENCE'S *LIFE OF HARRIET TUBMAN* SERIES (1939–40)

"I was very much excited . . . by the heroes . . . of the blacks, and I wanted to do something in painting about it."[84] So explains Jacob Lawrence regarding the inspiration for his various multiple narrative series dramatizing Black heroic figures. These include not only his works devoted to Louverture and Douglass but also his *Life of Harriet Tubman,* a thirty-one panel work he created in 1939 and 1940 to raise awareness within the black community regarding the political and social realities of otherwise marginalized female histories. Lawrence's groundbreaking epic reflects a widespread determination among African American artists such as William H. Johnson, Aaron Douglas, Elizabeth Catlett, Faith Ringgold, Barbara Ward, and Charles White "to put the Negro back where he belongs in American history," specifically by dramatizing Black female icons such as Tubman as representative embodiments of an exceptional heroism.[85]

In stark contrast to these other artists, however, Lawrence chose not to create a single work but a multipanel narrative series, in which, he explains, "You can tell a story, you can tell many episodes. *It's like chapters in a book.*" As he emphasizes, "What I couldn't do in one painting I could do in a series of paintings. "[86] Thus Lawrence's strategies of aesthetic experimentation not only openly dramatize the importance of his storytelling practices but also expose the inefficacy of linear narratives to memorialize black heroism with any degree of complexity. Slippery and signifying relationships are at work between pictorial image and textual caption in this series. Across these panels, Lawrence extrapolates ambiguities otherwise elided in dominant white representations, which tend toward eradicating black female heroism. As a multilayered and experimental work, Lawrence's *Life of Harriet Tubman* series relies on symbolic tableaux to dramatize a multiplicity of hidden histories of black female heroism immortalized solely within a black folkloric memory. As Patricia Hills observes, Lawrence's work demonstrates his role as "the pictorial *griot* . . . of his own African-American community."[87] "His narrative also conforms to other conventions of slave narratives, which generally downplay the narrator's personal feelings," she writes.[88] Clearly, Lawrence's pared-down techniques heighten the emotional and political impact of his work by endorsing a minimalist approach. Inspiring audiences to identify with his subject matter, he requires his viewers to engage imaginatively and empathetically with Tubman's multifaceted histories.

Lawrence's *Life of Harriet Tubman* series not only reinserts otherwise hidden black female experiences into the white historical record but also works as a corrective to the masculine biases on offer in his other narrative series, including *The Life of Toussaint L'Ouverture* (1939), *The Life of Frederick Douglass* (1938–39) and *The Life of John Brown* (1941). As he explains, "The Negro woman has never been included in American History."[89] In terms of African American art history more generally, Lawrence's work can be usefully compared to Aaron Douglas's mural *Spirits Rising*, painted nearly ten years earlier in 1930–31, in which, as Douglas acknowledges, "I used Harriet Tubman to idealize a superior type of Negro womanhood."[90] In his *Life of Harriet Tubman* series, Lawrence sought not only to dramatize a "superior type" but also a more multifaceted representation of black female heroism. He maintained that this work possessed "more pictorial drama" than his epics devoted to black masculinity because "I don't think the black woman has been heralded or thought of—even less so than the black male."[91] Not shying away from the elliptical distortions characterizing representations of black female heroism within white official records, Lawrence's symbolic use of color and composition creates dramatic vignettes designed emotionally to provoke as well as educate his viewer. As Ellen Harkins Wheat argues, the "emotional tone ranges from drama to wit, epic grandeur to intimate psychological insight."[92] Ultimately, Lawrence's series sought to redress the fact that enslaved Black women as well as men had been "taken out, just excluded, or put aside" from white sites of American memory.[93]

The first two panels of Lawrence's *Life of Harriet Tubman* series provide startlingly contrasting representations of black enslaved life. In panel 1, he depicts a group of laboring but erect Black men and women as they carry baskets, wood bundles, and buckets of water against the repetitive monotony of a gray-black sky and brown earth. Faceless, anonymous, and only partially clothed, the naked and emaciated backs of enslaved men are fully on view. The angular stylization of their tessellated bodies suggests synchronized patterns of movement to communicate not only black survival through solidarity but also the perils of conformity, as they collectively had no choice but to participate in oppressive cycles of enforced labor. More specifically, their physical subjugation supports Lawrence's caption, in which he quotes the white abolitionist Henry Ward Beecher's denunciation of the injustices of slavery: "With sweat and toil and ignorance he consumes his life, to pour the earnings into channels from which he does not drink."[94] However, Lawrence's painting does not constitute a conciliatory exploration of enslaved black suffering but instead a radical affirmation of incendiary protest. In an otherwise realist, if abstract-figurative, representation of individual black bodies in this first panel, therefore, the arms of Lawrence's subjects are truncated, as if to register his protest against white tendencies toward black dehumanization. Thus these Black men and women carry their burdens with squared abstract stumps that, crucially, resemble militant fists rather than real-life hands. Clearly, while such anatomical details offer a disturbing indictment of slavery as a source of mutilation and violation, as enslaved peoples were routinely denied both the labor, and even the ownership, of their bodies, Lawrence's image powerfully bear witness to black agency by transforming their mutilated hands into militant fists.

A haunting, hanging black body constitutes a radical tour de force in Lawrence's second panel (see plate 13). Such a terrifying spectacle of black suffering powerfully contrasts with Lawrence's accompanying caption, in which he quotes the white politician Henry Clay, a figure noted for his racist candor: "I am no friend of slavery, but I prefer the liberty of my own country to that of another people."[95] As a violated spectacle of black mutilation, this unidentified and iconic black body documents the insidious racism of Clay's self-preservationist, white-supremacist ideology. Equally, Lawrence's graphic exhibition of the anonymous suffering of an elongated, gender-ambiguous body reveals how a nonmilitant and self-interested yet seemingly antislavery position actually legitimized, if not outright authorized, acts of racist persecution. No less faceless than the laboring Black figures in panel 1, the stark nakedness of this unidentifiable black body distorted by torture is as shocking as the emaciated limbs of the anonymously laboring bodies. Hanging with arms upraised and legs closed together, this black body replicates Christ's position on the cross, embodying Nathaniel Turner's plea, "Was not Christ crucified." Drawing explicit parallels between black suffering and religious iconography in this work, Lawrence condemns the escalation of lynchings in the late nineteenth and early twentieth centuries. Blood streams down this black body in three diagonal streaks cut across the figure's lacerated back. Collapsing temporal boundaries, Lawrence's graphic portrayal bears witness to untold histories of enslaved and post-emancipation suffering in much the same way as the welts on Gordon's skin in the infamously captioned original photograph, *The Scourged Back*.

Remarkably, Tubman is conspicuously absent from Lawrence's first two panels. Instead, he provides a social and historical context within which to politicize and radicalize his iconic exemplar by narrating the otherwise hidden histories of enslaved women and men whose resistance not only existed in stark contrast to but acted as the inspiration for Tubman's monumental heroism. Thus Lawrence's aesthetic practice testifies to his determination to contextualize Tubman's acts of liberation by narrating the plight of anonymous enslaved women and men in order to restore lost histories. More powerfully still, he critiques the ability of any exemplary Black heroic figure to function as a representative of multifaceted black experiences during slavery. "She felt the first sting of slavery when as a young girl she was struck on the head with an iron bar by an enraged overseer."[96] So reads the caption accompanying Lawrence's fifth panel, in which he dramatizes Tubman's rites of passage. Risking aggrandizing Tubman's martyrdom rather than her agency, in this work he replicates Bradford's technique of withholding details regarding Tubman's militant protection of an enslaved runaway. Yet, in a stark manipulation of the picture plane, he accentuates the horror of her prostrate body by visually recalling the elongated figure of panel 2. Thus Tubman's victimized body lies graphically on view, while only the black trousers and pink fleshy hand of the white "overseer" appear. Here, Lawrence condemns white racist authority by including this barbarous figure only as an absent presence. A key concern of Lawrence's image is therefore Tubman's vulnerability, as she covers her face with one hand, while the other, reaching toward the overseer in a seeming plea for justice, resembles a tree limb with its elongated and distorted fingers. The branch-like contortions of her hand palpably resonate with the treelike body of panel 2 to dramatize a continuum of black agency, which encompasses not only sacrificial martyrdom but also physical protest. Exposing Tubman's frailty as a dispossessed and suffering body in these and other panels, Lawrence replaces myths of black female vulnerability with the spectacle of iconic invincibility. Thus, across this series, he maps her transformation into an empowered yet nonidealized embodiment of a multifaceted heroism.

The vertical wooden slats to the left of this panel function metonymically to dramatize Tubman's potential martyrdom, as they stand in a visual call-and-response relationship to the horizontal cabin boards of Lawrence's next work in this series, in which three sepia-colored, semiprostrate enslaved women appear in positions of desperate supplication (see figure 30). Hauntingly, their raised hands petition a beastlike figure carrying a whip, whose associations with a white demonic masculinity are unmistakable. Lawrence heightens the horror of his experimental representation of these faceless, abstract Black female figures by accentuating their unreadable expressions and contorted shadowy bodies silhouetted against a bare cabin wall. The anonymity of their histories provides an additional context for Tubman's long legacy of resistance, which was inspired by genealogies of black female suffering. As the caption reads, "Harriet heard the shrieks and cries of women who were being flogged in the Negro quarter. She listened to their groaned-out prayer, 'Oh Lord, have mercy.'"[97]

In this, one of Lawrence's most experimental and hard-hitting works, he relies upon an abstract-figurative style to bear witness to the spectacle of black female torture. At the same time, he urges historical accuracy, relying on sepia-colored tones that operate as an authenticating device testifying to the legitimacy of his portrayal of enslaved experiences. Lawrence's experimental use of visual imagery not only documents the "shrieks and cries of women who were being flogged" but also critiques the possibility of graphic portrayals of white-on-black violence ever to do justice to unspeakable atrocities. Clearly, Lawrence recognized the risk that uncensored exhibitions of black mutilated bodies, as provided in panel 2, may lead only to emotional catharsis from viewers and no mandate for social and political change. As a result, across this series Lawrence requires his audiences not only to decipher the aesthetic dynamics of particular works but also to interpret across these panels as he cultivates thematic and symbolic relationships between individual "chapters." In this particular work, he projects distorted and seemingly magnified bodies onto the cabin wall in an ironic denunciation of white genteel traditions of eighteenth-century silhouette portraiture. In so doing, he exposes the subversive possibilities of a historical art form that portrayed white bodies as black. Thus he provides a displaced aesthetic framework within which to highlight racist practices of exclusion. Here, he condemns the fact that official portraits of Black families remained beyond the pale for white racist societies. Across this series, Lawrence's poetics of ellipsis and fragmentation not only rejects white tendencies toward black objectification but also denies audiences any real emotional closure.

Refusing to trade in the graphic display of black female suffering, Lawrence relies on experimental aesthetic techniques that obscure rather than explicate the interior lives of his Black female subjects. Intent upon inspiring audiences to acts of reimagining, he foregrounds lacunae by barely documenting their hidden histories. Thus Lawrence actively resists white mainstream slave narrative conventions, which effected sentimental conversion solely by engaging in didactic explication. His self-reflexive approach complicates Hills's view that "the narration also conforms to conventions of slave narratives in which the narrator generally downplays his or her personal feelings."[98] Just as enslaved narrators themselves experimented with language to reject white attempts to confine black testimonies, so too Lawrence adopts a visual aesthetics of rupture and distortion to betray his anger and virulent protest against twentieth-century racist injustices.

FIGURE 30. Jacob Lawrence, panel 6, *The Life of Harriet Tubman* series (1939–40). (Collection of Hampton University Museum, Hampton, Va.; © ARS, NY and DACS, London 2011)

In his seventh panel, Lawrence revises his earlier portrayal of Tubman's victimization as a child (see plate 14). In this later work, and in stark contrast to the earlier portrait, he unequivocally exalts in her exemplary musculature to suggest that she was reborn into a life of black female heroism. According to his vision, she resists not only her own suffering but also that of countless anonymous enslaved victims. Here, a physically empowered adult Tubman saws wood, while Lawrence's caption reads—"Harriet Tubman worked as water girl to field hands. She also worked at plowing, carting, and hauling logs."[99] An ironic slippage emerges, which condemns white racist discourse by emphasizing the contrast between Lawrence's literary description of Tubman as a "girl" and his aggrandized image depicting this historical figure as an adult woman remarkable for her exceptional musculature. Replacing her earlier tree-limb-like, mutilated hands with the enlarged hands of an exceptional laborer, he vindicates her exemplary skills. Moreover, the green stripes of Tubman's dress draw attention to the intricate patterns upon her head scarf to celebrate her individualism in the face of debilitating, conformist labor. Rather than contemplating the viewer, Lawrence's Tubman here is intent upon her task, retaining psychological complexity in the face of the widespread penchant for dramatizing a physical exhibition of her herculean prowess.

"Like a half-crazed sybilline creature, she began to haunt the slave masters, stealing down in the night to lead a stricken people to freedom."[100] So reads the caption to panel 17, a work that replaces earlier representations of Tubman as a biblical figure clothed in white and leading enslaved men and women to freedom (panels 12, 13, and 14) with an angular Tubman portrayed as a contorted and faceless Black female subject. Sepia-colored and holding both hands upraised as if in a gesture of fear, Lawrence's new representation of Tubman recalls his earlier abstract-figurative depictions of black female suffering as in panel 6 but with a key difference. No longer begging for mercy, as an abstract-figurative model of black womanhood, Tubman symbolizes apocalyptic vengeance in her association with a spectral vision of gothic "haunting." More generally, throughout his *Life of Harriet Tubman* series, Lawrence consistently emphasizes her representative status in order to aggrandize her importance as a heroic composite representing all black womanhood. Thus she occupies the foreground of this image, while the half-hidden faces of varyingly clothed Black women, all possessing contrasting physiognomies, stand directly behind her. The indistinguishable bodies of these enslaved women merge with Tubman's physical frame to insist on her significance as an exemplary, representative leader whose wealth of experiences speak to and for an array of anonymous enslaved Black women. As Hills argues, "Lawrence's style seems especially fitting for such depersonalized epics from African-American history."[101] For "depersonalized," read experimental and nonsentimental, as Lawrence's bold and abstract-figurative style provides symbolic and metaphorically laden representations of black female heroism in order to encourage an analytical and yet an emotive engagement by his viewers.

Lawrence's final panel of this series renders his historical, political, and aesthetic engagement with diverse forms of black female memorialization yet more explicit. As the caption explains, "When she died, a large mass meeting was held in her honor. And on the outside of the county courthouse, a memorial tablet of bronze was erected."[102] Yet the accompanying image depicts only three barren trees in an otherwise desolate landscape populated solely by barely etched stars and a dark blue night sky. Thus he conveys not only the difficulties but also the failures of any "tablet of bronze" to represent barely fathomable black female histories. The symbolic call-and-response relationships he establishes between panels in this series is particularly telling here. These three trees symbolically resonate with the three bloodied wounds that scar the anonymous black body dramatized in the second panel in order to indict a continuity of conflict in ongoing cycles of oppression. Determined to expose the dangers of white historical, political, and cultural misrememberings of black history, Lawrence includes various symbolic landscapes to testify to Tubman's hidden histories in this series. In this abstract work, stripped of graphic representations of physical suffering, he exalts in the imaginative possibilities of black female psychological, metaphorical, and historical protest legacies.

Painted at the end of World War II, William H. Johnson's portrait *Harriet Tubman* (see plate 15) appears in his *Freedom-Fighters* series (1945), a multifaceted sequence of paintings that also includes *Nat Turner*, as he experiments with multifaceted constructions of black male and female heroism. Borrowing heavily from Darby's militant woodcut, Johnson's portrait *Harriet Tubman* depicts this armed heroic figure in an almost identical pose and wearing similar clothing. At the same time, however, he riffs off symbolic details by transforming her satchel buckle into a cross in order to accentuate her martyrdom, a fascination no less at work in the symbolism of his painting of Nathaniel Turner. Equally, he experiments in dramatic ways with a surreal use of color symbolism. Whereas bloodred brushstrokes smear an apocalyptic sky in his portrait of Turner as if to reinforce the militant leader's endorsement of violence, Johnson's Harriet Tubman appears before an oppressive gray-blue sky distinguished by two setting suns and a luminous star. For Johnson, such a dual horizon may reflect his metaphorical reimagining of the divergent possibilities for black male and female heroism. Johnson may also have intended to juxtapose black male and female heroism during the American Civil War with black valor in World War II. Clearly, he dramatizes a continuum of diverse forms of black militancy, ranging from the spectacle of Turner's hanging body to the armed resistance of Tubman's erect figure. Whereas in his painting of Nathaniel Turner he evokes a national backdrop by including an homage to Arlington National Cemetery, here he paints Tubman's striped skirt red and white and her overcoat a vivid dark blue, directly resonating with the U.S. flag as he works to reclaim black female heroism as a site of national patriotism.

Startlingly, Johnson defies realist conventions to include not one but two Tubmans in this work, as he powerfully juxtaposes his portrayal of a militant Civil War Tubman with the head-and-shoulders close-up of a much older Tubman. Compellingly coming to grips with her multifaceted identities, Johnson's portrayal of an elder Tubman highlights historical veracity by encouraging the view that this portrait may well have been inspired by her many photographs. It is no stretch of the imagination to suggest that Johnson may also have been inspired by photographs of Sojourner Truth in his re-creation of Tubman's physiognomy, as he sought to endorse a continuum of black female radicalism. Such a decision ran the risk, however, of minimizing rather than aggrandizing diverse feats of black female heroism by conflating two very different historical icons. Regardless of these ambivalences, however, William Johnson's symbolic strategies testify to aesthetic, political, and social conflicts no less relevant to Jacob Lawrence's extrapolation of Harriet Tubman as a touchstone within a diverse continuum of black female heroisms.

CENSORSHIP, EXPERIMENTATION, AND SYMBOLISM IN JACOB LAWRENCE'S *HARRIET AND THE PROMISED LAND* (1968)

"Isn't it sad that the oppressed often find themselves grotesque and ugly and find the oppressor refined and beautiful?" So Jacob Lawrence replied to a librarian who had challenged his seemingly "grotesque" portrayal of Harriet Tubman in *Harriet and the Promised Land,* his picture book for children published decades later in 1968. In forceful ways, Lawrence's response not only contests racially circumscribed aesthetic standards but also critiques the insidious effects of internalized racism. In one bold sweep, he undermines the nefarious assumptions generated by ignorance regarding the untold realities of black female histories. As Lawrence insisted to the librarian, "If you had walked in the fields, stopping for short periods to be replenished by underground stations; if you couldn't feel secure until you reached the Canadian border, you, too, madam, would look grotesque and ugly."[103] The repeated refrain "if you" asks the librarian not only to empathize with but to reimagine the horrific realities that confronted Tubman in her exceptional acts of black liberation. As this challenge to his work reveals, Lawrence faced the same battles encountered by John Biggers in his determination to dramatize the lives of Sojourner Truth and Harriet Tubman for the YWCA.

Before examining this work, it is important to note that Lawrence's *Harriet and the Promise Land* is just one of a great number of twentieth- and twenty-first-century picture books, novels, and poetical works commemorating Tubman's heroism for children and young adults. As Julia Mickenberg argues, "Using the cloak of history, personalized as biography, writers on the left taught children African American history in a way that implicitly challenged post-war racial hierarchies, communicated radical ideas about citizenship, and made a direct connection between past struggles against slavery and present struggles for civil rights."[104] Yet these works are important not only because of their forceful political protest but also because they celebrate diverse forms of aesthetic experimentation. As Romare Bearden and Harry Henderson argue, Lawrence struggled with profound difficulties in his determination to publish Harriet Tubman's history for children. "Lawrence's initial portrayal was too grim for some people," they explain, as "the publisher felt that in a book for children blood should not be depicted and Harriet Tubman should not be shown carrying a gun."[105] No less afflicted by censorship issues than Alewitz in his murals produced decades later, Lawrence painted radical, no-holds-barred works testifying to multiple, militant Tubmans. Even though none of these incendiary images made it into his picture book, they satisfied his desire for an "uncensored version for himself."[106] A particularly stark example is *Forward,* a work he painted in 1967 as a haunting memorial to Tubman's "liberty or death" philosophy (see plate 12). Betraying Lawrence's radical gender politics, this work preempts Alewitz's murals by dramatizing Tubman as an armed, exemplary freedom fighter. In this work, she not only protectively leads Black men, women, and children into freedom but also physically pushes a half-naked Black man "forward." At the same time, this unknown man fearfully covers his face with his hand as if to shore up Lawrence's determination to contrast a weakened spectacle of black masculinity with an idealized vision of black female heroism. Clearly speaking to the civil rights era, the title of this painting, *Forward,* works in conjunction with his representation of Harriet Tubman's leadership to provide a rallying cry to grassroots activism in the pursuit of black equal rights.

As *Harriet and the Promised Land* demonstrates, by 1968 Lawrence's experimental search for a new aesthetic language had substantially evolved, particularly in his development of a newly minimalist and symbolic use of textual and visual languages. Comparing his picture book to his *Life of Harriet Tubman* series painted decades earlier, he explains, "I have developed a degree of selectivity which I did not have then. I think it's just a more subtle thing. And I think technically it's a better series."[107] Yet, in contrast to his earlier narrative series, Lawrence's picture book has suffered from widespread critical neglect. As Audrey Thompson, one of the few scholars to examine this work, argues, "Words in *Harriet and the Promised Land* play an integral role in the artistic construction of meaning." However, she criticizes the fact that "the resulting story is perhaps a little *too* abstract," as she remains convinced that the work "suffers somewhat from its concessions to what is deemed appropriate for children."[108] Yet, irrespective of the omission of his incendiary "out-takes," Lawrence's *Harriet and the Promised Land* remains a forceful, haunting work. Fearlessly confronting difficult issues regarding black female heroism, slavery, and resistance, Lawrence created this work not only to heighten political consciousness but also to develop an aesthetic awareness among his child audiences.

Lawrence prefaces his picture book, dedicated "to the courageous women of America," by radically stating, "The United States is a great country" not in spite of but precisely because of its heroic dissidents. "It is a great country because of people like John Brown, Frederick Douglass, Abraham Lincoln, Sojourner Truth, and Harriet Tubman," he explains. Situating Tubman within a black and white, male and female heroic continuum of resistance, Lawrence contests the boundaries not only of white American nationalism and patriotism but also of the tendency among African American writers and artists to focus exclusively upon typically masculinized models of heroism. As further evidence of his similarities with John Biggers's and Charles White's memorializations of black female resistance, his dramatic explorations of Tubman were inspired by acts of storytelling within his own childhood experiences. "I recall learning of Harriet Tubman from my mother," he remembers.[109]

Lawrence's early works in *Harriet and the Promised Land* dramatize differing forms of grueling labor in order to convey the horrifying realities of slavery. At the same time, his use of a historical lens provides a displaced forum within which he succeeds not only in documenting the struggles of his own family as they endured a contemporary "economic slavery" but also in exposing the militant foundation of a long struggle for civil rights. Thus, one of the first double-page spreads in this work contrasts a vigorously strong Tubman digging earth in a rural southern context with the barely distinguishable forms of enslaved men and women as they labor in the background. As they are engaged in this grueling labor, the other half of the spread offers intimate access to the diminutive and hunched-over body of Tubman as she washes hardwood floors within a stark domestic interior. Such a seemingly timeless and unperiodized image resists historical specificity to indict the ongoing suffering of Black women as they perform debilitating labor across the nineteenth, twentieth, and twenty-first centuries. Lawrence's accompanying lyrical text confirms the "integral role" played by literary language as an interpretative guide to the child reader: "Harriet, grow bigger. / Harriet, grow stronger. / Harriet, work harder. / Harriet, work longer."[110] Clearly, his poetic text works against exclusive representations of solitary heroism to reimagine Tubman's exceptionalism within the context of collective experiences within the black community. Thus he complicates his otherwise uncensored display of black female bodies as sites of trauma by reassuring his young audiences of Tubman's future role as a heroic icon destined to perform exceptional feats of bravery. As Lawrence's artful juxtapositions in this work reveal, he counters potentially dehumanizing exposés of black female subjugation by emphasizing transgressive relationships between text and image.

Another early image in Lawrence's picture book dramatizes an enslaved Tubman tilling a burnished earth, not to belittle but to aggrandize the labor of faceless and anonymous enslaved women and men similarly carrying burdens and yet relegated to the distance. Moreover, his decision to decorate Tubman's apron with red and blue flowers and to include a multicolored cricket and small pig—the former distinctive for its expressive eyes, the latter for it curious snout—mitigate against the severity of her struggles by endorsing hope as symbolized through black female agency. According to Lawrence's reimagining, Tubman resisted forces of dehumanization not only through her labor but also in her artistry, as she has decorated her apron in order to contest its symbolism as a signifier of her physical suffering. According to this image, Tubman worked purposefully to grow "bigger" and "stronger" as she fought the conditions of her enslavement to journey toward the "Promised Land." Lawrence includes a jagged piece of wood at her feet, possibly to symbolize the apocryphal possibilities of black female heroism. This piece of wood assumes the silhouetted shape of a rifle as if to prophesy her later militancy, a subject he fully explored in paintings such as *Forward* but excluded from this text. Signifying on the symbolic possibilities of everyday objects, Lawrence circumvents taboo and censorship difficulties. Here, he communicates his ambiguous narratives by relying on the detailed attentiveness of child audiences, whom he knew were habitually intent upon transgressing, if not entirely abandoning, linear and surface narratives as they gave free reign to their imagination.

Yet, immediately countering any such problematic associations of black female identity with radical militancy, in the companion painting of this double-page spread, Lawrence represents an almost faceless Tubman kneeling on a vertical expanse of wooden boards. Here, the linear rigidity of his backdrop suggests both captivity and imprisonment via a grid-like intensity, while the raised knuckles of her enlarged brown hands clutch a white rag, the same color as her clothing, as if to suggest she has no less become a tool of her own labor. Yet in a seeming condemnation of the dystopian and "grotesque" hardships of oppressive labor, he replaces the blue horizon of the other panel with a small rectangular window to provide a symbolic engagement with the difficulties besetting black female heroism. Regardless of obstacles, Lawrence ultimately aggrandizes Tubman's "self-made woman" status by evoking parallels with Sojourner Truth's history of labor and activism. For Lawrence, both Black female icons succeed in carving out a space beyond the dehumanizing limits of their surroundings.

A year following the publication of Lawrence's *Harriet and the Promised Land,* the African American artist and activist Emory Douglas includes a powerful homage to Harriet Tubman in a cartoon that appeared in the *Black Panther* newspaper on September 13, 1969. Without mentioning Tubman by name, he dramatizes a militant Black female figure wearing a shawl while holding a machine gun, thereby signifying very much within the tradition of representations of Tubman as popularized by J. C. Darby. In a radical reversal, however, according to Douglas's visualization, she overshadows the militancy of the Black man standing beside her as, hunched over her weaponry, her facial expression remains impenetrable proof of her authoritative status. Choosing to accentuate both subterfuge and disguise in his construction of this Tubman-like figure, Douglas insists on the urgent necessity of historical models as catalysts to contemporary radicalism, especially made clear by the fact that her pins read one of the lessons of the hour, "Seize the Time."[111] Douglas's decision to omit Tubman's name here minimizes iconic narratives of black female heroic exceptionalism in favor of re-creating archetypal role models and reusable icons. For Douglas, Tubman's memory cuts across historical and social barriers to inspire Black male and female audiences to activism by raising their awareness of their own contexts of political ferment and struggle during a long civil rights era.

"Black women have a history of the use and sharing of power, from the Amazon legions of Dahomey through the Ashanti warrior queen Yaa Asantewaa and the freedom fighter Harriet Tubman, to the economically powerful market-women guilds of present West Africa," Audre Lorde writes. Taking a different approach than Jacob Lawrence, John Biggers, Charles White, and even Elizabeth Catlett, Lorde situates Harriet Tubman in relation to African female rather than white or African American male forms of resistance. Constructing a competing model for black female heroism, Lorde foregrounds her preference not for an isolationist individualism but for acts of resistance based on "the sharing of power." "Do we reenact these crucifixions upon each other, the avoidance, the cruelty, the judgments, because we have not been allowed Black goddesses, Black heroines?" Lorde asks. Across her writings she provides a candid exposure of the ways in which a denial of black female heroism has typically resulted in self-hatred, psychological splitting, and an annihilation of any politicized form of "sisterhood" in a twentieth-century context. Thus, Lorde's perceptive analysis returns us to Lawrence's lament "Isn't it sad that the oppressed often find themselves grotesque and ugly and find the oppressor refined and beautiful?" as she categorically states that "one of the functions of hatred is certainly to mask and distort the beauty which is power in ourselves."[112]

For African American writers and essayists ranging from Jacob Lawrence to Audre Lorde and from William Johnson to Emory Douglas, the memory of Harriet Tubman's life and activism signifies as a powerful defense against the apathy and self-hatred generated among Black men, women, and children by the ongoing effects of internalized racism. "I'm glad Harriet Tubman did not know she had no 'role model' and lead [sic] the slaves to freedom,"[113] writes the poet Nikki Giovanni, exalting in Harriet Tubman's memory as a symbol of empowerment and resistance regardless of annihilating forces. Ultimately, Lawrence's multifaceted representations of a radical and militant Tubman for both child and adult audiences resonate with, at the same time that they depart from, adaptations by writers such as Margaret Walker in her groundbreaking feminist celebrations of a no-holds-barred heroism. In her poem "Harriet Tubman," written in 1944, Walker reimagines this historical figure as a literary protagonist who not only could but actually did commit murder: "I killed that overseer."[114]

"Harriet Tubman was brave and strong and she was black like me. I think it was the first time I thought of wanting to be called Harriet—I wanted to *be* Harriet." So speaks Margaret, the central protagonist of the Caribbean writer Marlene Nourbese Philip's award-winning novel, *Harriet's Daughter*, published in 1988 and written for a young adult audience. Philip's powerful text dramatizes the lives of two Black child protagonists, Margaret and Zulma, as they navigate the difficulties of a first- and second-generation Caribbean Canadian context. According to Philip, Harriet Tubman's memory lies at the heart of their struggles for historically and politically empowered identities. Margaret protests against her father's repeated insistence that she should be returned to the Caribbean for some "Good West Indian discipline" by embarking on a search for agency. Her strategies of subversive resistance remain inextricable from her imaginative engagement with Tubman's history. She devises the "Underground Railroad Game" to re-create and reimagine Harriet Tubman's epic feats of heroism.[115] In forceful ways, acts of self-reflexive play and interactive performance operate as survival mechanisms by which Margaret and Zulma fight to transcend their oppressive contexts in a contemporary era.

The novel opens by plunging the reader into the immediacy of a reimagined history via one of Margaret's powerful reenactments of Tubman's escape attempts. Here, Philip highlights the educational and political use of play and the imagination as her young adult protagonists re-create and adapt Tubman's life as a childhood game in order to provide a displaced forum for their search for an autonomous selfhood. According to Samuel Hopkins Adams, writing in the early twentieth century, such a childhood pastime has historical precedent. "While other youngsters of the late 1870's played Scouts and Indians, our standard make-believe was Slaves and Overseers, with Harriet as heroine," he explains, adding, "Competition for the star part was rancorous."[116] Irrespective of whether it was "Slaves and Overseers" as created by white American children in the late nineteenth century or the "Underground Railroad Game" as devised by African Caribbean young adults toward the end of the twentieth century, imaginative play and performative reenactment remain integral to acts and arts of memorializing Harriet Tubman's political and historical legacies across diverse generations and transnational contexts. Here, Philip transgresses differences of race, nationality, identity, and familial history to universalize Tubman's memory as a source of imaginative empowerment in a novel she dedicates to "all of Harriet's children."

A rich and provocative work, Philip's *Harriet's Daughter* dramatizes an archetypal rites-of-passage story. At the same time, she modifies this generic model by borrowing from moments within African American history to map her protagonists' emergence from childhood tendencies toward assimilation to teenage nonconformity. For Margaret, the Underground Railroad Game provides not only an outlet for her frustration regarding her confined sense of self but also a way of liberating herself from an internalized sense of inferiority. Clearly, her relationship with Zulma, a recently arrived migrant from Tobago, proves crucial to her own emotional and psychological development. While others dismiss Zulma as "a dumb island kid," Margaret not only is open to her diverse forms of knowledge but also recognizes the nefarious problems caused by national barriers. Many key themes of this novel relate to psychological and emotional no less than historical and physical conditions of exile and displacement. These major issues include the difficulties of communication between adults and children, as Zulma's sense of grief is misinterpreted by adults who, intentionally or not, belittle childhood suffering by referring to her sorrow as simply "homesickness," a condition that "always passed." Recognizing the failures of language, Margaret admits, "There was no word I knew of that described what Zulma felt, except plain old loss." As a result of her heightened empathy and awareness, Margaret assumes Tubman's role of psychological as well as physical liberator when she tells Zulma, "I promise you, by the end of the year you will be back in Tobago," a resolution she ultimately keeps. Thus her actions testify not only to her politicized consciousness but also to the enduring influence of Tubman as a historical figure playing a key role in contemporary diasporic struggles.[117]

Engaging directly with nineteenth-century slave narrative conventions, Margaret's struggle for a new identity initially remains bound up with her determination to find a new name. At the height of her struggles against the confinements of family life and her powerlessness to help Zulma, Margaret attempts to gain control over her life through a politicized act of naming. She explains that she "first started thinking of changing my name, from boring old Margaret, to Harriet" after a white Jewish woman, Mrs. Harriet Blewchamp, for whom her mother had worked, had been kind to her. "I want a name that means something," she explains. She is drawn to the name Harriet for its symbolism: "Mrs Blewchamp had really lived, she was in the war, in a concentration camp, and had escaped and she wanted *me* to have her name." Initially, therefore, "Harriet" signifies upon white female heroism by evoking a fictional Jewish character who had liberated herself from twentieth-century Nazi persecution. Ultimately, however, Margaret's search for a new name leads her to the discovery of Harriet Tubman. Almost immediately, Margaret's investigation into Tubman's legacy becomes a part of the symbolic landscape of her unconscious by entering her dreams: "I could see Harriet Tubman's dress—her skirt—it had her face on it. . . . I stood against a wall facing a firing squad except that there weren't any soldiers: just my parents. . . . I screamed at them: 'My name is not Margaret, it's . . .' but each time I tried to say my name nothing came out."[118] Tubman's memory functions as an emotional catalyst to self-realization in Philip's text not only by testifying to the struggles of black female identity politics but also by inspiring Margaret's search for a new sense of self as unfettered by familial and social influences. Tubman's historical legacy encourages Margaret to confront nihilism and nonbeing as a liberating portal through which to strip away externally imposed identities. In this regard, the fact that Margaret says "nothing" can be interpreted as a positive rather than negative start to her existential quest for a new sense of selfhood. For Margaret, Tubman's reusable memory offers a way of articulating agency irrespective of anxieties of family influence.

Margaret's construction of the Underground Railroad Game in *Harriet's Daughter* provides a displaced and imaginative forum within which to confront the problems in her own life. For Margaret, Tubman is a simultaneously knowable and unknowable figure engaged in performative acts of disguise for survival. Significantly, Margaret compounds similarities between Tubman and her own mother by using her mother's clothing to assume the identity of the historical icon. As Margaret explains, "It was when I was tying my head one day in my room that I got my chance to talk to her about calling me Harriet."[119] According to Philip, Tubman's memory operates as a touchstone for cross-generational bonding between mother and daughter via a shared realization regarding their collective sense of disempowerment. Margaret's mother reassures her daughter by confessing her equal dislike of her own name, which she associates with duty, obligation, and a lack of free will. As a result, her mother capitulates to her daughter's choice of a new name, a decision that establishes their newfound empathy and identification. As Margaret tells her mother, "I'll be Harriet, and you will be—what? I know, Hatshepsut, like Queen Hatshepsut of Egypt—she was a pharaoh. You're big and black and beautiful, just like her."[120] Thus Tubman's history operates as a lens through which Margaret not only gains insight into her mother's struggles but also realizes her significance as a "black and beautiful" role model who makes her own transformation to a new sense of a multifaceted self-hood possible.

While the Underground Railroad Game serves a significant function in reconciling otherwise fraught mother-daughter relationships, tensions soon emerge in its repeated performances. Imaginative play betrays the extent to which historically rooted injustices and psychological tensions can survive into the contemporary era. "I heard Maria Rao, a slave, call another kid . . . a dog," Margaret admits. As a punishment for the disruptions the game causes by dividing children across racial and national categories, her father orders her to Barbados. Her immediate response is to stage her first major act of rebellion, as she explains her refusal to go by evoking a sense of place ("this is my home") and laying claim to her newfound racial identity: "I'm black, black, black!"[121] Margaret's acts and arts of self-liberation are made possible only by her active engagement with the problematic legacies of a history of slavery in general and of the struggles of Harriet Tubman in particular.

As a powerful historical precedent, Tubman's memory inspires Margaret's realization that the only way to return Zulma to her home is to help her become a runaway. Yet she is dissuaded from such a decision by bearing witness to contemporary acts of black female heroism as her friend "Mrs B" shares her own contemporary slave narrative of fleeing oppression in the U.S. South to effect her own freedom in the Canadian north. Margaret calls "Mrs B" is a "a modern-day Harriet Tubman," to which the latter replies, "Well I may be a Harriet, but there's nothing about you that reminds me of a slave." Yet the nuanced understanding of history by which Margaret engages imaginatively with Tubman's legacy refutes such a categorical demarcation between slavery and freedom: "I feel so helpless, not having any rights or power. Slaves must have felt something like that, don't you think?"[122] Thus, Philip draws powerful analogies in this radical passage between the confining limitations of young adulthood in a contemporary era and the horrors of a history of slavery. She also dramatizes the difficulties facing Margaret's mother's generation, who no less experience psychological, emotional, and physical confinement in the early twentieth century. At the same time, she is careful not to lose sight of the distinction between metaphorical slavery and chattel slavery.

As a result of her ultimate success in assisting Zulma to return home, which she effects by galvanizing the protest power of a radicalized sisterhood and by recruiting "Mrs B" and her mother to her cause, Margaret resolves her own identity conflicts and succeeds in no longer conflating the physical, legal, and psychological realities of slavery with its social and cultural legacies. She becomes independent not only of paternal influence but also of Tubman's memory. As she admits regarding her final choice of naming, "I wasn't so sure any more if I wanted to change it to Harriet. I mean I had done something as Margaret, hadn't I?"[123] For Philip, Tubman's memory is significant only in so far as it acts as a springboard to the formation of a new black female sense of self via creative play, active engagement, and artful reimagining. While Sernett argues, "If we must judge by the plethora of books about Tubman in the field of juvenile literature . . . Harriet Tubman is the all-comprehending black hero of our time," Philip's *Harriet's Daughter* tells a more complex story regarding reusable black female histories and their role in black female rites of passage.[124] Philip refracts Tubman's legacy as an ambiguous, fragmentary, and elusive figure through her child protagonist's coming to consciousness of radical self-definition. Anything but an "all-comprehending black hero," Philip's Tubman signifies as a catalyst to ongoing struggles for psychological and emotional self-realization in a contemporary era.

"FOLK LIVE IN MA BONES": HARRIET TUBMAN, THE MIDDLE PASSAGE, AND MEMORIALIZATION

"*I would have freed thousands mo, / If dey had known dey were slaves.*" So reads the seemingly historically accurate quotation by an imaginary Harriet Tubman that opens "faithless," a poem in Quraysh Ali Lansana's collection *They Shall Run: Harriet Tubman Poems,* published in 2004. As an experimental skein of anonymous voices, Lansana's work dramatizes Tubman's multiple heroic personae. In no way rooted in any historically verifiable testimony as recorded by Tubman, Lansana's imaginary quotation nonetheless comes to grips with tensions regarding black emotional and psychological experiences during slavery. Lansana's collection focuses upon Tubman's symbolic importance as a historical and spiritual repository for communal memory. As he writes in "burdens," "folk live in ma bones."[125] Lansana's collection interweaves poems documenting Tubman's heroism with a series of "dreamprints" in order to evoke the transatlantic horrors of the Middle Passage. Favoring a stripped-down and minimalist poetic style, he foregrounds lacunae and fragmentation to transgress the boundaries of language and engage with the unspeakable traumas experienced by enslaved Africans incarcerated on slave ships. Cryptic, nonlinear, and refusing to tell, these emotionally charged fragments testify to lost histories by dramatizing split-apart and hidden lives. Thus Lansana's poetic technique in this collection relies on an improvised pattern of quilted voices. Creating thought-provoking and emotionally charged vignettes, he interweaves archetypal and anonymous feats of heroism to dramatize a continuum of diverse experiences during slavery. For Lansana, Tubman signifies as a metaphorical and imaginative locus for black female resistance as he provides an inspirational reimagining of her ancestral origins.

"Does the flesh-and-blood Harriet Tubman measure up to the heavily romanticized heroine whose symbolic power many and varied constituencies have invoked in their search for a usable past?" Sernett asks in his expert study.[126] Yet this question regarding Tubman's success or failure in "measuring up" to her own mythology remains less significant than the imaginative and intellectual need for scholars to continue to search for ways in which to understand her historical representations as inextricably intertwined with her signifying status as a mythological symbol. As Larson argues, "The legend of Harriet Tubman as a heroic figure was constructed and established even during her own lifetime."[127] As a brief exploration of Tubman's multiple incarnations in diverse visual and textual materials reveals, the most important architect and artful originator of competing mythologies of black female heroism was Harriet Tubman herself. "These stories have come down to us largely because Tubman was 'in the right place at the right time' to become a black female hero," Jean Humez observes of Tubman's extensive oral archive.[128] However, any attempt to associate black female heroism with expediency is difficult to substantiate in light of Tubman's exceptional attributes, which have merited her recovery regardless of oppressive social, political, or historical contexts. Anything but a form of historical opportunism, Tubman's memory endures as a site not only for her own iconic feats of exceptional heroism but also as the locus for reimagining the anonymous lives and deaths of those born into slavery for whom no written, visual, or archaeological evidence remains. The performances of Harriet Tubman, no believer herself in the white literary imagination as any accurate way of communicating "de *real ting*," testify to her belief in the Black woman's right to her mythology and symbolism on the grounds that she was the only authoritative interpreter of her own history. For white audiences who felt they had any more profound knowledge regarding mythopoetic renderings of a multiplicity of black female experiences during slavery, Harriet Tubman powerfully testifies to her authority by declaring, "I know what a dreadful condition slavery is."[129]

CONCLUSION "PORTALS, CONTAINERS,

TIME CAPSULES, AND BRIDGES" ACTS

AND ARTS OF BLACK HEROISM IN TEXTUAL

AND VISUAL ARCHIVES

Appearing in 2002, Debra Priestly's mixed-media series *Strange Fruit* dramatizes black male and female strategies of psychological, physical, aesthetic, spiritual, and political resistance. As a thought-provoking series that places the onus upon the viewer to interpret from the fragments, Priestly's *Strange Fruit* series is composed of rows of canning jars into each of which she inserts haunting iconography. Following extensive research into the textual and visual archives of North American and transatlantic slavery, she generates emotional and aesthetic force by selecting fine-art portraits, plantation inventories, slave narrative frontispieces, photographs, propaganda broadsides, and abolitionist diagrams as multifaceted backdrops to these works. Adopting a self-reflexive and experimental approach, she includes visual and textual representations of all the historical figures examined in this book. More powerfully still, she juxtaposes diverse representations of iconic and anonymous Black men, women, and children with pseudoscientific illustrations of iron shackles, neck yokes, whips, and other implements of bodily torture. Refusing to shy away from a graphic engagement with disturbingly matter-of-fact reproductions of the shocking paraphernalia of the trade, Priestly's *Strange Fruit* series bears witness to black male and female bodies as sites and sights not only of trauma but also of empowerment.

As a series originally created for inclusion in an exhibition titled "Slave Routes: The Long Memory" at Kenkeleba House, New York, Priestly's *Strange Fruit* series self-reflexively interrogates any illusory belief in a singular, redemptive, and cathartic journey from slavery to freedom. "I chose images that would tell a complex narrative about the transatlantic slave trade," she explains. "Collectively, the images tell a narrative and in some cases, where images are layered there are smaller narratives within the whole," Priestly emphasizes. Coming to grips with thematic and formal ambiguities across this series, she cultivates a multiplicity of textual and visual possibilities. Relying upon narrative layering and symbolic juxtapositions, an array of ambiguous vignettes expose the failures of any single artwork or artifact to dramatize elided Black subjectivities and histories. A key concern of Priestly's series, therefore, is to do justice to her politics and poetics of selectivity. "It is haunting how many images exist," she admits, explaining, "I was never at a loss for images so I had to edit." Adopting a self-appointed role not only as an editor but also as an artist, she engages in recycling diverse textual and visual fragments, which she reappropriates from dominant white archives. Repeatedly, Priestly juxtaposes interrelated yet frequently undocumented and even unimagined "routes" of black memorialization, representation, and cross-generational exchange. "'Strange Fruit' explores fragments of historical events in American History," she summarizes.[1]

More particularly, Priestly reproduces the Cuban painter Enrique Caravia's portrait of Toussaint Louverture in the top left-hand corner of *Strange Fruit 2* (see plate 16), an especially provocative and stimulating work in this series. Selecting this African Caribbean icon as a point of origin for her diverse representations of black male and female heroism, Priestly foregrounds Louverture's frequently elided "founding father" status within black diasporic histories of resistance. Fascinatingly, however, she problematizes Caravia's envisioning of Louverture's exceptional status by positioning this image beside an "Address of John Brown" and above Wedgwood's "Am I Not a Man and A Brother?" icon. Resituated within a context of both radical and capitulatory strategies of white abolitionism, therefore, Priestly's Louverture resignifies not only as an archetypal model of black masculinity but also as a multifaceted figure whose legendary feats influenced the actions of subsequent Black, as well as white, freedom fighters. At the opposite end of the same row, Priestly inserts an anonymously produced nineteenth-century caricatured drawing purporting to represent Nathaniel Turner and his followers next to a facsimile reproduction of the title page of Turner and Thomas Gray's *Confessions of Nat Turner*. Signaling her rejection of the power of either text or image to encapsulate this controversial figure's slippery legacies, Priestly encourages her audiences not only to read but to visualize against the grain. Thus she urges her viewers to come to grips with Turner's revolution by reproducing Turner and Gray's title page above and across from problematic spectacles of black martyrdom. These include not only her reproduction of the daguerreotype showing the self-emancipated fugitive turned soldier, Gordon's scarred back, but also a historical drawing depicting an unknown enslaved subject as horrifically confined by a metal head brace and neck restraints. At war against the monolithic racism of white power, Priestly bears witness to the fact that black diasporic acts and arts of heroism exist in an ideologically, morally, and existentially charged no-man's-land vis-à-vis mainstream memorializations.

Priestly's decision to represent Turner via both textual and pictorial bodies of evidence, deliberately foregrounding experimental relationships between text and image as well as between known and unknown forms of black heroism, works against the legitimacy of any single representation over and above any other. "Each work references moments in time, a channel, a course, a means of access, a road, a route, or an opening," Priestly argues. Opting for a visual and textual poetics of interrelation and integration, she creates multiple narratives according to which "the jars become portals, containers, time capsules and bridges."[2] Constantly circulating and far from fixed, Priestly's re-appropriation of an eclectic array of textual and visual materials compellingly results in the proliferation of Black male and female heroic figures as slippery icons, ambiguous myths, and contestable symbols. Across *Strange Fruit 2*, therefore, Priestly's symbolic compositions consist of interrelated and layered visual and textual testimonies. As she explains, these vignettes are "to be read like the words on a page." "The precise grid the jars form suggests a strong steady rhythm that moves laterally from edge to edge," she declares.[3] Yet while Priestly seemingly prefers to present her hard-hitting material within uniform compositions, she nonetheless creates a powerful and jarring disjuncture between a "strong steady rhythm" on the one hand and the messy and horrifying realities of the traumatic content of her imagery on the other. Operating in a similar vein to Jacob Lawrence's juxtaposition of individual panels in his various narrative series produced decades previously, these jars function not only as mainstream and marginal "chapters" but also as installments testifying to the elided complexities of African, African American, and African Caribbean histories no less than heroisms.

Recognizing the difficulties and distortions presented by any potentially unequivocal endorsement of black male resistance in particular, in *Strange Fruit 2* Priestly relies on a series of vignettes to contest dominant models of black male heroism. Explicitly complicating her otherwise all-male pantheon, she includes an "Am I Not a Woman and a Sister?" engraving next to her reproduction of Wedgwood's "Am I Not a Man and a Brother?" medallion. Furthermore, she inserts photographic reproductions of Sojourner Truth and Harriet Tubman, one positioned below the other, not only to suggest black female solidarity but also to argue for the importance of a genealogical framework within which to reconstruct diverse feats of black female heroism. Yet more revealingly, Priestly's historical photograph of Truth represents one of the rare images in which she is dressed in patterned clothing.

She purposely selected this image in which Truth's clothing is "patterned after the American flag" in order to introduce key debates surrounding black female representation, nationalism, and identity construction. Thus she offers a powerful point of contrast to the plain clothes of the anonymous Black female figure who appears in the photograph to the left of Truth's portrait. Perhaps more in keeping with typical portraits of victimized black womanhood, this unknown Black woman undertakes strenuous and debilitating domestic labor. Troubling these multifaceted representations of black female heroism yet further, Priestly inserts a scarcely legible document to the right of Truth that consists of a "bill of sale listing human slaves." In forceful ways, this historical artifact refuses to bear witness to an uplifting testament to black female heroism by exposing the dehumanizing violations enacted by slavery's "chattel records."

Refusing to shy away from black female bodies as sites of militancy as well as martyrdom, Priestly inserts an empowering and inspirational historical portrait of Tubman in this work by reproducing H. B. Lindsley's famous photograph of this historical figure. More groundbreakingly still, she includes a copy of an early drawing of Sengbe Pieh, the "congolese chief" to the left of this photograph. In stark contrast, therefore, while she situates Truth within a context of black female labor and an itemized list of men and women sold into slavery, Priestly overtly positions Tubman within a black heroic male freedom-fighting tradition. Destabilizing monolithic constructions and transgressing dominant gender categorizations, she exposes the illusory foundations of artificial polarizations of black male and black female heroisms across this work. Furthermore, Priestly memorializes Sengbe Pieh within a context not of African but of African American resistance: she positions this portrait next to an illustration showing Crispus Attucks's martyrdom as the first man to fall during the American Revolutionary War. Appealing to white national sympathies, she ultimately minimizes Pieh's transatlantic context of black resistance instead to recuperate this Sierra Leonean–born leader within an explicitly African American heroic paradigm. Finally, a photograph of Frederick Douglass as an elder statesman appears on the bottom row of *Strange Fruit 2* and as a backdrop to an illustration from his final autobiography, *Life and Times,* in which he is shown as a young man engaged in armed combat with a white violent mob. Challenging one-dimensional representations of Douglass as the officially sanctioned and conciliatory elder statesman, Priestly returns viewers to Louverture's and Turner's militancy by reinforcing rather than refuting multifaceted relationships between black masculinity and revolutionary violence.

According to Priestly's aesthetic vision, any visual and textual archive of black male and female heroism must necessarily encompass not only martyrdom, via spectacles of violation and subjugation, but also a self-reliant and empowered individualism, via the radical display of acts and arts of agency and resistance. Celebrating black exceptional prowess and redemptive feats of self-transformation across her symbolic "chapters" in Strange Fruit 2 no less than in her other works in the series, Priestly dramatizes multiple political, social, and historical journeys from slavery to freedom. In a powerful move, and typical of her determination to deny audiences any emotional catharsis, however, Priestly's last "chapter" in this work testifies to the "Strange Fruit" of Billie Holiday's song by reproducing a lynching photograph as a provocative talisman through which she exposes the unspeakable horrors generated by repeated spectacles of hanging black bodies. Deliberately concluding on an ambivalent and hauntingly disturbing image, she establishes her rejection of any one-dimensional, teleological narratives of black male and female heroism. In palpable ways, this horrifying photograph takes us back to the start of this book by returning us to William Johnson's representation of Turner as a lynched and martyred figure in his psychologically layered portrait. Regardless of their many formal and thematic differences, therefore, both Priestly and Johnson represent the black body as a locus not only of struggle and protest but also of sacrifice and persecution. In clear-cut terms, Priestly's Strange Fruit 2 refuses to provide an all-encompassing and self-explanatory, socially didactic vision of black heroism. In stark contrast to the widespread proliferation of reductive representations of Black men and women within white dominant iconography, she shares Johnson's evocation of multifaceted, ambiguous, and contradictory reimagings to ensure that the signifying possibilities of black heroism are constantly "kept open."

For Priestly, the decision to insert textual and visual spectacles of Black male and female historical figures onto canning jars is no accident, as these domestic artifacts are integral to her aesthetic and political vision. "I am interested in the way common rituals, such as the preparation and consumption of food, and the everyday objects used in these rituals can inspire dialogue," she writes, observing that "the simple act of taking tea or the mere presence of a tea cup, a spoon, or a canning jar can become an important vehicle in the preservation and transmission of personal memory, ancestral knowledge and historic events."[4] As artifacts intended for "everyday use"—as of course is also the case for Missouri Pettway's quilt discussed in the introduction to this book—these jars signify as public and private touchstones of hidden and elided acts and arts of black male and female heroism. As mixed-media images simultaneously dramatizing "personal memory, ancestral knowledge and historic events," Priestly's *Strange Fruit* series constitutes a powerful tour de force. Coming to grips with the politics and poetics of amnesia versus memorialization, her visual and textual installments trace the lives and deaths of Louverture, Turner, Pieh, Truth, Douglass, and Tubman not only to exalt in their exceptionalism but also to denounce the widespread subjugation and annihilation of the multifaceted histories of millions of unknown Black women, children, and men. "In part, I do consider 'Strange Fruit 2' to be about heroism," she concedes.[5] And yet her concession that this work is an examination of heroism only "in part" speaks to Priestly's recognition of the importance of acknowledging lacunae, distortion, and misrepresentation even to begin to reimagine a multifaceted continuum of black male and female heroism.

In forceful ways, fragmentation, ellipses, and lacunae are brought no less powerfully to the fore in the mixed-media collages and installations recently emerging on the other side of the Atlantic and created by the contemporary Black British artists Lubaina Himid and Yinka Shonibare. No less relying upon experimental aesthetic strategies directly to confront the racist realities of white transatlantic sites of amnesia, both artists share Priestly's determination to debate a multitude of black diasporic heroisms, both iconic and unknown. Rather than inserting historical images onto rows of individual domestic artifacts that they then suspend before a metaphorical and geographical "no place," however, Himid and Shonibare specifically return us to one physical space in particular: the especially symbolic epicenter of imperial power with which I began this book, London's Trafalgar Square and its particularly iconic statue, Nelson's Column, in the U.K. Politicizing yet further William Wells Brown's joyous discovery of an anonymous "full-blooded African" on one of the bronze panels at the base of this monument in 1854 over one hundred fifty years later in 2009, Himid situates the aggrandized physique of Toussaint Louverture in powerful visual dialogue with Lord Nelson's iconic statue in her mixed-media work titled *London Guidebook: Soho and Trafalgar Square*.[6]

Appearing in revisionist guise as a quintessential symbol of black rather than white heroism, Himid's historical cutout bears witness to a revolutionary Louverture as clothed in full military regalia. Subversively recuperating Louverture within a white British national imaginary, she relies upon experimental aesthetic techniques to collage this centuries-old illustration of Louverture onto a contemporary photograph, which she then inserts as one of a number of reimagined, newly commemorated iconic sites in her London

Guidebook series created in 2009. Titling this particular vignette *London Guidebook: Soho and Trafalgar Square,* Himid inserts a black rather than white icon of heroism as the archetypal default within a newly envisioned national imaginary. Thus she accompanies her radical mixed-media image of Louverture with the following description: "Trafalgar Square, London's main venue for rallies and outdoor public meetings, was conceived by John Nash and was mostly constructed in the 1830s. As part of the drive at that time to end Britain's key role at the center of the slave trade, a large painted bronze statue was erected of Toussaint L'Ouverture the leader of the only successful slave revolt in the Caribbean, who had died in 1803, after having defeated the greatest armies of the day, including the forces of the French, the English and the Spanish."[7] Accentuating rather than minimizing the ideological biases nefariously at work within seemingly objective, populist descriptions of nationally renowned tourist sites, Himid's revisionist visual and textual narratives bear witness to radical acts and arts of black heroism. Inspiring her viewers to reimagine a far different memorial than is currently on view in Trafalgar Square, she destabilizes the hegemonic force of white public narratives and official histories by problematizing the self-indulgent, jubilantly jingoistic language of the typical tour guide, a no-holds-barred repository of national amnesia. Powerfully reversing the widespread penchant among white Britons for engaging in racist whitewashings of black British and black transatlantic and diasporic histories, Himid's transgressive act of black memorialization challenges audience expectations by marginalizing, if not entirely displacing, seemingly monolithic representations of white heroism: according to her reimagining, it is Nelson rather than Louverture who has been elided, distorted, and annihilated in the public domain.

Presented not in isolation but as part of a series, Himid's reimagined Toussaint Louverture statue is one of a number of images and tableaux that make up her radically reconceptualized *London Guidebook.* Reimagined as a powerful counterarchive, these interrelated works vouchsafe her determination not only to confront the marginalized histories of iconic Black liberators, such as Louverture, but also of the anonymous enslaved Black women, children, and men whose lives and deaths have otherwise existed beyond the pale of white official commemoration. "Greenwich is best known as the place from which the world's time is measured," Himid declares in the textual excerpt accompanying her collage titled *London Guidebook: Greenwich and Blackheath,* as she again evokes the pseudofactual tone generally typifying tourist guidebooks to expose their politically charged fallacies. "It marks the historic eastern approach to London by land and water and is home to the

National Maritime Museum," she writes, unequivocally observing, "The sea has always played an extremely important role in British history, as a means of both defense and expansion, and the museum magnificently celebrates this sea faring heritage. There are rooms devoted to trade and empire, but an exterior highlight for visitors is the massive wooden slave ship, marooned on the grass. Every weekend and summer weekday, dozens of children take part in chaotic, staged reenactments of the rescue and repatriation of thousands of soon-to-be enslaved Africans and the subsequent trial and punishment of their captors."[8] Across her *London Guidebook* series, therefore, Himid not only experiments with collaging techniques to reimagine missing monuments but also relies upon a symbolic use of literary language to generate slippery commemorative narratives. More tellingly still, as characterized not by an encyclopedic omniscience but by self-reflexive play, Himid's use of "marooned" in particular works to problematize any potential associations of her reimagined slave ship monument solely with victimization, sacrifice, and martyrdom. Juxtaposing this haunting image with a multilayered use of language, she unites the memory of the slave ship and the Middle Passage with the multiple heroisms enacted by formerly enslaved yet anonymous Black men and women as they lived and survived in marooned communities throughout the diaspora. Refusing to shy away from the historical and political realities of black diasporic dissidence and resistance, she no less relies upon performative discourse—"staged reenactments"—to expose the artificial failures embedded within any seemingly authentic attempts to do justice to the personal stories of millions of "enslaved Africans." For Himid, therefore, a multilayered narrative technique works in conjunction with an array of collaged images to extrapolate the elided legacies of iconic leaders such as Louverture and to confront the annihilated and distorted histories of metonymic objects—such as the slave ship—which resonate as imaginative touchstones for otherwise displaced and distorted black histories. As Alan Rice perceptively argues, Himid's "collaged images" signify "as a kind of graffiti, an underground dialogisation that subverts the majority story of triumphant lily-white imperial progress."[9] Nonlinear, anticathartic, and nonredemptive, Himid's mixed-media works protest against the sanitized, censored, and "invisibilizing" forces at work within white mainstream memorials and as embedded within the national psyche and imaginary.[10]

An artist no less intent upon resisting the confines of Trafalgar Square as an exclusive repository of only white memory, Yinka Shonibare designed his epic-sized installation *Nelson's Ship in a Bottle* similarly for insertion on this civil space's empty fourth plinth in 2010.[11] Rice celebrates this public sculpture, a monumental work commemorating Nelson's "flagship *Victory*, on which he died during the Battle of Trafalgar in October 1805," as a "multifaceted piece" in which Shonibare "complicates the traditional history of Nelson and Trafalgar" by creating "new narratives and images that refuse to be hidebound by the dead hand of imperial closure."[12] As open-ended and unresolved as Himid's *London Guidebook* series, Shonibare's *Ship in a Bottle* confronts the fraught legacies of slavery, colonialism, and empire by commemorating white acts of heroism through a prism of black diasporic creativity. In a bold move, Shonibare substitutes the customary white cloth typically adorning a nineteenth-century British battleship's sails with a multicolored and multipatterned fabric that carries numerous associations, both mythical and real. "We think of these fabrics as African textiles," Shonibare states, conceding, however, that "in fact these are Indonesian textiles produced by the Dutch for the African market." As a result of their hybridized circulation, he explains, "I'm interested therefore in their global nature, in the Indonesian, Dutch and indeed British connections, since they were also manufactured in Manchester."[13] Transgressing regional and national boundaries, Shonibare's installation deconstructs any clear-cut presumptions surrounding the seemingly fixed authenticity of soi-disant African textiles to expose the emergence of these fabrics within the interstices of global power. Hidden in plain sight, Shonibare's insertion of numerous multicolored and multipatterned African textiles as sails on the deck of Nelson's *Victory* symbolizes the individualized yet elided experiences of Black men, women, and children crammed into no less invisibilized slave ship holds. In contrast to Arlonzia Pettway's quilt, a work that generates emotional and political force as a private testament to black familial life, Shonibare's public sculpture exists as a public memorial to white amnesia. Bearing witness to ongoing white failures regarding black commemoration, Shonibare's *Victory* is a slippery rather than a fixed signifier. Far from a site of white sacrifice and martyrdom, his *Ship in a Bottle* operates in forceful ways as a stimulus to postcolonial, postempire, and postslavery black heroisms as enacted across a diasporic context and a transatlantic geographical, social, and political locale. Regardless of their relationship to iconic versus unknown acts and arts of black heroism, therefore, the mixed-media installations of contemporary artists Debra Priestly, Lubaina Himid, and Yinka Shonibare challenge white dominant iconographies and discourses by reconceptualizing and reappropriating black diasporic histories as sites and sights of political subversion, artistic play, and symbolic reimagining.

Just as Toussaint Louverture, Nathaniel Turner, Sengbe Pieh, Sojourner Truth, Frederick Douglass, and Harriet Tubman all engaged in multiple performances self-reflexively to originate and define the parameters for their own malleable symbolism in the face of reductive representations, subsequent authors, artists, and activists such as Priestly, Himid, and Shonibare among countless others, have no less interpreted a politicized aesthetics and aestheticized politics as equally integral to their fight to keep their memories alive. In forceful ways, the political, social, and aesthetic lives and deaths of multiple Louvertures, Turners, Piehs, Truths, Douglasses, and Tubmans betray no safe ground regarding their varied embodiments of a black male and female heroic tradition. Circulating as multifaceted signifiers over the centuries and across a transatlantic milieu, they have continued to define and redefine the parameters of a black diasporic heroic continuum. As a tradition characterized by paradox and ambiguity, however, these compelling uncertainties are a source not of despair but of hope. Diverse representations of enslaved forms of black male and female heroism proliferate in the transatlantic imagination not only to transgress boundaries but also to implode seemingly safe historical, social, and political demarcations. Recognizing the futility of the search for any safe ground in the contemporary era, the African American artist Betye Saar powerfully declares, "That slave ship imprint is on all of us."[14] Yet, as the lives and works of these six individuals demonstrate, theirs is not only a "slave ship imprint" but also a "characters of blood" legacy. For such an array of Black heroic figures, diverse acts and arts of radical self-representation remain no less precious currency in the twentieth and twenty-first centuries. At war with racist imaginings no less than imaginings of individual and collective heroism within a transatlantic milieu, as I argue in these pages, Toussaint Louverture, Nathaniel Turner, Sengbe Pieh, Sojourner Truth, Frederick Douglass, and Harriet Tubman have all defied the finality of their mortality not only to live but to live on.

We never look at just one thing; we are always looking
at the relation between things and ourselves.
—John Berger, *Ways of Seeing* (1973)

Celeste-Marie Bernier's *Characters of Blood: Black Heroism in the Transatlantic Imagination* grapples with the vexed legacy of race and representation in ingenious, imaginative, and innovative ways. Bernier's bold interdisciplinary study reveals the impossibility of innocent representations of race.
It also delineates the many different ways that Black artists, activists, and intellectuals have used diverse visual and verbal representations as a means of
talking back to power, as a creative form of self-representation designed to
interrupt, invert, and subvert the power and authority of the dominant racial order. Bernier traverses decades, centuries, countries, and continents to
select her primary objects of study, investigating how visual and textual cre-
ations by artists and authors in North America, Europe, the Caribbean, and
Africa have represented the long and as yet unfinished legacy of slavery. Her
diverse research objects cohere clearly around core concerns and questions
about what she calls "the inextricable relationship between coded systems of
signification and overt enactments of violence."

Bernier's focus on heroic imagery leads her to explore how Nathaniel Turner, Toussaint Louverture, Sengbe Pieh, Sojourner Truth, Frederick Douglass, and Harriet Tubman consciously attempted to influence the
ways they were represented by others in order to make their fame and/or
notoriety provide clues to a lost reality. They helped fashion an archive of
the occluded and distorted history of Afro-diasporic struggle against white
supremacy. Their successes provide Bernier with a second set of research
objects: the rearticulations of these representations and histories by Black
artists, authors, activists, and intellectuals in subsequent times of political
and social danger. She shows how images of struggle against slavery have
served important ends for aggrieved Afro-diasporic communities during the
Great Depression, the civil rights period, and the present era, when they are

needed as much as ever. Although our own time is sometimes referred to as a postracial period, it is actually a time permeated by proclamations of postracial color-blindness but plagued by practices of intensified racial subordination and exploitation. Bernier shows that these embattled representations from the past never disappear completely. Even if misunderstood in their own time, disregarded by succeeding gatekeepers of dominant cultural memory, and kept alive only in marginal, alternative, and underground institutions and practices, these images and ideas have been reiterated and recontextualized over and over again, repositioned as resources for the black freedom struggle, just as their creators hoped. *Characters of Blood* demonstrates that the past is never truly over. The book's approach to history evokes Paul Ricoeur's observation that "the temporal distance separating us from the past is not a dead interval but a transmission that is generative of meaning."[1] Each generation renegotiates its relationship to the past in response to its needs in the present. Bernier's genealogy of Afro-diasporic representations of slave rebellions and black heroism positions each new work of art inside a dialogue already in progress, part of a conversation in which there are no monologues and no one has the first or last word. This is a discursive context in which the image, the symbol, the story, and the word are "always half someone else's," to use Bakhtin's memorable formulation of the dialogic imagination in literature.[2]

Bernier's work enables us to see how Afro-diasporic aesthetics reject the post-Renaissance binary opposition between art and social life. With some notable exceptions, art in the Western tradition has generally occupied a separate sphere devoted to elevation, refinement, and ornamentation. It has functioned as a form of reparation and consolation for the injuries and injustices of competitive economic life. Afro-diasporic art, on the other hand, generally functions as a node in a network of social practices designed to create new social relations and to imbue the world with the ability to make right things come to pass.[3] In this artistic world, aesthetic objects perform practical political, social, and psychological work. Consistent with the traditional Yoruba belief that participation in aesthetic performance trains people to recognize significant communications, Frederick Douglass believed that political reform was partly an aesthetic project. He favored the retrieval of heroic histories and the performance of heroic identities as ways to insert into the everyday lives of ordinary people what Bernier calls "personal reflections of an ennobled selfhood." Douglass saw participation in art production and reception as an important means of cultivating empathy, understanding, self-confidence, and self-activity. Artistic practice could turn people treated as objects into knowing subjects, transform surveillance into display, and replace passive resignation with active agency. Where the Western art tradition has generally honored the created object, the Afro-diasporic tradition has emphasized the creative act. Perhaps most important in the context of this book, aesthetic work expands the sphere of politics. People without political representation can still make political representations in art. Those powerless to control the nation can still influence the imagination. Images of black heroism answer absences in the official historical record by recovering what Bernier calls lost "patterns of influence" that persist in collective memory even though they have "been written out of official testimonies." This is an art that is far more than the creation of individual "geniuses"; it is, rather, a visible manifestation of shared social grammars and vocabularies of resistance and affirmation. This art has meaningful work to do in the world. It serves as a repository of collective memory, a site of moral instruction, and a way of calling a community into being through performance, expression, articulation, and contestation.

Turning art, display, and performance into terrains of struggle was not merely a matter of choice. Works of art and other visual representations have long functioned as weapons of white supremacy. Bernier notes that the slave system at its core turned people into property, a process that required displaying black bodies as objects for sale. It should not be surprising that such a system also commodified and displayed black bodies in other ways: as objects of scientific study and anthropological investigation and as sources of entertainment. Slavery staged its own spectacles. Slaves parading to the auction block were tied together with rope like animals in a coffle and forced to sing "happy" songs as part of what Saidiya Hartman describes as "the obscene theatricality of the slave trade."[4] The coffle had practical purposes. It was intended to make slaves feel the humiliation of their subordination, to enact their own descent from human beings into chattel, and to "advertise" their attributes to potential purchasers. It was a form of subjection designed to produce compliant subjects. The coffle also served ideological ends. As Hartman argues, "The festivity of the [slave] trade and the pageantry of the coffle were intended to shroud the violence of the market and deny the suffering of those sold and their families."[5]

The end of legal slavery increased rather than diminished the importance of demeaning representations of Blacks as a way to preserve white privilege and power. Under slavery, white supremacy was protected by the full force and authority of the federal government. After emancipation, armed with the guarantees of the Thirteenth, Fourteenth, and Fifteenth Amendments and the 1866 Civil Rights Act, Blacks appeared for the first time to have the potential to become full-fledged competitors with whites. Blacks offered the hand of friendship to whites, working with them in state after state to secure benefits for both groups. Alliances between newly freed Blacks and poor whites created new democratic institutions and practices, enabling ordinary citizens for the first time to serve on juries, send their children to free public schools, be treated for medical problems in hospitals, and see tax money expended on internal improvements that opened up opportunities for all rather than merely subsidizing those who were already wealthy. Threatened by this egalitarian democracy, elites in the North and South recruited poor whites into an orchestrated campaign designed to criminalize and demonize black freedom. Vigilante violence, lynchings, and rapes were used to terrorize free Blacks. The sharecropping system replicated the social relations of slavery in new guises. Mass incarceration of Blacks for petty (and often purely fabricated) "crimes" like vagrancy and loitering freed white workers from having to compete with blacks, while the convict lease system provided business with a captive and inexpensive labor force. Jim Crow segregation relegated Blacks to separate but completely unequal schools and public accommodations.

These new economic and political relationships required ideological legitimation. Whites needed to make black subordination seem natural, necessary, and inevitable, to render ridiculous the idea of black citizenship. White property depended on the denial of black humanity. White artists, advertisers, and authors flooded the nation with demeaning images of degraded blackness, drawing from a deep well of racist images that circulated in the antebellum period and punctuating them with renewed fervor fueled by anxieties of a newly industrializing society. This visual order quickly established the core vocabulary of emerging new forms of visual representation including the photograph, the lithograph, and the feature film. Advertisements and figurines featured Black mammies, minstrels, and servants with wide-open mouths, enormous lips, toothy grins, and bulging eyes. Sunday school classes taught by solid citizens were brought on "field trips" to witness lynchings of blacks. Photographs and postcards depicting the dismemberment of black bodies circulated to satisfy the sadistic pleasure of those who missed the opportunity to observe them in person. Body parts of lynched blacks were preserved and put on display to warn blacks against insubordination and to reassure even the most degraded and exploited whites that there was a floor below which they could not fall. The relentless performativity of white supremacy entailed obsessive repetition of these images to the degree that it became almost impossible for anyone to see them without feeling they had seen them before.[6]

The spectacle of degraded and dehumanized blackness was more than a matter of race. In the nineteenth century, the rise of industrialization, urbanization, and state building led to new patterns of behavior that shook up social life. Mechanized production created new forms of alienated labor. Shopping districts, public transportation vehicles, and amusement parks produced new kinds of public spaces that generated new anxieties about interactions with strangers. Polarities of wealth and poverty produced an upper class for whom property was no longer connected to propriety and a lower class filled with resentments and anger. In such a society, as Peter Stallybrass and Allon White argue, the socially peripheral often becomes symbolically central.[7] Demeaning images of nonnormative outsiders define the boundaries of respectability for those on the inside. The array of servile Sambos, matronly mammies, and manically active minstrels in the visual economy of late nineteenth- and early twentieth-century America contrasted sharply with the images, icons, and ideals of white male heroism and prosperity. These images helped reassure whites while encouraging them to project their anger and resentments onto Blacks. In a world where the black body served as the master sign of inferiority, images of degraded blackness were essential to the perpetuation of not only white supremacy but also middle-class respectability and normativity. The phantasmagoria of superior white identities only worked when supplemented by representations of inferior black existences. Whites uncertain about their own autonomy needed the "not free" to be clearly the "not me." As Toni Morrison argues about American literature, "the Africanist character" is both a surrogate and an enabler. "Africanism," Morrison explains, "is the vehicle by which the American self knows itself as not enslaved, but free; not repulsive, but desirable; not helpless, but licensed and powerful; not history-less, but historical; not damned, but innocent; not a blind accident of evolution, but a progressive fulfillment of destiny."[8]

It is this context that makes Bernier's evidence and arguments so important. In a society where heroic images were reserved for whites, with an endless stream of degrading images defining blackness, the image became a highly charged terrain. Blacks could not choose to avoid imagery. Pictures of themselves pervaded white society and served to disqualify them as witnesses even before they could begin to speak. As W. E. B. Du Bois observed, white supremacy has no falsifiable hypotheses; all facts function to confirm black inferiority. "Everything Negroes did was wrong," Du Bois wrote in *Black Reconstruction in America*. "If they fought for freedom, they were beasts; if they did not fight, they were born slaves. If they cowered on the plantations, they loved slavery; if they ran away, they were lazy loafers. If they sang, they were silly; if they scowled, they were impudent."[9]

Even the whites who opposed slavery and raised modest objections to the system of segregation that supplanted it had no room for black self-activity or agency, much less heroism. They savored images of Blacks as suffering helpless victims in need of rescue by sympathetic whites. Bernier notes the transatlantic origins of these images, from the famous eighteenth-century image by Josiah Wedgwood of a kneeling slave framed by the question "Am I Not a Man and Brother?" on the official seal of the London-based Committee for the Abolition of the Slave Trade to the innocent suffering faithful souls in Harriet Beecher Stowe's mid-nineteenth century U.S. novel *Uncle Tom's Cabin*. These images served important historical purposes in promoting opposition to slavery, but they posed the issue as more a matter of saving white souls than one of saving black lives. They ignored the histories of slave resistance and rebellion embodied in the lives and actions of figures like Toussaint Louverture, Nathaniel Turner, Sengbe Pieh, Sojourner Truth, Harriet Tubman, and Frederick Douglass.

Black activists and artists faced seemingly insurmountable obstacles in the face of the omnipresence of representations that misrepresented their bodies and their history. How could they speak for themselves when they had already been spoken for? How could they represent themselves in the face of their widespread misrepresentation by both their enemies and their allies? How could they bring into visibility events, ideas, and actions that had been erased systematically from the historical record? Bernier's book teaches us that, like the physicians of antiquity or the generations of Afro-diasporic community healers that preceded them, black creators of new images of themselves operated from a different premise: things that can kill can also cure if they are deployed in the right ways. Precisely because racial subordination persisted through the validation and justification it received from a seemingly endless stream of representations, symbols, and significations, Blacks felt compelled to create an equally long and complicated chain of countersymbols through images of their own.[10] They sought to turn poison into medicine, to transform humiliation into honor. Louverture, Turner, Pieh, Truth, Tubman, and Douglass recognized that they could not control completely the images of themselves that white society circulated. But each of them also recognized that some images and representations could be manipulated to work to their advantage. As Bernier says in regard to Douglass, "the infinite possibilities of textual symbolism" could transcend "the finite fixity of physical suffering."

Bernier creates a new archive of black self-activity by excavating the historical record and finding much that previous scholars have missed. She identifies the importance of Toussaint's rejecting his slave name and calling himself "Louverture," which means "the opening." Similarly, when Isabella Baumfree renamed herself Sojourner Truth, when Frederick Augustus Washington Bailey took the name Frederick Douglass, when the man known to whites as Joseph Cinque knew himself as "Sengbe Pieh," and when Harriet Tubman was transformed from a hunted criminal into a biblical redeemer by the simple act of being called Moses by her people, they authored and authorized new identities different from those that whites had imposed on them. Because respectable family names given to Black slaves and their descendants served as markers of histories of rape, brutality, and exploitation, these namings and renamings also exposed and challenged what Bernier describes accurately as the "tangled skeins of black and white genealogies."

Bernier finds artistic agency in unexpected places. Frederick Douglass understood the aesthetic properties of photography so well that he crafted his poses to create images that emphasized his dignity and humanity. This kind of agency would not have been possible if he sat for portraits and had to surrender complete control of his image to a painter. Sojourner Truth challenged the ruling modes of representation of Black women by creating an elaborate visual archive that emphasized her activism and agency. Like Harriet Tubman, she cultivated an image of heroic action to undercut images of the abject female body as simply an invitation to white sympathy or a catalyst for Black male action. Having already been commodified and objectified by the slave system and its enduring legacies, these individuals embraced intentionally a certain kind of objectification and commodification as a tool to turn themselves into emblems of opposition, into icons of self-respect and self-activity. Without becoming painters, photographers, or sculptors, they crafted and sculpted their own public images. Even those who could not write often created stories that established their identities as memorable and heroic characters. Of course these ruses did not always work. People attempting to fool the enemy can sometimes deceive themselves. Louverture created a new name and a dramatic persona to challenge the idea that Black people were merely property. Yet these acts of self-assertion also created a kind of brand equity. Painters who had never seen Louverture's face found that adding the revolutionary hero's name to a portrait of any black male face increased its value and enabled it to circulate as a successful and lucrative commodity.

Bernier shows that the historical record also contains an answer to Amiri Baraka's rhetorical question "What if Nat Turner painted?" As far as we know, Turner did not paint, and no life portrait of him has been found. But he crafted his jailhouse "confession" to Thomas Gray in a way designed to provide powerful images for future generations of Blacks, while at the same time confusing whites. Having already been demonized as a sign of Black savagery, Turner turned that notoriety into a mystery, narrating an identity that quickly became a subversive sign and a sign of subversion. He turned his black body into a unique body of evidence. While awaiting his execution and confined in a jail cell, Turner talked to a white man, Thomas Gray. These stories circulated freely in the future in a series of paintings, poems, plays, and works of fiction. Bernier underscores the enduring power of Turner's story to vex white supremacy across the centuries through subsequent representations of his life in works as diverse as a Sterling Brown poem and a William Johnson painting. Brown wrote his poem in 1939 in response to his failed efforts as an employee of the Works Progress Administration to cultivate an appreciation of black history's relevance for the present. In the poem, as in his work for the WPA, Brown finds that rhetorical fictions and falsehoods obscure the actual historical record of black struggle. He laments the collective amnesia that has led people to forget Turner's heroism. Yet this very lament played an important role in reviving curiosity about the things about Turner that had been forgotten. Brown taught this poem to generations of his students at Howard University, several of whom went on to become prominent activists in the black freedom struggle. In 1945, William Johnson painted a picture of himself in the role of the executed Nathaniel Turner hanging from a gallows with a rope around his neck. The painting also evoked things about Turner that had been forgotten. Created in the wake of the lynching of Cleo Wright in Sikeston, Missouri, in 1943, as well as in the midst of the rising tide of black activism for jobs, justice, rights, resources, and recognition that would eventually produce the civil rights movement and related struggles for black freedom, Johnson's painting depicted weapons, gunpowder, and white sheets of paper on the ground near Turner. In his jailhouse conversation with Thomas Gray, Turner had explained that he had learned to make paper. Johnson's painting seemed to indicate that an important part of the historical record had been left blank, that words could be used as weapons, that important parts of both the past and the future remained unwritten.

The very suppression of Turner's heroism also imbued his name with a menacing power it might not have had otherwise. Bernier demonstrates this power by recounting the frenzied reaction of some self-proclaimed descendants of Confederate soldiers to spray-painted graffiti on the Alabama Confederate Memorial in Montgomery in 2007. The message that defaced the monument read "N.T. 11 11 31." Despite the brevity of the cryptic message, the offended Confederate sympathizers recognized it as a reference to Turner, who was executed on November 11, 1831. These defenders of the legacy of slavery offered a reward for information leading to the arrest and conviction of the perpetrator of this act, which they labeled "a hate crime."

Like Turner's, the heroism of Sengbe Pieh reached across generations. Accounts of his actions leading the successful revolt on the slave ship *Amistad* have not always been accurate, but they have been frequent. Stories originally written in newspapers engendered subsequent wax models, panoramas, public lectures, dioramas, poems, paintings, plays, murals, historical reenactments, street art, and (for better or worse) Hollywood films. These iterations and reiterations encompass a broad range of aesthetic intentions and achievements that also served significant social purposes. In Bernier's analysis, art functions as the alternative archive of the oppressed. It is a deep well from which future generations draw ideas, images, stories, and symbols otherwise unavailable to them. This archival dimension of African American art is especially important because so much of black history has been expunged from the official archives. Bernier relates how W. E. B. Du Bois was dissuaded by publishers from writing a book about Nathaniel Turner. She explains that no contemporaneous life portraits were painted of Pieh, Louverture, or Turner. She describes the responses by film producers to Danny Glover's proposal to make a motion picture about the life of Toussaint Louverture. Conceding that the saga of the first successful slave revolt in history was a gripping story, the producers declined to finance the film because it had no white hero.

True to the best possibilities of interdisciplinary scholarship, Bernier argues that the aestheticized politics of Louverture, Turner, Pieh, Truth, Tubman, Douglass, and those who followed in their footsteps also produced a politicized aesthetics organized around indirection, fragmentation, ellipsis, masquerade, and disguise. People lacking the power to articulate their ideas openly become masters of allusion, allegory, metaphor, and metonymy. Necessitated by asymmetrical relations of power in the diaspora, these aesthetic affinities also referenced traditional understandings of artistry in Africa. In his study of the staggered patterns and colors that create a kind of visual syncopation in textiles made by people of African ancestry in Haiti and the southern states of the United States, Robert Farris Thompson argues that they reflect the sensibility of a Senegambian proverb: "Evil travels in straight lines."[11] For Black artists, the long way around could sometimes be the shortest way through. Bernier shows that these aesthetic ideals forged by aggrieved individuals and communities out of their necessary struggle have significance that goes far beyond the pleasures they deliver as art and entertainment or even their important utility as mechanisms enabling people to refuse what Franklin Rosemont aptly terms "the shameful limits of an unlivable destiny."[12] The aesthetic ideals developed and deployed by the artists and activists that Bernier examines in this book reveal how our aesthetic problems are also social problems, how our political problems and moral problems are also problems of knowledge. Bernier's interdisciplinarity is not incidental to her achievement in *Characters of Blood*; it is its essential ingredient. By studying political reform as an aesthetic project, examining aesthetics as a social force, questioning the authority of the archive and the artificiality of temporal periodization, exposing visual imagery as a mechanism for racialization and individuation, and connecting the circulation of signs to the structures that shape social identities, Bernier exposes the limits of dominant disciplinary frames. The established archives are incomplete and unreliable. Works of expressive culture contain unacknowledged ideological and social hierarchies. Visual images encode unjust social relations. Celebrations of black art and Black artists obscure their connections to histories of black militancy. We need to produce new kinds of art and to become new kinds of people, but we cannot do so unless we recognize that we can be imprisoned by ideas, images, stories, and sentiments as easily as we can be imprisoned by stone walls and iron bars. In fact, we can be imprisoned *more* easily by the things we cannot see, like ideas, images, stories, and sentiments, than by the stone walls and iron bars that at least can be seen. We will not create new ways of being until we develop new ways of seeing.

The ways of seeing that produce the fatal couplings of violence and signification at the heart of Bernier's book have a long history. In so many ways, the problems of the past impede our progress in the present. Long after the abolition of slavery, the sadistic affective pleasures slavery promoted persist. They are deployed every day in support of new inequalities and injustices. Louverture, Turner, Pieh, Truth, Tubman, Douglass, and the artists and activists who followed in their footsteps were not merely confronting isolated, individual, or aberrant incidents of prejudice, exclusion, exploitation, and subordination. Rather, they challenge the logical consequences of an entire epistemology and its attendant visual economy, which had deep roots in the knowledge paradigms of the Enlightenment. Immanuel Kant, for example, believed that the black body constituted proof of intellectual and moral inferiority. In one memorable passage, Kant dismissed a comment made by an African because "this fellow was quite black from head to foot, a clear proof that what he said was stupid."[13] Kant's statement was no slip of the tongue or momentary lapse in judgment. For more than forty years he conducted research in anthropology and geography that persuaded him that white Europeans were the only race capable of progress in the arts and sciences. Blacks could be educated, he acknowledged, but only as servants, and he advised that training them necessitated corporal punishment. Kant recommended flogging blacks with a split bamboo cane rather than a whip because the cane inflicted more pain and opened up wounds that allowed blood to escape from what he perceived to be the thick skin of the Negro.[14] Thus the most important moral philosopher of the modern period was convinced that skin color encoded and codified a person's capacity for reason. As Charles Mills concludes, the philosopher known as the champion of "universal" personhood was also one of the architects of the modern concept of race with its insistence on the differentiated subpersonhood of Blacks.[15] For an individual or even a representative intellectual of the eighteenth century to harbor such notions may seem merely antiquated. But these are not limited individual notions. The ways of seeing that Kant learned from his culture—and the belief system he helped build in part because of them—have for centuries grounded links between visual representations and racial identities.

The racial dimensions of Kant's anthropology, geography, and philosophy have been largely ignored in the disciplines. As Cedric Robinson notes, "Racial regimes are unrelentingly hostile to their exhibition."[16] Yet the ways of seeing that Kant absorbed from his society continue to shape the contours of visual representations of race because they revolve around what Donald Lowe has named "bourgeois perception." During the Renaissance, artists developed geometric techniques of linear perspective that produced illusions of depth. Oil painting enabled a two-dimensional canvas to evoke a three-dimensional space filled with objects rich with color and texture receding before the eye into a seemingly infinite space.[17] Portraiture simulated another kind of depth by seeming to represent in visual form the deep interiority and personal character of heroic individuals. The modern bourgeois subject was founded in part on the practice of displaying people and the objects they owned in portraits, fueling grandiose aspirations for wholeness and plenitude, for both autonomy from other people and for dominance over them.[18] As Nancy Armstrong notes about the relationship between the novel and the bourgeois subject, once it was codified through cultural representation, this modern subject continuously reproduced itself, not only among writers and readers and painters and viewers, but also in law, medicine, philosophy, biography, history, and science.[19] The particular qualities that Armstrong associates with the modern subject called into being by the novel have particular relevance to Bernier's discussions of white desire for images of innocent suffering Blacks. The ability to display empathy for the suffering of others marked the modern subject as a person of virtue. Yet that virtue was thought to be private, personal, and interior. The desire for private virtue was premised on a phobic relationship with the social aggregate and a fear of being engulfed by it. For the individual to remain an individual, he or she could feel, but not act. Black suffering titillated viewers. It promoted pity, but not solidarity. Rather than serving as an impetus to action, it confirmed the modern subject's conviction that personal probity was needed as a shield against the corruptions of society. According to Lowe, bourgeois perception in painting also helped promote *the process of seeing* as "primarily a distancing, judgmental act."[20] The full and fatal consequences of that distancing are on clear display in Bernier's book. Racism is poisonous enough by itself. Because it is a crucible in which many other cruelties are learned and legitimated, it takes on even more toxic dimensions because of its utility as a justification for power.

Characters of Blood: Black Heroism in the Transatlantic Imagination shows us why we need to turn to the aesthetics, archives, imaginaries, and epistemologies embodied in the freedom dreams of Black people, past and present. These sources can be chaotic and contradictory, complex and confusing. They do not produce what Jurgen Habermas calls "the ideal speech situation,"[21] a sober dialogue among equals characterized by scientific detachment and instrumental reason. Forged in the midst of struggles with dominant power, replete with ellipsis and indirection, and dialogically referring to what came before and what will follow afterward, this archive is less an ideal speech situation than an unruly and unpredictable conversation among many different kinds of texts. But there is a reason for that, a reason related directly to Bernier's understanding of the links between overt enactments of violence and coded systems of signification. As the Black philosopher Charles Mills explains, "The 'ideal speech situation' requires our absence, since we are, literally, the men and women *who know too much, who*—in that wonderful American expression—*know where the bodies are buried* (after all, so many of them are our own)."[22]

Yet *Characters of Blood* also helps us see that the powerful knowledge regimes that discipline our ways of seeing are also inherently unstable, riddled with contradictions, and susceptible to critique and contestation. The alternative archive that Bernier documents; the collective, cumulative, and continuing struggles that she reveals; and the indispensible interdisciplinary framework that she provides advance the struggle that her book chronicles. Her book shows that the black body—used so often and so ignobly as proof of black inferiority—also contains a body of evidence of value to everyone. The history of the uses of the black body as proof is essentially a history of the tragic consequences of Western culture's anxieties about difference. It is a history of false subjects needing false objects. It is a history of how race has been used as an excuse for power. It is a history of how post-Enlightenment ways of seeing have inhibited the development of more democratic and humane ways of being. But Bernier's book also shows us that the things that can kill us can also cure us if we use them in the right way. By opening herself up to the insights of the black radical tradition, by moving deftly across the disciplines to ask and answer important questions, Bernier confirms the beat poet Bob Kaufman's observation that sometimes people whom society sees as "way out" actually know the way out.

George Lipsitz

NOTES

PREFACE

1. Qtd. in Holt, "Primitives."
2. Pinder, "Our Father," 227.
3. Hunton and Johnson, *Two Colored*, 233.
4. La Roche and Blakey, "Seizing," 84.
5. Rothstein, "Burial."
6. Higginson, *Black*, 165.
7. Powell, *Cutting*, 12.
8. Anon., "Fears," 35.
9. Qtd. in Berlin, "After Nat," 150.
10. Douglass, "Mission," 4
11. Baraka, "Fearful Symmetry," 37.
12. Ibid., 38.
13. Ibid.
14. Dial, *I Am a Man, I Always Am* (1994), http://www.artnet.com/artwork/424459225/423841944/i-am-a-man-i-always-am.html.
15. hooks, *Art*, 4.

INTRODUCTION

1. Brown, "Visit," 70.
2. Ibid., 70–71.
3. Ibid., 71.
4. Ibid., 71, 71–72.
5. Caulkins, *Stone*, 59–60.
6. Qtd. in Kaplan and Kaplan, *Black*, 56. Unfortunately, the authors provide no citation for the quotation.
7. Wood, *Terrible*.
8. Wood, *Horrible*, 126, 109.
9. Du Bois, *Correspondence*, 64.
10. Conrad, *Harriet*, v.
11. Foster, *Witnessing*, xxix.
12. Jacobs, *Incidents*, 317.
13. Bradford, *Harriet, the Moses*, 96.

14. Carby, *Race Men*, 129.
15. Carlyle, *On Heroes*, 3, 4.
16. Carlyle, "Occasional," 308.
17. Emerson, "Heroism," 228.
18. Ibid., 229.
19. Ibid., 234.
20. Emerson, "Character," 774.
21. Carlyle, *Chartism*, 60.
22. Kaplan, "Black Heroes," 34.
23. Abrahams, "Some Varieties," 341.
24. Kaplan, "Black Heroes," 34.
25. Bryant, *Victims*, 3.
26. Lambert, "Blood and Dream," 353.
27. Ibid., 354.
28. Cubitt, introduction to *Heroic Reputations*, 2.
29. Ibid., 3.
30. Ibid., 7.
31. Roberts, *Trickster*, 1.
32. Van Deburg, *New Day*, 4
33. Moses, *Black*, xi.
34. Baldwin, *To Make*, 26.
35. See Cone, *Martin & Malcolm*.
36. As the diverse materials examined in this book demonstrate, eighteenth- and nineteenth-century developments in print cultures and burgeoning forms of reproductive technologies were integral both to the marketing of these historical figures and to their experimental strategies of self-representation (see Lapsansky, "Graphic Discord"; Newman, "Writing"; DeLombard, "African American"; and Wood, *Blind*; Wood, *Exploding*; Wood, *Terrible*).
37. Quilts of Gee's Bend Catalog.
38. Walker, *Everyday*.

39. Bernier, *African American,* 93ff.

40. Ibid., 2.

41. Douglass to Henry C. Wright, 189.

42. Hughes, "Need," 225.

1. "I SHED MY BLOOD"

1. Ellison, "Mister Toussan," 26.

2. Ibid., 22.

3. Ibid., 25, 26.

4. Wood, *Slavery,* 257.

5. Belasco, "Harriet Martineau's," 175.

6. Forsdick, "Travelling," 152.

7. Parkinson, *Gilded,* 71.

8. Kaplan, "Black Heroes," 35, 36.

9. Ibid., 52–53.

10. Honour, *Image,* 106.

11. Pierrot, "Our Hero," 584.

12. Wilson, *Specters,* 146; Ethiop, "Afric-American," 87.

13. Ethiop, "Afric-American," 87.

14. Reproduced in Daguillard, *Enigmatic,* 13, 22.

15. Ibid., 7.

16. Ibid., 9.

17. Ibid.

18. Ibid.

19. Aravamudan, *Tropicopolitans,* 303.

20. Daguillard, *Enigmatic,* 21.

21. Rainsford, *Historical,* 252–53.

22. Daguillard, *Enigmatic,* 21.

23. Powell, *Cutting,* 60.

24. Daguillard, *Enigmatic,* 21.

25. Ibid., 21, 15, 32.

26. Parkinson, *Gilded,* 71.

27. Daguillard, *Enigmatic,* 29, 49.

28. Hopkins, *Daughter,* 14.

29. Elliott, *St. Domingo,* 26.

30. Nesbitt, *Toussaint,* xxiii.

31. Beard, *Life,* 296–329.

32. Dubois, *Avengers,* 173.

33. Parkinson, *Gilded,* 61.

34. James, *Black Jacobins* (1938), 129, 168.

35. Jenson, "Kidnapping(s)," 162.

36. Desormeaux, "First," 131.

37. Beard, *Life,* v, vi, 23, 136–37, 280.

38. Ibid., 295.

39. Ibid.

40. Ibid., 299.

41. Ibid., 209, 303, 308.

42. Ibid., 308, 309.

43. Ibid., 311, 314, 318.

44. Ibid., 319.

45. Rainsford, *Historical,* 216.

46. Beard, *Life,* 319.

47. Ibid., 320.

48. Ibid., 321.

49. Ibid., 323.

50. Ibid., 324, 324–25.

51. Ibid., 325.

52. Ibid., 328.

53. Desormeaux, "First," 137.

54. Louverture, "Address," 28; Louverture, "Letter," 34–35.

55. "Frenchmen React to Toussaint," in Tyson, *Toussaint,* 84.

56. Douglass, "Haiti."

57. Douglass, "Toussaint"; see Bernier, "Emblems."

58. Dash, *Haiti,* 5–6.

59. Clavin, "Second," 145.

60. Dain, "Haiti," 139–40.

61. Tyson, *Toussaint,* 137.

62. Kachun, "Antebellum," 252.

63. Clavin, "Second," 118, 119.

64. Brown, *St. Domingo,* 33, 3, 6.

65. Ibid., 12.

66. Ibid., 13.

67. Ibid., 16.

68. Ibid., 23, 32.

69. Ibid., 32.

70. Ibid., 36, 37, 38.

71. Holly, "Negro Race," 296, 299.

72. Smith, "Toussaint."

73. Langston, "World's Anti-slavery."

74. Clavin, "Second," 118.

75. Phillips, "Toussaint."

76. Ibid.

77. Ibid.

78. Ibid.

79. Ibid.

80. Emerson, "Character," 330.

81. See Clavin, *Toussaint*, 2010.

82. Wood, *Slavery*, 286.

83. Beard, *Life*, vi.

84. Higginson, *Army*, 78.

85. Child, *Appeal*, 161–62.

86. Tufts, "American," 54.

87. Hill, *Toussaint*, 7–8, 8.

88. Nesbett and DuBois, *Jacob Lawrence*, 28.

89. Lawrence, *Toussaint*, 11.

90. Ibid., 13.

91. Ibid., 14.

92. Kaplan, "Black Heroes," 56.

93. Hills, *Painting*, 61.

94. Ibid., 60.

95. Spradling, introduction to Lawrence, *Toussaint*, 4.

96. Qtd. in Lawrence, *Toussaint*, 10.

97. Ibid., 31.

98. Nesbett and DuBois, *Jacob Lawrence*, 28.

99. Ibid.

100. For a full reproduction of Lawrence's *Migration of the Negro* series, see Nesbett and DuBois, *Jacob Lawrence*.

101. Hills, *Painting*, 61, 75.

102. Nesbett and DuBois, *Jacob Lawrence*, 20.

103. Ibid., 29, 32.

104. Ibid., 29, 30.

105. Ibid., 30.

106. Powell, *Cutting*, 62.

107. Ibid., 63.

108. Bontemps, *Drums*, 91, 170–71.

109. James, *Black Jacobins: Toussaint* (1938), xv, xvi, xviii.

110. Ibid., xix.

111. Geggus, *Haitian*, 16.

112. James, *Black Jacobins: Toussaint* (1938), xix.

113. Ibid., xv, xvi.

114. Ibid., 79.

115. Qtd. in Tyson, *Toussaint*, 157.

116. Césaire, *Notebook*, 16.

117. Ibid., 15, 25.

118. Dash, *Haiti*, 19.

119. Césaire, *Collected Poetry*, 63. As the translators Eshleman and Smith explain, while their first translation "was based on the French text in Vol. I of Césaire's *Oeuvres complètes*, ed. by Jean-Paul Césaire," the "1976 text of the poem has a number of misprints that we reproduced in our 1983 translation" (ibid., 54).

120. Depestre, "Interview," 137–38.

121. Depestre, *Rainbow*, 45.

122. Ibid.

123. Kaisary, "Impact," 80.

124. Forsdick, "Refiguring," 268.

125. Glissant, *Monsieur*, 17, 21, 18, 19.

126. Banham, Hill, and Woodyard, *Cambridge*, 149, 150.

127. Clark, "Tragic," 240, 241.

128. Silenieks, introduction to Glissant, *Monsieur*, 8, 17, 17–18.

129. Ibid., 24.

130. Bell, *Toussaint*, 298.

131. Glissant, *Monsieur*, 25, 26.

132. Cohen, "Lamartine's," 261.

133. Ibid., 263.

134. Glissant, *Monsieur*, 26, 31, 33.

135. Ibid., 11, 41, 43.

136. Ibid., 48, 53, 59, 84.

137. Euba, "Theatre," 479.

138. Hansberry, "Toussaint," 51.

139. Glissant, *Monsieur*, 78.

140. Shangee, *For Colored*, 28.

141. Johnson, "Report," 64.

142. Qtd. in Chiappini, *Jean-Michel Basquiat*, 40, 48, 163, 66, 68.

143. Marshall, *Jean-Michel Basquiat*, 66.

144. Qtd. in Middelanis, "Blending," 113.

145. Brown, *Tracing*, 76.

146. Cosentino, *Divine*, 17.

147. Brown, *Tracing*, 83.

148. Rpt. in Brown, "Art," 49.

149. Anon., "Danny."

150. Kaisary, "Impact," 18.

151. Depestre, "What Can?," 169, 172.

2. "N.T. 11 11 31"

1. Anon., "NT 11 11 31."

2. Tragle, *Southampton*, 12.

3. Hunter, "Alabama."

4. Wheatley, *Collected*, 66.

5. Savage, *Standing*, 4.

6. Wood, *Horrible*, 61.

7. Ibid., 77.

8. Floyd, "Governor's Proclamation," 423.

9. Higginson, *Black*, 168.

10. Anon., "Capture of Nat Turner," 38.

11. Brown, "Nat Turner Insurrection," 350.

12. Higginson, *Black*, 164.

13. Williams, *History*, 85.

14. Weeks, "Slave Insurrection," 67.

15. Drewry, *Slave*, 27.

16. Garnet, "Address."

17. Douglass, "Black Hero," 134.

18. Rpt. in Foner, *Nat Turner*, 148.

19. Aptheker, "Event," 46.

20. Harding, *A River*, 98.

21. Bennett, *Pioneers*, 83.

22. Greenberg, *Nat Turner*, 3.

23. Warner, *Authentic*, 280–300.

24. Higginson, *Black*, 166.

25. Douglass, *Heroic*, 175.

26. Warner, *Authentic*, 282.

27. Tragle, *Southampton*, i, iii, iv.

28. Reproduced in Tragle, *Southampton*, 159; reproduced in Furstenberg, "Beyond Freedom," 1320.

29. Greenberg, *Nat Turner*, xviii.

30. Higginson, *Black*, 205.

31. Andrews, *To Tell*, 73.

32. Davis, *Nat Turner*, 4.

33. Rommel-Ruiz, "Vindictive Ferocity," 64.

34. Rucker, *The River*, 187.

35. Wood, *Horrible*, 384, 162, 160, 161.

36. Plummer, *Dying*.

37. Ibid.

38. Wood, *Horrible*, 161.

39. Mountain, *Sketches*, 19; Arthur, *Life*.

40. Tragle, *Southampton*, iv.

41. Gray, *Confessions*, 20.

42. King, introduction, xxv.

43. Wolf, *Freedom's*, 7.

44. King, introduction, xxvii, xxxi.

45. Gray, *Confessions*, 11, 12.

46. Styron, "Nat Turner Revisited," 73.

47. Greenberg, *Nat Turner*, 8.

48. Davis, *Nat Turner*, 75.

49. Stone, *Return*, 34.

50. Sundquist, *To Wake*, 37.

51. Anon., "To the Editors," 143.

52. Gray, *Confessions*, 4.

53. Wheatley, *Collected*, 134.

54. Sundquist, *To Wake*, 39.

55. Gray, *Confessions*, 18.

56. Yellin, *Women*, 187.

57. Gray, *Confessions*, 4.

58. Ibid., 4, 7.

59. Ibid., 7.

60. Ibid.

61. Ibid., 8, 3.

62. Ibid., 8.

63. Ibid., 8, 8–9.

64. Ibid., 9.

65. Ibid., 10.

66. Ibid., 10, 11.

67. King, introduction, xxxv.

68. Moses, *Black*, 65.

69. Wood, *Horrible*, 163.

70. Gray, *Confessions*, 12, 14, 16.

71. Joyner, Khalifah, and Magee, *Nat Turner*, 18.

72. Gray, *Confessions*, 18, 19.

73. Anderson, *A Voice*, 8.

74. Gray, *Confessions*, 19.

75. Davis, *Nat Turner*, 63, 241–42.

76. Andrews, *To Tell*, 77.

77. Trodd and Stauffer, *Meteor*, 217.

78. Smith, "Brown & Nat Turner," 219.

79. Brown, *The Negro*, 354.

80. Moore, "Slave Revolt," 13.

81. Coles, "Nat Turner," 10.

82. Brown, "Interview," 797.

83. Brown, "Remembering," 725.

84. Ibid.

85. Brown, "Interview," 797.

86. Ibid.

87. Stone, *Return*, 236–37.

88. Hayden, *Collected Poems*, 56.

89. Hayden, *Collected Prose*, 179.

90. Hayden, *Collected Poems*, 57–58.

91. Hayden, *Collected Prose*, 179.

92. Styron, "Nat Turner Revisited," 67.

93. Styron, "William Styron," 40.

94. Styron, "Nat Turner Revisited," 68.

95. Gray, *Confessions*, 19; Styron, *Confessions*, 262.

96. Styron, "Nat Turner Revisited," 68.

97. Foley, "History," 401.

98. Joyner, Khalifah, and Magee, *Nat Turner*, 68.

99. Styron, "Quiet," 125.

100. Greenberg, *Nat Turner*, 17.

101. Davis, *Nat Turner*, 10.

102. Brown, "Interview," 796–97.

103. Ellison et al., "A Discussion," 154.

104. Murray, *The Omni-Americans*, 134.

105. Harding, "Vincent Harding," 231.

106. Qtd. in Sokolov, "Nat Turner," 47.

107. Lester, *Look Out*, 39–40.

108. Styron, "Interview with William Styron," 222.

109. Aptheker, "Cataclysm," 117.

110. Styron, *Confessions*, ix.

111. Joyner, "Styron's Choice," 181.

112. Lipsitz, *Possessive*, vii.

113. Styron, *Confessions*, 11, 14, 16, 29.

114. Ibid., 23, 24, 35, 47; Styron, "Nat Turner Revisited," 67.

115. Styron, "Nat Turner Revisited," 67.

116. Qtd. in Sokolov, "Nat Turner," 46.

117. Styron, *Confessions*, 128, 139, 180.

118. Ibid., 227, 379.

119. Gray, *Confessions*, 18.

120. Styron, *Confessions*, 299, 227, 300.

121. Clarke, *Ten Black Writers*.

122. Styron, "Nat Turner Revisited," 72.

123. Kaiser, "Failure," 98; Poussaint, "Interview," 236.

124. Bennett, "Nat's Last," 4.

125. Harding, "You've Taken," 25.

126. Killens, "Confessions of Willie Styron," 35.

127. Clarke, introduction to *Ten Black Men*, iii.

128. Panger, *Ol' Prophet*, 10, 12, 19.

129. Davis, *Turner*, 207.

130. Stone, *Return*, 183.

131. Panger, *Ol' Prophet*, 136.

132. Anon., "Dig," 9.

133. Neal, *Shine*, 639–40.

134. Cleaver, "Radio Address," 4.

135. Cleaver, "Happy Birthday," 3.

136. Butterfield, "Search," 91, 98, 99.

137. Bodkin, translator's note to Hermary-Vieille, *Tragic Search,* 7.

138. Ibid., 5.

139. Hermary-Vieille, *Tragic Search,* 13, 16, 13, 28, 44, 46.

140. Ibid., 54, 58, 66, 93, 92.

141. Ibid.,92–93, 193, 260, 267.

142. Ibid., 352.

143. Celestine, *Confessions.*

144. Baker, *Nat Turner,* 6, 208, 6.

145. Qtd. in O'Shea, "Creator."

146. Baker, *Nat Turner,* 7.

147. Baker, "I Make."

148. Baker, *Nat Turner,* 7.

149. Ibid., 6.

150. Douresseaux, review of *Nat Turner.*

151. Cederlund, "History."

152. Baker, *Nat Turner.*

153. See bibliography for online availability of Weems's series *From Here I Saw What Happened and I Cried.*

154. Baker, *Nat Turner,* 33, 34, 36.

155. Ibid., 40, 44.

156. Ibid., 41, 43, 45, 47, 57.

157. See Douglass, "Haiti." As he vociferously proclaims, "It was once said by the great Daniel O'Connell, that the history of Ireland might be traced, like a wounded man through a crowd, by the blood. The same may be said of the history of Haiti as a free state."

158. Gray, *Confessions,* 12.

159. Baker, *Nat Turner,* 116–17, 116, 121.

160. Sherman, "Graphic."

161. Baker, *Nat Turner,* 186, 195, 196, 197.

162. Sherman, "Graphic."

163. Baker, *Nat Turner,* 202.

164. Williams, *History,* 92.

165. Rpt. in Foner, *Nat Turner,* 7.

166. Williams, *History,* 91.

167. Johnson, *Nat Turner,* 166.

168. Malcolm X, *Malcolm X,* 267, 268, 271.

169. Angelou, *I Know,* 175, 175–76.

170. Joyner, Khalifah, and Magee, *Nat Turner,* 5, 11.

171. Bennett, *Pioneers,* 84.

172. Qtd. in Burnett, *Nat Turner.*

3. "NO RIGHT TO BE A HERO"

1. Hamilton, "Making."

2. Hamilton, *Birth,* 87.

3. Rice, *Creating,* 15.

4. Hamilton, *Birth,* 87–89.

5. Dalzell, "Representing."

6. Morrison, *Beloved,* 23.

7. See Osagie, *Amistad;* and Rediker, *Amistad.*

8. Osagie, *Amistad,* xii.

9. Dalzell, "Representing."

10. Osagie, *Amistad,* xiv.

11. Powell, "Cinque," 73; Jones, "Mutiny," 12; Horton and Horton, *In Hope,* 244, 245.

12. Kelley, "No Coons," 401.

13. Powell, "Cinque," 64.

14. Jones, *Mutiny,* 42.

15. Alexander, "Portrait," 39.

16. Anon., "Long, Low," *New York Journal of Commerce,* Sep. 2, 1839.

17. While Sheffield's illustration is reproduced in this volume (see figure 12), the textual caption remains difficult to read. For interested readers, an enlarged version of this image and text can be found online at http://www.loc.gov/exhibits/odyssey/archive/01/012600ir.jpg.

18. Barber, *History,* 20.

19. Ibid.; Newton, *Thoughts,* 248.

20. Barber, *History,* 9.

21. Ibid., 8.

22. Ibid., 9.

23. Kaplan, "Black Mutiny," 494.

24. Fowler, "Phrenological."

25. Ibid.

26. Rokela, "Page," 288.

27. Powell, "Cinque," 50.

28. Anon., "Priceless."

29. Ibid.

30. Alexander, "Portrait," 31, 43.

31. Ibid., 31.

32. Powell, "Cinque," 53.

33. Alexander, "Portrait," 45.

34. Anon., "Priceless Picture."

35. Ibid.

36. Anon., "Cinque and Heroes."

37. Sale, *Slumbering*, 66.

38. See various articles from these sources listed in the bibliography.

39. Anon., *New York Journal of Commerce*, Aug. 30, 1839.

40. Anon., "Captured Africans," Sep. 18, 1839: 2.

41. Anon., *New York Morning Herald*, Sep. 10, 1839: 2.

42. Anon., "Captured Africans of the Amistad," Oct. 4, 1839: 2.

43. Anon., "Plans."

44. Anon., "African Testimony," 2.

45. Sale, *Slumbering*, 76.

46. Anon., "Long, Low," *Charleston Courier*.

47. Ibid.

48. Sale, *Slumbering*, 76.

49. Child, *Letters*, 212–13.

50. Anon., "On Cinques," 1.

51. Anon., "Amistad Case."

52. Newman, "Writing," 185.

53. Anon., "On Cinques," 1.

54. Whitfield, *America*, 20–21.

55. Osagie, *Amistad*, 76.

56. Peterson, "Legendary," 374.

57. Osagie, *Amistad*, xv.

58. Du Bois, "The Saga," 4.

59. Dodson, "Who Has Seen," 20.

60. Woodruff, "Interview," 74–75.

61. Ibid., 75.

62. Gaither, "Mural," 131.

63. Bearden and Henderson, *History*, 214.

64. See bibliography for online reproductions of these murals.

65. Gaither, "Mural," 132.

66. Ibid., 133.

67. Porter, *Modern*, 110.

68. Gaither, "Mural," 134.

69. Ibid.

70. LeFalle-Collins and Goldman, *Spirit*, 53.

71. Gaither, "Mural," 134.

72. Ibid., 133.

73. Dodson, "Play Script," 51.

74. Ibid., 51, qtd. in Gaither, "Mural," 133.

75. Qtd. in Bearden and Henderson, *History*, 212.

76. Gaither, "Mural," 133; Dodson, "Play Script," 97.

77. Gaither, "Mural," 133; Dodson, "Play Script," 102.

78. Dodson, "Play Script," 102.

79. Gaither, "Mural," 133; Dodson, "Play Script," 104.

80. Gaither, "Mural," 135.

81. Ibid., 142.

82. Woodruff, "Interview," 77.

83. Hayden, *Collected Poems*, 51.

84. Ibid., 53–54.

85. Ibid., 54.

86. Fetrow, "Middle Passage," 306–7.

87. Hayden, *Collected Prose*, 74–75.

88. Ibid., 75.

89. Ibid., 80, 117, 106, 115, 120–21.

90. Hayden, *Collected Poems*, 50, 51.

91. Ibid., 51, 52.

92. Kutzinski, "Changing Permanences," 182.

93. Qtd. in Schwartzman, *Romare Bearden,* 121.

94. Bearden, "Hofstra," 4.

95. Spielberg, Angelou, and Allen, *Amistad,* 6.

96. Kabba et al., *Sierra Leonean,* 30.

97. Osagie, *Amistad,* xii–xiii.

98. Opala, "Ecstatic Renovation!," 197, 217.

99. See Equiano, *Interesting.*

100. Osagie, *Amistad,* 53.

101. McFeely, *Frederick Douglass,* 950.

102. Opala, "Ecstatic Renovation!," 202.

103. Ibid., 201.

104. Ibid., 216, 217.

105. Osagie, *Amistad,* xvi.

106. Haffner, *Amistad,* 1, 3, 4.

107. Osagie, *Amistad,* 108.

108. Haffner, *Amistad,* 4.

109. Ibid., 10, 18, ellipses in original.

110. Ibid., 4, 6, 7, 12, 14.

111. Osagie, *Amistad,* xvi.

112. DeSouza-George, "Broken," 3.

113. Ibid., 4–5, 5, 6.

114. Ibid., 22, 27.

115. Ibid., 6.

116. Ibid., 33.

117. Qtd. in Wyatt-Brown, "Amistad," 1174.

118. Spielberg, Angelou, and Allen, *Amistad,* 9.

119. Rael, "Why This Film," 387.

120. Forbes, "On the Film," 383.

121. Lemisch, "Black," 57.

122. Ibid., 60.

123. Qtd. in Spielberg, Angelou, and Allen, *Amistad* 54.

124. Qtd. in ibid., 55.

125. Gilroy, *Against Race,* 25–26.

126. Qtd. in Spielberg, Angelou, and Allen, *Amistad,* 56.

127. Hamilton, "Making."

4. "TICKETY-UMP-UMP-NICKY-NACKY"

1. Qtd. in Strzemien, "Michelle Obama."

2. Vale, *Fanaticism,* 1:9, 62, 63.

3. Painter, "Difference," 461.

4. Sánchez-Eppler, "Bodily," 151.

5. Santamarina, *Belabored,* 35.

6. Haraway, "Ecce," 98.

7. Joseph, "Sojourner," 35, 36.

8. Douglass, *Heroic,* 220.

9. Bennett, *Pioneers,* 116.

10. Foster, *Witnessing,* 67.

11. Harding, *A River,* 98; Haraway, "Ecce," 91.

12. Hopkins, *Daughter,* 131.

13. Truth with Titus, *Narrative,* 201.

14. Wood, *Terrible.*

15. Stauffer, "Creating," 263.

16. Painter, *Sojourner,* 187.

17. Glass, *Courting,* 29, 28.

18. Holmes, *Soundings,* 5.

19. Collins, "Shadow," 184.

20. Rohrbach, "Profits," 248.

21. Griebel, "West African," 211.

22. Powell, *Cutting,* 43.

23. Truth with Titus, *Narrative,* 128.

24. Pauli, *Her Name,* 168.

25. Painter, *Sojourner,* 194.

26. Collins, "Shadow," 183.

27. Painter, "Difference," 485.

28. Qtd. in Stanton, "Sojourner Truth on the Press," 927.

29. Mirzoeff, "Shadow," 118.

30. Stauffer, "Creating," 263.

31. Collins, "Shadow," 183.

32. Rohrbach, "Profits," 253.

33. Qtd. in anon., "Speech," 898.

34. Grimké, *Appeal,* 33, 32.

35. Qtd. in anon., "Speech," 898.

36. Painter, *Sojourner,* 188; Collins, "Shadow," 190.

37. Anon., "Speech," 898.

38. Painter, *Sojourner,* 188.

39. Ibid.; Collins, "Shadow," 190.

40. Mirzoeff, "Shadow," 117.

41. Stetson and David, *Glorying,* 42.

42. Wood, *Terrible.*

43. Wood, *Blind,* 81.

44. Regarding eighteenth-century white abolitionists' iconographic and discursive representations of black enslaved male and female bodies as "iron arguments" or evidential proofs against the horrors of slavery, see the discussion in Bernier, "Arguments," 57ff.

45. Stetson and David, *Glorying,* 42.

46. Painter, "Difference," 470–71.

47. Mirzoeff, "Shadow," 118.

48. Wood, *Terrible.*

49. Rohrbach, "Profits," 249.

50. For a reproduction of the anonymously produced photograph of Harriet Powers, see http://xroads.virginia .edu/~ug97/quilt/harriet.html.

51. Reproduced in Bernier, *African American,* n.p. [color plate].

52. Powell, *Cutting,* 46.

53. Peterson, *Doers,* 40.

54. Washington, *Sojourner,* xxxi.

55. Mabee, "Sojourner," 68.

56. Rohrbach, "Profits," 244, 245.

57. Qtd. in anon., "First Annual Meeting," May 10, 1867, 129.

58. Ibid.

59. Campbell, "Style," 436.

60. Lipscomb, "Sojourner," 227.

61. Joseph, "Sojourner," 37.

62. Yellin, *Women,* 77.

63. Accomando, "Demanding," 62.

64. Fitch and Mandziuk, *Sojourner,* 39.

65. Campbell, "Style," 444.

66. Rohrbach, "Profits," 248.

67. Fitch and Mandziuk, *Sojourner,* 3.

68. Yellin, *Women,* 78.

69. Qtd. in Truth with Titus, *Narrative,* 131–32.

70. Qtd. in ibid., 133.

71. Qtd. in ibid., 133–34.

72. See Welter, "Cult."

73. Truth with Titus, *Narrative,* 134.

74. Painter, "Difference," 152.

75. Qtd. in Truth with Titus, *Narrative,* 134.

76. Anon., "Women's Rights Convention," 107.

77. Anon., "American Woman Suffrage Association," 175.

78. Qtd. in Stanton, "Sojourner Truth on the Press," 926.

79. Davis, *Women,* 60, 60–61.

80. Haraway, "Ecce," 97.

81. Truth with Titus, *Narrative,* 40.

82. Qtd. in anon., "First Annual Meeting," May 9, 1867, 121.

83. Piepmeier, *Public,* 92.

84. Riley, *Am I That Name?,* 1.

85. McDowell, "Transferences," 111.

86. Fitch and Mandziuk, *Sojourner,* 94.

87. Qtd. in anon., "Proceedings," July 4, 1854, 115.

88. Truth, "She Pleadeth," 213.

89. Stowe, "Libyan."

90. Painter, "Difference," 476.

91. Yellin, *Women,* 82.

92. See Bernier, "Arguments."

93. Stowe, "Libyan."

94. Ibid.

95. Peterson, *Doers,* 38.

96. Qtd. in James, *William Wetmore Story,* 70.

97. Ibid., 70–71.

98. See the bibliography for their availability online.

99. Murray, *Emancipation,* 8.

100. Stowe, "Libyan."

101. Collins, "Shadow," 186.

102. Savage, *Standing*, 59.

103. Ibid., 11, 14.

104. Qtd. in Truth with Titus, *Narrative*, 174.

105. Biggers, "Negro," 4, iv, 11.

106. Weismann et al., *Black Art*, 62.

107. Biggers, "Negro," 12.

108. Ibid., 112.

109. Short, "Strength," 142.

110. Biggers, "Negro," 13, 50, 23.

111. Short, "Strength," 139.

112. Biggers, "Negro," 25.

113. Ibid., 3, 10, 13.

114. Weismann et al., *Black Art*, 6.

115. Biggers, "Negro," 48.

116. Ibid., 60–61.

117. Ibid., 107, letters obscured in original.

118. Ibid., 37, 48–49.

119. Ibid., 54.

120. Bernier, *African American*, 130ff.

121. Biggers, "Negro," 50, 134.

122. See Charles White, *General Moses (Harriet Tubman)*, 1965, http://www .charleswhite-imagesofdignity.org/40 .html.

123. Jordan, "Sojourner."

124. Wallace, *Black*, 166.

125. Jordan, "Problems of Language," 231.

126. Ibid., 36.

127. Jordan, "Sojourner."

128. See Herzog, *Catlett*.

129. Jordan, "Sojourner."

130. Anon., "George Truman and Sojourner Truth," 186.

131. Jordan, "Sojourner."

132. Hayden, *Collected Poems*, 136.

133. Maracle, *Sojourner's Truth*, 11.

134. Ibid., 11, 13.

135. Ibid, 13.

136. Eigenbrod, *Travelling*, 191, 193.

137. Maracle, *Sojourner's Truth*, 122–23.

138. Eigenbrod, *Travelling*, 195.

139. Maracle, *Sojourner's Truth*, 124, 125, 126.

140. Eigenbrod, *Travelling*, 194.

141. Maracle, *Sojourner's Truth*, 129, 124.

142. Ibid., 131.

143. Ibid.

144. Eigenbrod, *Travelling*, 198.

145. Maracle, *Sojourner's Truth*, 132.

146. Koeninger, "Sojourner," 119.

147. Painter, "Representing," 480.

148. Qtd. in Terry, "Sojourner," 441.

149. Mabee and Newhouse reprint the phrase recorded by Olive Gilbert as "Is God gone?" (*Sojourner*, 85). Writing in his final autobiography, Frederick Douglass himself recorded Truth's question as follows: "Speaking at an antislavery convention . . . I expressed this apprehension that slavery could only be destroyed by blood-shed, when I was suddenly and sharply interrupted by my good old friend Sojourner Truth with the question, 'Frederick, is God dead?' 'No.' I answered, and 'because God is not dead slavery can only end in blood.' My quaint old sister was of the Garrison school of non-resistants, and was shocked at my sanguinary doctrine, but she too became an advocate of the sword, when the war for the maintenance of the Union was declared" (Douglass, *Life and Times*, 342).

150. Douglass, *Why Is the Negro?*, 20.

151. Truth with Titus, *Narrative*, v.

152. Qtd. in Stetson and David, *Glorying*, 135.

153. Frederick Douglass, "I Speak," 276.

154. Truth with Titus, *Narrative*, 253.

5. "A WORK OF ART"

1. Douglass, "American Prejudice," 66.

2. Qtd. in Voss, *Majestic*, xiv.

3. Moses, *Creative Conflict*, 60.

4. Martin, "Images," 271.

5. Trodd, "Reusable," 25.

6. Moses, "Honor," 178.

7. Levine, "Identity," 43–44.

8. Powell, *Cutting*, 12.

9. Moses, "Honor," 186, 188.

10. Gates, *Figures*, 108.

11. Obama, *Dreams*, 302; Douglass, *Heroic*, 175, 176.

12. Douglass, *Heroic*, 175.

13. Douglass, *My Bondage*, 177.

14. Douglass, *Life and Times*, 620.

15. Douglass, "Pictures and Progress," 460.

16. Ibid.

17. See Douglass, *Narrative*, 6. Douglass's dramatization of the "blood-stained gate" functioned as an allegorical, apocalyptic, and metonymic signifier in his first narrative as he sought to initiate readers into the "hell of slavery."

18. Lee, *Cambridge*, 5.

19. Lester, *Look Out*, 42.

20. Douglass, "Pictures and Progress," 453, 454, 455.

21. Sekula, "Body," 7.

22. Sontag, *Photography*, 149.

23. Barthes, *Camera*, 38.

24. Douglass, "Claims," 290.

25. Trachtenberg, "Photography," 17, 20.

26. Frank, *Love*, 1.

27. Wood, *Terrible*.

28. Gates, *Figures*, 103, 108.

29. Bernier, Stauffer, and Trodd, *Picturing*.

30. The daguerreotype held by the Moorland Spingarn Center is online at http://www.howard.edu/library/scholarship@howard/legacy/12.htm.

31. Sweeney, *Frederick*, 132.

32. Stauffer, "Creating," 258.

33. Westerbeck, "Frederick," 148, 156.

34. Douglass, "Pictures and Progress," 456.

35. Westerbeck, "Frederick," 152.

36. See anon., *Frederick Douglass*, ca. 1845, http://www.common-place.org/vol-02/no-02/fried/fried-2.shtml.

37. Douglass, "Pictures and Progress," 457.

38. Ibid., 461.

39. Painter, *Creating*, 84.

40. Tanner, *The Banjo Lesson*. See the bibliography for availability online.

41. Douglass, "Lecture on Pictures."

42. Douglass, *Heroic*, 188.

43. See Bernier, "Dusky."

44. Ibid.

45. Stauffer, "Creating," 262.

46. Stauffer, "Frederick," 120.

47. Qtd. in Lohmann, *Radical*, 68.

48. Stepto, "Storytelling," 359; Stauffer, "Frederick Douglass," 124.

49. McFeely, *Frederick Douglass*, 175.

50. Douglass, "American Prejudice," 66.

51. Andrews, "Novelization," 28.

52. Douglass, *Heroic*, 175.

53. Ibid.

54. Lawson, "Douglass," 123, 130.

55. Douglass, *Heroic*, 176.

56. Ibid.

57. Ibid., 177, 178.

58. Ibid., 179.

59. Ibid., 235.

60. Ibid., 220, 221.

61. See Bernier, "Emblems."

62. Douglass, "Black Hero," 134.

63. Douglass, "Fighting Rebels," 152–53.

64. Malcolm X, *By Any Means Necessary*, 155.

65. Tilton, *Sonnets*, 152, 155, 156, 157.

66. Lawrence, "Statement," 14.

67. Ibid.

68. Unpublished interview (April and May 1972), Jacob Lawrence Papers, Archives of American Art.

69. In Wheat, *Jacob Lawrence, American Painter* 58.

70. Cobby, "Emperors," 7.

71. Ibid., 7–8.

72. Qtd. in Wheat, *Jacob Lawrence, American Painter,* 40.

73. Qtd. in ibid.

74. Qtd. in Williams, "Now," 111.

75. Ibid., 110, 111.

76. Qtd. in Martin, "Images," 279.

77. Branch, *Splendid*, 198.

78. Lester, *Look Out*, 40.

79. Carmichael and Hamilton, *Black Power*, xii.

80. Martin, "Images," 280.

81. Ibid., 281.

82. Forman, *Making*, 109, 109–10.

83. Hayden, *Collected Poems*, 62.

84. Ibid.

85. Hughes, *Collected Poems*, 549.

86. Lester, *Look Out*, 44.

87. Alston, "Frederick," 1.

88. Lester, *Look Out*, 42.

89. Qtd. in Prigoff and Dunitz, *Walls*, 29.

90. Martin, "Images," 282.

91. Rolston, "Brothers," 447.

92. O'Kelly, *Cambria*, 2.

93. Sweeney, *Frederick*, 3.

94. Moynihan, *Other People's*, 4.

95. Sweeney, "Other Peoples'," 141, 143.

96. O'Kelly, *Cambria*, 4, ellipses in original.

97. Ibid.

98. Ibid., 5.

99. For an example of Barack Obama's use of Douglass's statement, see: http://www.necn.com/Boston/Politics/Obama-Change-never-comes-without-a-fight-/1224524817.html.

100. O'Kelly, *Cambria*, 5, ellipses in original.

101. Ibid., 8.

102. Moynihan, *Other People's*, 29.

103. O'Kelly, *Cambria*, 45, 46, 11.

104. Ibid., 5, 52.

105. Sweeney, "Other Peoples'," 146.

106. O'Kelly, *Cambria*, 20.

107. Adichie, *Half*, 360.

108. Muniz, *Frederick*, 207.

109. Gates, *Figures*, 124.

110. Bradford, *Scenes*, 7.

6. "i've seen de real ting"

1. Alewitz, "Dreams."

2. Stiehm, "Nothing."

3. Alewitz, Buhle, and Sheen, *Insurgent*, 130.

4. Alewitz, "Dreams."

5. Ibid.

6. Qtd. in Stiehm, "Nothing."

7. Rimensnyder, "Disarming."

8. Qtd. in Cheney, "Moses," 459.

9. Larson, *Bound*, xiv.

10. Brickler to Conrad.

11. See Anon., *Liberator,* July 16, 1859.

12. Sernett, *Harriet*, 178.

13. Blight, *Race*, 332.

14. Sernett, *Harriet*, 8, 182–83.

15. Larson, *Bound*, xix.

16. Sernett, *Harriet*, 67.

17. Braxton, *Black*, 73.

18. Bennett, *Pioneers*, 133.

19. Larson, *Bound*, xxi.

20. Bradford, *Scenes*, 22.

21. Humez, "Search," 166.

22. Adams, *Grandfather*, 275.

23. Bradford, *Harriet, the Moses*, 48.

24. Humez, *Harriet*, 158.

25. McGowan, "Harriet," 16.

26. In Bradford, *Scenes*.

27. Sernett, *Harriet*, 117.

28. Rpt. in Humez, *Harriet*, 199.

29. Ibid., 201.

30. Ibid., 202.

31. Conrad, *Harriet*, 203.

32. Humez, "Search," 163.

33. Sernett, *Harriet*, 4.

34. Bradford, *Scenes*, 7.

35. Humez, *Harriet*, 7.

36. Truth with Gilbert, *Narrative*, 30.

37. Bradford, *Scenes*, 9–10.

38. Adams, *Grandfather*, 277.

39. Bradford, *Harriet, the Moses* (1901), 152–53.

40. Bradford, *Scenes*, 10.

41. Ibid., 13.

42. Rpt. in Humez, *Harriet*, 209.

43. Truth with Titus, *Narrative*, 26.

44. Rpt. in Humez, *Harriet*, 210.

45. Bradford, *Scenes*, 13.

46. Ibid., 13–14.

47. Rpt. in ibid., 74.

48. Bradford, *Harriet, the Moses*, 96.

49. Rpt. in Humez, *Harriet*, 211, 206.

50. Rpt. in ibid., 206.

51. Rpt. in ibid., 209, 210.

52. Douglass, *Heroic*, 95.

53. Adams, *Grandfather*, 274.

54. Bradford, *Scenes*, 14–15.

55. Rpt. in Humez, *Harriet*, 209.

56. Qtd. in Bradford, *Scenes*, 17, 18, 25.

57. Qtd. in ibid., 26–27.

58. Cheney, "Moses," 462–63, rpt. in Humez, *Harriet*, 264.

59. Bradford, *Scenes*, 57.

60. Ibid., 58.

61. Rpt. in Humez, *Harriet*, 237.

62. Bradford, *Harriet, the Moses*, 148–49.

63. Bradford, *Scenes*, 21, 24–25.

64. Douglass, *Life and Times*, 342.

65. Rpt. in Humez, *Harriet*, 236.

66. Larson, *Bound*, 264.

67. Qtd. in Drew, *North-Side*, 30.

68. Qtd. in Sernett, *Harriet*, 93.

69. Rpt. in Humez, *Harriet*, 316, 199, 200, 339.

70. Bradford, *Scenes*, 81.

71. This photograph is also available online: http://z.about.com/d/womenshistory/1/0/k/b/2/harriet_tubman_1887_a.jpg.

72. In Bradford, *Scenes*.

73. Humez, *Harriet*, 353.

74. Adams, *Grandfather*, 276.

75. Humez, *Harriet*, 3.

76. Adams, *Grandfather*, 276.

77. Rpt. in Humez, *Harriet*, 233.

78. Bradford, *Scenes*, 85.

79. Wood, *Terrible*.

80. Bradford, *Scenes*, 110.

81. Wood, *Terrible*.

82. Murray, *Emancipation*, 103.

83. Blight, *Race*, 332.

84. Qtd. in Grant, "Image," 523.

85. Lawrence, "Interview."

86. Qtd. in Grant, "Image," 523.

87. Hills, "Jacob Lawrence," 42.

88. Hills, *Painting*, 77.

89. Lawrence, "Interview."

90. Qtd. in anon., "Aaron Douglas Fresco," 449.

91. Qtd. in Wheat, *Jacob Lawrence, American Painter* 41.

92. Ibid., 31.

93. Lawrence, "Interview."

94. In Wheat, *Jacob Lawrence, American Painter* 81.

95. In ibid., 82.

96. In ibid., 85.

97. In ibid., 86.

98. Hills, "Jacob Lawrence," 46.

99. In Wheat, *Jacob Lawrence, American Painter* 87.

100. In ibid., 97.

101. Hills, "Jacob Lawrence," 46.

102. In Wheat, *Jacob Lawrence, American Painter,* 111.

103. Qtd. in Bearden and Henderson, *A History,* 309.

104. Mickenberg, "Civil Rights," 65.

105. Bearden and Henderson, *A History,* 309.

106. Ibid., 310.

107. Lawrence, "Interview."

108. Thompson, "Harriet Tubman," 90, 91, 92.

109. Lawrence, *Harriet and the Promised Land.*

110. Ibid.

111. Reproduced in Durant, *Black Panther,* 90.

112. Lorde, "Eye to Eye," 151, 164–65.

113. Giovanni, *Sacred,* 86.

114. Walker, "Harriet Tubman," 327.

115. Philip, *Harriet's Daughter,* 3.

116. Adams, *Grandfather,* 269.

117. Philip, *Harriet's Daughter,* 7, 4–5, 9–10.

118. Ibid., 25, 26, 36.

119. Ibid., 46.

120. Ibid., 48.

121. Ibid., 82, 83, 91.

122. Ibid., 105.

123. Ibid., 130.

124. Sernett, *Harriet,* 11.

125. Lansana, *They Shall Run,* 10, 14.

126. Sernett, *Harriet,* 291.

127. Larson, *Bound,* 216.

128. Humez, *Harriet,* 193.

129. Qtd. in Drew, *North-Side,* 30.

CONCLUSION

1. Priestly, "Interview."

2. Ibid.

3. Ibid.

4. Online at http://www.debra priestly.net/page1/page1.html.

5. Priestly, "Interview."

6. Reproduced in Rice, "Tracing Slavery," 255.

7. Himid, "Who Are Monuments For?," 2.

8. Ibid., 5; image reproduced in Rice, "Tracing Slavery," 257.

9. Rice, "Tracing Slavery," 255–56.

10. As Himid powerfully explained to Rice, "I am interested in the politics of representation, how when something is there you can talk about it, write about it, paint about it, but when something isn't there what can you say, how can you make something of it, how can it not have been in vain, if you like. So that idea for memorialising came from trying to visualize the invisible." (Himid, "Interview"). As Himid's *London Guidebook* series demonstrates, her determination to "visualize the invisible" remains powerfully to the fore in her ongoing artistic recuperation not only of iconic but of anonymous forms of black diasporic heroism.

11. Illustration available at http:// www.artfund.org/ship/the-campaign.

12. Rice, "Tracing Slavery," 258, 260.

13. Qtd. in Higgins, "Yinka Shonibare."

14. Saar, "Interview," 19.

AFTERWORD

1. Ricouer, *Time,* 221.

2. Bakhtin, *Dialogic,* 293.

3. Thompson, *Flash.*

4. Hartman, *Scenes,* 17.

5. Ibid., 36.

6. Rawick, *From Sundown,* 125–49; Huggins, *Harlem,* 244–301.

7. Stallybrass and White, *Politics,* 5–6.

8. Morrison, *Playing,* 52.

9. Du Bois, *Black Reconstruction,* 125.

10. Mulvey, "Myth," 3.

11. Brothers, *Louis,* 50–51.

12. Qtd. in Woods, *Development,* 38.

13. Qtd. in Eze, "Color," 119.

14. Ibid., 116–17.

15. Mills, *Racial,* 70–71.

16. Robinson, *Forgeries,* xii.

17. Berger, *Ways,* 88–89.

18. Noble, *Death,* vi.

19. Armstrong, *How Novels,* 3.

20. Lowe, *History,* 7.

21. Habermas, *Philosophical Discourse,* 323.

22. Mills, *Racial,* 132.

SELECTED BIBLIOGRAPHY

Abrahams, Roger D. "Some Varieties of Heroes in America." *Journal of the Folklore Institute* 3, no. 3 (1966): 341–62.

Accomando, Christina. "Demanding a Voice among the Pettifoggers: Sojourner Truth as Legal Actor." *MELUS* 28, no. 1 (2003): 61–86.

Adams, Samuel Hopkins. *Grandfather Stories*. New York: Random House, 1947.

Adichie, Chimamanda Ngozi. *Half of a Yellow Sun*. London: Harper Perennial, 2006.

Adisa, Opal Palmer. "In Celebration of Women." *Frontiers: A Journal of Women Studies* 13, no. 1 (1992): 156–59.

Alewitz, Mike, Paul Buhle, and Martin Sheen.

Insurgent Images: The Agitprop Murals of Mike Alewitz. New York: Monthly Review Press, 2002.

———. "What Are 'The Dreams of Harriet Tubman?'" 2000. Hartford Web Publishing. http://www .hartford-hwp.com/archives/45a/ 304.html.

Alexander, Eleanor. "A Portrait of Cinque." *Connecticut Historical Society Bulletin* 49 (1984): 30–51.

Alston, Charles. "Frederick Douglass." *Crisis* 76, no. 2 (Feb. 1969): 1.

Anderson, Osborne Perry. *A Voice from Harper's Ferry*. Boston: printed for the author, 1861.

Andrews, William L. "The Novelization of Voice in Early African American Narrative." *PMLA* 105, no. 1 (1990): 23–34.

———. *To Tell a Free Story: The First Century of Afro-American Autobiography, 1760–1865*. Urbana: University of Illinois Press, 1986.

Angelou, Maya. *I Know Why the Caged Bird Sings*. New York: Bantam Books, 1969.

Anon. "The Aaron Douglas Fresco of Harriet Tubman." *Crisis* 39, no. 1 (Jan. 1932): 449.

———. "African Testimony." *New York Journal of Commerce* (Jan. 10, 1840): 2.

———. "American Woman Suffrage Association." May 11, 1870. In *Sojourner Truth as Orator: Wit, Story, and Song,* ed. Suzanne Pullon Fitch and Roseann M. Mandziuk, 175. Westport, CT: Greenwood, 1997.

———. "Amistad Case as Revolution." *Colored American* (Oct. 5, 1839): n.p.

———. "The Capture of Nat Turner." *Richmond Enquirer,* November 8, 1831. Rpt. in *The Nat Turner Rebellion: The Historical Event and the Modern Controversy,* ed. John B. Duff and Peter M. Mitchell, 36–38. New York: Harper and Row, 1971.

———. "The Captured Africans." *New York Morning Herald* (Sep. 17, 1839): 2.

———. "The Captured Africans." *New York Morning Herald* (Sep. 18, 1839): 2.

———. "The Captured Africans of the Amistad." *New York Morning Herald* (Oct. 4, 1839): 2.

———. "Cinque and Heroes of the American Revolution." *Colored American* (Mar. 27, 1841): n.p.

———. "Danny Glover's Slavery Film Lacked 'White Heroes,' Producer Said." Breitbart TV website, Jul. 25, 2010. http://www.breitbart.com/article.php?id=080725061939.qkti45ek&show_article=1.

———. "Dig on This." *Black Panther* 1, no. 6 (Nov. 23, 1967): 9.

———. "The Douglass Memorial." *Crisis* 14, no. 4 (Aug. 1917): 166.

———. "Fears of a General Insurrection: A Communication to the *Richmond Whig*." Rpt. in *The Nat Turner Rebellion: The Historical Event and the Modern Controversy*, ed. John B. Duff and Peter M. Mitchell, 34–36. New York: Harper and Row, 1971.

———. "First Annual Meeting." May 9, 1867. In *Sojourner Truth as Orator: Wit, Story, and Song*, ed. Suzanne Pullon Fitch and Roseann M. Mandziuk, 121–22. Westport, CT: Greenwood, 1997.

———. "First Annual Meeting of the American Equal Rights Association." May 10, 1867. In *Sojourner Truth as Orator: Wit, Story, and Song*, ed. Suzanne Pullon Fitch and Roseann M. Mandziuk, 129. Westport, CT: Greenwood, 1997.

———. "George Truman and Sojourner Truth in Orange." 1874. In *Sojourner Truth as Orator: Wit, Story, and Song*, ed. Suzanne Pullon Fitch and Roseann M. Mandziuk, 185–86. Westport, CT: Greenwood, 1997.

———. *Harriet Powers*. http://xroads.virginia.edu/~ug97/quilt/harriet1.html.

———. *Joseph Cinquez, Leader of the Gang of Negroes Who Killed Captain Ramon Ferrers and the Cook on Board the Spanish Schooner Amistad.* 1839. Wilson's Almanac. http://www.wilsonsalmanac.com/images2/cinque_j1.jpg.

———. "The Long, Low, Black Schooner." *Charleston Courier* (Sep. 5, 1839): n.p.

———. "The Long, Low Black Schooner." *New York Journal of Commerce* (Sep. 2, 1839): n.p.

———. "The Nat Turner Insurrection." *Weekly Anglo-African* (Dec. 31, 1859), n.p.

———. "NT 11 11 31." http://www.daylife.com/photo/0c0qc2139K3Dn.

———. "On Cinques." *Colored American* (Oct. 19, 1839): 1.

———. "Plans to Educate the Amistad Africans in English." *New York Journal of Commerce* (Oct. 9, 1839): n.p.

———. "A Priceless Picture: History of Sinque, the Hero of the Amistad." *Philadelphia Inquirer* (Dec. 26, 1889): n.p.

———. "Proceedings at the Anti-Slavery Celebration." July 4, 1854. In *Sojourner Truth as Orator: Wit, Story, and Song*, ed. Suzanne Pullon Fitch and Roseann M. Mandziuk, 115. Westport, CT: Greenwood, 1997.

———. "Sojourner Truth." In *History of Woman Suffrage*, vol. 1, *1848–1861*, ed. Elizabeth Cady Stanton, Susan B. Anthony, Matilda Joslyn Gage, and Ida Husted Harper,, 567–68. New York: Fowler and Wells, 1881.

———. "Speech by Miss Susan B. Anthony." Appendix to *History of Woman Suffrage*, vol. 2, *1861–1876*, ed.

Elizabeth Cady Stanton, Susan B. Anthony, Matilda Joslyn Gage, and Ida Husted Harper, 898–99. New York: Susan B. Anthony, 1881.

———. "Stowage of the British Slave Ship *Brookes* under the Regulated Slave Trade Act of 1788." Learn NC. http://www.learnnc.org/lp/media/uploads/2008/07/slaveshipposter.jpg.

———. "To the Editors of the Enquirer." *Richmond Enquirer,* Nov. 25, 1831. Rpt. in *The Southampton Slave Revolt of 1831: A Compilation of Source Material,* ed. Henry Irving Tragle, 143–50. Amherst: University of Massachusetts Press, 1971.

———. Untitled article. *New York Journal of Commerce* (Aug. 30, 1839): n.p.

———. Untitled article. *New York Morning Herald* (Sep. 10, 1839): 2.

———. Untitled article. *Liberator* (July 16, 1859).

———. "Women's Rights Convention." *Anti-Slavery Bugle* (May 28, 1851). Rpt. in *Sojourner Truth as Orator: Wit, Story, and Song,* ed. Suzanne Pullon Fitch and Roseann M. Mandziuk, 107–8. Westport, CT: Greenwood, 1997.

Aptheker, Herbert. "The Event." Rpt. in *Nat Turner: A Slave Rebellion in History and Memory,* ed. Kenneth S. Greenberg, 45–58. Oxford: Oxford University Press, 2004.

———. "Truth and Nat Turner: An Exchange." Rpt. in *The Nat Turner Rebellion: The Historical Event and the Modern Controversy,* ed. John B. Duff and Peter M. Mitchell, 195–202. New York: Harper and Row, 1971.

Aravamudan, Srinivas. *Tropicopolitans: Colonialism and Agency, 1688–1804.*

Durham, NC: Duke University Press, 1999.

Armstrong, Nancy. *How Novels Think: The Limits of Individualism from 1719–1900.* New York: Columbia University Press, 2005.

Arthur. *The Life and Dying Speech of Arthur, a Negro Man; Who Was Executed at Worcester. . . .* Boston: Milk Street, 1768.

Baker, Kyle. "I Make People Laugh: Our Exclusive Interview with Kyle Baker." By Kristen Brennan. Jitterbug Fantasia, 1999. http://www.moon gadget.com/baker/index.html.

———. *Nat Turner.* New York: Abrams, 2008.

Bakhtin, Mikhail. *The Dialogic Imagination.* Austin: University of Texas Press, 1982.

Baldwin, Lewis V. *To Make the Wounded Whole: The Cultural Legacy of Martin Luther King, Jr.* Minneapolis: Fortress, 1992.

Banham, Martin, Errol Hill, and George Woodyard. *The Cambridge Guide to African and Caribbean Theatre.* Cambridge: Cambridge University Press, 1994.

Baraka, Amiri. "Fearful Symmetry: The Art of Thornton Dial." In *Thornton Dial: Image of the Tiger,* ed. Amiri Baraka and Thomas McEvilley, 33–64. New York: H. N. Abrams, 1993.

Baraka, Amiri, and Thomas McEvilley, eds. *Thornton Dial: Image of the Tiger.* New York: H. N. Abrams, 1993.

Barber, John W. *A History of the Amistad Captives: Being a Circumstantial Account of the Capture of the Spanish Schooner* Amistad. New Haven, CT: E. L. and J. W. Barber, 1840.

Barthes, Roland. *Camera Lucida: Reflections on Photography*. London: Vintage, 1982.

Beard, John R. *The Life of Toussaint L'Ouverture, the Negro Patriot of Hayti*. London: Ingram, Cooke, 1853.

———. *Toussaint L'Ouverture: A Biography and Autobiography*. Boston: J. Redpath, 1863.

Bearden, Romare. "Hofstra." 1982. Romare Bearden Papers, Archives of American Art, Washington, DC.

Bearden, Romare, and Harry Henderson. *A History of African-American Artists: From 1792 to the Present*. New York: Pantheon Books, 1993.

Behn, Aphra. *Oroonoko; or, The Royal Slave: A True History*. Ed. Joanna Lipking. 1688. New York: W. W. Norton, 1997.

Belasco, Susan. "Harriet Martineau's Black Hero and the American Antislavery Movement." *Nineteenth-Century Literature* 55, no. 2 (2000): 157–94.

Bell, Madison Smartt. *Toussaint Louverture: A Biography*. New York: Pantheon Books, 2007.

Benjamin, Walter. *Illuminations*. Ed. Hannah Arendt. London: Fontana, 1992.

Bennett, Lerone, Jr. "Frederick Douglass: Father of the Protest Movement." *Ebony* (Sep. 1963): 50–58.

———. *Pioneers in Protest*. Chicago: Johnson, 1968.

Berger, John. *Ways of Seeing*. London: Penguin, 1973.

Berlin, Ira, ed. "After Nat Turner: A Letter from the North." *Journal of Negro History* 55, no. 2 (Apr. 1970): 144–51.

Bernier, Celeste-Marie. *African American Visual Arts: From Slavery to the Present*. Chapel Hill: University of North Carolina Press, 2008.

———. "'Arms Like Polished Iron': Representing the Black Slave Body in Narratives of a Slave Revolt." *Slavery and Abolition* 23, no. 2 (2002): 91–106.

———. "A Comparative Exploration of Narrative Ambiguities in Frederick Douglass' Two Versions of *The Heroic Slave* (1853, 1863?)." *Slavery and Abolition* 22, no. 2 (2001): 69–86.

———. "'Dusky Powder Magazines': The *Creole* Slave Ship Revolt in Nineteenth Century American Literature." Ph.D. diss., University of Nottingham, 2002.

———. "'Emblems of Barbarism': Black Masculinity and Representations of Toussaint L'Ouverture in Frederick Douglass' Unpublished Manuscripts." *American Nineteenth Century History* 4, no. 3 (2003): 97–120.

———. "'The Face of a Fugitive Slave': Representing and Reimagining Frederick Douglass in Popular Illustrations, Fine Art Portraiture and Daguerreotypes." In *Life Writing and Political Memoir*, ed. Magnus Brechtken. Göttingen: V&R Unipress, 2012.

———. "From Fugitive Slave to Fugitive Abolitionist: The Oratory of Frederick Douglass and the Emerging Heroic Slave Tradition." *Atlantic Studies: Literary, Cultural and Historical Perspectives* 3, no. 2 (2006): 201–24.

———. "'His Complete History?': Revisioning, Recreating and Reimagining Multiple Lives in

Frederick Douglass's *Life and Times* (1881, 1892)." Forthcoming, *Slavery and Abolition.*

———. "'Iron Arguments': Spectacle, Rhetoric and the Slave Body in New England and British Antislavery Oratory." *European Journal of American Culture* 26, no. 1 (2007): 57–78.

Bernier, Celeste-Marie, John Stauffer, and Zoe Trodd, eds. *Picturing Frederick Douglass.* Foreword by Henry Louis Gates Jr., afterword by Bill E. Lawson, image consultancy by Sally Pierce. New York: W. W. Norton, forthcoming 2015.

Biggers, John T. *Contribution of the Negro Woman to American Life and Education.* 1952. Accessed Aug. 2009. http://www.legaciesandthelivingarts .com/llajohnthomasbiggers.html.

———. "The Negro Woman in American Life and Education: A Mural Presentation." Ph.D. diss., Pennsylvania State University, 1954.

Blight, David. *Race and Reunion: The Civil War in American Memory.* Cambridge, MA: Harvard University Press, 2001.

Bodkin, Robert Orr. Translator's note to *Nat Turner's Tragic Search for Freedom: From Deprivation to Vengeance,* by Catherine Hermary-Vieille. Victoria, BC: Trafford, 2002.

Bontemps, Arna. *Drums at Dusk: A Novel.* London: Harrap, 1940.

Bradford, Sarah. *Harriet, the Moses of Her People.* New York: Geo. R. Lockwood and Son, 1886. Rpt. with additional materials, New York: J. J. Little, 1901.

———. *Scenes in the Life of Harriet Tubman.* Auburn, NY: W. J. Moses, 1869.

Brady, Mathew. "Gordon." Smithsonian National Museum of African American History and Culture. http://nmaahc.si.edu/section/ programs/view/10.

Branagan, Thomas. *Avenia; or, A Tragical Poem, on the Oppression of the Human Species; and Infringement on the Rights of Man.* Philadelphia: S. Engles, 1805.

Branch, William. *In Splendid Error.* 1955. In *Black Heroes: Seven Plays,* ed. Errol Hill, 123–204. New York: Applause Theatre Book Publishers, 1989.

Brawley, Benjamin. *Negro Builders and Heroes.* Chapel Hill: University of North Carolina Press, 1937.

Braxton, Joanne M. *Black Women Writing Autobiography: A Tradition within a Tradition.* Philadelphia: Temple University Press, 1989.

Brickler, Alice H. Letter to Earl Conrad. July 19, 1939. In Earl Conrad/Tubman Collection 1939–1940. 2 microfilm reels. Vol. 1. Wilmington, DE: Scholarly Resources, Schomburg Center for Research in Black Culture, 1995.

Brothers, Thomas. *Louis Armstrong's New Orleans.* New York: W. W. Norton, 2006.

Brown, Karen McCarthy. "Art and Resistance: Haiti's Political Murals, October 1994." *African Arts* 29, no. 2 (1996): 46–57, 102.

———. *Tracing the Spirit: Ethnographic Essays on Haitian Art.* Seattle: University of Washington Press, 1998.

Brown, Sterling A. "'Let Me Be with Old Jazzbo': An Interview with Sterling A. Brown." By Charles H. Rowell. *Callaloo* 21, no. 4 (1998): 789–809.

———. "Remembering Nat Turner." 1939. *Callaloo* 21, no. 4 (1998): 725–26.

Brown, William Wells. *The Black Man, His Antecedents, His Genius, and His Achievements.* 1863. Rpt. New York: Kraus Reprint, 1969.

———. "The Nat Turner Insurrection." In *The Southampton Slave Revolt of 1831: A Compilation of Source Material,* ed. Henry Irving Tragle, 329–54. Amherst: University of Massachusetts Press, 1971.

———. *The Negro in the American Rebellion: His Heroism and His Fidelity.* 1867. Rpt. New York: Johnson Reprint, 1968.

———. *The Rising Son; or, the Antecedents and the Advancement of the Colored Race.* 1874. Rpt. New York: Johnson Reprint, 1970.

———. *St. Domingo: Its Revolutions and Its Patriots, A Lecture.* Boston: Bela Marsh, 1855.

———. "Visit of a Fugitive Slave to the Grave of Wilberforce." In *Autographs for Freedom,* ed. Julia Griffiths, 70–76. Rochester, NY: Wanzer, Beardsley, 1854.

Bryant, Jerry. *Victims and Heroes: Racial Violence in the African American Novel.* Amherst: University of Massachusetts Press, 1997.

Burnett, Charles. *Nat Turner: A Troublesome Property.* Documentary film. San Francisco: California Newsreel, 2002.

Butterfield, Roger. "Beginning a New Series: Search for a Black Past." *Life* 65, no. 21 (Nov. 22, 1968): 90–122.

Campbell, Joseph. *The Hero with a Thousand Faces.* 1949. Rpt. Princeton, NJ: Princeton University Press, 2004.

Campbell, Karlyn Kohrs. "Style and Content in the Rhetoric of Early Afro-American Feminists." *Quarterly Journal of Speech* 72, no. 4 (1986): 434–45.

Carby, Hazel V. *Race Men.* Cambridge, MA: Harvard University Press, 1998.

Carlyle, Thomas. *Chartism.* Boston: Charles C. Little and James Brown, 1840.

———. *On Heroes, Hero-Worship, and the Heroic in History.* 1840. In *Thomas Carlyle's Collected Works,* vol. 12. London: Chapman and Hall, 1869.

———. "Occasional Discourse on the Nigger Question." 1853. New School for Social Research. http://homepage.newschool.edu/het//texts/carlyle/odnqbk.htm.

Carmichael, Stokely, and Charles V. Hamilton. *Black Power: The Politics of Liberation in America.* London: Jonathan Cape, 1967.

Caulkins, Frances Manwaring. *The Stone Records of Groton.* Ed. Emily S. Gilman. Norwich, CT: Free Academy Press, 1903.

Cederlund, Scott. "History Lessons—a Review of *Nat Turner* by Kyle Baker." *Wednesday's Haul,* 2008.http://wednesdayshaul.com/wordpress/2008/07/28/history-lessons-a-review-of-nat-turner-by-kyle-baker/.

Celestine, Alfred. *Confessions of Nat Turner.* London: Many Press, 1978.

Césaire, Aimé. *Aimé Césaire, the Collected Poetry.* Trans. Clayton Eshleman and Annette Smith. Berkeley: University of California Press, 1983.

———. *Notebook of a Return to the Native Land.* Trans. and ed. Clayton Eshleman and Annette Smith, introduction by André

Breton. Middletown, CT: Wesleyan University Press, 2001.

Cheney, Ednah. "Moses." 1865. In *Slave Testimony: Two Centuries of Letters, Speeches, Interviews, and Autobiographies,* ed. John Blassingame, 457–65. Baton Rouge: Louisiana State University Press, 1977.

Chiappini, Rudy, ed. *Jean-Michel Basquiat.* Milan: Skira Editore, 2005.

Child, Lydia Maria. *An Appeal in Favor of That Class of Americans Called Africans.* 1833. Ed. Carolyn L. Karcher. Amherst: University of Massachusetts Press, 1996.

———. "The Iron Shroud, 1842." In *A Lydia Maria Child Reader,* ed. Carolyn L. Karcher, 216–22. Durham, NC: Duke University Press, 1997.

———. *Letters from New York.* 1843. Ed. Bruce Mills. Athens: University of Georgia Press, 1998.

———. "Through the Red Sea into the Wilderness." 1865. In *A Lydia Maria Child Reader,* ed. Carolyn L. Karcher, 279–83. Durham, NC: Duke University Press, 1997.

Clark, VèVè A. "Haiti's Tragic Overture: (Mis) Representation of the Haitian Revolution in World Drama (1796–1975)." In *Representing the French Revolution,* ed. James A. W. Heffernan, 237–60. New Haven, CT: Yale University Press, 1992.

———. "When Womb Waters Break: The Emergence of Haitian New Theater (1953–1987)." *Callaloo* 15, no. 3 (1992): 778–86.

Clarke, John Henrik, ed. *William Styron's Nat Turner: Ten Black Writers Respond.* Baltimore: Black Classic, 1968. Rpt. as *The Second Crucifixion of Nat Turner.* Baltimore: Black Classic, 1997.

Clavin, Matthew. "American Toussaints: Symbol, Subversion, and the Black Atlantic Tradition in the American Civil War." *Slavery and Abolition* 28, no. 1 (2007): 87–113.

———. "A Second Haitian Revolution: John Brown, Toussaint Louverture, and the Making of the American Civil War." *Civil War History* 4, no. 2 (June 2008): 117–45.

———. *Toussaint Louverture and the American Civil War: The Promise and Peril of a Second Haitian Revolution.* Philadelphia: University of Pennsylvania Press, 2010.

Cleaver, Eldridge. "Happy Birthday Huey." *Black Panther* 4, no. 13 (Feb. 28, 1970): 3.

Cleaver, Kathleen. "Kathleen Cleaver: From New York Radio Address." *Black Panther* 2, no. 19 (Jan. 4, 1969): 4.

Cobby, Rebecca. "'Emperors of Masculinity': The Representation of Male Heroism in African American Culture." Ph.D. diss., University of Nottingham, 2010.

Cohen, Henry. "Lamartine's *Toussaint Louverture* (1848) and Glissant's *Monsieur Toussaint* (1961): A Comparison." *Studia Africana* 1, no. 3 (1979): 255–69.

Coles, Joseph C. "Nat Turner, the Revolutionist." *Chicago Defender* (Aug. 12, 1933): 10.

Collins, Kathleen. "'Shadow and Substance': Sojourner Truth." *History of Photography* 7, no. 3 (1983): 183–205.

Cone, James H. *Martin & Malcolm & America: A Dream or a Nightmare.* New York: Orbis Books, 1993.

Conrad, Earl. Earl Conrad/Tubman Collection 1939–1940. 2 microfilm reels. Wilmington, DE: Scholarly Resources, Schomburg Center for Research in Black Culture, 1995.

———. *Harriet Tubman.* Washington, DC: Associated Publishers, 1943.

———. *Harriet Tubman, Negro Soldier and Abolitionist.* New York: International Publishers, 1942.

Cosentino, Donald J. *Divine Revolution: The Art of Édouard Duval-Carrié.* Los Angeles: UCLA Fowler Museum of Cultural History, 2004.

Cubitt, Geoffrey. Introduction to *Heroic Reputations and Exemplary Lives,* ed. Geoffrey Cubitt and Allen Warren, 1–28. Manchester: Manchester University Press, 2000.

Daguillard, Fritz. *Enigmatic in His Glory: An Exhibit Commemorating the Bicentennial of the Death of Toussaint Louverture.* Port-au-Prince: Musée du Panthéon National Haïtien, 2003.

Dain, Bruce. "Haiti and Egypt in Early Black Racial Discourse in the United States." *Slavery and Abolition* 14, no. 3 (1993): 139–61.

Dalzell, Frederick. "Dreamworking *Amistad*: Representing Slavery, Revolt, and Freedom in America, 1839 and 1997." Review of *Amistad,* directed by Steven Spielberg. *New England Quarterly* 71, no. 1 (1998): 127–33.

———. "Representing Cinque: Man and Image." 2007. Accessed May 4, 2010. http://www.amistadamerica.org/content/view/183/100/.

Dash, J. Michael. *Haiti and the United States: National Stereotypes and the Literary Imagination.* Basingstoke, Hampshire, UK: Macmillan, 1988.

———. "The Theater of the Haitian Revolution / The Haitian Revolution as Theater." *Small Axe* 9, no. 2 (2005): 16–23.

Davis, Angela Y. *Women, Race and Class.* New York: Vintage Books, 1981.

Davis, Mary K. *Nat Turner before the Bar of Judgment: Fictional Treatments of the Southampton Slave Insurrection.* Baton Rouge: Louisiana State University Press, 1999.

DeLombard, Jeannine Marie. "African American Cultures of Print." In *A History of the Book in America,* vol. 3, *The Industrial Book, 1840–1880,* ed. Scott E. Casper et al., 360–73. Chapel Hill: University of North Carolina Press, 2007.

Depestre, René. "France Reads Haiti: An Interview with René Depestre." By Joan Dayan. *Yale French Studies* 83 (1993): 136–53.

———. *A Rainbow for the Christian West.* Trans. Jack Hirschman. Fairfax, CA: Red Hill, 1972.

———. "What Can Toussaint Louverture Do for the Haitians of 2004?" In *Reinterpreting the Haitian Revolution and Its Cultural Aftershocks,* ed. Martin Munro and Elizabeth Walcott-Hackshaw, 168–84. Kingston, Jamaica: University of the West Indies Press, 2006-.

Desormeaux, Daniel. "The First of the (Black) Memorialists: Toussaint Louverture." *Yale French Studies* 107 (2005): 131–45.

DeSouza-George, Raymond. "The Broken Handcuff (Give Me Free)." Unpublished manuscript. 1994.

Dial, Thornton. *I Am a Man, I Always Am.* 1994. http://www.artnet.com/

artwork/424459225/423841944/
i-am-a-man-i-always-am.html.

Dodson, Owen. "Play Script
Commissioned by Talladega
College Performed There April, 1939
Amistad." Unpublished. Second
holograph. Box 1, folder 30. Owen
Dodson Collection, Beneicke Rare
Book Library, Yale University.

———. "Who Has Seen the Wind?
Playwrights and the Black
Experience." *Black American
Literature Forum* 11 (1977): 108–16.

Douglass, Frederick. "American
Prejudice against Color." 1845. In *The
Frederick Douglass Papers, Series One:
Speeches, Debates, and Interviews*, vol.
1, ed. John Blassingame, 59–70. New
Haven, CT: Yale University Press,
1979.

———. "A Black Hero." 1861. In *The Life
and Writings of Frederick Douglass*, vol.
3, ed. Philip S. Foner, 132–34. New
York: International Publishers.

———. "Dedication of Douglass
Institute, Baltimore." 1865. In *The Life
and Writings of Frederick Douglass*, vol.
4, ed. Philip S. Foner, 179–80. New
York: International Publishers, 1950.

———. "Fighting Rebels with Only
One Hand." In *The Life and Writings
of Frederick Douglass*, vol. 3, ed.
Philip S. Foner, 151–54. New York:
International Publishers, 1950.

———. *The Heroic Slave*. 1853. In
Autographs for Freedom, ed. Julia
Griffiths, 174–239. Boston: John P.
Jewett, 1854.

———. "I Speak to You as an American
Citizen: An Address." Oct. 15, 1870. In
*The Frederick Douglass Papers, Series
One: Speeches, Debates, and Interviews*,
vol. 4, ed. John W. Blassingame, 272–
77. New Haven, CT: Yale University
Press, 1991.

———. "Lecture on Haiti." 1893.
The Louverture Project. http://
thelouvertureproject.org/index.
php?title=Frederick_Douglass_
lecture_on_Haiti_(1893).

———. "Lecture on Pictures." Speech,
Article, and Book File, A: Frederick
Douglass, Frederick Douglass Papers,
Library of Congress.

———. Letter to Henry C. Wright. Dec.
22, 1846. In *The Frederick Douglass Papers*,
vol. 1, *Correspondence*, ed. John R.
McKivigan, 183–90. New Haven, CT:
Yale University Press, 2009.

———. *Life and Times of Frederick
Douglass, Written by Himself*. Boston:
De Wolfe, 1892.

———. "Men of Color, To Arms!" 1863.
In *The Oxford Frederick Douglass
Reader*, ed. William L. Andrews,
223–35. Oxford: Oxford University
Press, 1996.

———. "The Mission of the War: An
Address Delivered in New York, New
York." Jan. 13, 1864. In *The Frederick
Douglass Papers, Series One: Speeches,
Debates, and Interviews*, vol. 4, ed.
John W. Blassingame, 3–24. New
Haven, CT: Yale University Press,
1991.

———. *My Bondage and My Freedom*.
New York: Miller, Orton and
Mulligan, 1855.

———. *Narrative of the Life of Frederick
Douglass, an American Slave. Written
by Himself*. Boston: Anti-Slavery
Office, 1845.

———. "The Negro Exodus from the
Gulf States." 1880. University of

Virginia Electronic Text Center. http://etext.virginia.edu/toc/ modeng/public/DouGulf.html.

———. "Pictures and Progress." 1861. In *The Frederick Douglass Papers, Series One: Speeches, Debates, and Interviews,* vol. 3, ed. John W. Blassingame, 452–73. New Haven, CT: Yale University Press, 1979.

———. "Toussaint L'Ouverture." 2 folders. Speech, Article, and Book File, C: Frederick Douglass, Undated and Untitled, Frederick Douglass Papers, Library of Congress.

———. "The Trials and Triumphs of Self-Made Men." 1860. In *The Frederick Douglass Papers, Series One: Speeches, Debates, and Interviews,* vol. 3, ed. John W. Blassingame, 289–300. New Haven, CT: Yale University Press, 1979.

———. "A Tribute for the Negro." 1849. In *The Life and Writings of Frederick Douglass,* vol. 1, ed. Philip S. Foner, 379–84. New York: International Publishers, 1950.

———. "West India Emancipation." 1857. In *The Life and Writings of Frederick Douglass,* vol. 2, ed. Philip S. Foner, 426–39. New York: International Publishers, 1950.

———. *Why Is the Negro Lynched?* Bridgwater, UK: John Whitby and Sons, 1895.

Douglass, Helen. *In Memoriam: Frederick Douglass.* 1897. Rpt. New York: Books for Libraries, 1971.

Douresseaux, Leroy. Review of *Nat Turner,* no. 1, by Kyle Baker. Comic Book Bin, 2005. http://www.comicbookbin.com/natturner001.html.

Drew, Benjamin. *A North-Side View of Slavery.* 1857. Rpt. New York: Negro Universities Press, 1968.

Drewry, William Sidney. *Slave Insurrections in Virginia (1830–1865).* Washington, DC: Neale, 1900.

Duberman, Martin. "Historical Fictions." In *William Styron's "The Confessions of Nat Turner": A Critical Handbook,* ed. Melvin J. Friedman and Irving Malin, 112–16. Belmont, CA: Wadsworth, 1970.

Dubois, Laurent. *Avengers of the New World: The Story of the Haitian Revolution.* Cambridge: Harvard University Press, 2004.

Du Bois, W. E. B. *Black Reconstruction in America: 1860–1880.* New York: Harper Collins, 1993.

———. *The Correspondence of W. E. B. Du Bois.* Vol. 1, *Selections, 1877–1934.* Ed. Herbert Aptheker. Amherst: University of Massachusetts Press, 1973.

———. *John Brown.* 1909. Ed. David Roediger. Rpt. New York: Random House, 2001.

———. "The Saga of L'Amistad." *Phylon* 2, no. 1 (1941): 1–4.

———. *The Suppression of the African Slave Trade to the United States of America, 1638–1870.* 1896. Rpt. New York: Cosimo, 2007.

Duff, John B., and Peter M. Mitchell, eds. *The Nat Turner Rebellion: The Historical Event and the Modern Controversy.* New York: Harper and Row, 1971.

Durant, Sam, et al. *Black Panther: The Revolutionary Art of Emory Douglas.* New York: Rizzoli, 2007.

Edmonds, Randolph. *Nat Turner.* 1935.

In *Black Heroes: Seven Plays,* ed. Errol Hill, 77–100. New York: Applause Theatre Book Publishers, 1989.

Eigenbrod, Renate. *Travelling Knowledges: Positioning the Im/migrant Reader of Aboriginal Literatures in Canada.* Winnipeg: University of Manitoba Press, 2005.

Elliott, Charles W. *St. Domingo: Its Revolutions and Its Hero, Toussaint Louverture.* New York: J. A. Dix, 1855.

Ellison, Ralph. "The Art of Romare Bearden." In *The Collected Essays of Ralph Ellison,* ed. John Callahan, 688–97. New York: Modern Library, 2003.

———. "Mister Toussan." In *Flying Home, and Other Stories,* ed. John F. Callahan, 22–32. New York: Vintage, 1998.

Ellison, Ralph, William Styron, Robert Penn Warren, and C. Vann Woodward. "A Discussion: The Uses of History on Fiction." *Southern Literary Journal* 1, no. 2 (1969): 57–90. Rpt. in *Conversations with Ralph Ellison,* ed. Maryemma Graham and Amritjit Singh, 141–72. Jackson: University Press of Mississippi, 1995.

Emerson, Ralph Waldo. "Address: Emancipation in the British West Indies." 1844. In *The Essential Writings of Ralph Waldo Emerson,* ed. Mary Oliver, 753–78. New York: Modern Library, 2000.

———. "Character." 1844. In *The Essential Writings of Ralph Waldo Emerson,* ed. Mary Oliver, 327–40. New York: Modern Library, 2000.

———. "Heroism." 1841. In *The Essential Writings of Ralph Waldo Emerson,* ed. Mary Oliver, 225–35. New York: Modern Library, 2000.

Equiano, Olaudah. *The Interesting Narrative of the Life of Olaudah Equiano, or Gustavus Vassa, the African.* 1790. Rpt., ed. Vincent Carretta. London: Penguin Books, 1995.

Ethiop. "Picture VII—Toussaint L'ouverture: Afric-American Picture Gallery—Second Paper." *Anglo-African Magazine* (Mar. 1859): 87.

Euba, Femi. "The Theatre of Édouard Glissant: Resolving the Problems of *Monsieur Toussaint* at LSU Theatre." In *Horizons D'Édouard Glissant,* ed. Yves-Alain Favre and Antonio Ferreira de Brito, 473–82. Pau, France: J and D Editions, 1990.

Eze, Emmanuel Chukwudi. "The Color of Reason: The Idea of 'Race' in Kant's Anthropology." In *Postcolonial African Philosophy: A Critical Reader,* ed. Emmanuel Chukwudi Eze, 103–31. Cambridge, MA: Blackwell, 1997.

Fetrow, Fred. "Middle Passage: Robert Hayden's Anti-Epic." *CLA Journal* 22, no. 4 (1979): 304–18.

Fitch, Suzanne Pullon, and Roseann M. Mandziuk, eds. *Sojourner Truth as Orator: Wit, Story, and Song.* Westport, CT: Greenwood, 1997.

Floyd, John. "The Governor's Proclamation of a Reward for the Capture of Nat Turner." In *The Southampton Slave Revolt of 1831: A Compilation of Source Material,* ed. Henry Irving Tragle, 421–23. Amherst: University of Massachusetts Press, 1971.

Foley, Barbara. "History, Fiction, and the Ground Between: The Uses of the Documentary Mode in Black Literature." *PMLA* 95, no. 3 (May 1980): 389–403.

Foner, Eric, ed. *Nat Turner.* Englewood Cliffs, NJ: Prentice-Hall, 1971.

Forbes, Robert P. "On the Film's Distinct Aesthetic Style." *History Teacher* 31, no. 3 (1998): 382–83.

Forman, James. *The Making of Black Revolutionaries, a Personal Account.* New York: Macmillan, 1972.

Forsdick, Charles. "Refiguring Revolution: The Myth of Toussaint L'Ouverture in C. L. R. James and Édouard Glissant." *New Comparison* 27, no. 28 (1999): 259–72.

———. "The Travelling Revolutionary: Situating Toussaint Louverture." In *Reinterpreting the Haitian Revolution and Its Cultural Aftershocks,* ed. Martin Munro and Elizabeth Walcott-Hackshaw, 150–67. Kingston, Jamaica: University of the West Indies Press, 2006.

Foster, Frances Smith. *Witnessing Slavery: The Development of Ante-Bellum Slave Narratives.* Madison: University of Wisconsin Press, 1994.

Fowler, L. N. "Phrenological Developments of Joseph Cinquez, Alias Ginqua." *American Phrenological Journal* 2 (1840). http://tdl.org/txlor-dspace/bitstream/handle/2249.3/937/Phrenological%20Study%20of%20Cinque.pdf?sequence=99.

Foxe, John. *Book of Martyrs: Select Narratives.* Ed. John N. King. Oxford: Oxford University Press, 2009.

Frank, Robin Jaffee. *Love and Loss: American Portrait and Mourning Miniatures.* New Haven, CT: Yale University Press, 2000.

Franklin, John Hope. "Rebels, Runaways and Heroes: The Bitter Years of Slavery." *Life* 65, no. 21 (Nov. 22, 1968): 90–123.

French, Scot. "Mau-Mauing the Filmmakers: Should Black Power Take the Rap for Killing *Nat Turner* the Movie?" In *Media, Culture, and the Modern African American Freedom Struggle,* ed. Brian Ward, 233–54. Gainesville: University Press of Florida, 2001.

———. *The Rebellious Slave: Nat Turner in American Memory.* Boston: Houghton Mifflin, 2004.

Furstenberg, François. "Beyond Freedom and Slavery: Autonomy, Virtue, and Resistance in Early American Political Discourse." *Journal of American History* 89, no. 4 (Mar. 2003): 1295–1330.

Fusco, Coco, and Brian Wallis, eds. *Only Skin Deep: Changing Visions of the American Self.* New York: International Center of Photography in association with Harry N. Abrams, 2003.

Gage, Frances. "Reminiscences by Frances D. Gage: Sojourner Truth." In *History of Woman Suffrage,* vol. 1, *1848–1861,* ed. Elizabeth Cady Stanton, Susan B. Anthony, and Matilda Joslyn Gage, 115–17. New York: Fowlers and Wells, 1881.

Gaither, Edmund Barry. "The Mural Tradition." In *A Shared Heritage: Art by Four African Americans,* ed. William E. Arnould-Taylor and Harriet G. Warkel, 124–42. Bloomington: Indiana University Press, 1996.

Garnet, Henry Highland. "An Address to the Slaves of the United States of America." 1843. Blackpastorg. http://www.blackpastorg/?q=1843-henry

-highland-garnet-address-slaves-united-states.

Gates, Henry Louis, Jr. *Figures in Black: Words, Signs, and the "Racial" Self.* New York: Oxford University Press, 1987.

Geggus, David. *Haitian Revolutionary Studies.* Bloomington: Indiana University Press, 2002.

Gilroy, Paul. *Against Race: Imagining Political Culture beyond the Color Line.* Cambridge, MA: Harvard University Press, 2000.

Giovanni, Nikki. *Sacred Cows and Other Edibles.* New York: W. Morrow, 1988.

Glass, Kathy L. *Courting Communities: Black Female Nationalism and "Syncre-Nationalism" in the Nineteenth Century.* London: Routledge, 2006.

Glissant, Édouard. *Monsieur Toussaint: A Play.* Translated by Juris Silenieks. Washington, DC: Three Continents, 1981.

Grant, Nathan. "Image and Text in Jacob Lawrence." *Black American Literature Forum* 23, no. 3 (1989): 523–37.

Gray, Thomas R., ed. *The Confessions of Nat Turner, the Leader of the Late Insurrection in Southampton, Virginia.* Baltimore: Thomas R. Gray, 1831.

Greenberg, Kenneth S., ed. *Nat Turner: A Slave Rebellion in History and Memory.* Oxford: Oxford University Press, 2004.

Griebel, Helen Bradley. "The West African Origins of the African-American Headwrap." In *Dress and Ethnicity Change across Space and Time,* ed. Joanne B. Eicher, 207–26. Washington, DC: Berg, 1995.

Grimké, A. E. *Appeal to the Christian Women of the South.* New York: American Antislavery Society, 1836.

Habermas, Jürgen. *The Philosophical Discourse of Modernity: Twelve Lectures.* Ed. Frederick G. Lawrence. Cambridge, MA: MIT Press, 1987.

Haffner, Charlie. *Amistad Kata Kata.* Unpublished play in the repertoire of the Freetown Players Theater Group, 1988.

Hamilton, Ed. "The Amistad Memorial, New Haven, Connecticut." http://edhamiltonworks.com/amistad.htm.

———. *The Birth of an Artist: A Journey of Discovery.* Louisville, KY: Chicago Spectrum, 2006.

———. "The Making of the Amistad Memorial." http://edhamiltonworks.com/making_of_amistad.htm.

Hansberry, Lorraine. "Toussaint: A Drama: Excerpt from Act I of a Work in Process." 1961. In *9 Plays by Black Women,* ed. Margaret B. Wilkerson, 41–68. New York: New American Library, 1986.

Haraway, Donna. "Ecce Homo, Ain't (Ar'n't) I a Woman, and Inappropriate/d Others: The Human in a Post-Humanist Landscape." In *Feminists Theorize the Political,* ed. Judith Butler and Joan W. Scott, 87–101. New York: Routledge, 1992.

Harding, Vincent. "Beyond Chaos: Black History and the Search for the New Land." In *Amistad I: Writings on Black History and Culture,* ed. John A. Williams and Charles F. Harris. New York: Random House, 1970.

———. *There Is a River: The Black Struggle for Freedom in America.* New York: Harcourt Brace Jovanovich, 1981.

———. "You've Taken My Nat and Gone." In *The Second Crucifixion of*

Nat Turner, ed. John Henrik Clarke, 23–33. Baltimore: Black Classic, 1997.

———. "Vincent Harding and Eugene D. Genovese—An Exchange on Nat Turner." In *The Nat Turner Rebellion: The Historical Event and the Modern Controversy,* ed. John B. Duff and Peter M. Mitchell, 217–27. New York: Harper and Row, 1971.

Hartman, Saidiya. *Scenes of Subjection: Terror, Slavery, and Self-Making in Nineteenth-Century America.* New York: Oxford University Press, 1997.

Hayden, Robert. *The Collected Poems of Robert Hayden.* Ed. Frederick Glaysher. New York: Liveright, 1985.

———. *The Collected Prose.* Ed. Frederick Glaysher. Ann Arbor: University of Michigan Press, 1984.

———. "Middle Passage." *Phylon* 6, no. 3 (1945): 247–53.

Healy, Mary Aquinas. "The Contributions of Toussaint L'Ouverture to the Independence of the American Republic, 1776–1826." *The Americas* 9, no. 4 (1953): 413–51.

Hermary-Vieille, Catherine. *Nat Turner's Tragic Search for Freedom: From Deprivation to Vengeance.* 1998. Trans. and ed. Robin Orr Bodkin. Victoria, BC: Trafford, 2002.

Herzog, Melanie. *Elizabeth Catlett: In the Image of the People.* Chicago: Art Institute of Chicago, 2005.

Hicks, Kyra. *This I Accomplish: Harriet Powers' Bible Quilt and Other Pieces.* N.p.: Black Threads, 2009.

Higgins, Charlotte. "Yinka Shonibare Celebrates Victory on Trafalgar Square's Fourth Plinth." *Guardian* (May 25, 2010).

Higginson, Thomas W. *Army Life in a Black Regiment.* 1869. Rpt. Boston: Houghton, Mifflin, 1900.

———. *Black Rebellion: Five Slave Revolts.* 1889. Ed. James McPherson. New York: Arno, 1969.

Hill, Errol, ed. *Black Heroes: Seven Plays.* New York: Applause Theatre Book Publishers, 1989.

Hill, Leslie Pinckney. *Toussaint L'Ouverture: A Dramatic History.* Boston: Christopher Publishing House, 1928.

Hills, Patricia. "Jacob Lawrence as Pictorial Griot: The 'Harriet Tubman' Series." *American Art* 7, no. 1 (1993): 40–59.

———. *Painting Harlem Modern: The Art of Jacob Lawrence.* Berkeley: University of California Press, 2009.

Himid, Lubaina. "Interview with Lubaina Himid." By Alan Rice, 2009. http://www.uclan.ac.uk/ahss/ journalism_media_communication/ literature_culture/abolition/ lubaina_himid_interview.php.

———. "Who Are Monuments For?" Unpublished typescript. 2009.

Holly, James T. "The Negro Race, Self-Government, and the Haitian Revolution." 1857. In *Lift Every Voice: African American Oratory, 1787–1900,* ed. Philip S. Foner and Robert J. Branham, 288–304. Tuscaloosa: University of Alabama Press, 1998.

Holmes, Oliver Wendell. *Soundings from the Atlantic.* Boston: Ticknor and Fields, 1864.

Holt, Nora. "Primitives on Exhibit." 1946. In William H. Johnson Papers, Archives of American Art, Smithsonian Archives, reel 3829.

Holt, Rosa Belle. "A Heroine in Ebony." *Chautauquan* 23 (July 1896): 459–62.

Honour, Hugh. *The Image of the Black in Western Art*, vol. 4, *From the American Revolution to World War I: Slaves and Liberators*. Cambridge, MA: Harvard University Press, 1989.

hooks, bell. *Art on My Mind: Visual Politics*. New York: New Press, 1995.

Hopkins, Pauline E. *Daughter of the Revolution: The Major Nonfiction Works of Pauline E. Hopkins*. Ed. Ira Dworkin. New Brunswick, NJ: Rutgers University Press, 2007.

Horton, James O., and Lois E. Horton. *In Hope of Liberty: Culture, Community, and Protest among Northern Free Blacks, 1700–1860*. New York: Oxford University Press, 1997.

Huggins, Nathan Irvin. *Harlem Renaissance*. 1971. Rpt. New York: Oxford University Press, 2007.

Hughes, Langston. *The Collected Poems of Langston Hughes*. Ed. Arnold Rampersad and David Roessel. New York: Vintage Books, 1994.

———. *Famous Negro Heroes of America*. New York: Dodd, Mead, 1958.

———. "The Need for Heroes." *Crisis* 48 (June 1941): 184–85.

Humez, Jean. *Harriet Tubman: The Life and the Life Stories*. Madison: University of Wisconsin Press, 2003.

———. "In Search of Harriet Tubman's Spiritual Autobiography." *National Women's Studies Association Journal* 5, no. 2 (1993): 162–82.

———. "Reading the Narrative of Sojourner Truth as a Collaborative Text." *Frontiers* 16 (Spring 1996): 29–52.

Hunt, Alfred N. *Haiti's Influence on Antebellum America: Slumbering Volcano in the Caribbean*. Baton Rouge: Louisiana State University Press, 1988.

Hunter, Desiree. "Alabama Capitol's Confederate Monument Vandalized." *Decatur Daily News* (Nov. 15, 2007). http://legacy.decaturdaily.com/ decaturdaily/news/071115/cap.shtml.

Hunton, Addie W., and Katherine M. Johnson. *Two Colored Women with the American Expeditionary Forces*. New York: Brooklyn Eagle, 1920.

Jacobs, Harriet A. *Incidents in the Life of a Slave Girl: Written by Herself*. Enlarged ed., 1861. Ed. Jean Fagan Yellin. Rpt. Cambridge, MA: Harvard University Press, 2009.

James, C. L. R. *The Black Jacobins*. 1936. In *The C. L. R. James Reader*, ed. Anna Grimshaw, 67–111. Oxford: Blackwell, 1992.

———. *The Black Jacobins: Toussaint L'Ouverture and the San Domingo Revolution*. London: Penguin Books, 1938.

James, Henry. *William Wetmore Story and His Friends: From Letters, Diaries, and Recollections*. 1903. Rpt. London: Adamant Media, 2007.

Jenson, Deborah. "From the Kidnapping(s) of the Louvertures to the Alleged Kidnapping of Aristide: Legacies of Slavery in the Post/ Colonial World." *Yale French Studies* 107 (2005): 162–86.

Johnson, Charles. "A Report from St. Domingue." In *Soulcatcher, and Other Stories*, 59–66. San Diego: Harcourt, 2001.

Johnson, F. Roy. *The Nat Turner Slave Insurrection*. Murfreesboro, NC: Johnson, 1966.

Johnstone, Abraham. *The Address of*

Abraham Johnstone, a Black Man, Who Was Hanged at Woodbury. Philadelphia: Printed for the purchasers, 1797.

Jones, Howard. "*Amistad:* Movie, History, and the Academy Awards." *History Teacher* 31, no. 3 (1998): 380–82.

———. "Cinque of the *Amistad* a Slave Trader? Perpetuating a Myth." *Journal of American History* 87, no. 3 (2000): 923–39.

———. *Mutiny on the* Amistad. New York: Oxford University Press, 1987.

———. "Mutiny on the *Amistad:* 'All We Want Is Make Us Free.'" In *The* Amistad *Incident: Four Perspectives,* ed. James U. Rundle, 7–25. Middletown: Connecticut Humanities Council, 1992.

Jordan, June. "In the Spirit of Sojourner Truth." Unpublished manuscript, 1978. June Jordan Papers, 1936–2002, Schlesinger Library, Radcliffe Institute, Harvard University.

———. "Problems of Language in a Democratic State." In *Some of Us Did Not Die: New and Selected Essays of June Jordan,* 223–33. New York: Basic Books, 2002.

Joseph, Gloria I. "Sojourner Truth: Archetypal Black Feminist." In *Wild Women in the Whirlwind: Afra-American Culture and the Contemporary Literature Renaissance,* ed. Joanne M. Braxton and Andrée Nicola McLaughlin, 35–47. New Brunswick, NJ: Rutgers University Press, 1990.

Joyner, Alexis, H. Khalif Khalifah, and James Magee. *Nat Turner and the Southampton Campaign of the Black Liberation Army in 1831.* N.p.: United Brothers and Sisters, 1998.

Joyner, Charles. "Styron's Choice: A Meditation on History, Literature, and Moral Imperatives." In *Nat Turner: A Slave Rebellion in History and Memory,* ed. Kenneth S. Greenberg, 179–213. Oxford: Oxford University Press, 2004.

Kabba, Muctaru R. A., et al., eds. *Sierra Leonean Heroes: Fifty Great Men and Women Who Helped to Build Our Nation.* London: Commonwealth, 1987.

Kachun, Mitchell A. "Antebellum African Americans, Public Commemoration and the Haitian Revolution: A Problem of Historical Mythmaking." *Journal of the Early Republic* 26, no. 2 (2006): 249–73.

Kaisary, Philip James. "The Literary Impact of the Haitian Revolution." Ph.D. diss., University of Warwick, 2008.

Kaiser, Ernest. "The Failure of William Styron." In *William Styron's "The Confessions of Nat Turner": A Critical Handbook,* ed. Melvin J. Friedman and Irving Malin, 92–103. Belmont, CA: Wadsworth, 1970.

Kaplan, Cora. "Black Heroes / White Writers: Toussaint L'Ouverture and the Literary Imagination." *History Workshop Journal* 46, no. 33 (1998): 32–62.

Kaplan, Sidney. "Black Mutiny on the *Amistad.*" *Massachusetts Review* 10, no. 3 (Summer 1969): 493–532.

Kaplan, Sidney, and Emma Nogrady Kaplan. *The Black Presence in the Era of the American Revolution.* Amherst: University of Massachusetts Press, 1989.

Kelley, Robin D. G. "There Are No Coons Here." *History Teacher* 31, no. 3 (1998): 399–402.

Killen, John Oliver. "The Confessions of Willie Styron." In *The Second Crucifixion of Nat Turner,* ed. John Henrik Clarke, 34–44. Baltimore: Black Classic, 1997.

King, John N. Introduction to *Book of Martyrs: Select Narratives,* by John Foxe, xi–xl. Oxford: Oxford University Press, 2009.

Koeninger, Kainoa. "Sojourner Truth Sings to the Woman Spirit." *Frontiers: A Journal of Women Studies* 15, no. 2 (1994): 119.

Kramer, Hilton. "Chronicles of Black History." *New York Times* (May 17, 1974): 17.

Kutzinski, Vera M. "Changing Permanences: Historical and Literary Revisionism in Robert Hayden's 'Middle Passage.'" *Callaloo* 26 (Winter 1986): 171–83.

Lambert, David. "'Part of the Blood and Dream': Surrogation, Memory and the National Hero in the Postcolonial Caribbean." *Patterns of Prejudice* 41, nos. 3–4 (2007): 345–71.

Langston, John Mercer. "The World's Anti-slavery Movement: Its Heroes and Its Triumphs." 1858. http://www.oberlin.edu/external/EOG/LangstonSpeeches/world.htm.

Lansana, Quraysh Ali. *They Shall Run: Harriet Tubman Poems.* Chicago: Third World, 2004.

Lapsansky, Philip. "Graphic Discord: Abolitionist and Antiabolitionist Images." In *The Abolitionist Sisterhood: Women's Political Culture in Antebellum America,* ed. Jean Yellin and John C. Van Horne. Ithaca, NY: Cornell University Press, 1994: 201–30.

La Roche, Cheryl J., and Michael L. Blakey. "Seizing Intellectual Power: The Dialogue at the New York African Burial Ground." *Historical Archaeology* 31, no. 3 (1997): 84–106.

Larson, Kate Clifford. *Bound for the Promised Land: Harriet Tubman, Portrait of an American Heroine.* New York: Ballantine Books, 2004.

———. "'From the Nature of Things': The Influence of Racial, Class and Gender Proscriptions on the Collective Memory of Harriet Tubman." In *Monuments of the Black Atlantic: Slavery and Memory,* ed. Joanne M. Braxton and Maria I. Diedrich, 45–52. Munster: Lit Verlag Münster, 2004.

Lavédrine, Bernard. *Photographs of the Past: Process and Preservation.* Los Angeles: Getty Conservation Institute, 2009.

Lawrence, Jacob. *The Frederick Douglass and Harriet Tubman Series of 1938–40.* Ed. Ellen Harkins Wheat. Hampton, VA: Hampton University Museum; Seattle: University of Washington Press, 1991.

———. *Harriet and the Promised Land.* New York: Simon and Schuster, 1968.

———. *The Migration Series* Ed. Elizabeth Hutton Turner. Washington, DC: Rappahannock Press, 1993.

———. "Oral History Interview with Jacob Lawrence." By Carroll Greene Jr. Oct. 26, 1968. Archives of American Art, Smithsonian Institution. http://www.aaa.si.edu/collections/

oralhistories/transcripts/lawren68
.htm.

———. "Statement by Jacob Lawrence,
May 10th 1978." In *The Legend of John
Brown*, ed. Ellen Sharp, 14. Detroit:
Detroit Institute of Arts, 1978.

———. *The Toussaint L'Ouverture Series:
A Visual Narration of the Liberation
of Haiti in 1804 under the Leadership
of General Toussaint L'Ouverture*. Ed.
James Buell and David C. Driskell.
New York: United Church Board for
Homeland Ministries, 1982.

Lawson, Bill E. "Douglass among the
Romantics." In *The Cambridge
Companion to Frederick Douglass*, ed.
Maurice S. Lee, 118–31. Cambridge:
Cambridge University Press, 2009.

Lee, Maurice S., ed. *The Cambridge
Companion to Frederick Douglass*.
Cambridge: Cambridge University
Press, 2009.

LeFalle-Collins, Lizzetta, and Shirfa M.
Goldman. *In the Spirit of Resistance:
African American Modernists and the
Mexican Muralist School*. New York:
American Federation of Arts, 1996.

Lemisch, Jesse. "Black Agency in the
Amistad Uprising; or, You've Taken
our Cinque and Gone." *Souls: A
Critical Journal of Black Politics,
Culture, and Society* 1, no. 1 (Winter
1999): 57–70.

Lester, Julius. *Look Out, Whitey! Black
Power's Gon' Get Your Mama!* New
York: Grove, 1968.

Levine, Robert S. "Identity in the
Autobiographies." In *The Cambridge
Companion to Frederick Douglass*, ed.
Maurice S. Lee, 31–45. Cambridge:
Cambridge University Press, 2009.

Lewis, Edmonia. *Cleopatra*. 1876.

http://farm1.static.flickr.com/129/
422647174_8a18f8c9c7.jpg.

———. *Forever Free*, 1867. http://farm4
.static.flickr.com/3198/2343882964
_78f064469e_o.jpg.

Lezra, Esther. "Representations of
Solitude: Transatlantic Transmissions
of Freedom Fighters." *Kalfou*,
forthcoming.

Lipscomb, Drema R. "Sojourner Truth:
A Practical Public Discourse." In
*Reclaiming Rhetorica: Women in the
Rhetorical Tradition*, ed. Andrea A.
Lunsford. Pittsburgh: University of
Pittsburgh Press, 1995.

Lipsitz, George. *The Possessive Investment
in Whiteness: How White People Profit
from Identity Politics*. Philadelphia:
Temple University Press, 2006.

Lohmann, Christopher, ed. *Radical
Passion: Ottilie Assing's Reports from
America and Letters to Frederick
Douglass*. New York: Canterbury,
1999.

Lorde, Audre. "Eye to Eye: Black
Women, Hatred, and Anger." In
Sister Outsider: Essays and Speeches.
Berkeley, CA: Crossing, 2007.

Louverture, Toussaint. "Address to
Soldiers for the Universal Destruction
of Slavery." 1797. In *Toussaint
L'Ouverture: The Haitian Revolution*,
ed. Nick Nesbitt, 28. London: Verso,
2008.

———. "Letter to the French Directory."
1797. In *Toussaint L'Ouverture: The
Haitian Revolution*, ed. Nick Nesbitt,
32–36. London: Verso, 2008.

Lowe, Donald M. *History of Bourgeois
Perception*. Chicago: University of
Chicago Press, 1982.

Lowry, Beverly. *Imagining a Life: A*

Biography of Harriet Tubman. New York: Doubleday, 2007.

Mabee, Carlton. "Sojourner Truth, Bold Prophet: Why Did She Never Learn to Read?" *New York History* 69 (1980): 55–77.

Mabee, Carleton, and Susan Mabee Newhouse. *Sojourner Truth: Slave, Prophet, Legend.* New York: New York University Press, 1993.

Maracle, Lee. *Sojourner's Truth, and Other Stories.* Vancouver: Press Gang, 1990.

Marshall, Richard, ed. *Jean-Michel Basquiat.* New York: Harry N. Abrams, 1992.

Martin, Waldo E., Jr. "Images of Frederick Douglass in the Afro-American Mind: The Recent Black Freedom Struggle." In *Frederick Douglass: New Literary and Historical Essays,* ed. Eric J. Sundquist. Cambridge: Cambridge University Press, 1990.

————. *The Mind of Frederick Douglass.* Chapel Hill: University of North Carolina Press, 1984.

Martineau, Harriet. *The Hour and the Man: An Historical Romance.* 1841. Rpt. Middlesex: Echo Library, 2008.

McDowell, Deborah. "Transferences— Black Feminist Discourse: The 'Practice' of 'Theory.'" In *Feminism Beside Itself,* ed. Diane Elam and Robyn Wiegman. New York: Routledge, 1995.

McFeely, William S. "Cinque, Tall and Strong." *Journal of American History* 87, no. 3 (2000): 949–50.

————. *Frederick Douglass.* New York: W. W. Norton, 1991.

McGowan, James A. "Harriet Tubman: According to Sarah Bradford." *Harriet Tubman Journal* 2 (Jan. 1994): 1–10.

Melville, Herman. *Benito Cereno.* 1855. Rpt. London: Nonesuch, 1926.

Mickenberg, Julia. "Civil Rights, History, and the Left: Inventing the Juvenile Black Biography." *MELUS* 27, no. 2 (2002): 65–93.

Middelanis, Carl Hermann. "Blending with Motifs and Colors: Haitian History Interpreted by Édouard Duval-Carrié." *Small Axe* 9, no. 2 (Sep. 2005): 109–23.

Mills, Charles. *The Racial Contract.* Ithaca, NY: Cornell University Press, 1997.

Mirzoeff, Nicholas L. "The Shadow and the Substance: Race, Photography, and the Index." In *Only Skin Deep: Changing Visions of the American Self,* ed. Coco Fusco and Brian Wallis, 111–28. New York: International Center of Photography in association with Harry N. Abrams, 2003.

Moore, George Coleman. "Slave Revolt over Virginia." *Chicago Defender* (Dec. 9, 1940): 13.

Morrison, Toni. *Beloved.* London: Chatto and Windus, 1987.

————. *Playing in the Dark: Whiteness and the American Literary Imagination.* New York: Vintage, 1993.

Moses, Wilson J. *Creative Conflict in African American Thought.* Cambridge: Cambridge University Press, 2004.

————. "Where Honor Is Due: Frederick Douglass as Representative Black Man." *Prospects* 17 (1992): 177–89.

Mountain, Joseph. *Sketches of the Life of Joseph Mountain, a Negro, Who Was*

Executed at New-Haven. New Haven, CT: T. and S. Green, 1790.

Moynihan, Sinéad. *"Other People's Diasporas": Negotiating Race in Contemporary Irish and Irish-American Culture.* Syracuse, NY: Syracuse University Press, 2012.

Mulvey, Laura. "Myth, Narrative, and Historical Experience." *History Workshop* 23 (Spring 1984): 3.

Muniz, Vik. *Frederick Douglass.* In *Only Skin Deep: Changing Visions of the American Self,* ed. Coco Fusco and Brian Wallis, 207. New York: International Center of Photography in association with Harry N. Abrams, 2003.

Munro, Martin, and Elizabeth Walcott-Hackshaw. "Introduction: Reinterpreting the Haitian Revolution and Its Cultural Aftershocks." *Small Axe* 9, no. 2 (2005): viii–xiii.

———, eds. *Reinterpreting the Haitian Revolution and Its Cultural Aftershocks.* Kingston, Jamaica: University of the West Indies Press, 2006.

Murray, Albert. *The Omni-Americans: Some Alternatives to the Folklore of White Supremacy.* New York: Da Capo, 1970.

Murray, Freeman Henry Morris. *Emancipation and the Freed in American Sculpture.* Washington, DC: published by the author, 1916.

Neal, Larry. *And Shine Swam On.* Ed. LeRoi Jones. New York: Morrow, 1968.

Nesbett, Peter T., and Michelle DuBois. *Jacob Lawrence: Paintings, Drawings, and Murals (1935–1999): A Catalogue Raisonné.* Seattle: University of Washington Press, 2000.

Nesbitt, Nick, ed. *Toussaint L'Ouverture: The Haitian Revolution.* Introduction by Jean-Bertrand Aristide. London: Verso, 2008.

Newman, Judith. "Writing against Slavery: Harriet Beecher Stowe." In *Women, Dissent and Anti-Slavery in Britain and America, 1790–1865,* ed. Elizabeth J. Clapp and Julie Roy Jeffrey, 175–96. Oxford: Oxford University Press, 2011.

Newton, John. *Thoughts upon the African Slave Trade.* 1788. In *The Posthumous Works of the Late Rev. John Newton,* vol. 2. Philadelphia: W. W. Woodward, 1809.

Noble, David W. *Death of a Nation: American Culture and the End of Exceptionalism.* Minneapolis: University of Minnesota Press, 2002.

Obama, Barack. *Dreams from My Father: A Story of Race and Inheritance.* New York: Random House, 1995.

O'Brien, Glenn, and Diego Cortez. *Jean-Michel Basquiat 1981: The Studio of the Street.* New York: Deitch Projects, 2007.

O'Kelly, Donal. *The Cambria: Frederick Douglass' Voyage to Ireland 1845.* Playography Ireland, 2005. http://www.irishplayography.com/.

Opala, Joseph A. "'Ecstatic Renovation!': Street Art Celebrating Sierra Leone's 1992 Revolution." *African Affairs* 93, no. 371 (1994): 195–218.

Osagie, Iyunolu Folayan. *The Amistad Revolt: Memory, Slavery, and the Politics of Identity in the United States and Sierra Leone.* Athens: University of Georgia Press, 2000.

O'Shea, Tim. "Creator, Publish Thyself: Kyle Baker." *Comics*

Bulletin, n.d. Accessed May 2010. http://www.comicsbulletin.com/features/106385753331986.htm.

Painter, Nell Irvin. *Creating Black Americans: African-American History and Its Meanings, 1619 to the Present*. New York: Oxford University Press, 2006.

———. "Difference, Slavery, and Memory: Sojourner Truth in Feminist Abolitionism." In *The Abolitionist Sisterhood: Women's Political Culture in America*, ed. Jean Fagan Yellin and John C. Van Horne, 139–58. Ithaca, NY: Cornell University Press, 1994.

———. "Representing Truth: Sojourner Truth's Knowing and Becoming Known." *Journal of American History* 81, no. 2 (Sep. 1994): 461–92.

———. *Sojourner Truth: A Life, a Symbol*. New York: W. W. Norton, 1996.

———. "Sojourner Truth in Life and Memory: Writing the Biography of an American Exotic." *Gender and History* 2, no. 1 (1990): 3–16.

Panger, Daniel. *Ol' Prophet Nat*. Greenwich, CT: Fawcett, 1967.

Parkinson, Wenda. *"This Gilded African": Toussaint L'Ouverture*. London: Quartet Books, 1978.

Pauli, Hertha. *Her Name Was Sojourner Truth*. New York: Appleton-Century-Crofts, 1962.

Peterson, Bernard L., Jr. "The Legendary Owen Dodson." *Crisis* 86, no. 9 (Nov. 1979): 373–78.

Peterson, Carla. *"Doers of the Word": African-American Women Speakers and Writers in the North (1830–1880)*. New Brunswick, NJ: Rutgers University Press, 1998.

Philip, Marlene Nourbese. *Harriet's Daughter*. Oxford: Heinemann, 1988.

Phillips, Wendell. "Toussaint L'Ouverture." Lecture given in New York and Boston, 1861. The Louverture Project. http://thelouvertureproject.org/index.php?title='Toussaint_L'Ouverture'_A_lecture_by_Wendell_Phillips_(1861).

Piepmeier, Alison. *Out in Public: Configurations of Women's Bodies in Nineteenth-Century America*. Chapel Hill: University of North Carolina Press, 2004.

Pierrot, Grégory. "'Our Hero': Toussaint Louverture in British Representations." *Criticism* 50, no. 4 (2008): 581–607.

Pinder, Kimberly N. "'Our Father, God; Our Brother, Christ; or Are We Bastard Kin?': Images of Christ in African American Painting." *African American Review*, 31, no. 2 (1997): 223–33.

Plummer, Jonathan. *The Dying Confession of Pomp, A Negro Man*. Newburyport, MA: Blunt and March, 1975.

Poe, Edgar Allan. "The Daguerreotype." 1840. American Studies at the University of Virginia website. http://xroads.virginia.edu/~hyper/POE/daguer.html.

Porter, James. *Modern Negro Art*. 1943. Ed. David C. Driskell. Washington, DC: Washington Project for the Arts, 1992.

Poussaint, Alan F. "Interview with Alan F. Poussaint." By Kenneth S. Greenberg. In *Nat Turner: A Slave Rebellion in History and Memory*, ed. Kenneth Greenberg, 228–42. Oxford: Oxford University Press, 2004.

Powell, Richard J. "Cinque: Antislavery Portraiture and Patronage in Jacksonian America." *American Art* 11, no. 3 (1997): 48–73.

———. *Cutting a Figure: Fashioning Black Portraiture*. Chicago: University of Chicago Press, 2008.

———. *Homecoming: The Art and Life of William H. Johnson*. New York: W. W. Norton, 1991.

Powers, Hiram. *The Greek Slave*. 1846. http://www.corcoran.org/collection/images/73.4.jpg.

Priestly, Debra. "Debra Priestly." http://www.debrapriestly.net/.

———. Interview with the author. Nov. 2010.

Quilts of Gees Bend Catalog. http://www.auburn.edu/academic/other/geesbend/explore/catalog/slideshow/index.htm.

Prigoff, James, and Robin J. Dunitz. *Walls of Heritage, Walls of Pride: African American Murals*. Warwick: Pomegranate Europe, 2000.

Rael, Patrick. "Why This Film about Slavery?" *History Teacher* 31, no. 3 (1998): 387.

Rainsford, Marcus. *An Historical Account of the Black Empire of Hayti*. London: Cundle and Chapple, 1805.

Rawick, George P. *From Sundown to Sunup: The Making of the Black Community*. Westport, CT: Greenwood, 1973.

Rediker, Marcus. *The Amistad Rebellion: A Sea Story of Slavery and Freedom*. New York: Viking-Penguin, 2012.

Reinhardt, Thomas. "200 Years of Forgetting: Hushing Up the Haitian Revolution." *Journal of Black Studies* 35, no. 4 (2005): 246–61.

Rice, Alan. *Creating Memorials, Building Identities: The Politics of Memory in the Black Atlantic*. Liverpool: Liverpool University Press, 2010.

———. "Tracing Slavery and Abolition's Routes and Viewing inside the Invisible: The Monumental Landscape and the African Atlantic." *Atlantic Studies* 8, no. 2 (2011): 253–74.

Ricouer, Paul. *Time and Narrative*. Vol. 3. Chicago: University of Chicago Press, 1990.

Riley, Denise. *"Am I That Name?": Feminism and the Category of "Women" in History*. Basingstoke, Hampshire, UK: Macmillan, 1998.

Rimensnyder, Sara. "Disarming Harriet Tubman." *Reason* (Dec. 2000). http://findarticles.com/p/articles/mi_m1568/is_7_32/ai_67589538/.

Roberts, John W. *From Trickster to Badman: The Black Folk Hero in Slavery and Freedom*. Philadelphia: University of Pennsylvania Press, 1989.

Robinson, Cedric. *Forgeries of Memory and Meaning: Blacks and Regimes of Race in American Theater and Film before World War II*. Chapel Hill: University of North Carolina Press, 2007.

Rodgers, Kenneth G. *Climbing Up the Mountain: The Modern Art of Malvin Gray Johnson*. Durham: North Carolina Central University Museum, 2002.

Rohrbach, Augusta. "Profits of Protest: The Market Strategies of Sojourner Truth and Louisa May Alcott." In *Prophets of Protest: Reconsidering the History of American Abolitionism*, ed. Timothy Patrick McCarthy and John

Stauffer, 235–55. New York: New Press, 2006.

Rokela. "A Page of History: One of the Tragedies of the Old Slavery Days." *Godey's Magazine* (Mar. 1898): 233.

Rolston, Bill. "'The Brothers on the Walls': International Solidarity and Irish Political Murals." *Journal of Black Studies* 39, no. 3 (2009): 446–70.

Rommel-Ruiz, Bryan. "'Vindictive Ferocity': Virginia Responds to the Nat Turner Rebellion." In *Enemies of Humanity: The Nineteenth-Century War on Terrorism,* ed. Isaac Land, 63–78. New York: Palgrave Macmillan, 2008.

Rothstein, Edward. "A Burial Ground and Its Dead Are Given Life." *New York Times* (February 26, 2010). http://www.nytimes.com/2010/02/26/arts/design/26burial.html.

Rubin, Louis D., Jr. "William Styron and Human Bondage." In *William Styron's "The Confessions of Nat Turner": A Critical Handbook,* ed. Melvin J. Friedman and Irving Malin, 72–83. Belmont, CA: Wadsworth, 1970.

Rucker, Walter C. *The River Flows On: Black Resistance, Culture, and Identity Formation in America.* Baton Rouge: Louisiana State University Press, 2006.

Saar, Betye. "Betye Saar: An Interview." By M. J. Hewitt. *International Review of African American Art* 10, no. 2 (1992): 7–23.

Sale, Maggie M. *The Slumbering Volcano: American Slave Ship Revolts and the Production of Rebellious Masculinity.* Durham, NC: Duke University Press, 1997.

Sánchez-Eppler, Karen. "Bodily Bonds: The Intersecting Rhetorics of Feminism and Abolitionism." *Representations* 24 (1998): 28–59.

Santamarina, Xiomara. *Belabored Professions: Narratives of African American Working Womanhood.* Chapel Hill: University of North Carolina Press, 2005.

Sartain, John, *Cinque.* ca. 1840. http://www.npg.si.edu/img2/amistad/lgcinq.jpg.

Savage, Kirk. *Standing Soldiers, Kneeling Slaves: Race, War, and Monument in Nineteenth-Century America.* Princeton, NJ: Princeton University Press, 1997.

Schwartzman, Myron. *Romare Bearden: His Life and Art.* New York: Harry N. Abrams, 1990.

Sekula, Allan. "The Body and the Archive." *October* 39 (1986): 3–64.

Sernett, Milton C. *Harriet Tubman: Myth, Memory, and History.* Durham, NC: Duke University Press, 2007.

Shangee, Ntozake. *For Colored Girls Who Have Considered Suicide When the Rainbow Is Enuf.* London: Methuen, 1978.

Sherman, Bill. "Graphic Novel Review: *Nat Turner—Volume Two* by Kyle Baker." 2007. Blogcritics. http://blogcritics.org/books/article/graphic-novel-review-nat-turner-volume/.

Short, Alvia Jean Wardlaw. "Strength, Tears, and Will: John Biggers' 'Contribution of the Negro Woman to American Life and Education.'" *Callaloo* 2, no. 1 (1979): 135–43.

Silenieks, Juris. Introduction to *Monsieur Toussaint: A Play,* by Édouard Glissant. Washington, DC: Three Continents, 1981.

Smith, James McCune. "Brown & Nat Turner: An Editor's Comparison." In *Meteor of War: The John Brown Story,* ed. Zoe Trodd and John Stauffer, 217–19. New York: Brandywine, 2004.

———. "Toussaint L'Ouverture and the Haytian Revolution." 1841. The Louverture Project. http://thelouvertureproject.org/index.php?title=Toussaint_L'Ouverture_and_the_Haytian_Revolutions.

Sokolov, Raymond A. "Into the Mind of Nat Turner." In *William Styron's "The Confessions of Nat Turner": A Critical Handbook,* ed. Melvin J. Friedman and Irving Malin, 42–50. Belmont, CA: Wadsworth, 1970.

Sontag, Susan. *On Photography.* London: Penguin, 1978.

Spielberg, Steven, Maya Angelou, and Debbie Allen. *Amistad: "Give Us Free"; A Celebration of the Film by Steven Spielberg.* New York: Newmarket, 1998.

Spradling, Grant. Introduction to *The Toussaint L'Ouverture Series: A Visual Narration of the Liberation of Haiti in 1804 under the Leadership of General Toussaint L'Ouverture,* by Jacob Lawrence. Edited by James Buell and David C. Driskell. New York: United Church Board for Homeland Ministries, 1982.

Stallybrass, Peter, and Allon White. *The Politics and Poetics of Transgression.* Ithaca, NY: Cornell University Press, 1986.

Stanton, Elizabeth Cady. "Sojourner Truth on the Press." In *History of Woman Suffrage,* vol. 2, *1861–1876,* ed. Elizabeth Cady Stanton, Susan B. Anthony, Matilda Joslyn Gage, and Ida Husted Harper, 926–28. New York: Susan B. Anthony, 1881.

Stauffer, John. *The Black Hearts of Men: Radical Abolitionists and the Transformation of Race.* Cambridge, MA: Harvard University Press, 2002.

———. "Creating an Image in Black: The Power of Abolition Pictures." In *Prophets of Protest: Reconsidering the History of American Abolitionism,* ed. Timothy Patrick McCarthy and John Stauffer, 256–67. New York: New Press, 2006.

———. "Frederick Douglass and the Aesthetics of Freedom." *Raritan* 25, no. 1 (2005): 114–36.

———. *Giants: The Parallel Lives of Frederick Douglass and Abraham Lincoln.* New York: Twelve, 2008.

Stepto, Robert B. "Storytelling in Early Afro-American Fiction: Frederick Douglass' *The Heroic Slave.*" *Georgia Review* 36 (Summer 1982): 355–68.

Stetson, Erlene, and Linda David. *Glorying in Tribulation: The Lifework of Sojourner Truth.* East Lansing: Michigan State University Press, 1994.

Stiehm, Jamie. "Nothing Will Stop This Historic Endeavor; Tubman Mural with Musket Is Rejected." *Baltimore Sun* (June 2000). Accessed at Hartford Web Publishing. http://www.hartford-hwp.com/archives/45a/306.html.

Stone, Albert. *The Return of Nat Turner: History, Literature, and Cultural Politics in Sixties America.* Athens: University of Georgia Press, 1992.

Stowe, Harriet Beecher. *Dred: A Tale of the Great Dismal Swamp.* 1856.

Ed. Robert S. Levine. Chapel Hill: University of North Carolina Press, 2006.

———. "The Libyan Sibyl." 1863. Electronic Text Center, University of Virginia Library. http://etext.virginia .edu/toc/modeng/public/StoSojo .html.

———. *Uncle Tom's Cabin: A Tale of Life among the Lowly*. 1852. Ed. Ann Douglas. New York: Penguin, 1981.

Strzemien, Anya. "Michelle Obama Honors Sojourner Truth, Wears Striped Skirt." *Huffington Post,* May 29, 2009. http://www.huffingtonpost .com/2009/04/28/michelle-obama -honors-soj_n_192427.html.

Styron, William. *The Confessions of Nat Turner*. 1967. Rpt. London: Picador, 1994.

———. "Interview with William Styron." By Kenneth Greenberg. In *Nat Turner: A Slave Rebellion in History and Memory,* ed. Kenneth Greenberg, 214–27. Oxford: Oxford University Press, 2004.

———. "Nat Turner Revisited." *American Heritage* (Oct. 1992): 64–73.

———. "This Quiet Dust." In *The Nat Turner Rebellion: The Historical Event and the Modern Controversy,* ed. John B. Duff and Peter M. Mitchell, 120–40. New York: Harper and Row, 1971.

———. "William Styron: A Shared Ordeal." Interview by George Plimpton. In *William Styron's "The Confessions of Nat Turner": A Critical Handbook,* ed. Melvin J. Friedman and Irving Malin, 36–41. Belmont, CA: Wadsworth, 1970.

Sullivan, Edward J., ed. *Continental Shifts: The Art of Édouard Duval Carrié*. Miami: American Art Corporation, 2007.

Sundquist, Eric J. *To Wake the Nations: Race in the Making of American Literature*. Cambridge, MA: Harvard University Press, 1993.

Sweeney, Fionnghuala. *Frederick Douglass and the Atlantic World*. Liverpool: Liverpool University Press, 2007.

———. "Other Peoples' History: Slavery, Refuge and Irish Citizenship in Donal O'Kelly's *The Cambria*." In *Public Art, Memorials and Atlantic Slavery,* eds. Celeste-Marie Bernier and Judie Newman, 140–52. London: Routledge, 2009.

Tanner, Henry Ossawa. *The Banjo Lesson*. 1893. http://georgiainfo.galileo.usg. edu/banjo_lesson.jpg.

Terry, Esther. "Sojourner Truth: The Person Behind the Libyan Sibyl." *Massachusetts Review* 26 (Summer–Fall 1985): 425–44.

Thompson, Audrey. "Harriet Tubman in Pictures: Cultural Consciousness and the Art of Picture Books." *The Lion and the Unicorn* 25, no. 1 (Jan. 2001): 81–114.

Thompson, Robert Farris. *Flash of the Spirit: African and Afro-American Art and Philosophy*. New York: Vintage Books, 1984.

Tilton, Theodore. *Sonnets to the Memory of Frederick Douglass*. 1895. In *In Memoriam: Frederick Douglass,* ed. Helen Douglass, 149–57. New York: Books for Libraries, 1971.

Trachtenberg, Alan. "Photography:

The Emergence of a Key Word." In *Photography in Nineteenth-Century America,* ed. Martha A. Sandweiss. New York: H. N. Abrams, 1991.

Tragle, Henry Irving. *The Southampton Slave Revolt of 1831: A Compilation of Source Material.* Amherst: University of Massachusetts Press, 1971.

Trodd, Zoe. "The Reusable Past: Abolitionist Aesthetics in the Protest Literature of the Long Civil Rights Movement." Ph.D. diss., Harvard University, 2009.

Trodd, Zoe, and John Stauffer, eds. *Meteor of War: The John Brown Story.* New York: Brandywine, 2004.

Truth, Sojourner. "My Friends." In *History of Woman Suffrage,* vol. 2., *1861–1876,* ed. Elizabeth Cady Stanton, Susan B. Anthony, Matilda Joslyn Gage, and Ida Husted Harper, 193–94. New York: Susan B. Anthony, 1881.

———. "She Pleadeth for Her People." In *Sojourner Truth as Orator: Wit, Story, and Song,* ed. Suzanne Pullon Fitch and Roseann M. Mandziuk, 213–14. Westport, CT: Greenwood, 1997.

Truth, Sojourner, with Olive Gilbert. *Narrative of Sojourner Truth, a Northern Slave, Emancipated from Bodily Servitude by the State of New York, in 1828.* Boston: J. P. Yerrington and Sons, 1850.

Truth, Sojourner, with Frances W. Titus. *Narrative of Sojourner Truth; a Bondswoman of Olden Time, Emancipated by the New York Legislature in the Early Part of the Present Century; with a History of Her Labors and Correspondence, Drawn from Her "Book of Life."* 1878. Ed.

Jeffrey C. Stewart. New York: Oxford University Press, 1991.

Tufts, Eleanor. "An American Victorian Dilemma, 1875: Should a Woman Be Allowed to Sculpt a Man?" *Art Journal* 51, no. 1 (Spring 1992): 51–56.

Tyson, George F., Jr., ed. *Toussaint L'Ouverture.* Englewood Cliffs, NJ: Prentice-Hall, 1973.

Vale, Gilbert. *Fanaticism: Its Source and Influence.* 2 vols. New York: G. Vale, 1835.

Van Deburg, William L. *New Day in Babylon: The Black Power Movement and American Culture, 1965–1975.* Chicago: University of Chicago Press, 1992.

Voss, Frederick S. *Majestic in His Wrath: A Pictorial Life of Frederick Douglass.* Washington, DC: Smithsonian Institution Press, 1995.

Wagner, Gerard A. "Sojourner Truth: God's Appointed Apostle of Reform." *Southern Journal of Speech* 28 (1962): 123–38.

Walcott, Derek. *The Haitian Trilogy.* 1954. Rpt. New York: Farrar, Strauss and Giroux, 2001.

Walker, Alice. *Everyday Use.* Ed. Barbara Christian. New Brunswick, NJ: Rutgers University Press, 1994.

Walker, David. *Walker's Appeal.* 1829. Rpt. New York: Arno, 1969.

Walker, Margaret. "Harriet Tubman." *Phylon* 5, no. 4 (1994): 326–30.

Wallace, Michele. *Black Macho and the Myth of the Superwoman.* New York: Dial, 1979.

Warner, Samuel. *An Authentic and Impartial Narrative of the Tragical Scene Which Was Witnessed in Southampton County.* In *The*

Southampton Slave Revolt of 1831:
A Compilation of Source Material,
ed. Henry Irving Tragle, 280–300.
Amherst: University of Massachusetts
Press, 1971.

Washington, Margaret. "Introduction:
The Enduring Legacy of Sojourner
Truth." In *Narrative of Sojourner Truth*,
ed. Margaret Washington, ix–xxxiii.
New York: Vintage Books, 1993.

———. *Sojourner Truth's America*.
Urbana: University of Illinois Press,
2009.

Wedgwood, Josiah. "Am I Not a Man
and a Brother?" BBC News website,
2007. http://www.bbc.co.uk/stoke/
content/images/2007/01/24/slave
_medallion_main_203x152.jpg.

Weeks, Stephen Beauregard. "Slave
Insurrection in Virginia, 1831." In *The
Nat Turner Rebellion: The Historical
Event and the Modern Controversy,* ed.
John B. Duff and Peter M. Mitchell,
66–76. New York: Harper and Row,
1971.

Weems, Carrie Mae. *From Here I Saw
What Happened and I Cried.* 1995–96.
http://carriemaeweems.net/.

Weismann, Donald, John Biggers,
Carroll Simms, and John Edward
Weems. *Black Art in Houston: The
Texas Southern University Experience.*
College Station: Texas A&M
University Press, 1978.

Welter, Barbara. "Cult of True
Womanhood." *America Quarterly* 18,
no. 2, pt. 1 (Summer 1966): 151–74.

Westerbeck, Colin L. "Frederick
Douglass Chooses His Moment." *Art
Institute of Chicago Museum Studies*
24, no. 2 (1999): 144–61, 260–62.

Wheat, Ellen Harkins. *Jacob Lawrence,
American Painter.* Seattle: University
of Washington Press, 1986.

———, ed. *Jacob Lawrence: The Frederick
Douglass and Harriet Tubman Series
of 1938–40.* Hampton, VA: Hampton
University Press, 1991.

Wheatley, Phillis. *The Collected Works
of Phillis Wheatley.* 1887. Ed. John
Shields. New York: Oxford University
Press, 1988.

White, Charles. *Five Great American
Negroes.* 1939–40. http://www.charles
white-imagesofdignity.org/30.html.

———. *General Moses (Harriet
Tubman).* 1965. http://www
.charleswhite-imagesofdignity.org/
40.html.

White, Walter. "Sojourner Truth: Friend
of Freedom." *New Republic* 118 (May
24, 1948): 15–18.

Whitfield, James Monroe. *America, and
Other Poems.* New York: James S.
Leavitt, 1853.

Whittier, John Greenleaf. "Toussaint
L'Ouverture." 1833. http://www
.humanitiesweb.org/human. hp?s
=l&p=c&a=p&ID=21148&c=333.

Williams, George Washington. *History of
the Negro Race in America.* 2 vols. 1883.
Rpt. New York: Bergman, 1968.

Williams, Melvin G. "Now and Then:
William Branch's *In Splendid Error.*"
Black American Literature Forum 12,
no. 3 (Autumn 1978): 110–12.

Wilson, Ivy G. *Specters of Democracy:
Blackness and the Aesthetic of Politics in
the Antebellum U.S.* New York: Oxford
University Press, 2011.

Wolf, Hazel Catherine. *On Freedom's
Altar: The Martyr Complex in the
Abolition Movement.* Madison:
University of Wisconsin Press, 1952.

Wood, Marcus. *Blind Memory: Visual Representation of Slavery in England and America, 1780–1865.* Manchester: Manchester University Press, 2000.

———. *Exploding Archives: Meditations on Slavery, Brazil, America and the Limits of Cultural Memory.* Athens: University of Georgia Press, forthcoming.

———. *The Horrible Gift of Freedom: Atlantic Slavery and the Representation of Emancipation.* Athens: University of Georgia Press, 2010.

———. *Slavery, Empathy, and Pornography.* Oxford: Oxford University Press, 2003.

———. *Terrible Beauty: Visual Cultures of Slavery in Brazil and America.* New York: Oxford University Press, forthcoming.

Woodruff, Hale. "An Interview with Hale Woodruff." By Albert Murray. In *Hale Woodruff: Fifty Years of His Art,* ed. Mary Schmidt Campbell, 71–88. New York: Studio Museum in Harlem, 1979.

———. *The Mutiny aboard the Amistad; The Amistad Slaves on Trial at New Haven Connecticut, 1839; and The Return to Africa, 1842.* 1939. University of Missouri–Kansas City School of Law. http://www.law.umkc.edu/faculty/projects/ftrials/amistad/ami_imag.htm.

Woods, Clyde. *Development Arrested: The Blues and Plantation Power in the Mississippi Delta.* New York: Verso, 1998.

Wyatt-Brown, Bertram. "*Amistad* by Steven Spielberg." *Journal of American History* 85, no. 3 (1998): 1174–76.

X, Malcolm. *By Any Means Necessary.* Ed. Betty Shabazz. New York: Pathfinder, 1970.

———. *Malcolm X on Afro-American History.* Ed. Steve Clark. New York: Pathfinder, 1970.

Yellin, Jean Fagan. *Women and Sisters: The Antislavery Feminists in American Culture.* New Haven, CT: Yale University Press, 1987.

INDEX

Italicized page and color plate numbers refer to illustrations.